CROSSOVERS 1
EXPANDED
A Secret Chronology of the World

CROSSOVERS 1 EXPANDED

A Secret Chronology of the World

(Dawn of Time–1939)

Sean Lee Levin

Meteor House

Crossovers Expanded, Volume 1
Copyright © 2016 by Sean Lee Levin

Cover art and design copyright © 2016 by Keith Howell. All Rights Reserved.

Foreword copyright © 2016 by Win Scott Eckert. All Rights Reserved.

The Crossover Universe™ is a trademark of Win Scott Eckert,
used herein under license to Sean Lee Levin. All Rights Reserved.

Meteor House
ISBN 978-0-9905673-9-4
First Trade Edition

*For Steven Levin and Janet Takehara,
who nurtured my creative spark*

Acknowledgments

As Win Scott Eckert so correctly stated in the Acknowledgments of the original *Crossovers* volumes, "no work of this volume is created in a vacuum." Indeed, the present volumes owe much to the input of other people. Jay Lindsey provided much info on contemporary horror crossovers. Pete Rawlik filled in many of the gaps in my knowledge regarding some of the connections in his work. George Henry Smathers, Jr., aka "Henry Zeo Covert," provided me with much of the soap opera crossover info included in the appendix on television crossovers. Rick Lai's extensive knowledge of the pulps and other forms of popular fiction was invaluable. Chuck Loridans and Mark Brown's creative mythographic research regarding Dracula and Frankenstein forms the framework for many of the entries regarding those particular Children of the Night. Rather than list each specific piece of data I've received from people over the past few years, I will simply thank the following:

Matthew Baugh, James Bojaciuk, Andrew Brook, Dave Brzeski, Loki Carbis, Anthony R. Cardno, Salvatore Cucinotta, John L. French, Martin Gately, Greg Gick, Micah Harris, Andrew Henry, Matt Hickman, Matthew Ilseman, Rick Lai, Jay Lindsey, Brad Mengel, Bobby Nash, Adrian Nebbett, Jess Nevins, Kim Newman, Dennis E. Power, Pete Rawlik, Josh Reynolds, Charles R. Rutledge, Andrew Salmon, I. Ronald Schablotski, Art Sippo, B. L. Sisemore, John Allen Small, George Henry Smathers, Jr., aka "Henry Zeo Covert," Luke Van Horn, Alejandro Vasquez, and Chris Wike.

Thanks as well to my fellow members of the New Wold Newton Meteoritic Society, for their unwavering support and valuable feedback on my work. You're the best friends a guy could ask for. I owe Meteor House and its masterminds, Michael Croteau, Paul Spiteri, and Win Scott Eckert, for giving my first two books a home. In particular, Win has been my strongest supporter, and I am honored that he chose me to continue his amazing work with the original volumes. Win, you are a true friend, and it's a pleasure, as well as a privilege, to follow in your footsteps. Thanks are also due to Keith Howell for his stunning covers.

I cannot understate the impact the work of Philip José Farmer has had on my life. Phil, I miss you a great deal. I, Win, and many others owe you more than I can possibly say.

Last, but never least, I want to thank my parents, who believed in my abilities as a writer long before I did. Thank you for encouraging my creativity. It has all led up to these two massive books.

Sean Lee Levin

Foreword

World-Building, Fictional Biographies, and Crossovers

Fictional Biographies

I've long been fascinated by the genre called "fictional biographies," in which the character is treated as if he or she were real. As one can see from the list below, the fictional biography is a fairly small, and yet intriguing, phenomena, especially when one excludes reference books or articles that commingle pure fictional biographical details with "real world details" (e.g., Doyle based the character of Sherlock Holmes on Joseph Bell, and so on).

As I stated in the Foreword to the Bison Books edition of Philip José Farmer's *Tarzan Alive: A Definitive Biography of Lord Greystoke* (University of Nebraska Press Bison Books, 2006), the fictional biography genre was birthed from

> ... The Sherlockian tradition in which the object of the fictional biography is treated as a real person. Sherlockian biographical scholarship (commonly called the "Game") arose as a response to a myriad of discrepancies in Watson's writings of the master detective, Sherlock Holmes. In the Sherlockian Game Holmes' amanuensis, Dr. Watson, is also treated as a real person. As Dr. Watson narrates the cases, Arthur Conan Doyle is relegated to the status of Watson's "editor."

Game players then write critical essays that resolve the chronology of the Sherlock Holmes canon and otherwise provide explanations for inconsistencies in Watson's work. Sometimes the inconsistencies are explained as resulting from Watson's carelessness, whereas in other instances we are told that Watson deliberately changed certain details, times, and names to protect innocent parties and prevent delicate information from being uncovered through his writings.

Occasionally Game players go so far as to research and write complete biographies of their subjects.

The Sherlockian Game brings us to this list of fictional biographies, which forms the basis of the continuity I call the "Crossover Universe." Some of the fictional biographies themselves have crossovers, as noted below.

- *America's Secret Service Ace: The Operator 5 Story* by Nick Carr
- *Biggles: The Authorized Biography* by John Pearson
- *Confessions of a Teen Sleuth*, an autobiography by Nancy Drew, edited by Chelsea Cain (mega-crossover with other teen sleuths that Nancy Drew meets throughout her lifetime: Frank and Joe Hardy, the Hardy

Boys; Nurse Cherry Ames; Vicki Barr, Flight Stewardess; Louise and Jane Dana, the Dana Girls; Tom Swift, Sr.; aviator Ted Scott; Bert, Freddie, and Flossie Bobbsey, from the Bobbsey Twins; Tom Swift, Jr. and his pal Bud Barclay; Christopher Cool, Geronimo Johnson, and Spice Carter, TEEN agents; Foxy Belden-Frayne, daughter of Trixie Belden; Kim Aldrich, secretary at WALCO, Inc.; Judy Bolton; Donna Parker; Encyclopedia Brown; and Jupiter, Pete, and Bob, the Three Investigators)

- *Doc Savage: His Apocalyptic Life* by Philip José Farmer (mega-crossover with countless other heroes, villains, adventurers, and detectives, as part of the Wold Newton Family Tree)
- "Edgar Rice Burroughs: A Brief Biographical Sketch" by John Flint Roy in his *A Guide to Barsoom*
- *Four-&-Twenty Bloodhounds*. Like *Sleuths* (see below), there is a mini-biography of each detective along with each short story. The detectives featured are Shadrack Arnold, Senator Brooks U. Banner, Jim Burgess, Dr. Gideon Fell, Mortimer Death, Dr. Mary Finney, Dr. Sam: Johnson, Scott Jordan, Johnny Liddell, Inspector Magruder, John & Suzy Marshall, Merlini, Miss Rachel Murdock, the Mysterious Traveler, Nick Noble, O'Reilly Sahib, Ben Pedley, Solar Pons, Ellery Queen, Mike Shayne, Henry Smith, Dr. Paul Standish, Lieut. Timothy Trent, Jeff & Haila Troy, and Hildegarde Withers. Nearly every detective has a "Detective's Who's Who" entry provided by his creator. The only detectives who do not have entries are Ellery Queen, Mike Shayne, and the Mysterious Traveler. Ellery Queen provides a letter containing a vague summation of his life: "I was born, I have lived, and I'm going to hang on as long as I can." Mike Shayne's creator, Brett Halliday, provides a brief biography which is short on actual biographical details. The Mysterious Traveler writes Boucher a letter so disconcerting that it is unprintable, which Boucher forwards to the archives of Miskatonic University, thus establishing a crossover with H. P. Lovecraft's Cthulhu Mythos
- *The Flying Spy: A History of G-8* by Nick Carr
- "An Informal Biography of Conan the Cimmerian" by Clark, Miller, and de Camp in *The Blade of Conan*
- *The Great Detectives: Seven Original Investigations* by Julian Symons. Each of the investigations is a short biographical sketch in the form of a short story, first person narration, or interview. The detectives covered are Sherlock Holmes, Miss Marple, Nero Wolfe and Archie Goodwin, Hercule Poirot, Maigret, Ellery Queen(s), and Philip Marlowe
- *Holmes and Watson* by June Thomson
- *James Bond: The Authorized Biography of 007* by John Pearson

- *Jeeves: A Gentleman's Personal* Gentleman by C. Northcote Parkinson (crossover with Father Brown, Hercule Poirot, and Lord Peter Wimsey)
- *John Steed: An Authorized Biography, Volume 1: Jealous In Honour* by Tim Heald (crossover with James Bond)
- "Jonathan Swift Somers III, Cosmic Traveller in a Wheelchair: A Short Biography by Philip José Farmer (Honorary Chief Kennel Keeper)" in *Myths for the Modern Age: Philip José Farmer's Wold Newton Universe* (crossover with Edgar Lee Masters' *Spoon River Anthology*)
- *Leopold Bloom: A Biography* by Peter Costello
- *The Life and Exploits of the Scarlet Pimpernel* by John Blakeney
- *The Life and Times of Hercule Poirot* by Anne Hart
- *The Life and Times of Horatio Hornblower* by C. Northcote Parkinson
- *The Life and Times of Miss Jane Marple* by Anne Hart
- "Michael Shayne as I Know Him" by Brett Halliday in *Four-&-Twenty Bloodhounds*
- *Nero Wolfe of West Thirty-Fifth Street: The Life and Times of America's Largest Private Detective* by William S. Baring-Gould (crossover with Sherlock Holmes)
- "The Obscure Life and Hard Times of Kilgore Trout," by Philip José Farmer in *The Book of Philip José Farmer*, reprinted in *Venus on the Half-Shell and Others*
- *The Official World of Austin Powers* by Andy Lane
- *The Private Life of Dr. Watson: Being the Personal Reminiscences of John H. Watson, M.D.* by Michael Hardwick
- *The Private Lives of Private Eyes, Spies, Crime Fighters, and Other Good Guys* by Otto Penzler. Lew Archer, Modesty Blaise, James Bond, Father Brown, Nick Carter, Charlie Chan, Nick and Nora Charles, Bulldog Drummond, C. Auguste Dupin, Mike Hammer, Sherlock Holmes, Jules Maigret, Philip Marlowe, Miss Jane Marple, Perry Mason, Mr. Moto, Hercule Poirot, Ellery Queen, The Shadow, John Shaft, Sam Spade, Dr. Thorndyke, Philo Vance, Lord Peter Wimsey, and Nero Wolfe
- *Radio's Captain Midnight: The Wartime Biography* by Stephen A. Kallis, Jr.
- *Sherlock Holmes of Baker Street: The Life of the World's First Consulting Detective* by William S. Baring-Gould (crossover with Nero Wolfe)
- *Sherlock Holmes: My Life and Crimes* by Michael Hardwick
- *Sleuths: Twenty-Three Great Detectives of Fiction and Their Best Stories*. Each story features a short biography of the detective in the story; many biographies are by the characters' authors, providing canonicity. The twenty-three detectives are: C. Auguste Dupin, Sherlock Holmes, Martin Hewitt, Eugene Valmont, The Thinking Machine, The Old Man in the Corner, Craig Kennedy, Uncle Abner, Dr. Thorndyke, Father

Brown, Astro, Philip Marsham Trent, Max Carrados, William Dawson, Mr. Reginald Fortune, Hercule Poirot, Jim Hanvey, Superintendent Wilson, Lord Peter Wimsey, Dr. Hailey, J. G. Reeder, Detective Duff, and Henry Poggioli
- *Tarzan Alive: A Definitive Biography of Lord Greystoke* by Philip José Farmer (mega-crossover with countless other heroes, villains, adventurers, and detectives, as part of the Wold Newton Family Tree)
- *The Wimsey Family* by C. W. Scott-Giles
- *Yankee Lawyer: The Autobiography of Ephraim Tutt* by Arthur Train

The Crossover Chronology

For perhaps even longer than I've followed the genre of fictional biographies, I've been a fan of crossovers. It was originally my deep interest in Wold Newton studies which sparked these obsessions, and first led me to seek out and document crossover stories involving characters whom Philip José Farmer had placed in his Wold Newton Family Tree. The idea has since expanded well beyond that basis, leading to my idea of creating and building a consistent universe out of a chronology of crossovers.

The *Crossover Chronology* builds a universe using the fictional biographies listed above as its platform. Put another way, the *Crossover Chronology* plays a "six degrees of separation" game, with the characters from the fictional biographies as the first degree. Given the role of Sherlockian studies in this metafictional Game, it should surprise no one to learn that Sherlock Holmes is, without a doubt, the most crossed-over character in history. It is possible that Count Dracula runs a distant second. H. P. Lovecraft's Cthulhu Mythos also ranks high in the crossover count.

The *Crossover Chronology* also honors the basic tenant of fictional biographies, treating the universe it documents as a series of real, historical events. Of course, this universe only resembles our real world on the surface. Dig deeper, and one finds crimefighters and villains of extraordinary ability and scope, Lovecraftian entities, covered-up alien visitations, and innumerable spy and counter-spy cartels. Still, to the ordinary Joe on the street, this universe very much resembles the world outside our window.

In order to maintain the real-world appearance, crossovers are incorporated using a set of rules and guidelines. I documented these guidelines in *Myths for the Modern Age: Philip José Farmer's Wold Newton Universe* (MonkeyBrain Books, 2005). Although the universe shown in these crossover events has grown many degrees beyond the original Wold Newton mythos, those original guidelines still prove instructive, and are reproduced here, with amendments and revisions. (These guidelines also appeared in my books which kicked off the Crossover Universe in print: *Crossovers: A Secret Chronology of the World*, Volumes 1 & 2, Black Coat Press, 2010.)

The *Crossover Chronology* is a timeline of crossover stories in which two or more literary characters, situations, universes, or, in some rare cases, actual historical personages, are linked together.[1] A very good example is *The Rainbow Affair*, which brings together Sherlock Holmes, Fu Manchu, Nayland Smith, James Bond, Miss Marple, and The Avengers, (all already in the Crossover Universe [CU], based on the list of fictional biographies), with The Men From U.N.C.L.E (Napoleon Solo and Illya Kuryakin), The Saint, Inspector West, and Department Z (all added to the CU per this crossover).

Noncanonical pastiche is the rule, not the exception. This book is not for Sherlockians who devoutly subscribe only to the Canon of the original four novels and fifty-six short stories by Sir Arthur Conan Doyle. Nor is it for fans of *Star Trek* who religiously restrict themselves to the televised episodes and films (and ignore *Star Trek: The Animated Series*).

Derivations from media other than the original are acceptable, as long as they do not explicitly contradict the information in the original source. If a seemingly contradictory story can be shown to fit into the continuity after all, through a scholarly essay, piece of research, or a reconciling theory, so much the better.

Again, when evaluating crossovers, I looked for stories that involve two or more fictional characters and that do not involve contradictions (that are too difficult to resolve) with what is already included. Examples of the latter would be the otherwise enjoyable *Sherlock Holmes and the Hentzau Affair*, and *Superman: War of the Worlds*. These stories are mentioned instead in an appendix on *Alternate Universe Crossovers, Parodies, and Farces*.[2]

---

[1] Fan fiction is not included. An exception to this policy is fiction that is written by professionally published authors, but which goes unpublished for some reason. This exception allows for the inclusion of the following tales, the crossover entries for which appeared in the original two-volume *Crossovers* books:

- *The Final Affair* by David McDaniel (who has many other published *Man From U.N.C.L.E.* novels to his credit);
- *Tarzan on Mars* by "John Bloodstone" aka Stuart J. Byrne (not authorized by ERB, Inc. but Byrne is a professionally published science-fiction author);
- *Farewell Pellucidar* by Allan Howard Gross (author of the ERB, Inc. authorized Sunday *Tarzan* strip and several *Tarzan* comics published by Dark Horse); and
- *Red Axe of Pellucidar* by John Eric Holmes (author of the ERB, Inc.-authorized *Mahars of Pellucidar*, as well as *Mordred*, the authorized sequel to Philip Francis Nowlan's *Armageddon 2419 A.D.*).

[2] Regarding parodies, I am much more likely to include a parody that uses original characters to spoof a genre, such as Derek Flint spoofing the genre of spy films, than I am to include parodies that substantially change preexisting characters, such as those which cast Sherlock Holmes as an addle-headed bumbler, or James Bond as a crossdresser. Nevertheless, I have doubtless bent or broken this "rule" once or twice.

On Historical Figures

When I first began to catalog crossovers, I often used a fictional character meeting an historical character as a way of linking in different fictional characters. After a while, though, it became obvious that certain historical characters made this problematic, Adolph Hitler and Jack the Ripper being two prime examples. Who hasn't met them in some fictional tale? This was too easy. Therefore, I concluded that no more fictional characters should be added on that basis, although I would not retroactively exclude characters previously brought in that way. A side rule to this is that fictional descendants and/or relatives of fictionalized versions of real people can be used to make additions to the Crossover Universe, because this type of crossover is not as over-utilized as the fictional-character-meets-real-person scenario. An example of the fictional relative crossover is a character on the television program *Alias* who states that he is the great-nephew of Harry Houdini. Since a strongly fictionalized version of Houdini exists in the CU, this brings in *Alias*.

Furthermore, if an historical person becomes a bona fide character in a fictional series, then we are dealing with the Crossover Universe version of that person. Therefore, Peter Heck's "Mark Twain-as-a-sleuth" series of mystery books come in through Twain's meeting with Inspector Lestrade, because this is not "our" universe's Mark Twain, it's the CU version of Twain. The same goes for Harry Houdini's numerous appearances in the CU, as well as the historical highwaymen Dick Turpin, Tom King, Cartouche, John "Sixteen String Jack" Rann, and Claude Duval, versus the romanticized, fictionalized versions, and so on.

On Superheroes and Comic Book Universes

The Crossover Universe is not a superhero universe. The CU is grounded in the literary trick that everything being discussed is real and takes place in our world. If an event or characters appear outlandish in real-world terms, then perhaps the events or characters are concealed from the world at large, so that those of us living our day-to-day lives have no idea of the secret history occurring all around us, all the time. Or perhaps the events depicted in the story have been fictionalized and somewhat exaggerated beyond the real events.

If one accepts that the CU at least appears to be the real world, if it is not actually the real world, then one would not expect to see too many superheroes. A supposedly "real world" universe filled with superheroes is not believable. A universe containing only a few superheroes operating in secret (or not operating in secret, but nevertheless regarded as urban legends) is much more believable if one wishes to maintain the premise that, to the general observer, the Crossover Universe is the real world.

This means not only limiting the number of superheroes or "mystery men," but also that these characters must be alternate universe (AU) versions of their comic-universe selves. This is important in order to avoid importing the whole history, continuity, and character set of the comic universe. This applies in particular to the overly "retconned" and continuity-laden DC Comics and Marvel Comics Universes, in which extraterrestrial beings are a fact of life well known to all inhabitants of Earth in the 20th and 21st centuries, and which have a very different sociopolitical dynamic (Marvel's Civil War and the widespread hatred directed towards the mutants of the X-Men, to name but two examples) than the real world does. Earth-CU, to use a comic book naming convention, is not subject to alien invasions and attacks every other month, as seems to occur in the DC and Marvel Universes.

Additionally, it should be assumed across the board that the Crossover Universe versions of superheroes operated for less time than as portrayed by comic book publishers, that they were much less powerful than as described in the exaggerated comics, and that their adventures were considerably less cosmic and earthshaking. This means that there is a preference for superhero references that are set in the particular superhero's original general time frame, such as Superman in the 1930s–40s, or Spider-Man in the 1960s–70s. In a "real-world" continuum like the Crossover Universe, it is unlikely, though not impossible, that Spider-Man would still be operating in the early 21st century, absent an *elixir vitae* such as Fu Manchu's. Therefore, less weight will be given to superhero crossover references that take place late in a particular hero's publishing career and particularly after superhero-universe "reboots" or in the context of a superhero-universe "retcon." Obviously, viable explanations will be considered, such as interpreting the 1986 Batman/Sherlock Holmes crossover as a meeting between Batman III and Holmes.

Having thus established the necessity for limiting the inclusion of superheroes when building a universe that resembles the real world, some general Rules, Guidelines, and Exceptions follow.

The basic rule of the Crossover Universe is: Very few superheroes. This is not because I find some of the powers unbelievable (although some are), but because large numbers of high-powered superheroes would change the nature and outcome of events in this continuity. The goal of the CU is to emulate the real world. This is clearly not the goal of superhero universes such as the DC and Marvel Universes. Too many superheroes make the Crossover Universe less and less similar to the real world. And too many super-powered heroes also overshadow the other heroes like Philip Marlowe and Travis McGee.

The exception to the basic rule is: Superheroes will be admitted if they appear in a crossover with a character already in the Crossover Universe. For example: Batman appears through Tarzan and Sherlock Holmes crossovers. Captain America is in through the appearance in a Green Hornet story. Elongated Man appears through a meeting with Sherlock Holmes, and Plastic Man appears though a connection with The Spirit. Spider-Man comes in because he shared adventures with Red Sonja, King Kull, and Doc Savage.

Rule: Superheroes do not automatically bring in other superheroes through crossovers that take place within their own regular universes, especially the highly continuity-burdened DC and Marvel Universes which are overflowing with superheroes. Instead, these are taken on a case-by-case basis. This rule also applies to non-superheroes from superhero universes. Examples: The Elongated Man does not imply the existence of the Silver Age Flash in the Crossover Universe. The X-Men cannot be added just because they met Captain America. The presence of "Hop" Harrigan does not mean that all the members of the Justice Society of America are in the CU. Red Sonja's battle with Kulan Gath, an evil wizard in Marvel Comics, does not mean that other Marvel superheroes that battled Kulan Gath are incorporated into the CU. Shang Chi does not bring in the other Marvel heroes. The Prowler (who is not technically a superhero anyway) can bring Airboy (also not a superhero) into the CU, but these characters will not necessarily bring the Eclipse Comics Universe's superheroes into the CU. The Shadow's meeting with the Ghost does not necessarily bring in the rest of Dark Horse Comics' superheroes.

Rule: Appearances or cameos of a superhero's alter ego are enough to place that alter ego in the CU, but are not enough to substantiate the presence of the actual superhero. Examples: The mention of Billy Batson in "The New York Review of Bird" is not enough to bring in Captain Marvel. The appearance of Freddy Freeman in Lin Carter's *The Earth-Shaker* does not bring in Captain Marvel Jr. The mention of Donald Blake in the Doc Savage/Thing crossover does not bring in Thor. The mention of Carol Danvers in the Red Sonja/Spider-Man crossover is not sufficient to bring in Ms. Marvel. The appearance of Bruce Wayne in the Prince Zarkon novels is not enough to bring in Batman (but Batman comes in anyway through his meetings with Tarzan and Sherlock Holmes). The appearance of Clark Kent in a Green Hornet story does not suffice to link in Superman (but Superman does come in via more solid Crossover Universe links in the stories "Three Men, a Martian, and a Baby" and "War Between Two Worlds").

Exception: Even though technically only Steve Rogers appears in the Green Hornet crossover, he is definitely Captain America; otherwise, he would be portrayed as quite scrawny and emaciated.

Rule: Once a superhero is already validly included, that superhero can bring in other characters, as long as the other characters are not from an overly continuity-laden universe like the DC and Marvel Universes. Examples: A reference to the *Daily Star* newspaper from Superman is sufficient to bring in a pulp-like African-American hero, Captain Gravity. Likewise, the appearance of the *Daily Planet* newspaper in a Jon Sable comic serves to substantiate Sable's presence in the CU.

Rule: Characters such as Dracula and the Frankenstein Monster are not automatically valid crossover links; many different comic publishers (and films, for that matter) have portrayed conflicting versions of Dracula and so they must be evaluated on a case-by-case basis. Example: Although Dracula is a character in the Crossover Universe, the Marvel Comics Universe version of Dracula does not automatically bring in every Marvel superhero that Dracula ever met. If the Marvel version of Dracula meets another Marvel character who has a valid, independent link to the Crossover Universe, then that crossover can also be interpreted as valid. For example, a version of Dr. Strange exists in the Crossover Universe via a reference in a Dr. Zarnak tale, "The Deep Cellars;" since Marvel's *The Tomb of Dracula* series fits well with CU continuity, via links to Alexandre Dumas' Count Cagliostro and Robert E. Howard's King Kull, it is likely that the Dracula-Dr. Strange clash depicted in the pages of Marvel Comics also occurred in the CU.

Rule: Inter-company crossovers from independent publishers (i.e. not DC or Marvel) that are based on promotional marketing strategies will be evaluated on a case-by-case basis to determine if they mesh with or violate continuity. Example: Vampirella's promotional crossovers with characters from other publishers, such as ShadowHawk, Lady Death, Purgatori, and Shi, are taken on a case-by-case basis to ensure that they fit into continuity; many do, and many do not. The same goes for the many crossovers involving Tomb Raider, Shi, Darkchylde, Witchblade, Spawn, Cyblade, Darkness, Avengelyne, Glory, the 10th Muse, Pandora, etc.

Rule: Superhero teams, particularly from the DC and Marvel Universes, are generally excluded. There is not enough time in a realistic chronology of a hero's life to have all of his/her own adventures and have regular adventures with a formally organized superteam. Additionally, the menaces superteams face are almost always cosmic or at least earth-shattering in scope. One cannot theorize the concealment of all these events from the public in the hopes of maintaining the facade of a "real" world—the sheer numbers are too great.

Exception 1: "Family" superhero teams like the Fantastic Four are more likely. Besides the family connections and going through the origin of their superhero powers together, they tend to have most of their adventures together and not individually. Cameos of superhero teams in individual hero's comic books can be excluded as cross-promotional ploys designed to encourage readers to try other comics. This leaves out the following examples:

- The brief appearance of a Marvel Comics superteam, The Avengers, in an Iron Man comic book which features Fu Manchu; the Iron Man/Fu Manchu connection remains intact; and
- The appearance of Scott Summers and Jean Grey (from The X-Men) in an Iron Fist comic which features Del Floria's Tailor Shop (from *The Man From U.N.C.L.E.*); the Iron Fist/U.N.C.L.E. connection remains intact.

Exception 2: A commando type of superteam, expressly brought together for one, or perhaps two missions, is more realistic—as long as the characters who are part of the team have valid, independent links into the Crossover Universe which follow the rest of these guidelines. In this way, perhaps a Crossover Universe version of the World War II team code-named "The Invaders" (comprised of Captain America, Bucky, and the Sub-Mariner, who all have valid independent CU links) performed one or two assignments, although certainly not all the ongoing missions depicted in forty-one issues of the original *Invaders* comic series from Marvel Comics. Likewise, so many Golden Age DC Comics heroes have valid connections to the CU, independent of crossovers with other DC superheroes, that one might be tempted to postulate that in the Crossover Universe they banded together and performed one or two missions under the direction of President Franklin D. Roosevelt, calling themselves the "Justice Society of America." However, the JSA as an ongoing superteam, and their intertwined continuity with the DC Universe, must be dismissed as contradictory with mainstream Crossover Universe continuity.

Rule: Multiversal connections: There are so many Cthulhu Mythos references throughout Marvel and DC comics that they cannot be treated as an automatically valid connector, or else the combined DC/Marvel Universes would subsume the CU. Therefore, the Cthulhu Mythos will be treated as existing across multiple universes, when it comes to superhero crossovers from DC Comics and Marvel Comics. Likewise, there are a few Predator and Aliens stories that have strong connections to the Crossover Universe, but many tales are not in continuity. The Predators and Aliens are treated as races which exist in many parallel universes.

Any crossover that appears to be valid and passes these rules and guidelines must still pass the bar of being non-contradictory with existing Crossover Universe continuity. Therefore, even if a comic book hero meets a character from one of the listed fictional biographies, or a character in a valid crossover chain, it is not necessarily a genuine crossover for purposes of Crossover Universe continuity.

For instance, there have been several G.I. Joe/Transformers crossovers in comics. G.I. Joe is nominally in the Crossover Universe because Action

Force, the European counterpart to the G.I. Joe team, met Shang Chi, and CU primary links Fu Manchu and Nayland Smith were mentioned in the story. So far, this is a valid crossover chain. However, the alien giant robots featured in the *Transformers* violate the overall guiding principle that the Crossover Universe, on the surface, must resemble the world outside our window, and thus they are excluded. As with all crossovers, the settings, characters, and time placement must harmonize with whole of the Crossover Universe.

Some might argue that the inclusion of mystical characters such as Witchblade, H. G. Wells' Martian Invasion, occult monsters like Dracula, or Lovecraftian entities violates the real world premise—that in fact they do not harmonize with the continuity of the Crossover Universe—in the same way that the inclusion of all of DC and Marvel's costumed super-powered heroes would. Granted that such creatures of the night and events are not part of our real world, inhabitants of the Crossover Universe would also maintain that such creatures are not part of their world, or are urban legends. The world at large would not know of the 1898 Martian Invasion, which was covered up or is now dismissed as an event that "never really happened." It would be hard to similarly cover up or dismiss giant alien robots using Earth as a battleground for twenty years running.

Conversely, inhabitants of the DC or Marvel Universes would know about and readily report on events such as the Superhuman Registration Act in the aforementioned Civil War event from Marvel Comics. Average citizens of Earth would know that at least something was up with the multiple Crises that routinely afflict their world in the DC Universe. They would know about the worldwide devastation meted out in Marvel's World War Hulk series. The Marvel and DC Universes are increasingly about yearly colossal, world-changing events with lasting sociopolitical repercussions.

Thus, seemingly unrealistic characters or events can be included in the Crossover Universe, as long as, again, the CU appears to the average Joe to be the world outside our window.

Besides, who's to say that clandestine and mystical cabals like the Illuminati and the Nine Unknown really haven't been secretly ruling the world since time immemorial?

Conjecture

As previously mentioned, sometimes crossover stories or events are included in the Crossover Universe which, on their face, appear to be mutually exclusive or contradictory. Sometimes crossover characters are included on the basis of a genealogical relationship with a prior included character, but the exact familial relationship is not mapped out. These circumstances require, or at least open the door to, a limited integration of conjecture in order to reconcile these disconnects or gaps. The conjecture is included on three bases:

- For the purpose of filling in genealogical "holes";[3]
- For reconciling seemingly conflicting information;[4] and
- For answering "burning questions" which are raised by different elements of the Crossover Universe.[5]

It should be noted that conjectural theories are not used to create a crossover which is not otherwise a crossover on its face. The crossovers listed herein are from documented appearances in published media—books, comics, film, television, and so on. They are crossovers on their own merits, not constructed based on creative theorizing.[6]

---

[3] As an example, the inclusion of the character Clive Reston (*Master of Kung Fu* comic series) left open the question of his parentage. It was established in the series that James Bond was Reston's father, and his great-uncle was Sherlock Holmes. Matthew Baugh postulated that Mycroft Holmes was Reston's grandfather, and that Mycroft Holmes had a daughter who had an affair with James Bond. As seen in the short story "The Eye of Oran" (*Tales of the Shadowmen Volume 2: Gentlemen of the Night*, Black Coat Press, 2006) I named the daughter "Shrinking" Violet Holmes, married her off to British agent Charles Reston, killed off Reston, and gave Violet and Bond a child: Clive Reston. The crossover entry for "The Eye of Oran" is in *Crossovers: A Secret Chronology of the World, Volume 2*.

[4] An example of reconciliation is my explanation in the *Crossover Chronology* of the history of Professor Moriarty and Captain Nemo, and the inclusion of Rick Lai's "The Secret History of Captain Nemo" (*Myths for the Modern Age: Philip José Farmer's Wold Newton Universe*, MonkeyBrain Books, 2005). Lai views some events as completely fictional, while Prof. H. W. Starr and Philip José Farmer believe other events to be fictional. My explanation, found in the original *Crossovers* volumes from Black Coat Press, views all the recorded events as having happened, and attempts to meld them together, thus rescuing the Prince Dakkar character and the events of Jules Verne's *The Mysterious Island* from the fictional oblivion to which Starr consigned them.

[5] An example here is my answer to the burning question raised by the inclusion of H. G. Wells' Martian Invasion from his novel *The War of the Worlds* (via Sherlock Holmes and *League of Extraordinary Gentlemen* crossovers), *Superman*, and *The X-Files* (connected to the Cthulhu Mythos): if humanity has a past history of contact with extraterrestrial beings, why is Dana Scully such a disbeliever in alien life? My answer, seen in the original *Crossovers* books, is certainly conjecture, but it is conjecture within the established facts and boundaries of the Crossover Universe.

[6] That said, these are my own editorial metafictional musings and dot-connectings, not necessarily an authoritative bible to the original intent of the many authors whose works I cite. For instance, Philip José Farmer took extreme care never to claim that Sahhindar, the Gray-Eyed God from *Hadon of Ancient Opar* and *Flight to Opar*, was Tarzan. In the addenda to *Hadon*, he intentionally infers that Sahhindar is the time traveler from *Time's Last Gift*, nowhere mentioning an Edgar Rice Burroughs connection.

Some creative mythological essays or conjectural theories are referred to as background info, in order to explain published crossovers which are contradictory. For instance, Chuck Loridans' "soul-clone" theory is cited in order to explain a multitude of contradictory Dracula crossovers which otherwise would not fit into one continuity.

Put another way, the crossovers themselves do not emanate from speculative theories; speculative theories are used to explain some of them. If the amount of speculation needed to reconcile strains believability (and believability is subjective, of course), then the crossover is listed in the Alternate Universes Appendix since it is not in mainstream Crossover Universe continuity.

There are some ambiguous references that could be interpreted either as to a fictional or pop culture figure, or to a real person within continuity. There is a preference for the latter interpretation, as it allows for more inclusions, but is usually applied regarding pop cultural references to figures or series which already have strong, valid ties to Crossover Universe continuity, such as Sherlock Holmes: "He's a regular Sherlock Holmes!"

The Handoff

Accurately documenting thousands of crossovers stories and reconciling them into a single continuity is a mammoth effort. Even as my original two-volume *Crossovers* was hot off the presses in 2010, I knew it was out of date. There were many tales of which I was aware, but hadn't had room to include. Other crossover comics and novels had been announced, but were not published in time to include. And, of course, more new tales came out every year.

And yet the thought of acceding to fans' requests and devoting another several years to follow-up books filled me with a dread of Lovecraftian proportions. I love crossovers, obviously, but was ready to spend my creative energies in new areas.

Enter Sean Lee Levin. I had known Sean online for several years as a devotee of Philip José Farmer's Wold Newton mythos. His posts showed a clear head and strong understanding of the subject matter. Sean was always able to dig up that obscure fact or citation, even those of which I only had a vague recollection.

In many Wold Newton discussion forums, it is also natural to discuss crossovers, even though they are generally separate (if adjacent) topics. Sean occasionally posted crossovers write-ups of new stories utilizing my own *Crossovers* format.

It only took a few such posts to know that Sean *got* my Crossover Universe continuity. Lock, stock, and barrel.

And it took zero arm-twisting to convince him to step into my shoes and write the next two books.

Little did he know . . .

Sean has devoted the past several years to identifying, collating, and documenting as many crossovers as possible in preparation for these new volumes—*Crossovers Expanded*—perfectly following the conventions and standards established in my original *Crossovers* books. His meticulous research will prove to be an essential resource to fans of crossovers, metafiction, and pop culture.

And on a more personal note, it has been a pleasure getting to know Sean better and working with him over the past several years, including annual meet-ups at PulpFest/FarmerCon, in Columbus, OH, where we and many other fans have a chance to come together and renew our geek cred with one another.

Without further ado, I present you with *Crossovers Expanded*. Enjoy the feast!

Win Scott Eckert
Monroe, Louisiana
April 2016

Introduction

Even as a child, I was aware of what crossovers were. Like many kids, my first exposure to the concept was through comic books. When I was about four- or five-years-old, and intrigued by comics even before I'd fully learned to read, my father bought the trade paperback collection *DC/Marvel Crossover Classics*, which reprinted the various stories published in treasury editions and one-shots in the 1970s and 1980s in which DC Comics and Marvel Comics had their heroes teaming-up, beginning with Superman joining forces Spider-Man to fight Lex Luthor and Doctor Octopus, and culminating with the New Teen Titans and the X-Men battling Darkseid, who sought to resurrect the Dark Phoenix. I found something indefinably cool about the idea of these characters who would otherwise never meet having adventures together. I had further exposure to the idea of crossovers through contemporary comics stories and the odd television show, including reading the first volume of Alan Moore and Kevin O'Neill's *The League of Extraordinary Gentlemen* in my early teens. When I discovered Philip José Farmer's Wold Newton writings (which had in fact influenced Moore and other writers) in 2002, my interest in crossovers increased tenfold. The idea that characters from different works of fiction, pulp heroes and Great Detectives, cowboys and secret agents, could conceivably meet each other, was immensely appealing to me. When my dear friend and fellow Farmerphile Win Scott Eckert's magnum opus *Crossovers: A Secret Chronology of the World* was published in two volumes by Black Coat Press in 2010, I was one of the first to purchase copies, and devoured each of the two volumes in a couple of days. It was also gratifying to have my name listed in the acknowledgments of both volumes for providing Win with several pieces of crossover info.

In December 2011 and early 2012, I posted *Crossovers*-style write-ups of several works not included in those books on a Wold Newton group on Yahoo that Win and I both belonged to. He was so impressed by these that he brought up the possibility of me doing a follow-up to his own work. Four years of near-daily research later, you hold this book in your hands. It was through my love of crossovers that I discovered the Wold Newton Universe, and through that cultivated friendships with other Farmer and Wold Newton fans, especially Win. The Crossover Universe as outlined by Win and myself is a rich tapestry crossing mediums and genres, where P. G. Wodehouse's Bertie Wooster can become involved in H. P. Lovecraft's Cthulhu Mythos. and the jungle lord can team up with Sherlock Holmes.

As the title suggests, *Crossovers Expanded* builds on Win's timeline, rather than beginning even further into the future from when *Crossovers* ends. Both pairs of books cover the history of the Crossover Universe from the dawn of time to the far future, and are therefore best read in conjunction to get a full picture of that history. To know all the details of what happened in the Crossover Universe (CU) in 1935, one should consult the listings for that year in *Crossovers Volume 1* and *Crossovers Expanded Volume 1*, respectively. Only then can you begin to appreciate the larger-than-life (albeit not publicly known) history of this vast shared universe.

The Latest and Greatest

The Crossover Universe is ever expanding as new connections are forged by writers, artists, filmmakers, and others, some working deliberately within the framework of the Universe, and many more adding to it without even realizing the fact. *Crossovers Expanded* is split into two volumes. The first encompasses the Dawn of Time to 1939, with accompanying appendices covering TV crossovers brought in by "six degrees" reasoning, and Kim Newman's works in the "*Anno Dracula* Universe and Character Guide." The second volume covers 1940 to the far future, and includes an appendix outlining various Alternate Universe stories that, for various reasons, cannot be included in the main timeline.

Although every effort has been made to make these books as complete as possible, there are a number of works with crossover references that could not be included due to space and timing issues. These include much of the interconnected fiction of Stephen King, Kim Newman's *The Secrets of Drearcliff Grange School*, the Sackett series and related works by Louis L'Amour, Talbot Mundy's various works set on the Indian subcontinent, and several stories published by Black Coat Press.

In addition to these, the following crossovers have been announced, but could not be included in the present volumes due to the aforementioned matters of space and time.

- A story by Larry Correia and Jonathan Maberry, whose title has not yet been announced, teaming Agent Franks from Correia's *Monster Hunter International* series with Maberry's series character Joe Ledger, included in *Urban Allies*, an upcoming anthology of collaborative stories by urban fantasy authors crossing over their respective characters
- *Aliens/Vampirella*, miniseries by Corinna Bechko and Javier Garcia-Miranda, Dynamite Entertainment
- *Angels of Music, or: Phantom Ladies Over Paris* by Kim Newman, a novel melding Newman's stories "Angels of Music," "Angels of

Music II: The Mark of Kane," and "Guignol," featuring various female characters of the late 19th and early 20th centuries acting as agents of the Phantom of the Opera, in the style of *Charlie's Angels*
- *Kolchak Double Feature*, a collection of two novellas by Chuck Miller, featuring Kolchak encountering Domino Patrick (the Domino Lady's daughter) and Zero, a character created by Miller and based on the original pulp hero Captain Zero
- *Kolchak: The Phoenix Rising* by Paul Kupperberg and David Bryant, in which Kolchak meets Bennu, the main character of the 1982 television series *The Phoenix*
- *Kolchak, the Night Stalker/Dan Shamble: Zombie P.I.*, one-shot comic by Kevin J. Anderson, Richard Dean Starr, and Sergio Ibanez
- *Lords of the Jungle*, a miniseries by Corinna Bechko and Roberto Castro, featuring Tarzan and Sheena
- *Sherlock Holmes and the Servants of Hell* by Paul Kane, in which Holmes battles the Cenobites of the *Hellraiser* film series.

In the pages that follow, you will discover the history of a world resembling the one outside our window on the surface, but which has a hidden wellspring of fantastic events and individuals. It is our mundane world made extraordinary. The Land of Fiction is a massive realm, and these books are effectively a map to it. Hopefully it will lead the readers to explore this universe and the works contained within it further, just as Win's books prompted me to do.

Sean Lee Levin
Chicago, Illinois
January 2016

Crossovers Expanded Volume 1: Dawn of Time–1939

10,812 B.C.E.–10,810 B.C.E.

EXILES OF KHO

The priestess Lupoeth leads a band of her fellow Khokarsan exiles on a journey which results in the fulfillment of a prophecy she will found a great city. The god Sahhindar accompanies them, and says the city founded by Lupoeth and her companions will be very important to him. The foreword states the bulk of the story is derived from the recently discovered notebooks of Sir Beowulf William Clayton, the Oxford linguist who provided a partial translation of Phileas Fogg's secret diary. The story has been reconstructed from Clayton's translation of a tablet enigmatically designated "Holly 27-A." Sahhindar refers to the  star-shaped being from which the roots of the Tree of Kho emanate. Sahhindar and other members of Lupoeth's group, including the priest Methquth, are captured by the K'goroshanaka tribe. Sahhindar later tells Lupoeth ingesting the *nethkarna*, the seed of the Tree, caused Methquth to experience visions of the future of Khokarsa.

 Novella by Christopher Paul Carey, Meteor House, 2012. *Exiles of Kho effectively serves as a prequel to Philip José Farmer's Ancient Opar series, detailing how Lupoeth arrives at the site where she will build the city of Opar, from Edgar Rice Burroughs' novels about Lord Greystoke. Sahhindar is the immortal, time-traveling Greystoke himself, as readers of the Opar books and Farmer's* Time's Last Gift *will recognize. Sir Beowulf William Clayton, a distant cousin of the jungle lord, is from Farmer's* The Other Log of Phileas Fogg. *Holly is a reference to Ludwig Horace Holly from H. Rider Haggard's novel* She *and its sequels. In* She, *Ayesha states her oracular powers only encompass events in Africa; her ability is derived from the same source as Methquth's. According to Farmer, Ayesha's native city, Kôr, was founded by Kohr, the son of Hadon of Opar. The star-shaped being is from Farmer's translation and adaptation of J.-H. Rosny aîné's* Ironcastle. *The K'goroshanakas are the ancestors of the Goura-Zannkas from* Ironcastle.

c. 10,000 B.C.E.

WITCHBLADE/RED SONJA

Red Sonja battles the fallen angel Ragniel alongside Nissa, wielder of the powerful Witchblade. Thanks to the actions of 21st century Witchblade host Sara Pezzini, the weapon joins with Sonja, who kills several of Ragniel's minions with it, and returns it to Nissa, who finally imprisons Ragniel within his own tomb.

Five-issue miniseries by Doug Wagner and Cezar Razek, Dynamite Entertainment, 2012. Both Witchblade and Red Sonja have strong independent links to the CU; this crossover confirms they exist in the same universe. Sara's own battle with Ragniel takes place in 2011.

THE CRIMSON WELL

Red Sonja battles a time-traveling Dracula, who turned her into a vampire during their previous encounter in 2012.

Red Sonja: She-Devil with a Sword #76-80 by Brandon Jerwa and Sergio Fernandez Davila, Dynamite Entertainment, 2013. Sonja met Dracula when she was transported through time to the year 2012 in the miniseries Prophecy. *This Dracula is a "soul-clone" of the true Lord of the Vampires, and has had several run-ins with Vampirella.*

GROO VS. CONAN

Conan finds himself in battle with a dimwitted wandering swordsman named Groo.

Four-issue miniseries by Mark Evanier, Sergio Aragonés, and Thomas Yeates, Dark Horse Comics, 2014. This crossover brings Evanier and Aragonés' character Groo into the CU. The Groo stories are set in an unspecified era in the distant past that could conceivably be an exaggerated version of the Hyborian Age. The framing sequences featuring Evanier and Aragonés themselves take place in an alternate reality to the CU.

CONAN/RED SONJA

Conan and Red Sonja join forces to battle Thoth-Amon, who seeks to overrun the world with the deadly Bloodroot.

Four-issue miniseries by Gail Simone, Jim Zub, and Dan Panosian, Dark Horse Comics, January–April 2015.

RED SONJA/CONAN

Red Sonja and Conan battle the sorcerer Kal'Ang, who has acquired the same Bloodroot previously used by Thoth-Amon.

Four-issue miniseries by Victor Gischler and Roberto Castro, Dynamite Entertainment, 2015. This story is a sequel to Conan/Red Sonja.

c. 2400 B.C.E.

KING OF THE BASTARDS

A barbarian king battles Meeble of the Thirteen.

Novel by Brian Keene and Steven Shrewsbury, Apex Publications, 2015. The Thirteen are the main villains of Keene's Labyrinth cycle. The year is conjecture, based on a mention these events take place before the Great Flood.

1336 B.C.E.

DREAM'S END

Barbarella pursues Duran-Duran from the 40th century to ancient Egypt, and encounters the Time Traveler and Manse Everard of the Time Patrol in the process. Weena, the Eloi, the Danellians, Professor Ping, and the Morlocks are mentioned, and Lord Dianthus, Dard Kelm, and Sinahu appear.

Short story by Paul Hugli in Tales of the Shadowmen Volume 11: Force Majeure, *Jean-Marc and Randy Lofficier, eds., Black Coat Press, 2014. Barbarella appeared in French science fiction comics by Jean-Claude Forest. Duran-Duran, Professor Ping, and Lord Dianthus are from Roger Vadim's film version of Forest's comic. Barbarella's future timeline is but one of many possible futures for the CU. The Time Traveler, Weena, the Eloi, and the Morlocks are from H. G. Wells' novel* The Time Machine. *Manse Everard, the Time Patrol, the Danellians, and Dard Kelm appear in a series of books by Poul Anderson. Sinahu (or Sinuhe) is from Mika Waltari's novel* The Egyptian.

29 CE

Jesus Christ vs. Ob, Lord of the Siqqusim, in Brian Keene's short story "The Resurrection and the Life."

41

THE WEDDING OF SHEILA-NA-GOG

Simon of Gitta visits Regio Averonum, an area of Gaul. He finds himself aligned with a tribe called the Averoni, who worship a god named Sadoqua and command large black cats. Fighting Simon and his allies are the Black Goat Druids, adherents of the goddess Sheila-na-gog, who was originally in Acheron and Hyperborea. Simon throws a corrupt Roman official into Sheila-na-gog, and she gives birth to a monster who "was small and had the shape of a rat, but its pallid bearded face and handlike forepaws were evilly human."

Story by Richard L. Tierney and Glenn Rahman in Crypt of Cthulhu #29. *Rick Lai writes, "Regio Averonum is a chronologically earlier version of the region of France later known as Averoigne in 'The Holiness of Azéderac' and other stories by Clark Ashton Smith. Sadoqua is an alias which Smith used for his demon-god Tsathoggua. The name Regio Averonum and the black cats were actually ideas of H. P. Lovecraft's, which were given to Smith in the correspondence between the two authors (see Lovecraft's* Selected Letters IV: 1932-1934, *letters #669, 674, and 685). Lovecraft also came up with the idea of a tribe called the Averones, whose name was changed to Averoni in the Simon of Gitta story. Acheron is from Robert E. Howard's 'Black Colossus' and* Conan the Conqueror, *while Hyperborea is a polar continent described by Clark Ashton Smith. Sheila-na-gog has the form of a pool which gives birth to monsters. The appearance and nature of Sheila-na-gog are virtually identical with Abhoth the Unclean, the Hyperborean deity from Clark Ashton Smith's 'The Seven Geases.' I don't think Sheila-na-gog and Abhoth are the same deity. I suspect that they are either father and daughter, or sister and brother, or son and mother. The monsters spawned by Sheila-na-gog only have a long life span if a human being is thrown into Sheila-na-gog first. The goddess devours a human and fashions a spawn from his flesh. Sheila-na-gog's spawn in this story could be Brown Jenkin from Lovecraft's 'The Dreams in the Witch-House.'*

48

THE GARDENS OF LUCULLUS

Simon of Gitta battles Empress Messalina of Rome alongside gladiator Rufus Hibernicus. Messalina is a priestess of the Magna Mater ("Great Mother"), who is identified with Shupnikkurat. Ikribu and Rebathoth are mentioned.

This novel by Richard L. Tierney and Glenn Rahman connects Rahman's gladiator Rufus Hibernicus, the protagonist of Heir of Darkness, to Tierney's Simon of Gitta, and therefore to the Crossover Universe. Rick Lai writes, "Linking Rufus to Simon raises an apparent contradiction between the two series. Both Rahman's Heir of Darkness and Tierney's 'The Ring

of Set' are set in 37 CE and deal with the death of Emperor Tiberius. In Heir of Darkness, Tiberius' nephew, Caligula, conspires with the sorcerer Zenodotus to bring about the Emperor's death through black magic. Zenodotus gives Tiberius the ring of Andvaranaut, a magical ring linked to the Nordic goddess Heid, who is identified as an alias for Shupnikkurat (an alias for H. P. Lovecraft's Shub-Niggurath which is also used in Tierney's 'The Seed of the Star-god.') Tiberius touches the ring, but decides not to wear it. The ring still causes him to die under unrecorded circumstances during the night. After his death is announced by Caligula, the ring briefly reanimates Tiberius' corpse to warn his nephew that the Great Old Ones will demand a price for their assistance. In 'The Ring of Set,' Tiberius puts on the ring of Thoth-Amon (from Robert E. Howard's 'The Phoenix on the Sword'), and a demon from this ring kills the Emperor. The theory which I have to reconcile the discrepancy is that the ring of Andvaranaut influenced Tiberius to put on the ring of Thoth-Amon and consequently die from the other ring's effects. The ring of Andvaranaut is clearly more powerful than the ring of Thoth-Amon.

"According to Tierney's 'The Seed of the Star-god,' Shupnikkurat's husband, Assatur (aka August Derleth's Hastur the Unspeakable), has sent various meteors or meteorites to Earth to be used by his wife's worshippers in magical rites. These magical meteors are known as Ajar-Alazwats. One Ajar-Alazwat was battled by Red Sonja in Star of Doom (a collaboration between Tierney and David C. Smith), and then combated by Simon in 'The Seed of the Star-god.' This Ajar-Alazwat became buried in the Arabian Desert in 31 CE. In The Gardens of Lucullus, Simon and Rufus come into contact with another Ajar-Alazwat in Rome. Tierney probably intends some connection between these Ajar-Alazwats and the meteor from Lovecraft's 'The Color Out of Space.' The Ajar-Alazwat in Star of Doom affects the Hyborian countryside in ways similar to the manner in which Lovecraft's meteor affected an area of the Miskatonic Valley.

"In Seabury Quinn's 'The Hand of Glory,' an archaeologist discovers an artifact identified as the Sacred Meteorite of the Magna Mater in Syria, and brings it to Harrisonville, New Jersey, where it is stolen by evil cultists. This object is supposed to be a meteorite covered by clay. Jules de Grandin supposedly destroys this occult symbol in a rite of exorcism which causes an abandoned church to collapse. De Grandin claims that this symbol of the Magna Mater was just clay, and no meteorite was inside it. All the clay is found shattered and nothing else is found. There may really have been a meteorite inside this relic. I suspect that the meteorite could have been an Ajar-Alazwat, and that the meteorite buried itself deep within the ground of Harrisonville as a result of the exorcism. Ikribu was created by David C. Smith in his Attluma/Oron series, and Red Sonja came into conflict with the deity in The Ring of Ikribu. Rebathoth is described in detail in Rahman's 'The Sun of God' from the fanzine Nyctalops #14."

c. 500

ST. GEORGE

Prince Valiant and Aleta's daughters Karen and Valeta rescue Aleta's soul from the netherworld to which it had been banished by the sorceress Maldubh, and in the process also rescue a heroic blond stranger who had helped Aleta in the realm of banished souls. Aleta dubs the amnesiac stranger St. George. He introduces a sport identical to the 20th century's polo to the people of Camelot, and wears a tunic with a symbol of a sun on it. After helping Valiant and company defeat a rampaging golem, St. George remembers his true name. However, before he can utter it, a bolt of lightning strikes, and "the blond warrior disappears—in a flash!"

Story by Mark Schultz in the Prince Valiant Sunday strip, December 2011–March 2012. "St. George" is Alex Raymond's interplanetary hero Flash Gordon, who was a famous polo player before he traveled to Mongo. The sun symbol on "St. George's" tunic is associated with Mongo. When and how he ended up in the land of lost souls is unknown, but it can be presumed time flows differently in that realm, hence Flash ending up in the time of King Arthur. This story ran untitled.

SURELY YOU JOUST

Sir Dagonet, jester and Knight of the Round Table, and the mage Ganieda (Gani for short), Merlin's twin sister, journey to the kingdom of Lyonese to recruit a knight of its court to join the knights of Camelot, but wind up nearly being sacrificed to Father Dagon. The knights of Lyonese ride Byakhee. Gani gives Dagonet an amulet inscribed with the Elder Sign.

Short story by Patrick Thomas in Cthulhu Unbound Volume 2, Thomas Brannan and John Sunseri, eds., Permuted Press, 2008. Sir Dagonet (aka the Infinite Jester) appears in Thomas' Murphy's Lore series and its spin-offs. Father Dagon and the Elder Sign are from H. P. Lovecraft's Cthulhu Mythos tales. The Byakhee are from Mythos stories by August Derleth. The connection to the Mythos cements the Murphy's Lore Universe as part of the larger CU.

616–617

THE SHIP FROM ATLANTIS

Gwalchmai, the half-Aztec son of the Roman centurion Ventidius Varro and the godson of Merlin, meets Corenice, an Atlantean who prolonged her life by transferring her soul into a body made of orichalcum. Corenice's account of Atlantis' fall mentions Valusia and Cimmeria.

The second novel in H. Warner Munn's Merlin's Godson *series, which consists of* King of the World's Edge, The Ship from Atlantis, *and* Merlin's Ring. *The references to Valusia (from Robert E. Howard's Kull stories) and Cimmeria (from Howard's Conan tales) bring this series into the CU.*

900

Winter
CASTLE ATLANTE

Jirel of Joiry encounters the sorcerer Malagigi, who reveals he brought her to Castle Atlante on her way back to her native time period. Malagigi asks Jirel if she is the Eternal Champion. Malagigi believes Jirel has been sent by the Cosmic Balance to protect the Castle from the forces of the Dark Tower. Meanwhile, noticing the Castle and the Tower, Doctor Omega decides to investigate. Malagigi gives Jirel the sword of Bradamante. At the same time, the Master of the Dark Tower begins to awaken. This being has held many identities: Rasalom, Randall Flagg, Voilodion Ghagnasdiak, and Nyarlathotep. He chooses Wampus as his current form. Jirel, Omega, and Malagigi are greeted by Sir Agilulf, the Nonexistent Knight. Suddenly, all four of them are attacked by the Hounds of Tindalos. Malagigi says the Atlanteans' knowledge of science was already ancient when the ancestors of the Babylonians faced the Xipehuz, and it predates the Kingdom of Valusia. Jirel finds herself in a shared dream with her old acquaintance, 20th century native Jules de Grandin.

Short story by Olivier Legrand *in* Doctor Omega and the Shadowmen, *Jean-Marc and Randy Lofficier, eds., Black Coat Press, 2011; reprinted in French in* Les Compagnons de l'Ombre (Tome 8), *Jean-Marc and Randy*

Lofficier, eds., Rivière Blanche, 2011. *Jirel of Joiry is a female warrior created by C. L. Moore. This story serves as a sequel to Legrand's "Lost in Averoigne" (*Tales of the Shadowmen Volume 8: Agents Provocateurs, *Jean-Marc and Randy Lofficier, eds., Black Coat Press, 2011). Malagigi, Castle Atlante, and Bradamante are from Ludovico Ariosto's epic poem* Orlando Furioso. *The Eternal Champion, a being with many incarnations in the works of Michael Moorcock, is chosen by the Cosmic Balance. Voilodion Ghagnasdiak, also created by Moorcock, appears in* The Sleeping Sorceress *(aka* The Vanishing Tower*) and* The King of the Swords, *and is mentioned in* The Bull and the Spear *and* The Quest for Tanelorn. *The Dark Tower is from the series of novels of the same name by Stephen King. Randall Flagg appears in that series, as well as several other novels by King. Rasalom appears in F. Paul Wilson's Adversary Cycle of novels. Nyarlathotep, aka "The Crawling Chaos," is from the Cthulhu Mythos fiction of H. P. Lovecraft. Wampus is a French comic book character created by Franco Frescura and Luciano Bernasconi. In King's* The Stand, *Nyarlathotep is listed as one of Flagg's other names. The revelations about Flagg's origins in the final Dark Tower novel make it unlikely he is actually the same being as Nyarlathotep, but Flagg may have "borrowed" the identities of the Crawling Chaos and the other beings in the course of his own evil deeds. Sir Agilulf is from Italo Calvino's novel* The Nonexistent Knight. *The Hounds of Tindalos are from the titular short story by Frank Belknap Long. The Xipehuz are from J.-H. Rosny aîné's short story "Les Xipéhuz." The Kingdom of Valusia is from Robert E. Howard's Kull stories. Jules de Grandin is Seabury Quinn's occult detective.*

1225

Summer
LOST IN AVEROIGNE

The priest Azedarac swears by the Black Goat with a Thousand Young and is assaulted by the female warrior Jirel of Joiry. Azedarac flees to 1925, only to find Jirel has followed him. Jirel is later returned to her own time by Jules de Grandin.

Short story by Olivier Legrand appearing in Les Compagnons de l'Ombre (Tome 6), *Jean-Marc and Randy Lofficier, eds., Rivière Blanche, 2010, and in English in* Tales of the Shadowmen Volume 8: Agents Provocateurs, *Jean-Marc and Randy Lofficier, eds., Black Coat Press, 2011. Azedarac is from Clark Ashton Smith's story "The Holiness of Azédarac." Shub-Niggurath, "the Black Goat with a Thousand Young," is from H. P. Lovecraft's Cthulhu Mythos. Jules de Grandin is an occult investigator featured in stories by Seabury Quinn.*

1227

June
QUEST OF THE STARSTONE

Jirel of Joiry steals the Starstone jewel from the sorcerer Franga, who summons the outlaw Northwest Smith and his Venusian companion Yarol from the future to retrieve it for him.

Short story by C. L. Moore and Henry Kuttner in Weird Tales, *November 1937. The 1500 date given for this story does not fit with references to weapons of the Middle Ages in this and other Jirel stories by Moore, or with her appearance in the year 1225 in Olivier Legrand's story "Lost in Averoigne," and must be considered an error. Moore's Northwest Smith stories take place in a future where mankind has colonized other worlds, all of which are inhabitable. This would place Smith's adventures in an alternate reality to the CU, Jirel's native world.*

1300

ARMY OF DARKNESS/VAMPIRELLA

Ash Williams encounters Vampirella, who was dragged along when he was sent back in time by the *Necronomicon Ex Mortis*, and together they battle the Deadites.

Four-issue miniseries by Mark Rahner and Jethro Morales, Dynamite Entertainment, 2015. This story takes place during the events of the original film Army of Darkness.

1470–1477

VAMPIRE RENAISSANCE

A quote from Armand Tesla's *The Supernatural and Its Manifestations* is given. Count Marcian Gregoryi attempts to scalp his unfaithful wife, the Countess Addhema, but is killed by Addhema and her lover, Janos Szandor.

Addhema's maiden name is Yorga. King Matthias Corvinus later assigns Count Szandor to be Prince Dracula's aide-de-camp. Szandor says his and Addhema's son will be cared for by his brother-in-law, Count Yorga. Dracula reveals to Addhema he is descended from the Draconic Adder, also known as the Drac. The Adder's parents were Yiggurath, Father of Serpents, and Tiamit, the Dragon of Arabu. The Lemurians worshiped the Adder under the name Slidith. Minions of the other Great Old Ones preyed on Dracula's ancestors. Yiggurath also mated with Adana the Snake Mother, producing Set, the Great Serpent, who in turn spawned the Serpent Men of Hyperborea, who warred on humanity alongside the Werewolf Folk and the winged Akaana. Slidith empowered a group of mortals as the Red Brotherhood to wage war on the Serpent Men and their allies. The Brotherhood was aided by Slidith's offspring, the Dragon Kings. Records of Slidith were unearthed in Stygia by a sorcerer named Rammon. Rammon inducted Princess Akivasha into Slidith's service. The Viceroy of Slidith is also referred to as the Great Vampire. Simon the Mage killed Pontius Pilate, who had become the Viceroy. Dracula bought a knife from French warlock Gilles Grenier.

Short story by Rick Lai in Tales of the Shadowmen Volume 8: Agents Provocateurs, *Jean-Marc and Randy Lofficier, eds., Black Coat Press, 2011; reprinted in French in* Les Compagnons de l'Ombre (Tome 11), *Jean-Marc and Randy Lofficier, eds., Rivière Blanche, 2013, and* L'Almanach des Vampires, *Jean-Marc and Randy Lofficier, eds., Rivière Blanche, 2014; and in* The Vampire Almanac (Volume 1), *Jean-Marc and Randy Lofficier, eds., Black Coat Press, 2015. Armand Tesla is from the film* The Return of the Vampire. *Count Gregoryi, Countess Addhema, and Count Szandor are from Paul Féval's novel* The Vampire Countess. *Count Yorga is from the films* Count Yorga, Vampire *and* The Return of Count Yorga. *Dracula is, of course, from the novel by Bram Stoker. Yiggurath is from Robert Bloch's Cthulhu Mythos story "The Grinning Ghoul"; Lai identifies Yiggurath with Yig, who first appeared in "The Curse of Yig," a posthumous collaboration between Zealia Bishop and H. P. Lovecraft. Tiamit (or Tiamat) is from Robert E. Howard's story "The House of Arabu." Slidith is from Lin Carter's tales of Thongor of Lemuria; here, he is identified with Draco from Peter Tremayne's trilogy of novels consisting of* Dracula Unborn *(aka* Bloodright), The Revenge of Dracula, *and* Dracula, My Love, *and the Drac from Sylvie Miller and Philippe Ward's novel* The Song of Montsegur. *Richard L. Tierney's novel* The House of the Toad *implied Draco was one of the Great Old Ones from the Cthulhu Mythos. Adana is from A. Merritt's novel* The Face in the Abyss. *Set is from Robert E. Howard's Conan stories; L. Sprague de Camp and Lin Carter conflated Set with the Great Serpent worshipped* by the Serpent Men in Howard's *King Kull* stories. Clark Ashton Smith linked the Serpent Men to the Great Old Ones. The Werewolf Folk are from Howard's poem "A Song of the Werewolf Folk." The Akaana are from Howard's Solomon Kane story "Wings in the Night." The Red Brotherhood and the Dragon Kings are from the Thongor stories. Rammon is mentioned in the Conan story "The Phoenix on the Sword." Akivasha is from the Conan novel The Hour of the Dragon. *In Louis Feuillade's film serial* Les Vampires, *the leader of the titular gang is called the Great Vampire. Simon the Mage is better known as Simon of Gitta from Richard L. Tierney's collection* The Scroll of Thoth; *he slew the vampirized Pontius Pilate in "The Dragons of Mons Fractus." Gilles Grenier is from Clark Ashton Smith's story "The Mandrakes."*

1520

Spring
TEQUILA'S SUNRISE

A fourteen-year-old Aztec boy named Chalco is given access to the Labyrinth so he can kill Hernán Cortés before he arrives in the New World, and prevent the fall of the Aztec Empire. The *Daemonolateria* is quoted: "To open doors, one must first know how to find them." The Thirteen are mentioned, including Behemoth, Leviathan, Api, and Ob, Lord of the Siqqusim. Huitzilopochtli, the Aztec god of war, mentions several different names for the being known as Quetzalcoatl, including "Jesus of Nazareth, Adonis, Mohammad, Buddha, Divimoss, Kurt Cobain, Prosper Johnson, Benj—." While traveling the Labyrinth, Chalco sees into different worlds and time periods, witnessing a flooded world from which giant tentacles attack him, several people sealed inside a strange metal room, a group of pig-faced humanoids, a world where "the dead get up and hunt the living," a planet overcome with living darkness, a tribe of goat-men who dance around a fire and rut with terrified human women, people on an island fleeing from savage monsters, and a coastline overrun with crab-lobster-scorpion monsters. After reaching his destination, Chalco is attacked by Meeble, the planned assassination of Cortés fails, and history continues as recorded.

Short story by Brian Keene, found in his collections Unhappy Endings, Tequila's Sunrise, *and* Blood on the Page. *The Labyrinth is a recurring location in Keene's works, an other-dimensional realm that connects all the various realities and parallel universes; this story provides the most extensive glimpse into the Labyrinth. All the worlds connected by the Labyrinth are threatened by a group of beings known as the Thirteen, pre-Universal monsters that travel from reality to reality destroying Earths. These beings are Ob, Ab, Api, Leviathan, Behemoth, Kandara, Meeble, Purturabo, Nodens, Shtar, Kat, Apu, and one more unknown to readers at this time. Ob, Ab, and Api are from Keene's novels* The Rising, City of the Dead, *and* Clickers vs. Zombies, *as well as several short stories; these all take place in an alternate reality to the CU, with the exception of Keene's "The Resurrection and the Life." Leviathan and Behemoth appear in Keene's novels* Earthworm Gods, Deluge: Earthworm Gods II, Earthworm Gods: Selected Scenes form the End of the World, *and* Clickers III: Dagon Rising, *all also alternate realities. Although Leviathan is conflated by Keene with Cthulhu and Dagon, in the reality of the CU, they are separate beings. Kandara appears in Keene's story "Babylon Falling"; its name is a reference to the Kandarian demons from the* Evil Dead *movies. Meeble appears in this story, and its minions are the villains of Keene's novel* A Gathering of Crows. *Purturabo appears in Keene's story "Caught in a Mosh." Nodens is the villain of Keene's novels* Ghost Walk *(which takes place in the CU) and* Darkness at the Edge of Town *(which doesn't). Shtar appears in Keene's story "The Cage." The* Daemonolateria *is a fictional book of magic that appears in a number of Keene's works, including "Caught in a Mosh,"* Dark Hollow, *and* Ghost Walk; *it is not to be confused with a real-world book called the* Daemonolatreia. *Prosper Johnson is a minor character mentioned in several Keene stories, most importantly in "Slouching in Bethlehem." "Benj-" is Benjy from Keene's novel* Terminal, *which is also the source of the people in the strange metal room (a bank vault). The pig-faced humanoids are a shout-out to William Hope Hodgson's novel* The House on the Borderland. *The world of the living dead could be any of Keene's various zombie universes: the worlds seen in his* The Rising *series, his novels* Dead Sea *and* Entombed, *or his comic* The Last Zombie. *The planet overcome with living darkness is from Keene's novel* Darkness at the Edge of Town. *The goat-men are a reference to the satyr from Keene's novel* Dark Hollow. *The island monsters are from Keene's novel* Castaways, *and the crab-lobster-scorpion creatures are from Keene and J. F. Gonzalez'* Clickers *trilogy (though the first book was written by Gonzalez and Mark Williams) and* Clickers vs. Zombies, *all different levels of the Labyrinth to the CU.*

1582

BLOOD QUEEN VS. DRACULA: WORLD PAINTED BLOOD
Dracula encounters Elizabeth Bathory, also known as the Blood Queen.

Four-issue miniseries by Troy Brownfield and Kewber Baal, *Dynamite Entertainment*, 2015. This crossover features the version of Elizabeth Bathory seen in the Dynamite comic Blood Queen. At some point after this series, Elizabeth becomes a vampire herself, as seen in the movie Daughters of Darkness *and other accounts.*

1598

June 22–23
QUEST OF THE VOURDALAKI
A group of vampires including Yvgeni, Vseslav, Hella, and Gorcha ride the Steppes in pursuit of two men, one of whom is a sorcerer or alchemist. Vseslav instructs Yvgeni to infiltrate the Cossack camp their targets have arrived at, and make contact with another minion of his who has infiltrated it named Boris Liatoukine. Yvgeni is greeted by a Cossack named Ayub. Liatoukine tells Yvgeni the Koshovoi Ataman ordered the men he is seeking be placed in the stocks. Khlit convinces Liatoukine and Yvgeni not to kill the two captives. Ivan Sabalinka releases the men from the stocks. The sorcerer identifies himself as Quentin Moretus Cassave, and tells the Cossacks a group of witches are planning to raise the demon Chernabog to Earth, which he will take over. Menelitza says Khlit, his godfather, will lead the group seeking to prevent this. The other members of the expedition include Ayub; Sabalinka; Zaroff (who prefers a Tartar warbow to pistols); his servant, a huge man named Ivanushka; Taras and his brother Doroscha; and Cassave and his companion, whom he refers to as "Magister."

Short story by Matthew Baugh in Tales of the Shadowmen Volume 10: Esprit de Corps, *Jean-Marc and Randy Lofficier, eds., Black Coat Press, 2013; reprinted in French in* Les Compagnons de l'Ombre (Tome 15), *Jean-Marc and Randy Lofficier, eds., Rivière Blanche, 2014, and* L'Almanach des Vampires, *Jean-Marc and Randy Lofficier, eds., Rivière Blanche, 2014; and in* The Vampire Almanac (Volume 1), *Jean-Marc and Randy Lofficier, eds., Black Coat Press, 2015. Yvgeni is the narrator of Baugh's story "The Heart of the Moon," which takes place in 1790. Vseslav is an historical Russian prince who was reputed to be a vampire and werewolf. Hella is from Mikhail Bulgakov's novel* The Master and Margarita. *The Magister is the Master of the book's title, who is actually Satan. Gorcha is an ancestor of Gorcha, the title character of Alexei Tolstoy's novella* The Family of the Vourdalak. *Boris*

Liatoukine is the title character of Marie Nizet's novel Captain Vampire, which has been translated for Black Coat Press by Brian Stableford. Ayub, the Koshovoi Ataman, Khlit, and Menelitza are from pulp stories by Harold Lamb. Ivan Sabalinka (originally spelled Sablianka) is from Robert E. Howard's "The Road of the Eagles." Quentin Moretus Cassave is from Jean Ray's novel Malpertuis. Zaroff and Ivanushka are ancestors of General Zaroff and Ivan from Richard Connell's "The Most Dangerous Game." Taras and his brother Doroscha are from Nikolai Gogol's novella Taras Bulba.

1604

Summer
THE LAST OF THE GUARANYS

Immortal time traveler John Gribardsun rescues a beautiful young woman named Cecilia from attackers. He tells her he is Peri, the only survivor of the decimated Guarany tribe.

Short story by Octavio Aragão and Carlos Orsi in The Worlds of Philip José Farmer 3: Portraits of a Trickster, Michael Croteau, ed., Meteor House, 2012; reprinted in Tales of the Wold Newton Universe, Win Scott Eckert and Christopher Paul Carey, eds., Titan Books, 2013. Gribardsun, one of the main characters of Farmer's novel Time's Last Gift, was strongly implied to be the jungle lord whose tales were told by Edgar Rice Burroughs. This story in turn reveals the character of Peri from Brazilian author José de Alencar's novel O Guarani was really Gribardsun pretending to be the last surviving Guarany Indian.

1639–1641

FIAT LUX!
In 1965, Quentin Travers reports to the Watchers Council about Marquis Henri-Jean de Sainte-Claire's duel in 1639 with Cyrano de Bergerac. Injured by Cyrano, the Marquis is tended to by Comte de Rochefort, and discovers

he now has the ability to see in the dark. A footnote states, "Historical records indicate that some members of the Sainte-Claire family later shortened their name to Saint-Clair during the French Revolution, when Louis-Jean de Sainte-Claire, a friend of the notorious Sir Percy Blakeney, helped save numerous members of the French aristocracy from the blade of the guillotine." Henri-Jean routs a plot against France whose conspirators include two alleged Spaniards whose fourth fingers are bent, and who possess an unusual vehicle and weaponry. Travers suggests these may in fact have been Invaders from another world. He also notes the Greek historian Manetho's papyrus details a warrior caste created by Aten's high priest Merira, the leader of which was endowed by Aten with the ability to see in the dark. This man was able to transfer this power to his descendants. Travers suggests Henri-Jean may have been a descendant of this warrior, and he may in turn have passed the ability onto his own descendant Leo Saint-Clair, aka the Nyctalope, just as there has been a line of Slayers since time immemorial.

Report by Quentin Travers, edited by Emmanuel Gorlier in Tales of the Shadowmen Volume 7: Femmes Fatales, *Jean-Marc and Randy Lofficier, eds., Black Coat Press, 2010; reprinted in French in* Les Compagnons de l'Ombre (Tome 7), *Jean-Marc and Randy Lofficier, eds., Rivière Blanche, 2011; and in* The Nyctalope Steps In, *Jean-Marc and Randy Lofficier, eds., Black Coat Press, 2011. Quentin Travers, the Watchers Council, and the Slayers are from the television series* Buffy the Vampire Slayer. *Marquis Henri-Jean de Sainte-Claire is the ancestor of Jean de La Hire's hero the Nyctalope. The Comte de Rochefort appears in Alexandre Dumas' novels* The Three Musketeers *and* Twenty Years After. *Sir Percy Blakeney is, of course, better known as the Scarlet Pimpernel. The "Spaniards" are actually members of the titular alien race from the 1960s television series* The Invaders. *Manetho is a historical figure, but his papyrus is from Edgar P. Jacobs' Belgian comic book series* Blake and Mortimer.

1655

July
THE BROTHERHOOD OF MERCY
The Comte d'Artagnan and a group of his fellow Musketeers ride ahead of a carriage bearing the coat of arms of the Archdiocese of Vyones in Averoigne. Inside the carriage is Archbishop Henri de Ximes. After the Archbishop's assassination, d'Artagnan meets with Cardinal Mazarin alongside a group of men which includes Henri-Jean de Sainte-Claire, Cyrano de Bergerac, and Baron d'Ylourgne. Cyrano prevented an attempt on the life of

the Duc de Nevers by his old foe, the Comte de Duras, and other members of the Brotherhood of Mercy. Cyrano dies in the arms of a woman in a convent.

Short story by Emmanuel Gorlier in Tales of the Shadowmen Volume 10: Esprit de Corps, *Jean-Marc and Randy Lofficier, eds., Black Coat Press, 2013; reprinted in French in* Les Compagnons de l'Ombre (Tome 13), *Jean-Marc and Randy Lofficier, eds., Rivière Blanche, 2014. D'Artagnan is a historical figure whose life was fictionalized by Alexandre Dumas in* The Three Musketeers *and its sequels. Vyones, Averoigne, Ximes, and Ylourgne are from supernatural fiction by Clark Ashton Smith. Henri-Jean de Sainte-Claire is the ancestor of Jean de La Hire's hero Leo Saint-Clair, aka the Nyctalope; Henri-Jean shares his descendant's ability to see in complete darkness. Cyrano de Bergerac is another historical figure whose life was dramatized by Edmond Rostand in a play. The woman in the convent is Cyrano's beloved Roxane. The Duc de Nevers is an ancestor of the Duc seen in Paul Féval's* Le Bossu.

1667

Summer. Captain Henry Morgan helps the Three Musketeers rescue the Man in the Iron Mask (*Unter Schwarze Flagge*, 1908).

1685; 1625; 1685

THE SCREECHING OF TWO RAVENS
Captain Peter Blood and his crewman Jeremy Pitt find themselves sixty years in the past, where they encounter Milady Clarice de Winter. Blood mentions Governor Bishop.
Short story by Bradley H. Sinor in Tales of the Shadowmen Volume 7:

Femmes Fatales, *Jean-Marc and Randy Lofficier, eds., Black Coat Press, 2010; reprinted in French in* Les Compagnons de l'Ombre (Tome 8), *Jean-Marc and Randy Lofficier, eds., Rivière Blanche, 2011. Captain Peter Blood, Jeremy Pitt, and Governor Bishop are from the Captain Blood books by Rafael Sabatini. Milady Clarice de Winter is from Alexandre Dumas'* The Three Musketeers.

1756

Spring
FORT OF SKULLS

In the Miscatonic Valley, Hawkeye, Uncas, and Chincachgook lead a group of British Redcoats to a fort, where the soldiers begin to be picked off by the cannibalistic Misqas tribe. Trooper McCrothy states, "You've heard the stories too, though, sarge... You must have, back in Ipswich. Strange lights under the sea at Dunwich point. That siren they saw on the Manuxet River by the Inns-Mouth. That island in the Miscatonic with the sacrifice stone. Those dug-up graves on Hangman's Hill."

Story by I. A. Watson in Pride of the Mohicans, *Van Allen Plexico, ed., White Rocket Books, 2014, connecting James Fenimore Cooper's Leatherstocking Tales to H. P. Lovecraft's Cthulhu Mythos.*

1766

Autumn
THE DARKNESS IN THE WOODS

Doctor Joseph Balsamo travels to New Orleans, where he is asked by Louisiana's acting governor to investigate a rash of murders of local Indians. Some of the natives say the killings are the work of the *Jibbenainosay*, which translates as "Spirit That Walks." Balsamo questions a little girl named Atala who survived one of the killer's attacks. Atala was named after a woman with whom her ancestor was deeply in love. Two potential suspects are a pirate captain named Clegg and a Quaker called Wandering Nathan. Clegg's ship is called the *Imogene*. Clegg, whose true name is Christopher Syn, claims to have killed Black Satan. The killer turns out to be Wandering Nathan, whose last name is Slaughter. The watch commander on duty when Balsamo and Clegg captured Slaughter was named Childress. Balsamo and Clegg discover a makeshift man made of twigs, branches, and a human skull, dressed in a pale, yellow cloak. They realize there was a second killer.

Short story by Nathan Cabaniss in Tales of the Shadowmen Volume 11: Force Majeure, *Jean-Marc and Randy Lofficier, eds., Black Coat Press, 2014.*

Joseph Balsamo, Count Cagliostro, *is an historical figure who also appeared in novels by Alexandre Dumas, and was identified as the founder of a villainous branch of the Wold Newton Family in* Doc Savage: His Apocalyptic Life. *Nathan Slaughter (aka the* Jibbenainosay*) is from Robert Montgomery Bird's novel* Nick of the Woods. *Atala is a descendant of the Natchez Chactas, whose love for the earlier Atala was chronicled in François-René de Chateaubriand's novel named for the latter. The Reverend Doctor Christopher Syn (aka Captain Clegg), the* Imogene, *and Black Satan appear in novels by Russell Thorndike. Childress, implicitly the second killer, is the ancestor of serial killer Errol Childress from the television series* True Detective, *who was connected to the Yellow King of Carcosa from Robert W. Chambers'* The King in Yellow.

1770

Summer
DECAPITATOR ASAEMON

Yamada Asaemon, sword-tester for the *shogun*, is dispatched to kill Ogami Ittō, the *shogun*'s executioner turned *ronin*. Asaemon does not survive the battle.

Chapter 27 of Kazuo Koike and Goseki Kojima's manga (comic book) Lone Wolf and Cub. *Koike and Kojima would later chronicle Yamada's life prior to his battle with Ogami in the manga* Samurai Executioner. *Since* Lone Wolf and Cub *takes place in the CU through references in stories by Rick Lai, so does* Samurai Executioner.

1776

Winter
WHAT LURKS IN ROMNEY MARSH?

Doctor Omega's companions Denis Borel and Fred are stranded in the village of Dymchurch, near Romney Marsh. Omega's other companion, the Martian Tiziraou, is mentioned. Fred refers to other time travelers, such as Omega's friend from Oxford, the madman Rotwang, Doctor Moses Nebogipfel, and an Englishman whose name he cannot recall. Denis requests the aid of the Vicar of Dymchurch, Doctor Christopher Syn, as well as his sexton Mister Mipps. Denis and Fred end up battling the alien Red Lectroids alongside the Scarecrow of Romney Marsh, an older version of Fred himself, and Josie Bauer.

Short story by Travis Hiltz in Tales of the Shadowmen Volume 9: La Vie en Noir, *Jean-Marc and Randy Lofficier, eds., Black Coat Press, 2012; reprinted in French in* Les Compagnons de l'Ombre (Tome 14), *Jean-Marc and Randy Lofficier, eds., Rivière Blanche, 2014. Doctor Omega, Denis Borel, Fred, and Tiziraou are from Arnould Galopin's novel* Doctor Omega. *Jean-Marc and Randy Lofficier's adaptation and translation of Galopin's book implied that Omega was actually the CU counterpart of the Doctor of* Doctor Who *fame. Omega's friend at Oxford is Professor Chronotis from the unfinished* Doctor Who *serial "Shada," written by Douglas Adams, and Adams' novel* Dirk Gently's Holistic Detective Agency. *Rotwang is from Thea von Harbou's novel* Metropolis *and its classic silent film adaptation by von Harbou's husband Fritz Lang. Doctor Omega encountered Rotwang in Hiltz's story "The Robots of Metropolis" (*Tales of the Shadowmen Volume 7: Femmes Fatales, *Jean-Marc and Randy Lofficier, eds., Black Coat Press, 2010). Doctor Nebogipfel is from H. G. Wells' tale "The Chronic Argonauts"; Doctor Omega encountered him in Martin Gately's "Wolf at the Door of Time," which is also collected in* Tales of the Shadowmen Volume 9. *The Englishman whose name Fred cannot recall is the Time Traveler from H. G. Wells'* The Time Machine. *Doctor Christopher Syn is also known as the pirate Captain Clegg and the smuggler the Scarecrow of Romney Marsh in novels by Russell Thorndike; Mr. Mipps, besides being Doctor Syn's sexton, aids Syn's alter egos as well. The Red Lectroids are from the film* The Adventures of Buckaroo Banzai Across the Eighth Dimension. *Josie Bauer is the adopted daughter of Philip José Farmer and an agent of the Time Police in Spider Robinson's* Callahan's Crosstime Saloon *books; per Dennis E. Power's story "Bronze Lady Down," (*Doctor Omega and the Shadowmen, *Jean-Marc and Randy Lofficier, eds., Black Coat Press, 2011), Josie is also the biological granddaughter of Doctor Omega.*

1777

Spring
HE WHO LAUGHS LAST

Two smugglers who are members of the Gentlemen of the Night (aka the Brotherhood of Mercy) are killed by the Scarecrow of Romney Marsh (aka Dr. Christopher Syn and Captain Clegg). The Scarecrow's beloved Charlotte is mentioned. The Scarecrow is confronted by the leader of the

Gentlemen, Colonel Bozzo-Corona, who threatens him by saying should any harm come to him, his minions will expose Syn's comrades Mr. Mipps and Jimmie Bone as smugglers.

Short story by Matthew Dennion in Tales of the Shadowmen Volume 10: Esprit de Corps, *Jean-Marc and Randy Lofficier, eds., Black Coat Press, 2013; reprinted in French in* Les Compagnons de l'Ombre (Tome 15), *Jean-Marc and Randy Lofficier, eds., Rivière Blanche, 2014. The Gentlemen of the Night are from Paul Féval's* The Mysteries of London. *The Brotherhood of Mercy and Colonel Bozzo-Corona are from Féval's series of books featuring the criminal conspiracy known as the Black Coats. The Scarecrow of Romney Marsh (aka Dr. Christopher Syn and Captain Clegg), Charlotte Cobtree, Mr. Mipps, and Jimmie Bone are from a series of books by Russell Thorndike.*

1779

July–October 3
THE HIDDEN CHILDREN

An American soldier in the Revolutionary War named Loskiel learns he was discovered as an orphaned infant by three Mohican Indians, Mayaro, Uncas, and the Great Serpent, in 1757, during the French and Indian War.

1914 novel by Robert W. Chambers. Mayaro seems to be Chambers' creation, but Uncas and the Great Serpent (Chingachgook) are major characters in James Fenimore Cooper's novel The Last of the Mohicans. *Philip José Farmer identified Uncas and Chingachgook's companion Natty Bumppo as the ancestor of a branch of the Wold Newton Family in* Doc Savage: His Apocalyptic Life. *This novel is part of a series that also includes* Cardigan *(1901),* The Maid-at-Arms *(1902),* The Reckoning *(1905),* The Little Red Foot *(1920), and* America; or, The Sacrifice *(1924).*

1789

Spring
THE REVOLUTIONARY AND THE BRIGAND

Albert Lecoq, Philippe Buonarroti, and Pasquale Paoli discuss the *Veste Nere*, which is described as "a brotherhood of brigands, like the Camorra in Southern Italy, or the Beati Paoli in Sicily." The *Veste Nere*'s leader is known only as the All-Father. Paoli was allied with him once, in the days of Rinaldo Rinaldini and Nicolas Patropoli. Buonarroti tells the All-Father he does not agree with the views of his fellow Illuminati, such as Gerolstein and Lebrenn.

Short story by Jared Welch in Tales of the Shadowmen Volume 11: Force Majeure*, Jean-Marc and Randy Lofficier, eds., Black Coat Press, 2014. Albert Lecoq is from Philip José Farmer's biography* Tarzan Alive; *he is the father of Lecoq de la Perière of the Black Coats ("Veste Nere" in Italian), a criminal society featured in novels by Paul Féval, and the grandfather of Emile Gaboriau's sleuth Monsieur Lecoq. The Black Coats' leader is Colonel Bozzo-Corona, also known as the All-Father. Nicolas Patropoli is also from the Black Coats series. The Beati Paoli is from a book by Luigi Natoli, although it may have been based on a real group of that name. Rinaldo Rinaldini is from* Rinaldo Rinaldini, the Robber Captain *by Christian Vulpius. Gerolstein is from Eugène Sue's* The Mysteries of Paris, *while Lebrenn is from Sue's* The Galley Slave's Ring.

Spring 1792–Summer 1794; Summer 1996

A SHARPNESS ON THE NECK

In Revolutionary France, Vlad Dracula repays a debt of honor to Philip Radcliffe, illegitimate son of Benjamin Franklin, who has been sentenced to the guillotine through the machinations of Vlad's brother Radu as retribution for saving Vlad's unlife. Radu was revived by a group of grave-robbers that included Jerry Cruncher. Imprisoned alongside Radcliffe in *La Conciergerie* are Percy Blakeney and Charles Darnay. Vlad's companion and fellow *nosferatu* Constantia tells him an Englishman, "Barton or Garton, or some name like that" switched places with Darnay, and went to the guillotine in his stead. As the prisoners are being loaded into the tumbrils, it is discovered Blakeney has escaped. Madame Defarge is one of the *tricoteuses* present at Radcliffe's seeming execution. Radcliffe's lover, Melanie Romain, has a 10-year-old illegitimate son named Auguste by a deceased former lover named Charles Dupin. Vlad reveals after Radcliffe and the Romains fled to London, "little Auguste fell in with his paternal grandfather, himself a successful refugee. Old Monsieur Dupin conceived a liking for this youngster, wanted him to bear the family name, and more or less adopted him. I have heard that Melanie's child, like many another exile, returned in a few years to France, at a time when Bonaparte promised glory and that in later life he formed some vague connection with the Parisian police." Two centuries later, Vlad saves Philip Radcliffe's descendant and namesake and his wife June from Radu's vengeance.

Novel by Vlad Dracula, edited by Fred Saberhagen, 1996. Vlad is not the Dracula of Bram Stoker's novel, but rather one of his "soul-clones"; see Dennis E. Power's article "Best Fangs Forward" (found at the Wold Newton Universe: A Secret History *website) for more information. Jerry Cruncher, Charles Darnay, the Englishman (Sydney Carton), and Madame Defarge are from Charles Dickens'* A Tale of Two Cities. *Sir Percy Blakeney is the alter ego of the Scarlet Pimpernel; Sir Percy must have devised a way to preserve his dual identity after escaping from prison. At first glance, Auguste would appear to be the detective C. Auguste Dupin, from the stories by Edgar Allan Poe; however, his age and genealogy do not fit with the information given by Philip José Farmer in* Tarzan Alive. *We must assume Saberhagen's Auguste (note the absence of the first initial) Dupin was a relative of Poe's Dupin, and the person who inspired him to become a detective.*

1793

Spring
HOPE FOR FORGIVENESS
The Scarlet Pimpernel attempts to provide safe passage out of France to a woman named Lenore (who, unbeknownst to him, is a vampire), but is prevented from doing so by Captain Kronos.

Short story by Matthew Dennion in The Vampire Almanac (Volume 1), *Jean-Marc and Randy Lofficier, eds., Black Coat Press, 2015; reprinted in French in* L'Almanach des Vampires (Tome 2), *Jean-Marc and Randy Lofficier, eds., Rivière Blanche, 2015. The Scarlet Pimpernel is from Baroness Orczy's novels. Lenore is the title character of a ballad by Gottfried August Bürger, first published in 1774. Captain Kronos is from the Hammer film* Captain Kronos–Vampire Hunter.

1795

November 19–23
NADINE'S INVITATION

Lady Marguerite Blakeney writes to Countess Nadine Carody, inviting her to winter with her and her husband, Sir Percy, at Blakeney Hall, near Would Newton. She mentions Alice, and names some of the other people that will be joining them: the Darcys (including Lizzie), the Duke of Holdernesse, Baron Tennington, and M. and Mme. Delagardie. Nadine writes a letter to Colonel Bozzo-Corona announcing her attendance, and asks him to chastise his man Lecoq for ogling her. Lecoq writes to the Colonel from the Calyx Bar about Nadine's eccentric behavior. Dr. Siger Holmes writes to Sir Percy he trailed Lecoq to the Bar and the *Cordon Jaune* brothel. Holmes reminds Sir Percy the Colonel and the Brothers of Mercy aided them in the de Musard matter by supplying Alice and Marguerite with the Heart of Ahriman. Nadine writes to her master, who has Brides and a Transylvanian stronghold.

Collection of letters by Marguerite, Lady Blakeney; Countess Nadine Carody; Colonel Bozzo-Corona; Lecoq; and Dr. Siger Holmes, edited by Win Scott Eckert in Tales of the Shadowmen Volume 7: Femmes Fatales, *Jean-Marc and Randy Lofficier, eds., Black Coat Press, 2010; reprinted in French in* Les Compagnons de l'Ombre (Tome 9), *Jean-Marc and Randy Lofficier, eds., Rivière Blanche, 2012, and* L'Almanach des Vampires, *Jean-Marc and Randy Lofficier, eds., Rivière Blanche, 2014; and in* The Vampire Almanac (Volume 2), *Jean-Marc and Randy Lofficier, eds., Black Coat Press, 2015. This story is the second in Eckert's Wold Newton Origins series, which elaborate upon the circumstances of the gathering at Wold Newton on December 13, 1795. Sir Percy Blakeney (aka the Scarlet Pimpernel) and his wife Marguerite are from novels by Baroness Orczy. The Darcys are Fitzwilliam Darcy and his wife Elizabeth (née Bennet) from Jane Austen's* Pride and Prejudice. *According to* Tarzan Alive, *they, along with Sir Percy,* were present at the meteor strike. Countess Nadine Carody is from Jesús Franco's film Vampyros Lesbos; her master is Count Dracula. Colonel Bozzo-Corona and the Brothers of Mercy are from Paul Féval's novels about the criminal conspiracy known as Les Habits Noirs (aka the Black Coats). The Calyx Bar is from Louis Feuillade's serial Judex. The Cordon Jaune brothel is from Casino Royale, the first James Bond novel by Ian Fleming. The de Musard matter was the subject of Eckert's story "Is He in Hell?" (Tales of the Shadowmen Volume 6: Grand Guignol, Jean-Marc and Randy Lofficier, eds., Black Coat Press, 2010). De Musard is an ancestor of Baron de Musard from Philip José Farmer's authorized Doc Savage novel Escape from Loki. The Heart of Ahriman is from Robert E. Howard's Conan novel The Hour of the Dragon. Other references from Tarzan Alive: Alice is Alice Clarke Raffles, Sir Percy's future second wife and the great-great-aunt of A. J. Raffles; the Duke of Holdernesse is meant to be John William Clayton, 3rd Duke of Greystoke and great-great-grandfather of the jungle lord (H. W. Starr's essay "A Case of Identity, or, The Adventures of the Seven Claytons" identified the 6th Duke of Holdernesse from the Sherlock Holmes story "The Adventure of the Priory School" with the 6th Duke of Greystoke, a theory adapted by Farmer); Baron Tennington is the ancestor of both the jungle lord and his cousin Edward from The Return of Tarzan; M. and Mme. Delagardie are Honoré Delagardie and his wife Philippa (née Drummond; both are ancestors of Lord Peter Wimsey, while Philippa is a collateral ancestor of Bulldog Drummond); Lecoq is Albert Lecoq, father of Lecoq de la Perière of Les Habits Noirs and grandfather of Monsieur Lecoq; and Dr. Siger Holmes is Sherlock Holmes' great-grandfather.

December 11–13
THE WILD HUNTSMAN

John Gribardsun and XauXaz of the Nine (aka Larsen and Baron von Hessel) have a fateful encounter revolving around a meteor strike in the village of Wold Newton. Appearing or mentioned are: Sir Percy Blakeney; General Sir Hezekiah Fogg; Dr. Siger Holmes; Colonel Bozzo-Corona; Albert Lecoq; Sir Hugh Drummond; Honoré Delagardie; Iain Bond; William de Winter; Gerolstein; Philippa Delagardie; Fitzwilliam Darcy; George Edward Rutherford, the 11th Baron Tennington; John Clayton, the 3rd Duke of Greystoke; Countess Nadine Carody; the Calyx Bar; Marguerite, Lady Blakeney; Alice Clarke Raffles; the Brothers of Mercy; the Heart of Ahriman; Baron de Musard; Elizabeth Darcy; Miss Caroline Bingley; Alicia, Lady Greystoke; Lady Tennington; Violet Clarke Holmes; Elizabeth de Winter; Lady Drummond; another Baron de Musard in the late 1500s in

France; Gustavas Kramm; Miss Bingley's brother; Louis Lupin; Arthur Blake; Etienne Austin; the Capelleans and Eridaneans; the *H. G. Wells I*; Khokarsa; the Door of Kho; a massive crystalline root system; Dr. Jacob Moishe; the Gokako; Lupoeth; Sahhindar, the Grey-Eyed Archer God; the *nethkarna*; the Tree of Kho; a time distorter; a Royal Jelly treatment; Sherlock Holmes; the Oil of Life; a Mastermind from the Far East; James Clarke Wildman; the "human magnetic moment"; a pulp hero with moldable white skin; Shraask; Anana; Iwaldi; Ebnaz XauXaz and Thrithjaz; John Cloamby, Lord Grandrith; Doctor James Caliban; Wildman's wife; a private clinic in New York; and Wildman's daughter, Patricia.

Short story by *Win Scott Eckert in* The Worlds of Philip José Farmer 3: Portraits of a Trickster, *Michael Croteau, ed., Meteor House, 2012; reprinted in* Tales of the Wold Newton Universe, *Win Scott Eckert and Christopher Paul Carey, eds., Titan Books, 2013. This story explains the reason why so many people were at the remote village of Wold Newton when a meteor fell there in 1795. XauXaz, the Nine, Anana, Iwaldi, Ebnaz XauXaz, Thrithjaz, John Cloamby, Lord Grandrith; and Doctor James Caliban are featured in Farmer's trilogy of novels consisting of* A Feast Unknown, Lord of the Trees, *and* The Mad Goblin. *In these novels, XauXaz is portrayed as the inspiration for legends of the Norse god Wotan. In* Tarzan Alive, *Farmer noted Wotan was an ancestor of the jungle lord, and suggested he may have been responsible for the meteor coming to Earth in Wold Newton. Shraask is from the unpublished fourth book in the Grandrith/Caliban series,* The Monster on Hold. *The latter novel implies, and this story confirms, Grandrith and Caliban's exploits occur in a parallel universe to the CU. Characters from Farmer's* Tarzan Alive *and* Doc Savage: His Apocalyptic Life *include: Dr. Siger Holmes and his wife Violet Clarke, ancestors of Sherlock Holmes; Albert Lecoq, father of Lecoq of the Black Coats and grandfather of Monsieur Lecoq; Sir Hugh Drummond and his wife, Lady Georgia Dewhurst, ancestors* of Bulldog Drummond; Honoré Delagardie and his wife Philippa Drummond, ancestors of Lord Peter Wimsey; Alice Clarke Raffles, companion of Sir Percy and Marguerite Blakeney, and Sir Percy's future second wife; George Edward Rutherford, 11th Baron Tennington and his wife Elizabeth Cavendish, ancestors of the jungle lord; John William Clayton, 3rd Duke of Greystoke, and his wife Alicia Rutherford, also ancestors of the jungle lord; and Arthur Blake, ancestor of Sexton Blake. The Capelleans and the Eridaneans are warring alien races from Farmer's novel The Other Log of Phileas Fogg, which is also the source of the distorter. Another time distorter, albeit operating on different principles, is used by Farmer himself in stories by Paul Spiteri. General Sir Hezekiah Fogg was mentioned as the great-grandfather of Phileas Fogg (from Jules Verne's Around the World in Eighty Days) in the Have Gun–Will Travel episode "Fogg Bound." However, according to The Other Log of Phileas Fogg, Phileas' stepfather Sir Heraclitus Fogg was an Old Eridanean, a native member of the race rather than an adoptee. Therefore, Eckert proposed in "A Chronology of Major Events Pertinent to The Other Log of Phileas Fogg" (found in the 2012 Titan Books edition of Other Log) Sir Hezekiah was a prior alias used by Sir Heraclitus himself, who later posed as his own descendant. John Gribardsun, the H. G. Wells I, Project Chronos, and Jacob Moishe are from Farmer's novel Time's Last Gift; Gribardsun was implied to be the jungle lord, who received an immortality elixir from a grateful witch doctor according to Edgar Rice Burroughs' novel Tarzan and the Foreign Legion. The timeline was split into two divergent realities when the H. G. Wells I's second trip to 14,000 B.C. was diverted to 26,000 B.C. by Gribardsun's presence in their intended time period, as chronicled by John Allen Small in his story "Into Time's Abyss" (The Worlds of Philip José Farmer 2: Of Dust and Soul, Michael Croteau, ed., Meteor House, 2011). Sir Percy Blakeney and his wife Marguerite are from Baroness Orczy's Scarlet Pimpernel novels. Percy, Alice and Marguerite battled Baron de Musard in Eckert's story "Is He in Hell?" (Tales of the Shadowmen Volume 6: Grand Guignol, Jean-Marc and Randy Lofficier, eds., Black Coat Press, 2010). The Baron de Musard in that story is an ancestor of the Baron de Musard referred to in Farmer's Doc Savage novel Escape from Loki. Gribardsun's battle with a member of that family in the 1500s was alluded to in Farmer and Eckert's novel The Evil in Pemberley House. Colonel Bozzo-Corona and his Brothers of Mercy are from Paul Féval's novels about the criminal conspiracy known as the Black Coats. Iain Bond is an ancestor of British Secret Service agent James Bond. William de Winter and his wife Elizabeth Richmond are from Jean-Marc Lofficier's articles "Will There Be Light Tomorrow?" (Shadowmen: Heroes and Villains of French Pulp Fiction, Black Coat Press, 2003) and "The Tangled Web: Genealogies of the Members of the French Wold

Newton Families–Rocambole and Fantômas" (found at The French Wold Newton Universe *website*); William is descended from Milady from Alexandre Dumas' The Three Musketeers. Gustavas Kramm is the ancestor of Dr. Cornelius Kramm from Gustave Le Rouge's Le Mystérieux Docteur Cornelius, while the surviving Gerolstein brother is the father of Rodolphe de Gerolstein from Eugène Sue's The Mysteries of Paris; both were identified as present at the meteor strike by Lofficier in "Will There Be Light Tomorrow?" which also first proposed the reason why those present at the meteor strike were gathered together. Fitzwilliam Darcy, his wife, the former Elizabeth Bennet; Elizabeth's sister-in-law, Miss Caroline Bingley; and Caroline's brother Charles are from Jane Austen's Pride and Prejudice. Countess Nadine Carody is from the film Vampyros Lesbos. The Calyx Bar is from Louis Feuillade's film serial Judex. The Heart of Ahriman is from Robert E. Howard's Conan novel The Hour of the Dragon. Etienne Austin was identified as present at the Wold Newton meteor strike by Cheryl L. Huttner in her creative mythographic essay "Name of a Thousand Blue Demons" (Myths for the Modern Age: Philip José Farmer's Wold Newton Universe, *Win Scott Eckert, ed., MonkeyBrain Books, 2005*); he is an ancestor of Professor Challenger's chauffeur-butler Austin as well as Seabury Quinn's occult detective Jules de Grandin. Dennis E. Power revealed Sexton Blake was related to the Scarlet Pimpernel in his series of articles "The Wold, Wold West" (found at the Wold Newton Universe: A Secret History *website*), a theory that was adopted by Eckert for his essay "The Blakeney Family Tree" (The Worlds of Philip José Farmer 1: Protean Dimensions, *Michael Croteau, ed., Meteor House, 2010*). Khokarsa is featured in the Ancient Opar series by Farmer and/or Christopher Paul Carey: the latest editions are Hadon of Ancient Opar *(Titan Books, 2012);* Flight to Opar *(Meteor House, 2015);* The Song of Kwasin *(coauthored with Christopher Paul Carey, Meteor House, 2015); and* Hadon, King of Opar *(by Carey, Meteor House, 2015).* Another book in the series, Blood of Ancient Opar, *is forthcoming from Carey and Meteor House.* The Gokako are also from the Opar books, and Greystoke/Gribardsun appears in the series under the name Sahhindar. The Temple of Kho also appears in the Opar books. The nethkarna *and the Door and Tree of Kho appear in Christopher Paul Carey's novella* Exiles of Kho. *Lupoeth is mentioned in the Opar books, and her founding of Opar (originally from Burroughs' books about Lord Greystoke) is depicted in* Exiles of Kho. Dr. Sebastian Noel is from Rick Lai's essay "The Secret History of Captain Nemo" *(Myths for the Modern Age);* he is the father of Dr. Noel from Robert Louis Stevenson's "The Suicide Club" and the grandfather of Professor Moriarty. The crystalline root system is from Eckert and Carey's story "Iron and Bronze" *(Tales of the Shadowmen Volume 5: The Vampires of Paris, Jean-Marc and Randy Lofficier, eds., Black Coat Press, 2009).*

The root system is an extension of the star-shaped mineral-vegetable king from J.-H. Rosny aîné's novel L'Étonnant Voyage d'Hareton Ironcastle, translated and adapted by Farmer as Ironcastle, *and is also related to the Crystal Tree of Time, which the jungle lord encountered in 1918 during the events of Farmer's* The Dark Heart of Time: A Tarzan Novel *(based on ideas from "Crystal Corridors in the Farmerian Monomyth," presentation by Christopher Paul Carey and Dennis E. Power, FarmerCon III, Peoria, Illinois, July 26, 2008). Wolf Larsen is from Jack London's* The Sea Wolf, *and was identified as Doc Wildman's grandfather in* Tarzan Alive. *Baron von Hessel is from* Escape from Loki; *Christopher Carey identified Larsen*  *and von Hessel as aliases for XauXaz in his essay "The Green Eyes Have It–Or Are They Blue? or Another Case of Identity Recased" (*Myths for the Modern Age*). The Royal Jelly treatment was created by Sherlock Holmes, as revealed in William S. Baring-Gould's biography* Sherlock Holmes of Baker Street. *XauXaz's attempt to retrieve a shard of the Wold Newton meteor was chronicled in Watson and Eckert's story "The Adventure of the Fallen Stone" (*Sherlock Holmes: The Crossovers Casebook, *Howard Hopkins, ed., Moonstone Books, 2012), which also revealed the British Secret Service's interest in the "human magnetic moment," first identified in* Tarzan Alive. *The Oil of Life was created by Dr. Fu Manchu, who was identified by Farmer as the grandson of the 3rd Duke of Greystoke in* Doc Savage: His Apocalyptic Life. *Wildman's wife is Adélaïde Johnston Lupin, who appears in Eckert's stories "The Eye of Oran" (*Tales of the Shadowmen Volume 2: Gentlemen of the Night, *Jean-Marc and Randy Lofficier, eds., Black Coat Press, 2005) and "Les Lèvres Rouges" (*Tales of the Shadowmen Volume 3: Danse Macabre, *Jean-Marc and Randy Lofficier, eds., Black Coat Press, 2006). Their daughter is Patricia Clarke Lupin Wildman, the protagonist of* The Evil in Pemberley House. *The man with the moldable skin is Paul Ernst's avenging pulp hero; Eckert has chronicled his battles with XauXaz in a trilogy of stories for Moonstone Books' anthologies featuring the character. The private clinic is Doc Wildman's Crime College.*

1797

February 14, 1797–February 14, 1798
SAILS ON THE HORIZON
    The *Louisa*, commanded by Charles Edgemont, encounters a small boat whose passengers consist of Lieutenant Horatio Hornblower and some of the shipwrecked crew of a Spanish privateer he has rescued. Edgemont offers to take on Hornblower, who has been imprisoned in Ferrol since February 1797, as an officer, but the Lieutenant declines, saying he is on parole and sworn to return to Spain.
    Novel by Jay Worrall. Edgemont returned in two sequels, Any Approaching Enemy *and* A Sea Unto Itself. *This crossover brings him into the CU. Edgemont's encounter with Hornblower takes place in December 1797, during the final chapter of* Mr. Midshipman Hornblower.

1798

April 1–August 1
ANY APPROACHING ENEMY
    Lieutenant Jack Aubrey of the *Leander* delivers two mast sticks to the ship *Louisa*, captained by Charles Edgemont.
    Novel by Jay Worrall. The appearance of Patrick O'Brian's naval hero Jack Aubrey further confirms Edgemont's presence in the CU.

Autumn
MARGUERITE'S TEARS
    Dr. Siger Holmes and his wife Violet discuss the recent death of Lady Marguerite Blakeney. Marguerite had been in ill health since a winter visit to her husband Sir Percy's place at Would Newton. Violet wonders if the rock from the sky that came down near their carriages had a deleterious effect on Lady Blakeney. Marguerite had three children after the Would Newton conclave, Violet Yvonne being the youngest. Earlier in the evening, Siger chats with Sir Percy and Fitzwilliam Darcy, mentioning the latter's wife, and suggests they invite Colonel Bozzo-Corona and his man Lecoq to the funeral service. He also reminds them he observed Lecoq meeting with Countess Nadine Carody at the Calyx Bar in Paris. Percy says the Countess was enamored of both Alice and Marguerite. Darcy mentions Lupin's half-brother. Holmes realizes Nadine's true nature after reading *The Ruthvenian*, and recalls being told of Sir Percy, Marguerite, and Alice's battle with the wizard de Musard. The Duke of Holdernesse aids Holmes in attending to Marguerite's body. Guests at her funeral included the eleventh Baron Tennington, M.

Delagardie, Drummond, Balsamo, Kramm, de Winter, Gerolstein, Sir John Gribson or Grebson, Charles Bingley, Lord Richard Selwick, George Knightly, and a man with a monocle and a snuff-box with obscure symbols on it, who bows in a Germanic fashion. Percy and Marguerite's children Hélène, Jack, George, and Violet remained at the manor, as did Percy and Alice's children, Percy Armand and newborn twins Serena and Suzanne.

Short story by Win Scott Eckert in Tales of the Shadowmen Volume 8: Agents Provocateurs, Black Coat Press, 2011; reprinted in French in Les Compagnons de l'Ombre (Tome 12), Jean-Marc and Randy Lofficier, eds., Rivière Blanche, 2013, and L'Almanach des Vampires, Jean-Marc and Randy Lofficier, eds., Rivière Blanche, 2014; and in The Vampire Almanac (Volume 2), Jean-Marc and Randy Lofficier, eds., Black Coat Press, 2015. Sir Percy and Lady Marguerite Blakeney are from the Scarlet Pimpernel novels by Baroness Orczy. Violet Yvonne Blakeney and her brothers Jack and George are from John Blakeney's biography The Life and Exploits of the Scarlet Pimpernel (aka A Gay Adventurer). Violet Yvonne also appears in Eckert's story "Zorro's Rival" (More Tales of Zorro, Richard Dean Starr, ed., Moonstone Books, 2011). Fitzwilliam Darcy, his wife Elizabeth Bennet Darcy, and Charles Bingley are from Jane Austen's novel Pride and Prejudice. Colonel Bozzo-Corona is the leader of the Black Coats, the criminal conspiracy chronicled by Paul Féval. Countess Nadine Carody is from Jesús Franco's film Vampyros Lesbos. The Calyx Bar is from Louis Feuillade's serial Judex. The Ruthvenian is a vampire bible that appears in several works by author and filmmaker Donald F. Glut, named for Lord Ruthven from John Polidori's "The Vampyre." Ruthven would not yet have become a vampire in 1798. This discrepancy was resolved in Eckert's story "Violet's Lament" (Tales of the Shadowmen Volume 9: La Vie en Noir, Jean-Marc and Randy Lofficier, eds., Black Coat Press, 2012). De Musard is an ancestor of Baron de Musard from Philip José Farmer's Doc Savage novel Escape from Loki. Sir Percy, Marguerite, and Alice encountered the earlier de Musard in Eckert's story "Is He in Hell?" (Tales of the Shadowmen Volume 6: Grand Guignol, Black Coat Press, 2010; reprinted and expanded *in* The Worlds of Philip José Farmer 1: Protean Dimensions, *Michael Croteau, ed., Meteor House, 2010). The man with the snuff-box is Baron von Hessel from* Escape from Loki. *Kramm is the ancestor of Dr. Cornelius Kramm from Gustave Le Rouge's novel* Le Mystérieux Docteur Cornélius. *De Winter is a descendant of Milady from Alexandre Dumas'* The Three Musketeers. *Balsamo is Joseph Balsamo, both a historical figure and the title character of a novel by Dumas. Gerolstein is the father of Rodolphe de Gérolstein from Eugène Sue's novel* Les Mystères de Paris. *Sir John Gribson is the immortal time traveler John Gribardsun from Farmer's novel* Time's Last Gift; *Farmer strongly implies "Gribardsun" is actually the jungle lord of Burroughs' tales. Lord Richard Selwick is from Lauren Willig's Pink Carnation novels. George Knightly is from Jane Austen's novel* Emma. *Dr. Siger Holmes, Violet Holmes, Lecoq (Albert Lecoq), Alice (Alice Clarke Raffles, Sir Percy's future second wife), the Duke of Holderness (actually Greystoke; in his essay "A Case of Identity, or, The Adventure of the Seven Claytons," H. W. Starr identified the 6th Duke of Holdernesse from the Sherlock Holmes story "The Adventure of the Priory School" as the 6th Duke of Greystoke, a theory adopted by Farmer), Lupin (Louis Lupin), the eleventh Baron Tennington, M. Delagardie (Honoré Delagardie), Drummond (Sir Hugh Drummond), Percy Armand Blakeney, Suzanne Blakeney, and Serena Blakeney are all from Farmer's seminal biography* Tarzan Alive. *In Ponson du Terrail's Rocambole novels, the mother of Armand de Kergaz and his half-brother Andrea de Felipone (aka Sir Williams) is the former Hélène Durand; Jean-Marc Lofficier theorized Hélène was a daughter of Sir Percy and Marguerite Blakeney in his essay "The Tangled Web: Genealogies of the Members of the French Wold Newton Families–Rocambole and Fantômas" (found at* The French Wold Newton Universe *website). The circumstances under which Violet Yvonne herself took the name Durand are revealed in "Violet's Lament." Hélène must have later adopted the name herself.*

1799

January 15, 1799; October 8–10, 1893
WHAT DOESN'T DIE

In the 18th century, Victor Frankenstein's Monster tries to complete his creator's work on a bride, but is only partially successful, though he believes he has failed completely. In 1893, the Bride, "Eve," arrives in Chicago for the World's Fair, where she hopes Nikola Tesla can make her "whole." She is defeated by Doctor Omega, who refers to having been exiled from his people.

Short story by Thom Brannan in Tales of the Shadowmen Volume 7:

Femmes Fatales, *Jean-Marc and Randy Lofficier, eds., Black Coat Press, 2010;* reprinted in in Doctor Omega and the Shadowmen, *Jean-Marc and Randy Lofficier, eds., Black Coat Press, 2011;* and in French in Les Compagnons de l'Ombre (Tome 9), *Jean-Marc and Randy Lofficier, eds., Rivière Blanche, 2012.* Victor Frankenstein and his monster are, of course, from Mary Shelley's novel. The Bride from the novel, whose construction Victor left uncompleted, is not to be confused with the Bride of the monster created by Victor's descendant Henry Frankenstein. Doctor Omega is the title character of a novel by Arnould Galopin. The reference to Omega being exiled from his people is meant to imply he is the CU counterpart to the time and space-traveling Doctor, of Doctor Who fame, as suggested in Jean-Marc and Randy Lofficier's translation and adaptation of Galopin's novel.

March–May
SHARPE'S TIGER

Private Richard Sharpe infiltrates the army of Tippoo Sultan. One of the jewels the Sultan wears is a dagger with a large yellow-white diamond. The French colonel that advises the Sultan says the diamond is called the Moonstone, and supposedly brings misfortune to anyone who steals it. Sharpe does just that.

Novel by Bernard Cornwell, Harper Collins, 1997. *The appearance of the Moonstone (from Wilkie Collins' novel of the same name) reinforces Sharpe's presence in the CU.*

July 20, 1799–November 13, 1817
THE THOUSAND AUTUMNS OF JACOB DE ZOET

Housekeeper Satsuki Miyake is a native of Yakushima. A carpenter named Con Twomey reveals his real name is Fiacre Muntervary. A young sailor aboard the *Profetes* named Boerhaave also appears, as does a blacksmith's son named Buntaro.

Novel by David Mitchell. *Joe Hill's book* NOS4A2, *which takes place in the CU, has an appearance by Sigmund de Zoet, implicitly a descendant of Jacob de Zoet. Satsuki Miyake is a collateral ancestor of Yakushima native Eiji Miyake, the protagonist of Mitchell's novel* number9dream. *Buntaro is probably the ancestor of Eiji's landlord Buntaro. Fiacre Muntervary is an ancestor of Mo Muntervary, one of the main characters of Mitchell's* Ghostwritten. *The* Profetes *(or* Prophetess*) and Boerhaave are from another of Mitchell's novels,* Cloud Atlas.

1800

May 1800–June 1802
A JOYOUS ADVENTURE
   Martin Saint-Denys, a former member of the League of the Scarlet Pimpernel, becomes involved in a scheme to restore the royal house of Bourbon to the throne of France.
   The Scarlet Pimpernel is mentioned several times in this standalone novel by Baroness Orczy, bringing it into the CU.

1803

Winter
HOARE AND THE FROG PRINCE
   Lieutenant Bartholomew Hoare investigates the death of a member of French royalty. An offhand comment by Lieutenant Horatio Hornblower gives Hoare the epiphany that enables him to solve the case.
   Short story by Wilder Perkins in Alfred Hitchcock's Mystery Magazine, *February 1999. The appearance by Horatio Hornblower brings Perkins' naval mysteries featuring Bartholomew Hoare into the CU.*

1805

October–November 6
HOARE AND THE HEADLESS CAPTAINS
   One of Captain Bartholomew Hoare's men uses the phrase "the lesser evil," reminding him of "the jape invented by one of the more successful frigate captains—Bolitho? Cochrane? He was wont to challenge a new acquaintance to a wager upon which of two beetle larvae, chosen at random from among those tapped from a piece of ship's biscuit, would be the first to reach the edge of the table. The unwitting newcomer naturally chose the larger grub. When it lost, as it always did, Captain Whoever would joyfully advise the stranger 'always to select the lesser of two weevils' and nearly burst his breeches with laughter at his own paltry jest. Aubrey. That was the joker's name. Lucky Jack Aubrey, they called him, from the wealth of prize money he had won at sea—and squandered ashore."
   Novel by Wilder Perkins, Thomas Dunne Books, 2000. Hoare is already in the Crossover Universe through an encounter with Horatio Hornblower in 1803. Patrick O'Brian's naval hero Jack Aubrey is also in the CU. This crossover brings in Alexander Kent's character Richard Bolitho. Aubrey's quote about the lesser of two weevils originally appeared in O'Brian's The Fortune of War.

November 18, 1805–April 1, 1806
HOARE AND THE MATTER OF TREASON

Captain Bartholomew Hoare makes conversation with Horatio Hornblower, who has just come out of the Port Officer's office. Vice Admiral Sir Hugh Abercrombie asks Hoare to look into the disappearance of one of his senior confidential clerks, after his underling Lestrade fails to turn up any results. Abercrombie also has a meek clerk named Cratchit. Hoare and his gunner's mate, Titus Thoday, find a figurine of a falcon inside the missing man's room. Hoare "had seen a similar figurine before, somewhere in the Med, in ninety-one or thereabouts—in Malta, if memory served him correctly."

Novel by Wilder Perkins, Thomas Dunne Books, 2001. Hoare previously met Hornblower in Perkins' story "Hoare and the Frog Prince," which was set in 1803. Lestrade is probably an ancestor of Inspector G. Lestrade from the Sherlock Holmes stories. Both Lestrades are described as resembling ferrets, adding to the strength of this genealogical connection. Cratchit must be a relative of the equally mild-mannered clerk Bob Cratchit from Charles Dickens' A Christmas Carol. The figurine Hoare saw in Malta in 1791 is the Maltese Falcon, from Dashiell Hammett's titular novel.

1808–1810

GODS OF THE UNDERWORLD

Aubert Lecoq and his sons are imprisoned under the Convent de la Merci alongside Colonel Bozzo-Corona. Their jailer is Marcel Draco, who is planning to kill the Colonel for refusing to share the Treasure of the Black Coats with the rest of the High Council. Draco and his fellow rebels play cards to determine who gets to kill the Colonel; Doctor Lerne wins the game. However, the Colonel manages to escape, and the Lecoqs wind up being rescued. A year later, at the Callyx Bar in Paris, Bibi-Lupin, who has stolen the Empress Joséphine's necklace, asks Trompe-la-Mort to dispose of it, but he refuses. Joseph Fouché, Napoleon's Minister of Police, discusses Bibi-Lupin with Jean Henry, the chief of the Paris police. Bibi-Lupin was arrested for treason in 1793 by Citizen Chauvelin, but escaped execution and fled to England, becoming a coachman for Sir Percy Blakeney, who married an actress who was Saint-Just's cousin. Monsieur Jackal, a former criminal recently recruited as an informer, has assured Henry Bibi-Lupin acted only out of greed. Anne de Breuil argues with the Colonel, who remarks Anne inherited her namesake's beauty. Claude Verdier states Napoleon betrayed the Colonel. Lawyer Portal-Giraud came up with the Black Coats' doctrine of "paying the law." The Colonel declares a toast using a bottle of La Frenaie wine. Trompe-la-Mort murders Verdier, leaving behind the *Botte de Nevers*, the mark of Lagardère. He forces the Colonel to give him the Scapular of the Black Coats. However, he scratches himself on a replica of a dragon's fang on the box containing the Scapular, which the Colonel reveals was coated with a poison derived from the black scorpion of India. Trompe-la-Mort is really Jacques Collin, who took the fall for his comrade Franchessini's forgery. Rather than killing him, the black scorpion poison tossed Collin into a cataleptic state. The Colonel is considering replacing the poison with a Brazilian drug called the "Mato Grosso Pestilence." At the Colonel's orders, a man named Toussac whips Collin. Henri de Lagardère learned the *Botte de Nevers*, invented by the great fencing master Delapalme, from his friend the Duc de Nevers. Anne de Breuil is also known as Jacqueline Collin, Jacques' aunt. The Collins' forebear, Milady de Winter, was Cardinal Richelieu's most accomplished agent. The box containing the Scapular is kept in a concealed wall alcove alongside a book called *Les Chroniques de Nemedea*. The book features an illustration of a box similar to the one bearing the Scapular alongside an account of a legendary killer who encountered said box. Monsieur Jackal has heard Trompe-la-Mort is currently infatuated with a youth named Alexis Ladeau. Trompe-la-Mort attempts to convince six fellow convicts who were also betrayed by the Black Coats, including Fil-de-Soie, Le Biffon, and Auguste, they must band together to defeat the Colonel. After his fellow convicts escape, Trompe-la-Mort plans to recruit more men, including La Pouraille. Trompe-la-Mort dubs this new alliance the Society of the Ten Thousand. Later that night, he decides upon his new alias: Vautrin.

Short story by Rick Lai in Tales of the Shadowmen Volume 9: La Vie en Noir, *Jean-Marc and Randy Lofficier, eds., Black Coat Press, 2012; reprinted in French in* Les Compagnons de l'Ombre (Tome 13), *Jean-Marc and Randy Lofficier, eds., Rivière Blanche, 2014. Aubert Lecoq is meant to be coachman Albert Lecoq, father of future Black Coats member Lecoq de la Perière and grandfather of Emile Gaboriau's policeman and sleuth Monsieur Lecoq, from Philip José Farmer's biography* Tarzan Alive. *The Convent de la Merci, Colonel Bozzo-Corona, the Black Coats, their Treasure and Scapulary, and Portal-Giraud are featured in the Black Coats novels by Paul Féval. Marcel Draco is an ancestor of Union Corse leader Marc-Ange Draco and his daughter Tracy from Ian Fleming's James Bond novel* On Her Majesty's Secret Service. *Doctor Lerne is an ancestor of the title character of Maurice Renard's novel* Doctor Lerne. *Jacques Collin (aka Trompe-la-Mort and Vautrin), Franchessini, Le Biffon, Fil-de-Soie, Auguste, La Pouraille, and the Society of the Ten Thousand are from Honoré de Balzac's interconnected cycle of novels* La Comédie

Humaine. *The Callyx Bar is from Louis Feuillade's serial* Judex. *Bibi-Lupin is also from* La Comédie Humaine; *here, he is conflated with coachman Louis Lupin from* Tarzan Alive, *the ancestor of Maurice Leblanc's gentleman thief Arsène Lupin. Jacqueline Collin, Vautrin's aunt, also appears in the* La Comédie Humaine *novels. Here, she is romantically involved with Aubert Lecoq, and conflated with an unidentified beautiful woman who appeared as a member of the Black Coats' Council in the novel* The Cadet Gang, *both story elements being based on theories proposed by Jean-Marc Lofficier. Sir Percy Blakeney; his wife, the former Marguerite St. Just; and Citizen Chauvelin are from Baroness Orczy's Scarlet Pimpernel novels. Monsieur Jackal is from Alexandre Dumas'* The Mohicans of Paris; *here, he is conflated with the historical Eugène François Vidocq, reformed criminal turned founder of the French Sûreté. Claude Verdier is an ancestor of Satanas from Louis Feuillade's silent film serial* Les Vampires; *in the English language version of the serial, Satanas' real name is given as Claude Dupont-Verdier. La Frenaie wine is from Clark Ashton Smith's Averoigne stories. Henri de Lagardère, the Duc de Nevers, the* Botte de Nevers, *and Delapalme are from Féval's swashbuckling novel* Le Bossu. *According to Sax Rohmer's* The Golden Scorpion, *the drug F. Katalepsis, used by the Si-Fan, the organization led by Dr. Fu Manchu, has as its chief ingredient the venom of the black scorpion of India. The Mato Grosso Pestilence is from Harold A. Davis' Doc Savage pulp novel* The Green Death. *Toussac is the brother of the Toussac that appears in Arthur Conan Doyle's* Uncle Bernac. *Robert E. Howard claimed he learned of the Hyborian Age and the barbarian Conan's exploits through a tome called* The Nemedian Chronicles. *Conan encountered a box similar to that containing the Scapular of the Black Coats in* The Hour of the Dragon *(aka* Conan the Conqueror*). Alexis Ladeau is from Howard's Cthulhu Mythos story "The Black Stone."*

1809

Spring 1809–March 10, 1815
BLACK AJAX

Tom Molineaux, a freed black American slave, becomes a successful boxer in Britain, initially under the patronage of Captain Buckley "Mad Buck" Flashman. Young Bob Logic and his friends Tom and Jerry witness one of Molineaux's fights.

Novel by George MacDonald Fraser, Harper-Collins, 1997. Tom Molineaux was a real person. In Robert E. Howard's story "The

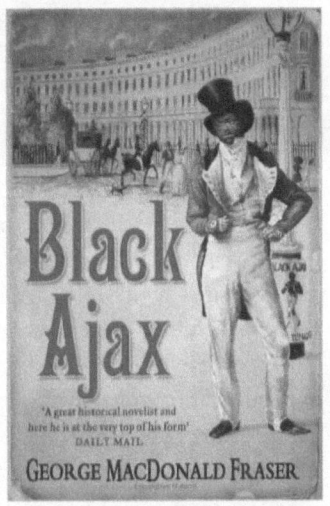

Apparition in the Prize Ring," Molineaux's ghost appears to a black boxer named Ace Jessel, whom Matthew Baugh brought into the CU in his story "The Tournament of the Treasure." Captain Flashman is the father of Fraser's most famous character, Harry Flashman. Bob Logic and his friends Corinthian Tom and Jerry Hawthorn are from Pierce Egan's book Life in London. *Interestingly, Egan himself appears as a character in* Black Ajax, *and a footnote mentions his authorship of* Life in London, *which must have been based on the real exploits of Bob, Tom, and Jerry.*

1810

September
SHARPE'S ESCAPE
   One of the members of Captain Richard Sharpe's South Essex Regiment Light Company is Rifleman Matthew Dodd, who is separated from the regiment at the Battle of Bussaco.
   Novel by Bernard Cornwell, Harper Collins, 2004. Rifleman Matthew Dodd is from C. S. Forester's novel Death to the French.

1812

Winter
ALL ROADS LEAD TO MARS
   Doctor Omega, his handyman Fred, two versions of his companion Denis from different time periods, members of the Time Brigade (which Omega often confuses with the Time Patrol), and some Black Lectroids prepare for battle with the Red Lectroids. The Time Brigade's commander is Jason Spell. Captain Spencer, an English World War I soldier, gives Omega a message from Spell. Omega enters a rift, and finds himself on Mars, where he spots a black pyramid, and encounters a dying Setissi, as well as John Carter, the planet's warlord, who calls it Barsoom, and invites Omega to accompany him to Helium. Omega is scooped up in another rift, and finds himself on another version of Mars, uninhabited except for Rovers. He tells a disembodied robot head named Thea it has more than earned its place aboard the *Cosmos*. Another rift takes Omega to a third Mars, where he meets Sorns who refer to their world as Malacandra, and speak for the Oyarsa, saying Omega's predicament was caused by the "bent" Oyarsa (or Eldil) of Thulcandra, who has channeled the energy of the chrono-synclastic infundibulum that covers Malacandra. Omega rescues his Martian companion Tiziraou from Loompaland, but not before giving the Oompa Loompas some cocoa beans.

Short story by Travis Hiltz in Tales of the Shadowmen Volume 11: Force Majeure, *Jean-Marc and Randy Lofficier, eds., Black Coat Press, 2014. Doctor Omega, Fred, Denis, the Setissi, the Cosmos, and Tiziraou are from Arnould Galopin's novel* Doctor Omega. *Jean-Marc and Randy Lofficier's adaptation and translation of the novel implied Omega was the CU counterpart of the time-and-space-traveling Doctor from the long-running British science fiction television series* Doctor Who. *Similarly, the Setissi were implied to be counterparts to the Ice Warriors encountered by the Doctor. The black pyramid is from the Doctor Who serial "The Pyramids of Mars." The Time Brigade and its commander, Jason Spell, are from French comics by Claude Legrand and Edmond Ripoll. The Time Patrol is featured in stories by Poul Anderson. The Black and Red Lectroids are from the movie* The Adventures of Buckaroo Banzai Across the Eighth Dimension. *The previous chapters of Omega's conflict with the Red Lectroids are Hiltz's stories "What Lurks in Romney Marsh?" (*Tales of the Shadowmen Volume 9: La Vie En Noir, *2012) and "The Next Omega" (*Tales of the Shadowmen Volume 10: Esprit de Corps, *Black Coat Press, 2013). Captain Eliot Spencer will later become the Cenobite known as Pinhead, as seen in the* Hellraiser *horror film series. The warlord of Mars, Barsoom, and Helium are from the works of Edgar Rice Burroughs. Thea is meant to be the robot from Thea von Harbou's science fiction novel* Metropolis *and its film adaptation directed by Fritz Lang. Doctor Omega acquired Thea's head during the events of Hiltz's story "The Robots of Metropolis" (*Tales of the Shadowmen Volume 7: Femmes Fatales, *Black Coat Press, 2010). Malacandra (Mars), the Sorns, the Oyarsa, the Bent Oyarsa (or Eldil), and Thulcandra (Earth) are from C. S. Lewis' novel* Out of the Silent Planet. *Various pastiches indicate Barsoom is actually the Mars of an alternate universe to the CU. The Mars inhabited solely by Rovers is the Mars of the CU, which closely resembles our universe's Mars. This story establishes Malacandra is also the Mars of an alternate universe. The chroni-synclastic infundibulum is from Kurt Vonnegut, Jr.'s novel* The Sirens of Titan. *Loompaland and the Oompa Loompas are from Roald Dahl's book* Charlie and the Chocolate Factory.

1815

February 28–April
VIOLET'S LAMENT

Dr. Siger Holmes enters the library at Blakeney Manor, home of Sir Percy Blakeney, where he reads the *Ruthvenian*. The book was written over a hundred years ago by Armand Tesla, a researcher on vampires and the occult, and primarily focuses on the Ruthven family, which according to Tesla has a long history of vampirism. Holmes wonders if the present Lord Ruthven has himself joined the ranks of the undead. He thinks of Sir Percy's deceased first wife, Marguerite's own return from the grave as a vampire. He is joined by Sir Percy and Marguerite's daughter Violet, who was named after Holmes' wife. Holmes and Sir Percy are close as brothers, and Holmes' wife and Sir Percy's second wife Alice are sisters. Holmes and Violet discuss the gathering at Would Newton in December of 1795 held by Violet's parents, where a fiery stone fell from the sky. Holmes wishes to track down Countess Nadine Carody, who was responsible for Marguerite's death and subsequent undeath, and Violet insists on accompanying him. Twenty years ago, Sir Percy and Holmes suspected Countess Carody and Colonel Bozzo-Corona were in league. A month prior to the Would Newton Conclave, Holmes saw the Colonel's man, Lecoq, at the Countess' Parisian townhouse. Agreements with the Colonel and the Brothers of Mercy were made at the Conclave. In the Etsch Valley two months later, Holmes and Violet are saved by a female vampire called Ziska from another *nosferatu* called the Giaour. Four men approach the duo: Leo Lecoq (son of the Colonel's henchman), Durand, Thénardier, and Mondego. Lupin's half-brother Bonaparte is mentioned. The Colonel and the Countess are holed up in the Castle of Monteleone. Three murders happened during the Conclave, all signaled by the sound of a bell tolling nine times. The Colonel's contingent at that time included the elder Lecoq, Kramm, Carody, and Gerolstein. A vampire called Count Aubri attacks Holmes, Violet, and Lecoq and his men. Thénardier and Mondego perish in the assault. Reaching the Castle at last, the survivors come face to face with the Countess, Ziska, and another vampire, Count Yorga. The Colonel offers Violet a place in his organization. He has long been planning to expand his operations into Spanish California, and he wishes Violet to pose as Durand's daughter as part of this expansion.

Short story by Win Scott Eckert in Tales of the Shadowmen Volume 9: La Vie en Noir, *Jean-Marc and Randy Lofficier, eds., Black Coat Press, 2012; reprinted in French in* Les Compagnons de l'Ombre (Tome 13), *Jean-Marc and Randy Lofficier, eds., Rivière Blanche, 2014, and* L'Almanach des Vampires, *Jean-Marc and Randy Lofficier, eds., Rivière Blanche, 2014; and in* The Vampire Almanac (Volume 2), Jean-Marc and Randy Lofficier, eds., Black Coat Press, 2015. *Sir Percy Blakeney, his first wife Marguerite, and Blakeney Manor are from the Scarlet Pimpernel novels by Baroness Orczy. Dr. Siger Holmes and his wife, the former Violet Clarke (the great-grandparents of Sherlock Holmes); Alice, Sir Percy's second wife (the former Alice Clarke Raffles, Violet Holmes' sister); the elder Lecoq (Albert Lecoq, grandfather of Emile Gaboriau's sleuth Monsieur Lecoq); and Lupin (Louis Lupin, great-great-grandfather of Arsène Lupin) are from Philip José Farmer's seminal biography* Tarzan Alive. *Sir Percy and Marguerite's*  *daughter, Violet Yvonne Blakeney, is from John Blakeney's biography* The Life and Exploits of the Scarlet Pimpernel *(aka* A Gay Adventurer*). The* Ruthvenian *is a book of vampiric lore featured in many interconnected books, comics, and films by Donald F. Glut. It is named after the Ruthven family, the most famous member of whom is the Lord Ruthven featured in John Polidori's "The Vampyre." Armand Tesla is the occult scholar and vampire played by Bela Lugosi in the film* The Return of the Vampire. *The trip to Would Newton (or Wold Newton, as it is better known), along with the murders occurring prior to same, were depicted in Eckert's story "The Wild Huntsman" (*The Worlds of Philip José Farmer 3: Portraits of a Trickster*, Michael Croteau, ed., Meteor House, 2012; reprinted in* Tales of the Wold Newton Universe*, Win Scott Eckert and Christopher Paul Carey, eds., Titan Books, 2013). The Countess Nadine Carody is from Jesús Franco's horror film* Vampyros Lesbos. *Colonel Bozzo-Corona, Leo Lecoq (aka Lecoq de la Perière, Monsieur Lecoq's father), and the Castle of Monteleone are from the Black Coats novels by Paul Féval. Ziska is from Alexandre Dumas père's play* The Vampire. *Mondego is a relative of Fernand Mondego from Dumas' novel* The Count of Monte Cristo. *The Giaour is from the poem of the same name by Lord Byron. Durand is the future alleged father of Violet Yvonne and her sister Hélène. M. Durand and Violet's activities in Spanish California are detailed in Eckert's story "Zorro's Rival" (*More Tales of Zorro*, Richard Dean Starr, ed., Moonstone Books, 2011). Hélène Durand is the mother of Andrea de Felipone (aka Sir Williams) and his half-brother Armand de Kergaz in Ponson du Terrail's Rocambole novels. Jean-Marc*

Lofficier identified Hélène as Violet's sister in his article "The Tangled Web: Genealogies of the Members of the French Wold Newton Families– Rocambole and Fantômas" (found on The French Wold Newton Universe website). Thénardier is a relative of Madame Thénardier and her son from Victor Hugo's classic novel Les Misérables. Kramm is the ancestor of Dr. Cornelius Kramm from Gustave le Rouge's Le Mystérieux Dr. Cornélius. Gerolstein is the father of Rodolphe de Gerolstein from Eugène Sue's Les Mystères de Paris. Count Aubri is from Peter Josef von Lindpaintner and Cäsar Max Hegel's opera Der Vampyr. Count Yorga is from the films Count Yorga, Vampire and The Return of Count Yorga. Given his reappearance in the 1970s, Yorga must have been resurrected sometime after his death at Dr. Holmes' hands in this story.

March 20–June 18
THE BRONZE EAGLE

The Comte de Cambray and his family were rescued from the guillotine by the League of the Scarlet Pimpernel.

The references to the Scarlet Pimpernel bring this standalone novel by Baroness Orczy, which begins with Napoleon's return from exile and ends on the date of the Battle of Waterloo, into the CU.

1820

Autumn
MELMOTH RECONCILED

The immortal wanderer John Melmoth makes a deal with an embezzling cashier, who takes on Melmoth's curse and all the power that goes with it. Melmoth dies in peace. The cashier works for the banker Baron Nucingen, and observes Nucingen's wife flirting with the unscrupulous Rastignac. Also appearing are prostitutes Aquilina and Euphrasie and devious money lender Charles Claparon.

Novel by Honoré de Balzac, 1835. This crossover connects Charles Robert Maturin's Melmoth the Wanderer *to Balzac's* La Comédie Humaine *cycle of novels. Madame Nucingen and Rastignac began their affair in Balzac's* Père Goriot. *Aquilina and Euphrasie first appeared in* The Magic Skin, *while Charles Claparon went on to appear in* César Birotteau.

1822

Winter
SECRETS

Senor Alejandro Raposa travels to Montreuil-sur-Mer, France, where he earns the wrath of the members of the gang known as the Wolves by killing their leader. The mayor of Montreuil, Monsieur Madeleine, allows Raposa to stay at his house. Raposa recounts a story the priest Monsieur Myriel told him of an escaped convict named Jean Valjean. The two are attacked by the vengeful Wolves. Raposa's swordplay reminds Madeleine of the legendary *Botte de Nevers*. Raposa promises the Mayor his secret is safe with him. "Raposa" is actually Don Diego de la Vega.

Short story by Roberto Lionel Barreiro *in* Tales of the Shadowmen Volume 7: Femmes Fatales, *Jean-Marc and Randy Lofficier, eds., Black Coat Press, 2010; reprinted in French in* Les Compagnons de l'Ombre (Tome 8), *Jean-Marc and Randy Lofficier, eds., Rivière Blanche, 2011. Don Diego de la Vega is better known as Zorro. Don Diego must have gone on a brief mission to France before returning to California and being unmasked and imprisoned later in the year, as shown in the opening scene of the film* The Mask of Zorro. *The Wolves are from Paul Féval's novel* Le Loup Blanc *(*The White Wolf*). Jean Valjean, aka Monsieur Madeleine, and Monsieur Myriel are from Victor Hugo's classic novel* Les Misérables. *The* Botte de Nevers *is a sword-stroke used by Lagardère in Féval's swashbuckling novel* Le Bossu.

1830

Autumn
CITY OF THE NOSFERATU

Boris Liatoukine meets with Count Dracula at the latter's castle. They discuss the Sepulchre, also known as Selene, the Vampire City. Liatoukine refers to an expedition to Selene a few years back which was led by an Englishwoman, causing chaos and the death of Otto Goetzi. Liatoukine refers to a fellow vampire named Orlok. Riding into Zagreb, Liatoukine is brought before Commander Sponsz. He discovers Orlok has plans to extend Selene's influence throughout Europe. Entering Selene, Liatoukine meets the Vampire Council: Count Szandor, Baron Iskariot and Baroness Phryne, the second Otto Goetzi, and Graf Orlok himself. The second Goetzi was formerly a young village woman named Polly Bird, who was transformed by the original Goetzi into a duplicate of himself. A phonograph recording by Van Helsing from August 10, 1901, describes Orlok's activities in Wisborg, Germany in 1838, during which Ellen Hutter, wife of Thomas Hutter, sacrificed herself in order to destroy Orlok.

Short story by Brian Gallagher in Tales of the Shadowmen Volume 10: Esprit de Corps, *Jean-Marc and Randy Lofficier, eds., Black Coat Press, 2013; reprinted in French in* Les Compagnons de l'Ombre (Tome 15), *Jean-Marc and Randy Lofficier, eds., Rivière Blanche, 2014, and* L'Almanach des Vampires, *Jean-Marc and Randy Lofficier, eds., Rivière Blanche, 2014; and in* The Vampire Almanac (Volume 1), *Jean-Marc and Randy Lofficier, eds., Black Coat Press, 2015. Boris Liatoukine is the title character of Marie Nizet's novel* Captain Vampire. *Dracula and Van Helsing are, of course, from Bram Stoker's novel. Selene, Otto Goetzi, Baron Iskariot, Baroness Phryne, and Polly Bird are from Paul Féval's* Vampire City. *Count Szandor is from Féval's* The Vampire Countess. *Graf Orlok, Ellen Hutter, and Thomas Hutter are from the silent film* Nosferatu. *Orlok was also portrayed as residing in Selene in Matthew Baugh's story "The Heart of the Moon." That tale's narrator, Yvgeni, described Orlok as the oldest vampire of whom he was aware, and therefore one would assume his turning predates Dracula's. However, Gallagher's story reveals Orlok was a Transylvanian nobleman transformed by Dracula into a doppelganger of the vampire lord himself. This theory evokes both an ability displayed by Otto Goetzi in* The Vampire City *and the "soul-clone" theory proposed by Chuck Loridans to explain the myriad contradictory versions of Dracula across different media. Perhaps Orlok was transported into the distant past (likely via supernatural means) at some point after his transformation by Dracula, and continued his unlife for centuries before his encounter with Yvgeni. Commander Sponsz is an ancestor of Colonel Sponsz, head of the Bordurian Secret Police in Hergé's Tintin stories.*

1839

Winter
ALL THE TEA IN CHINA
 Carolus Mortdecai "Karli" van Cleef arrives in England with the intention of selling fine china, and is befriended by John Jorrocks, MFH, merchant of Great Coram Street. Karli's first customer is a Lord Windermere. Mr. Jorrocks is proud of having established an Honourable Wooster as a customer of his own.
 Novel by Kyril Bonfiglioli, 1978. Karli is the ancestor of Bonfiglioli's series

character Charlie Mortdecai. Mr. Jorrocks is from R. S. Surtees' Jorrocks' Jaunts and Jollities. Lord Windermere must be an ancestor of the holder of that title seen in Oscar Wilde's Lady Windermere's Fan. The Honourable Wooster must be related to Bertie Wooster.

1842

Spring
CASTLE EPPSTEIN
The narrator of the introduction, telling ghost stories, says, "Certainly Hoffmann believed in the reality of his characters: he had seen Master Floh and had known Coppelius."

An 1843 Gothic novel by Alexandre Dumas. This reference implies Master Floh (from E. T. A. Hoffman's novel Master Flea: A Fairy-Tale in Seven Adventures of Two Friends) and Coppelius (from Hoffmann's story "The Sandman") exist in the same universe as the characters in this novel. "The Sandman" has already been established as taking place in the Crossover Universe, and therefore both this novel and Master Flea take place in the CU as well. While the introduction takes place contemporaneously with this book's publication, the rest of the novel happens during the time of Napoleon.

Summer
THE MOON HAG
A metaphysician named Professor Quercus encounters Elsa Karnstein and her daughter Carmilla aboard a ship, and ultimately becomes their servant. Elsa and Carmilla initially claim to be Madame and Malicarla Strenkin of the House of Dolingen.

Short story by Professor Quercus, edited by Martin Gately in The Vampire Almanac (Volume 1), Jean-Marc and Randy Lofficier, eds., Black Coat Press, 2015; reprinted in French in L'Almanach des Vampires (Tome 2), Jean-Marc and Randy Lofficier, eds., Rivière Blanche, 2015. Carmilla is the title character of the classic vampire story by J. Sheridan Le Fanu. Carmilla's mother Elsa and Professor Quercus also appear in Le Fanu's story, though neither are referred to by name. The House of Dolingen is a reference to the vampire Countess Dolingen of Gratz from Bram Stoker's story "Dracula's Guest," generally believed to be the deleted original first chapter of Dracula.

1845

Spring
THE GRUESOME AFFAIR OF THE ELECTRIC BLUE LIGHTNING

C. Auguste Dupin battles Johann Conrad Dippel, who transferred his soul into an ape's body centuries ago, and is trying to unleash the Old Ones using the *Necronomicon*.

Short story by Joe R. Lansdale in Beyond Rue Morgue: Further Tales of Edgar Allan Poe's 1st Detective, *Paul Kane and Charles Prepolec, eds., Titan Books, 2013, connecting Edgar Allan Poe's sleuth C. Auguste Dupin to H. P. Lovecraft's Cthulhu Mythos. Johann Conrad Dippel is a historical alchemist. Despite his apparent death in this story, Dippel must have eventually had his soul placed back in his human body, or an exact replica thereof, as seen in Christopher Farnsworth's novel* Blood Oath *and other accounts.*

1846

February
VALDEMAR'S DAUGHTER

C. Auguste Dupin and his unnamed companion search for the remains of Ernest Valdemar, which have been stolen en route to his daughter Jana. The Comte de Saint-Germain, the leader of the Philosophical Harmonic Society, appears.

Novella by Brian Stableford included in Wildside Double #10, *Wildside Books, 2010. Farmer's* Tarzan Alive *identified Edgar Allan Poe's detective C. Auguste Dupin as a Wold Newton Family member. Therefore, this crossover brings the events of Poe's story "The Facts in the Case of M. Valdemar" into the Crossover Universe. It is unclear whether this Comte de Saint-Germain is the historical figure who has appeared in a number of works of fiction or an imposter.*

May
THE MAD TRIST
   The Comte de Saint-Germain gives C. Auguste Dupin's companion a copy of Sir Launcelot Canning's *The Mad Trist*, the allegedly cursed book Roderick Usher read from right before his death and the destruction of his home, in the hopes he will pass the book on to Dupin. However, the detective's amanuensis is unable to give it to him directly, as he is bound for England, where he reads the book to a bibliophile friend and his sisters.
   Novella by Brian Stableford included in Wildside Double #10, *Wildside Books, 2010. Sir Launcelot Canning's* The Mad Trist *and Roderick Usher are from Edgar Allan Poe's "The Fall of the House of Usher," bringing that story into the CU. As noted above, this Comte de Saint-Germain may or may not be the genuine historical figure that has appeared in many works of fiction.*

1849

Spring
THE PURL OF THE PACIFIC
   Mad Amos Malone contends with an evil *Kahuna* (sorcerer) in Hawaii. He pays for a ship's anchor chain with a scrimshawed tooth from a white sperm whale, which was given to him by a harpooner named Queequeg. He mentions a man named Herman who is writing a book about the story of the white whale.
   Short story by Alan Dean Foster in Mad Amos, *Del Rey, 1993. Mad Amos Malone is a mountain man who has many semi-occult adventures, somewhat in the vein of Manly Wade Wellman's Silver John. Queequeg and the white whale are from Herman Melville's* Moby-Dick, *although how Queequeg survived the destruction of the* Pequod *has yet to be revealed.*

1850

Summer
KAPITÄN STÜRMER FAHRTEN UND ABENTEUER ZU WASSER UND ZU LANDE
   Captain Fred Stürmer of the *Albatross* enters the same subterranean world later explored by Professor Otto Lidenbrock.
   Kapitän Stürmer Fahrten und Abenteuer zu Wasser und zu Lande *by Harry Strong, 1906. The connection to Jules Verne's* Journey to the Center of the Earth *brings Captain Stürmer into the CU. The* Albatross *is not to be confused with the airship of the same name used by Verne's science pirate Robur.*

November 7, 1850–December 28, 1998
CLOUD ATLAS

The same soul is incarnated in a number of individuals over more than a century, including composer Robert Frobisher, writer Luisa Rey, and publisher Timothy Cavendish. All of these incarnations bear a comet-shaped birthmark. Timothy has a double Kilmagoon at a pub after escaping from a nursing home.

Novel by David Mitchell. Robert Frobisher and his Cloud Atlas *sextet are both mentioned in Joe Hill's novel* NOS4A2, *which takes place in the Crossover Universe via ties to the works of Stephen King. Luisa Rey and Timothy Cavendish first appeared in Mitchell's novel* Ghostwritten; *in that book, Katy Forbes had a comet-shaped birthmark, marking her as another iteration of the same soul. Since Cavendish, Luisa, and Katy's lifespans partially overlap, the soul must have somehow been split between the three of them. Kilmagoon whiskey recurs in Mitchell's fiction. The sections of the book entitled "An Orison of Sonmi~451" and "Sloosha's Crossin' an' Ev'rythin' After" take place in future eras inconsistent with the known future of the CU, and therefore must take place in an alternate reality. In "An Orison of Sonmi~451," the title character mentions having read Ireneo Funes'* Remembrances, *a reference to Jorge Luis Borges' short story "Funes the Memorious," and refers to a fabricant living doll of Zizzi Hikaru, a Japanese virtual sex symbol from Mitchell's novel* number9dream.

1855

Summer
PIERCING THE VEIL OF ISIS

The Chevalier Auguste Dupin's new assistant is Reginald Goodwin, who flirts with Juliette Saint-Fond. Juliette's potential employer, Comte Jacques de Carignan, shows Dupin some of the grimoires in his personal library, including *De Vermis Mysteriis,* the *Book of Eibon, Unaussprechlichen Kulten,* and John Dee's personal copy of the *Necronomicon,* authored by Abdul Alhazred, "the Mad Arab." The Comte and Dupin discuss the Illuminati. The Comte says the Director of the city museum, Dr. Ponnonmer, procured the mummy of Allamistako from his cousin, Captain Arthur Sabretash. The Comte once believed Cagliostro was his father. Edme-François Jomard had the Comte spy on Ethan Gage; one of these assignments happened while Gage was searching for his love, Astiza. The Comte tells Dupin the *Habits Noirs* (aka the Black Coats) are also seeking the secret of life over death. The Comte says Colonel Bozzo-Corona, the leader of the High Council of the Black Coats, is his true father. One of Bozzo-Corona's cronies, Dr. Samuel, stole the secret of re-animation from the Comte, intending to use it to resurrect the mummy Pha-ho-tep, which he would control with a golden ankh.

Short story by Paul Hugli in Tales of the Shadowmen Volume 10: Esprit de Corps, *Jean-Marc and Randy Lofficier, eds., Black Coat Press, 2013; reprinted in French in* Les Compagnons de l'Ombre (Tome 16), *Jean-Marc and Randy Lofficier, eds., Rivière Blanche, 2015. The Chevalier C. Auguste Dupin is from Edgar Allan Poe's tales "The Murders in the Rue Morgue," "The Mystery of Marie Rogêt," and "The Purloined Letter." Dr. Ponnonmer (originally spelled Ponnonner), Allamistako (originally Allamistakeo), and Captain Arthur Sabretash are from Poe's "Some Words with a Mummy." Reginald Goodwin is an ancestor of Nero Wolfe's legman and biographer Archie Goodwin. Juliette Saint-Fond is a descendant of the wealthy Saint-Fond from the Marquis de Sade's novel* Juliette. *De Sade's Juliette is the sister of the title character of his book* Justine, *bringing that novel into the CU as well. Abdul Alhazred's* Necronomicon, *created by H. P. Lovecraft, is a staple of his Cthulhu Mythos.* De Vermis Mysteriis, *the* Book of Eibon, *and* Unaussprechlichen Kulten *are Mythos tomes created by Robert Bloch, Clark Ashton Smith, and Robert E. Howard respectively. The CU version of the Illuminati has had encounters with many adventurers, including Gary Seven and his companion Roberta Lincoln, as well as Lara Croft, and has also appeared in a series of novels by Robert Anton Wilson. Count Cagliostro is a historical figure who was identified as the ancestor of a villainous branch of the Wold Newton Family by Philip José Farmer. He also appeared in novels by Alexandre Dumas. Ethan Gage and his lover Astiza are from novels by William Dietrich. The* Habits Noirs, *Colonel Bozzo-Corona, and Dr. Samuel are from the works of Paul Féval. Pha-ho-tep and the golden ankh are from the Spanish horror film* Assignment Terror, *part of a series of movies featuring Paul Naschy as werewolf Waldemar Daninsky; the Colonel will use the mummy for his own nefarious ends in Christofer Nigro's "Death of a Dream" (*Tales of the Shadowmen Volume 9: La Vie en Noir, *2012).*

1857

Winter
THE NEXT OMEGA

An old man seeking a younger fellow who claims to be Doctor Omega remarks, "A Morlock would feel right at home in this neighborhood." The older man, who is also known as Doctor Omega, carries a robot head in a hatbox he acquired in the future, in the city of Metropolis. His companion Fred is mentioned. The two Doctors' carriage is driven by Eugene Papillon. The duo discovers a card bearing the name Maupertuis. The older Omega refers to Lecoq and "that Marple woman." The Omegas find themselves pursued by robed men that appear to be followers of the Ubasti. The elder Omega tells the younger how a wave of radioactive turbulence separated him and his traveling companions, and asks if he has been to Quinnis in the fourth universe. The apparent Ubasti cultists work for Baron Oscar Maupertuis. Omega refers to a suppressed account by Watson. They are attacked by the robed men, who turn out to actually be Red Lectroids. The younger Omega shows his elder namesake a crystal, which the latter identifies as from Metebelis-Three. The young Omega regains his memory of traveling to the Moon, where he met one of the Lunian Immortals, and realizes he is really balloonist Antoine Gerpré. Omega recognizes Maupertuis as Ozer, one of many immortals claiming to be the Wandering Jew. Omega departs with Helvetius, his fellow traveler in space and time.

Short story by Travis Hiltz in Tales of the Shadowmen Volume 10: Esprit de Corps, *Jean-Marc and Randy Lofficier, eds., Black Coat Press, 2013; reprinted in French in* Les Compagnons de l'Ombre (Tome 16), *Jean-Marc and Randy Lofficier, eds., Rivière Blanche, 2015. Doctor Omega is from Arnould Galopin's novel of the same name, as are Fred and Helvetius. The Lofficiers' translation and adaptation of Galopin's book implied the Doctor was the Crossover Universe counterpart of the time and-space-traveling Doctor from the television series* Doctor Who. *Quinnis in the fourth universe is mentioned in the* Doctor Who *serial "The Edge of Destruction," while Metebelis-Three is from the serials "The Green Death" and "Planet of the Spiders." The Morlocks are from H. G. Wells'* The Time Machine. *The robot and the city of Metropolis are from Fritz Lang's film* Metropolis. *Doctor Omega visited Metropolis in Hiltz's story "The Robots of Metropolis" (*Tales of the Shadowmen Volume 7: Femmes Fatales, *2011). Lecoq is Emile Gaboriau's sleuth. Eugene Papillon is from Gaboriau's novel* Monsieur Lecoq. *Baron Maupertuis is mentioned in the Sherlock Holmes story "The Adventure of the Reigate Squire"; here, he is conflated with Ozer from Paul Féval's novel* The Wandering Jew's Daughter. *"That Marple woman" is Agatha Christie's detective Miss Jane Marple. The*

Cult of Ubasti is from the serial The Return of Chandu, *and has also appeared in Hiltz's stories "The Treasure of the Ubasti" (*Tales of the Shadowmen Volume 6: Grand Guignol, *2009) and "In the Caves of the Serpent" (*Tales of the Shadowmen Volume 8: Agents Provocateurs, *2011). The serial was based on the radio series* Chandu the Magician, *which spawned a spin-off,* Omar the Mystic. *After being separated from Omega, Fred found himself in the year 1776, where he also encountered Red Lectroids, as seen in Hiltz's tale "What Lurks in Romney Marsh?" (*Tales of the Shadowmen Volume 9: La Vie En Noir, *2012). The Lunian Immortals and Antoine Gerpré are from Alfred Driou's book* The Adventures of a Parisian Aeronaut in the Unknown Worlds, *which has been translated by Brian Stableford for Black Coat Press.*

1857–1868

KEMOSABE

Young John Reid rescues and befriends a Potawatomi boy named Tonto. Ben Reid, John's father, is a member of the Texas Rangers alongside Al King, Bobby Stuart, and Jake Cutter. A man named Favor appears. Tonto honed his tracking skills under a Kickapoo scout who often worked for the Rangers. Over a decade later, a grown Tonto comes to the aid of John Reid, now a Ranger himself, who has been wounded and his comrades killed in an ambush at Bryant's Gap.

Short story by Matthew Baugh in The Lone Ranger Chronicles, *Matthew Baugh and Tim Lasiuta, eds., Moonstone Books, 2012. This story recounts the first meeting between John Reid, the future Lone Ranger, and his faithful companion Tonto. Al King is a reference to Allen King, the Ranger's alter ego in the 1938 film serial* The Lone Ranger; *obviously, the CU version of King is a distinct individual from the Ranger. Bobby (or Bob) Stuart is also from* The Lone Ranger *serial. Texas Ranger Jake Cutter is from Paul Wellman's Western novel* The Comancheros, *and was played by John Wayne in the 1961 film version. Favor is Gil Favor, the trail boss from the television series* Rawhide. *The Kickapoo scout is Famous Shoes from Larry McMurtry's* Lonesome Dove *novels.*

1858

Winter 1858–Spring 1859
DJANGO UNCHAINED

Django Freeman's wife is Broomhilda von Shaft. One of the members of Smitty Bacall's gang is Crazy Craig Koons. A man and his daughter watch from a window as Django and King Schultz ride into town.

Feature film directed by Quentin Tarantino, 2012. Django and Broomhilda are ancestors of Ernest Tidyman's private eye John Shaft. This Django is named after, but otherwise unrelated to, the gunslinger played by Franco Nero in Django *and* Django Strikes Again. *Crazy Craig Koons is an ancestor of Captain Koons from* Pulp Fiction. *The man and his daughter are played by Russ Tamblyn and his own daughter Amber, who are credited as "Son of a Gunfighter" and "Daughter of a Son of a Gunfighter," respectively. Tamblyn starred as Johnny Ketchum in the 1965 Western* Son of a Gunfighter. *Since that film takes place in 1877, it is impossible for the older man in* Django Unchained *to be Johnny himself, but perhaps he is his maternal grandfather.*

1860

Summer 1860; Late November–December 24, 1828
CHRISTMAS AT SCHÖNBRUNN

Père Tabaret reads a diary entry to Lecoq that was written by his former pupil's father, Lecoq de la Perière, in 1828. The entry describes how the elder Lecoq and his master, Colonel Bozzo-Corona, traveled to Austria to attempt to convince Franz, Duke of Reichstadt, to assume the throne and create a Second Empire. Henri de Belcamp is mentioned. Manse Everard, a Time Patrol agent masquerading as Franz's English tutor, sends a memo to Colonel Graigh, saying the divergent Second Empire timeline has been eliminated.

Short story by Jean-Marc and Randy Lofficier in Tales of the Shadowmen Volume 10: Esprit de Corps, *Jean-Marc and Randy Lofficier, eds., Black Coat Press, 2013; reprinted in French in* Les Compagnons de l'Ombre (Tome 15), *Jean-Marc and Randy Lofficier, eds., Rivière Blanche, 2014. Lecoq and his mentor, Père Tabaret, are from the works of Emile Gaboriau. Lecoq de la Perière and Colonel Bozzo-Corona are from the Black Coats novels by Paul Féval. Henri de Belcamp is from Féval's book* John Devil, which is set in the same continuity as the Black Coats series. Manse Everard is an agent of the Time Patrol in stories by Poul Anderson, while Colonel Graigh commands an identically-named organization in Henri Vernes' novels about adventurer Bob Morane. Emmanuel Gorlier's story "Out of Time" (Tales of the Shadowmen Volume 6: Grand Guignol, 2010) conflated the two Time Patrols.

1861

December
DAMNED NATION

A Confederate monster hunter mentions he knows Rhett Butler, whom he describes in the following manner: "Nice fellow, strange ears, bad taste in women."

This novel by Nick Pollotta serves as a prequel to Pollotta's three Bureau 13 novels, based on the role-playing game Bureau 13: Stalking the Night Fantastic, *and is set eight months after the start of the Civil War. Rhett Butler is from Margaret Mitchell's novel* Gone with the Wind; *this crossover brings Bureau 13 into the CU.*

1864

Winter
TROUBLED WATERS (EAUX TROUBLES)

Rocambole unsuccessfully attempts to steal the plans for the *Nautilus* from Captain Nemo in order to give them to the French government.

Short story by Patrick Lorin appearing as "Eaux Troubles" in Les Compagnons de l'Ombre (Tome 12), *Jean-Marc and Randy Lofficier, eds., Rivière Blanche, 2013, and in English in* Tales of the Shadowmen Volume 10: Esprit de Corps, *Jean-Marc and Randy Lofficier, eds., Black Coat Press, 2013. Rocambole is the villain-turned-hero of a series of novels by Ponson du Terrail. Captain Nemo is from Jules Verne's* 20,000 Leagues Under the Sea *and* The Mysterious Island.

1865

Spring
A MAN CALLED HORSE

Wagon master Major Seth Adams meets Horse, a Bostonian who was abducted as an infant by Crow Indians and eventually inducted into the tribe.

Episode of the television series Wagon Train *broadcast March 26, 1958. See the 1874 entry for* Alias Jesse James *for an explanation of how* Wagon Train *fits into the CU. This crossover brings in the events of Dorothy M. Johnson's short story "A Man Called Horse."*

THE TIDES OF KREGEN

Dray Prescot is an Earthman who has been transported several times to the planet Kregen by alien super beings known as the Star Lords. While there, he has had many swashbuckling adventures and married a princess. After rebelling against the Star Lords' dictates, he is sent back to Earth for twenty years as punishment. He spends time in America fighting for the Union in the Civil War. At the end of the war, he meets a man from Virginia who he believes would like a life like his.

Novel by Alan Burt Akers (pseudonym for Kenneth Bulmer). The man from Virginia is intended to be the warlord of Mars from Edgar Rice Burroughs' Mars series. Kregen may be in the Edgar Rice Burroughs Alternate Universe (ERB-AU).

Summer
OUR MIDNIGHT VISITOR

This story about a stolen diamond takes place on the island of Uffa.

Short story by Archie McDonald, edited by Arthur Conan Doyle. Dr. Watson, in "The Five Orange Pips," refers to "the singular adventures of the Grice Patersons in the island of Uffa."

Summer 1865–1873
HELL COME SUNDOWN

The Dark Ranger, Sam Hell (born Sam Yoakum), is an ex-Texas Ranger who has been transformed into a vampire. He spends his existence tracking down supernatural creatures and destroying them. Hell advertises his services in a penny dreadful called *Pickman's Illustrated Serials*, which also has ads for "Dr. Mirablis's Amazing Electric Truss" and a dime novel called "The Tortuga Gang Rides Again."

Story by Nancy A. Collins in Dead Man's Hand: Five Tales of the Weird West, *2004. Pickman's Illustrated Serials is probably published by relatives of Richard Upton Pickman from H. P. Lovecraft's "Pickman's Model." Rick Lai's story "The Last Vendetta" refers to the publishers as Pickman and Sons. Dr. Mirablis is from Collins' story "Lynch." The dime novel "The Tortuga Hill Gang Rides Again" will prompt a monster to join the Tortuga Gang many years later, as seen in Collins' "The Tortuga Hill Gang's Last Ride."*

1867

Spring. Young Johnny Brainerd creates a steam-powered automaton and embarks upon a series of adventures with a group of friends, as recounted by Edward S. Ellis in "The Steam Man of the Prairies," *Beadle's American Novel*, August 1868.

1868

Spring
LONGARM AND THE LONE STAR LEGEND
Deputy U.S. Marshal Custis "Longarm" Long meets cattle heiress Jessie Starbuck and her half-Japanese partner and bodyguard Ki, who are hunting down a European crime cartel responsible for the deaths of Jessie's parents.

Longarm Giant *#1 by Tabor Evans, 1982. Jessie Starbuck and Ki appeared in the first ten* Longarm Giant *books, as well as their own series, the* Lone Star *books, written under the pen name Wesley Ellis. Several later Longarm novels refer to his friendship with Jessie and Ki. Since Longarm is in the CU, so are Jessie and Ki.*

1869

Summer
SECRET OF THE DEAD
Former police Sergeant Richard Cuff investigates a pair of murders that appear to be related alongside a visiting fifteen-year-old named Sherlock Holmes.

Short story by David Stuart Davies in The Mammoth Book of Best British Crime 11, *Maxim Jakubowski, ed., Robinson, 2014. Sergeant Cuff is from Wilkie Collins' novel* The Moonstone. *Holmes and Cuff met again* during the 1872 events of Thomas Kent Miller's The Great Detective at the Crucible of Life, *though for some reason they did not mention their prior meeting in front of that book's narrator, Allan Quatermain.*

c. 1870s

WHAT ROUGH BEAST

Jonathan Crowley and the axe-wielding Kharrn battle a pack of werewolves.

Chapbook by James A. Moore and Charles R. Rutledge, White Noise Press, 2015. The immortal barbarian Kharrn appeared alongside Thomas Carnacki in Rutledge's story "The Beautiful Lady Without Pity: A Carnacki the Ghost-Finder Adventure," and was mentioned in Moore and Rutledge's novel Congregations of the Dead. *Jonathan Crowley, also an immortal, is a recurring character of Moore's, and encountered one of H. P. Lovecraft's Deep Ones in the book* Writ in Blood.

1870

Winter
JÜRGEN PETERS DER SCHIFFSJUNGE

A young German sailor, Jürgen Peters, encounters the Curupuri, sails aboard the *Grampus*, travels the same route as Dr. Samuel Ferguson, and meets "the New Robinson," a German sailor shipwrecked in the South Pacific.

Jürgen Peters der Schiffsjunge *#1–448, 1914–1923. The connections to the Curupuri (from Arthur Conan Doyle's* The Lost World*), the* Grampus *(from Edgar Allan Poe's* The Narrative of Arthur Gordon Pym of Nantucket*) and Dr. Ferguson (from Jules Verne's* Five Weeks in a Balloon*) bring Jürgen Peters into the CU, and in turn bring in the New Robinson, who appeared in Heinz Waldau's pulp* Ein Neuer Robinson *#1–60, 1912–1913.*

SOMEONE ELSE'S TROUBLE

Clint Adams, the Gunsmith, teams up with Ki to track down a gang who stole a katana in the custody of a friend of Clint's, killed the man's wife, and kidnapped his daughter. Clint's friendship with Secret Service agent Jim

West is mentioned. Clint has heard about Ki, the partner and bodyguard of rancher Jessie Starbuck, from Marshal Custis Long.

The Gunsmith #345 by "J. R. Roberts" (Robert J. Randisi), Jove Publications, 2010. Jessie Starbuck and Ki appeared alongside Marshal Custis "Longarm" Long in the first ten Longarm Giants by Tabor Evans, as well as their own series, the Lone Star books by Wesley Ellis. The katana is the same one seen in the film Red Sun, which takes place immediately after this novel. The movie's opening caption says it takes place around 1870. Several of the Gunsmith books refer to Clint's friendship with Jim West, who is from the classic TV western The Wild Wild West. Clint's friend Talbot Roper, a Pinkerton and recurring character in the Gunsmith books, appears as the main character of two novels by Randisi, Bullets and Lies and The Reluctant Pinkerton.

1871

Mid Spring–Late Summer. The events of Zane Grey's novel Riders of the Purple Sage.

1872

Autumn
RETURN TO THE CENTER OF THE EARTH
Professor Otto Lidenbrock and his nephew Axel once again embark on a voyage to the Earth's core, this time at the orders of Chancellor von Bismarck, in order to reach the crust before the Gun Club. Accompanying them are Captain Von Horst, Hans Bjelke, and Ned Land. The Lidenbrocks, Hans, and Ned eventually discover Pellucidar. Axel's wife Gretchen and the Professor's maid Martha appear, and Professor Aronnax, Captain Nemo, and Arne Saknussemm are mentioned. Among the races inhabiting Pellucidar are the *tarags, jaloks, thags*, Mahars, Sagoths, *lidis*, and *thipdars*. Eventually, the Lidenbrocks discover the Gun Club did visit the Arctic Circle, but not to travel to the Earth's core.

Serial by John Peel beginning in Tales of the Shadowmen Volume 10: Esprit de Corps, Jean-Marc and Randy Lofficier, eds., Black Coat Press, 2013, and concluding in Tales of the Shadowmen Volume 11: Force Majeure, Jean-Marc and Randy Lofficier, eds., Black Coat Press, 2014. Professor Lidenbrock, his nephew Axel, Hans Bjelke, Gretchen (or Gräuben), Martha, and Arne Saknussemm are from Jules Verne's novel Journey to the Center of the Earth. Evidently, the account of Axel's death earlier this year in Thos. Kent Miller's The Great Detective at the Crucible of Life was an exaggeration. *The Gun Club is from Verne's novels* From the Earth to the Moon *and* Around the Moon. *A footnote at the end of the second part of this story claims this voyage to the Arctic Circle by the Gun Club is that seen in Verne's novel* The Purchase of the North Pole. *However, that novel takes place in 1885–1886, not 1872. The Gun Club must have made an earlier trip to the Arctic for an unknown reason. Ned Land, Professor Aronnax, and Captain Nemo are from Verne's* 20,000 Leagues Under the Sea. *Pellucidar is the world at the Earth's core depicted in novels by Edgar Rice Burroughs. The various races named are all from the Pellucidar novels. Captain Von Horst is an ancestor of a character from the novels* Tarzan at the Earth's Core *and* Back to the Stone Age.

December 2–7, 1872; 1873
BEING AN ACCOUNT OF THE DELAY AT GREEN RIVER, WYOMING OF MR. PHILEAS FOGG, WORLD TRAVELER

At the *Casa del Gato* brothel in Oakland, California, the Lone Ranger,  disguised as bounty hunter Bret Reagan, finds that the man he has been pursuing has been killed by members of a tong called the Sublime Order of the White Peacock, which wishes to end the oppression of Chinese laborers on the railroads and coal mines. A sheriff sends a message to the Ranger, who uses the name Allen King for communication purposes. Later, on a train ride to Green River, Wyoming, the Ranger meets Phileas Fogg of Savile Row, England, his traveling companion Aouda, and his manservant Passepartout. Fogg, who has made a substantial bet that he can circumnavigate the entire globe in eighty days or less, had a confrontation with a Colonel Proctor on the Oakland ferry, causing him and his companions to be late. They returned to San Francisco and checked at the British Consulate, where they were referred to a gentleman gunfighter who resides at the Hotel Carlton, who escorted them to Reno. Along the way, the Colonel's brother, Major Proctor, repeatedly tried to goad this man in black into a gunfight, and the San Franciscan was forced to shoot him. Passepartout carries an oversized silver watch with esoteric markings on the cover. The Sublime Order of the White Peacock's leader, Shan Ming Fu, wishes to acquire Passepartout's watch, and claims that he and Fogg share paternity. Shan tells the Ranger that he will follow his progress, and that of his descendants and their descendants. A year later, the Ranger and Tonto meet the gentleman gunfighter in San Francisco. Their new acquaintance recounts the story of how he was requested to escort a bigwig from Seattle back to California. The man in black describes his charge: "Former mayor of Seattle, now a US Representative of the Washington Territory. Wife was plain, but adoring. Apparently lost some big bet about marrying off brides when he met her. Biddy was her name." The Ranger and Tonto received orders from Colonel Richmond of the Secret Service. They are supposed to meet Secret Service men, Agents W. and G. in Omaha, where the ex-mayor of Seattle will be speeded to hearings in the capital by a specially appointed, private Service train. The Representative says that "celestial men" are planning to meet with the President and congressional leaders, and he must stop them.

Short story by Win Scott Eckert in a forthcoming volume of Lone Ranger stories, Matthew Baugh, ed., Moonstone Books. Thomas Hewitt Edward Cat, the protagonist of the TV series T.H.E. Cat, *will later adopt the name of the* Casa del Gato *for his nightclub in San Francisco, California in the 1960s. The Lone Ranger's guise as Bret Reagan is from the movie* The Lone Ranger and the Lost City of Gold, *starring Clayton Moore, while the Ranger used the name Allen King in a 1938 film serial. Shan Ming Fu is meant to be Sax Rohmer's villain Doctor Fu Manchu, whose birth name was revealed by Dennis E. Power in his essay "The Devil Doctor: The Early History of Fu Manchu" (found on the* Wold Newton Universe: A Secret History *website). The Sublime Order of the White Peacock is from Rohmer's novels. Phileas Fogg, Aouda, Passepartout, and Colonel Stamp Proctor are from Jules Verne's novel* Around the World in Eighty Days. *The Hotel Carlton is the home of Paladin, the refined gunslinger featured in the television series* Have Gun – Will Travel, *who escorted Fogg, Aouda, and Passepartout to Reno in the episode "Fogg Bound." In "A Chronology of Major Events Pertinent to* The Other Log of Phileas Fogg,*" included in Titan Books' reissue of Philip José Farmer's novel, Eckert adopted a theory, originally proposed by Dennis E. Power, that the Major Proctor seen in "Fogg Bound" was the brother of Colonel Proctor from Verne's novel. In* The Other Log of Phileas Fogg, *Farmer revealed that Passepartout's watch contained a distorter, one of the teleportation devices used by the extraterrestrial Eridaneans of which he, Fogg, and Aouda are agents, as well as by their bitter rivals, the Capelleans. Shan Ming Fu's interest in acquiring a distorter was first revealed in Eckert and Matthew Baugh's novel* Honey West and T.H.E. Cat: A Girl and Her Cat. *Philip José Farmer's* Doc Savage: His Apocalyptic Life *identified Phileas Fogg and Fu Manchu as half-brothers, both being sons of Sir William Clayton. The Devil Doctor encountered the Lone Ranger's collateral descendant, the Green Hornet, in Eckert's stories "Fang and Sting" (*The Green Hornet Chronicles, *Joe Gentile and Win Scott Eckert, eds., Moonstone Books, 2010) and*

"Progress" (The Green Hornet: Still at Large, *Joe Gentile, Win Scott Eckert, and Matthew Baugh, eds., Moonstone Books, 2012). The Representative from Seattle is Aaron Stempel from the television series* Here Come the Brides. *The revelation that he married Biddie Cloom after losing the bet comes from Barbara Hambly's* Star Trek *novel* Ishmael, *which finished the show's unresolved storylines. The celestial men are the alien Karsids from* Ishmael. *Colonel Richmond, Agent W. (James West), Agent G. (Artemus Gordon), and the train are from the classic television series* The Wild, Wild West.

December 7–8
PASSING THROUGH THE HANDS OF STEEL
Jean Passepartout, accompanying his master Phileas Fogg on his eighty-day trip around the world, is captured by a trio of Germans disguised as Indians. The "Indians" are under the employ of Herr Doktor Schultze, who is based out of Steel City. Passepartout frees himself and their other captive, young hunchbacked inventor Johnny Brainerd, who asks Passepartout if Mr. Henry sent him. Johnny mentions his late friend Baldy. One of the "Indians" is a German named Santer. Schultze wants Brainerd to redesign and mass-produce the Steam-Man he created. Passepartout asks his captors if they are members of the Reform Club that wish to sabotage Fogg's voyage, and wonders if Colonel Stamp Proctor was an agent of Schultze's. In his youth, Passepartout aided Chief Inspector Gevrol and the Chevalier Dupin on several occasions. Passepartout and Brainerd manage to defeat the "Indians" with the aid of German-American cowboy Old Shatterhand and his Mescalero companion Winnetou.

Short story by Dennis E. Power in Tales of the Shadowmen Volume 8: Agents Provocateurs, *Jean-Marc and Randy Lofficier, eds., Black Coat Press, 2011; reprinted in French in* Les Compagnons de l'Ombre (Tome 12), *Jean-Marc and Randy Lofficier, eds., Rivière Blanche, 2013. Passepartout, Fogg, the Reform Club, and Colonel Proctor are from Jules Verne's novel* Around the World in Eighty Days. *Power's story elaborates on Passepartout's activities while separated from Fogg in Chapter 30 of Verne's novel. Herr Doktor Schultze and the Steel City are from Verne's novel* The Begum's Millions. *Johnny Brainerd, his friend Baldy Bicknell, and his Steam-Man are from Edward S. Ellis' dime novel story "The Steam Man of the Prairies." Old Shatterhand and Winnetou, their nemesis Santer, and Mr. Henry appear in Western novels by German author Karl May. Chief Inspector Gevrol appears in Emile Gaboriau's novels* L'Affaire Lerouge *and* Monsieur Lecoq. *The Chevalier C. Auguste Dupin is the sleuth created by Edgar Allan Poe. The date of December 10 given for this story is incorrect.*

1873

August
ALLAN QUATERMAIN AT THE DAWN OF TIME

Allan Quatermain and his Hottentot companion Hans encounter a group of scientists that are attempting to learn the true nature of the Star of Bethlehem. Impey Barbicane is the group's chief engineer. The group uses a pair of submarines based on technical details about Captain Nemo's *Nautilus* told to Barbicane by Professor Aronnax. This tale is framed as a letter by Lady Luna Holmes Ragnall to her cousin, recounting to him how Quatermain told her the story in 1882. Annotations and apicultural commentary written in 1905 are provided by men identified as "M" and "SS." A pair of footnotes state, "Some authorities have argued from internal evidence that 'M' is the initial of a pseudonymous name used by a certain Great Detective during his retirement in Sussex," and, "The same authorities sometimes suggest that 'SS' are the initials of a neighbor, fellow honey fancier, and occasional assistant of M during this late interlude." A clipping from a newspaper story by E. D. Malone about the third expedition by Professor Challenger to South America in 1915 appears.

From a memoir by Allan Quatermain, recorded by Lady Luna Holmes Ragnall, and edited by Thos. Kent Miller, Rosemill House, 2014. Allan Quatermain, Hans, and Lady Luna Holmes Ragnall are from the novels of H. Rider Haggard. Impey Barbicane is from Jules Verne's From the Earth to the Moon *and* Around the Moon. *Professor Aronnax, Captain Nemo, and the* Nautilus *are from Verne's* 20,000 Leagues Under the Sea. *"M" is a reference to Mr. Mycroft, the elderly beekeeping sleuth featured in novels and stories by H. F. Heard, who is heavily implied to be Sherlock Holmes using an alias. "Mycroft's" sidekick and fellow apiarist is named Sidney Silchester. E. D. Malone and Professor Challenger appear in* The Lost World *and other tales by Arthur Conan Doyle.*

Late Autumn
THE TREASURE OF EVERLASTING LIFE

Miguelito Loveless and his henchman Voltaire confront Allan Quatermain at his home in Africa. Loveless states his rhinoceros-shaped vehicle is based on a steel elephant that was used to explore India several decades ago.

Loveless is a member of the Black Coats, led by Colonel Bozzo-Corona. Loveless believes the Treasure of the Black Coats is the secret of eternal life. Loveless wishes Quatermain to lead him to the city of Kor, ruled by Ayesha. When Quatermain scoffs at the concept of immortality, Loveless cites other stories of incredible longevity in Africa, including the Phantom of Bangalla (aka the Ghost Who Walks) and Solomon Kane's writings about Queen Nakari. Loveless forces a group of Waziri tribesmen to join his expedition. The Colonel is extorting Doctor Dolittle, who has the ability to communicate with animals, into assisting him against Loveless. Dolittle communicates with the King of the Elephants, as well as another elephant named Cornelius. At the conclusion of the battle that follows, the Colonel instructs Loveless to create a sanctuary in California for the children of those killed by his personal executioner, the Marchef. Quatermain's Hottentot companion Hans also appears.

Short story by Matthew Dennion in Tales of the Shadowmen Volume 9: La Vie en Noir, *Jean-Marc and Randy Lofficier, eds., Black Coat Press, 2012; reprinted in French in* Les Compagnons de L'Ombre (Tome 13), *Jean-Marc and Randy Lofficier, eds., Rivière Blanche, 2014. Miguelito Loveless and Voltaire are from the television series* The Wild Wild West. *Allan Quatermain, Hans, the city of Kor, and Ayesha are from the novels of H. Rider Haggard. Allan encountered Ayesha in the summer of this year during the events of Haggard's* She and Allan. *The steel elephant is from Jules Verne's* The Steam House. *The Black Coats and their Treasure, as well as Colonel Bozzo-Corona and the Marchef, appear in novels by Paul Féval. The Phantom of Bangalla is, of course, from Lee Falk's classic comic strip. Solomon Kane is a wandering Puritan adventurer featured in stories by Robert E. Howard; the story in which Nakari appears is "The Moon of Skulls." The Waziri are the same tribe that will later be led by the jungle lord. Doctor Dolittle is featured in a series of books by Hugh Lofting. The elephants must be non-anthropomorphic CU counterparts of Babar and Cornelius from the books by Jean de Brunhoff.*

1874

Spring
ALIAS JESSE JAMES
 A posse tracking down Jesse James includes Marshal Matt Dillon, Major Seth Adams, Annie Oakley, Wyatt Earp, Davy Crockett, Roy Rogers, and Tonto.
 1959 feature film. Matt Dillon and Tonto are already in the CU. Wyatt Earp is played by Hugh O'Brian, who played the historical lawman on the

television series The Life and Legend of Wyatt Earp, *which is also in the CU. Major Seth Adams is from the television series* Wagon Train. *Annie Oakley was a real person, of course, but she is portrayed in this film by Gail Davis, who played Annie in the television series* Annie Oakley. *Therefore, that series must depict the life of Annie's CU counterpart. The historical Davy Crockett lived from 1786–1836, but perhaps the character seen here is his son or grandson. The Roy Rogers seen in this film may be the same Roy who appeared as the main character in several period Westerns, and an ancestor of the version of Roy seen in several set in the modern day. Matthew Baugh writes, "The date is speculative, and was chosen because it fits well with the careers of Jesse James and with most of the other characters appearing in the story." A reference to the 1892 bout between Gentleman Jim Corbett and John L. Sullivan and an appearance by a young Harry S. Truman (born in 1884) are clear anachronisms. It is worth noting Bret Maverick appears in a deleted scene.*

Autumn
THE HUNTING PARTY
    The Masked Rider has a friend who lives at the Carlton Hotel in San Francisco.
    Novella by Roman Leary in The Masked Rider: Tales of the Wild West, Volume Two, *Ron Fortier, ed., Airship 27 Productions, 2014. The Masked Rider appeared in the pulp magazine* The Masked Rider Western *from 1934–1953. His friend in San Francisco is Paladin from the radio and television western* Have Gun–Will Travel. *This reference brings the Rider into the CU. The Masked Rider met Jackson Cole's Navajo Tom Raine, Arizona Ranger, in C. W. Harrison's story* "Boothill Beller Box" *(Exciting Western Volume 8 #2, October 1944), while Raine crossed over with Steve Reese from the pulp Range Riders in* "Rawhide Ranger" *(Exciting Western Volume 7 #2, April 1944). The year is conjecture.*

1875

March
STUFF OF DREAMS

Haakon Jones is lured into a blizzard by a beautiful red-golden haired girl. It is suggested Ithaqua may have caused the blizzard.

Story by Aaron B. Larson in The Weird Western Adventures of Haakon Jones, Battered Silicon Dispatch Box, *1999. The girl is clearly Atali, the title character of Robert E. Howard's Conan story "The Frost Giant's Daughter." It is possible the frost giant and Ithaqua (from August Derleth's Cthulhu Mythos story of the same name) are the same being.*

1876

Summer
THE LAST ROUNDUP

In Algeria, Captain Hector Servadac and his adjutant Laurent Ben Zoof are thrown to the ground by the impact of an object crashing to the ground. Suddenly, Servadac and Ben Zoof are stationed instead in Tombstone, Arizona, and the same object collides with the earth. Aboard the *Cosmos*, Doctor Omega tells his companions Denis Borel and Fred something is seriously wrong. The Doctor wishes to return to 1905, where his friend the Sâr Dubnotal will consult with Serge Myrandhal on his Mars-bound vessel, which uses a psychic-powered propulsion drive. Meanwhile, Lucky Luke gallops into Tombstone aboard his horse Jolly Jumper. He is greeted by U.S. Marshal Hickok and his deputy, Jingles P. Jones. At the Silverado Saloon, General Custer is introduced by Major Blueberry. Luke tells Custer they are fighting against Mexican units supported by Franco-Imperial forces under General Vicomte de Blissac. Accompanying Custer are federal agents Jim West and Artemus Gordon. Custer came to Arizona with the Seventh Cavalry and the Fighting Blue Devils of the 101st Cavalry from Fort Apache. Custer wants the masked man and his Potawatomi friend to destroy the balloon unit among the enemy troops, and tells Gordon to have his engineer friend,

Frank Reade, meet with him to discuss building war machines for the forthcoming battle. Tucson Smith, Stony Brooke, and Lullaby Joslin, collectively known as the Three Mesquiteers, offer to reconnoiter for Custer. Doctor Omega discovers Denis altered history by fathering a child in 1865 by Empress Carlotta of Mexico. West rides out with Frederick Altamont Cornwallis "English Freddie" Twistleton, younger son of the fourth Earl of Ickenham, who has a Beadle dime novel, a fictionalized adventure of Deadwood Dick and Calamity Jane, tucked in his gun belt. West warns Freddie about a con man at the saloon named Slick. West and Freddie discover their opponents have Steam House technology, much like Engineer Barnes designed for Munro in India. West realizes the engine of destruction was created by his old foe, Doctor Miguelito Loveless, who is accompanied by his gigantic mute servant. West and Freddie are captured and questioned by Colonel Henri Marquis de Prerolles and Don Pedro O'Sullivan, who are accompanied by an Indian named Perro-Rojo. After they leave, West tells Freddie he believes "O'Sullivan" was actually the Ranger, and Perro-Rojo his Potawatomi companion, noting "O'Sullivan" called the latter "*tonto*." Alcide Jolivet tries to interview Servadac. Servadac was recommended for this assignment by his old science professor, Palmyrin Rosette. Jolivet asks Servadac about stories ethnologists have discovered a mountain valley filled with extinct reptiles called *valle del guangi*. Frank Reade is building a Steam Man to turn the tide of the battle.

Short story by Stuart Shiffman in Doctor Omega and the Shadowmen, *Jean-Marc and Randy Lofficier, eds., Black Coat Press, 2011; reprinted in French in* Les Compagnons de L'Ombre (Tome 10), *Jean-Marc and Randy Lofficier, eds., Rivière Blanche, 2012. Hector Servadac, Laurent Ben Zoof, and Palmyrin Rosette are from Jules Verne's novel* Hector Servadac *(aka* Off in a Comet*). The Steam House, Engineer Banks, and Munro are from Verne's* The Steam House. *Alcide Jolivet is from Verne's* Michel Strogoff: The Courier of the Czar. *The* Cosmos, *Doctor Omega, Denis Borel, and Fred are from Arnould Galopin's novel* Doctor Omega, *which has been adapted and translated by the Lofficiers. The Sâr Dubnotal is an occult investigator in a series of French pulp novels by an anonymous author, possibly Norbert Sévestre. Serge Myrandhal is from* Les Aventures Merveilleuses de Serge Myrandhal sur la Planète Mars *by Henri Gayar. Lucky Luke and Jolly Jumper are from the Belgian comic book series created by "Morris" (Maurice de Bevere). Wild Bill Hickok is an historical figure; however, his deputy Jingles P. Jones is from the radio and television series* Adventures of Wild Bill Hickok. *Major Michael Steven "Blueberry" Donovan appeared in a Franco-Belgian comic series by Jean-Michel Charlier and Jean "Moebius"*

Giraud. *The Vicomte de Blissac appears in P. G. Wodehouse's novel* Hot Water. *Frederick Altamont Cornwallis Twistleton is better known as Uncle Fred, who appears in several books and stories by Wodehouse. Jim West, Artemus Gordon, and Doctor Loveless are from the television series* The Wild Wild West; *Loveless' giant mute assistant is Voltaire from the same series. Matthew Dennion's story "The Treasure of Everlasting Life" (*Tales of the Shadowmen Volume 9: La Vie En Noir*, Jean-Marc and Randy Lofficier, eds., Black Coat Press) also shows Loveless using Steam House technology. The Fighting Blue Devils of the 101st Cavalry and Fort Apache are from the television series* The Adventures of Rin Tin Tin. *The masked man (aka the Ranger) and his Potawatomi friend are the Lone Ranger and Tonto. Don Pedro O'Sullivan is from "The Return of Don Pedro O'Sullivan," an episode of* The Lone Ranger *television series. In that episode, the Ranger impersonated the real Don Pedro after he was shot. In the episode "Outlaw Masquerade," Tonto posed as an outlaw named "Red Dog" ("Perro Rojo" in Spanish). Frank Reade is one of the most famous boy inventors in American dime novels. The Three Mesquiteers appeared in a series of Western novels by William Colt MacDonald, which were adapted into a series of "B"-films. Deadwood Dick and a fictionalized version of Calamity Jane appeared in dime novels by Edward L. Wheeler. Calvin "Slick" Stanhope is from the movie* Silverado. *Henri Marquis de Prerolles is from Philippe de Massa's novel* Zibeline. *The valle del guangi is a reference to the film* The Valley of Gwangi.

August
BELFRY'S IN YOUR BATS!

Haakon Jones thwarts a bizarre plot on the life of President Grant. He is assisted by a Secret Service agent named Jim who dresses in a tight suit and vest, and carries an explosive material in his boot heel.

Story by Aaron B. Larson in The Weird Western Adventures of Haakon Jones, *Battered Silicon Dispatch Box, 1999; reprinted in* Showdown at Midnight, *David B. Riley, ed., Science Fiction Trails, 2011. Jim is Jim West from* The Wild Wild West, *thus reinforcing Haakon Jones' inclusion in the CU.*

Autumn 1876–Winter 1877
LYNCH

Johnny Pearl, an ex-Confederate farmer, is lynched by members of the U.S. Cavalry, who also murder his pregnant Indian wife. Pearl is restored to life by Dr. Anton Mirablis and given the name of "Lynch." Mirablis is nearly 100-years-old and studied medicine in the 1790s with Frankenstein. Mirablis has some of Frankenstein's notebooks. According to Mirablis, he and Frankenstein were working to create life together, until they went their separate ways when they disagreed on the method. Frankenstein was interested in electricity, but Mirablis was interested in creating a serum. Eventually, Mirablis combined both methods.

Story by Nancy A. Collins, originally published as a chapbook in 1992, reprinted in Dead Man's Hand: Five Tales of the Weird West, *2004. Rick Lai writes, "Mirablis claims that Mary Shelley altered events for her classic novel. He says that Frankenstein's real name was Viktor von Frankenstein, and that the two of them studied at the University of Vienna (rather than Ingolstadt). Mirablis also claims that both Frankenstein and the Monster perished differently than in the novel. Mirablis is an untrustworthy person, and could be lying for his own reasons."*

1877

Spring
A KNIGHT DOES NOT A PAWN MAKE

Haakon Jones finds himself on the opposite side of a range war from an expensive hired gun. The man is unnamed, but dresses all in black, has a holster decorated with a silver chess knight, charges $1000 for his services, quotes classical authors, and gives his address as the Hotel Carlton in San Francisco.

Story by Aaron B. Larson in The Weird Western Adventures of Haakon Jones, *Battered Silicon Dispatch Box, 1999. The hired gun is Paladin from the television series* Have Gun–Will Travel.

Summer
THE BLACK TRAIL

Tales of outlaws such as Jed Herne, Edge, Jack Ryker, Cuchillo Oro, and Crow are mentioned. Crow has a creed that requires killing enemies before they have a chance to kill him, "which meant he didn't have any enemies. Like a nervy shootist named Lee once said. Lee had gotten himself killed swatting some flies away from a little village south of the border against Calveras. With Chris and a half-dozen others. He'd said he had no enemies. Alive."

Crow #5 *by James W. Marvin, Corgi Books, 1980.* George G. Gilman's *Edge is already in the CU. Therefore, this crossover brings in several other Western series characters: Marvin's Crow, John J. McLaglen's Jed Herne (aka Herne the Hunter), Charles C. Garrett's John "Jack" Ryker (featured in the* Gunslinger *series), and William M. James' Cuchillo Oro (the protagonist of the* Apache *series). Lee, Calvera (spelled Calveras here), and Chris are from the film* The Magnificent Seven. Crow #1: The Red Hills *also contains a reference to Edge, and both Cuchillo Oro and Edge are mentioned in* Crow #7: One-Eyed Death *and* Crow #8: A Good Day. A Good Day *also mentions Herne.* Crow #3: *Tears of Blood also references Cuchillo Oro. Edge was also mentioned in each of the first three* Gunslinger *novels:* The Massacre Trail, The Golden Gun, *and* White Apache. *Edge is also mentioned in* Herne the Hunter #5: Apache Squaw, Herne the Hunter #7: Death Rites, Herne the Hunter #11: Silver Threads, Herne the Hunter #21: Pony Express, *and* Herne the Hunter #24: The Last Hurrah. *Both* Herne the Hunter #1: White Death *and* Apache Squaw *mention Nathan Brittles from the movie* She Wore a Yellow Ribbon. Apache Squaw *also refers to the Ringo Kid from* Stagecoach. *Both characters were played by John Wayne, and both films were directed by John Ford. Both* Silver Threads *and* The Last Hurrah *also contain references to Crow. Also mentioned in* Silver Threads *is Caleb Thorn, who appeared in five novels by "L. J. Coburn" (Laurence James and John Harvey). Edge appeared alongside another George G. Gilman series character, Adam Steele, in the novels* Two of a Kind, Matching Pair, *and* Double Action, *and also appeared in Charles R. Pike's* Jubal Cade #6: The Burning Man. *In* Breed #15: *Slaughter Time by James A. Muir, a girl remembers being taken to see a traveling carnival that had a block of gold protected by a tiger, a reference to* Edge #14: The Big Gold. *The same novel also mentioned Chato's hunt for revenge, referring to the movie* Chato's Land. *In* Breed #8: Blood Debt, *Breed meets Ethan Edwards and Martin Pawley from the movie* The Searchers.

1878

April 1–19
MURDER ON THE LEVIATHAN
Erast Fandorin becomes embroiled in a murder mystery aboard the steamship *Leviathan*. One of the other passengers, Reginald Milford-Stokes, writes in a letter to his wife, "The *Leviathan* is the largest passenger ship in the history of the world, with the single exception of the colossal *Great Eastern*, which has been furrowing the waters of the Atlantic Ocean for the last 20 years. When Jules Verne described the *Great Eastern* in his book

The Floating City, he had not seen our *Leviathan*—otherwise he would have renamed the old *G.E.* 'the floating village.' That vessel now does nothing but lay telegraph cables on the ocean floor, but *Leviathan* can transport 1,000 people and in addition 10,000 tons of cargo."

Novel by Boris Akunin. Erast Fandorin is already in the CU, and so this crossover brings in Verne's novel The Floating City. *Rick Lai writes, "In Verne's* The Floating City, *there is a passenger, Dean Pitferge, who intends to always sail on the ship until it sinks. The novel concludes with Pitferge sending a telegram in 1868 that the* Great Eastern *was 'ship-wrecked' near Auckland Rocks, New Zealand. Pitferge has been rescued by another ship. I can only assume that the* Great Eastern *was later salvaged and re-fitted."*

Spring
THE FALLEN ANGEL OF DODGE CITY
   The Lone Ranger answers a summons from actor Eddie Foy, who says, "I also wired an old friend of mine in San Francisco, but have received no reply–I must assume he is already engaged. I understand, though, that you, like he, are a paladin of sorts, if you are familiar with the expression." Foy requests the Ranger come to the aid of his friend Dora Hand in Dodge City, and speaks derisively of the town's lawmen, including Bat Masterson, Bill Tilghman, Charlie Bassett, Wyatt Earp, and Doc Holliday, comparing them to "that big damn fella that was marshal there for so long . . . but he retired and disappeared off the face of the earth." When Dora is murdered, the Ranger and Tonto work with the Dodge lawmen to bring her killer to justice. Doctor Chapman is mentioned as having performed Dora's autopsy.
   Short story by Troy D. Smith in The Lone Ranger Chronicles, *Matthew Baugh and Tim Lasiuta, eds., Moonstone Books, 2012. Foy's friend in San Francisco is Paladin from the radio and television series* Have Gun–Will Travel. *The big man that was a marshal in Dodge City is Matt Dillon from the radio and TV shows* Gunsmoke. *Dillon's retirement and disappearance must have been short-lived, as he continued to defend Dodge until the mid 1880s. Dr. John Chapman briefly replaced Galen "Doc" Adams as Dodge's primary physician in six episodes of* Gunsmoke *aired in 1971.*

August
DEAD IN THE WEST

The Reverend Jebidiah Mercer battles zombies in Mud Creek, a town in East Texas. The town doctor has copies of *The Necronomicon, Mysteries of the Worm* (aka *De Vermis Mysteriis*), *Nameless Cults, Caballa of Saboth, Cultes des Goules, The Black Book of Doches,* and *Compendium Maleficarum.*

This short novel by Joe R. Lansdale is reprinted along with the other Reverend Jebidiah Mercer stories in Deadman's Road, *Subterranean Press, 2010. The references to various books from the Cthulhu Mythos bring the Reverend into the CU. The town of Mud Creek appears in a number of Lansdale's novels and short stories, including "Bubba Ho-Tep," which has previously been included in the CU due to a reference to tana leaves from Universal Studios' original series of Mummy films. The Book of Doches also appears in another Mercer story, "The Crawling Sky," Lansdale and Timothy Truman's comic book miniseries* Jonah Hex: Two-Gun Mojo, *and Lansdale and Peter Bergting's comic book adaptation of Lovecraft's "The Dunwich Horror," which updates the story to the 21st century, and thus must take place in an alternate universe. The year is conjecture, although the chronological references in the book suggest a 1870s setting. Furthermore, Mercer at one point refers to Wild Bill Hickok in the past tense, suggesting a placement after Hickok's death in 1876.*

1879

Winter
THE BLOOD LIBEL

The Hassidic gunslinger known as the Merkabah Rider comes to the town of Delirium Tremens, which has a sign from Drucker and Dobbs Mining Company welcoming newcomers. He winds up rescuing Reverend Shallbetter's daughter from Molech-worshipping cultists whose leader refers to the Great Old Ones.

Short story by Edward M. Erdelac in Merkabah Rider: Tales of a High Planes Drifter, *Damnation Books, 2009. The connection to the Cthulhu*

Mythos brings the Merkabah Rider stories into the CU. Future stories have more Mythos references, as well as other crossovers. The town of Delirium Tremens has appeared in other works by Erdelac, including the story "The Blood Bay" and the independent film Meaner Than Hell. Reverend Shallbetter's daughter, Carrie, is also from "The Blood Bay." Drucker and Dobbs Mining Company is meant to evoke gold prospector Fred C. Dobbs from B. Traven's novel The Treasure of the Sierra Madre and John Huston's film adaptation. Since both the book and the movie take place in the 1920s, the Dobbs that co-owns the mining company must be a relative of Fred's.

Summer
THE NIGHTJAR WOMEN

The Merkabah Rider battles Lilith, the Queen of Demons, in the town of Tip Top, Arizona. Lilith hints at the coming of certain "things," which the Rider suspects might be the Elder Gods.

Short story by Edward M. Erdelac in Merkabah Rider: Tales of a High Planes Drifter, *Damnation Books, 2009. The reference to the Elder Gods of the Cthulhu Mythos once again confirms the Rider's place in the CU.*

Late September–October 2
TEN LORDS A-LEAPING

Friedrich Engels brings Lord Beckworth, a friend of a friend, to meet Karl Marx. Beckworth tells the two nine generations of Beckworths before him have fallen to their death. Two days later, when they pay call on him, Inspector Bucket tells them Beckworth has taken a fatal fall. Marx and Engels finally expose the killer, whom Bucket takes into custody. A week later, Engels meets with Marx outside the British Museum, where the latter says goodbye to a young man with a tweed cap of a type Engels does not recognize. The youth has recently left university and currently resides in Montague Street. He is interested in criminology, and Marx discerns from their conversation he wishes to be a detective. Marx adds, "He is working on a puzzle presented to him by a high-born friend of his from college, a superstitious observance of an ancient family known as 'the Musgrave Ritual.'"

Short story by Friedrich Engels, edited by Jake Arnott in The Best British Mysteries 2006, *Maxim Jakubowski, ed., Allison & Busby. Engels and Marx were both real people, and among the first major leaders of the modern Communist party. Inspector Bucket is from Charles Dickens'* Bleak House. *Bucket, middle-aged during the events of Dickens' novel, must be pushing hard against retirement in this story. The young man is, of course, Sherlock Holmes. The dates of this story are based on William S. Baring-Gould's dating of "The Adventure of the Musgrave Ritual."*

1880

Summer
THE INFERNAL NAPOLEON
The Merkabah Rider has a clay Cheyenne horse talisman given to him by the great shaman Misquamacus. Doctor Sheardown, the current pupil of the Rider's former master Adon, is working with Adon to bring about the Hour of Incursion, in which the Great Old Ones will be unleashed upon the world. The Rider finds among Sheardown's belongings a book called *The Wisdom and Sacred Magic of Zylac the Mage* and a rejection letter from a Dr. Allen Halsey, the dean of a new medical school opening in Massachusetts.

Short story by Edward M. Erdelac *in* Merkabah Rider: The Mensch with No Name, *Damnation Books, 2010. The Great Old Ones are from H. P. Lovecraft's Cthulhu Mythos. Dr. Allen Halsey is the dean of Miskatonic University's medical department in Lovecraft's "Herbert West—Reanimator." Misquamacus is from August Derleth's short Mythos novel* The Lurker at the Threshold *and the Manitou novel series by Graham Masterton.* The Wisdom and Sacred Magic of Zylac the Mage *was created by Joseph S. Pulver, though Zylac himself is from Cthulhu Mythos stories by Clark Ashton Smith.*

THE DAMNED DINGUS
The Merkabah Rider reads *The Wisdom and Sacred Magic of Zylac the Mage*, which mentions beings by the names of Tsathoggua, Shub-Niggurath, Eibon, and Milaab, and places named Commorion and Phenquor, as well as Hyperborea. Serpent men societies and toad gods dwelled in Hyperborea, and it also bore an enchanted tower on the peninsula of Mhu Thulan. The book has many glyphs and runes for the binding of and protection against Azathoth, and frequently mentions the Great Old Ones. One glyph in the book shows the Elder Sign. The Rider meets Professor Alfred William Wallace Spates, who is working on a field catalog of hitherto unknown creatures. The Rider's late enemy Dr. Sheardown sought the Star-Stones of Mnar. Mysterious Dave Mather and his brother were tattooed with the Elder Sign by a drunken sailor when they were aboard the *Hetty*. Spates learned of the Elder Sign from sources such as Von Junzt and Al-Hazred, author of the *Necronomicon*, and once consulted a colleague in Boston about inscriptions on a woodblock print of an Atlantean tablet depicting a shoggoth. He identified the inscriptions as being written in the written language of the Hyperboreans, Tsath-yo.

Short story by Edward M. Erdelac *in* Merkabah Rider: The Mensch with No Name, *Damnation Books, 2010. Shub-Niggurath and Azathoth are* among the Great Old Ones of H. P. Lovecraft's Cthulhu Mythos. The Elder Sign *is a means by which to ward off the Great Old Ones. The ship* Hetty *is from Lovecraft's "The Shadow over Innsmouth"; the drunken sailor is probably Zadok Allen. Abdul Al-Hazred, the* Necronomicon, *and the shoggoth are also from Lovecraft's Mythos stories. The Tsath-yo language is from Lovecraft and E. Hoffmann Price's "Through the Gates of the Silver Key." Zylac, Tsathoggua (the toad god), Eibon, Milaab, Commorion, Phenquor, Hyperborea, the serpent men societies (aka the Serpent People), and Mhu Thulan are all from the works of Clark Ashton Smith, another contributor to the Mythos. The Wisdom and Sacred Magic of Zylac the Mage appears in Mythos fiction by Joseph S. Pulver. "Spates' catalog" is a list of supernatural entities mentioned in the movie* Ghostbusters. *The Star-Stones of Mnar are from August Derleth's* The Lurker at the Threshold. *Mysterious Dave Mather is a historical figure who has also battled the Great Old Ones in a series of stories by Matthew Baugh. Von Junzt is Friedrich Wilhelm von Junzt, the author of* Unaussprechlichen Kulten *in Cthulhu Mythos stories by Robert E. Howard.*

WHO REALLY WAS THAT MASKED MAN?

In the 1930s framing sequence, a Texas Ranger says he recently brought cattle rustlers to justice in cooperation with ranchers from the B-Bar-B in Big Bend County, the TM Bar in Dobie County, and the Bar 20, as well as an Arizona rancher-pilot who is a kind of "king" of the sky and a mystery-loving Texan detective called "Doc." The Ranger's horse is named Charcoal, and other horses ridden during the operation include Amigo, Tony, and Topper III. The Ranger was sent a historical puzzle a few months back by a daily newspaper called the *Sentinel.* The stack of documents sent to him by the paper's publisher includes stories torn from the *London Times.* The documents describe the true story of a former Ranger who became a legend in the Old West. In the tale, a Dodge City Marshal talks with his Deputy and a man who has a gray steel and rainbow mother-of-pearl six-shooter in his holster. The man with the gun is planning to go shooting with Ted, an old friend of his from Tennessee who owns a "squirrel gun," and recently spent some time with a Mountie and his remarkable dog in the Yukon Territory. The Marshal is friends with a sheriff in Canyon County. The man with the six-shooter mentions "that lovely lady down at

the Longbranch." A Masked Man and his Indian companion ride into town to turn Deuce Cavendish, a cousin of an infamous outlaw they once brought to justice, over to the Marshal. The Masked Man volunteers to take Cavendish to Doc's office. The Marshal has Wanted posters of two Mexicans, one of whom is trim and handsome and calls himself "Kid," while the other is fat and almost slovenly. The Masked Man has a friend who is a Cavalry Captain at Fort Laramie. The Mexicans, who ride horses named Diablo and Loco, come across the Masked Man and the Indian. The Kid says he knows of only one man who is not a bandito and who wore a mask, and the Masked Man is not El Zorro. A red-haired man and a young Indian boy ride to Dodge City from Painted Valley to get a birthday present for the Duchess. Three men meet in an outpost some distance from Dodge: a man with dark, somewhat wavy hair and a thick mustache; a cattleman with silver hair and a neckerchief clasp in the shape of a steer's head; and an Englishman who seems to be a kind of frontier gentleman, and who bears an uncanny resemblance to the dark-haired man. The silver-haired man, who calls himself Bill, has an elderly sidekick. The two come across the cave of a Comanche and his grizzled companion, and Bill notices the Comanche resembles a rancher they recently encountered.

Short story by Don Glut in Radio Western Adventures, *Bill Cunningham, ed., Pulp 2.0 Press, 2010. This story is a tour-de-force crossover between the main characters of many radio Westerns. The Texas Ranger is Jayce Pearson from* Tales of the Texas Rangers. *The B-Bar-B ranch and Amigo are from* Bobby Benson and the B-Bar B Riders. *The TM Bar and Tony are from* Tom Mix Ralston Straight Shooters. *The Bar 20 is from* Hopalong Cassidy, *based on short stories by Clarence E. Mulford. The silver-haired man is Hopalong himself, while his sidekick is California Carlson. Topper III is a descendant of Hopalong's horse Topper. The Arizona rancher-pilot is the title character of* Sky King, *while the Texan detective is "Doc" Long from* I Love a Mystery. *The* Sentinel *is the newspaper published by Britt Reid, aka the Green Hornet. The former Texas Ranger of the Old West is John Reid, aka the Lone Ranger. The* Green Hornet *radio series established Britt Reid was John Reid's great-nephew. The Ranger's Indian companion is Tonto, while Deuce Cavendish is the cousin of his foe Butch Cavendish. The* London Times *is from* Frontier Gentleman. *The title character of that show is* Times *reporter J. B. Kendall. The Marshal and his Deputy are Matt Dillon and Chester from* Gunsmoke. *"That lovely lady at the Longbranch" and Doc are Miss Kitty Russell and Galen "Doc" Adams from that series. The man with the colorful gun is Britt Ponset from* The Six Shooter. *"Ted" is a typo for "Jed," and the reference is actually to Tennessee Jed Sloan from* Tennessee Jed. *The Mountie and his dog are Sgt. Preston and King from* Challenge of the Yukon. *The Sheriff of Canyon County* is Mark Chase of Death Valley Sheriff. *The Kid and his sidekick* are the Cisco Kid and Pancho. The radio version of the Cisco Kid is much more good-natured than the character's original version in O. Henry's tale "The Caballero's Way." Also, Henry's Cisco Kid was a white man whose last name was Goodall, rather than a Mexican. The radio Kid likely assumed his literary namesake's alias for reasons of his own. Diablo and Loco are the Kid and Pancho's horses, respectively. The Lone Ranger's friend is Captain Lee Quince from Fort Laramie. Zorro is self-explanatory. The red-haired man from Painted Valley is the title character of Red Ryder, based on the comic strip of the same name, while his sidekick is Little Beaver. The Duchess is Red's aunt. The dark-haired man is Paladin from Have Gun–Will Travel. Both Paladin and J. B. Kendall were played on radio by John Dehner. The Comanche is the title character of *Straight Arrow,* who has a secret identity as rancher Steve Adams. His sidekick is Packy McCloud. The year is conjecture.

November
THE OUTLAW GODS

The Merkabah Rider was dubbed "Rider Who Walks" by the Indian shaman Misquamacus. A group of Indians leads the Rider to Chaksusa, disciple of Shar-Rogs pa the Ancient One, the blue abbot of Shambhala. The Black Goat Man, who sent a creature to attack the Rider and his traveling companions, is the high priest of Shub-Niggurath, one of the Great Old Ones, which are also known as the Outer Gods, and were worshipped by the people of K'n-yan in the Kingdom of Aztlan. The Great Old Ones' servants, the *Mexica,* were liberated and led to Texcoco by Shar-Rogs pa's brother Mun Gsod, who corrupted himself and took the name Huitzilopochtli, and was worshipped by the same people he saved. Shub-Niggurath is consort to Yig, whose minions are the Cold Ones, one of which was the creature that attacked the Rider and the others. The Rider recently read the book of Zylac, which contained the Elder Sign, among other glyphs and wards. Chaksusa says the Red House is the ruins of a citadel of a lost colony of K'n-yan, which worshipped the Not to Be Named One, also known as the *Magnum Innominandum.* Chaksusa has made arrows from one of the Greater Star-Stones of Mnar. The Black Goat Man read about Shub-Niggurath in a long lost copy of Ostanes' *Sapientia Magorum.*

Short story by Edward M. Erdelac in Merkabah Rider: The Mensch with No Name, *Damnation Books, 2010. Misquamacus is from August Derleth's* The Lurker at the Threshold, *as well as the Manitou novels by Graham Masterton. The Star-Stones of Mnar are also from* The Lurker at the Threshold. *Shub-Niggurath is among the Great Old Ones of Lovecraft's Cthulhu Mythos stories. Yig is from Lovecraft's revision of Zealia Bishop's "The Curse of Yig," while K'n-yan is described in Lovecraft's revision of Bishop's "The Mound," and is also mentioned in "The Whisperer in Darkness" and his revision of Hazel Heald's "Out of the Aeons." The Magnum Innominandum is also from "The Whisperer in Darkness." In Lovecraft's stories, the Elder Sign is a defense against the Great Old Ones. "Shar-Rogs Pa" and "Mun Gsod" are Tibetan approximations of "Darkness Slayer" and "East-helper," the English translations of the names of the Blue Wizards Morinehtar and Rómestámo from J. R. R. Tolkien's epic fantasy saga* The Lord of the Rings. *The Cold Ones and Zylac appear in Cthulhu Mythos fiction by Clark Ashton Smith. Zylac's book,* The Wisdom and Sacred Magic of Zylac the Mage, *appears in Cthulhu Mythos stories by Joseph S. Pulver. Ostanes'* Sapientia Magorum *is from Richard L. Tierney's "The Seed of the Star-God."*

1881

January
THE PANDÆMONIUM RIDE

The Merkabah Rider, shaken by his recent encounter with the Great Old One known as Shub-Niggurath, accompanies the African Kabede to meet Lucifer. Kabede possesses the Rod of Aaron, which was previously in the hands of a Christian adventurer, who is said to have died using it to defeat a great evil some two hundred years ago, though Kabede removed the image of a cat-headed god the Egyptians placed upon it. The Rider shows Lucifer one of the Star-Stones of Mnar, which has the Elder Sign upon it, and tells him the symbol warded off Yig.

Short story by Edward M. Erdelac in Merkabah Rider: The Mensch with No Name, *Damnation Books, 2010. The Great Old Ones, Shub-Niggurath, the Elder Ones, and Yig are from H. P. Lovecraft's Cthulhu Mythos. The Christian adventurer is Robert E. Howard's wandering heroic puritan Solomon Kane, who was identified as a Wold Newton Family member by Philip José Farmer. The long-lived Kane actually met his end in 1790 during the events of Matthew Baugh's story "The Heart of the Moon" (*Tales of the Shadowmen Volume 3: Danse Macabre, *Jean-Marc and Randy Lofficier, eds., Black Coat Press, 2006). Kabede probably heard a false account of Kane's death in the 17th century. Also, the cat's head fetish* must have been reattached to the Rod of Aaron at some point after the 1882 events of the last Merkabah Rider book, Once Upon a Time in the Weird West, as it adorns the top of the staff in Robert M. Price's Anton Zarnak story "Dope War of the Black Tong," which takes place in 1938. The Star-Stones of Mnar are from August Derleth's short novel The Lurker at the Threshold.

THE LONG SABBATH

The Merkabah Rider and his companion Kabede fight parasitic spawn of the Great Old Ones that have incubated inside the soldiers at a fort alongside Sgt. Dick Belden, the Rider's friend and comrade from the Civil War. The Rider remembers leaving San Francisco with his best friend Abe Lillard to join the army. When the Rider was a boy, Rabbi Belinski renamed him at his mother's request. Some of the etchings on the talismans worn by the Rider's foe Jacobi remind the Rider of characters in the *Book of Zylac* and lettering in Sheardown's correspondences, lettering Professor Spates had called Tsath-yo. The Rider also recalls battling reptilian Yiggians recently. He took a Star-Stone of Mnar, which had the Elder Sign etched upon it, from a cave in New Mexico.

Short story by Edward M. Erdelac in Merkabah Rider: Have Glyphs Will Travel, *Damnation Books, 2011. The Great Old Ones and the Elder Sign are from the Cthulhu Mythos of H. P. Lovecraft. The Yiggians are minions of the Great Old One known as Yig, from Lovecraft's revision of Zealia Bishop's "The Curse of Yig." The Tsath-yo language is from Lovecraft and E. Hoffmann Price's "Through the Gates of the Silver Key." Rabbi Avram Belinski is from the film* The Frisco Kid. *Abe Lillard is the son of Tommy Lillard from the same movie, and was named after Avram. Zylac is from Cthulhu Mythos fiction by Clark Ashton Smith. His book is* The Wisdom and Sacred Magic of Zylac the Mage, *from Cthulhu Mythos stories by Joseph S. Pulver. Professor Spates is based on a reference to "Spates' catalog" in the film* Ghostbusters. *The Star-Stones of Mnar are from August Derleth's* The Lurker at the Threshold. *This story takes place immediately after "The Pandæmonium Ride."*

February
A VOLUME IN VERMILION

Archie Stamford introduces Colonel Sebastian Moran to Professor James Moriarty, who recruits Moran into his criminal organization. They are promptly hired by Enoch Drebber and Joseph Stangerson of Utah to assassinate Jim Lassiter, Jane Withersteen, and Fay Larkin. Bishop Dyer, Elder Tull, and Jefferson Hope are mentioned during their conversation. The Old Jago and Strelsau are mentioned later on.

Short story by Colonel Sebastian Moran, edited by Kim Newman in Sherlock Holmes Mystery Magazine #3, Marvin Kaye, ed., Wildside Press, 2009; reprinted in Professor Moriarty: The Hound of the d'Urbervilles, Titan Books, 2011. Moran and Moriarty are from Doyle and Watson's Sherlock Holmes stories. Enoch Drebber, Joseph Stangerson, and Jefferson Hope are from the first Holmes novel, A Study in Scarlet. "Archie Stamford, the forger" is mentioned in the Holmes story "The Adventure of the Solitary Cyclist." Moriarty and Moran previously collaborated on a mission for the Capelleans in 1872, as seen in Philip José Farmer's novel The Other Log of Phileas Fogg. Moran must have omitted any mention of this previous encounter in order to conceal the existence of extraterrestrial life. Jim Lassiter, Jane Withersteen, Fay Larkin, Bishop Dyer, and Elder Tull are from Zane Grey's novel Riders of the Purple Sage. The Old Jago is from Arthur Morrison's novel A Child of the Jago. Strelsau is the capital of Ruritania in Anthony Hope's novels The Prisoner of Zenda and Rupert of Hentzau.

HELL STREET

The Lone Ranger and Tonto team up with the Cisco Kid to apprehend the Kid's enemy Sandridge.

Short story by Joe Gentile in The Lone Ranger Chronicles, Matthew Baugh and Tim Lasiuta, eds., Moonstone Books, 2012. The Cisco Kid and Sandridge are from O. Henry's story "The Caballero's Way." The Kid previously met the masked man and his faithful companion in the comic book miniseries The Cisco Kid: Gunfire & Brimstone, which was also published by Moonstone. In the comic story "Master of the World," the

Cisco Kid and his sidekick Pancho (spelled "Poncho" in the story) teamed up with the Rook and Sherlock Holmes, among others, in 1909. However, the Kid in that story is based on the film, radio, television, and comic version of the character, which is considerably more good-natured than Henry's ruthless version. He must be an impostor using the O. Henry character's alias for more benevolent purposes.

Spring
LONGARM AND THE DEVIL'S BRIDE
In the library of Grant Stockton's house, Deputy U.S. Marshal Custis Parker "Longarm" Long finds thick, leather-bound books whose authors have foreign-sounding names that he doesn't recognize, such as Alhazred and Von Junzt.

Longarm #311 *by "Tabor Evans" (James Reasoner). Longarm is already in the CU through a meeting with his fellow Western series characters Clint Adams (of the* Gunsmith *series) and Slocum. Abdul Alhazred is the author of the* Necronomicon *in H. P. Lovecraft's Cthulhu Mythos. Friedrich Wilhelm von Junzt, the author of* Unaussprechlichen Kulten, *is from Robert E. Howard's own contributions to the Cthulhu Mythos. The time of year is given as spring, while the 1881 date is based on Longarm's surprise Stockton doesn't have a copy of Governor Lew Wallace's new book* Ben-Hur, *which was first published on November 12, 1880.*

Summer
THE FLOWERS OF UTAH
Sherlock Holmes and Dr. Watson travel to Utah to track down Tom Dennis, Jefferson Hope's accomplice. There, Watson encounters Lucy Ferrier Hope, who reveals with Dennis' assistance she is helping young Mormon women wishing to avoid polygamy flee to Wyoming. She further says she would do it alone if she could, or be a Masked Rider like her old friend Bess Erne.

Short story by Dr. Watson, edited by Robert Pohle in Sherlock Holmes in America, *Martin H. Greenberg, Jon L. Lellenberg, and Daniel Stashower, eds., Skyhorse Publishing, 2009. Tom Dennis, Jefferson Hope, and Lucy Ferrier are from the first Sherlock Holmes novel,* A Study in Scarlet. *This story reveals both the true identity of Hope's accomplice who used the alias "Mrs. Sawyer," and that Lucy Ferrier's apparent death was a deception. Bess Erne is from Zane Grey's Western novel* Riders of the Purple Sage, *thus bringing that classic work into the CU. The year is based on the fact James A. Garfield is president; Garfield became president on March 4, 1881, and was assassinated on September 19 of that year.*

KING SOLOMON'S MINES

Upon discovering King Solomon's treasure, Allan Quatermain exclaims, "We are the richest men in the world. Monte Cristo was a fool to us." Later, Quatermain, Sir Henry Curtis, and Captain John Good discover Curtis' brother Sir George, who tells them he and his native guide have lived "like a second Robinson Crusoe and his man Friday" for nearly two years.

The first Allan Quatermain novel by H. Rider Haggard. Quatermain, the Count of Monte Cristo, and Robinson Crusoe and Friday have all been established as existing in the CU, and therefore it can be assumed the references are to real people rather than literary characters.

Summer 1881–Winter 1884
WYLLARD'S WEIRD

Mademoiselle Beauville, a female fashion designer, has "cherished one bitter and unappeasable hatred, and that was against Messrs. Spricht, Van Klopen, and the whole confraternity of men-milliners." Later Beauville boasts about a client, "I made all her gowns, and I was proud that she could challenge comparison with actresses who squandered their thousands upon such impostors as Spricht and Van Klopen." Hilda Heathcote "had read of gentlemanlike murderers—assassins of good bearing and polished manners—Eugene Aram, Count Fosco, and many more of the same school."

Novel by Mary Elizabeth Braddon, originally serialized 1884–1885. Rick Lai notes, "Van Klopen was the criminal fashion designer who was part of the Mascarot blackmail ring in Emile Gaboriau's Lecoq series. Van Klopen was still at liberty in Gaboriau's non-Lecoq mystery novels set in the early 1870s. Eugene Aram was a real-life murderer from the 18th century. His life was fictionalized in Edward Bulwer-Lytton's novel Eugene Aram. *Count Fosco is the villain of* The Woman in White *by Wilkie Collins. Mentioning Fosco alongside Aram implies that both were historical criminals whose lives were fictionalized."*

Autumn
THE WAR SHAMAN

The Merkabah Rider gives his ally Kabede a pistol with the Elder Sign imprinted on its side. Kabede refers to their conflict with the Great Old Ones. The two of them, along with the Rider's old friend Dick Belden, are visited by Shar-rogs pa, the blue abbot of Shambhala, aka Faustus Montague. The monk Chaksusa told the Rider of the abbot when he'd battled Shub-Niggurath, the Yiggians, and the Black Goat Man. Faustus' brother is Mun Gsod. Faustus tells the Rider, Kabede and Belden of stories that are true: a whaler with an Indian figurehead pursuing a pale leviathan to the doom of her crew and her scarred captain; a young boy putting his hand on a sword and drawing it lightly from a stone, becoming the greatest king the world has ever known; and thirteen heroes with two hearts between them, who set themselves between an insignificant world and all the evil that time and space can muster. He further states a word Chaksusa taught to the Rider, when combined with the Star-Stones of Mnar, is doubly detrimental to the Great Old Ones. The Apache Piishi has seen the Rider's old acquaintance Misquamacus. Ten of Faustus' disciples died battling Adon's Creed on a mesa at a place called Stallions Gate in New Mexico. Among the allies of the Merkabah Riders are the Kun-Sun-Dai and the Watchers. Faustus thinks Misquamacus may be serving Nyarlathotep. The Rider's own claustrophobia reminds him of his boyhood friend Aloysius Monkowitz's many phobias. The Rider and Piishi faced Shub-Niggurath and the Cold Ones together. Misquamacus has manipulated the Billington family in the past. The geometric patterns in sand-images made by a group of skinwalkers remind the Rider of the diagrams in the *Book of Zylac*. Misquamacus summons Ossodagowah.

Short story by Edward M. Erdelac in Merkabah Rider: Have Glyphs Will Travel, Damnation Books, 2011. *The Elder Sign, the Great Old Ones, Shub-Niggurath, and Yig are from H. P. Lovecraft's Cthulhu Mythos. The Star-Stones of Mnar are from August Derleth's* The Lurker at the Threshold. *Misquamacus is from both* The Lurker at the Threshold *and Graham Masterton's* Manitou *novels. The Lurker at the Threshold mentions both Misquamacus' devotion to Nyarlathotep and his conjuring of Ossodagowah. The Billington family is also from* The Lurker at the Threshold. *"Shar-rogs pa" and "Mun Gsod" are Tibetan approximations of "Darkness Slayer" and "East-helper," the English translations of the names of the blue wizards Morinehtar and Rómestámo from J. R. R. Tolkien's* The Lord of the Rings. *This story reveals Rómestámo and Misquamacus are the same being. The whaler is the* Pequod *from Herman Melville's* Moby-Dick. *The boy who drew the sword from the stone is King Arthur. The thirteen heroes with two* hearts between them are the various incarnations of the Doctor, of Doctor Who fame. While most of the Doctor's exploits take place in an alternate universe, it has been established the Doctor has a CU counterpart, who often goes by the name of Doctor Omega. Stallions Gate, New Mexico, is the future site of Project Quantum Leap, from the television series Quantum Leap. *The Watchers (more properly the Watchers' Council) are from the television series* Buffy the Vampire Slayer, *while the Kun-Sun-Dai (whose full name is the Order of the Kun-Sun-Dai) are from the "Awakening" and "Calvary" episodes of the* Buffy *spin-off* Angel. *Aloysius Monkowitz is an ancestor of obsessive-compulsive private investigator Adrian Monk from the television series* Monk. *The Cold Ones and Zylac appear in Cthulhu Mythos fiction by Clark Ashton Smith. Zylac's book,* The Wisdom and Sacred Magic of Zylac the Mage, *appears in stories by Joseph S. Pulver.*

1882

March
THE GREEN FLAG

The Royal Mallows, an Irish regiment, fights to protect a green Fenian flag during the Mahdist War.

Short story by Arthur Conan Doyle in The Green Flag and Other Stories, *1900. In "The Adventure of the Crooked Man," Sherlock Holmes investigates the death of Colonel Barclay, the former commander of the fictional Royal Mallows, which is replaced with the real Royal Munsters in many American editions. The connection to the Holmes canon brings the events of "The Green Flag" into the CU. The year is conjecture.*

Spring
THE MULES OF THE MAZZIKIM

The Merkabah Rider parts ways with his allies Kabede and Dick Belden, who are going to meet with Professor Spates in Tombstone. The Rider doubts his ability to combat the Great Old Ones, and remembers Kabede telling him a Christian once wielded the Rod of Aaron, which is now in Kabede's own hands. The Rider remembers Rabbi Belinski raising a cup of wine and shouting *"Mazeltov!"* at his *bar mitzvah* and Abe Lillard lying dead from a Texas sharpshooter's bullet. Marshal Books arrests the Rider for murder.

Short story by Edward M. Erdelac in Merkabah Rider: Have Glyphs Will Travel, *Damnation Books, 2011. Professor Spates is based on a reference to "Spates' catalog" in the movie* Ghostbusters. *The Great Old Ones are from the Cthulhu Mythos tales of H. P. Lovecraft. The Christian who once wielded the Rod of Aaron is Solomon Kane, whose exploits were chronicled by Robert E. Howard. Rabbi Avram Belinski is from the film* The Frisco Kid. *Abe Lillard (who was named after Avram) is the son of Tommy Lillard, who is also from* The Frisco Kid. *Marshal Books is J. B. Books from Glendon Swarthout's novel* The Shootist *(and its 1976 film adaptation starring John Wayne), or else his brother.*

THE MAN CALLED OTHER

The Merkabah Rider has been jailed by Marshal Books. He asks his guardian angel what the Great Old Ones are. After being transferred to prison, he wonders if his allies Kabede and Dick have heard from Spates yet. The Rider discovers the prison's deputy superintendent is possessed by his former teacher Adon, who was once a disciple of Nyarlathotep. The Rider thinks of other Great Old Ones he knows of, including Shub-Niggurath, Ossodagowah, and others mentioned in the *Book of Zylac*. Adon mentions reading *The Kitab al-Azif*, aka the *Necronomicon*. The Rider reflects his friend Abe Lillard helped prevent him from being corrupted by Adon. Adon drugs the Rider with a narcotic distilled from the Black Lotus. The Rider later finds himself reunited with Kabede and Faustus Montague.

Short story by Edward M. Erdelac in Merkabah Rider: Have Glyphs Will Travel, *Damnation Books, 2011. Marshal Books is either J. B. Books from Glendon Swarthout's novel* The Shootist *or his brother. The Great Old Ones, Nyarlathotep, Shub-Niggurath, and the* Necronomicon *are from H. P. Lovecraft's Cthulhu Mythos. Spates is based on a reference to "Spates' catalog" in the movie* Ghostbusters. *Ossodagowah is from August Derleth's* The Lurker at the Threshold. *Zylac is from Cthulhu Mythos fiction by Clark Ashton Smith, while his book,* The Wisdom and Sacred Magic of Zylac the Mage, *appears in stories by Joseph S. Pulver. Abe Lillard is the son of Tommy Lillard from the movie* The Frisco Kid, *and is named after another character from the film, Rabbi Avram Belinski. The Black Lotus is from Robert E. Howard's stories about Conan the barbarian and detective Steve Harrison. Faustus Montague is meant to be Morinehtar from J. R. R. Tolkien's* The Lord of the Rings.

WILDTÖTER

The German immigrant frontiersman Deerslayer meets the New Robinson, the Robinsons, and Winoga.

Wildtöter #1–300, 1915–1917 and 1920–1924. Since the New Robinson is in the CU, so is Deerslayer, who is not to be confused with Natty Bumppo, who also used that name. The Robinsons, a German family lost in the American frontier, appeared in Robinsons im Wilden West #1–20. Winoga, who appeared in Winoga, der Letzte Mohikaner #1–90, 1921–1924, is himself in the CU through a link to Bumppo's companion Chingachgook.

May 25
THE FIRE KING TRIUMPHANT

The Merkabah Rider now trusts his ally Faustus Montague, despite his previous close-mouthedness about his brother Misquamacus. Faustus and Kadebe, another ally of the Rider's, were given a letter from Professor Spates by Sadie Marcus. The trio goes to Tombstone to meet with Spates and his colleague Warren Rice. Rice has confirmed the letters the Rider gave to Spates do indeed feature Tsath-yo characters. Several tomes associated with the Great Old Ones are mentioned in their discussion, including the *Book of Eibon*, the *Cthaat Aquadingen*, the *Necronomicon*, the *Book of Karnak*, the *Testament of Carnamagos*, the *Ponape Scripture*, *De Vermis Mysteriis*, and the *Scroll of Thoth-Amon*. Nyarlathotep is also mentioned, along with Abdul Alhazred and Prinn.

Short story by Edward M. Erdelac in Merkabah Rider: Have Glyphs Will Travel, *Damnation Books, 2011. Faustus Montague is actually Morinehtar from J. R. R. Tolkien's* The Lord of the Rings. *Misquamacus is from August Derleth's* The Lurker at the Threshold; *the Merkabah Rider stories conflate Misquamacus with Morinehtar's fellow Blue Wizard Rómestámo. The Great Old Ones (including Nyarlathotep) are from H. P. Lovecraft's Cthulhu Mythos, as are the* Necronomicon *and its author, Abdul Alhazred. Warren Rice is from Lovecraft's "The Dunwich Horror." Professor Spates is based on a reference to "Spates' catalog" in the movie* Ghostbusters. *The Tsath-yo language is from the Hyperborea stories of Clark Ashton Smith. The* Book of Eibon *and the* Testament of Carnamagos *are Cthulhu Mythos tomes created by Smith. The* Cthaat Aquadingen *appears in Mythos stories by Brian Lumley. The* Book of Karnak *appears in Mythos fiction by Henry Kuttner. The* Ponape Scripture *is from Lin Carter's "Out of the Ages." De Vermis Mysteriis and its author, Ludwig Prinn, are from Robert Bloch's "The Shambler from the Stars." The* Scroll of Thoth-Amon *(aka* The Book of Thoth*) is from Richard L. Tierney's stories of Simon of Gitta. This* *story depicts a historical fire that occurred in Tombstone, Arizona on May 25, 1882.*

May 25–September 23
MERKABAH RIDER: ONCE UPON A TIME IN THE WEIRD WEST

The Merkabah Rider and his allies set forth to at long last prevent the Hour of Incursion, in which the Great Old Ones will be unleashed upon the world. Appearing or mentioned are: the Dreamlands; the *Liber Damnatus Damnationum*; Delirium Tremens; the *Scroll of Thoth*; Misquamacus; Azathoth; Faustus Montague; an African witch-doctor; a Christian adventurer; the Drucker and Dobbs Mining Company; Professor Spates; Miskatonic University; Arkham; Warren Rice; the Tsath-yo language; New Valusia; Yoth; Yig; Tsathoggua; the Elder Sign; Nyarlathotep (aka the Abhorred Dread); Ossadagowah; Stallions' Gate; the *Book of Zylac*; the Cold Ones; Shub-Niggurath; the Star Stones of Mnar; Pnakotus; the flying polyps; the Aklo language; Picaro Jake Gonnoff; the Hyperboreans; the Black Lotus; a barefoot man, possibly a Chinaman, playing a bamboo flute; Dunn & Duffy; the Flying Graysons; Cooger & Dark's Pandemonium Shadow Show; Noah Whateley; Yog-Sothoth; Dunwich; the shoggoth; Zorro; Gallo del Cielo; Slim Reezer; Jesse McLaughlin; Oscar Diggs; Richard Wilkins III; Lin McAdams; High Spade; Freddie Sykes; Dog Kelly; John Russell; an "*electricista y aventurero*"; Danny Caine; a masked gunman; the *Pnakotic Manuscripts*; the *Seven Books of Hsan*; the *History of G'harne*; the Naacal language; and the Elder Script.

Novel by Edward M. Erdelac, Damnation Books, 2013. *The Great Old Ones, the Dreamlands, Azathoth, Miskatonic University, Arkham, Warren Rice, Yig, the Elder Sign, Shub-Niggurath, Pnakotus, the Great Race of Yith, the flying polyps, Yog-Sothoth, Dunwich, the shoggoth, the* Pnakotic Manuscripts, *and the* Seven Cryptical Books of Hsan *are from the Cthulhu Mythos of H. P. Lovecraft. Nyarlathotep is also from Lovecraft's Mythos; Erdelac conflates him with Sauron (aka the Abhorred Dread) from J. R. R.*

Tolkien's epic fantasy trilogy The Lord of the Rings. *The Tsath-yo and Naacal languages are from Lovecraft and E. Hoffmann Price's "Through the Gates of the Silver Key." Yoth is from Lovecraft and Zealia Bishop's "The Mound." The Aklo language originally appeared in Arthur Machen's "The White People," and was also used by Lovecraft in his stories "The Dunwich Horror" and "The Haunter of the Dark." Noah Whateley is meant to be Old Whateley from "The Dunwich Horror"; his first name was given as Noah in the role-playing game* Call of Cthulhu. *The* Liber Damnatus Damnationum *is from Richard L. Tierney's Mythos novel* The House of the Toad. *The* Scroll of Thoth *is from Tierney's tales of Simon of Gitta. The town of Delirium Tremens appears in several works by Erdelac, including the film* Meaner Than Hell. *Picaro Jake Gonnoff is also from* Meaner Than Hell. *Misquamacus, Ossadagowah, and the Star Stones of Mnar are from August Derleth's short novel* The Lurker at the Threshold; *here, Misquamacus is conflated with the Blue Wizard Rómestámo from* The Lord of the Rings. *Faustus Montague is meant to be Rómestámo's fellow Blue Wizard Morinehtar. The Christian adventurer is Robert E. Howard's Solomon Kane, while the African witch-doctor is Kane's ally N'Longa. New Valusia is named after the kingdom of Valusia from Howard's King Kull stories. The Black Lotus is from Howard's stories of the barbarian Conan and police detective Steve Harrison. The Drucker and Dobbs Mining Company alludes to gold prospector Fred C. Dobbs from B. Traven's novel* The Treasure of the Sierra Madre *and its film adaptation; since both versions of the story take place in the 1920s, the Dobbs who co-owns the mining company must be a relative of Fred's. Professor Spates is based on a reference to "Spates' catalog" in the movie* Ghostbusters. *Tsathoggua, Zylac, the Cold Ones, the Hyperboreans, and the Elder Script appear in fiction by Clark Ashton Smith. Stallions' Gate, New Mexico is from the television series* Quantum Leap. *The Book of Zylac (aka* The Wisdom and Sacred Magic of Zylac the Mage*) appears in Cthulhu Mythos fiction by Joseph S. Pulver. The barefoot Chinaman is Kwai Chang Caine from the television series* Kung Fu; *Danny Caine is his older half-brother. The Dunn & Duffy Combined Circus is from the film* Indiana Jones and the Last Crusade. *The Flying Graysons are a family of acrobats that died out in the 1940s when young Dick Grayson's parents were murdered, resulting in his adoption by Batman and becoming the first Robin. Cooger & Dark's Pandemonium Shadow Show is from Ray Bradbury's novel* Something Wicked This Way Comes. *It is worth noting Green Town, Illinois, the setting of* Something Wicked This Way Comes, *is also the town in which Bradbury's books* Dandelion Wine, Farewell Summer, *and* Summer Morning, Summer Night *take place. Gallo del Cielo is from Tom Russell's song of the same name, as is Zorro. Both are roosters, and therefore* this Zorro is no relation to any of the many heroes that have used that name. Slim Reezer and Jesse McLaughlin are from the movie House II: The Second Story. *"Electricista y aventurero" is Spanish for "electrician and adventurer,"* which is how the character Bill Towner describes himself in House II. *Oscar Diggs is better known as the Wizard of Oz. The immortal Richard Wilkins III is the Mayor of Sunnydale, California on the television series* Buffy the Vampire Slayer. *Lin McAdams and High Spade are from the film* Winchester '73. *Freddie Sykes is from the film* The Wild Bunch. *Dog Kelly is from Sam Raimi's Western* The Quick and the Dead. *John Russell is from the film* Hombre. *The masked gunman is the Lone Ranger. The* History of G'Harne *(aka the* G'harne Fragments*) appears in Cthulhu Mythos fiction by Brian Lumley.*

Early June–Early September
THE ISSUE OF DR. JEKYLL
Several English professors travel to Massachusetts, where they wind up examining a comet that landed on the Gardner farm. Appearing or mentioned are: Doctor George Edward Rutherford; Doctor Henry Jekyll; Mr. Banks; Mr. Darling; Professor Henry Higgins; Doctor Moreau; Doctor Perry; Denton; Causton; Arkham; Evangeline West's uncle; Miskatonic University; Witch's Hollow; Bolton; Kingsport; Innsmouth; Derrie; Axel Lidenbrock; Ammi Pierce; Nahum Gardner and his wife Nabby; Chapman's Brook; Professor Selwyn Cavor; Karel Colceag; Herbert West; and Gabriel Utterson.

Short story by Pete Rawlik at the HorrorTalk *website. Doctor George Edward Rutherford is meant to be Arthur Conan Doyle's Professor George Edward Challenger; Farmer revealed the Professor's true last name was Rutherford in* Tarzan Alive. *Doctor Henry Jekyll and Gabriel Utterson are from Robert Louis Stevenson's* The Strange Case of Dr. Jekyll and Mr. Hyde. *Mr. George Banks is from P. L. Travers'* Mary Poppins *books, while Mr. George Darling is from J. M. Barrie's* Peter Pan. *Professor Henry Higgins is from George Bernard Shaw's play* Pygmalion. *Doctor Moreau is from H. G. Wells'* The Island of Doctor Moreau. *Moreau's first name is given as Jean-Paul in this story, whereas he is identified as Alphonse Moreau in* The League of Extraordinary Gentlemen, Volume II *and other sources. The Jean-Paul reference must be considered an error. Doctor Perry may be from Edgar Rice Burroughs'* Pellucidar *novels. Denton is the English town* where R. D. Wingfield's Jack Frost novels and the television series A Touch of Frost *take place*. *The English town of Causton is the setting of the Chief Inspector Barnaby novels by Caroline Graham, as well as the television series* Midsomer Murders. *Arkham and Miskatonic University are staples of H. P. Lovecraft's Cthulhu Mythos. Evangeline West's uncle is James West from the television series* The Wild Wild West. *Witch's Hollow is from the story of the same name by August Derleth. Bolton and Herbert West are from Lovecraft's "Herbert West—Reanimator." Kingsport is from Lovecraft's "The Festival." Innsmouth is from another Lovecraft story, "The Shadow over Innsmouth." The town of Derry (spelled "Derrie" here), Maine appears in many of Stephen King's novels and short stories. Axel Lidenbrock is from Jules Verne's* Journey to the Center of the Earth. *Ammi Pierce, Nahum and Nabby Gardner, and Chapman's Brook are from Lovecraft's "The Colour Out of Space." Professor Cavor is from Wells'* The First Men in the Moon; *his first name was given as Selwyn in* The League of Extraordinary Gentlemen, Volume I. *Karel Colceag is modeled after Carl Kolchak, although the two are not meant to be the same character.*

Summer
TEXAS IRON

Brothers Evan, Jubal, and Sam McCall return to their hometown of Vengeance Creek, Texas seeking justice for the murder of their parents. Sam asks his friend, federal marshal Page Murdock, to recommend another marshal who can investigate.

Novel by Robert J. Randisi, Dorchester Publishing, 1991. Page Murdock, the protagonist of a series of books by Loren D. Estleman, was brought into the CU by a reference in Randisi's Gunsmith novel Death Times Five. *Bat Masterson is described as not yet thirty-years-old. Masterson was born in 1853.*

1883

Winter
THE DEAD OF WINTER

Cora and Ben Oglesby, a married couple who hunt monsters for a living, battle a wendigo in Leadville, Colorado. Afterwards, an English occult scholar named James Townsend hires them to deal with a coven of vampires holed up in a mine. Townsend learned vampires were real from a friend of his, a Dutch physician and occult expert who has hunted the undead in the past, and has taught some of the art to Townsend.

Novel by Lee Collins, Angry Robot Books, 2012. *The Dutch physician is Abraham Van Helsing from Stoker's* Dracula, *bringing Cora Oglesby, who returned in the 2013 novel* She Returns from War, *into the CU.*

March
THE ADVENTURE OF THE LOCKED CARRIAGE
Actor Henry Clarendon tells Sherlock Holmes he considers him "the preeminent detective in London today, far outstripping the likes of Hewitt and that foreign chap Dupin." Holmes thanks him, but adds "modesty forbids my agreement with your judgment."

Short story by Dr. Watson, edited by Stuart Douglas in Encounters of Sherlock Holmes, *George Mann, ed., Titan Books, 2013. Martin Hewitt is Arthur Morrison's sleuth, while C. Auguste Dupin was created by Edgar Allan Poe. Holmes disparaged Dupin's abilities in "A Study in Scarlet," but there are a few instances in the Holmes stories of Holmes putting up a modest front despite thinking very highly of his own abilities. Watson, writing his account of this case circa 1919, claims Holmes is long dead by that time. This is obviously misinformation, given Holmes' numerous post-1919 appearances.*

Autumn
THE EVIL OF DRACULA
Dracula comes to Dr. Abraham Van Helsing seeking a cure for his vampirism. Van Helsing's friend Dr. Henry Jekyll shares with Dracula the formula that turns him into Edward Hyde. Unfortunately, the serum has an unexpected effect on Dracula, who swears revenge on Van Helsing.

Story by Martin Powell in Vampires: Dracula and the Undead Legions, *Dave Ulanski and Garrett Anderson, eds., Moonstone Books, 2009; reprinted in* Startling Stories–Summer 2012, *Ron Hanna, ed., Wild Cat Books. Dracula seeks a cure for his bloodlust because he believes he will be eternally damned. This seems out of character for Stoker's Dracula, and therefore this story likely features a "soul-clone" who is rebelling against the real vampire lord's wishes.*

1884

Spring
NEMO AT R'LYEH

Captain Nemo and the crew of the *Nautilus* explore the resurfaced island of R'lyeh, and narrowly avoid an encounter with the dreaded Cthulhu himself. Robur is also mentioned.

Short story by Joshua Reynolds in Cthulhu Unbound Volume 2, *Thomas Brannan and John Sunseri, eds., Permuted Press, 2008. Captain Nemo is from Jules Verne's* 20,000 Leagues Under the Sea *and* The Mysterious Island. *Cthulhu is the most famous of H. P. Lovecraft's Great Old Ones. Cthulhu slumbers in sunken island of R'lyeh, which resurfaces from time to time. Robur is from Verne's novels* Robur the Conqueror *and* Master of the World. *The year is conjecture.*

Summer
ATOMIC ROBO AND THE KNIGHTS OF THE GOLDEN CIRCLE

Atomic Robo has spent the last fourteen years in the Old West after accidentally being transported there from June 2013. Robo, Doc Holliday, and Bass Reeves encounter the younger version of Robo's foe Heinrich von Helsingard. Robo says, "Old colleague of mine, he used to say, 'wherever you go, there you are.' I think it works with whenever too." In the epilogue, Secret Service Agents James West and Artemus Gordon discover the wreckage of Helsingard's airship.

Five-issue miniseries by Brian Clevinger and Scott Wegener, Red 5 Comics, April–October 2014. Robo was transported to 1870 at the end of the miniseries Atomic Robo and the Savage Sword of Dr. Dinosaur. *Robo's old colleague is Dr. Buckaroo Banzai. James West and Artemus Gordon are from the television series* The Wild Wild West, *of course.*

1885

Spring
DEATH TIMES FIVE

Clint Adams, the Gunsmith, is asked by Judge Parker to track down a gang of young men, none older than nineteen, who are committing a string of murders, rapes, and general hell-raising. Until Parker tells him the son of an old friend of his is believed to be part of the gang, Clint refuses, saying, "So, send someone to stop them. Send Bass. Or that fellow Murdoch you're so all-fired proud of." The sheriff of Jay City, Felix Leiter, is smitten with saloon girl Jenny Morse, and the attraction seems to be mutual.

The Gunsmith *#209* by "J. R. Roberts" (Robert J. Randisi). Bass is Bass Reeves, who historically was one of the first African-American deputy U.S. Marshals. "Murdoch" is a reference to Page Murdock, a deputy U.S. Marshal featured in novels by Loren D. Estleman. Since Clint Adams is in the CU, this crossover brings in Murdock. Sheriff Felix Leiter and Jenny Morse are probably the great-grandparents of James Bond's friend, CIA-agent turned Pinkerton Felix Leiter.

Summer
SHERLOCK HOLMES AND THE HORROR OF FRANKENSTEIN

Sherlock Holmes and Dr. Watson meet the Frankenstein Monster and Dr. Pretorius.

Graphic novel by Luke Kuhns and Marcie Klinger, MX Publishing, 2013. The Monster seen here is the original, from Mary Shelley's novel. Dr. Pretorius is from the Universal film *The Bride of Frankenstein*.

October
THE HOUND OF THE D'URBERVILLES

Professor Moriarty and Colonel Moran are hired by Jasper Stoke-d'Urberville, nephew of Simon Stoke-d'Urberville, to kill Red Shuck, the spectral hound that has allegedly haunted the d'Urberville family for generations. Appearing or mentioned are: the village of Trantridge; the Chase; Simon's son Alexander; Theresa "Tess" Durbeyfield-Clare; Tess' son Sorrow and siblings Abraham and Modesty; the city of Wintoncester; Selden; Desperado Dan'l; a terrifying Fat Man in Whitehall; Doctor Jack Quartz; Dr. Nikola; the Si-Fan; the Lord of Strange Deaths; the Grand Vampire; *Les Vampires*; Wessex; Diggory Venn; Parson Tringham; Car Darch; Sir Pagan d'Urberville; Melchester; Lord John Roxton; Casterbridge; the Ranee of

Ranchipur; Blind Herder; Arnsworth Castle; Jim Lassiter; John Durbeyfield; the parish of Kingsbere; Sherton Abbas; Singapore Charlie; Marlott Churchyard; and Elizabeth-Louise Durbeyfield.

Short story by Colonel Sebastian Moran, edited by Kim Newman in Professor Moriarty: The Hound of the d'Urbervilles, *Titan Books, 2011. The village of Trantridge, Simon Stoke-d'Urberville, the Chase, Simon's son Alexander, Theresa "Tess" Durbeyfield-Clare, Sorrow Durbeyfield, Abraham Durbeyfield, Modesty Durbeyfield, the city of Wintoncester, Parson Tringham, Car Darch, Sir Pagan d'Urberville, John Durbeyfield, the parish of Kingsbere, Marlott Churchyard, and Elizabeth-Louise (or Eliza-Louisa) Durbeyfield are from Thomas Hardy's novel* Tess of the d'Urbervilles. *Diggory Venn is from Hardy's novel* The Return of the Native. *Wessex is a fictional region of England that appears in most of Hardy's novels. Melchester is from Hardy's* Two on a Tower *and* Jude the Obscure. *Casterbridge is from Hardy's* The Mayor of Casterbridge. *Sherton Abbas is from Hardy's* The Woodlanders. *Selden is from Doyle and Watson's* The Hound of the Baskervilles. *The terrifying Fat Man in Whitehall is Mycroft Holmes, Sherlock's brother. Blind Herder is the blind mechanic Von Herder from the Holmes story "The Adventure of the Empty House." "The Arnsworth Castle business" is an untold Holmes case mentioned in "A Scandal in Bohemia." Desperado Dan'l is inspired by (though not the same person as) the British comic book cowboy Desperate Dan. Doctor Jack Quartz is the arch nemesis of dime novel detective Nick Carter. Dr. Nikola is from the series of novels by Guy Boothby. The Si-Fan and Singapore Charlie are from the Fu Manchu novels by Sax Rohmer; the Lord of Strange Deaths is Fu Manchu himself. Les Vampires are from the titular film serial directed by Louis Feuillade, as is their leader, the Grand Vampire. Lord John Roxton is from Doyle's Professor Challenger stories. Ranchipur is from the film* The Rains of Ranchipur. *Jim Lassiter is from the novel* Riders of the Purple Sage *by Zane Grey. The month is given, but the year is conjecture based on the facts Moran has worked for Moriarty for some time and Selden is next seen as an escaped convict in 1888.*

1886

Spring
BOUNTY ON A BARON
The bounty hunter known only as Decker tracks down a hired killer called the Baron. A federal marshal working Wyoming-Montana named Murdock is mentioned.

Novel by "Joshua Randall" (Robert J. Randisi), PaperJacks, 1987. Murdock is Deputy U.S. Marshal Page Murdock, the protagonist of a series of books by Loren D. Estleman, who was brought into the CU by a reference in Randisi's Gunsmith novel Death Times Five. *This crossover brings in Decker.*

Summer
SAINT OF KILLERS

Several famous figures of the Old West are named, including J. B. Books, Josey Wales, Ethan Edwards, Woodrow Call and Gus McCrae, and William Munny.

Four-issue Preacher Special *mini-series* by Garth Ennis, Steve Pugh, and Carlos Ezquerra, DC Comics, August–November 1995. J. B. Books is from Glendon Swarthout's novel The Shootist. Josey Wales is from Forrest Carter's novels Gone to Texas *and* The Vengeance Trail of Josey Wales. *Ethan Edwards is from the movie* The Searchers. *Woodrow Call and Gus McCrae are from Larry McMurtry's* Lonesome Dove *novels. William Munny is from the movie* Unforgiven. *Since Books, Edwards, and Call and McCrae are in the CU, so are Wales and Munny. Matthew Baugh writes, "The* Preacher *universe is difficult to reconcile with the CU. It features a unique characterization of God that is at odds with that of many established CU stories.* Preacher *also takes place in a universe where the American President (implicitly Bill Clinton) had a nuclear weapon dropped on the Navajo and Hopi reservations. Since a nuclear strike in Arizona is incompatible with other CU stories set in the late 20th century, I have taken the (admittedly odd) position that the 19th century events [in* Saint of Killers*] may be included, but the 20th century events take place in an alternate universe." In the* Peacemaker *novels by William S. Brady, it is established the protagonist, John T. McLain, served with Josey Wales under Bloody Bill Anderson during the Civil War, and Wales was the one who suggested to McLain he go to Texas afterwards. It is also stated in that series McLain was the one who taught the title character of Brady's* Hawk *series to handle weapons, and gave him the swan-down Meteor shotgun he wears in a special belt holster.*

Late November
CARNACKI AND THE PRESIDENT'S VAMPIRE

Thomas Carnacki comes to the aid of the future American president, Theodore Roosevelt, when his fiancée mysteriously falls ill. Carnacki resolves to call in his friend Professor Huxley, although the Indian medicine chief Red Dog remarks this seems to be more a matter for Professor Van Helsing. Carnacki mentions his friend Sherlock Holmes was involved in an investigation which revolved around the church of St. George's, Hanover Square.

Short story by Robert Pohle in Carnacki: The New Adventures, *Sam Gafford, ed., Ulthar Press, 2013. Carnacki's exploits were chronicled in short stories by William Hope Hodgson. Professor Abraham Van Helsing is from Bram Stoker's Dracula. In Doyle and Watson's "The Adventure of the Noble Bachelor," Sherlock Holmes investigated the disappearance of Hatty Doran, which happened immediately after her marriage to Lord Robert St. Simon at St. George's Church.*

1887

Winter
THE SOLDIER LEGACY'S STRANGE TALES: NIGHT OF THE WARRIOR

The Soldier encounters Dr. Nikola.

Backup feature by Christopher Sequeira and Paul Mason in The Dark Detective: Sherlock Holmes *#7–9, Black House Comics; reprinted as a one-shot. Guy Boothby's villain Dr. Nikola is already in the CU; therefore, this crossover brings in the Soldier. The 1942 and 2011 bearers of the name and mask of the Soldier appear in Mason's comic* The Soldier Legacy, *also published by Black House Comics. In 1942, the Soldier fights the Japanese in Papua, New Guinea. The 2011 incarnation, the grandson of the 1940s Soldier, is a street-level vigilante on the streets of Brisbane.*

LONGARM AND THE OUTLAW EMPRESS

Longarm and his old acquaintances Jessie Starbuck and Ki find themselves separately drawn to the town of Zamora, a haven for criminals, seeking justice. Zamora is under the control of a new version of the Cartel Jessie and Ki once battled.

Longarm Giant #25 by "Tabor Evans" (James Reasoner). Jessie Starbuck and Ki appeared alongside Longarm in the first ten Longarm Giant *books, and also battled the Cartel solo in their own series of books, the* Lone Star series written under the pen name Wesley Ellis. The Cartel becomes a recurring element of Reasoner's Longarm Giants with this book. The year is conjecture based on a reference to the historical XIT Ranch, which began operating in 1885.

Spring
LONGARM AND THE GOLDEN EAGLE SHOOT-OUT
Longarm works alongside former Pinkertons Raider and Doc Weatherbee.
Longarm Giant #26 by "Tabor Evans" (James Reasoner). This crossover brings in the main characters of J. D. Hardin's Doc and Raider series.

April 4–5
THE HOUR OF THE TORTOISE
Chelone Burchell, an illegitimate offspring of the Calipash family, writes a pornographic story that mentions Miss Coote's Academy for Young Women of Breeding and Promise. The family's Private Library included a copy of a book entitled *Nameless Cults*. Chelone once had sex with Lord Crim-Con.
Short story by Molly Tanzer in The Book of Cthulhu 2, Ross E. Lockhart, ed., Night Shade Books, 2012; reprinted in A Pretty Mouth, Lazy Fascist Press, 2012. Miss Coote is a reference to Rosa Coote, a character who appeared in the Victorian pornographic magazine The Pearl. Rosa was confirmed to exist in the CU in The League of Extraordinary Gentlemen, Volume I, which depicted her as having taken over the Correctional Academy for Wayward Gentlewomen she attended in the original stories. Chelone must have known the real Rosa Coote, and incorporated her into her story. Lord Crim-Con is from another serial in The Pearl, "Lady Pokingham, or They All Do It"; Lady Pokingham was mentioned in The League of Extraordinary Gentlemen as visiting the Academy. Friedrich von Juntz's book Nameless Cults (or Unaussprechlichen Kulten) appears in Cthulhu Mythos stories by Robert E. Howard. These links bring the connected stories in A Pretty Mouth, featuring several generations of the Calipash family, into the CU.

Summer
LONGARM AND THE VALLEY OF SKULLS
Longarm teams up with the soldiers of Easy Company and John Fury to bring down a mob of hooded killers preying on settlers in the Valley of Skulls in the Wyoming Territory.

Longarm Giant *#27 by "Tabor Evans" (James Reasoner). This crossover brings in two more Western series: John Wesley Howard's* Easy Company *books and Jim Austin's* Fury *novels.*

Autumn
LONGARM AND THE LONE STAR TRACKDOWN
Longarm comes to the rescue of a kidnapped Jessie Starbuck. Raider lends a helping hand.

Longarm Giant *#28 by "Tabor Evans" (James Reasoner). Jessie Starbuck and Ki appeared in the first ten* Longarm Giants, *plus the* Lone Star *books by Wesley Ellis. Raider and his partner Doc Weatherbee were Pinkertons featured in novels by J. D. Hardin.*

1888

Winter
LONGARM AND THE RAILROAD WAR
Longarm investigates sabotage on a railroad line being built in Wyoming, and encounters Jessie Starbuck and Ki once more in the process.

Longarm Giant *#29 by "Tabor Evans" (James Reasoner).*

Spring
THE MUTINY OF THE MAVERICKS
An Irish-American revolutionary seals his own fate when he attempts to stir Her Majesty's Royal Loyal Musketeers, aka the Mavericks, an Irish regiment stationed in Afghanistan, into mutiny.

Short story by Rudyard Kipling in Mine Own People, *United States Book Company, March 1891. The father of the title character of Kipling's novel* Kim *was a member of the Mavericks, thus bringing this story into the CU.*

April 24
THE ADVENTURE OF THE AMATEUR MENDICANT SOCIETY
Holmes and Watson investigate the reappearance of the formerly missing Colonel Oliver Pendleton-Smythe, who is a member of the Amateur Mendicant Society. Pendleton-Smythe tells them about a meeting the club held in a pub called the Slaughtered Lamb.

Short story by Dr. Watson, edited by John Gregory Betancourt in The Resurrected Holmes, *St. Martin's Press, 1996; revised and reprinted in* The Mammoth Book of New Sherlock Holmes Adventures, *Carroll & Graf, 1997. The Slaughtered Lamb pub is from the film* An American Werewolf in London. *Although this case is dated to Tuesday, April 24, 1887, Doyle and Watson's tale "The Adventure of the Reigate Squires" has been dated by Baring-Gould to April 14–April 26, 1887. Additionally, April 24, 1887, was a Sunday, not a Tuesday. However, April 24 did fall on a Tuesday in 1888. Baring-Gould has Watson gaining his second wound (the one in his leg mentioned in*

The Sign of Four*) and the little affair of the Vatican cameos in late April of that year, and suggests these may even have been the same case; Betancourt's story must have happened shortly before or after those events.*

July
BLOOD TO THE BONE
Sherlock Holmes and Dr. Watson are hired by female bare-knuckle boxer Eby Stokes to investigate the disappearance of her husband, who is also her tag team partner. After seeing his body in the morgue, Holmes, Watson, and Eby visit the Waggon and Horses, a bar frequented by boxers.

A Fight Card *novella written by Dr. Watson, and edited by Andrew Salmon under the pen name "Jack Tunney," Fight Card Books, 2014. The Waggon and Horses is from Arthur Conan Doyle's Gothic novel* Rodney Stone. *This novel concludes on the evening of a real total lunar eclipse which occurred on July 23, 1888.*

Late September. On behalf of his friend Sir Richard Francis Burton, Algernon Swinburne hires Sherlock Holmes to investigate the theft of a new translation of a chapter of *The Perfumed Garden* omitted from Burton's own translation. ("The Loss of Chapter Twenty-One" by Dr. Watson, edited by Mark Hodder in *Encounters of Sherlock Holmes*, George Mann, ed., Titan Books, 2013.) Holmes and Watson first met Burton earlier in the month, as recorded in "The Adventure of the Arabian Knight," edited by Loren D. Estleman. Watson must have had good reason to omit any reference to this initial encounter. Hodder has also written a series of novels featuring Burton and Swinburne, which so far consists of *The Strange Affair of Spring Heeled Jack*, *The Curious Case of the Clockwork Man*, *Expedition to the Mountains of the Moon*, *The Secret of Abdu El-Yezdi*, and *The Return of the Discontinued Man*; however, these are set in an alternate universe in which Queen Victoria was assassinated in 1840, amongst other differences between that world and the CU.

Autumn
THE ADVENTURE OF THE SIX MALEDICTIONS
Professor Moriarty and Colonel Moran are hired by Major Humphrey "Mad" Carew to protect him from the *mi-go*, which seek to retrieve the gem known as the Green Eye of the Little Yellow God from him. Moriarty's plan involves hiring a group of master thieves to steal similar cursed items. Appearing or mentioned are: Ted Baldwin; the Vermissa Valley Scowrers; Birdy Edwards, aka John McMurdo and John Douglas; Birlstone Manor; the Assassination Bureau, Ltd.; "that Limehouse Chinese with the marmoset"; the Moonstone; the Eye of Klesh; the All-Seeing Eye of the Goddess of Light; the Crimson Gem of Cyttorak; the Pink Diamond of Lugash; Lukundoo; a Zuni fetish; "a naked Porroh man"; the Barlow rubies; the Rosenthall diamonds; the Mirror of Portugal; the Agra treasure; Azathoth; Tabanga; St. Custard's; Amaryllis Framington; Giles Conover; the Ingestre Necklace; Mrs. Lovett's Fleet Street pie shop; the Herncastle Heirloom; the Black Pearl of the Borgias; the Hoxton Creeper; "the cricketing ponce"; the Falcon of the Knights of St. John; the Jewels of the Madonna of Naples; the Jewel of Seven Stars; the Eye of Balor; Simon Carne; Fat Kaspar; the Grand Vampire; *Les Vampires*; Abel Trelawny; Margaret Trelawny; Gennaro; King Brian of the Leprechauns; Bianca Castafiore; Alf Bassick; Don Rafaele Corbucci; Irene Adler; "Dynamite" Desmond Mountmain and his son Tyrone; Malvoisin's Mirror; the Monkey's Paw; Cap'n Flint's treasure; Sir Michael Sinclair's Door; Marshall Alaric Molina de Marnac; Vokins; Malilella; Henry Wilcox; Queen Tera; Mrs. Sarah "The Black Widow of Lauder" Stewart; and Hagar "Thieving Pikey" Stanley.
Short story by Colonel Sebastian Moran, edited by Kim Newman in Gaslight Arcanum: Uncanny Tales of Sherlock Holmes, *J. R. Campbell and Charles Prepolec, eds., EDGE Science Fiction and Fantasy Publishing, 2011; reprinted and revised in* Professor Moriarty: The Hound of the d'Urbervilles, *Titan Books, 2011. Professor Moriarty, Colonel Moran, and Irene Adler are from the Sherlock Holmes stories. Ted Baldwin, the Vermissa Valley Scowrers, Birdy Edwards, and Birlstone Manor are from the Holmes*

novel The Valley of Fear. *The Agra treasure* is from the Holmes novel The Sign of Four. *The Black Pearl of the Borgias* is from the Holmes story "The Adventure of the Six Napoleons." In "The Adventure of the Empty House," Holmes states "the death of Mrs. Stewart, of Lauder, in 1887" was likely perpetrated by Moran. Mad Carew, the Green Eye of the Little Yellow God and Amaryllis Framington are from J. Milton Hayes' poem "The Green Eye of the Little Yellow God," although in the poem Amaryllis is only identified as "the Colonel's daughter." Azathoth is one of the Great Old Ones from H. P. Lovecraft's Cthulhu Mythos. The mi-go are also from the Mythos. The Assassination Bureau, Ltd.  is a novel by Jack London, completed posthumously by Robert L. Fish. "That Limehouse Chinese with the marmoset" is Dr. Fu Manchu. The Moonstone (aka the Herncastle Heirloom) is the subject of a novel by Wilkie Collins. The Eye of Klesh is from Lord Dunsany's one-act melodrama A Night at an Inn. The All-Seeing Eye of the Goddess of Light is from the 1940 film The Thief of Bagdad. The Crimson Gem of Cyttorak is from the exploits of Marvel Comics' Doctor Strange. Although the gem is best known as the power source of the X-Men villain Juggernaut, it is unlikely it empowered Cain Marko in the CU. The Pink Diamond of Lugash is better known as the Pink Panther, from the film series of the same name. Lukundoo is from the short story of the same name by Edward Lucas White. The Zuni fetish is from Richard Matheson's story "Prey," later adapted as "Amelia," the third segment of the made-for-television film Trilogy of Terror. The "naked Porroh man" is from H. G. Wells' story "Pollock and the Porroh Man." The Barlow rubies are from Patrick Hamilton's play Gas Light. "The cricketing ponce" is E. W. Hornung's Raffles. The Rosenthall diamonds are from the Raffles story "A Costume Piece." Don Rafaele Corbucci is Raffles' nemesis Count Corbucci from "The Fate of Faustina" and "The Last Laugh." Rick Lai gives the Count the first name Salvatore in his own fiction. Perhaps his full name is Salvatore Rafaele Corbucci. The Mirror of Portugal is from Arthur Morrison's story "The Case of 'The Mirror of Portugal,'" found in the collection The Dorrington Deed Box. *Tabanga is from the film* From Hell It Came. *St. Custard's is the school attended by Nigel Molesworth in books written by Geoffrey Willans and illustrated by Ronald Searle. Giles Conover and the Hoxton Creeper are from the Sherlock Holmes film* The Pearl of Death. *The Creeper was played by Rondo Hatton, who also portrayed a character called the Creeper in the films* House of Horrors *and* The Brute Man; *perhaps the latter-day Creeper is a descendant of his Victorian namesake and look-alike. The Ingestre Necklace and Mrs. Lovett's Fleet Street pie shop are from the penny dreadful story* "The String of Pearls: A Romance," *which formed the basis for the stage musical* Sweeney Todd: The Demon Barber of Fleet Street. *The Falcon of the Knights of St. John is the titular statue from Dashiell Hammett's novel* The Maltese Falcon; *Fat Kaspar is Casper Gutman. The Jewels of the Madonna of Naples, Genarro, and Malilella (usually spelled without the second "l") are from Ermanno Wolf-Ferrari's opera* The Jewels of the Madonna. *The Jewel of Seven Stars, Abel Trelawny, Margaret Trelawny, and Queen Tera are from the novel* The Jewel of Seven Stars *by Bram Stoker. The Eye of Balor is from Celtic mythology. Simon Carne is from the collection* A Prince of Swindlers *by Guy Boothby. The Grand Vampire and* Les Vampires *are from Louis Feuillade's serial named for the latter. King Brian of the Leprechauns is Brian Connors from the film* Darby O'Gill and the Little People. *Bianca Castafiore is from the Tintin comics by Hergé. Alf Bassick is from William Gillette's play* Sherlock Holmes. *Desmond and Tyrone Mountmain are undoubtedly relatives of the Mountmain family which appears in Newman's serial novel* Seven Stars. *Malvoisin's Mirror is from a titular story by Chris Lowder and Brian Lewis in the British comic magazine* Halls of Horror *#12. The Monkey's Paw is the subject of the short story of the same name by W. W. Jacobs. Cap'n Flint's treasure is from* Treasure Island *by Robert Louis Stevenson. Sir Michael Sinclair's Door is from* "The Door," *a segment of the British horror anthology film* From Beyond the Grave. *Marshall Alaric Molina de Marnac is likely a descendant of Alaric de Marnac, the 15th century warlock played by Paul Naschy (née Jacinto Molina Álvarez) in the films* Horror from the Tomb *and* Cries of Terror. *Vokins is Charles Vokins from* "The Horizontal Witness," *an episode of the television series* Cribb, *based on Peter Lovesey's series of novels about a Victorian era Police Sergeant. Henry Wilcox is from E. M. Forster's novel* Howards End. *Hagar Stanley is from the collection* Hagar of the Pawn-Shop: The Gypsy Detective *by Fergus Hume. The original version of this tale had references to the Emeralds of Suliman (from Edgar Wallace's J. G. Reeder tale "The Green Mamba") and Sylvia Marsh (from Ken Russell's 1988 film version of Bram Stoker's* The Lair of the White Worm*).*

1889

Spring
FORTUNEHEAD!

The heroic gunslinger Johnny Thunder (aka John Tane) rescues his father, Sheriff Bill Tane, from a criminal named Rand. A flashback shows Johnny preventing a bank robbery as Rand rides into town. Rand asks a witness who the hero is; the man begins telling a story of a group of Texas Rangers who were massacred. The only survivor swore a vow. Another bystander contradicts him, saying Thunder "wasn't thet guy." As this discussion takes place, an image of a masked cowboy clad in blue and wearing a badge is shown.

Story by Elliot S. Maggin, Alan Weiss, and Dick Giordano in Secret Origins #50, August 1990, DC Comics. *The bystander has confused Johnny Thunder with his fellow lawman, the Lone Ranger. Presumably, he has heard rumors of the Ranger's origins. In any case, this crossover brings the Western hero Johnny Thunder, who appeared in* All-American Comics *(later renamed* All-American Western*) and* All-Star Western*, into the CU. The year of this story is conjecture, though Johnny's mother's tombstone says she died in 1882.*

Summer
SURF CITY, HERE I COME

Haakon Jones is a passenger aboard a ship that encounters the island of R'lyeh in the South Seas. Haakon fights the Deep Ones and briefly glimpses Cthulhu.

Story by Aaron B. Larson in The Weird Western Adventures of Haakon Jones, Battered Silicon Dispatch Box, 1999.

THE SILENCE

Officer Jonas Drake asks Michel Ardan to help him investigate a sniper attack on a lawyer. The attorney's law partner is named Mr. Dickson. Later, at the Baltimore Gun Club, Ardan discusses the case with his fellow club member McDonald Boothroyd. Boothroyd remarks he wishes another club member, Impey Barbicane, could help them, but he and some of the other members are in Tampa Town, Florida, investigating the place as a possible site for a secret project the club has under development. Ardan suggests they enlist Artemus Gordon's help, but Boothroyd says, "He headed out west several years ago, something about helping to design a very special train." Boothroyd deduces the bullet came from an airgun designed by the blind German mechanic Von Herder, and introduces Ardan to Colonel Sebastian Moran. Moran's boss has been christened the Napoleon of Crime by a detective. Moran has been making inquiries about the estate of one of the law firm's clients, a supposedly late Captain from Virginia. The Captain, who is very much alive, helps Ardan defeat Moran.

Short story by Bradley H. Sinor in Tales of the Shadowmen Volume 9: La Vie en Noir*, Jean-Marc and Randy Lofficier, eds., Black Coat Press, 2012; reprinted in French in* Les Compagnons de l'Ombre (Tome 13)*, Jean-Marc and Randy Lofficier, eds., Rivière Blanche, 2014. Officer Jonas Drake is an ancestor of private investigator Paul Drake from Erle Stanley Gardner's* Perry Mason *books. Michel Ardan, the Baltimore Gun Club, and Impey Barbicane are from Jules Verne's novels* From the Earth to the Moon *and* Around the Moon. *In* From the Earth to the Moon, *the lunar expedition is launched from Tampa Town, Florida. However, Verne's book is set in 1865. Therefore, the secret project of 1889 must be a separate mission, possibly a follow-up to the journey of more than two decades ago. Mr. Dickson may be a relative of detective Harry Dickson, "the American Sherlock Holmes," who appeared in German, Dutch, Belgian, and French pulp magazines. McDonald Boothroyd is an ancestor of Major Boothroyd from Ian Fleming's* James Bond *novels. Artemus Gordon is from the television series* The Wild Wild West. *Colonel Sebastian Moran is Professor Moriarty's second in command in the Sherlock Holmes story "The Adventure of the Empty House," which is also the source of Von Herder. The Virginian Captain may be the warlord of Mars from Edgar Rice Burroughs' novels.*

Autumn
THE HOUSE OF A THOUSAND MIRRORS
In Deadwood, Haakon Jones nearly loses his soul to a witch's enchanted mirrors.

Story by Aaron B. Larson in The Weird Western Adventures of Haakon Jones, *Battered Silicon Dispatch Box, 1999. The mirrors are clearly meant to be those seen in Robert E. Howard's Kull story "The Mirrors of Tuzun Thune." In Howard's story, Tuzun Thune is assisted by a girl. Rick Lai speculates the witch who encountered Haakon Jones is an older version of that same girl.*

PHILEAS FOGG AND THE WAR OF SHADOWS

The prologue of this tale is a letter written by "V." in October 1975 to a woman named Patricia. V. hopes Patricia can decipher some journals she has discovered at the Fogg Shaw Barrow in Derbyshire, saying she considered letting Jeperson's coterie try to do it, but the Diogenes Club isn't what it was in better days. V. refers to Patricia's involvement in "that Xibumian affair," and mentions M... The journals were found in a time capsule that also included photographs V. has sent to the Wilmarth Foundation. The handwriting in the journals closely resembles that in the Savile Row papers Sir Beowulf Clayton translated, copied, and passed on to V. and Patricia's mutual friend Philip José Farmer. V. tells Patricia, "I have no doubt that you will decipher those journals the moment you turn your little gray cells to the task, as that obstreperous little Belgian was wont to say." In 1889, Phileas Fogg's aid is forcibly enlisted by Captain Nemo and Colonel Sebastian Moran to help them stop whoever is kidnapping and torturing former agents of the warring alien Eridanean and Capellean races in an attempt to discover the secrets of their distorter technology. Nemo, who once served the Capelleans as Fogg served the Eridaneans, now goes by the name of Professor James Moriarty. Fogg thinks of parties that would risk anything to discover the secrets of the distorter, including Dr. Nikola and the Si-Fan. Aboard a ship carrying him and Fogg to France, Moran carries one of the deadly airguns designed by the blind gunsmith Von Herder, mentions Vandeleur, and refers to himself as Tiger Jack. They are attacked by a young man named Gurn, whom Moran says nearly pushed Fred Porlock off a platform at King's Cross. Later, Fogg has a battle with a young woman named Irma. Moriarty's enemies include rival organizations and individuals with names like Quartz, Kramm, Nikola, and Bozzo-Corona, as well as the Si-Fan and the Red Hand, the Golden Chrysanthemum, and the Black Coats. Fogg and Moran are captured by Gurn's employer, the Phantom

of the Paris Opera House, who now also controls the gang known as *Les Vampires*, having killed the previous leader after hunting him across the rooftops of the Rue d'Auseil. A Persian named Nadir and his servant, Darius, are mentioned. The Phantom tells Fogg they say his father was a veritable beast. In a letter to Violet (V.), sent from Pemberley House in Lambton in November 1975, Patricia refers to Fogg's further adventures after his exploit in Paris, including an affair in Ruritania. Patricia adds the strange carvings Fogg found in the barrow in 1889 correspond to similar markings found in Antarctica by the Pabodie Expedition of 1930, and to those found in Australia's Great Sandy Desert a year later, both of which her father paid some special attention to. She reminds Violet of the journals she found at that Kensington flat during the Persano Affair, and refers to Violet's involvement in the "Eye of Oran" debacle. Patricia also mentions the events at Wardenclyffe Tower in 1903 involving something called a "Thoan," the disappearance of Harley Warren in 1924, and the Finnegan Manuscript.

Novella by Josh Reynolds, Meteor House, 2014. "V." is "Shrinking" Violet Holmes, daughter of Mycroft Holmes ("M . . .") and niece of Sherlock Holmes. Violet was co-created by Matthew Baugh and Win Scott Eckert. Patricia is Patricia Clarke Wildman from Philip José Farmer and Eckert's novel The Evil in Pemberley House *and Eckert's novella* The Scarlet Jaguar, *which depicted "that Xibumian affair." Patricia's father is James Clarke Wildman Jr., aka Doc Wildman. Pemberley House itself and the village of Lambton are from Jane Austen's* Pride and Prejudice. *The Diogenes Club is from the Sherlock Holmes stories, and was proposed as a front for a branch of the British Secret Service in Billy Wilder's film* The Private Life of Sherlock Holmes. *Jeperson is Richard Jeperson, a member of the Diogenes Club during the 1960s and 1970s in stories by Kim Newman. The Wilmarth Foundation is from Brian Lumley's Titus Crow novel series. "That obstreperous little Belgian" is Agatha Christie's detective Hercule Poirot. Phileas Fogg is from Jules Verne's* Around the World in Eighty Days. *In his article "A Submersible Subterfuge, or, Proof Impositive," H. W. Starr proposed*

Captain Nemo from Verne's 20,000 Leagues Under the Sea *was really Sherlock Holmes' archenemy Professor James Moriarty, a theory adopted and modified by Farmer for his novel* The Other Log of Phileas Fogg, *which identified Fogg and Moriarty as agents of alien races known as the Eridaneans and Capelleans, respectively. Win Scott Eckert has further modified Starr and Farmer's theories, showing that while Moriarty did use the name Captain Nemo and captain a submarine called the* Nautilus, *he was not the same Nemo whose exploits were chronicled by Verne. Colonel Sebastian Moran is Moriarty's second-in-command from Doyle and Watson's "The Adventure of the Empty House," which is also the source of Von Herder. In George MacDonald Fraser's novel* Flashman and the Tiger, *Moran's full name is given as John Sebastian "Tiger Jack" Moran. Dr. Nikola is a criminal mastermind and scientist in novels by Guy Boothby. The Si-Fan is the criminal organization controlled by Sax Rohmer's Dr. Fu Manchu. Vandeleur appears in* The Other Log of Phileas Fogg, *but is originally from Robert Louis Stevenson's "The Rajah's Diamond." Gurn will later become the vicious criminal mastermind Fantômas, as seen in novels by Marcel Allain and Pierre Souvestre. Fred Porlock is Sherlock Holmes' informant within Professor Moriarty's organization in Doyle and Watson's* The Valley of Fear. *In Louis Feuillade's 1915 film serial* Les Vampires, *Irma Vep is a member of the eponymous gang. Rick Lai's story "All Predators Great and Small" portrayed Irma as a child in 1895, six years after the events of this novel. The 1889 Irma Vep must be an earlier holder of the nom de guerre. Dr. Jack Quartz is a mad scientist and foe of the dime novel detective Nick Carter. Dr. Cornelius Kramm is the leader of the Red Hand gang in Gustave Le Rouge's* Le Mystérieux Docteur Cornélius. *The Black Coats are a criminal conspiracy run by Colonel Bozzo-Corona in novels by Paul Féval. The Golden Chrysanthemum (whose full name is revealed as the Brotherhood of the Golden Chrysanthemum in Reynolds' story "The Pnakotic Puzzle") may be related to the Sons of the Golden Chrysanthemum, a Chinese tong in Derrick Ferguson's Dillon novels and stories. The Phantom of the Paris Opera House is from Gaston Leroux's novel* The Phantom of the Opera. *The Persian and Darius are also from Leroux's novel. The Persian was given the name Nadir in Susan Kay's novel* Phantom. *Jean-Marc and Randy Lofficier's short story "His Father's Eyes" identified the Phantom as the son of the monster created by Victor Frankenstein in Mary Shelley's classic novel. The Rue d'Auseil is from H. P. Lovecraft's short story "The Music of Erich Zann." The Pabodie Expedition to Antarctica was depicted in Lovecraft's* At the Mountains of Madness. *The Great Sandy Desert reference is to Lovecraft's story "The Shadow Out of Time." Harley Warren is from Lovecraft's Dream Cycle stories; his disappearance was depicted in "The Statement of*

Randolph Carter." Ruritania is from Anthony Hope's The Prisoner of Zenda and Rupert of Hentzau. The Persano Affair must be a sequel incident to Farmer's "The Problem of the Sore Bridge–Among Others," which takes place in May of 1895. The "Eye of Oran" debacle was depicted in Eckert's story "The Eye of Oran." The Thoan, a humanoid race who are able to create their own artificial pocket universes, are featured in Farmer's World of Tiers novels. The Finnegan Manuscript was presumably written by or about one of the two main characters of the World of Tiers series, Paul Janus Finnegan, aka Kickaha, Fogg's great-nephew. This novella takes place several months into the historical Exposition Universelle in Paris, which ran from May 6 to October 31, 1889.

c. 1890s

MILORD SIR SMIHT, THE ENGLISH WIZARD

Dr. Eszterhazy is a special agent of the government of Scythia-Pannonia-Transbalkania who undertakes various missions for the government involving mysteries and supernatural encounters. Oberzee-leutnant-commander Adler has written a monograph on the deep-sea fishes. Scythia-Pannonia-Transbalkania's neighboring countries include Ruritania and Graustark. A young student in Prague who thought he had turned into a giant cockroach is mentioned.

Short story by Avram Davidson in The Enquiries of Doctor Eszterhazy. *In Doyle and Watson's "A Scandal in Bohemia," Irene Adler's biography is sandwiched between that of a Hebrew rabbi and that of a staff-commander who had written a monograph upon the deep-sea fishes in Sherlock Holmes' index. Ruritania is from Anthony Hope's* The Prisoner of Zenda *and* Rupert of Hentzau, *while Graustark is from the series by George Barr McCutcheon. The young student in Prague who thought he had turned into a giant cockroach is Gregor Samsa from Franz Kafka's "The Metamorphosis." However, Gregor was a traveling salesman rather than a student, and he actually did turn into a cockroach. According to Davidson, Gregor's case was investigated by the local government of Prague. The government must have distorted the* true details of the case in order to avoid the public learning the grisly details of Gregor's transformation, making Kafka's account the more accurate one. This crossover brings Doctor Eszterhazy and Gregor Samsa into the CU.

1890

January
THE ADVENTURE OF THE ETHICAL ASSASSIN

Sherlock Holmes is hired by the King of Bohemia once again, this time to protect him from an assassin. After preventing one such attempt, Holmes discovers the would-be assassin is a member of the Assassination Bureau, Ltd., led by Ivan Dragomilov. The assassin's weapon is a device invented by the Russian hunter Zaroff.

Short story by Dr. Watson, edited by Matthew Baugh in Sherlock Holmes: The Crossovers Casebook, Howard Hopkins, ed., Moonstone Books, 2012. The Bureau and Dragomilov (originally Dragomiloff) are from Jack London's novel The Assassination Bureau, Ltd, completed posthumously by Robert L. Fish. Zaroff is from Richard Connell's short story "The Most Dangerous Game." This story takes place three years after Holmes and Watson's first encounter with the King in "A Scandal in Bohemia."

Spring
THE TRAGIC CASE OF THE CHILD PRODIGY

Sherlock Holmes and Dr. Watson attempt to rescue young violin *virtuoso* Arthur Tremayne's mother from the influence of occultist William Frawley. Back in Baker Street, Holmes tells Watson he will fetch Billy the page and see if young Mr. Pons is interested in learning the proper way to play the violin.

Short story by Dr. Watson, edited by William Patrick Maynard in Gaslight Grotesque: Nightmare Tales of Sherlock Holmes, J. R. Campbell and Charles Prepolec, eds., EDGE Science Fiction and Fantasy Publishing, 2009. Watson is married to Mary Morstan, which places this story before the Great Hiatus. August Derleth's sleuth Solar Pons studied the art of detection under Holmes, who must have taught the ten-year-old Pons how to play the violin as well.

April 24–May
THE CASE OF THE PORTUGEUSE SONNETS

Sherlock Holmes investigates a case related to a collection of books and papers of great literary worth once owned by the now-deceased poet Jeffrey Aspern.

Short story by Dr. Watson, edited by Donald Thomas in Sherlock Holmes and the King's Evil, *Pegasus Books, 2009. Jeffrey Aspern is from Henry James' novella* The Aspern Papers.

Summer
JACKALOPE

Mad Amos Malone takes "Lord Guy Ruxton" hunting Jackalope in the Bitterroot Range of the Rocky Mountains.

Short story by Alan Dean Foster in Mad Amos, *Del Rey, 1993. Considering his physical description, his skill with firearms and his reputation as a big game hunter, "Lord Guy Ruxton" must really be Lord John Roxton from Arthur Conan Doyle's Professor Challenger stories. The year is conjecture based on Roxton's reputation already being established and a reference to the day of the mountain man being long past.*

THE CURIOUS AFFAIR OF THE ITALIAN ART DEALER

Sherlock Holmes and Dr. Watson investigate the theft of a painting by Titian and the beating of the man who was planning to have the painting authenticated, but Miss Amelia Butterworth of Buffalo, New York solves the mystery before Holmes can.

Short story by Dr. Watson, edited by Sara Paretsky in In the Company of Sherlock Holmes, *Laurie R. King and Leslie S. Klinger, eds., Pegasus Books, 2014. Amelia Butterworth appeared in three detective novels by Anna Katherine Green.*

Autumn
BY A HAIR'S BREADTH

Sleuth Paul Beck encounters his rival Murdoch Rose. Rose is "tall and lithe, with a long clever face," and has an unnamed companion "who walked a little lame." Said companion is described as "shorter, stouter, and duller looking." Rose is dismissed by his client after falsely accusing the man's wife and Beck takes up the case himself.

Story by M. McDonnell Bodkin in Paul Beck the Rule of Thumb Detective, *1898. "Murdoch Rose" and his unidentified companion are clearly meant to be Sherlock Holmes and Dr. Watson. "Rose" was first mentioned* in "The Vanishing Diamonds," a story in the same collection. Since Holmes would not accuse someone of a crime without good reason to believe them guilty, Beck must have distorted the truth when recounting the details of the case to Bodkin. Paul Beck is already in the CU through references in G. L. Gick's "The Werewolf of Rutherford Grange" and Barbara Roden's "The Things That Shall Come Upon Them." Queen Victoria's Jubilee is mentioned as a past event; Victoria had Jubilees in 1887 and 1897.

THE STUFF OF NIGHTMARES

Sherlock Holmes and Dr. Watson team up with Baron Cauchemar, a vigilante in a remarkable suit of armor, to battle a megalomaniac seeking to rule the world. The villain's main henchman, Abednego Torrance, lost an arm to a giant rat on an expedition in Sumatra with Professor George Challenger.

Novel by Dr. Watson, edited by James Lovegrove, Titan Books, 2013. Although Watson says here he has been married to his wife Mary for two years, Baring-Gould places their wedding in 1889. Therefore, they have only been married for one year at the time of the novel.

1891

Early January
THE GREEK INVERTEBRATE

Professor Moriarty and Colonel Moran are asked by the Professor's brother, Colonel James Moriarty, to ignore a summons from the third Moriarty brother, stationmaster James. The Professor and Moran defy his orders, and become involved with espionage and a new machine with which to wage war. Appearing or mentioned are: Sir Augustus Moran; the Club of the Damned; the Mausoleum Club; a chandelier falling on the audience of the Paris Opera during the jewel song from *Faust*; Fal Vale Junction; Greyfriars; the *kuripuri*; the Grand Vampire; *Les Vampires*; a German rival of Moriarty's who sometimes assumes the guise of "a shock-haired, stooped alienist with mesmeric eyes"; Irma Vep; Palliser; Nevil Airey Stent; Fred Porlock; the Lord of Strange Deaths; R. G. Sanders; Eduardo Lucas; Thomas Carnacki; Cursitor Doone; Monsieur Sabin; Ilse von Hoffmansthal, aka Madame Gabrielle Valladon; Flaxman Low; Hugo Oberstein; Sophy Kratides; Malilella of the Stiletto; Irene Adler; Lady Yuki Kashima; Mad Margaret Trelawny; Dr. Syn; Partington; Paul Finglemore, alias Colonel Clay; and Ram Singh.

Short story by Colonel Sebastian Moran, edited by Kim Newman in Professor Moriarty: The Hound of the d'Urbervilles, Titan Books, 2011. Professor Moriarty, Colonel Moran, and Irene Adler are from Doyle and

Watson's Sherlock Holmes stories. Colonel Moriarty is mentioned in "The Final Problem." Stationmaster Moriarty and Fred Porlock are from The Valley of Fear. Sir Augustus Moran, the Colonel's father, is mentioned in "The Adventure of the Empty House." Eduardo Lucas is from the Holmes story "The Adventure of the Second Stain"; since Lucas died in that story, which Baring-Gould has dated to October 1886, the Lucas in Newman's story must be a cousin of Doyle's character who is also involved in espionage. Hugo Oberstein is mentioned in both "The Adventure of the Second Stain" and "The Adventure of the Bruce-Partington Plans," which is also the source of Partington. Sophy Kratides is from the Holmes tale "The Adventure of the Greek Interpreter." The Club of the Damned is from the 1970s British television series Supernatural. The Mausoleum Club is from the 1980s BBC radio comedy series Tales from the Mausoleum Club. The chandelier falling on the audience of the Paris Opera during the jewel song from Faust is a reference to The Phantom of the Opera by Gaston Leroux. Fal Vale Junction is from Arnold Ridley's play The Ghost Train. Greyfriars is the school attended by Billy Bunter in stories written by Charles Hamilton under the pen name Frank Richards. The kuripuri (originally spelled curupuri) is from Doyle's novel The Lost World. Les Vampires are from Louis Feuillade's film serial of the same name, as are their leader, the Grand Vampire, and Irma Vep. This Grand Vampire's predecessor, who appeared in "The Adventure of the Six Maledictions," must be the one murdered by Erik, the Phantom of the Opera, in 1889, as mentioned in Josh Reynolds' Phileas Fogg and the War of Shadows. Rick Lai's "All Predators Great and Small" has Irma as a child in 1895; perhaps the alias "Irma Vep" is used by whoever serves as Les Vampires' primary female operative at any given time. This is likely the same Irma seen in Phileas Fogg and the War of Shadows. Moriarty's German rival is Dr. Mabuse, the master criminal who appeared in fiction by Norbert Jacques and three films directed by Fritz Lang. Palliser is Plantagenet Palliser, the protagonist of a series of novels by Anthony Trollope. The Palliser novels are connected to the Chronicles of Barsetshire series, as well as several non-series novels by Trollope. Stent is from H. G. Wells' The War of the Worlds. The Lord of Strange Deaths is Fu Manchu. R. G. Sanders is Edgar Wallace's Sanders of the River. Sanders and another of Wallace's characters, Lieutenant Bones, appear in each other's series. Thomas Carnacki, "the Ghost-Finder," was created by William Hope Hodgson. Cursitor Doone's name is meant to evoke the British comic book character Cursitor Doom. Monsieur Sabin is from E. Phillips Oppenheim's novels Mysterious Mister Sabin and The Yellow

Crayon. *Ilse Von Hoffmansthal (originally spelled without the second "h"), aka Gabrielle Valladon, is from Billy Wilder's film* The Private Life of Sherlock Holmes. *Flaxman Low is from the collection* Ghosts; Being the Experiences of Flaxman Low, *by "E. and H. Heron" (Hesketh V. Prichard and Kate O'Brien Ryall Prichard). Malilella (usually spelled without the second "l") is from Ermanno Wolf-Ferrari's opera* The Jewels of the Madonna. *Lady Yuki Kashima is better known as the title character of Kazuo Koike and Kazuo Kamimura's* manga Lady Snowblood. *Margaret Trelawny is from Bram Stoker's* The Jewel of Seven Stars. *Dr. Syn is from novels by Russell Thorndike. Paul Finglemore, aka Colonel Clay, is from Grant Allen's* An African Millionaire. *Ram Singh is from the film* Sherlock Holmes and the Secret Weapon. *Several details given about the Moriarty family in this story contradict their established CU history: the Colonel is younger than the Professor, the father of all three brothers was named James, and the Professor implicitly killed his own parents. Moriarty must have had an ulterior motive for lying to Moran.*

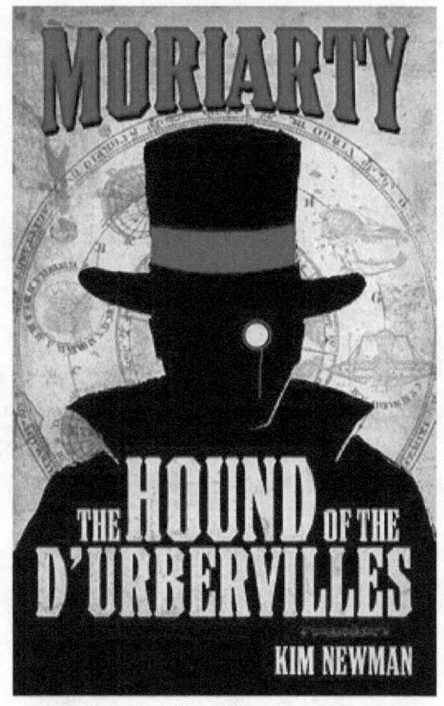

Early January–May 4
THE PROBLEM OF THE FINAL ADVENTURE
Colonel Sebastian Moran recounts the events leading to Professor Moriarty's battle with Sherlock Holmes at the Reichenbach Falls. Appearing or mentioned are: Watson; Colonel Moriarty; the third James Moriarty; "an Irish spinster scribbler"; the Fat Man of Whitehall; the Diogenes Club; Billy the Page; Charlie Vokins; Lestrade; Mackenzie; MacDonald; Simon Carne; the Ranee of Ranchipur; the Lord of Strange Deaths; Fal Vale; Sophy Kratides; Harold Latimer and Wilson Kemp; Charles Milverton; Dan Levy; *Les Vampires*; the Grand Vampire; Irma Vep; Kingstead Cemetery; *La Castafiore*; Thomas Carnacki; Van Helsing; Bulstrode & Sons; Baron Maupertuis; quap; Mr. Beebe; the Daughter of the Dragon; Doctor Nikola;

Madame Sara; Margaret Trelawny; the Hoxton Creeper; Doctor Mabuse; Alraune ten Brincken; Arthur Raffles and Bunny Manders; Théophraste Lupin and Joséphine Balsamo, Countess Cagliostro; Doctor Jack Quartz and Princess Zanoni; Rupert of Hentzau; Irene Adler; the Si-Fan; Queen Tera; the Jewel of Seven Stars; the Black Pearl of the Borgias; the Duke of Shires; Dr. Syn; Barchester Cathedral; the Forsyte tomb; Colonel Clay; Jim Lassiter; Diggory Venn; Sir Augustus Moran; Von Herder; a skull-faced "ghost" in the *khanum*'s palace at Mazenderan; Parker; the Reverend John Jago; the Mountmains; Colonel Sapt; Princess Flavia; Birdy Edwards; Grimesby Roylott; John Clay; Bert Stevens; Fred Porlock; Birlstone Manor; Paul Kratides; Ruritania; Rudi; Michael; Rassendyll; *The Englischer Hof*; and Peter Steiler. The endnotes to the story reveal Kate Reed ghosted for her friend and later lover, Charles Beauregard, and the Diogenes Club traded as Universal Exports in the 1950s. Paul Forrestier is mentioned in the same endnote.

Short story by Colonel Sebastian Moran, edited by Kim Newman in Professor Moriarty: The Hound of the d'Urbervilles, Titan Books, 2011. Moriarty, Moran, Holmes, Watson, the Fat Man of Whitehall (Sherlock's brother Mycroft), the Diogenes Club, Billy the Page, and Lestrade are from the Sherlock Holmes stories. Further references from the Holmes stories: Colonel Moriarty, Inspector Patterson, the Englischer Hof, and Peter Steiler from "The Final Problem"; the third James Moriarty (the stationmaster, later known as the second Professor Moriarty), MacDonald, Birdy Edwards, Fred Porlock, and Birlstone Manor from The Valley of Fear; Sophy Kratides, Harold Latimer, Wilson Kemp, and Paul Kratides from "The Adventure of the Greek Interpreter"; Charles Milverton from "The Adventure of Charles Augustus Milverton"; Baron Maupertuis, mentioned in "The Adventure of the Reigate Squire"; the Black Pearl of the Borgias from "The Adventure of the Six Napoleons"; Sir Augustus Moran, Von Herder, and Parker from "The Adventure of the Empty House"; Grimesby Roylott from "The Adventure of the Speckled Band"; John Clay from "The Adventure of the Red-Headed League"; and Bert Stevens from "The Adventure of the Norwood Builder." Moran's claim he shot Moriarty as the latter grappled with Holmes at Reichenbach must be considered spurious; Holmes would *surely have noticed, and* The League of Extraordinary Gentlemen *depicts Moran and Campion Bond tending to Moriarty after his plunge down the falls. Moran must have lied to conceal the fact the Professor survived his painful fall. The "Irish spinster scribbler" is Kate Reed, a "deleted" character from* Dracula *who appears in several stories by Newman, and also has a counterpart in the Anno Dracula Universe. Charlie Vokins is from "The Horizontal Witness," an episode of the television series* Cribb. *Arthur Raffles, Bunny Manders, and Mackenzie are from the Raffles stories by E. W. Hornung. Dan Levy is from the novel* Mr. Justice Raffles. *Moran indicates Raffles and Bunny are gay. Given that Philip José Farmer identified Raffles as the father of Arthur Upfield's Inspector Napoleon Bonaparte, and Dennis E. Power has theorized he also fathered Simon Templar, it is more likely Raffles is actually bisexual. Simon Carne is from Guy Boothby's collection of stories* A Prince of Swindlers. *Ranchipur is from the film* The Rains of Ranchipur. *The Lord of Strange Deaths is Fu Manchu; the Si-Fan is the criminal organization Fu Manchu runs. The Daughter of the Dragon is presumably meant to be Fu Manchu's daughter, Fah Lo Suee; however, this conflicts with Fah's established birthdate of 1896. Fu must have had another daughter before Fah Lo Suee. Fal Vale is from Arnold Ridley's play* The Ghost Train. *Les Vampires, the Grand Vampire, and Irma Vep are from Louis Feuillade's serial* Les Vampires. *Kingstead Cemetery and Van Helsing are from Stoker's* Dracula. *La Castafiore is Bianca Castafiore from Hergé's Tintin comics. Thomas Carnacki, "the Ghost-Finder," was created by William Hope Hodgson. Bulstrode & Sons is a reference to the British sitcom* That's Your Funeral. *Quap is a radioactive compound from H. G. Wells' novel* Tono-Bungay. *Mr. Beebe is from E. M. Forster's novel* A Room with a View. *Doctor Nikola is the master criminal created by Guy Boothby. Madame Sara is from L. T. Meade and Robert Eustace's* The Sorceress of the Strand. *Rick Lai has identified Madame Sara as the mother of Miss Warrender from Doyle's short story "Uncle Jeremy's Household" in his own fiction, and therefore she is probably bisexual like Raffles, rather than a lesbian as Moran thinks. Margaret Trelawny, Queen Tera, and the Jewel of Seven Stars are from Bram Stoker's* The Jewel of Seven Stars. *The Hoxton Creeper is from the Sherlock Holmes film* The Pearl of Death. *Doctor Mabuse is the subject of fiction by Norbert Jacques, as well as a film trilogy by Fritz Lang. Alraune ten Brincken is from the novel* Alraune *by Hanns Heinz Ewers. Théophraste Lupin is the father of Maurice Leblanc's gentleman thief Arsène Lupin, while Joséphine Balsamo is Arsène's future nemesis. Doctor Jack Quartz and Princess Zanoni are foes of dime novel detective Nick Carter. Rupert of Hentzau, Colonel Sapt, Princess Flavia, Ruritania, Rudi (Rudolf V), Michael (Black Michael), and Rassendyll (Rudolf Rassendyll) are from* The Prisoner of

Zenda *and* Rupert of Hentzau *by Anthony Hope*. The Duke of Shires is from the Sherlock Holmes film A Study in Terror. *Dr. Syn, aka the Scarecrow of Romney Marsh and Captain Clegg, is from the series of novels by Russell Thorndike. Barchester Cathedral is from Anthony Trollope's* Chronicles of Barsetshire *novels.* The Forsyte Saga *is a series of novels by John Galsworthy. Colonel Clay is from the novel* An African Millionaire *by Grant Allen. Jim Lassiter is from Zane Grey's novel* Riders of the Purple Sage. *Diggory Venn is from Thomas Hardy's* The Return of the Native. *The skull-faced "ghost" in the khanum's palace at Mazenderan is the Phantom of the Opera, from the novel by Gaston Leroux. The Reverend John Jago is an ancestor of Anthony Jago from Newman's novel* Jago, *and also has a counterpart in the Anno Dracula Universe. Paul Forrestier is also from* Jago. *The Mountmains are likely kin to the Mountmains who appear in Newman's* Seven Stars. *Charles Beauregard is from Newman's Diogenes Club stories, and has a counterpart in the Anno Dracula Universe. In Billy Wilder's film* The Private Life of Sherlock Holmes, *the Diogenes Club was portrayed as a front for the British Secret Service, a theory Newman has adopted for his own fiction; here, it is revealed the Club eventually became Universal Exports, the front for the BSS in Ian Fleming's James Bond novels. However, the BSS must have still privately used the Club's name at times, as demonstrated by Richard Jeperson's exploits.*

1892

Spring
DR. WATSON'S AMERICAN ADVENTURE

Dr. John Watson and his wife Mary travel to America to visit Mary's recently discovered relatives. The *New York Comet* prints a misleading story about Watson's visit. Watson and Mary meet Theodore "T. R." Roosevelt and his friend Robert Van Loan. The Blackhawk Insurance Company is mentioned. Discussing the exaggerations found in dime novels, Watson says, "The fictional accounts of the very real Sexton Blake suffer from similar 'enhancement.'" Buffalo Bill Cody refers to the *New York Clarion* and its new owner, Franklin Havens. T. R. tells Watson they must pass through the Bar 20 ranch to get to Mary's cousin's ranch. Watson and T. R. drive off some highwaymen with the help of the gunslinger Deadwood Dick. Soon after, they meet Mr. Stanley, editor of the *South Dakota Clarion*, who once used the name Deadwood Dick himself, with the original's permission. Watson recalls the supposedly deceased Sherlock Holmes' lecture to Professor Higgins' Linguistics class, and soon after meets Commander Renwick of the Royal Navy and Lieutenant Hurricane of the Royal Marines.

Novel by Erwin K. Roberts, Airship 27 Productions, 2012. The New York Comet newspaper will later employ Rex Parker, aka the Masked Detective, a pulp hero created by Norman A. Daniels. Robert Van Loan is the father of Richard Curtis Van Loan, aka the title character of the pulp magazine The Phantom Detective. *Franklin Havens' son Frank will later become the owner of the* New York Clarion *himself, and his daughter Muriel will become Richard Curtis Van Loan's girlfriend. The Blackhawk Insurance Company is from the television series* The Man from Blackhawk. *Sexton Blake is one of the most famous British penny dreadful detectives. The Bar 20 Ranch is from Clarence E. Mulford's Hopalong Cassidy novels. Deadwood Dick appeared in dime novel stories by Edward L. Wheeler. Mr. Dick Stanley is from the 1940 serial* Deadwood Dick. *Professor Henry Higgins is from George Bernard Shaw's* Pygmalion, *the basis for the musical* My Fair Lady. *Commander Renwick is probably a relative of one of the aides of a golden-eyed pulp hero known as "Doc." Lieutenant Hurricane is an ancestor of Captain Hercules Hurricane, a superhumanly strong Royal Marine active during World War II, who appeared in the British comic* Valiant *from 1972 to 1976.*

Summer
WANTED: SEÑORITA SCORPION

Bounty hunter Bellem pays a call on Anse Hawkman at the advice of Waxahachie Smith. Hawkman wants Bellem to track down the outlaw Señorita Scorpion, who is said to shoot faster than Dusty Fog. Bellem dented his rifle pistol-whipping a man he was paid to track down by a banker in Yellowdog.

Short story by Brad Mengel in The New Adventures of Señorita Scorpion, *Percival Constantine, ed., Pro Se Press, 2013. Waxahachie Smith, Dusty Fog, and the town of Yellowdog are from the Floating Outfit novels by J. T. Edson, which are already firmly in the CU. Therefore, this crossover brings in Les Savage, Jr.'s Señorita Scorpion, who appeared in eight stories in the pulp magazine* Action Stories *from 1944 to 1949.*

1893

Spring
JACK WRIGHT AND FRANK READE JR., THE TWO YOUNG INVENTORS; OR, BRAINS AGAINST BRAINS. A THRILLING STORY OF A RACE AROUND THE WORLD FOR $10,000

Young inventors Frank Reade Jr. and Jack Wright make a $10,000 bet to prove whether Jack's *Sea Serpent* submarine can circumnavigate the globe faster than Frank's airship, the *Storm King*.

Story by "Noname" (Luis Senarens) in Happy Days #1–8, October 20–December 15, 1894. Luis Senarens wrote both the Frank Reade Jr. stories and the Jack Wright tales. Frank Reade is already in the CU, and therefore this crossover brings in Jack Wright.

Summer
WORLD'S GREATEST SLEUTH!

Big Red and Old Red Amlingmeyer enter a detective contest at the 1893 Chicago World's Fair. Also in attendance are William Pinkerton, Old King Brady, Young King Brady, and Eugene Valmont. A Johan Sigerson congratulates Old Red on winning the contest.

A novel by Big Red Amlingmeyer, edited by Steve Hockensmith. William Pinkerton is a historical figure. Old King Brady and Young King Brady are dime novel characters. In this novel, Young King Brady is an actor hired to impersonate Old King Brady since Old King is not as handsome as the pictures in the dime novels make out. Whether this is actually true has yet to be determined. Eugene Valmont was created by Robert Barr. Nick Carter is mentioned as being fictional in an exposé. This demonstrates that even during their own careers, many of the great detectives of the CU were considered fictional. A note by Big Red confirming Sherlock Holmes' existence appears at the beginning of the novel, so it's ironic he's misled into thinking Carter is fictional. Johan Sigerson is implicitly the then-believed dead Sherlock Holmes.

WITH CAT-LIKE TREAD

Zachary Quinn (aka Lancelot du Lac) attends a performance of *The Pirates of Penzance* alongside Lady Alana Williams, her sister DeLinda, and DeLinda's companion Raoul d'Andrésy. He recognizes the actor playing the Pirate King as a vampire like himself. Quinn meets with Mycroft Holmes at 221B Baker Street, and tells him the place is being watched. Mycroft says the eavesdropper acts as an enforcer for several local loan sharks, such as Scrooge, Marley, and Cratchet. Quinn asks where Mrs. Hudson is, and suggests Mycroft's brother may still be alive, contrary to the good doctor's account entitled "The Final Problem." The Diogenes Club and Lestrade are also mentioned. Mycroft asks Quinn to prevent the theft of a collection of items that includes D'Artagnan's sword and baton. Gossip columnist Dietrich Hollister refers to "that mathematics professor who was consulting with a lot of different gangs." The owner of the collection tells his secretary to send Professor Challenger a telegram letting him know he will be able to have dinner with him that evening, and to ask Professor Helvetius if he might be able to join them. Quinn intercepts d'Andrésy, who is planning to steal a stone possessed by the collector. D'Andrésy, who reveals his true name is Arsène Lupin, says he was told of the stone, which is called a god-stone, by a stage magician named Pickmann.

Short story by Bradley H. Sinor in The Many Faces of Arsène Lupin, *Jean-Marc and Randy Lofficier, eds., Black Coat Press, 2012. Lancelot du Lac, one of the Knights of the Round Table, appears as a vampire in other stories by Sinor. Nigel Bennett and P. N. Elrod have also chronicled the vampiric Lancelot's activities in the 1990s and 2000s under the alias of Lord Richard d'Orleans. Arsène Lupin is the gentleman thief created by Maurice Leblanc. Lupin would encounter a Père Dulac, implied to be the immortal Lancelot, during the 1931 events of Matthew Baugh's "Ex Calce Liberatus" (*Tales of the Shadowmen Volume 2: Gentlemen of the Night, *Jean-Marc and Randy Lofficier, eds., Black Coat Press, 2005; reprinted in* The Many Faces of Arsène Lupin*), but Dulac seems very different in personality from Quinn, and Lupin showed no signs of recognizing Dulac in 1931. Sinor's Lancelot stories are written in a way that makes it clear Quinn is definitely the legendary knight. My theory is that Père Dulac was actually a descendant of the original Lancelot, who fathered a child sometime before he was turned into one of the undead. For reasons of his own, Dulac tricked Lupin into thinking he was his own ancestor. Since Lupin never learned Quinn was in fact Lancelot, he was taken in by this deception. Pickmann is from the Lupin story "The Wedding Ring," included in* The Confessions of Arsène Lupin. *Another god-stone appears in the Lupin story "The Island of Thirty Coffins."*

The vampire appearing as the Pirate King is Dracula, who played the role in Sinor's story "Places for Act Two!" Mycroft Holmes is Sherlock's older brother, and an agent of the British government. The Diogenes Club and Inspector Lestrade are also from the Holmes stories. This story takes place during the Great Hiatus, when Holmes was believed dead by the world after his battle with Professor Moriarty during the events of "The Final Problem." Mrs. Hudson is Sherlock's landlady, while the good doctor is Dr. Watson. Professor Challenger is from The Lost World *and other works by* Doyle. The firm of Scrooge, Marley, and Cratchet is from Charles Dickens' classic A Christmas Carol. D'Artagnan is from Dumas' The Three Musketeers *and sequels*. Professor Helvetius is from Arnould Galopin's novel Doctor Omega, *which has been translated and adapted by Jean-Marc and Randy Lofficier. The introduction to the story states Lupin is seventeen during these events. Since Lupin was born in 1874, that would suggest a placement in 1891. However, this cannot be the case, as "Places for Act Two!" takes place in 1893, during Dracula's second trip to England.*

September 7–14
THE DIARY OF DESOLATION

Appearing or mentioned are: Sabine Absalom (aka Sabine Balsamo); Irene Chupin; Victoire Chupin; Lothaire Stepphun; Josine; Leonard; Arsène; Joseph Balsamo; Cagliostro's grandson; the Black Coats; Marguerite Chavain; Jillian Blake; Urania Caber and her father; Sherlock Holmes; the All-Father; Saladin; Sebastian Moran; Noel Moriarty and his wife, Catarina; Arthur Gordon; the Marie Gilbert School; Raquel Valencia; Madame Fourneau's College for Young Women; Noel and Catarina Moriarty's son; Louis Fourneau; St. Swithin's Medical School; Dr. Arthur Spratt; Paul Cato; Emanuel Medjora; Horace Dorrington; the Sanctuary Club; Anatole Cerral; Teresa Grévin; a tall man with a beard and burning eyes; and Antonio Nikola.

Short story by Rick Lai *in* Sisters of the Shadows: The Cagliostro Curse, *Black Coat Press, 2013. Sabine Absalom is Lai's own invention. Irene Chupin is meant to be Irene Tupin from the film* La Residencia *(aka* The

House That Screamed). *Marguerite Chavain, Madame Fourneau's College for Young Woman, Louis (or Luis) Fourneau,* and *Teresa Grévin are also from* La Residencia. *Victoire Chupin is from the Arsène Lupin novels by Maurice Leblanc. Josine is Joséphine Balsamo, one of Arsène's greatest foes. Leonard is from the Lupin novel* The Countess of Cagliostro, *Joséphine Balsamo's first appearance. "Lothaire Stepphun" is an anagrammatical alias for Théophraste Lupin, Arsène's father. Joseph Balsamo was a historical figure who also appeared in novels by Alexandre Dumas. Cagliostro's grandson is Count Cagliostro from the Mexican horror films* The Bloody Vampire *and* The Invasion of the Vampires. *The Black Coats, the All-Father, and Saladin appear in novels by Paul Féval. Jillian Blake is based on a reference to a Jill Fagin who married a Blake in Philip José Farmer's* Doc Savage: His Apocalyptic Life. *Urania Caber is meant to be Urania Moriarty from the same book. Lai's story "Urania's Babysitter" explains why she prefers to use her mother's surname, rather than that of her father, Professor James Moriarty, Sherlock Holmes' archenemy. Colonel Sebastian Moran, Professor Moriarty's second-in-command, appears in Doyle's "The Adventure of the Empty House." Noel Moriarty, the Professor's brother, is mentioned in* The Valley of Fear; *his full name is in fact James Noel Moriarty, and he will assume his brother's identity after the latter's seeming death. Catarina Moriarty is meant to be Madame Koluchy from L. T. Meade and Robert Eustace's* The Brotherhood of the Seven Kings. *The Sanctuary Club is from Meade and Eustace's novel of the same name, as is Dr. Paul Cato. Arthur Gordon is from Emile Gaboriau's novel* La Vie Infernale. *The Marie Gilbert School is from the movie* Madeline. *Raquel Valencia's name is meant to evoke Nina Valencia from Walter Gibson's Shadow novel* Washington Crime. *Noel and Catarina Moriarty's son is Dominick Medina, the villain of John Buchan's* The Three Hostages. *St. Swithin's Medical School is from Richard Gordon's Doctor novels; Dr. Arthur Spratt is an ancestor of Dr. Lancelot Spratt from that series. Emanuel Medjora is from Rodrigues Ottolengui's novel* A Modern Wizard. *Horace Dorrington is from Arthur Morrison's collection* The Dorrington Deed Box. *Dr. Anatole Cerral is the father of the surgeon from Maurice Renard's* The Hands of Orlac. *The tall man with a beard and burning eyes is Count Dracula. Dr. Antonio Nikola is a criminal mastermind featured in novels by Guy Boothby.*

Late December 1893–January 1895
RECALLED TO LIFE

Sherlock Holmes is in New York during the Great Hiatus. Using the alias Simon Greaves, he meets disgraced ex-police captain Robert Battle. The two attend the opera, where Battle points out Henry Ogden Slade, his ward, and Slade's best friend, Thaddeus Chadwick, who was responsible for Battle's downfall. Holmes forces Chadwick to clear Battle's name. Two years later, Battle and his wife visit Holmes and Watson in London, where Battle tells Holmes Chadwick was murdered by a young woman with whom he was living.

Short story by Dr. Watson, edited by Paula Cohen in Sherlock Holmes in America, Martin H. Greenberg, Jon L. Lellenberg, and Daniel Stashower, eds., Skyhorse Publishing, 2009. Henry Ogden Slade, his ward (Clara Adler), Thaddeus Chadwick, and the young woman (Lucy Pratt) are from Cohen's novel Gramercy Park. Watson wrote up this case after Holmes' retirement.

1894

Spring
PREDATORS AND PREY
The Earthman Gullivar Jones reluctantly teams up with the vampires of Mars to rescue Princess Heru from the equally bloodthirsty Erloor.

Short story by Matthew Dennion in The Vampire Almanac (Volume 1), Jean-Marc and Randy Lofficier, eds., Black Coat Press, 2015; reprinted in French in L'Almanach des Vampires (Tome 2), Jean-Marc and Randy Lofficier, eds., Rivière Blanche, 2015. Gullivar Jones and Princess Heru are from Edwin L. Arnold's novel Lieutenant Gullivar Jones: His Vacation. This story takes place a few days after the end of Arnold's novel. The vampires of Mars and the Erloor are from Gustave Le Rouge's novel The Vampires of Mars, which has been translated by Brian Stableford for Black Coat Press.

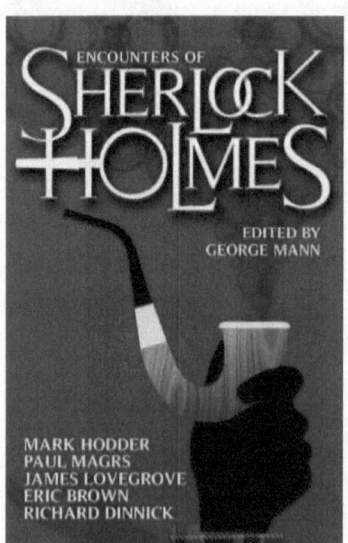

May
THE PROPERTY OF A THIEF
Sherlock Holmes investigates a theft at the home of a couple who are friends of Dr. Watson. He ultimately identifies the culprits as A. J. Raffles and Bunny Manders, but chooses to let the two go free and unexposed.

Short story by Dr. Watson, edited by Mark Wright in Encounters of Sherlock Holmes, George Mann, ed., Titan Books,

2013. The story is set in May, after Mary Watson's death, and therefore also after Holmes returned from the Great Hiatus in April 1894. Raffles faked his death in July 1895 during the events of Hornung's "The Gift of the Emperor," so "The Property of a Thief" must take place before that tale. 1894 is a more likely year for the story to occur than 1895, since Holmes and Raffles were both involved in the events of Farmer's "The Problem of the Sore Bridge–Among Others" in May 1895. Contrary to Watson's account, he and Holmes have encountered Raffles and Manders many times before the events of this story. The deception may be related to the fact Holmes was once married to Raffles' sister Marjorie, who died in childbirth.

Late May
THE ADVENTURE OF THE HANGING TYRANT

Sherlock Holmes investigates a case that involves Oswald Crawshay, who learned the art of housebreaking from his uncle, a suspect in the theft of the Melrose Necklace.

Story by M. J. Elliott in Curious Incidents 2: Being a Collection of the Further Adventures of Sherlock Holmes, *J. R. Campbell and Charles Prepolec, eds., Mad for a Mystery, 2003; reprinted in* Sherlock Holmes: The Game's Afoot, *David Stuart Davies, ed., Wordworth Editions, 2008, and* Sherlock Holmes in Pursuit, *MX Publishing, 2013. Oswald Crawshay's uncle is Reginald Crawshay from E. W. Hornung's Raffles stories "Gentlemen and Players" and "The Return Match," both of which are included in the collection* The Amateur Cracksman.

June
THE SECOND THEFT OF ALHAZRED'S MANUSCRIPT

Sir James Marsden, a member of a group dedicated to combating occult forces, hires Sherlock Holmes and Dr. Watson to investigate the theft of a portion of Abdul Alhazred's manuscript the *Al-Azif,* aka the *Necronomicon.*

Short story by Dr. Watson, edited by Bradley H. Sinor in Historical Lovecraft: Tales of Horror Through Time, *Silvia Moreno-Garcia and Paula R. Stiles, eds., Innsmouth Free Press, 2011. This story takes place two months after "The Adventure of the Empty House."*

Summer
THE CALDWELL GHOST

Occult detective Simon Feximal says the Third Line of the Saaamaaa Ritual, on which he and his fellow ghost-hunter Carnacki had done such perilous research.

Short story by Robert Caldwell, edited by K. J. Charles in the e-book The Casebook of Simon Feximal, *Samhain Publishing, 2015. The Saaamaaa Ritual and Carnacki are from William Hope Hodgson's* Carnacki the Ghost-Finder. *Since Carnacki is in the CU, so are Simon Feximal and his lover and biographer Robert Caldwell, whose first meeting is recounted in this story.*

Autumn
THE ADVENTURE OF THE IMAGINARY NIHILIST
    Colonel Richard Henry Savage hires Sherlock Holmes and Dr. Watson to help him find his former lover, nihilist Helene Marie Vanderbilt-Astor Gaines. Savage thinly veiled their relationship in a novel called *My Official Wife*.
    Short story by Dr. Watson, edited by Will Murray in Sherlock Holmes: The Crossovers Casebook, *Howard Hopkins, ed., Moonstone Books, 2012. Colonel Richard Henry Savage was a real person. Helene is referred to by that name in Savage's novel, although Savage himself is identified as Colonel Lenox. The comic book miniseries* Doc Savage: Doom Dynasty *claims Colonel Savage was the grandfather of Doc. However, this does not fit with the genealogy given for Doc in Philip José Farmer's biographies* Tarzan Alive *and* Doc Savage: His Apocalyptic Life. *It is more likely the Colonel is James Clarke Wildman, Sr.'s adoptive father, as proposed by Win Scott Eckert in "The Doc Savage Chronology" on the* An Expansion of Philip José Farmer's Wold Newton Universe *website. The year is conjecture based on the fact Savage's novel was published in 1891. Therefore, this story likely takes place after the Great Hiatus.*

November 4
REMEMBER, REMEMBER
    Mr. Lownie, editor of the *Chronicle*, tells Robert Caldwell that Simon Feximal is at Hartley House "with Miss Kay and Dr. Berry. Carnacki's in Ireland chasing some haunting, else he'd be there too, I hear." According to Robert, "that list encompassed the best-known ghost-hunters in England, with the exception of the reclusive Dr. Silence."
    Short story by Robert Caldwell, edited by K. J. Charles in the e-book The Casebook of Simon Feximal, *Samhain Publishing, 2015. Carnacki is from William Hope Hodgson's short story collection* Carnacki the Ghost-Finder, *while Dr. Silence is from Algernon Blackwood's collection* John Silence.

Late Autumn
SHERLOCK HOLMES AND THE GOLDEN BIRD

Sherlock Holmes and Dr. Watson investigate the theft of the Golden Bird, a statue of a roc made out of gold. Holmes' interest in Montenegro is noted several times, and Watson wonders if his friend spent any time there during the period the world believed him dead. A footnote to a passage about Holmes' interest in geography says, "It is interesting to note that a latter-day detective of widespread fame and girth who was born in Montenegro spent a great deal of time studying maps." Holmes says Jimmie Valentine is one of four burglars who could have stolen the Bird from a safe, but he is in America. Holmes compares the Chinese criminal Chu San Fu to a modern Monte Cristo.

Novel by Dr. Watson, edited by Frank Thomas, Pinnacle Books, 1979. Given its physical description and history, the Golden Bird is not the Maltese Falcon, despite what one might think. In his biographies Sherlock Holmes of Baker Street *and* Nero Wolfe of West Thirty-Fifth Street, *William S. Baring-Gould proposed Holmes had an affair with Irene Adler in Montenegro during the Great Hiatus, resulting in a child who would later be known as Nero Wolfe. Jimmie (or Jimmy) Valentine is from O. Henry's classic 1903 story "A Retrieved Reformation." Holmes refers to the Count of Monte Cristo as a real person. This novel takes place before* Sherlock Holmes and the Sacred Sword, *which has to take place in 1895 due to a reference to General Kitchener preparing for the reconquest of the Sudan. As he so often does, Watson causes deliberate chronological confusion by referring to cases that take place after 1894, such as "The Adventure of Charles Augustus Milverton." The death of Holmes' rival Barker from "The Adventure of the Retired Colourman" is also a distortion, as he appears alive and well in Win Scott Eckert's "No Ghosts Need Apply," which takes place during and after the events of "Charles Augustus Milverton."*

1895

Winter
THE SEASON OF THE SHARK

The man-shark known as the Hictaner explores a ship captained by Tobias Marsh of Innsmouth, Massachusetts. He thinks Marsh's name is not connected to Fulbert and Oxus, his creators. Marsh, who has allied with Fulbert, is a member of the Esoteric Order of Dagon. He invokes Cthulhu's name in an incantation. Fulbert sics half a dozen Deep Ones on the Hictaner.

Short story by Julien Heylbroeck in The Nyctalope Steps In, *Jean-Marc and Randy Lofficier, eds., Black Coat Press, 2011; reprinted in French in* Les Compagnons de l'Ombre (Tome 8), *Jean-Marc and Randy Lofficier, eds., Rivière Blanche, 2011. The Hictaner, Oxus, and Fulbert are from Jean de La Hire's* The Man Who Could Live Underwater. *Oxus went on to appear in de La Hire's* The Nyctalope on Mars. *The Marsh family, Innsmouth, the Esoteric Order of Dagon, and the Deep Ones are from H. P. Lovecraft's "The Shadow over Innsmouth." Cthulhu is one of the Great Old Ones in Lovecraft's Mythos.*

Spring
THE LONE RANGER: VENDETTA

The Lone Ranger battles Butch Cavendish's vengeful widow Laura Cavendish. Laura says she and Butch had a couple children.

Novel by Howard Hopkins, Moonstone Books, 2012. *One of Butch and Laura's children will grow up to have a son named John Cavendish. John's daughter, named Laura Cavendish after her great-grandmother, will continue the family feud by battling the Ranger's (John Reid) great-grandnephew, the Green Hornet (Britt Reid), as the Yellowjacket, as seen in Hopkins' stories "Flight of the Yellowjacket" (*The Green Hornet Chronicles, *Joe Gentile and Win Scott Eckert, eds., Moonstone Books, 2010), "Sting of the Yellowjacket" (*The Green Hornet Casefiles, *Joe Gentile and Win Scott Eckert, eds.,*

Moonstone Books, 2011), and "Revenge of the Yellowjacket" (The Green Hornet: Still at Large, *Joe Gentile, Win Scott Eckert, and Matthew Baugh, eds., Moonstone Books, 2012), as well as Matthew Baugh's story "Auld Acquaintance" (The Green Hornet Casefiles).*

December
THE WATERS OF DEATH
Sherlock Holmes and Dr. Watson are dispatched to Loch Ness by Holmes' brother Mycroft to prevent sabotage of the Bruce-Partington Submarine. In the process, they meet the Duke of Forgill at Forgill Castle. Tulloch Moor is also seen, and Commander Ralph Lethbridge-Stewart, Captain Harry Sullivan, and Lieutenant Philip Benton also appear.

Novella by Dr. Watson, edited by Kel Richards in Sherlock Holmes: Footsteps in the Fog and Other Stories, *Beacon Books, 2009. Forgill Castle and Tulloch Moor are from "Terror of the Zygons," a* Doctor Who *serial set in Loch Ness. The Duke of Forgill seen in this story must be the ancestor of the Duke that later encountered the Doctor. Commander Ralph Lethbridge-Stewart, Captain Harry Sullivan, and Lieutenant Philip Benton must be ancestors of* Doctor Who*'s Brigadier Alistair Lethbridge-Stewart, Lieutenant Harry Sullivan, and Sergeant Benton, respectively. This crossover provides further evidence a version of the Doctor exists in the CU.*

Late Autumn
DEVILS ON HORSEBACK
Simon Feximal is a member of the Diogenes Club, to which he had been nominated by one of his more peculiar acquaintances, a Government man whose intellectual capacity is matched only by his corpulence. Both Simon and his biographer and lover Robert Caldwell are members of a club called the Remnant, whose members include Dr. Silence, Thomas Carnacki, and Dr. Nikola.

Short story by Robert Caldwell, edited by K. J. Charles in the e-book The Casebook of Simon Feximal, *Samhain Publishing, 2015. The Diogenes Club is from the Sherlock Holmes stories, while the corpulent government man is Sherlock's brother Mycroft. Given that various sources portray the Diogenes Club as a front for the British Secret Service, it is likely Mycroft recruited Simon for the Club because he felt his expertise at ghost-hunting would come in handy. Dr. Silence is an occult detective created by Algernon Blackwood, while Thomas Carnacki (aka Carnacki the Ghost-Finder) was created by William Hope Hodgson. Dr. Nikola is a supervillain created by Guy Boothby.*

1896

Spring
THE ADVENTURE OF THE INFERNAL INHERITANCE

Sherlock Holmes and Dr. Watson investigate the death of Cecil Armitage, who put Professor Moriarty on the path to crime. Armitage was being tailed by Mycroft Holmes' operative Giles Waverly until Waverly's murder. Colonel Moran tells Holmes he is hoping to get into the good graces of the Technological Hierarchy, the current incarnation of Moriarty's criminal organization, by getting his hands on Armitage's recreation of a hypothetical proto-atom bomb Moriarty wrote about in *The Dynamics of an Asteroid.*

Short story by Greg Hatcher in Sherlock Holmes: Consulting Detective Volume 6, *Ron Fortier, ed., Airship 27 Productions, 2014. Giles Waverly is meant to be the brother of Alexander Waverly from the television series* The Man from U.N.C.L.E.*, as confirmed by Hatcher in his afterword to this story. Win Scott Eckert's essay "The Amazing Lanes" speculated Alexander (born 1892) was the son of Hester Lane, the niece of Robert Louis Stevenson's Dr. Henry Jekyll, from Robert Bloch and Andre Norton's novel* The Jekyll Legacy. *Hester was born in 1867, and could not possibly have had a grown son in 1896. Her husband Mr. Waverly (possibly the same Waverly who appears in Stuart Shiffman's story "The Milkman Cometh") must have had a much earlier marriage that resulted in Giles Waverly, who would in fact be Alexander's elder half-brother. David McDaniel's tie-in novel* The Dagger Affair *revealed U.N.C.L.E.'s primary nemesis, THRUSH, arose from the ashes of Professor Moriarty's organization, and the latter-day group's name stood for the Technological Hierarchy for the Removal of Undesirables and Subjugation of Humanity.*

Summer
SHERLOCK HOLMES AND THE TREASURE TRAIN

Sherlock Holmes and Dr. Watson attend a shooting competition whose announcer is Lord Arthur Seville. Lady Windermere and the Duchess of

Paisley are also in attendance. Watson says of financier Burton Hananish, "With a treasure like Monte Cristo's at his fingertips, he might well have pictured himself as the second coming of Moriarty."

Novel by Dr. Watson, edited by Frank Thomas, Pinnacle Books, 1985. Lord Arthur Seville (or Savile), Lady Windermere, and the Duchess of Paisley are from Oscar Wilde's story "Lord Arthur Savile's Crime." Lady Windermere may be the same woman seen in Wilde's play Lady Windermere's Fan. Watson's comment seems to suggest the Count of Monte Cristo is every bit as real as Hananish and Moriarty. This case takes place after Sherlock Holmes and the Sacred Sword *(1895) and before the death of Otto von Bismarck (1898).*

THE ALBINO'S TREASURE
Sherlock Holmes and Dr. Watson attempt to prevent two rival criminal masterminds, Zenith the Albino and the Chinese Lord of Strange Deaths, from getting their respective hands on a mysterious but precious item called "England's Treasure." Donald Petrie is the Secretary of the National Portrait Gallery.

Novel by Dr. Watson, edited by Stuart Douglas, Titan Books, 2015. Zenith the Albino is one of Sexton Blake's greatest foes. Although Zenith first battled Blake in a 1913 story, this novel demonstrates that he was already active well before then. "The Lord of Strange Deaths" is one of Fu Manchu's appellations. Donald Petrie may be a relative of Dr. Petrie from the Fu Manchu novels.

December
CUT THE BRANCH
Appearing or mentioned are: the Black Coats; Joséphine Balsamo; the House of Crafts; Dr. Antonio Nikola; Catarina Corbucci; Count Salvatore Corbucci; Professor James Moriarty; Madame Fourneau's College for Young Women; Norman Head; Noel Moriarty; Irina Putine; the Chupin Detective Agency; Urania Caber; the golden ram crest of the Cagliostro family; the Gentlemen of the Night; Orianne Coyatier; Rochelle Moreau; Ramirez; Professor Chavain; Madame Sara (aka Sarah Warrender); Colleen Pegler; the White Lodge; Frank Moran; Colonel Sebastian Moran; Patrick Dickson; Hamish Webb; Stangerson's *Disassociation of Matter Through Electricity*; the Brotherhood of the Seven Kings; Gordo Reloj; Pilar; Aguilar; the All-Father; Dominick Moriarty; Marga Sandorf; Aristide Orlowsky Sandorf; Baron Von Schulenberg; Manny Bennet; Solly Bennet; Corben Caine; Wilmot Rogers; Jefferson Gonzales; the Lanky Gunman; the Yankee Whistler;

a friend of Gordo's; Dupont-Verdier (aka Satanas); Jillian Blake; Leonard; Etienne Cressy Raimond D'Arcourt; Sharita; the Duchy of Strackenz; the Thuggee cult's alliance with Naga worshippers; Achmet Genghis Khan; Gruesome Clayton; Carfax Abbey; Dracula; and Ballmeyer.

Short story by Rick Lai in Sisters of the Shadows: The Cagliostro Curse, *Black Coat Press, 2013. The Black Coats are a criminal conspiracy featured in novels by Paul Féval. Orianne Coyatier is the granddaughter of Jean-François Coyatier (aka the Marchef), who acted as the Black Coats' executioner. The All-Father is the leader of the Black Coats. The Gentlemen of the Night are from Féval's* The Mysteries of London. *Joséphine Balsamo battled Arsène Lupin in Maurice Leblanc's* The Countess of Cagliostro. *Leonard is also from that novel. The House of Crafts is an allusion to the criminal organization known as Krafthaus in John Buchan's* The Power-House. *Dr. Antonio Nikola is a scientist and criminal mastermind featured in novels by Guy Boothby. Catarina Corbucci is meant to be Madame Koluchy from L. T. Meade and Robert Eustace's* The Brotherhood of the Seven Kings. *Norman Head is also from Meade and Eustace's novel. Madame Sara is from Meade and Eustace's* The Sorceress of the Strand; *her alias of Sarah Warrender is meant to imply she is the mother of Miss Warrender from Arthur Conan Doyle's "Uncle Jeremy's Household." Achmet Genghis Khan was identified as Miss Warrender's father in Doyle's tale. Count Salvatore Corbucci dueled with A. J. Raffles in E. W. Hornung's "The Fate of Faustina" and "The Last Laugh." Professor James Moriarty is Sherlock Holmes' archenemy. Noel Moriarty (whose full name is James Noel Moriarty) is the Professor's younger brother mentioned in* The Valley of Fear. *Colonel Sebastian Moran is Professor Moriarty's second-in-command from "The Adventure of the Empty House." In* The Power-House, *the Krafthaus' leader Andrew Lumley lives in a house called the White Lodge; the implication of the White Lodge reference in Lai's story is Lumley is actually Noel Moriarty. Madame Fourneau's College for Young Women is from the Spanish horror film* La Residencia. *Irina Putine is an alias for Irene Tupin from the same film. Professor Chavain is based on Madame Fourneau's reference to her former student, a noted botanist. The Chupin Detective Agency, run by Victor "Toto" Chupin, is from the works of Emile Gaboriau. Urania Caber is meant to be Urania Moriarty, the Professor's daughter, whose existence was revealed by Philip José Farmer in* Doc Savage: His Apocalyptic Life. *Jillian Blake is based on a reference to a Jill Fagin who married a Blake in Farmer's book. The golden ram crest of the Cagliostro family is from the animated Lupin III film* The Castle of Cagliostro. *Rochelle Moreau is the daughter of H. G. Wells' Dr. Moreau and the niece of Bernard Moreau, who is mentioned in* La Residencia. *Tuco Benedicto Pacifico Juan Maria Ramirez is from the film* The Good, the Bad and the Ugly. *"Colleen Pegler" is an alias for Peg Cullane from Louis L'Amour's* The Man Called Noon. *Frank Moran is Francis "Colt" Moran from the film* Today It's Me... Tomorrow You! *Patrick Dickson is meant to be Tricky the Gambler from the movie* The Fighting Fists of Shanghai Joe. *Hamish Webb is meant to be James Webb from the movie* Black Killer. *Stangerson's Disassociation of Matter Through Electricity is from Gaston Leroux's first Rouletabille novel,* The Mystery of the Yellow Room. *Ballmeyer is Rouletabille's father. Gordo Reloj is meant to be Gordo Watch from the film* Arizona Colt *(aka* The Man from Nowhere*); "reloj" is Spanish for*

"watch." Pilar and Aguilar are from the film A Stranger in Town. *Dominick Moriarty is meant to be Dominick Medina from John Buchan's* The Three Hostages. *Marga Sandorf is the niece of the title character of Jules Verne's novel* Mathias Sandorf. *Aristide Orlowsky Sandorf is meant to be the Hungarian villain Orlowsky from the movie* Django Strikes Again. *Baron Von Schulenberg is from the movie* The Big Gundown. *Manny Bennet is meant to be Manuel from the film* Cemetery Without Crosses. *Corben Caine and Wilmot Rogers are Ben Caine and Will Rogers from the same film. Solly Bennet is Solomon "Beauregard" Bennet from the movie* Face to Face. *Jefferson Gonzales is from the film* Ringo and His Golden Pistol. *The Lanky Gunman is Hank "Lanky" Fellows from the movie* A Taste for Killing. *The Yankee Whistler is the title character of the movie* Yankee. *Gordo's friend is Frank Talby from the movie* Day of Anger. *Satanas is from Louis Feuillade's film serial* Les Vampires; *in the English language translation of the serial, Satanas' real name is given as Claude Dupont-Verdier. Etienne Cressy Raimond D'Arcourt and Sharita are from Gardner F. Fox's novel* Woman of Kali. *The Duchy of Strackenz is from George MacDonald Fraser's* Royal Flash; *here, it is implied to be the same country as the Duchy of Cagliostro from* The Castle of Cagliostro. *The alliance between the Thuggee and Naga worshippers is from Emilio Salgari's Sandokan novels. Gruesome Clayton is Sir William Clayton from Farmer's* Tarzan Alive *and* Doc Savage: His Apocalyptic Life. *Carfax Abbey is from Bram Stoker's* Dracula.

1897

Early January
UNSEEN STRATAGEMS
Appearing or mentioned are: Dr. Malbodius; the Black Coats; Noel Moriarty; the White Lodge; Coswell; Bridau; Hallward; Jacques Saillard; Irina Putine; the Chupin Detective Agency; the Espionage Hotel; Madame Fourneau; Fritz Kramm; Joséphine Balsamo; the d'Arx family; Marga Sandorf; Madame Sara; Count Salvatore Corbucci; Acheron; Valusia; Count Cagliostro; Adana; Sithra; Ixcatl; Dr. Antonio Nikola; the Neptune Society; Dorcas Spode; a nobleman who owned the last unicorn on Earth; Claud and Jimmy Caber and their mother, Urania; Trickie Moriarty; the Nightingale Hierarchy; Professor Chavain; Hattori Hanzo III; Zatoichi; Daigoro and his father; Dr. Baian; Rochelle Moreau; Rochelle's uncle, a lawyer in Avignon; Dr. Noel; Madame Zéphyrine; the Northumberland Hotel Conference of 1895; Madame Vabre; the Sanctuary Club; Orianne Coyatier; Mary Holder; the Regenerator of Fashion; Suzanne Noel; Dr. Cerral; the Cavalier Arom; Coleen Pegler; Sabine Balsamo's maternal grandfather and his daughter Anna; Théophraste Lupin; Chief Inspector Jacques Lefevre; the Order of the Serpent Heart; Ace Sartana (aka Jake Silver); the House of Crafts; Transas Shipping; Martin Stedor; Lord Faber; and the Ripening Rubies.

Short story by Rick Lai in Sisters of the Shadows: The Cagliostro Curse, Black Coat Press, 2013. Dr. Malbodius is an alias for Dr. Mabuse from novels by Norbert Jacques and a long-running German film series. The Espionage Hotel is from the film The 1,000 Eyes of Dr. Mabuse. Transas Shipping is the precursor to the Transas Moving Company from The Invisible Claws of Dr. Mabuse; Martin Stedor is an ancestor of Martin Droste from the same film. Noel Moriarty is Professor Moriarty's younger brother from The Valley of Fear; his full name is James Noel Moriarty. Mary Holder is from Doyle and Watson's "The Adventure of the Beryl Coronet." In John Buchan's The Power-House, the villainous Andrew Lumley lives in a house called the White Lodge. The implication of this reference is "Lumley" is really Noel Moriarty. The House of Crafts is an allusion to the organization called Krafthaus controlled by Lumley in The Power-House. The Black Coats are a criminal conspiracy featured in novels by Paul Féval. The d'Arx family is also from the Black Coats series. Orianne Coyatier is the granddaughter of Jean-François Coyatier, aka the Marchef, the Black Coats' executioner. The Cavalier Arom is a reference to the Black Coats' leader, the All-Father, who sometimes used the alias of the Cavalier Mora. Josette du Pres' portrait on the television series Dark Shadows bore the signature "Coswell." The nobleman who owned the last unicorn on Earth is Count Petofi from that series. Joseph Bridau appears in several novels in Honoré de Balzac's La Comédie Humaine cycle. Basil Hallward is from Oscar Wilde's The Picture of Dorian Gray. Jacques Saillard is from E. W. Hornung's Raffles story "An Old Flame." Count Corbucci is from the Raffles tales "The Fate of Faustina" and "The Last Laugh." Irina Putine is the same character as Irene Tupin from the movie La Residencia. Madame Fourneau and Suzanne Noel are also from that film. Professor Marguerite Chavain and the lawyer Moreau are mentioned, but never seen, in La Residencia. The Chupin agency and its owner, Victor "Toto" Chupin, are from the works of Emile Gaboriau, as is the Regenerator of Fashion shop. Fritz Kramm is from Gustave Le Rouge's Le Mystérieux Dr. Cornélius. Joséphine Balsamo battled Arsène Lupin in Maurice Leblanc's The Countess of Cagliostro. Théophraste Lupin, Arsène's father, is also from The Countess of Cagliostro. Marga Sandorf is the niece of the title character of Jules Verne's novel Mathias Sandorf. Madame Sara is from L. T. Meade and Robert Eustace's The Sorceress of the Strand. Her alias of Sarah Warrender is meant to imply she is the mother of Miss Warrender from Arthur Conan Doyle's "Uncle Jeremy's Household." Catarina Moriarty is meant to be Madame Koluchy from Meade and Eustace's The Brotherhood of the Seven Kings. The Sanctuary Club is from Meade and Eustace's novel of the same name. Acheron is from Robert E. Howard's Conan novel The Hour of the Dragon, while Valusia is from Howard's Kull stories. Besides being a historical figure, Count Cagliostro was featured in novels by Alexandre Dumas. Adana the Snake Mother is from A. Merritt's novel The Face in the Abyss. Sithra and Ixcatl are from Richard L. Tierney's Simon of Gitta tale "The Dragons of Mons Fractus," as well as Tierney and David C. Smith's Red Sonja novel Against the Prince of Hell. Dr. Antonio Nikola is a criminal genius featured in the works of Guy Boothby. The Neptune Society is a precursor to the group of scientists seen in The Man from U.N.C.L.E. episode "The Neptune Affair." The Nightingale Hierarchy is the precursor to the Technological Hierarchy for the Removal of Undesirables and the Subjugation of Humanity, aka THRUSH, U.N.C.L.E's main opponent. The Northumberland Hotel Conference of 1895 is from David McDaniel's The Man from

U.N.C.L.E. novel The Dagger Affair. *Dorcas Spode is a relative of Roderick Spode from the Jeeves and Wooster tales by P. G. Wodehouse. Claud Caber is meant to be Bulldog Drummond's archenemy Carl Peterson, as well as Claud Darrell from Agatha Christie's Hercule Poirot novel* The Big Four. *Jimmy Caber is better known as the criminal mastermind Dr. Caber from Lord Dunsany's Jorkens books. Philip José Farmer identified Peterson and Caber's mother as Urania Moriarty, the Professor's daughter, in* Doc Savage: His Apocalyptic Life. *Lai's story "Urania's Babysitter" explains why Urania prefers to use her mother's surname. Trickie Moriarty is meant to be Patricia Donleavy, the Professor's daughter from Laurie R. King's* The Beekeeper's Apprentice. *Hattori Hanzo III is from the Japanese television series* Shadow Warriors. *The blind swordsman Zatoichi was played by Shintaro Katsu in a series of films. Daigoro Ogami and his father Itto are from Kazuo Koike and Goseki Kojima's comic book* Lone Wolf and Cub. *Dr. Fujieda Baian is from Shōtarō Ikenami's novels* Master Assassin *and* Bridge of Darkness, *as well as the television series* Baian the Assassin. *Rochelle Moreau's father is H. G. Wells' Dr. Moreau. Dr. Noel and Madame Zéphyrine are from Robert Louis Stevenson's story "The Suicide Club." Madame Vabre is from Émile Zola's book* Pot-Bouille. *Dr. Cerral is the father of the surgeon from Maurice Renard's* The Hands of Orlac. *Colleen Pegler is an alias for Peg Cullane from Louis L'Amour's* The Man Called Noon. *Sabine Balsamo's maternal grandfather is Count Cagliostro from the films* The Bloody Vampire *and* The Invasion of the Vampires. *The Count's daughter Anna is also from* The Bloody Vampire. *Chief Inspector Jacques Lefevre is from the movie* Bluebeard. *The Order of the Serpent Heart is meant to be the secret society from H. Rider Haggard's* Heart of the World. *Ace Sartana is a combination of Sartana, the hero of five Spaghetti Westerns, with the Ace of Hearts from the film* They Called Him Cemetery *and Silver from* The Price of Death; *actor Gianni Garko played all three roles. The Ripening Rubies are from Max Pemberton's short story of the same name, included in the collection* Jewel Mysteries I Have Known, *as is Lord Faber.*

Winter
A GUNFIGHT

Will Tenneray and Abe Cross, a pair of famous but aging and down on their luck gunslingers, agree to stage a gunfight in a bullfighting ring, with the ticket proceeds going to the winner. Tenneray has a conversation with his young son Bud, who tells of how folks in town talk about the time Tenneray outdrew the Ringo Kid.

A novelization by Phillip Rock of the 1971 film A Gunfight. *The Ringo Kid is from the classic Western* Stagecoach, *which was brought into the CU* by John Allen Small's story "Buck Mason Loses His Horse." *The year is conjecture, though the story clearly takes place in the dying days of the Old West.*

March
THE MINISTER'S MISSING DAUGHTER
Sherlock Holmes and Dr. Watson vacation in New York City, where they attend a dinner party at the home of Mr. and Mrs. Theodore Roosevelt. There, they meet Mrs. Sarah Brandt, who asks them to investigate the disappearance of Harriet Penny. Working on the case with them is Detective Sergeant Frank Malloy.
Short story by Dr. Watson, edited by Victoria Thompson in Sherlock Holmes in America, *Martin H. Greenberg, Jon L. Lellenberg, and Daniel Stashower, eds., Skyhorse Publishing, 2009. Brandt and Malloy are the protagonists of Thompson's* Gaslight Mysteries *series of novels; this crossover brings them into the CU. The date is not explicitly given, but can be deduced from a reference to William McKinley as "the newly-elected American president."*

Spring
FLASHMAN AND THE MOUNTAIN OF LIGHT
Harry Flashman tells his great-niece Selina the story of a man who lost a rifle in Paris and tripped over it in West Africa twenty years later.
Novel by George MacDonald Fraser. The man who lost the rifle is Captain Battreau from P. C. Wren's story "No. 187017," included in the collection Flawed Blades. *"No. 187017" and Wren's other books and stories involving the French Foreign Legion are interconnected, including* Beau Geste, *which Philip José Farmer referenced in* Doc Savage: His Apocalyptic Life. *The main events of Fraser's novel take place in 1845–1846, but the framing sequences, which refer to Flashman telling Battreau's story to Selina, were written by Flashman after 1894 and before 1902.*

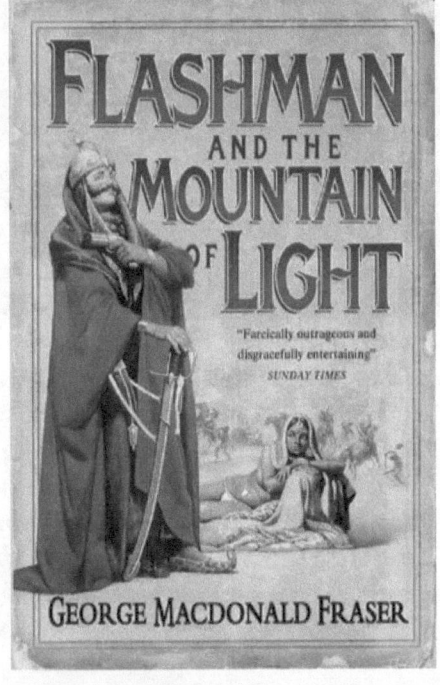

Summer
THE SCION OF FEAR
Sherlock Holmes and Dr. Watson work with Inspector Athelney Jones and Jonathan Small to investigate a pair of attacks apparently committed by an Andaman Islands native like Small's late confederate Tonga. Watson reveals to Mycroft Holmes the box which once held the Agra treasure has a hidden panel which opens to reveal three yellow diamonds. Mycroft says they are part of a series of four "moonstones" that adorned temple idols in India. He adds the fourth diamond was recovered years ago after much drama.

Short story by Dr. Watson, edited by Christopher Sequeira in Sherlock Holmes: The Crossovers Casebook, *Howard Hopkins, ed., Moonstone Books, 2012. Inspector Jones, Jonathan Small, and Tonga are from the Sherlock Holmes novel* The Sign of Four. *The diamonds are from Wilkie Collins' novel* The Moonstone.

September 20–22
SO MUCH LOSS
The Sâr Dubnotal assists Dr. Jack Seward and Arthur Holmwood, Lord Godalming in trying to cure Dexter Stratton's son Gavin, a former victim of Lucy Westenra who shows signs of vampirism. Mentioned are: Count Dracula; Harker; Quincey Morris; Harker's wife Mina and son Quincey; Van Helsing; Thomas Carnacki; Sherlock Holmes; Quincey Morris' son by his late wife; Celia Lytton and her new husband; and Dr. Watson.

Short story by Anthony R. Cardno in Tales of the Shadowmen Volume 10: Esprit de Corps, *Jean-Marc and Randy Lofficier, eds., Black Coat Press, 2013; reprinted in French in* Les Compagnons de l'Ombre (Tome 16), *Jean-Marc and Randy Lofficier, eds., Rivière Blanche, 2015, and* L'Almanach des Vampires (Tome 2), *Jean-Marc and Randy Lofficier, eds., Rivière Blanche, 2015; and in* The Vampire Almanac (Volume 2), *Jean-Marc and Randy Lofficier, eds., Black Coat Press, 2015. Dr. Jack Seward; Arthur Holmwood, Lord Godalming; Lucy Westenra; Count Dracula; Quincey Morris; Jonathan Harker; his wife Mina; their son Quincey; and Abraham Van Helsing are from Bram Stoker's* Dracula. *Thomas Carnacki is from William Hope Hodgson's* Carnacki the Ghost-Finder. *Sherlock Holmes and Dr. Watson are from Arthur Conan Doyle's stories. Quincey Morris' son and his deceased wife are from the Morris and Chastain Supernatural Investigations series by Justin Gustainis, which features Quincey's great-grandson and namesake acting as an occult detective. Gavin Stratton's father Dexter is the great-grandfather of Charlie Pace on the television series* Lost; *Gavin's younger brother Charles is* presumably Charlie's grandfather. Celia Lytton and her husband are from Penny Vincenzi's The Spoils of Time *trilogy of novels*. The Sâr Dubnotal is the main character of a French pulp series by an anonymous author.

October
CONSEQUENCES OF A FUNERAL

Appearing or mentioned are: Raffles; Dr. Nikola; Count Corbucci; the Black Coats; Noel Moriarty; Madame Koluchy; Kate Washburn; "the Queen of the Outlaws"; the Pallid Mask (aka Juan North and Dirk Gurn); Etienne Rambert; Stefano; Madame Sara; Joséphine Balsamo; Dr. Eric Malbodius; the Gentlemen of the Night; Marga Sandorf; Ignacz Djanko; Jeff Gonzales; Maricruz Juana (aka Mijanou); John Forest (aka Djanko); Angel-Face Brown; Death-Sentence Cash; the Von Schulenberg  family; Louise King; Leeman Bailey; Gunsight Eyes; Ballmeyer; Colonel Sebastian Moran; Ronald Adair; Julius Von Herder; Irina Putine; a distant American relative of Joséphine; Madame Vabre; the Chupin Detective Agency; the Iga ninjas; the Royal Palace Hotel; Ulthar; Coleen Pegler; Maître Durnais; Cornelia Vadarasse; and César Cascabel.

Short story by Rick Lai in Sisters of the Shadows: The Cagliostro Curse, Black Coat Press, 2013. A. J. Raffles *is the gentleman thief created by* E. W. Hornung. Count Corbucci *battled Raffles in* "The Fate of Faustina" *and* "The Last Laugh." Stefano *is also from* "The Fate of Faustina." Dr. Nikola *is a master criminal in Guy Boothby's novels. The* Black Coats *are a criminal conspiracy from the works of Paul Féval. The* Gentlemen of the Night *are from Féval's* The Mysteries of London. Noel Moriarty *(aka James Noel Moriarty, the second Professor Moriarty) is Professor Moriarty's younger brother mentioned in* The Valley of Fear. Colonel Sebastian Moran, Ronald Adair, *and* Julius Von Herder *are from Doyle's* "The Adventure of the Empty House." *Von Herder's first name, not given in Doyle's story, is meant to imply he is the father of the title character of Ian Fleming's James Bond novel* Dr. No. Madame Koluchy *is from L. T. Meade and Robert Eustace's* The Brotherhood of the Seven Kings. Madame Sara *is from Meade and Eustace's* The Sorceress of the Strand. Kate Washburn *is related to* Curly *and* Duke Washburn *from the movies* City Slickers *and* City Slickers II: The Legend of

Curly's Gold. *The "Queen of the Outlaws" is the title character of Roy Chanslor's novel* The Ballad of Cat Ballou. *The Pallid Mask is Marcel Allain and Pierre Souvestre's "Lord of Terror,"* Fantômas. *The Pallid Mask alias is derived from Robert W. Chambers'* The King in Yellow. *Etienne Rambert is the father of Charles Rambert, aka Jerôme Fandor, one of Fantômas' greatest foes. The Royal Palace Hotel is from the first Fantômas novel. Joséphine Balsamo is Arsène Lupin's archenemy. Dr. Eric Malbodius is meant to be Norbert Jacques' criminal mastermind Dr. Mabuse. Marga Sandorf is the niece of the title character of Jules Verne's novel* Mathias Sandorf. *Ignacz Djanko is the title character of the films* Django *and* Django Strikes Again. *Jeff Gonzales is from the film* Ringo and His Golden Pistol. *Maricruz Juana is meant to be a combination of Django/Djanko's lover Maria with Mijanou from the film* 10,000 Dollars Blood Money; *Loredana Nusciak played both roles. John Forest was played by Gianni Garko in the film* Vengeance Is Mine; *here, he is conflated with the Django played by Garko in* 10,000 Dollars Blood Money. *Angel-Face Brown is from the films* A Pistol for Ringo *and* The Return of Ringo. *Death-Sentence Cash is from the movie* Death Sentence. *The members of the Von Schulenberg family include Baron Von Schulenberg from the film* The Big Gundown. *Louise King is from the film* The Legend of Frenchie King. *Leeman Bailey is from the movie* Hannie Caulder. *Gunsight Eyes is the title character of the films* Sabata *and* The Return of Sabata *combined with Colonel Douglas Mortimer from* For a Few Dollars More; *Lee Van Cleef played both characters. Ballmeyer is the father of Gaston Leroux's detective Rouletabille. Irina Putine is the same character as Irene Tupin from the film* La Residencia. *Joséphine Balsamo's distant American relative is the title character of the film* The Great Silence. *Madame Vabre is from Émile Zola's book* Pot-Bouille. *The Chupin Detective Agency is from the works of Emile Gaboriau. A fictionalized version of the historical Iga ninja clan appeared in the Japanese television series* Shadow Warriors. *Ulthar is from H. P. Lovecraft's "The Cats of Ulthar." Coleen Pegler is an alias for Peg Cullane from Louis L'Amour's* The Man Called Noon. *Maître Durnais is from Cole Porter's musical* Can-Can. *César Cascabel is from Jules Verne's novel of the same name, as is Cornelia Vadarasse.*

THE ADVENTURE OF THE HAUNTED SHOWMAN

Inspector Lestrade brings a potential client to Sherlock Holmes. Holmes says he is engaged in a pressing affair involving an unclaimed rare book recently auctioned after the sale of the Al Hazred Collection, and he shall not be free until a courier returns from Amsterdam with a message he requires. After the woman and Lestrade leave, Holmes admits to Watson he was lying about the prior case.

Short story by Christopher Sequeira in Sherlock Holmes: The Game's Afoot, *David Stuart Davies, ed., Wordsworth Editions, 2008. Despite Holmes' falsehood, he must be aware of the real "Mad Arab" Abdul Alhazred, the author of the* Necronomicon *in H. P. Lovecraft's Cthulhu Mythos.*

1898

Winter
A PROFESSIONAL MATTER
In 1902, Adam Adamant tells Sherlock Holmes and Dr. Watson the tale of how Inspector Ganimard recruited him to apprehend Arsène Lupin four years ago. A Collector received a note warning Lupin would rob him of his green paste idol of Princess Hermonthis. Adamant meets Inspector Ledoux at the scene of a murder. The victims are members of the Diogenes Club, in Paris on orders from Mycroft Holmes. The Collector gives a grimoire to Griffin, an invisible English scientist who is currently in league with a cult of Nyarlathotep worshippers. The grimoire was written by Charles le Sorcier, an alchemist and magician, the son of Michel Mauvais. Adamant heard about Nyarlathotep and his follower Pharaoh Nephren-Ka from the Curator at Miskatonic University. Adamant receives a letter from Lupin, revealing the thief had impersonated the real Ledoux, who died in 1879 while hunting the Phantom of the Opera.

Short story by Sam Shook in Tales of the Shadowmen Volume 11: Force Majeure, *Jean-Marc and Randy Lofficier, eds., Black Coat Press, 2014. Adam Adamant is from the 1960s BBC television series* Adam Adamant Lives! *Sherlock Holmes, his brother Mycroft, Dr. Watson, and the Diogenes Club are from Arthur Conan Doyle's stories. The Collector and the idol of Princess Hermonthis are from Théophile Gautier's short story "The Mummy's Foot." Inspector Ledoux is from the 1925 film version of Gaston Leroux's novel* The Phantom of the Opera. *Griffin is from H. G. Wells' classic science fiction novel* The Invisible Man. *After escaping Adamant and Lupin's clutches in this story, Griffin returns to England, where he takes up residence in a private girl's school, as seen in* The League of Extraordinary Gentlemen, Volume I. *Nyarlathotep, Charles le Sorcier, Michel Mauvais, and Nephren-Ka are from the works of H. P. Lovecraft.*

Early Spring
KINGDOM OF THE BLIND

Appearing or mentioned are: Sylvia Pence; Count Salvatore Corbucci; Catarina Corbucci (aka the Blind Spinner); Noel Moriarty; the Gentlemen of the Night; the Black Coats; the Agnes de la Fere Athletic Club; Rochelle Moreau; Orianne Coyatier; Ecstasy Parker; Norman Head; Koutatsu of Shimosa Province; Sumeru Yuki; the Iga clan; Senzo; Marga Sandorf; the Order of the Serpent Heart; Baron Von Schulenberg; Colonel Skimmel; Aristide Sandorf; Dr. Eric Malbodius; Madame Sara's Perfumery; Senora Pilar Reloj; the Pallid Mask; the Chupin Detective Agency; Chief Inspector Jacques Lefevre; Irina Putine; Vathelos; Anna Beringer; Leonard Wolfe; Superintendent Ford; the Koga clan; the White Priest; the Countess Yalta Memorial Hospital; the Royal Palace Hotel; the Regenerator of Fashion; Joséphine Balsamo; Ace Sartana; Maude North; the hero of the dime novel *The Man from Minnesota*; Mary Holder; Sir George Burnwell; the *Old Fellow*; La Frenaie wine; Dr. Antonio Nikola; Tarao Hanzo; Inspector Justin Ganimard; Helen Lipsius; Cesarine Caoutchouc; Colonel Clay; Alexander Holder; a blade used by the legendary Yagyu family to slay demons; and Julius Von Herder.

Short story by Rick Lai in Sisters of the Shadows: The Cagliostro Curse, Black Coat Press, 2013. *Sylvia Pence is meant to be Madame Sylvia from L. T. Meade and Robert Eustace's story "Finger Tips," included in the collection* The Oracle of Maddox Street. *Catarina Corbucci is better known as Madame Koluchy, from Meade and Eustace's* The Brotherhood of the Seven Kings; *here, she is conflated with the Blind Spinner from John Buchan's* The Three Hostages. *Norman Head, Anna Beringer, and Superintendent Ford are also from* The Brotherhood of the Seven Kings. *Madame Sara's Perfumery is from another book by Meade and Eustace,* The Sorceress of the Strand. *Count Salvatore Corbucci dueled with A. J. Raffles in E. W. Hornung's "The Fate of Faustina" and "The Last Laugh." Noel Moriarty is Professor Moriarty's younger brother, who was mentioned in the Sherlock Holmes novel* The Valley of Fear. *Ecstasy Parker is the sister of Larry Parker from Doyle and Watson's "The Adventure of the Empty House." Julius Von Herder is also from that story, although his first name is Lai's invention, and is meant to imply he is the father of the titular villain of Ian Fleming's James Bond novel* Dr. No. *Mary Holder, Sir George Burnwell, and Alexander Holder are from another Holmes tale, "The Adventure of the Beryl Coronet." The Gentlemen of the Night are from Paul Féval's* The Mysteries of London. *The Black Coats are a criminal conspiracy featured in a series of novels by Féval. Orianne Coyatier's grandfather Jean-François Coaytier, also known as the Marchef, was the Black Coats' executioner. The Agnes de la Fere Athletic Club is named after the main character (also known as Dark Agnes de*

Chastillon) of Robert E. Howard's stories "Sword Woman," "Blades for France," and "Mistress of Death." Vathelos is from Howard's Conan story "Black Colossus." The experiments of Rochelle Moreau's father were chronicled in H. G. Wells' The Island of Doctor Moreau, *while her uncle Bernard is mentioned in the film* La Residencia. *Koutatsu of Shimosa Province and Senzo are from the movie* Zatoichi's Cane-Sword. *Sumeru Yuki is related to the Marquis Sumuru from Sax Rohmer's novels dealing with the Marquis' villainous widow. The Iga and Koga ninja clans are historical, but their feud formed the basis for the Japanese television series* Shadow Warriors. *Tarao Hanzo is also from that series. Marga Sandorf's uncle is the title character of Jules Verne's novel* Mathias Sandorf. *The Order of the Serpent Heart is meant to be the secret society from H. Rider Haggard's* Heart of the World. *Baron Von Schulenberg is from the film* The Big Gundown, *while Colonel Skimmel is from the movie* Adios Sabata. *Here, the Baron and the Colonel are identified as cousins; both were played by Gérard Herter. Aristide Sandorf is meant to be the villain Orlowsky from the movie* Django Strikes Again. *Dr. Eric Malbodius is meant to be Norbert Jacques' criminal mastermind Dr. Mabuse. Senora Pilar Reloj is Pilar from the film* A Stranger in Town; *Lai's story "Cut the Branch" revealed she married her fellow outlaw Gordo Reloj, who is meant to be Gordo Watch from the movie* Arizona Colt. *The Pallid Mask will later be known as Fantômas; his alias in this story is derived from Robert W. Chambers'* The King in Yellow. *The Royal Palace Hotel is from the first Fantômas book, while the* Old Fellow *is from the seventh novel in the series,* Le Pendu de Londres. *Maude North is the villain's late Boer wife mentioned in* The Daughter of Fantômas. *The Chupin Detective Agency, headed by Victor "Toto" Chupin, is from the works of Emile Gaboriau, as is the Regenerator of Fashion. Chief Inspector Jacques Lefevre is from the movie* Bluebeard. *Irina Putine is meant to be Irene Tupin from* La Residencia. *Leonard Wolfe is from R. Austin Freeman's Dr. Thorndyke tale "The Aluminium Dagger." The White Priest is Pai Mei of Chinese legend and film; his tendency to pluck out women's eyes is an allusion to the movie* Kill Bill: Vol. 2, *which features a flashback in which Pai Mei rips out Elle Driver's right eye. The Countess Yalta Memorial Hospital is named after a character from Fortuné du Boisgobey's* The Lost Casket *(aka* The Severed Hand*); at*

the end of the novel, there are plans to construct a hospital in the Countess' memory somewhere in France. Joséphine Balsamo is from Maurice Leblanc's Arsène Lupin books The Countess of Cagliostro and Countess Cagliostro's Revenge. Inspector Justin Ganimard is also from the Lupin tales. Ace Sartana is the Spaghetti Western hero Sartana combined with the Ace of Hearts from the movie They Called Him Cemetery; both were played by Gianni Garko. The hero of The Man from Minnesota is the title character of the film Minnesota Clay. La Frenaie wine is from the Averoigne tales by Clark Ashton Smith. Dr. Antonio Nikola was the subject of novels by Guy Boothby. Helen Lipsius is meant to be the Helen who worked for Dr. Lipsius in Arthur Machen's The Three Hostages; her usage of the doctor's surname is meant to suggest she is his mistress, just as Carl Peterson's mistress Irma is often referred to as Irma Peterson. Cesarine Caoutchouc and Colonel Clay are from Grant Allen's An African Millionaire. The Yagyu blade is from the film Samurai Reincarnation.

March. Harry Houdini hires Sherlock Holmes to accompany him to a séance given by Harker Bellamy, and to help him prove Bellamy is a fraud. ("The Adventure of the Magician's Meetings" by Dr. Watson, edited by Larry Engle and Kevin VanHook in *Sherlock Holmes: The Crossovers Casebook*, Howard Hopkins, ed., Moonstone Books, 2012.) Holmes and Houdini would meet several more times after this, though a number of Watson's written accounts of these events falsely purported to depict the duo's first meeting. Tiger Standish, the protagonist of a series of novels by Sydney Horler, is a British Intelligence agent reporting to Sir Harker Bellamy. Horler's Bellamy was also the main character of *The Curse of Doone* and *My Lady Dangerous*, which did not feature Standish. The Harker Bellamy appearing in "The Adventure of the Magician's Meetings" cannot be the same character, but is probably a relative and namesake of Standish's superior. Tiger Standish is already in the CU through a connection to Dr. Syn and an appearance in Erwin K. Roberts' novella "The Sons of Thor," thus adding some credence to this genealogical connection.

Summer
THE WRITING ON THE WALL
   Simon Feximal and Robert Caldwell encounter the occultist Karswell. Dr. Silence appears, and the Saaamaaa Ritual and John Watson are mentioned.
   Short story by Robert Caldwell, edited by K. J. Charles in the e-book The Casebook of Simon Feximal, *Samhain Publishing, 2015. Karswell is from M. R. James' story "Casting the Runes." Dr. John Silence is an occult detective created by Algernon Blackwood. The Saaamaa Ritual is from* Carnacki the Ghost-Finder *by William Hope Hodgson. Dr. John Watson is Sherlock Holmes' best friend and biographer.*

1899

January
REMNANT

Ghost hunter Simon Feximal and his biographer and lover Robert Caldwell join forces with visiting American scholar and sorcerer Percival Endicott Whyborne and his own partner, ex-Pinkerton Griffin Flaherty, to investigate an occult menace in England. Feximal reads a news story about Whyborne's visit that says he discovered the tomb of the pharaoh Nephren-ka. Whyborne looks at a drawing of an Egyptian tablet in his notebook and recognizes Apep, the serpent of chaos, who is sometimes associated with Nyarlathotep. Whyborne and Flaherty initially speculate Caldwell may be a

member of a cult called the Eyes of Nodens. Feximal and Caldwell later take Whyborne and Flaherty to a private club called the Remnant, run by the Hesselian Society of Occult Investigation. It is said one may meet the ghost-finder Thomas Carnacki at the Remnant on his usual storytelling Thursdays (which are best avoided), and Dr. Silence always takes one of the small bedrooms on his infrequent trips to town. Feximal snaps at Whyborne that the Saaamaaa Ritual is not sorcerous.

E-novella by K. J. Charles and Jordan L. Hawk. This story is a team-up between the occult detectives of Charles' The Secret Casebook of Simon Feximal *series and Hawk's* Whyborne & Griffin *series. Nephren-ka is from H. P. Lovecraft's Cthulhu Mythos tale "The Haunter of the Dark." In Lovecraft's Mythos fiction, Nyarlathotep is one of the malevolent Great Old Ones, while Nodens is a benevolent Elder God. The Hesselian Society of Occult Investigation is named after Dr. Martin Hesselius from J. Sheridan Le Fanu's short story collection* In a Glass Darkly, *considered by many to be one of the first occult detectives in fiction. Thomas Carnacki is from William Hope Hodgson's collection* Carnacki the Ghost-Finder, *while Dr. Silence is from Algernon Blackwood's collection* John Silence. *The Saaamaaa Ritual is from the Carnacki stories "The Gateway of the Monster," "The House Among the Laurels," and "The Whistling Room."*

Winter
LES ECUMEURS DE LA BOURSE
Ganimard unmasks a fake Lord Lister in Paris.
Short story by Yves Varende in Lord Lister, le Mystérieux Inconnu. *Inspector Justin Ganimard is Arsène Lupin's policeman nemesis.*

FIRST STEPS
Seeking a use for his newfound powers, Leo Saint-Clair begins debunking mediums alongside his friend Robert Champeau. He attends a séance held by the Prillants. Among those in attendance are the Baldwins and the pregnant Mrs. Anne Jones and her chaperone, Ms. Loveday Brooke. The medium is Simon Orne, who conjures a demonic being. Leo later discovers another attendee at the séance was Lily Flowers, a member of the gang called the Vampires. Leo and Robert meet the Sâr Dubnotal, who reveals Orne summoned the creature, Baal, using a page from the *Necronomicon*. Inspector Milfroid accompanies Leo to another séance in order to arrest Orne.
Short story by Travis Hiltz in Night of the Nyctalope, *Jean-Marc and Randy Lofficier, eds., Black Coat Press, 2012; reprinted in French in* Les Compagnons de l'Ombre (Tome 11), *Jean-Marc and Randy Lofficier, eds., Rivière Blanche, 2013. Leo Saint-Clair, aka the Nyctalope, is a hero in novels by Jean de La Hire. Robert Champeau and the Prillants are also from the Nyctalope stories. The Baldwins, Lily Flowers, and the Vampires are from Louis Feuillade's serial* Les Vampires. *Anne (or Anna) Jones is the mother of noted archaeologist Dr. Henry "Indiana" Jones, Jr. Since Indiana Jones was born in 1899, the date of 1900 assigned to this story must be incorrect. Loveday Brooke is from* The Experiences of Loveday Brooke, Lady Detective *by Catherine Louisa Pirkis. Simon Orne is from Lovecraft's* The Case of Charles Dexter Ward. *The* Necronomicon *is a mainstay of Lovecraft's Cthulhu Mythos. The Sâr Dubnotal appeared in his own self-titled pulp magazine penned by an anonymous author (possibly Norbert Sévestre). Baal is from the novel of the same name by Renée Dunan. Inspector Milfroid is from Gaston Leroux's* The Phantom of the Opera.

THE CASE OF THE DISPLACED DETECTIVE
A future version of Sherlock Holmes travels back in time and persuades Dr. Watson to prevent the Holmes of the doctor's era from discovering a working scale model of a time machine in a house in Richmond, knowing it will ultimately lead to Watson's death.
Short story by Roy Gill in Further Encounters of Sherlock Holmes, *George Mann, ed., Titan Books, 2014. The time machine seen here is a prototype of the one seen in H. G. Wells'* The Time Machine. *Obviously,*

the future Holmes' intervention resulted in his own timeline never coming to pass. *The story is set in winter, shortly after Harrods installed its moving stairway, which historically happened on November 16, 1898.*

Spring
A CABINET SECRET
   A mysterious secret society plotting to sabotage the British Empire rents Wiltshire House, a residence belonging to the Earl of Brewarden, to use as their London headquarters.
   1901 novel by Guy Boothby. Wiltshire House was the residence of the Duchess of Wiltshire in Boothby's collection A Prince of Swindlers. *The Duchess must have sold her home to the Earl of Brewarden sometime in the five years since the 1894 events of* A Prince of Swindlers. *Since* A Prince of Swindlers *takes place in the Crossover Universe, so does this novel. In* A Cabinet Secret, *the British Prime Minister is assassinated. Since no such event happened in 1899, this should be regarded as a distortion of the truth on Boothby's part.*

Summer
THE CASE OF THE LIMEHOUSE LAUNDRY

   The Baker Street Irregulars investigate the disappearance of a number of flower girls. One of the Irregulars, Rosie, is told of the disappearances by a flower girl named Eliza, the daughter of an alcoholic dustman. Eliza was recently approached by a gentleman who offered to teach her to speak like a proper lady. Professor Moriarty proves to be behind the vanishings.
   A Sherlock Holmes' Baker Street Boys novel by Anthony Read based on the 1980s British television series The Baker Street Boys. *Eliza is Eliza Doolittle from George Bernard Shaw's* Pygmalion. *The gentleman is Professor Henry Higgins. A boatman named Enoch claims the Chinese festival occurring in Limehouse during the climax of this novel is to celebrate "New Year or summat." However, Enoch is incorrect, as* Pygmalion *takes place in Summer 1899, and Chinese New Year (the beginning of the Year of the Pig) fell on February 10 in 1899. The Moriarty in this book must be the second Professor Moriarty; that is, the first Professor's younger brother, James Noel Moriarty, posing as his elder sibling.*

1900

Winter
FIGHTING ALASKA

At the Hotel Carlton in San Francisco, boxer Jean St. Vrain and his friend Pete Lally argue over Pete's idea of heading to Nome, Alaska to take over a gold claim, causing the Hotel's elderly owner to intervene.

A Fight Card novella by "Jack Tunney" (Duane Spurlock), Fight Card Books, 2015. The owner of the Hotel Carlton is Paladin from the radio and television series Have Gun–Will Travel, *who apparently took over the Hotel after merely being a permanent resident there in both series' original runs.*

Spring
THE QUALITY OF VENGEANCE

Jacques de Trémeuse refuses an offer of power to take vengeance on the banker Favraux from the demon Pazuzu.

Short story by Matthew Dennion in The Shadow of Judex, *Jean-Marc and Randy Lofficier, eds., Black Coat Press, 2013; reprinted in French in* L'Ombre de Judex, *Jean-Marc and Randy Lofficier, eds., Rivière Blanche, 2013. Jacques de Trémeuse will later take his own brand of revenge on Favraux as Judex. Pazuzu is from William Peter Blatty's novel* The Exorcist.

Summer
THE ADVENTURE OF THE NOBLE HUSBAND

Louise Hawkins Doyle visits Sherlock Holmes, asking him to investigate whether her husband Arthur Conan Doyle, Dr. Watson's editor and literary agent, is having an affair. Holmes suggests she consult Adrian Mulliner instead. Conan Doyle's sister Constance and her husband E. W. Hornung appear, as do Jean Leckie and P. G. Wodehouse.

Short story by Dr. Watson, edited by Peter Cannon in The Confidential Casebook of Sherlock Holmes, *St. Martin's Griffin, 1999. Adrian Mulliner* is the nephew of Wodehouse's series character Mr. Mulliner. Adrian appears in the stories "The Smile That Wins" and "From a Detective's Notebook." In the latter, he reaches the (obviously mistaken) conclusion Holmes and Moriarty were one and the same. Jean Leckie will become Conan Doyle's second wife after Louise's death. Although Watson identifies Hornung here as the author of the Raffles stories, in reality, he shared a relationship with A. J. Raffles' sidekick and amanuensis Harry "Bunny" Manders similar to his brother-in-law Conan Doyle's with Dr. Watson. Watson may have claimed the Raffles stories were fictional in order to conceal the fact Holmes was once married to A. J.'s sister Marjorie.

THE MYSTERY OF THE FLYING MAN

Music hall singer Emily Trelawney says of her captors, "Grant and his wretched father intend to take the money and flee England, settling in some obscure little European county like Ruritania or Graustark."

A Harry Challenge story by Ron Goulart in Sherlock Holmes Mystery Magazine #2, *Marvin Kaye, ed., Wildside Press, 2009.*

THE HEADLESS MONK

Sherlock Holmes and Dr. Watson investigate an apparent haunting on an island near Cornwall. Inspector Lestrade is also there, investigating events that occurred on the island twenty years ago alongside Constable Poldark of the Truro county police.

Novel by Dr. Watson, edited by Kel Richards, Beacon Communications, 1997. Winston Graham wrote a series of novels about a Cornish family named Poldark. We can assume the Constable is meant to be a member of Graham's Poldark family, if not directly descended from Ross Poldark and his wife Demelza.

Late August
NOT CRICKET

Sherlock Holmes receives a telegram that mentions his "unfortunate involvement with a member of the ruling house of Ruritania."

Short story by Dr. Watson, edited by L. F. E. Coombs in Sherlock Holmes at the Breakfast Table, *Robert Hale, 2013. Apparently, Holmes once had a case involving one of the Elphbergs, the royal family of the country of Ruritania from Anthony Hope's* The Prisoner of Zenda *and* Rupert of Hentzau.

1901

Winter
THE RAFFLES HUNT (aka RAFFLES AND THE AUTOMOBILE GANG)
Raffles and Bunny Manders encounter Smiler Bunn and his gang.

Short story by Barry Perowne (pseudonym for Philip Atkey) in Ellery Queen's Mystery Magazine, *January 1974, reprinted in* Raffles of the Albany, *1976. Smiler Bunn is a comedic thief-turned-detective appearing in short stories and novels by Perowne's uncle Bertram Atkey from 1911 to 1940.*

Spring
THE PROBLEM OF THE ELUSIVE CRACKSMAN
Harry Challenge deduces the gorilla-like thief who stole the Mirabilis Diamonds took a serum that could turn an average man into a large, powerful superhuman. Challenge's sidekick, the Great Lorenzo, recalls that a fellow named Dr. Henry Jekyll stumbled upon a similar concoction some years ago, and came to a bad end.

Story by Ron Goulart in The Magazine of Fantasy & Science Fiction, *November–December 2012.*

June 7–8
THE ADVENTURE OF THE SINISTER CHINAMAN
Dr. Watson, recovering from an illness, accompanies Sherlock Holmes to San Francisco, where they become embroiled in an investigation of a Chinese-American magician who has been accused of kidnapping a young girl who was helping him perform a trick. They are aided by another stage magician, Professor Oscar Zoroaster Diggs, who is also a balloonist. Diggs claims to have spent the last forty years in a magical realm, and built a City of Emeralds and done battle with the Wicked Witch of the East and her minions. After the resolution of the case, Watson learns Professor Diggs looked exactly the same when he returned as when he disappeared forty years ago, and concludes the Professor that he and Holmes met was an impostor. He notes the alleged Professor disappeared a year later on another ballooning expedition.

Short story by Dr. Watson, edited by Barbara Hambly in Sherlock Holmes: The Crossovers Casebook, *Howard Hopkins, ed., Moonstone Books, 2012. Professor O. Z. Diggs is better known as the Wizard of Oz. Of course, the Diggs who disappeared in the 1860s and the one who encountered Holmes and Watson are one and the same.*

1902

January
THE SECOND TREATY

The former Annie Harrison comes to Sherlock Holmes for assistance. Her husband Percy Phelps has been meeting with a delegation from Valletta to discuss unrest in the Mediterranean. One of the delegates has been assaulted and the treaty stolen. Holmes identifies the culprit and reveals the weapon used on the delegate was in fact the true object of the theft, rather than the treaty. He produces both the treaty and a black statue of a bird. Holmes says the latter is "a falcon, I suspect, Watson. I believe we will find that it holds some special significance for the people of Valletta— indeed, for the whole of the Maltese island. But that is neither here nor there. I was engaged to recover the treaty, and I have done so. As for this— this Maltese falcon, that I fear, is a problem for some other detective."

Short story by Dr. Watson, edited by Daniel Stashower in The New Adventures of Sherlock Holmes, *expanded edition, Martin H. Greenberg, Carol-Lynn Rossel Waugh, and Jon L. Lellenberg, eds., Carroll & Graf, 1999. Percy Phelps and Annie Harrison are from the Sherlock Holmes story* "The Adventure of the Naval Treaty." *The problem of the Falcon was taken up by private detective Sam Spade in November 1928, as seen in Dashiell Hammett's novel* The Maltese Falcon. *Holmes previously came in contact with the Falcon in 1877 ("The Adventure of the Impecunious Chevalier"), 1886 ("The Adventure of the* Rara Avis"), *and 1889 ("The Madness of Colonel Warburton"), although Watson treats this as his and Holmes' first encounter with the statue.*

September 3–16
THE ADVENTURE OF THE ILLUSTRIOUS CLIENT

The Cunard liner *Ruritania* is mentioned in this Sherlock Holmes adventure.

Short story by Dr. Watson, edited by Arthur Conan Doyle in The Strand Magazine, *February–March 1925, and reprinted in* The Case-Book of Sherlock Holmes, *1927*. *The* Ruritania *is named after the country depicted in Anthony Hope's* The Prisoner of Zenda, Rupert of Hentzau, *and* The Heart of Princess Osra.

1903

Early Spring
PETER AND WENDY

It is mentioned Bill Jukes served aboard the *Walrus* under Captain Flint. Captain Hook is described as the only person Barbecue ever feared, and even Flint feared Barbecue.

1911 novel by J. M. Barrie, based on his 1904 play Peter Pan; or, the Boy Who Wouldn't Grow Up. *Captain Flint and the* Walrus *are from Robert Louis Stevenson's* Treasure Island. *Barbecue is Long John Silver's nickname. In his speech "Captain Hook at Eton," Barrie revealed the pirate attended Eton in the late 19th century. Hook is also mentioned in the novel as having served as bo'sun to Blackbeard, who lived from c. 1680–1718. Hook must have been transported back in time somehow to the 18th century, and ceased to age under unrevealed circumstances, though they were probably related to his voyage into the past. He and his crew traveled to Neverland at some point between Flint and Silver's era and 1903.*

May 26
A CASE FOR LANGDALE PIKE

Sherlock Holmes comes to his friend Langdale Pike seeking help on a case. Mentioned are: Sir Harry Flashman; Miss Irene Adler; Enoch Soames; James Moriarty; Dr. John H. Watson; A. J. Raffles; the Diogenes; Isadora Klein (aka Lady Lomond); His Royal Highness Prince Florizel of Bohemia; Clarence, Lord Emsworth; Professor G. E. Challenger; the Doctors Nikola and Thorndyke; Mr. Oswald Bastable; Frederick, Lord Ickenham; Mr. A. V. Laider; Mr. Joseph Jorkens; the Darling children; Karswell; "that so-called ghost ship at Whitby"; Graustark; Ruritania; Van Dusen; an officious young waiter who is trying to better himself by reading Spinoza and memorizing Shakespeare and aspires to be a gentleman's gentleman, whose name starts with a J; Strether; Little Bilham; Isadora Klein; Spencer John; Grimpen Mire; Hewitt; young Wimsey; the Great Old Ones; and Miskatonic University.

Short story by Michael Dirda in On Conan Doyle; or, The Whole Art of Storytelling, *Princeton University Press, 2012*. Langdale Pike, Isadora Klein, and Spencer John are from Doyle and Watson's Sherlock Holmes story "The Adventure of the Three Gables." This story depicts Holmes' consultation with Pike on that case, which was only alluded to in the original tale. Irene Adler is from the Holmes story "A Scandal in Bohemia." Professor James Moriarty is Holmes' greatest foe. One member of the Diogenes Club is Sherlock's older brother Mycroft. Grimpen Mire is from the Holmes novel The Hound of the Baskervilles. Professor George Edward Challenger appears in The Lost World and other works by Doyle. Sir Harry Flashman is the antihero of a series of novels by George MacDonald Fraser. Enoch Soames and A. V. Laider are the respective title characters of two stories by Max Beerbohm, both of which are included in the collection Seven Men. A. J. Raffles is E. W. Hornung's gentleman thief. Prince Florizel of Bohemia is from Robert Louis Stevenson's books New Arabian Nights and The Dynamiter. Clarence, Lord Emsworth is from P. G. Wodehouse's Blandings Castle novels. Frederick, Lord Ickenham, better known as Uncle Fred, is the subject of another series by Wodehouse. The officious young waiter is Wodehouse's Reginald Jeeves, future valet to Bertie Wooster. Dr. Antonio Nikola is a master criminal created by Guy Boothby, while Dr. John Evelyn Thorndyke is a detective created by R. Austin Freeman. Oswald Bastable is from Edith Nesbit's books The Story of the Treasure Seekers, The Wouldbegoods, and The New Treasure Seekers. Joseph Jorkens is an explorer and raconteur created by Lord Dunsany. The Darling children are from J. M. Barrie's Peter Pan. Karswell is from M. R. James' story "Casting the Runes." The "so-called ghost ship at Whitby" is from Bram Stoker's Dracula. Graustark is a European monarchy appearing in novels by George Barr McCutcheon. The kingdom of Ruritania is from Anthony Hope's The Prisoner of Zenda and Rupert of Hentzau. Van Dusen is Professor Augustus S. F. X. Van Dusen, aka "the Thinking Machine," a sleuth created by Jacques Futrelle. Lambert Strether and Little Bilham are from Henry James' novel The Ambassadors. Private detective Martin Hewitt appeared in stories by Arthur Morrison. Young Wimsey is Dorothy L. Sayers' future sleuth Lord Peter Wimsey. The Great Old Ones and Miskatonic University are from H. P. Lovecraft's Cthulhu Mythos.

Summer
THE FOLLY OF FLIGHT
Arsène Lupin recruits Sherlock Holmes and Dr. Watson to help him apprehend the murderer of a French aeronaut who has invented a remarkable airship.

Short story by Dr. Watson, edited by Matthew Mayo in Sherlock Holmes: The Crossovers Casebook, *Howard Hopkins, ed., Moonstone Books, 2012. Both Lupin and Holmes are members of the Wold Newton Family. A reference to "Queen and country" indicates Queen Victoria is in power, which would place this story before her death on January 22, 1901. Holmes and Watson both say they have encountered Lupin more than once in the past. In Boris Akunin's novella "The Prisoner of the Tower, or, A Short But Beautiful Journey of Three Wise Men," Holmes and Watson first encountered Lupin on New Year's Eve, 1899. Holmes met Lupin again during the 1902 events of Maurice Leblanc's story "Sherlock Holmes Arrives Too Late." Therefore, I am treating the "Queen and country" reference as an error and placing this story in 1903, shortly before Holmes' semi-retirement to the Sussex Downs. Since Watson was not present for the events of "Sherlock Holmes Arrives Too Late," most likely he and Holmes had an unrecorded encounter with Lupin sometime between that tale and "The Folly of Flight."*

JUDEX AB CHAOS
Jacques de Trémeuse purchases Château-Rouge in order to use it as a base for his future vigilante activities. Losing consciousness, he finds himself in the past, with his mind in the body of the Black Knight, whose duel with Enguerrand de Sombreval is witnessed by Louis XI. The Knight's best friend Quentin Durward suggested the duel. Shortly after the Knight defeats Enguerrand, Jacques finds himself back in his own body and time, where he decides to adopt the name Judex after the Knight's family motto.

Short story by Emmanuel Gorlier in The Shadow of Judex, *Jean-Marc and Randy Lofficier, eds., Black Coat Press, 2013; reprinted in French in* L'Ombre de Judex, *Jean-Marc and Randy Lofficier, eds., Rivière Blanche, 2013. Judex (aka Jacques de Trémeuse) is from the film serial of the same name by Louis Feuillade. Quentin Durward is the title character of a historical novel by Walter Scott. This story takes place sometime between 1900 and 1910; the exact year is conjecture.*

Autumn
THE INAUDIBLE MAN
The Honourable Clarence Green, applying to join the Mausoleum Club, names the other clubs to which he already belongs, including the Club of Queer Trades.

First episode of the British radio series Tales from the Mausoleum Club, written by Ian Brown and James Hendrie, January 3, 1987. The Club of Queer Trades is from G. K. Chesterton's short story collection of the same name. The Mausoleum Club was brought into the Crossover Universe via a reference in Kim Newman's story "The Greek Invertebrate"; therefore, it follows the Club of Queer Trades is in as well.

1904

January 3–4
THE AFFAIR OF THE WRETCHED FLESH

Sherlock Holmes investigates a series of murders that are revealed to be the work of a dog-man serving Dr. Moreau. Holmes recognizes a brand of cigarette found at one of the crime scenes. The cigarettes are hand rolled by an old woman in Limehouse using a mixture of some unknown poppy and tobacco, and are called the Claws of the Manchu. Noting they are highly addictive, Holmes says he has often wondered about what dark genius created the Claws.

Short story by Dr. Watson, edited by Joshua Reynolds in Sherlock Holmes: Consulting Detective Volume Two, *Ron Fortier, ed., Cornerstone Book Publishers, 2010. Dr. Moreau is from H. G. Wells' classic science fiction novel* The Island of Doctor Moreau. *This story gives Moreau the same first name, Alphonse, used in* The League of Extraordinary Gentlemen, Volume II. *Apparently, Moreau is no longer working for the British government, as he did in that series. The creator of the Claws of the Manchu is Sax Rohmer's criminal mastermind Dr. Fu Manchu. Watson says Holmes' confrontation with Moriarty "a year or more" ago shook the Great Detective. At first glance, one might assume this refers to Holmes and Moriarty's duel at Reichenbach Falls in 1891. However, two facts argue against this. Firstly, Holmes did not return to England for three years following the events at Reichenbach, allowing the world to believe he was deceased during that time. Second, a reference to the events of "The Adventure of the Creeping Man" indicates this story takes place after 1903. Either Watson was engaging in his customary chronological obfuscation, or else he was referring to a later battle between Holmes and Moriarty.*

Winter
ACTION ON ARKHAM'S BOOT HILL
Haakon Jones visits Arkham, Massachusetts, where he meets Miskatonic University student Ward Phillips.

Story by Aaron B. Larson in The Weird Western Adventures of Haakon Jones, *Battered Silicon Dispatch Box, 1999. A character named Ward Phillips appeared in H. P. Lovecraft and E. Hoffmann Price's "Through the Gates of the Silver Key." Phillips was based on Lovecraft himself, whose full name was Howard Phillips Lovecraft. If Lovecraft and Price's Phillips is the same person as the Phillips who encountered Haakon Jones, he must be a few years older than Lovecraft, who was only fourteen-years-old in 1904.*

THE MAN WITH THE DEVIL'S EYES (DERR MANN MIT DEN TEUFELSAUGEN)
The domino-masked "Detective Nobody," a detective who travels around the world, from St. Petersburg to Monte Carlo to the South Seas, on behalf of *Worlds Magazine*, meets Dr. Nikola in Tibet.

Detektiv Nobody's Erlebnisse und Reiseabenteuer *#5 by Johannes Jühling. The connection to Guy Boothby's supervillain Dr. Nikola brings Detective Nobody into the CU.*

1905

August 1905–Spring 1926
WINNER TAKES ALL
Gervase Kent-Cumberland suggests to his mother they also have the Anchorages stay with them while Gervase's younger brother Tom, his fiancée, and his prospective father-in-law visit, but he later discovers they are staying with the Chasms.

Short story by Evelyn Waugh in The Strand, *March 1936; reprinted in* The Complete Stories of Evelyn Waugh, *Little, Brown and Company, 1998. The Anchorage and Chasm families first appeared in Waugh's novel* Vile Bodies, *and went on to appear in several more works.* Vile Bodies *takes place in the CU through appearances by characters from Waugh's first novel,*

Decline and Fall, *as well as the appearance of the ex-King of Ruritania, who must be the same former monarch of that country (originally from Anthony Hope's* The Prisoner of Zenda *and* Rupert of Hentzau*) that appears in some of P. G. Wodehouse's stories. Therefore, the rest of Waugh's interconnected fiction takes place in the CU as well.*

1906

Winter
THE SEEDS OF CASSIOPEIA
Doctor Omega, Tiziraou, and Denis Borel travel in the *Cosmos II* to the star system Cassiopeia in search of seeds that can save the life of the mortally wounded Professor Helvetius.

Part one of an as-yet uncompleted short story by Denis Borel, edited by Samuel T. Payne in Doctor Omega and the Shadowmen, *Jean-Marc and Randy Lofficier, eds., Black Coat Press, 2011. Doctor Omega, Tiziraou, Borel, the* Cosmos, *and Professor Helvetius are from Arnould Galopin's novel* Doctor Omega. *Cassiopeia is from C. I. Defontenay's novel* Star (Psi Cassiopeia). *This story takes place a year after* Doctor Omega.

Spring
THE ANGEL AND THE EXORCIST
Father Lankester Merrin learns a member of Baron Glo von Warteck's archaeological expedition he was led to believe was possessed is actually under von Warteck's mental domination. Von Warteck is seeking the Serpent Ring of Set, once wielded by the wizard Thoth-Amon. Father Merrin awakens the being known as Ogon Bat to defeat von Warteck.

Short story by Matthew Dennion in Night of the Nyctalope, *Jean-Marc and Randy Lofficier, eds., Black Coat Press, 2012; reprinted in French in* Les Compagnons de l'Ombre (Tome 11), *Jean-Marc and Randy Lofficier, eds., Rivière Blanche, 2013. Father Lankester Merrin is the title character of William Peter Blatty's novel* The Exorcist. *Merrin, elderly during the 1970s events of Blatty's novel, must be very young in this story. Baron Glo von Warteck is one of the foes of Jean de La Hire's hero the Nyctalope. Thoth-Amon and the Serpent Ring of Set are from "The Phoenix on the Sword," the first story by Robert E. Howard to feature the barbarian Conan. Although the Ring is apparently destroyed in this story, it must have been recreated sometime before its appearance in the year 1914 in Frank Schildiner's novel* The Quest of Frankenstein. *Ōgon Bat is a Japanese comic book and cartoon character created by Ichiro Suzuki and Takeo Nagamatsu.*

Autumn
LONDON'S BURNING
Quentin Collins investigates a series of deaths in London. At one point, he briefly disappears to consult "a friend in Baker Street."

A Dark Shadows audio drama written by Joseph Lidster and directed by Darren Gross, Big Finish Productions, 2010. Quentin's friend is, of course, Sherlock Holmes. Although Holmes owned his farm on the Sussex Downs by this time, he had not yet given up his rooms in Baker Street completely.

1907

Winter
JOHN WILSON, AUS DEM GEIHEMBUCH DES BERÜHMTEN AMERIKANISCHEN DETEKTIVS
The famous American detective John Wilson investigates the apparent murder of Nick Carter.

John Wilson, Aus dem Geheimbuch des Berühmten Amerikanischen Detektivs, 1908. The account of Nick Carter being "murdered" must have been a distortion of the actual events involving him and Wilson.

Autumn
RIGADIN CONTRE ARSÈNE LUPIN
French master thief Rigadin duels with his rival Arsène Lupin.

1908 silent film. Charles Prince played Rigadin in well over 200 French short films; this crossover brings him into the CU.

1908

Summer
THE CAPTURE OF PAUL BECK
Paul Beck crosses paths with his fellow sleuth Dora Myrl. The two ultimately marry.

Novel by M. McDonnell Bodkin, 1911. Dora Myrl previously appeared in Bodkin's Dora Myrl, the Lady Detective. *The year is based on a reference to Teddy Roosevelt choosing not to seek another presidential term.*

September 1908–1911
YOUNG BECK, A CHIP OFF THE OLD BLOCK
Paul Beck Jr., the son of sleuth Paul Beck, embarks upon his own detective career. There are references to a cricket-playing gentleman thief named Baffles, and Paul Jr.'s best friend, Charlie Kirkwood, remarks to Paul Sr., "I think I remember once, long before I had the pleasure of knowing you personally, reading a case of yours in which the famous Baffles imitated the finger marks of an absent burglar with India-rubber gloves." Paul Sr. also comments, "No monkey has turned up in a burglary since the mystery of the Rue Morgue, so it must be a man."

Collection of short stories written by Charles Kirkwood, edited by M. McDonnell Bodkin, 1912. "Baffles" is meant to be A. J. Raffles. The elder Beck's encounter with Raffles is unrecorded. Paul Sr.'s comments treat Poe's "Murders in the Rue Morgue" as an historical event. Paul Beck, Jr. is in his twenties, and is allegedly Paul Sr.'s son by Dora Myrl. However, Paul Sr. was identified as forty-one-years-old when he married Dora during the events of The Capture of Paul Beck, *which also took place in 1908. Rick Lai writes, "Paul is now in his early sixties while Dora is about forty. I suspect that Paul Sr. had an earlier marriage when he was about nineteen. For some reason, Paul Sr. didn't want this first wife discussed; possibly she was a crook. Kirkwood must have been instructed to make misleading chronological assertions and pretend that Paul Jr. was Dora's son."*

1909

January
DANGEROUS TERRITORY
The Nyctalope is traveling through Central Africa, where he has come into contact with a race of Great Apes unknown to science. He encounters a tribe whose chief, Mbonga, believing him to be a jungle spirit, asks him to avenge the death of his son, Kulonga, at the hands of a "White Ape Demon." The Nyctalope's foe Koynos appears and Mbonga decides the two will compete to slay the ape man. Discovering the object of his search is a feral human, the Nyctalope thinks of similar individuals of whom he has heard stories, including a young boy in India who had been raised by wolves, and ten-year-old George Villiers, who had been rescued by To-Ho, the leader of a peaceful tribe of ape-men in the jungles of Sumatra.

Short story by Matthew Dennion in Night of the Nyctalope, *Jean-Marc and Randy Lofficier, eds., Black Coat Press, 2012; reprinted in French in* La Nuit du Nyctalope, *Jean-Marc and Randy Lofficier, eds., Rivière Blanche, 2012. The exploits of Leo Saint-Clair, aka the Nyctalope, were chronicled by Jean de La Hire. The "White Ape Demon" is the jungle lord, and the Great Apes are the evolutionary offshoots of humanity that raised him. This story takes place shortly before the jungle lord's alleged first meeting with other whites. Apparently he never told either Burroughs or Farmer of his meeting with the Nyctalope and Koynos. Mbonga and Kulonga are from the first novel in Burroughs' series,* Tarzan of the Apes. *The young boy in India is Mowgli from Rudyard Kipling's* The Jungle Book. *George Villiers and To-Ho are from Jules Lermina's novel* To-Ho and the Gold-Destroyers, *which has been translated into English by Georges T. Dodds for Black Coat Press.*

1910

February 21–26, August 20
THE HOUSE ON MOREAU STREET
Sherlock Holmes is abducted by Augustus Moreau, nephew of the notorious Dr. Moreau, whose beast-men have committed a series of murders in the course of robberies to finance Augustus' experiments. Edward Prendick brought the elder Moreau's predations to the public's attention. Dr. John Thorndyke and Christopher Jervis, investigating the crimes independently from Holmes, wind up working with Dr. Watson to save Holmes. Thorndyke has Nathaniel Polton examine hair samples found at one of the crime scenes.

Short story by Dr. Watson, edited by Don Roff in Sherlock Holmes: The Crossovers Casebook, *Howard Hopkins, ed., Moonstone Books, 2012. Dr. Moreau and Edward Prendick are from H. G. Wells'* The Island of Doctor Moreau. *Thorndyke, Jervis, and Polton appear in a series of books by R. Austin Freeman.*

March 6, 1910–August 27, 1911
PROFESSOR PEASLEE PLAYS PARIS

In 1910, a group of men led by Count Ferenczy and Professor Peaslee uncover a meteor in the Tunguska region of Siberia. Peaslee claims because of Ferenczy's failure in 1795, they must struggle with men with remarkable skills, and says this meteor must not create another Holmes or Nemo. The following year, Peaslee requests the criminal Flambeau's aid in deceiving the criminal organization known as the *Habits Noirs*. Inspector Romaine visits the *Louvre*, from which the *Mona Lisa* has been stolen, and reflects Chief Aristide Valentin has committed suicide. The best and brightest of the police, including Broquet, Guichard, and Maigret, are attempting to deal with the massive crime-wave in Paris. Romaine meets with a man in an iron mask and his female aide, Joséphine. Peaslee asks a young girl named Nardi, recommended to him by Flambeau, to steal a stone. Peaslee compares that stone, the Tear of Azathoth, to the Heart of the Ocean, the Pink Panther, and the Maltese Falcon. Baron Cesare Stromboli, an agent of the Black Coats, tries unsuccessfully to purchase the *Mona Lisa* from the man who stole it. The current leader of the *Habits Noirs*, the Iron King, is furious when he learns of the thief's refusal. Exploring Paris' sewers, Nardi is caught by a group of men, one of whom remarks "Rats are getting bigger it seems. Regular Sumatra down here." The Colonel, previously believed dead, reclaims the mantle of leader from the Iron King.

Short story by Pete Rawlik in Tales of the Shadowmen Volume 9: La Vie en Noir, *Jean-Marc and Randy Lofficier, eds., Black Coat Press, 2012; reprinted in French in* Les Compagnons de l'Ombre (Tome 12), *Jean-Marc and Randy Lofficier, eds., Rivière Blanche, 2013. Count Ferenczy is from H. P. Lovecraft's* The Case of Charles Dexter Ward, *while Professor Nathaniel Wingate Peaslee is from Lovecraft's* "The Shadow Out of Time." *The Tunguska meteor strike was a real event that occurred in 1908, and has been linked to many curious events in the CU. The 1795 reference is to the Wold Newton meteor strike. According to Philip José Farmer, Sherlock Holmes is a member of the Wold Newton Family. In* The Other Log of Phileas Fogg, *Farmer claimed Jules Verne's Captain Nemo was actually Holmes' foe Professor James Moriarty. Later research has established Moriarty was indeed one of at least three men who used the name Nemo, though he was not the same person as Prince Dakkar, who used that alias in Verne's novels. The Nemo referred to by Peaslee is likely Moriarty, who was identified as a member of the Wold Newton Family in* Doc Savage: His Apocalyptic Life. *Flambeau and Aristide Valentin are from G. K. Chesterton's stories about the crime-solving priest Father Brown. Les Habits Noirs, aka the Black Coats, are featured in novels by Paul Féval, as is their leader, Colonel Bozzo-*

Corona. Inspector Romaine is from the film Charlie Chan in City in Darkness, *while Nardi is from* Charlie Chan in Paris. *Rawlik's story reveals Nardi is Flambeau's niece. Paulin Broquet is the policeman nemesis of the gypsy crime lord Zigomar in pulp novels by Léon Sazie. Commissaire Jules Maigret is featured in mystery novels by Georges Simenon. Chief Xavier Guichard was a real person who also appeared in the Maigret books. The Iron King is from Les Martin's novel* Young Indiana Jones and the Gypsy Revenge; *he is a descendant of the title character of Alexandre Dumas'* The Man in the Iron Mask. *Joséphine Balsamo is Arsène Lupin's greatest foe. Azathoth, "the blind idiot god," is one of the Great Old Ones of the Cthulhu Mythos. The Heart of the Ocean diamond is from the film* Titanic. *The Pink Panther gem is featured in the film of the same name. The statue known as the Maltese Falcon is from the novel of the same name by Dashiell Hammett. Baron Cesare Stromboli is a gentleman thief appearing in stories by Jose Moselli. In the Sherlock Holmes story "The Adventure of the Sussex Vampire," Holmes mentions "the giant rat of Sumatra, a story for which the world is not yet prepared." The tale of the giant rat is perhaps the most pastiched of the many unchronicled Holmes cases alluded to in the Canon.*

Spring
THE SECRET OF GRANT'S TOMB

Sherlock Holmes and Dr. Watson, visiting Inspector Lestrade, are drawn into Professor Van Dusen and his sidekick Hutchinson Hatch's investigation of the murder of a friend and fellow reporter of Hatch's. The quartet, along with Lestrade and Inspector Conway, apprehend the culprit, master thief Bradlee Cunnyngham Leighton.

Short story by Dr. Watson, edited by Joe Gentile in Sherlock Holmes: The Crossovers Casebook, *Howard Hopkins, ed., Moonstone Books, 2012. Professor Augustus S. F. X. Van Dusen and Hutchinson Hatch are featured in the Thinking Machine stories by Jacques Futrelle. Cunnyngham and Conway appear in the Thinking Machine story "Problem of the Missing Necklace." Although Hatch implies 1907 is the year of this adventure, Watson says he has not seen Holmes "since the summer before, right after the* Lion's Mane *affair." Although Holmes dates "The Adventure of the Lion's Mane" to 1907, meteorological evidence led William S. Baring-Gould to conclude this was a typographical error and the case actually took place in 1909. Therefore, I have adjusted the date of this story to 1910.*

KING OF THE MOON

Bedford, Professor Challenger, Ann Cavor and a pair of father-and-son American inventors rescue Ann's uncle from the Selenites.

Short story by Bedford, edited by Lawrence C. Connolly in Professor Challenger: New Worlds, Lost Places, *J. R. Campbell and Charles Prepolec, eds., EDGE Science Fiction and Fantasy Publishing, 2015. Bedford, Dr. Cavor, and the Selenites are from H. G. Wells'* The First Men in the Moon, *which is described as having taken place ten years ago. Bedford implies here he is the one who put Challenger in contact with Arthur Conan Doyle. Challenger must have introduced Doyle in turn to Edward Malone. Doyle became Malone's literary agent and editor, publishing the reporter's accounts of his adventures with Challenger under his own byline.*

Summer
WOLF AT THE DOOR OF TIME

Doctor Omega, traveling aboard the *Cosmos*, discovers a derelict time machine and its owner, Doctor Moses Nebogipfel. Omega believes Nebogipfel's machine is from the Arcadian Hegemony of the 42nd century. Nebogipfel was transporting a masonychid, a proto-wolf, in his conveyance, but the wolf escaped and is now bouncing through time. Annoyed with Nebogipel, Omega thinks he has been lucky in his choice of companions, including Fred, Borel, and Tizairou. In 1643, the masonychid attacks a man named Sir Hugo near the village of Grimpen on Dartmoor. In 1767, Omega convinces Joseph Balsamo to make a special cylinder Jean Chastel can use to destroy the masonychid, now known as the Beast of Gévaudan. In rural France in the 18th century, the wolf convinces a sabot-maker named Thibault it is Satan. Omega tells Nebogipfel masonychids are the ancestors of all land-based whales and dolphins, and his actions have altered the time stream so a race of sky-whales in the far future will never exist, and rather than the deity Zoomashmarta, the remaining humans will worship a wolf that devours human flesh. Thibault asks the masonychid to bring him all the women he has ever desired, including Agnelette, Madame Magloire, and the Comtesse de Mont-Gobert. The *Cosmos* is almost hit by an ionized meteorite, which will exit the void of time in 1795, and which Omega believes might cause beneficial mutations. Omega travels to the battlefield of Mons in 1916, where he encounters Captain Yeskes of the Fifth Northumberland Fusiliers, who is wounded by the masonychid. A Nurse Miller treats his wounds, and contemplates writing a book about the story Yeskes tells her of the attack. Omega reveals Nebogipfel is a brainwashed member of the same race to which Omega himself belongs. Omega does not believe Nebogipfel should continue his exile in the 19th or 20th centuries; otherwise, he would drop him off in "that rather lovely Italianate village in North Wales near Penrhyndeudrath." The Arcadian Hegemony was founded by a starship commander known as Captain Strange, who is at war with the Federation. Omega finally decides to place Nebogipfel in Randgrith Abbey near the Village of Wulnoth in the mid 11th century. In the 20th century, the Nyctalope battles the masonychid, now known as the King Wolf, and his legions at the request of Comrade Frunzoff. After he kills it and Omega takes a sample of its blood, the Nyctalope encounters Captain Gogol of Army Intelligence, who is accompanied by Oktobriana and Avakoum Zahov.

Short story by Martin Gately in Tales of the Shadowmen Volume 9: La Vie en Noir, *Jean-Marc and Randy Lofficier, eds., Black Coat Press, 2012; reprinted in French in* Les Compagnons de l'Ombre (Tome 14), *Jean-Marc and Randy Lofficier, eds., Rivière Blanche, 2014. Doctor Omega is from the novel of the same name by Arnould Galopin, as are the* Cosmos, Fred, Borel, *and* Tizairou. *The Lofficiers' translation and adaptation of Galopin's novel implied Doctor Omega was the CU universe counterpart of the Doctor of* Doctor Who *fame, a member of the extraterrestrial Time Lords of Gallifrey. Moses Nebogipfel is from H. G. Wells' story "The Chronic Argonauts," a precursor to his novel* The Time Machine, *and is here meant to be a counterpart of the Doctor's foe the Meddling Monk. Wulnoth, a village headman in the year 1066, appeared in the* Doctor Who *serial that introduced the Monk, "The Time Meddler." Arcadia, Captain Strange, and the Federation are from Sarah Brightman and Hot Gossip's song "I Lost My Heart to a Starship Trooper." It is worth noting the song mentions both Flash Gordon and Darth Vader as real people. Sir Hugo Baskerville and the village of Grimpen are from* The Hound of the Baskervilles, *arguably Sherlock Holmes' most famous exploit. Joseph Balsamo, Count Cagliostro, is a historical figure who also appears in novels by Alexandre Dumas; Philip José Farmer also identified him as the ancestor of a branch of the Wold Newton Family in* Doc Savage: His Apocalyptic Life. *Thibault, Agnelette, Madame Magloire, and the Comtesse de Mont-Gobert are from Dumas' story "The Wolf-Leader." The Beast of Gévaudan was a real creature whose exact nature is much debated; Jean Chastel is usually credited as having killed the monster. The sky-dolphins and Zoomashmarta are from Philip José Farmer's science fiction sequel to Herman Melville's* Moby-Dick, The Wind Whales of Ishmael. *According to Farmer's novel* A Feast Unknown, *the family of the jungle lord Lord Grandrith originally called themselves Randgrith. The Grandrith/Caliban novels take place in an alternate universe to the CU, but perhaps a version of the Randgrith family existed in the CU, one of whose members founded the abbey. However, John Cloamby, Lord Grandrith, himself never existed in the CU. The meteorite will arrive in the village of Wold Newton in 1795, where it will indeed, as Omega theorized, cause beneficial mutations in the offspring and descendants of those exposed to its ionization, as revealed by Farmer in* Tarzan Alive *and* Doc Savage: His

Apocalyptic Life. *The Fifth Northumberland Fusiliers were a real regiment whose CU equivalent counted Dr. John H. Watson among its numbers. Nurse Miller will later write novels under her married name of Agatha Christie; one of her stories, "The Hound of Death," was likely inspired by the tale Yeskes told her. The village in North Wales is the Village from the cult-classic television series* The Prisoner; *the village of Portmeirion, located in Penrhyndeudraeth, was used as the filming location for the Village. The Nyctalope (aka Leo Saint-Clair) is the night-sighted hero of a series of novels by Jean de La Hire. Comrade Frunzoff is Frunzoff Nosh from the Doc Savage novel* The Red Spider. *Captain Gogol is the future General Anatol Alexis Gogol from the James Bond films* The Spy Who Loved Me, Moonraker, For Your Eyes Only, Octopussy, *and* A View to a Kill. *Many of the Bond films are incompatible with the Fleming novels, and thus with the CU; however, despite using the titles of Fleming novels or stories, the five films in which Gogol appears are radically different from the works they are based on, and can be considered separate or sequel incidents for CU purposes. Oktobriana (or Octobriana) was created by Czech artist Petr Sadecký, and, not being under copyright, has appeared in a number of works by different artists and writers. Avakoum Zahov is a Bulgarian secret agent featured in Andrei Gulyashki's novels* The Zahov Mission *and* Avakoum Zahov versus 07. *The year is conjecture based on Doctor Omega's perspective, which is after the events of Galopin's novel.*

1911

Winter
RAFFLES CONTRO NAT PINKERTON
Gentleman thief A. J. Raffles engages in a duel of wits with detective Nat Pinkerton.
1912 Italian short film directed by Ubaldo Maria Del Colle.

THE WHITE LADY OF POURVILLE (LA DAME BLANCHE DE POURVILLE)

Detective Sexton Blake and his apprentice Harry Dickson travel to Pourville to investigate the appearance of what seems to be the legendary White Lady, whose gaze drives men mad. Dickson befriends Adèle Blanc-Sec. Dickson and Adèle travel to Tiffauges to research the history of Gilles de Rays, and are told about de Rays and Joan of Arc by Doctor Jules de Grandin of the Faculty of Forensic Medicine of Paris. A false de Rays proves to be the archcriminal Fantômas, who is told to surrender by a policeman named Juve. Fantômas' plan involved a Subatlantic locomotive, designed by the great French inventor, Arsène Golbert, and sabotaged by William Boltyn, the leader of the so-called "billionaires' conspiracy." The alleged White Lady is actually the mentally ill Paulette Arnaud, whose sister Thérèse works for the French Secret Service. Most of the cases of madness suffered by those who encountered Paulette were actually caused by an Indian poison called Rajaijah.

Short story by Michel Stéphan appearing as "La Dame Blanche de Pourville" in Les Compagnons de L'Ombre (Tome 10), *Jean-Marc and Randy Lofficier, eds., Rivière Blanche, 2012, and in English in* Harry Dickson vs. the Spider, *Jean-Marc and Randy Lofficier, eds., Black Coat Press, 2014. Harry Dickson, "the American Sherlock Holmes," was the subject of German, Dutch, Belgian, and French pulp magazines, the latter written by Jean Ray. Sexton Blake is one of the most famous British penny dreadful detectives. G. L. Gick's story "The Werewolf of Rutherford Grange" revealed Dickson served as an apprentice to Blake in his youth, before he struck out on his own as a detective. Adèle Blanc-Sec will later become a private investigator herself, as seen in Jacques Tardi's comic book*

The Extraordinary Adventures of Adèle Blanc-Sec. *Doctor Jules de Grandin is Seabury Quinn's occult detective, who appeared in the magazine* Weird Tales. *Fantômas and Juve are from the novels by Marcel Allain and Pierre Souvestre. Arsène Golbert and William Boltyn are from Gustave Le Rouge and Gustave Guitton's pulp serial* The Dominion of the World, *which has been translated and adapted in four volumes by Brian Stableford. Thérèse Arnaud is from Pierre Yrondy's* The Adventures of Thérèse Arnaud of the French Secret Service, *which has been translated by Nina Cooper for Black Coat Press. Rajaijah is from Hergé's Tintin comic* The Blue Lotus.

Spring
DAM BUSTERS OF MARS

On Mars, Leo Saint-Clair, aka the Nyctalope, overhears a conversation between his fellow Earthman Gullivar Jones and Martian scientist Samoht Yor. Yor refers to the Rock Snake Hills, the gargoyle-like insect folk, and Utopia Planitia Lake. When Saint-Clair first came to Mars, the only native species he knew of was the one described by historian H. G. Wells, who are now referred to as "Kephales." Saint-Clair teams up with Jones to prevent corrupt Martian scientist Ras Thavas from transferring the evil Ar-Hap's mind into a deadly creature.

Short story by Martin Gately in Night of the Nyctalope, *Jean-Marc and Randy Lofficier, eds., Black Coat Press, 2012; reprinted in French in* Les Compagnons de l'Ombre (Tome 11), *Jean-Marc and Randy Lofficier, eds., Rivière Blanche, 2013. The Nyctalope was the protagonist of French pulp stories by Jean de La Hire. Gullivar Jones and Ar-Hap are from Edwin L. Arnold's novel* Lieutenant Gullivar Jones: His Vacation. *Samoht Yor's name spelled backwards is "Roy Thomas," the name of one of the writers of Marvel Comics' adaptation of Arnold's novel. Thomas included a character called Lu-Pov in the adaptation, a nod to author Richard Lupoff. The Rock Snake Hills are a reference to the Rock Snake creatures from the movie* Thunderbirds Are Go. *The Rock Snake Hills were also used as a geographical location in Captain Scarlet stories in the British comic book* TV21. *Thunderbirds and Captain Scarlet take place in one of many alternate futures to the CU. The gargoyle-like insect folk are from the British television serial* Quatermass and the Pit. *Utopia Planitia is a real place that was also the site of the construction of the Enterprise-D on* Star Trek: The Next Generation. *H. G. Wells described the Martian invasion of Earth in his novel* The War of the Worlds. *Here, Wells' Martians (aka the Sarmaks) are conflated with the Kephales from de La Hire's pulp serial* Les Grandes Aventures d'un Boy Scout. *Ras Thavas is from Edgar Rice Burroughs' Mars novels. In Gately's story, Gullivar is surprised to learn of the Martian invasion of Earth in his absence. However,* The League of Extraordinary Gentlemen, Volume II *depicted him and the warlord of Mars unintentionally forcing the invaders to flee to Earth in the first place. Given that the invaders were all wiped out via biological warfare, Gullivar was likely unaware of what actually happened on his homeworld. This story is named after the movie* The Dam Busters, *which was based on true events. The death of the Zerlat in Gately's story is meant to parallel the death of Guy Gibson's dog in both real life and the film.*

THE LEGACY OF ARSÈNE LUPIN

Arsène Lupin, disguised as Prince Sernine, tells his biographer Maurice Leblanc a tale involving the Comte de Guy's ownership of d'Artagnan's sword, having heard rumors of how the Comte acquired it: "There's been talk of dealings with the Chinese fence, Hanoi Shan—his path has crossed Lupin's before—rumors of a murderous thug named Gurn . . . half-whispered rumors of Cagliostro, Saint-Germain, and the Englishman Barrington, who had defrauded the great Cagliostro of a fortune and the sword; talk that the sword had once been the trust of one Prince Rodolphe; that it was stolen by Colonel Bozzo-Corona or by that young rogue Rocambole; that that British cracksman took a shot at it; and there was a suggestion the Devil Doctor in Limehouse had shown an interest; Josephine Balsamo's name came up . . ." The sword was brought to Lupin's attention by the young journalist Rouletabille. The Comte asks Lupin, in his guise as M. Lenormand, head of the *Sûreté Nationale*, to guard his valuables at a masked ball. Lupin says, "Even old Lecoq might have found himself challenged by this problem!" and assures the Comte, "The cracksman Bunn is in Perth, by all accounts, and that Englishman Raffles who has plagued Scotland Yard has not been heard of since the Boer War." The Comte introduces "Lenormand" to his daughter, the Comtesse Emmeline de Guy. Lupin encounters a young boy who calls himself "Stephen Tarleton" and wishes to steal the sword from the Comte. The Comte stores his valuables in a safe made by the Dale company in New York, which the American called the Gray Seal had remarkable luck in cracking. Marie Antoinette's necklace was stolen by Cagliostro, then in England by George Barrington, the Picaroon, king of the London underworld, and from the Dreux-Soubize family by Lupin himself, as a boy. Lupin recognizes members of Paris' infamous *Vampires* and the Union Corse from Marseilles at the ball, as well as deadly enemies of the English cracksman, Cleek.

Short story by David L. Vineyard in Tales of the Shadowmen Volume 11: Force Majeure, *Jean-Marc and Randy Lofficier, eds., Black Coat Press, 2014. Arsène Lupin, the Dreux-Soubize family, and Josephine Balsamo are from Maurice Leblanc's novels. The Comte de Guy is one of the many aliases used by Carl Peterson, the archenemy of H. C. "Sapper" McNeile's adventurer*

Bulldog Drummond. The Comtesse Emmeline is Carl's niece and future mistress Irma. Lupin thinks "Emmeline" is no older than eighteen, if that. Irma would be ten-years-old in 1911, but perhaps she was physically mature enough to pass for a teenager. Hanoi Shan is from H. Ashton-Wolfe's Warped in the Making: Crimes of Love and Hate. *Hanoi Shan encountered Lupin in Vineyard's story "The Jade Buddha"* (Tales of the Shadowmen Volume 5: The Vampires of Paris, *Jean-Marc and Randy Lofficier, eds., Black Coat Press, 2009). Gurn is better known as Marcel Allain and Pierre Souvestre's villain Fantômas. Count Cagliostro was a historical figure, who also appeared in novels by Alexandre Dumas, and was identified as the founder of a villainous branch of the Wold Newton Family by Philip José Farmer. The Comte de Saint-Germain was also a real person, and has appeared in a number of works of fiction. George Barrington is from Ernest Dudley's novel* Picaroon. *Prince Rodolphe is from Eugène Sue's* The Mysteries of Paris. *Colonel Bozzo-Corona is the leader of the gang known as the Black Coats in novels by Paul Féval. Rocambole is the villain-turned-hero of novels by Ponson du Terrail. The British cracksman is E. W. Hornung's A. J. Raffles. The Devil Doctor is Sax Rohmer's Doctor Fu Manchu, whom Farmer conflated with Hanoi Shan in* Doc Savage: His Apocalyptic Life. *Apparently, it is not common knowledge Fu and Shan are the same person, and doubtless that is how the criminal mastermind prefers it. Rouletabille is a young reporter featured in novels by Gaston Leroux. Lecoq is Emile Gaboriau's detective. Smiler Bunn is a thief appearing in comedic stories by Bertram Atkey. "Stephen Tarleton" is really Simon Templar, who will later be known as the Saint, the "laughing Robin Hood of crime" created by Leslie Charteris. Lupin thinks Templar is fourteen-years-old. In fact, Templar would be ten-years-old in 1911. The Dale company is owned by Jimmie Dale, aka the Gray Seal, who appears in books by Frank L. Packard. The* Vampires *are from Louis Feuillade's silent film serial* Les Vampires. *The* Union Corse *is a real organization, but a fictionalized version of the group appears in Ian Fleming's James Bond novel* On Her Majesty's Secret Service. *Hamilton Cleek, "the man of forty faces," was the protagonist of books by Thomas W. Hanshew.*

June
THE PETRIFYING WELL

Sherlock Holmes accepts T. E. "Ned" Lawrence's request to investigate the bizarre death of a friend's brother. The planned Maracot expedition to the deep Atlantic is mentioned several times.

Short story by Sherlock Holmes, edited by Martin Gately in Sherlock Holmes: The Crossovers Casebook, Howard Hopkins, ed., Moonstone Books, 2012. This story takes place nearly two years after the events of "The Adventure of the Lion's Mane." Although Holmes claimed in that story its events happened in 1907, research by William S. Baring-Gould has demonstrated this was a typographical error, and the story actually took place in 1909. The Maracot expedition is a reference to Arthur Conan Doyle's The Maracot Deep, which takes place in 1926. Gately's story "Rouletabille and the New World Order" explains why the expedition seen in this story failed.

July
BEDLAM IN YELLOW

Carnacki investigates strange happenings at Bethlem Asylum involving an inmate who read the play *The King in Yellow*, and finds himself transported to Carcosa, where he encounters the King himself.

Story by William Meikle in In the Court of the Yellow King, Glynn Owen Barrass, ed., Celaeno Press, 2014.

Summer
LITTLE MORITZ ÉLÈVE DE NICK WINTER

Detective Nick Winter, with the help of his student Little Moritz, battles a gang attempting to rob a villa.

1912 French short film directed by Paul Garbagni. Maurice Schwarz played Little Moritz in twenty-three shorts. Since Nick Winter is in the CU, so is Little Moritz.

THE BEAST OF GLAMIS

During the course of a case, Carnacki consults *The Concordances of the Red Serpent*.

Short story by William Meikle in Carnacki: Heaven and Hell, Dark Regions Press, 2012. The Concordances of the Red Serpent *is from Meikle's novel of the same name. The Carnacki connection brings that novel into the CU.

August–November
THE KEW GROWTHS

Professor Challenger and Edward Malone join forces with Thomas Carnacki to combat the menace of giant fungi that threaten to overrun England. Carnacki tells Malone the fungi originated millennia ago on the high plains of Leng, and he found a fragment of a chant hidden in *The Concordances of the Red Serpent* which alluded to manipulation and control of their sporulation process.

Story by Edward Malone, edited by William Meikle in Professor Challenger: The Kew Growths and Other Stories, Dark Renaissance Books, 2014. *Professor Challenger and Edward Malone appear in the novel* The Lost World *and other stories by Arthur Conan Doyle. Thomas Carnacki is from William Hope Hodgson's short story collection* Carnacki the Ghost-Finder. *Leng is from H. P. Lovecraft's Cthulhu Mythos tales. The Concordances of the Red Serpent is from Meikle's novel of the same name.*

September 25
HOW THEY MET THEMSELVES

Thomas Carnacki knows of a fellow occult investigator from America who carries a silver-edged sword.

Short story by Charles R. Rutledge in Carnacki: The New Adventures, *Sam Gafford, ed., Ulthar Press, 2013. Thomas Carnacki appears in stories by William Hope Hodgson. The American occult investigator is Manly Wade Wellman's Judge Keith Hilary Pursuivant. Since Pursuivant was born in 1891, he must have begun delving into the supernatural at a young age. The month and year are given in the story, and a reference to the autumnal equinox being yesterday further pins the date down to September 25, 1911.*

October 31
THE SWINE OF GERASENE

Sâr Dubnotal and John Silence view a house that is said in Kraighten to be built by the Devil. Silence refers to two other psychic sensitives, a young girl in the Highlands named Crerar and a fellow named Vance in

London. Dubnotal says Count Magnus is no Crowley or Karswell, to be taunted. An Oxford don of Silence's acquaintance has theorized Magnus is a 17th century mystic of ill-repute, while an elderly theatre owner in London claims Magnus is the same individual who led the Tong of the Black Scorpion to its destruction in Queen Victoria's day. Magnus' Brotherhood of Gerasene has abducted Thomas Carnacki, the Ghost-Finder, who rescued a man named Baines from their dark plans. Magnus tells the assembled Brotherhood they will bring their master, the Hog, over the border on which the house sits. Magnus says he has made the Black Pilgrimage. A group of swine-things attack Dubnotal and Silence; the latter counters one with the Voorish Sign. Dubnotal possesses a cane that conceals a silver blade, inspired by his meeting with an American named Pursuivant. Dubnotal says Doctor Omega warned him about Magnus, whom he calls "Greel." Silence suggests using the Incantation of Raaaee or the Saaamaaa Ritual against the Hog. Dubnotal takes out a sliver of the gem known as the Blood of Belshazzar, which was retrieved from the fire column of Kor. Dubnotal says the flames of the Faltine lurk within the sliver.

Short story by Josh Reynolds in Tales of the Shadowmen Volume 10: Esprit de Corps, *Jean-Marc and Randy Lofficier, eds., Black Coat Press, 2013; reprinted in French in* Les Compagnons de l'Ombre (Tome 15), *Jean-Marc and Randy Lofficier, eds., Rivière Blanche, 2014; and in* Sâr Dubnotal 2: The Astral Trail, *Jean-Marc and Randy Lofficier, eds., Black Coat Press, 2015. The Sâr Dubnotal was the title character of a French pulp series by an anonymous author. John Silence is from Algernon Blackwood's titular collection of stories. The house, Kraighten, and the swine-things are from William Hope Hodgson's* The House on the Borderland. *Thomas Carnacki, Baines, the Hog, the Incantation of Raaaee, and the Saaamaa Ritual are from Hodgson's collection* Carnacki the Ghost-Finder. *Sheila Crerar appeared in stories by Ella Scrymsour, while Aylmer Vance is an occult detective created by Alice and Claude Askew. Count Magnus is from M. R. James' short story* of the same name, as are the Oxford don (Mr. Wraxall) and the Black Pilgrimage. Reynolds conflates Magnus with Magnus Greel from the Doctor Who serial "The Talons of Weng-Chiang," which is also the source of the elderly theatre owner (Henry Gordon Jago) and the Tong of the Black Scorpion. Although most of the Doctor's exploits take place in an alternate reality to the Crossover Universe, Jean-Marc and Randy Lofficier's translation and adaptation of Arnould Galopin's Doctor Omega implies Omega is the Doctor's CU counterpart. Greel most likely assumed the identity of the real Count Magnus de la Gardie, who may be distantly related to the Delagardie branch of the Wold Newton Family. Karswell is the villain of another M. R. James story, "Casting the Runes." The Voorish Sign is from Lovecraft's "The Dunwich Horror." Judge Keith Hilary Pursuivant is from the works of Manly Wade Wellman. The Blood of Belshazzar is from Robert E. Howard's Cormac Fitzgeoffrey story of the same name. Kor is the homeland of H. Rider Haggard's Ayesha, She-Who-Must-Be-Obeyed. The Faltine are from the tales of Marvel Comics' Sorcerer Supreme, Doctor Strange.

Autumn
THE PRICE OF A FAVOR

Arsène Lupin prevents Leland Gaunt from corrupting the people of an Arrondissement where Gaunt has set up shop.

Short story by Matthew Dennion in The Many Faces of Arsène Lupin, *Jean-Marc and Randy Lofficier, eds., Black Coat Press, 2012; reprinted in French in* Les Compagnons de L'Ombre (Tome 10), *Jean-Marc and Randy Lofficier, eds., Rivière Blanche, 2012. Arsène Lupin is Maurice Leblanc's gentleman thief. Leland Gaunt is the villain of Stephen King's novel* Needful Things.

Late December 1911–Spring 1912
THE FORGERS

The *New York Star* is mentioned in the first exploit of adventuress Constance Dunlap.

Short story by Arthur B. Reeve, 1913. The New York Star *is the newspaper that employs Walter Jameson, sidekick of Reeve's scientific detective Craig Kennedy. The Constance Dunlap story "The Embezzlers" also mentions the* Star. *The fictional Central American country Vespuccia is mentioned in both the Craig Kennedy story "The Artificial Paradise" and the Constance Dunlap story "The Gun Runners." Since Craig Kennedy is in the CU, so is Constance Dunlap.*

1912

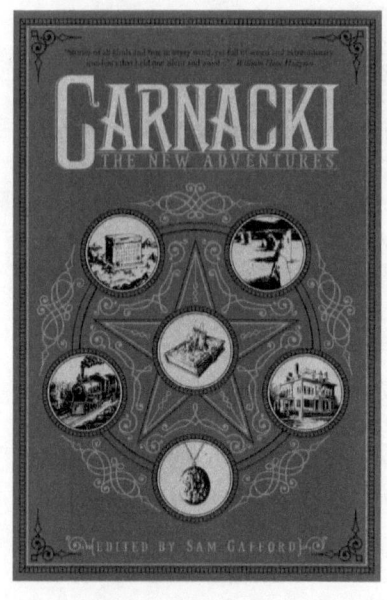

Winter
THE BRAES OF THE BLACKSTARR

Arkwright says he has long since given up on listening to John Silence's stories, preferring Carnacki's tales of his own cases instead.

Short story by Robert E. Jefferson in Carnacki: The New Adventures, Sam Gafford, ed., Ulthar Press, 2013. Thomas Carnacki and Dr. John Silence are occult detectives created by William Hope Hodgson and Algernon Blackwood, respectively.

TIME'S BLACK GULF

Professor Summerlee, Lord John Roxton, Edward Malone, and Thomas Carnacki battle Indrid Cold and other members of his race, who are part of a conspiracy to infiltrate the human race at every stage of its evolution along with an alien race that has swapped Professor Challenger's consciousness with that of one of their own people. Challenger has copies of *Cultes des Goules* and *Unaussprechlichen Kulten*. Carnacki refers to the Sigsand Manuscripts, the *Book of Eibon*, the Pnakotic texts, the Florentine monk Corsi, and Khephnes. The *Tind'Losi*, the Hounds of the Angles, appear. Dr. John Silence and Jessie Challenger ultimately save the day.

Short story by Josh Reynolds in Professor Challenger: New Worlds, Lost Places, *J. R. Campbell and Charles Prepolec, eds., EDGE Science Fiction and Fantasy Publishing, 2015. Professor Challenger, his wife Jessie, Professor Summerlee, Lord John Roxton, and Edward Malone are from Arthur Conan Doyle's* The Lost World *and other novels and stories. Thomas Carnacki and the Sigsand Manuscripts are from William Hope Hodgson's* Carnacki the Ghost-Finder. *Indrid Cold is a supposedly real person connected to the Mothman sightings of 1966–1967. Here, he is also a member of the race of creatures seen in H. P. Lovecraft's "The Festival." This version of Cold also appears in Reynolds' stories "The Pnakotic Puzzle" and "The Yoth Protocols." "The Pnakotic Puzzle" indicates this story happened "some years before the war." Although Malone seems unfamiliar with Carnacki here, they actually met each other the previous year, as seen in "The Kew Growths," and* so this must be chalked up to fictionalization. The consciousness-swapping alien race is the Great Race of Yith from Lovecraft's "The Shadow Out of Time." Bartolomeo Corsi and Khephnes are also from "The Shadow Out of Time." The Cultes des Goules *is a Cthulhu Mythos tome created by Robert Bloch.* Unaussprechlichen Kulten *is a Mythos tome created by Robert E. Howard. The* Book of Eibon *is from Clark Ashton Smith's contributions to the Mythos. The Pnakotic texts are a reference to Lovecraft's Pnakotic Manuscripts. The* Tind'Losi *are from Frank Belknap Long's story "The Hounds of Tindalos." Dr. John Silence is an occult detective featured in stories by Algernon Blackwood.*

Spring
A THEFT OF CHINA

Arsène Lupin and Calpurnia Pendergast visit the Rue Morgue, and he shows her the spot where the Chevalier Dupin had his most famous exploit. Lupin first met Calpurnia in the Black Moon Café, where she had been listening to a story told by his distant relative Emil. Lupin initially introduced himself to her as "Aristide Dupin." Besides the Rue Morgue, Lupin has also shown Calpurnia landmarks related to Erik, the Companions of Baal, Hanoi Shan, and Fantômas. Lupin points out the home of Baron Adelbert Gruner, who was once defeated by Sherlock Holmes, to Calpurnia. Lupin tells Calpurnia Gruner has claimed Britain's Archibald, Lord Wissex, tried to poison him, and it is said London's Assassination Bureau has a contract out on him. Lupin further claims Gruner is, along with Moriarty and MacHeath, one of the most ruthless criminals of their times. Lupin changes the subject by telling Calpurnia about other strange deaths in the Rue Morgue, including the experiments supposedly performed on humans by the alchemist Hubert de Mauvouloir. When Calpurnia commits suicide after being victimized by Gruner, Lupin meets with his old foe Inspector Ganimard, who recommends he contact Anton Le Brun. Le Brun tells Lupin about Gruner's English valet, Sebastian Jeeves. Gruner's scarred face reminds Lupin of a picture of an American gunfighter whose face had been similarly disfigured by Apache Indians.

Short story by Matthew Ilseman in The Many Faces of Arsène Lupin, *Jean-Marc and Randy Lofficier, eds., Black Coat Press, 2012; reprinted in French in* Les Compagnons de L'Ombre (Tome 10), *Jean-Marc and Randy Lofficier, eds., Rivière Blanche, 2012. Arsène Lupin is the gentleman thief created by Maurice Leblanc, of course. Inspector Justin Ganimard is Lupin's policeman nemesis. Calpurnia Pendergast is a relative of Aloysius Pendergast, a modern-day FBI Special Agent featured in novels by Douglas Preston* and Lincoln Child. *The Rue Morgue* and *the Chevalier C. Auguste Dupin* are from Edgar Allan Poe's "The Murders in the Rue Morgue." *The Black Moon Café* and *Emil Lupin* appeared in a regular feature in the British story magazine Bullseye. *Aristide Dupin* encountered Sexton Blake in Gwyn Evans' story "The League of Onion Men." Jess Nevins has argued "Dupin" is actually an alias for Lupin. Erik is the title character of Gaston Leroux's The Phantom of the Opera. *The Companions of Baal* are the subject of a French television miniseries of the same name, which is also the source of *Hubert de Mauvouloir*. *Hanoi Shan* is from H. Ashton-Wolfe's Warped in the Making: Crimes of Love and Hate *and* The Thrill of Evil. *Fantômas* is the "Lord of Terror" created by Marcel Allain and Pierre Souvestre. *Baron Gruner* and *Anton Le Brun* are from the Sherlock Holmes story "The Adventure of the Illustrious Client." *Professor James Moriarty* is Holmes' archenemy. *Archibald, Lord Wissex,* is a member of the House of Wissex, a line of British assassins that appears in the Destroyer novels Profit Motive *and* Fool's Gold. The Assassination Bureau, Ltd. *is a novel by Jack London, completed posthumously by Robert L. Fish.* MacHeath *is from Bertolt Brecht's musical* The Threepenny Opera. *Sebastian Jeeves is a relative of Bertie Wooster's valet Reginald Jeeves, from the books by P. G. Wodehouse. The American gunfighter who was disfigured by Apaches is DC Comics' bounty hunter Jonah Hex.*

AUDIENCE WITH THE GHOST FINDER

Dodgson expresses surprise Carnacki has requested his assistance, noting Jessop is very experienced with occult matters "after that business aboard the *Mortzestus.*"

Play by M. J. Starling *in* Carnacki: The New Adventures, *Sam Gafford, ed., Ulthar Press, 2013. Carnacki is William Hope Hodgson's occult detective. The* Mortzestus *is from Hodgson's novel* The Ghost Pirates. *Starling's play conflates the Jessop that narrates* The Ghost Pirates *with the Jessop that appears in the Carnacki stories. The year is given as 1912. Carnacki says he helped out Captain Hisgins "last year." However, he must have had a lapse of memory, since Carnacki encountered Hisgins in Hodgson's story "The Horse of the Invisible," which was first published in 1910.*

THE PETRIFIED FOREST

Professor Challenger and Edward Malone encounter winged, five-pointed, barrel-shaped creatures that drain life from other beings and chant "*Tekeli-Li!*"

Story by Edward Malone, edited by William Meikle *in* Professor

Challenger: The Kew Growths and Other Stories, *Dark Renaissance Books, 2014. The creatures are the Elder Things, which appear in H. P. Lovecraft's Cthulhu Mythos tales, notably* At the Mountains of Madness.

Summer
MORE IMAGINATIVE SINS

Thomas Carnacki comes to the aid of Agnes Cardinal at the Sâr Dubnotal's request. The source of Agnes' affliction is Madame Palmyre, who is trafficking with the otherworldly creature known as Baal.

Short story by Dodgson, edited by John Peel in Tales of the Shadowmen Volume 8: Agents Provocateurs, *Jean-Marc and Randy Lofficier, eds., Black Coat Press, 2011; reprinted in French in* Les Compagnons de l'Ombre (Tome 11), *Jean-Marc and Randy Lofficier, eds., Rivière Blanche, 2013. Thomas Carnacki, "the Ghost-Finder," appears in a series of stories by William Hope Hodgson. The Sâr Dubnotal is the protagonist of an anonymously-written French pulp series. Madame Palmyre and Baal are from Renée Dunan's novel* Baal.

TOM SHARK, DER KÖNIG DER DETEKTIVS

Tom Shark pursues but ultimately declines to apprehend Lord Lister.

Tom Shark, der König der Detektivs, *1937. This story confirms Tom Shark and Lord Lister coexist within the CU.*

September
CARNACKI: CAPTAIN GAULT'S NEMESIS

Thomas Carnacki aids Captain Gault in ridding his ship of the Babylonian god Oannes.

Short story by William Meikle in Carnacki: The New Adventures, *Sam Gafford, ed., Ulthar Press, 2013. William Hope Hodgson's "Ghost-Finder" Thomas Carnacki is already in the CU; therefore, this crossover brings in Hodgson's unscrupulous seaman Captain Gault. Most of the Gault stories are collected in* Captain Gault, Being the Exceedingly Private Log of a Sea-Captain.

Autumn. The insane Dr. Orloff kidnaps women of loose morals in order to use their flesh to restore the beauty of his fire-scarred daughter, as recounted in the movie *The Awful Dr. Orloff*.

Autumn
SHERLOCK HOLMES ROULÉ PAR RIGADIN (SHERLOCK HOLMES CHEATED BY RIGADIN)
The French master thief Rigadin does battle with Sherlock Holmes. *This 1914 short film reinforces Rigadin's presence in the CU.*

THE BLUE EGG
Carnacki accompanies Captain Gault on a voyage to acquire a blue jewel that has a powerful pull on those who come in contact with it.
Short story by William Meikle in Sargasso: The Journal of William Hope Hodgson Studies #1, Sam Gafford, ed., Ulthar Press, 2013. *This story is a crossover between two of William Hope Hodgson's characters, Thomas Carnacki, aka Carnacki the Ghost-Finder, and the unethical seaman and smuggler Captain Gault. This story takes place in autumn, "not long" after Carnacki and Gault's first meeting in Meikle's story "Carnacki: Captain Gault's Nemesis."*

December 25–26
THE BEAUTIFUL LADY WITHOUT PITY: A CARNACKI THE GHOST-FINDER ADVENTURE

Thomas Carnacki, staying overnight at an estate called the Elms after a Christmas party, teams up with another guest, a mysterious man named Kharrn, to deal with a ghost haunting a third partygoer.
Short story by Charles R. Rutledge in Widowmakers: A Benefit Anthology of Dark Fiction, *Pete Kahle, ed., 2014. Carnacki is from William Hope Hodgson's collection* Carnacki the Ghost-Finder. *The long-lived barbarian Kharrn was mentioned in Rutledge and James A. Moore's novel* Congregations of the Dead.

1913

Winter
THE GARGOYLES OF NOTRE-DAME

Judex, disguised as the corrupt banker Favraux's secretary Vallières, accompanies Madame Beaudin to a séance hosted by the Sâr Dubnotal and his assistant, the medium Gianetti Annunciata. Gianetti is briefly possessed by someone who challenges the Sâr. The Sâr swears by Mitra and Viritrilbia, and later identifies the individual who possessed Gianetti as Herr Doctor Von Meyer to the *abbé* of Notre-Dame cathedral. The *abbé* tells the Sâr about the gargoyles the cathedral has borrowed from another cathedral in Vyones. It is mentioned the four bells in Notre-Dame's South Tower have not been rung since the days of Quasimodo. The Sâr tells Judex the gargoyles were made by a stonecutter named Reynard.

Short story by Matthew Baugh in The Shadow of Judex, *Jean-Marc and Randy Lofficier, eds., Black Coat Press, 2013; reprinted in French in* L'Ombre de Judex, *Jean-Marc and Randy Lofficier, eds., Rivière Blanche, 2013; and in* Sâr Dubnotal 2: The Astral Trail, *Jean-Marc and Randy Lofficier, eds., Black Coat Press, 2015. Judex and Favraux are from Louis Feuillade's film serial* Judex. *The Sâr Dubnotal and his assistant Gianetti Annunciata were featured in a French pulp magazine written by an anonymous author. The deity Mitra is from Robert E. Howard's Conan tales, while Viritrilbia is another name for Mercury in C. S. Lewis' novel* That Hideous Strength. *Herr Doctor Von Meyer is from Seabury Quinn's Jules de Grandin tale "The Mansion of Unholy Magic." The gargoyles and their creator, Blaise Reynard, are from Clark Ashton Smith's "The Maker of Gargoyles," part of his Averoigne cycle of stories. Vyones is also from the Averoigne tales. Quasimodo is from Victor Hugo's* The Hunchback of Notre-Dame.

Spring
THE TRIAL OF VAN HELSING

General Boris Liatoukine, also known as "Captain Vampire," seeks to capture Professor Van Helsing and take him to the Sepulchre, also known as Selene, the Vampire City, in order to place him on trial for the murder of Count Dracula. In Transylvania, Van Helsing discusses Selene with Baron Vordenberg. Van Helsing refers to Selene's current ruler, Mircalla Karnstein. Mircalla was destroyed (apparently temporarily) decades ago; the Baron's grandfather was present at her death, and the accounts of Doctor Hesselius and Mircalla's descendant Laura confirm her destruction. Liatoukine is allied with Polly Bird, who was once for a time transformed by the vampire Otto

Goetzi into a duplicate of himself. Liatoukine refers to Dracula and Orlok as vampires of power who drove things too far, and ended up dead. Mircalla's lieutenant is the Countess Marcian Gregoryi, also known as the Countess Addhema. The Countess accuses Van Helsing and his allies of also killing the newly-created vampire Lucy Westenra and Dracula's three "Brides." With Van Helsing's help, Liatoukine exposes the false Mircalla as Laura, who became a vampire after her ancestor's destruction.

Short story by Brian Gallagher in Tales of the Shadowmen Volume 11: Force Majeure, *Jean-Marc and Randy Lofficier, eds., Black Coat Press, 2014; reprinted in French in* Les Compagnons de l'Ombre (Tome 16), *Jean-Marc and Randy Lofficier, eds., Rivière Blanche, 2015, and* L'Almanach des Vampires (Tome 2), *Jean-Marc and Randy Lofficier, eds., Rivière Blanche, 2015; and in* The Vampire Almanac (Volume 2), *Jean-Marc and Randy Lofficier, eds., Black Coat Press, 2015. Boris Liatoukine is from Marie Nizet's novel* Captain Vampire. *Professor Van Helsing, Count Dracula, Lucy Westenra, and Dracula's "Brides" are from Bram Stoker's novel* Dracula. *The Sepulchre (aka Selene), Polly Bird, and Otto Goetzi are from Paul Féval's novel* Vampire City. *Countess Marcian Gregoryi (aka Countess Addhema) is from Féval's* The Vampire Countess. Captain Vampire, Vampire City, *and* The Vampire Countess *have all been translated by Brian Stableford for Black Coat Press. Mircalla Karnstein, the earlier Baron Vordenberg, Doctor Hesselius, and Laura are from J. Sheridan Le Fanu's story "Carmilla." Graf Von Orlok is from the silent horror film* Nosferatu.

Summer
MONMOUTH'S GIANTS

Thomas Carnacki encounters Charles St. Cyprian and three of his friends, Florence, Bobbie, and Boko. Bobbie refers to "one of Runcible's tedious old parties," and asks if Carnacki is the fellow who went to Switzerland and fell over a waterfall. Carnacki corrects her, saying that was Sherlock Holmes.

Short story by Josh Reynolds in Carnacki: The New Adventures, *Sam Gafford, ed., Ulthar Press, 2013. Occult detective Thomas Carnacki was created by William Hope Hodgson. Charles St. Cyprian is the protagonist of Reynolds'* Royal Occultist *stories. St. Cyprian will become Carnacki's apprentice soon after this tale, and replace him as Royal Occultist in 1918. St. Cyprian's friends are Lady Florence Craye, Roberta "Bobbie" Wickham, and George "Boko" Fittleworth from P. G. Wodehouse's Jeeves books. Runcible is Agatha Runcible from Evelyn Waugh's novel* Vile Bodies. *Sherlock Holmes is self-explanatory.*

CHALLENGER'S TITANIC CHALLENGE

Sherlock Holmes and Dr. Watson visit Professor Challenger, ostensibly to help him with his research into the ultimate cause of the sinking of the steamer *Titanic* last year, but actually to prevent his assassination.

Short story by Gary Lovisi in Sherlock Holmes Mystery Magazine #12, Marvin Kaye, ed., Wildside Press, 2014. Despite appearances, this is not the first time Holmes and Watson have met Challenger. Also, a reference to the Professor's expedition to Maple White Land having taken place two years ago is incorrect, as the events of The Lost World occurred in 1908, not 1911.

Autumn

THE LAST TALE (LA DERNIÈRE HISTOIRE)

Thomas Carnacki relates to Dodgson, Jessop, and Arkright how he was recently introduced to Leo Saint-Clair by his colleague and neighbor, the Sâr Dubnotal. Saint-Clair told Carnacki about a creature called the Horla, which was the subject of a tale by Guy de Maupassant. The *Brigade des Maléfices*, a little known department of the *Sûreté*, has a folder on the creature, which includes a mention of it in the memoirs of a 16th century woman called Fausta. Saint-Clair indicates that another name for the Horla is the Lloigor. Carnacki interrupts his story when the Horla, which he has trapped inside his own body, begins to fight for dominance with him. His listeners arrange for him to be placed in Dr. Seward's private clinic.

Short story by Dodgson, edited by Olivier Legrand appearing as "La Dernière Historie" in Les Compagnons de l'Ombre (Tome 11), Jean-Marc and Randy Lofficier, eds., Rivière Blanche, 2013, and in English in Tales of the Shadowmen Volume 10: Esprit de Corps, Jean-Marc and Randy Lofficier, eds., Black Coat Press, 2013. Thomas Carnacki, Dodgson, Jessop and Arkright are from William Hope Hodgson's collection Carnacki the Ghost-Finder; since Carnacki appears in many stories set after 1913, seemingly none the worse for wear, the Horla must have left his body at some point. Leo Saint-Clair is better known as the Nyctalope, the hero of a series of novels by Jean de La Hire. The Sâr Dubnotal is an occult detective appearing in a French pulp series by an anonymous author. The Horla is from Guy de Maupassant's tale of the same name. The Brigade des Maléfices are from the 1971 television series of that name. Fausta is the anti-heroine of Michel Zevaco's swashbuckling novels about the Chevalier de Pardaillan; Fausta came in contact with the Horla in Micah S. Harris' tale "The Anti-Pope of Avignon" (Tales of the Shadowmen Volume 4: Lords of Terror, 2008). The Lloigor are from Colin Wilson's "The Return of the Lloigor." Dr. Seward is from Stoker's Dracula, of course.

1914

Winter
PATRICIDE

Erik the Opera Ghost tortures a member of the Red Hand, the criminal syndicate led by Dr. Cornelius Kramm. Gouroull, alias the Frankenstein Monster, attacks a group of young thugs. Bouzille informs Dr. Kramm of Gouroull's bloody rampage. Kramm tells his brother Fritz he intends to duplicate Dr. Pretorius' procedure for creating homunculi. The Kramm brothers are attacked by Erik's Angels of Music: Florence Drummond, Bri Warren, and Hélène Gurn. Florence boasts she is related to the slave trader Heinrich Von Drummond, captain of the *Mary Stewart*. Erik's servant Cochenille attacks Gouroull. Erik reveals to Gouroull he is the product of Gouroull's rape of a girl named Rosemary, who he says was an innocent like his beloved Christine. Officer Jules Maigret and Doctor Jules de Grandin investigate an explosion caused by Erik. De Grandin suggests the blast could have been the work of the Red Hand, the Black Coats, or the Vampires.

Short story by Chris Nigro *in* Tales of the Shadowmen Volume 8: Agents Provocateurs, *Jean-Marc and Randy Lofficier, eds., Black Coat Press, 2011; reprinted in French in* Les Compagnons de L'Ombre (Tome 10), *Jean-Marc and Randy Lofficier, eds., Rivière Blanche, 2012.* Erik and Christine Daae are from Gaston Leroux's novel The Phantom of the Opera. The Red Hand, Dr. Cornelius Kramm, and his brother Fritz are from Gustave Le Rouge's Le Mystérieux Docteur Cornélius. *The Frankenstein Monster is of course from Mary Shelley's novel, and appears under the name Gouroull in novels by Jean-Claude Carrière. Gouroull was briefly allied with the Kramms in Matthew Baugh's story "The Mask of the Monster"* (Tales of the Shadowmen Volume 1: The Modern Babylon, *Jean-Marc and Randy Lofficier, eds.,*

Black Coat Press, 2005). Two previous incarnations of the Angels of Music have appeared in stories by Kim Newman for the Tales of the Shadowmen anthologies. Florence Drummond is better known as the Flame, "the Girl with the Criminal Mind," from Carroll John Daly's stories about the incredibly hard-boiled P.I. Race Williams. Brianna "Bri" Warren is the great-great-great-aunt of the Halliwell sisters from the television series Charmed. Hélène Gurn is the daughter of Fantômas, the "Lord of Terror" created by Marcel Allain and Pierre Souvestre. Bouzille is also from the Fantômas books. Heinrich Von Drummond is from "The Ancestors," an episode of the television series Diff'rent Strokes. Cochenille is from Jacques Offenbach's opera The Tales of Hoffmann. Erik's parentage was revealed in Jean-Marc and Randy Lofficier's story "His Father's Eyes," which appeared as a bonus feature in their translated edition of The Phantom of the Opera. Jules Maigret is from the novels by Georges Simenon. Jules de Grandin is the protagonist of several stories by Seabury Quinn. The Black Coats are the criminal conspiracy featured in novels by Paul Féval. The Vampires are from Louis Feuillade's serial Les Vampires.

BLUE EYE

Turkish sleuth Avni's opponent is described as having a record better than that of Rocambole.

Found in Amanvermez Avni #2 by Ebüssüreyya Sami, 1914.

Spring
A JOB FOR CARNACKI

Carnacki comes to the aid of the Reverend Doctor Sidney Lampton, a divinity instructor at Brichester. Attempting to cure Lampton of his ailment, Carnacki chants the syllables of the Voola Ritual.

Short story by Robert M. Price in Carnacki: The New Adventures, Sam Gafford, ed., Ulthar Press, 2013. Brichester University is located in the town of Brichester, the site of a number of Cthulhu Mythos stories by Ramsey Campbell. The Voola Ritual appears in one such story, "The Mine on Yuggoth."

DRUMS IN THE DEEP

Professor Challenger and Edward Malone encounter a group of fish-men who chant the name Dagon.

Story by Edward Malone, edited by William Meikle in Professor Challenger: The Kew Growths and Other Stories, Dark Renaissance Books, 2014. The fish-men are the Deep Ones from Lovecraft's "The Shadow over Innsmouth."

Spring 1914–1918
THE QUEST OF FRANKENSTEIN

Gouroull, the truly inhuman creation of Victor Frankenstein, travels the world finding the components Herbert West needs to create a mate for the monster, who wishes to breed a new race that will replace humanity. Shortly before his first meeting with West, Gouroull has a battle with the deformed Creeper. Frankenstein was taught alchemy by the elderly Doctor Septimus Pretorius. West possesses a set of books that include Frankenstein's works, which previously belonged to a Baron de Musard. One of the items he acquires is the blood of a German soldier who is secretly a warlock, and possesses a serpent ring. A pale man gave the warlock power in exchange for the blood of those fallen in war. The sorcerer's underling, Yosef Vrolok, steals the ring after he is left catatonic. Gouroull crashes a vampire congress whose attendees include Count Karnstein and his daughter Countess Mircalla; Barnabas Collins and his relative Quentin, a werewolf; a Russian named Saushkin, who is accompanied by a witch; the Master of the Order of Aurelius (who Mircalla says reminds her of Orlok), accompanied by a blonde woman; Viktor and his raven-haired female underling; Padma and his weretiger servant; Princess Asa Vajda; Queen Akasha; and Dracula. Gouroull finds the next item he needs in Selene, the Vampire City. After that, he heads to the Greek island of Mykos, acquiring a piece of the city of the Deep Ones nearby. Gouroull than acquires Paracelsus' formula from Marie Moreau, who has created beast-men like her father before her. She allows the Russian Count Zaroff to hunt her creations. Lord Ruthven, who was once betrayed by an Englishman named Lord Wilmore, has seized control of the Camorra in Naples, the former home of the notorious *Veste Nere*. His rival, Sir Francis Varney, has allied with a Sicilian group called the Brotherhood of Silence. Gouroull offers Ruthven Varney's head in exchange for the location of the zombie Knights Templar known as the Blind Dead. An archaeologist performing a ritual in the tomb of the Blind

Dead has been to Miskatonic University. After the undead creatures attack, he vows to head for Dunwich. Gouroull sees a shell-shocked British soldier named Peter. Afterwards, he acquires the bones of Countess Wandessa de Nasdady. In Suffolk, he encounters Lavinia Morley, who is the high priestess of a worm cult that once had a battle with a Pictish king. Lavinia invokes Yog-Sothoth. Lady Sara Durwood, an emotional vampire, feeds on a man while his fellow Drones Club members Bertie, Tuppy Glossop, and Bingo Little cavort, with Bertie's butler attempting to maintain order. Gouroull encounters a witch who has been known by many names, including Louhi, Pannochka, and Atla the witch-woman of Dagon-moor. In Cairo, Herbert Fuchs, who is obsessed with the ancient Egyptian Queen Tera, consults the Scroll of Thoth-Amon. The Heart of Ahriman is mentioned. Fuchs acquires tana leaves, and drugs his daughter with the black lotus. Gouroull's final mission brings him to the African kingdom of Negari, which is at war with the nearby kingdom of Kor. Gouroull encounters the true Dracula, rather than the one he met before.

Novel by Frank Schildiner, Black Coat Press, 2015. Gouroull is the name by which Victor Frankenstein's monster is known in novels by Jean-Claude Carrière. Herbert West is from H. P. Lovecraft's story "Herbert West – Reanimator." The pale man is Nyarlathotep, one of the gods of Lovecraft's Cthulhu Mythos. The Deep Ones are from Lovecraft's "The Shadow over Innsmouth." Miskatonic University and Dunwich are recurring locales in Lovecraft's Mythos. Yog-Sothoth is another of Lovecraft's Great Old Ones. The Creeper is from the movies The Pearl of Death, House of Horrors, *and* The Brute Man. *Doctor Septimus Pretorius is from the movie* The Bride of Frankenstein. *Baron de Musard is from Philip José Farmer's authorized Doc Savage novel* Escape from Loki. *The Serpent Ring of Set is from Robert E. Howard's stories "The Phoenix on the Sword" and "The Haunter of the Ring." "The Phoenix on the Sword" is also the source of the Scroll of Thoth-Amon. Yosef Vrolok is also from the "The Haunter of the Ring." The worm cult encountered the Pictish king Bran Mak Morn in Howard's "Worms of the Earth." Atla is also from "Worms of the Earth." The Heart of Ahriman is from Howard's Conan story "The Hour of the Dragon." The Black Lotus appears in the Conan stories, as well as those of Howard's policeman Steve Harrison. Negari is from Howard's Solomon Kane story "The Moon of Skulls." The Karnsteins are from J. Sheridan Le Fanu's "Carmilla." Barnabas and Quentin Collins are from the TV series* Dark Shadows. *Saushkin and the witch are from Sergei Lukyanenko's* The World of the Watches *novel series. The* Necronomicon *appears in the second book in that series,* Day Watch. *The Master of the Order of Aurelius and his blonde companion Darla are from the TV series* Buffy the Vampire Slayer. *Orlok is from the silent horror film* Nosferatu. *Viktor and his underling Selene are from the Underworld film series. Padma and the weretiger are from Laurell K. Hamilton's* Anita Blake, Vampire Hunter *series, which takes place in a world where the existence of the supernatural is common knowledge. However, other crossovers establish that a version of Anita exists in the CU. Princess Asa Vajda is from the movie* Black Sunday. *Queen Akasha is from the novels of Anne Rice. This novel utilizes Chuck Loridans' "soul-clone" theory, which explains myriad contradictory versions of Dracula across various media. The Dracula at the congress is a soul-clone, while the one at the end of the book is Dracula-Prime. Selene is from Paul Féval's novel* The Vampire City. *The Veste Nere are also known as the Black Coats, a criminal society featured in other books by Féval. The Brotherhood of Silence are from Féval's novel* The Companions of Silence. *Marie Moreau's father is from H. G. Wells' novel* The Island of Doctor Moreau. *Count Zaroff is from Richard Connell's story "The Most Dangerous Game." Lord Ruthven is from John Polidori's "The Vampyre." Lord Wilmore is one of the aliases of Alexandre Dumas' Count of Monte Cristo, who encountered Ruthven in Micah Harris' story "May the Ground Not Consume Thee . . ." Sir Francis Varney is from J. M. Rymer's* Varney the Vampire. *The Blind Dead were featured in a series of Spanish horror films. Peter is Lord Peter Wimsey from Dorothy L. Sayers' detective novels. Countess Wandessa de Nasdady is from the Spanish horror movie* The Night of Walpurgis. *Lavinia Morley is from the movie* Curse of the Crimson Altar. *Lady Sara Durwood (or Durward) is from the movie* Captain Kronos – Vampire Hunter. *The Drones Club, Bertie Wooster and his valet Jeeves, Tuppy Glossop, and Bingo Little are from the works of P. G. Wodehouse. Louhi is from L. Sprague de Camp and Lin Carter's Conan story "Legions of the Dead." Pannochka is from Nikolai Gogol's story "Viy." Queen Tera and Margaret Fuchs are from the movie* Blood from the Mummy's Tomb. *Tana leaves are from Universal Studios' original series of Mummy films. Kor is from H. Rider Haggard's novels of Ayesha, She-Who-Must-Be-Obeyed.*

Summer
THE TWO DOCTORS
    Doctor Omega and the Sâr Dubnotal investigate the disappearance of everyone in Paris, with the Doctor refusing to believe a *djinn* is responsible. Eventually, the Sâr is proven right, and Omega wishes for hundreds of duplicates of himself to appear in order to resolve the situation.
    Short story by Neil Penswick in Doctor Omega and the Shadowmen, *Jean-Marc and Randy Lofficier, eds., Black Coat Press, 2011; reprinted in French in* Les Compagnons de l'Ombre (Tome 9), *Jean-Marc and Randy*

Lofficier, eds., Rivière Blanche, 2012. Doctor Omega is from the novel of the same name by Arnould Galopin. The Sâr Dubnotal is an occult detective who starred in a French pulp series. Though the story ends on an enigmatic note, it can be assumed the duplicates of the brilliant Doctor Omega worked with the Sâr to restore the population of Paris. The year of this story is conjecture.

SACREBLEU!

Irma Vep attempts to steal the Pink Panther gem from a museum. She thinks of rumors more of Moreau's vile concoctions are loose on the streets, and of her former mentor, Arsène Lupin. After ending up with a streak of white paint on the back of her body stocking, she is accosted by a giant skunk, who calls himself Pepé.

Short story by G. L. Gick in Harry Dickson and the Werewolf of Rutherford Grange, *Black Coat Press, 2011; reprinted in French in* Les Compagnons de l'Ombre *(Tome 9), Jean-Marc and Randy Lofficier, eds., Rivière Blanche, 2012. Irma Vep is from Louis Feuillade's 1915–1916 serial* Les Vampires. *The Pink Panther is from the movie of the same name and its sequels. Moreau is from H. G. Wells' novel* The Island of Doctor Moreau. *Arsène Lupin is Maurice Leblanc's gentleman thief. Pepé is the Crossover Universe counterpart of Pepé le Pew, an amorous French skunk appearing in Warner Brothers cartoons. This Pepé is obviously the result of one of Doctor Moreau's experiments.*

HOCHMULLER'S HOUND

Thomas Carnacki, the Royal Occultist, and his assistant Charles St. Cyprian battle a German scientist who has created a man-eating hound that is preying on the Allies. Carnacki's adventures once decorated the pages of *The Idler*, even as those of the Great Detective had appeared in *The Strand*.

Short story by Josh Reynolds in Blood Trails, *Miles Boothe, ed., Emby Press, 2014. Thomas Carnacki's stories in* The Idler *were written by William Hope Hodgson, and collected as* Carnacki the Ghost-Finder. *Charles St. Cyprian will succeed Carnacki as Royal Occultist near the end of the war, and appear in his own series of stories by Reynolds. The Great Detective is Sherlock Holmes, of course.*

October
THE JOURNAL OF MILO THATCH

Preston Whitmore, the financier of an expedition to find Atlantis, writes of the destruction of the submarine *Ulysses*, "Much like the crew of Captain Nemo's famous *Nautilus*, they had 'a plan for living, but also a plan for dying.'"

This book, a tie-in for the animated movie Atlantis: The Lost Empire, *brings that film into the CU via a reference to Captain Nemo as a real person. The quote attributed to Nemo is from Disney's film version of* 20,000 Leagues Under the Sea. *However, the literary Nemo could very well have said something similar at some point. The book tells the events of the movie from Milo Thatch's point of view, with additional commentary by Whitmore, and is edited by Jeff Kurtti. The sequel* Atlantis: Milo's Return *must take place in an AU, as it involves Atlantis rising to the surface, an event of which the whole world learns. It is worth noting the unaired spin-off TV series* Team Atlantis *would have had a crossover with the cartoon* Gargoyles *in the episode "The Last."*

Autumn
DIABOLICAL, MORE DIABOLICAL, AND THE MOST DIABOLICAL
Sherlock Holmes teams up with Nick Carter, Nat Pinkerton, and Nick Winter.

1915 short film produced by the French company Eclipse. Holmes, Carter, and Pinkerton are already firmly in the CU. This crossover brings in Nick Winter. According to Jess Nevins, "Nick Winter was created by Paul Garbagni and appeared in at least nineteen films from 1911 to 1921, beginning with Nick Winter et le Vol de la Joconde; *he also appeared in the Spanish pulp* Nick Winter, Memorias del Famoso Detective Ingles *#1–13 (1912?) and the Turkish pulp* Nick Vinter Serisi *#1–2? (1918). Nick Winter is a Great Detective modeled on Nick Carter."*

Late Autumn
THE CORNISH OWLMAN

Professor Challenger, Edward Malone, and Thomas Carnacki battle a supernatural owl-like creature in Cornwall.

Story by Edward Malone, edited by William Meikle in Professor Challenger: The Kew Growths and Other Stories, *Dark Renaissance Books*, 2014.

1915

Summer
THE SPAR: A STORY OF CARNACKI

Thomas Carnacki comes to the aid of a shop-keeper whose store is beset by otherdimensional beings that gain their substance in our world via a connection to a spar recovered as salvage from the sinking of the cargo ship *Mortzestus* on her last voyage from San Francisco. A colleague of Carnacki's acquaintance Dodgson wrote *The Ghost Pirates*, an account of the cursed ship's invasion by hellish beings from outside and its subsequent sinking into the Pacific Ocean, which was marketed as fiction because the public would never accept it as the truth.

Short story by Fred Blosser in Carnacki: The New Adventures, *Sam Gafford, ed., Ulthar Press, 2013. Occult sleuth Thomas Carnacki was the subject of a number of stories by William Hope Hodgson, who also wrote the book* The Ghost Pirates.

1916

February
WHAT ROUGH BEAST

During World War I, French Foreign Legionnaire Hugo Danner of Colorado is recruited for a dangerous mission by a man named Vallières. Vallières is aware of Danner's prodigious strength, which is the product of injections given to him in the womb by his father, Professor Abednego Danner, and of Hugo's leaving Webster University after accidentally killing a fellow football player. Hugo's orders are signed by General Broulard. Danner's allies in the mission are the mystic Sâr Dubnotal and his assistant, the medium Gianetti Annunciata, and the cloaked crime fighter Judex. They are to travel to the Château de Joiry and prevent Doctor Von Meyer from using the grimoire of Nathare of Vyones to sculpt reanimated soldiers into the Colossus that once laid waste to Ylourgne. Hugo mentions his deceased friend and comrade Tom Shayne. Von Meyer is served by several creatures, including dog-headed ghouls, a bat-winged reptilian creature shaped like a giant ape, and a small toad-skinned man with tentacles lining his mouth.

Short story by Matthew Baugh in Tales of the Shadowmen Volume 7: Femmes Fatales, *Jean-Marc and Randy Lofficier, eds., Black Coat Press, 2010; reprinted in French in* Les Compagnons de l'Ombre (Tome 9), *Jean-Marc and Randy Lofficier, eds., Rivière Blanche, 2012, and* L'Ombre de Judex, *Jean-Marc and Randy Lofficier, eds., Rivière Blanche, 2013; and in* The Shadow of Judex, *Jean-Marc and Randy Lofficier, eds., Black Coat Press, 2013, and* Sâr Dubnotal 2: The Astral Trail, *Jean-Marc and Randy Lofficier, eds., Black Coat Press, 2015. Hugo Danner, Professor Abednego Danner, Webster University, and Tom Shayne are from Philip Wylie's novel* Gladiator. *Judex (aka Vallières) is the title character of the film serial directed by Louis Feuillade. General Broulard is from Stanley Kubrick's film* Paths of Glory, *based on Humphrey Cobb's novel of the same name, in which Broulard's equivalent was named de Guerville. The Sâr Dubnotal and his assistant Gianetti Annunciata are from a French pulp series by an anonymous author (possibly Norbert Sévestre). Château de Joiry is the home of Jirel of Joiry, the heroine of historical fantasy stories by C. L. Moore. Von Meyer is from Seabury Quinn's Jules de Grandin story "The Mansion of Unholy Magic." Von Meyer previously encountered the Sâr and Judex in Baugh's tale "The Gargoyles of Notre-Dame," also included in* The Shadow of Judex. *The small toad-skinned man is Dewer from the de Grandin story "The Bride of Dewer." Nathare (or Nathaire) of Vyones, the Colossus, and Ylourgne are from Clark Ashton Smith's story "The Colossus of Ylourgne." The dog-headed ghouls are from H. P. Lovecraft's story "Pickman's Model." The bat-winged reptilian creature is from E. Hoffmann Price's Pierre d'Artois story "Spirit Murder."*

July
THE MARK OF THE RED LEECH
Private Henry Jones Junior is scolded for journaling by Captain Dickson, whom Colonel Renwick respects. Jones' journal entry refers to Pvt. Simpson. Dickson refers to Captain Spencer and the others, and doubts they will see Captain Ulysses Paxton again in this world. Jones says his father has met Dickson's famous mentor. The mark left on the corpses of a group of soldiers reminds Dickson of something in his mentor's files called the red leech, a case which his biographer never published. A maddened Major Richard Wentworth attacks Dickson and the others, but is subdued and calmed down. The killer proves to be the vampire Sir Francis Varney. Dickson says Dracula is real. Varney is killed by a man named Isaac, who is accompanied by a little girl. Several groups were investigating the soldiers' deaths, including one led by Colonel Renwick and one including Colonel Wyndham-Price.

Short story by Travis Hiltz in Harry Dickson vs. the Spider, *Jean-Marc and Randy Lofficier, eds., Black Coat Press, 2014. Private Henry Jones Junior is better known as Indiana Jones. Although this story is dated to 1914, Indiana Jones fan Luke Van Horn notes, "There is no way Indy was involved in World War I in 1914, as his adventures during that year are very well-documented. It has to be in 1916 after he joined the Belgian army. Since Indy is a private, this story has to take place between* The Young Indiana Jones Chronicles *episodes 'Love's Sweet Song' and 'Trenches of Hell,' since in the latter he has been promoted to corporal. My best guess is that this story probably takes place in June or July 1916." Captain Dickson is*  detective Harry Dickson, from pulp stories by Jean Ray and others. Colonel Renwick will later become an aide to a famous bronze-skinned pulp hero. Pvt. Simpson is meant to be an ancestor of the titular family from the animated sitcom The Simpsons. *However,* The Simpsons *is too absurd in its events to comfortably take place in the CU. Most likely, there is a Simpson family in the CU, but they have had very different misadventures from their cartoon counterparts. Also, they almost certainly do not have yellow skin and only four fingers. Captain Eliot Spencer will later become the Cenobite known as Pinhead, as seen in the movie* Hellraiser, *based on Clive Barker's story "The Hellbound Heart," and its sequels. Paxton is from Edgar Rice Burroughs' Mars novels. Burroughs'* The Master Mind of Mars *has Paxton being transported to Mars in 1917, not 1916, so Dickson's comment cannot be a reference to that. Most likely, Paxton and his troop resurfaced soon after this story. Dickson's mentor is Sherlock Holmes. Dr. Watson referred to Holmes' involvement in "the repulsive story of the Red Leech" in "The Adventure of the Golden Pince-Nez." Major Richard Wentworth will later fight crime as the Spider. Sir Francis Varney is from James Malcolm Rymer's* Varney the Vampire. *Dracula needs no introduction at this point. Isaac Laquedem (aka the Wandering Jew) and the little girl (Lotte) are from Paul Féval's novel* The Wandering Jew's Daughter. *Despite the different spellings, Colonel Wyndham-Price is meant to be an ancestor of Wesley Wyndam-Pryce from the television series* Angel.

LEVIATHAN CREEK

On assignment in New Jersey, Joseph Rouletabille witnesses a man being savagely wounded at a beach. Ambassador Jusserand tells Rouletabille his assignment involves a group of German saboteurs led by a former U-boat captain named Mors. Rouletabille is told to attend a costume party at General Herbert Brown's house. He dresses as the Phantom of the Opera. General Brown introduces Rouletabille to his wife Elena. Brown says his papers once belonged to Cyrus Smith, with whom he was stranded on the mysterious Pacific island Lincoln. Others on the island were Gideon Spilett, Neb Dobey, and Smith's dog Top. Brown possesses plans drawn up by both Captain Nemo and Robur. Neb Jr. is planning to leave Brown's service and become a police officer in Bay City, and asks Rouletabille to give him some pointers on detective work. Rouletabille says when he is through, they'll probably make Neb Jr. Captain of Detectives, and his descendants as well. Neb Jr. responds his son Harold is fond of playing cops and robbers. Rouletabille thinks of Professor Stangerson's disassociation of matter experiments. Mors has been using sharks to attack beachgoers. Admitting defeat, Mors permits Rouletabille to set the controls on the cylinders containing the sharks so they will open in decades, rather than a few weeks as originally planned. Rouletabille sets it for 690 months, figuring the sharks will all be dead by then, or else the beach fad will have long since passed. He leaves the Amity Point Lighthouse.

Short story by Martin Gately in Tales of the Shadowmen Volume 8: Agents Provocateurs, *Jean-Marc and Randy Lofficier, eds., Black Coat Press, 2011; reprinted in French in* Les Compagnons de L'Ombre (Tome 10), *Jean-Marc and Randy Lofficier, eds., Rivière Blanche, 2012. Joseph Josephin, aka Rouletabille is a journalist and sleuth appearing in novels by Gaston Leroux. Professor Stangerson is from the first Rouletabille novel,* The Mystery of the Yellow Room. *Captain Mors is a Nemo-like scientist from a series of German pulp novels. Captain Nemo is from Jules Verne's* 20,000 Leagues Under the Sea *and* The Mysterious Island. *Brown, Cyrus Smith, Spilett, Neb, and Top are also from* The Mysterious Island. *Elena Brown is the former Elena Fairchild from the 1961 film version of* The Mysterious Island. *Robur is from Verne's* Robur the Conqueror *and* The Master of the World. *Neb Jr.'s son Harold is Captain Harold Dobey from the television series* Starsky and Hutch, *which was set in Bay City, California; Harold was played by Bernie Hamilton, who also played Neb in the 1951 film version of* The Mysterious Island. *Despite Rouletabille's hopes, one of the sharks will survive to menace the town of Amity in the 1970s, as seen in Peter Benchley's novel* Jaws.

Autumn 1916; Autumn 1926
ROULETABILLE VS. THE CAT

A mysterious figure stalks the grounds of Glen Cliff Manor, home of Cyrus West. General Herbert Brown points out the mansion to Joseph Rouletabille. Rouletabille realizes West is the same man as Captain Cyrus Smith (aka Cyrus Harding), Brown's former commanding officer and fellow castaway on Lincoln Island in the Pacific. West's lawyer, Roger Crosby, tells them not to tarry. They are greeted at the door by West's maid, Missy-Lou Pleasant. West says he hates war as much as his old friend Prince Dakkar. West had many run-ins in Serbia with a cat-worshipping cult, from which his agents rescued a little girl who was intended to be a human sacrifice. The child is now being raised by a foster mother in Tarrytown. West possesses a carbine with the word *Natuilus* engraved upon it. West's nephew Charlie Wilder is staying with him. An individual called the Cat Man attacks the assembly and steals the necklace West wished Rouletabille to protect, whose gems came from the Crown of Jovan Nenad, the most revered object of the Serbian cat cult. Brown instructs Missy-Lou to get Dr. Trifulgas from the village in order to treat the badly wounded Cat Man. West decides to have the Cat Man placed in the nearby Fairview Asylum. Ten years later, Rouletabille returns to Glen Cliff for the reading of West's will. The detective reflects on some of his exploits over the past decade, including his encounter with the seemingly indestructible superhuman, Hugo Danner; the Affair of the Octopus; and the death of his beloved Ivana. Nearly two years after his first visit to Glen Cliff, Rouletabille received word from Elena Fairchild-Brown General Brown had died. Rouletabille is driven to Glen Cliff alongside Harry Blythe, Cicily Young, and Miss Susan Sillsby, blood relatives of West's. Annabelle West arrives soon after from Kingsport. Miss Sillsby mentions a scientist cousin of West's up in Massachusetts. Hendricks, the chief guard at Fairview, shows up to tell the gathered heirs the Cat Man has escaped. Dr. Trifulgas tells Rouletabille he is originally from a place called Ulthar. Rouletabille's foe Larsan is mentioned.

Short story by Martin Gately in Tales of the Shadowmen Volume 10: Esprit de Corps, *Jean-Marc and Randy Lofficier, eds., Black Coat Press, 2013; reprinted in French in* Les Compagnons de l'Ombre (Tome 14), *Jean-Marc and Randy Lofficier, eds., Rivière Blanche, 2014. Glen Cliff Manor,*

Roger Crosby, Missy-Lou Pleasant, Charlie Wilder, the Cat Man, Fairview Asylum, Harry Blythe, Cicily Young, Miss Susan Sillsby, Annabelle West, and Hendricks are from John Willard's play The Cat and the Canary. Willard evidently omitted the presence of Gaston Leroux's sleuth Joseph Rouletabille from his fictionalized retelling of these events. Rouletabille's late wife Ivana Vilitchkov, Frederic Larsan (aka Ballmeyer, the detective's father), and the Octopus are also from Leroux's books. Gately conflates Cyrus West with Cyrus Smith (Cyrus Harding in many English translations) from Jules Verne's The Mysterious Island, the sequel to his novel 20,000 Leagues Under the Sea. Prince Dakkar is better known as Captain Nemo from both books; the Nautilus is his remarkable submarine. Herbert Brown and Lincoln Island are also from The Mysterious Island; Brown's wife, the former Elena Fairchild, is from the 1961 film version of that book. Dr. Trifulgas is from Verne's story "Frritt-Flack" (aka "Dr. Trifulgas: A Fantastic Tale.") The Serbian cat-worshipping cult is from the movie Cat People. The little girl rescued from the cult, raised as Barbara Farren, appears in the sequel, Curse of the Cat People. Gately notes, "Her cat-like appearance is never explained in the movie, but Julia Farren, who appears to be in the early stages of dementia, says that she is not really her daughter, and that her real daughter died years ago (presumably true, but only half-remembered by Julia)." Hugo Danner is the protagonist of Philip Wylie's book Gladiator. Kingsport, Massachusetts is from the works of H. P. Lovecraft. Cyrus West's cousin, Dr. Herbert West of Arkham, Massachusetts, is from Lovecraft's "Herbert West—Reanimator." Ulthar is from Lovecraft's "The Cats of Ulthar."

1917

Spring
MEETING WITH THE MIR BEG

Rouletabille, the American adventurer Blaylock, and Houdini battle the Mir Beg, the priest of the Yezidee god Melek Taos. Rouletabille identifies the Mir Beg as Blaylock's old foe Belasco, who has a cousin named Emeric.

Short story by Micah S. Harris and Loston Wallace in Tales of the Shadowmen Volume 11: Force Majeure, *Jean-Marc and Randy Lofficier, eds., Black Coat Press, 2014. Journalist and amateur detective Joseph Rouletabille appeared in novels by Gaston Leroux. Blaylock is an original character created by Harris and Wallace. This is not the Houdini of the "real" word, but rather his CU counterpart, who has had several encounters with Sherlock Holmes, among others. Melek Taos is the actual god of the Yezidees, but this story uses the fictionalized version of the god and his worshippers seen in Robert E. Howard's fiction. Emeric Belasco is from Richard Matheson's novel* Hell House.

April
THE ADVENTURE OF THE FALLEN STONE

Dr. Watson's pregnant wife, Nylepthah, is staying with her cousin, Sir George Curtis. In 1919, Holmes would visit his old friend with a large financial payment from the English Lord of the Apes, the result of their adventure in Africa in 1916. Holmes' gardener, Black Mike Croteau, has been murdered. After examining the body, Holmes and Watson are met at the former's cottage by Harry Dickson, who has apprenticed with both Barker (Holmes' Surrey rival) and Blake. He takes them to the Diogenes Club, where Holmes accuses his brother Mycroft of knowing there was a possibility he and Watson would be blown off course during  the previous year's African expedition he sent them upon. Holmes suggests Mycroft knew all along the ape lord was actually impersonating his deceased cousin, "William Clayton, the 7th Duke of Grey—." Holmes points out Mycroft identified their flier, Leftenant John Drummond, as the great-nephew of Holmes' old acquaintance, the 6th Duke. However, if Mycroft had been unaware of the imposture, he would have identified the Leftenant as the 6th Duke's grandson. Mycroft reveals William Clayton was a government agent reporting directly to him, and William's alleged shipwreck in Africa was actually part of his investigation. When he died, the Duke's cousin, the ape lord, who had survived a prior shipwreck as an infant, assumed his identity, wishing to avoid the publicity attendant to the discovery of an English lord who had been reared and suckled by apes. The mission involved tracking down the German spy Von Bork and his bacillus. Holmes deduces Mycroft hoped he and Watson would encounter the ape lord and asks why. Holmes speculates it has to do with the many unlikely coincidences the ape man comes up against. Mycroft says their scientists call it "the human magnetic moment." Holmes' adversary, Dr. Shan Ming Fu, informed Holmes of the *lotus vitae* almost ten years ago. Holmes' encounter with the

ape man brought him into contact with the jungle man's "human magnetic" influence, causing him to discover the lotus in the hidden valley of Zu-Vendis, though he asked Watson to omit that discovery from his written account. The lotus has been stolen from Holmes' garden. Mycroft says if Holmes' bees can be induced to sample the lotus' nectar, a particular honey may result, which would be the key ingredient in a unique concoction. Holmes mentions the "Hellbirds" incident, in which Von Bork escaped, though Mycroft asked Watson to distort his account of these events so Von Bork fell to his death from the Eiffel Tower. Von Bork is being trailed by Sexton Blake. The mastermind of the theft is a man who has been known by many names, including Wolf Larsen, Karl Woldheim, and Carl Woldhaus; currently, he goes by the name of Baron Ulf Von Waldman. He is the Commandant of a seemingly inescapable German prison camp for those who have escaped from other camps and been recaptured. The Baron also conducts experiments on humans. There are rumors Von Waldman is the son of Professor Moriarty. Holmes, Watson, Dickson and Isis Vanderhoek travel to Blakeney House. Isis' father was Mr. Klaw, "the dreaming detective." Mycroft tells Sherlock that the Diogenes Club has recently become more focused on investigating outré and unexplainable matters that affect the Empire. The butler at Blakeney House gives Dickson a coded message from Blake, in which he says he has wired Peter Blakeney in Richmond (with whom he has common relatives dating back to the mid 17th century), and Blakeney House is at their disposal, with Blakeney Jr. off at war. Blake soon arrives with a captive Von Bork in tow. Holmes recalls the tale of Openshaw. Blake tells his comrades about several places of interest in the East Riding of Yorkshire, including the village of Wold Newton, where a meteor fell near Major Edward Topham's property, the Wold Cottage, in 1795. Holmes decides they must visit the Wold Cottage and the monument Topham had placed at the site of the meteor's fall. Holmes unmasks "Blake" as Von Waldman. Holmes and his allies free the true Blake, and discover some fragments of stone. Holmes concludes the Germans believe exposing the *lotus vitae* to the meteor fragments will result in the prolongation of human life. Isis mentions Holmes' own cultivation of the plant. Von Waldman escapes from his bonds, taking the plant with him; however, Holmes still has seeds to grow more. When Watson asks Holmes if he thinks Von Waldman is really the son of Professor Moriarty, Holmes replies that Mycroft's files on the Baron indicate that he was born in 1888, that he was investigating Moriarty quite thoroughly at that time, and that there was no indication of a child born to the Professor in that period. Dickson suggests Von Waldman may have been someone else, much older, who once had access to a similar elixir, but whose supply may have run out, leading him to attempt to find a means of duplicating it.

  Short story by Dr. Watson, edited by Win Scott Eckert in Sherlock Holmes: The Crossovers Casebook, *Howard Hopkins, ed., Moonstone Books, 2012. This story serves as a sequel to Watson's account* The Adventure of the Peerless Peer, *as edited by Philip José Farmer. Watson's wife Nylepthah and child are from that novel; Nylepthah is the daughter of Sir Henry Curtis from the Allan Quatermain stories (although Farmer says she is Curtis' granddaughter, Eckert's essay "Who's Going to Take Over the World When I'm Gone?: A Look at the Genealogies of Wold Newton Family Super-Villains and Their Nemeses"* [Myths for the Modern Age: Philip José Farmer's Wold Newton Universe, *Win Scott Eckert, ed., MonkeyBrain Books, 2005] argues she is in fact his daughter). Nylepthah's cousin, Sir George Curtis, is from Farmer's translation and adaptation of J.-H. Rosny aîné's* Ironcastle; *Farmer specifically identifies Sir George as Sir Henry's nephew. The ape lord is Lord Greystoke, of course. Harry Dickson is "the American Sherlock Holmes" who appeared in French pulp stories by Jean Ray and others. Holmes' rival Cecil Barker first appeared in the story "The Adventure of the Retired Colourman"; Dickson acted as his apprentice in Eckert's story "No Ghosts Need Apply" (*The Phantom Chronicles, Vol. 2, *Joe Gentile and Mike Bullock, eds., Moonstone Books, 2010). Sexton Blake is one of the longest-running British penny dreadful detectives; Dickson acted as his apprentice in Greg Gick's story "The Werewolf of Rutherford Grange" (originally published in two parts in* Tales of the Shadowmen Volume 1: The Modern Babylon, *Jean-Marc and Randy Lofficier, eds., Black Coat Press, 2005, and* Tales of the Shadowmen Volume 2: Gentlemen of the Night, *Jean-Marc and Randy Lofficier, eds., Black Coat Press, 2006; reprinted in* Harry Dickson and the Werewolf of Rutherford Grange, *Black Coat Press, 2011). William Clayton, the 7th Duke of Greystoke, appears in Edgar Rice Burroughs' novels* Tarzan of the Apes *and* The Return of Tarzan;

in his essay "A Case of Identity," H. W. Starr identified the 6th Duke of Holdernesse and his son Lord Saltire from the Holmes story "The Adventure of the Priory School" as the 6th and 7th Duke of Greystoke, respectively, a theory adapted by Farmer for his biography *Tarzan Alive*. Leftenant Drummond is the jungle lord's adopted son John Drummond-Clayton. Farmer identified the human magnetic moment in *Tarzan Alive*. Dr. Shan Ming Fu is Sax Rohmer's Fu Manchu; Dennis E. Power revealed the Devil Doctor's birth name in his essay "The Devil Doctor: The Early History of Fu Manchu," found on the Wold Newton Universe: A Secret History *website*. The *lotus vitae is the plant from which Fu Manchu's life-prolonging* Elixir vitae *is derived;* Fu Manchu told Holmes about the elixir in George Alec Effinger's story "The Adventure of the Celestial Snows." The honey is the Royal Jelly that, according to William S. Baring-Gould in his biography *Sherlock Holmes of Baker Street, has extended Holmes' natural lifespan.* The Hellbirds incident refers to Austin Mitchelson and Nicholas Utechin's Holmes pastiche Hellbirds. Wolf Larsen *is from Jack London's novel* The Sea Wolf; *in his essay "The Green Eyes Have It—Or Are They Blue? Or Another Case of Identity Recased" (*Myths for the Modern Age*), Christopher Paul Carey argued Larsen and Baron von Hessel (from Farmer's authorized Doc Savage novel* Escape from Loki*) were really aliases of XauXaz from Farmer's trilogy of novels about the evil secret society known as the Nine. In his essay "Asian Detectives in the Wold Newton Universe" (*Myths for the Modern Age*), Dennis E. Power instead offered the alternative theory Larsen was the son of Professor Moriarty. Isis and her father Moris Klaw are from Sax Rohmer's book* The Dream Detective. *The Diogenes Club's latter-day focus on outré matters is the subject of many stories by Kim Newman. Blakeney House is one of the holdings of the Blakeney family, whose most famous member is Sir Percy Blakeney, the Scarlet Pimpernel. Blakeney House previously appeared in Eckert's stories "Is He in Hell?" (*Tales of the Shadowmen Volume 6: Grand Guignol*, Jean-Marc and Randy Lofficier, eds., Black Coat Press, 2010; reprinted and revised in* The Worlds of Philip José Farmer 1: Protean Dimensions, *Michael Croteau, ed., Meteor House, 2010) and "Nadine's Invitation" (*Tales of the Shadowmen Volume 7: Femmes Fatales, *Jean-Marc and Randy Lofficier, eds., Black Coat Press, 2010). Peter Blakeney Jr. is Sir Percy's descendant from* The Pimpernel and Rosemary. *In his series of articles "The Wold Wold West" (found at the* Wold Newton Universe: A Secret History *website), Dennis E. Power argued Sexton Blake was distantly related to the Blakeney family, a theory Eckert adopted for his essay "The Blakeney Family Tree" (*The Worlds of Philip José Farmer 1*). Openshaw is from the Holmes story "The Five Orange Pips."*

April. John Masters' first adventure as the Lone Eagle, "No Man's Air" by "Lt. Scott Morgan" (Fred Rechnitzer), *The Lone Eagle,* September 1933. With no particular loyalties, Masters fights for each of the Allied countries in World War I; his greatest enemy is the German female spy known only as R-47. During World War II, a U-boat attack on an ocean liner he is aboard spurs Masters to come out of retirement. R-47's daughter, who uses her mother's codename, becomes his primary nemesis.

Summer
SCOURGE OF THE SKIES

Captain Philip Strange battles a mechanical pterodactyl developed by the Germans to terrify the Allies. Strange claims unnamed "scientists" believe in the existence of dinosaurs living in "an almost impassable jungle in South America." Strange even remembers Harmer, a Canadian explorer, who talked of a "lost world" in "the upper Amazon country."

Story by Donald E. Keyhoe in Flying Aces, *November 1932;* reprinted in The Compleat Adventures of Captain Philip Strange in Flying Aces, Volume 1, *Battered Silicon Dispatch Box, 2011, and* Captain Philip Strange: Strange War, *Age of Aces Books, 2011. Strange is referring to Maple White Land from Arthur Conan Doyle's* The Lost World.

July
THE HUNTERS OF MARS

Leo Saint-Clair (aka the Nyctalope) takes a transport to the Martian city of Helium, where his assistance has been requested by John Carter, Warlord of Mars (aka Barsoom). Carter managed to convince two other Martian races, the Sorns and the Hither People, to join forces with his to drive the invading Cephales from Mars. The Cephales fled to Earth, where they crushed England's armies before falling prey to the planet's bacteria. The surviving members of the colony returned to Mars, where Leo and Oxus prevented them from attacking the newly-created French colony. After the Cephales' defeat, the duo learned of other races on the Red Planet such as the Tharks and the Red Men of Helium. Oxus believes the radium used by the people of Helium might be able to revive an ancient capsule he has discovered in one of the nearby Martian ruins, which apparently contains secrets that could advance the cause of space travel by light years, and end the Great War within a few months. Leo meets with a group consisting of the Thark Tars Tarkas, Carter, and the latter's wife, Dejah Thoris, Princess of Helium. Reports are mentioned of a warrior resembling Carter in ancient Phoenicia, as well as a 13th century "Outlaw of Torn." Carter wishes Leo to investigate the mutilations of several Tharks. Kantos Kan and other Martians gather around the bodies of two murdered palace guards. Leo tells Carter the killer does not operate under the ethical codes of the Tharks, the Sorns, the Hross, the Hither People, or any other known race on Barsoom. He theorizes the killer is a hunter from another world collecting trophies. Leo is well versed in the hunting techniques of Quatermain and Roxton. The hunter, or Predator, is blown up by a device in its gauntlet after being killed, destroying a Thark incubation chamber in the process. Carter says he will take the sole surviving infant to Sola, who will care for him.

Short story by Matthew Dennion in The Nyctalope Steps In, *Jean-Marc and Randy Lofficier, eds., Black Coat Press, 2011; reprinted in French in* Les Compagnons de l'Ombre (Tome 8), *Jean-Marc and Randy Lofficier, eds., Rivière Blanche, 2011. The Nyctalope and Oxus appear in French pulp novels by Jean de La Hire. Helium, Carter, Barsoom, the Tharks, the Red Men, Tars Tarkas, Dejah Thoris, Kantos Kan, and Sola are from Edgar Rice Burroughs'* Mars *novels. The Sorns and the Hross are from C. S. Lewis'* Out of the Silent Planet. *The Hither People are from Edwin Arnold's* Lieutenant Gullivar Jones: His Vacation. *The Cephales (or Kephales) are from de La Hire's* The Great Adventures of a Scout; *here, they are conflated with the Martians from H. G. Wells'* The War of the Worlds. *George Alec Effinger's story "Mars: The Home Front" proposed Wells' Martians (aka the Sarmaks) came from Barsoom, while* The League of Extraordinary Gentlemen, Volume II *depicted Carter's alliance with the Sorns and the Hither People to drive off Wells' Martians. The Nyctalope and Oxus encountered Wells' Martians in de La Hire's* The Nyctalope on Mars. *The capsule is from the British television serial* Quatermass and the Pit. *The Phoenician warrior is the title character of another Edwin Arnold novel,* Phra the Phoenician, *whom Dennis E. Power and Dr. Peter Coogan conflated with the Warlord of Mars in their essay "John Carter: Torn from Phoenician Dreams (An Examination Into the Theories that John Carter was Phra the Phoenician and Norman of Torn)" (*Myths for the Modern Age: Philip José Farmer's Wold Newton Universe, Win Scott Eckert, ed., MonkeyBrain Books, 2005*). The Outlaw of Torn is from the novel of the same name by Burroughs; Philip José Farmer conflated him with Carter in his speech "The Arms of Tarzan," also reprinted in* Myths for the Modern Age. *Quatermain is H. Rider Haggard's Allan Quatermain, while Roxton is Lord John Roxton from Arthur Conan Doyle's* Professor

Challenger tales. The Predator race is featured in a series of science fiction films. The Predators have appeared in several crossover tales in comic books; however, only those crossovers involving Crossover Universe mainstays such as the jungle lord or Mycroft Holmes will be incorporated into CU continuity.

JUSTICE AND POWER

The Nyctalope returns to Earth after the destruction of his Martian colony and the death of his family. He is treated by Dr. Cerral, who objects to him being given a new assignment. The hero's bunkmate on this mission is the Belgian Remy Baudouin. The Nyctalope goes berserk, and the vigilante Judex uses a technique taught to him by the Sâr Dubnotal to rid his fellow hero of his traumatic memories.

Short story by Chris Nigro in Night of the Nyctalope, Jean-Marc and Randy Lofficier, eds., Black Coat Press, 2012; reprinted in French in La Nuit du Nyctalope, Jean-Marc and Randy Lofficier, eds., Rivière Blanche, 2012, and L'Ombre de Judex, Jean-Marc and Randy Lofficier, eds., Rivière Blanche, 2013; and in The Shadow of Judex, Jean-Marc and Randy Lofficier, eds., Black Coat Press, 2013. The Nyctalope is a forerunner to the modern superhero whose stories were written by Jean de La Hire. Dr. Cerral is from Maurice Renard's novel The Hands of Orlac. Remy Baudouin befriended Indiana Jones during World War I, as seen in the television series The Young Indiana Jones Chronicles. Judex is from the serial of the same name directed by Louis Feuillade. The Sâr Dubnotal is an occult investigator who was featured in a French pulp series by an anonymous author.

Summer 1917–Late September 1918
UNDER OUTLAW FLAGS

Roy Tacker's outlaw gang, captured during a bank robbery, is offered the choice of going to prison or joining the army. They choose the latter, and soon find themselves embroiled in a World War. Roy's brother Jace and another member of the gang, Aaron Gault, eventually join the Army Air Corps. Arriving at the Allied aerodrome, they are greeted by men named Wentworth and Allard, who soon depart for a special mission.

The appearance of Richard Wentworth (aka the Spider) and Allard Kent Rassendyll (the man who would become a shadowy pulp hero in novels written by Walter Gibson and others) brings this book by James Reasoner into the CU. Wentworth and Rassendyll are both described as pilots. However, while Allard was indeed a pilot during the entire length of his service in World War I, Wentworth served in the French Air Corps until the United States officially entered the war, at which point he joined the American infantry. Reasoner's novel is primarily narrated by Drew Matthews, another member of the Tacker Gang, in his old age. Drew was not present at Jace and Aaron's encounter with the two future vigilantes. Perhaps his friends heard about Wentworth's service in the French corps at some point, and assumed he was still in it, passing that false info on to Drew when they recounted their exploits to him. Alternatively, the "Wentworth" seen here may in fact be the noted World War I aviator G-8, Wentworth's half-brother and Rassendyll's brother, who did use his elder half-sibling's name at least once, as seen in Farmer's The Adventure of the Peerless Peer.

Autumn
THE BEAST WITHIN
Judex once again does battle with Dr. Cornelius Kramm, leader of the Red Hand, who has revived the werewolf Bertrand Calliet in order to use his blood to create super-soldiers.

Short story by Christofer Nigro in The Shadow of Judex, *Jean-Marc and Randy Lofficier, eds., Black Coat Press, 2013; reprinted in French in* L'Ombre de Judex, *Jean-Marc and Randy Lofficier, eds., Rivière Blanche, 2013. Judex is from Louis Feuillade's classic film serial. Dr. Cornelius Kramm and his criminal syndicate, the Red Hand, are from Gustave Le Rouge's* Le Mystérieux Dr. Cornélius. *Judex first encountered Kramm in Matthew Baugh's story "Mask of the Monster" (*Tales of the Shadowmen Volume One: The Modern Babylon, *Jean-Marc and Randy Lofficier, eds., Black Coat Press, 2005; reprinted in* The Shadow of Judex*). Bertrand Calliet is the title character of Guy Endore's novel* The Werewolf of Paris.

RAID OF THE RED REAPER
Captain Philip Strange battles an agent of a disfigured German scientist, Garst, who is trying to unleash the Red Death, a plague that had ravaged Europe in the Middle Ages.

Story by Donald E. Keyhoe in Flying Aces, *March 1935; reprinted in* The Compleat Adventures of Captain Philip Strange in Flying Aces, Volume 2, *Battered Silicon Dispatch Box, 2011, and* Captain Philip Strange: Strange Enemies, *Age of Aces Books, 2012. The Red Death is clearly the same plague* seen in Edgar Allan Poe's "The Masque of the Red Death," which is also referenced in The New Traveler's Almanac *text piece in* The League of Extraordinary Gentlemen, Volume II. *Rick Lai notes, "Garst is only mentioned in 'Raid of the Red Reaper.' Garst seems to be Von Garst, the disfigured villain who battled the Vanished Legion in Keyhoe's 'The Squadron of Forgotten Men.' The Vanished Legion was another World War I series by Keyhoe. All of the stories in this series were reprinted in* The Vanished Legion, *another Age of Aces collection."*

BLOOD AND FIRE

A libertine falls prey to two female vampires, one of whom is named Carody. The womanizer's friend Dr. Orlof was also bitten by the two women.

Short story by Artikel Unbekannt in The Vampire Almanac (Volume 1), *Jean-Marc and Randy Lofficier, eds., Black Coat Press, 2015; reprinted in French in* L'Almanach des Vampires (Tome 2), *Jean-Marc and Randy Lofficier, eds., Rivière Blanche, 2015. The Countess Nadine Carody is from Jesús Franco's film* Vampyros Lesbos, *while Dr. Orlof (also spelled Orloff) is from Franco's film* The Awful Dr. Orloff *and its sequels. The year is conjecture.*

1918

Winter
DEAD MEN'S BONES

Charles St. Cyprian, Sergeant Bass of the American 81st Infantry Division, and Thomas Carnacki are camped outside the fortress of Ylourgne in the province of Averoigne. St. Cyprian had to leave the company of a young woman he met at the cabaret in Vyones in order to go on this mission. Carnacki says he believes there is an oil painting of Ylourgne, or rather the Chateau de Faussesflammes, in the Louvre. The adventures of Carnacki, England's present Royal Occultist, appeared in the pages of *The Idler*, just as those of the Great Detective had

appeared in *The Strand*. Corpses throughout Averoigne are coming back as zombies, in places such as Vyones, Les Hiboux, and Ximes. The Isoile is mentioned. Professor Max Ewer tells the trio Ylourgne was the site of one of the greatest acts of alchemical diabolism in this age or any other, according to the writings of one Gaspard du Nord: a dwarf named Nathaire made a giant monster out of dead men's bones, which rampaged through Vyones. Carnacki refers to the 266 Squadron RFC.

Short story by Josh Reynolds in Kaiju Rising: Age of Monsters, Tim Marquitz and Nickolas Sharps, eds., Ragnarok Publications, 2014. Charles St. Cyprian is the protagonist of Reynolds' Royal Occultist stories, which take place after he has assumed the role previously played by Carnacki. Sergeant Bass is John Bass, an occult detective from Jackapo, South Carolina featured in several of Reynolds' stories. Thomas Carnacki appeared in stories by William Hope Hodgson published in The Idler, which were later collected as Carnacki the Ghost-Finder. Ylourgne, Averoigne, Vyones, the Chateau de Faussesflammes, Les Hiboux, Ximes, the Isoile River, Gaspard du Nord, and Nathaire are from the works of Clark Ashton Smith. This marks the second attempt by a madman to create their own version of Nathaire's Colossus during the Great War; the first was in 1916, as seen in Matthew Baugh's "What Rough Beast." The Great Detective is Sherlock Holmes. The 266 Squadron RFC, from W. E. Johns' Biggles books, is not to be confused with the real 266 Squadron RAF.

THE BLOOD OF FRANKENSTEIN

Dr. Herbert West tells Gouroull, the monster created by Victor Frankenstein, about his discovery of the notes of a nobleman named de Musard, and that they will need the blood of a vampire lord to create a mate for Gouroull. Gouroull suggests Dracula in Transylvania, or Karnstein in Styria. West says Dracula has created copies of himself in many parts of the world. Gouroull travels to China, and the village of Ping Kwei. Gouroull has heard tales of seven immortals called *Jiangshi* that live in a temple in the hills. A group of martial artists battles the seven golden vampires. Gouroull comes face to face with Dracula, who initially identifies himself as the high priest Kah.

Short story by Frank Schildiner in Tales of the Shadowmen Volume 10: Esprit de Corps, *Jean-Marc and Randy Lofficier, eds., Black Coat Press, 2013; reprinted in* The Vampire Almanac (Volume 1), *Jean-Marc and Randy Lofficier, eds., Black Coat Press, 2015; and in French in* L'Almanach des Vampires, *Jean-Marc and Randy Lofficier, eds., Rivière Blanche, 2014. Dr. Herbert West is from H. P. Lovecraft's "Herbert West—Reanimator." Victor Frankenstein and his creation are from Mary Shelley's novel* Frankenstein.

The monster was given the name Gouroull in stories by Jean-Claude Carrière. De Musard is a relative of Baron de Musard from Philip José Farmer's authorized Doc Savage novel Escape from Loki. Dracula needs no introduction at this point. Karnstein is from J. Sheridan Le Fanu's vampire tale Carmilla. *The village of Ping Kwei, the seven immortals, and Kah are from* the Hammer Dracula film The Legend of the 7 Golden Vampires. *In that film, Dracula transforms Kah into a duplicate of himself;* this served as the primary basis for Chuck Loridans' theory regarding Dracula creating "soul-clones" of himself in order to carry out his plans while he is lying dormant in his coffin filled with Transylvanian soil. *The various martial artists, all inspired by, but not actually meant to be, characters and actors from Chinese martial arts films, are Chien Fu (*Snake in the Eagle's Shadow*), Muscular Lo (*Kid with the Golden Arm*), Lady Swallow (*Come Drink with Me *and* Golden Swallow*), One-Armed Fang (*The One-Armed Swordsman *and* Return of the One-Armed Swordsman*), and Liu (*The 36th Chamber of Shaolin*). The events of this story take place during those of Schildiner's novel* The Quest of Frankenstein, *which spans the years 1914–1918, and therefore the 1925 date assigned to the story is incorrect.*

Spring
THE ADVENTURE OF THE NIGHT HUNTER

Sherlock Holmes and Professor Challenger battle an alien creature that literally hunts humans. It is stated Holmes "knew more about human speech than any man in London, except, perhaps, old Higgens, of course..."

Short story by Ralph E. Vaughan in The Great Detective: His Further Adventures, *Gary Lovisi, ed., Wildside Press, 2013. The Night Hunter is a member of the alien race seen in the* Predator *film series. The Predators have had crossovers with a number of other properties; only those involving characters that have already been established as existing in the CU are included here. "Old Higgens" is a reference to Professor Henry Higgins from George Bernard Shaw's play* Pygmalion, *adapted as the musical* My Fair Lady.

1919

January 15–16
BLACK AND GOLD

Leo Saint-Clair (aka the Nyctalope) meets with *Président du Conseil* Valenglay, who tells him about the Black Corsair, who in 1912 stole a revolutionary prototype submarine from the French military, something Lupin also did in 1902. The Black Corsair acquired a deadly strain of plague from the enigmatic Asian mastermind sometimes known as Doctor Natas.

Short story by Emmanuel Gorlier in Enter the Nyctalope, *Jean-Marc and Randy Lofficier, eds., Black Coat Press, 2009;* reprinted in French in Les Compagnons de L'Ombre (Tome 5), *Jean-Marc and Randy Lofficier, eds., Rivière Blanche, 2009. The Nyctalope is the hero of a series of novels by Jean de La Hire. The Black Corsair is from de La Hire's serial story* The Undersea Corsair. *Valenglay is from Maurice Leblanc's Arsène Lupin novels* 813 *and* The Teeth of the Tiger. *Lupin's 1902 submarine theft was chronicled in Leblanc's story "The Seven of Hearts." Doctor Natas is from Guy d'Armen's novel* Doc Ardan: City of Gold and Lepers. *Jean-Marc and Randy Lofficier's adaptation and translation of that book implied Natas was really Sax Rohmer's criminal mastermind Doctor Fu Manchu.*

Winter
DEAD MAN'S TONGUE

Harley Warren and Randolph Carter encounter a *rolang*, a living dead man created in Tibet. Carter, briefly thinking they have stumbled on a Nordic rite, expresses his eagerness to tell Conrad and Kirowan.

Short story by Josh Reynolds in The Dark Rites of Cthulhu, *Brian M. Sammons, ed., April Moon Books, 2014. Harley Warren and Randolph Carter are from H. P. Lovecraft's Dream Cycle stories. John Conrad and John Kirowan appeared in a series of stories by Robert E. Howard.*

Spring
IN THE CAVES OF THE SERPENT
Francis X. "El Borak" Gordon and his companion Masa encounter a woman named Orlando, who has been assigned to work with them. Orlando tells Gordon the desert is inhabited by the followers of Ubasti. The trio is attacked by a group of Serpent Men. Orlando swears by Crom. The man Orlando is trying to rescue is Issac Laquedem, the Wandering Jew. Issac is accompanied by his daughter, the spectral Lotte. Orlando says MacLeod, the Sâr Dubnotal, and Doctor Omega have also been searching for Issac. The Serpent Men serve Elder Gods, and wish to sacrifice Issac using a Hattori Hanzo sword once belonging to Orlando.

Short story by Travis Hiltz in Tales of the Shadowmen Volume 8: Agents Provocateurs, *Jean-Marc and Randy Lofficier, eds., Black Coat Press, 2011; reprinted in French in* Les Compagnons de L'Ombre (Tome 10), *Jean-Marc and Randy Lofficier, eds., Rivière Blanche, 2012. El Borak and Masa appear in several stories by Robert E. Howard. Orlando is the titular gender-switching immortal from Virginia Woolf's novel; his/her affiliation with British Intelligence in this story is consistent with his/her activities in Alan Moore and Kevin O'Neill's comic book series* The League of Extraordinary Gentlemen. *The Cult of Ubasti is from the serial* The Return of Chandu, *and also appears in Hiltz's story "The Treasure of the Ubasti" (*Tales of the Shadowmen Volume 6: Grand Guignol, *Jean-Marc and Randy Lofficier, eds., Black Coat Press, 2009). The Serpent Men are from Robert E. Howard's King Kull stories, while Crom is from Howard's Conan stories. Issac Laquedem and Lotte are from Paul Féval's novel* The Wandering Jew's Daughter. *MacLeod is Connor Macleod from the* Highlander *film series. The Sâr Dubnotal is an occult investigator from a French pulp series by an anonymous author. Doctor Omega is from the novel of the same name by Arnould Galopin, which has been adapted and translated into English by Jean-Marc and Randy Lofficier for Black Coat Press. The Elder Gods appear prominently in the Cthulhu Mythos. Hattori Hanzo is a historical figure, though both he and his descendants were portrayed by Sonny Chiba in the Japanese television series* Shadow Warriors. *In Quentin Tarantino's film* Kill Bill: Vol. 1, *Chiba played a modern-day swordsmith named Hattori Hanzo. Tarantino has confirmed the Hanzo in* Kill Bill *is a descendant of the Hanzo family featured in* Shadow Warriors. *The Hanzo who made Orlando's sword must be another member of the same family.*

THE UNWRAPPING PARTY

Charles St. Cyprian, the Royal Occultist, lives at 472 Cheyne Walk. St. Cyprian had been an apprentice to Thomas Carnacki before the Great War, just as Carnacki had been to Edwin Drood. St. Cyprian owns lurid artwork by Goya, Blake, and Pickman. The Royal Occultists' library once included books by Dee, Strange, and Subtle, as well as lost Pnakotic texts. St. Cyprian receives an invitation from the Esoteric Order of Thoth-Ra, which has poached members from the Mausoleum Club, the Bell Club, and the Drones. The self-proclaimed Grand Vizier of the Esoteric Order is Edward Bellingham. St. Cyprian remembers listening to Carnacki's stories with Dodgson and Arkwright and others. St. Cyprian refers to the ancient Egyptians' obsession with cats, including "whole temples devoted to Ulthar's own, what?" Going up against the Sisterhood of the Rats or the Si-Fan is not something St. Cyprian looks forward to. St. Cyprian recognizes the scent of a mixture of certain strange unguents, having been shown how to mix them by Carnacki, from a recipe recorded in the Sigsand Manuscript. Bellingham intends to unwrap the mummy of Nephren-Ka, the Black Pharaoh. The cult leader says Nephren-Ka was the equal to the sorcerer kings of the lost antediluvian kingdoms named in the Chaldean Fragments or the Cimmerian Scrolls. St. Cyprian learned how to open his spirit eye from a Tibetan lama of his acquaintance, who has what St. Cyprian considers an unhealthy fascination for the color green. St. Cyprian thinks that Nephren-Ka was already dead, "and what was dead could likely eternal lie, to misquote Alhazred."

Short story by Josh Reynolds in Pro Se Presents, Lee Houston, Jr., ed., *Pro Se Press, August 2012. Thomas Carnacki, "the Ghost-Finder," appeared in a series of stories by William Hope Hodgson. Carnacki lived at 472 Cheyne Walk in Hodgson's stories. The Carnacki stories were presented as tales being told by Carnacki to his friends, including Arkwright and Dodgson. The Sigsand Manuscript is also from the Carnacki tales. According to the Royal Occultist stories, Carnacki died at the hands of a sniper in Ypres in 1918. Given that several stories set after 1918 feature or refer to a still-living Carnacki, this was most likely a deception, after which Carnacki allowed St. Cyprian to take over his position as Royal Occultist and home at Cheyne Walk, letting only St. Cyprian and a few other allies know he was still alive. Edwin Drood is from Charles Dickens' unfinished novel* The Mystery of Edwin Drood. *Pickman is painter Richard Upton Pickman from H. P. Lovecraft's story "Pickman's Model." Pnakotic texts are a reference to the* Pnakotic Manuscripts, *which appear in several stories of Lovecraft's Cthulhu Mythos. Ulthar is from Lovecraft's story "The Cats of Ulthar." Nephren-Ka is from another Lovecraft story, "The Haunter of the Dark." In the Cthulhu Mythos, Abdul Alhazred is the author of the* Necronomicon, which includes the line "That is not dead which can eternal lie, and with strange aeons even death may die," as quoted in "The Call of Cthulhu." Strange is probably an ancestor of Dr. Stephen Strange, aka the Sorcerer Supreme, a character published by Marvel Comics. Subtle is from Ben Jonson's play The Alchemist. The Mausoleum Club is from the British radio comedy show Tales from the Mausoleum Club. The Bell Club is from the anthology Tales from the Bell Club, edited by Paul Mannering. The Drones Club counts many of P. G. Wodehouse's characters among its members. Some of the Drones Club stories were collected as Tales from the Drones Club. Edward Bellingham is from Arthur Conan Doyle's short story "Lot No. 249." The Si-Fan is the secret society run by Fu Manchu in Sax Rohmer's novels. Cimmeria is the home of Robert E. Howard's barbarian Conan. The Tibetan lama is Kendall Crossen's pulp hero the Green Lama.

May 5
REVENGE OF THE REANIMATOR

Robert Peaslee writes a letter to his wife Hannah describing his visit to Locus Solus in Montmartre, the estate of Dr. Martial Canterel. Peaslee, a native of Arkham, is met by a colleague of his, a young veteran named Gatsby. Peaslee mentions his father, Professor Nathaniel Peaslee. Canterel says he believes a goggle-eyed light fixture he owns to be a piece of Nemo's *Nautilus*. Canterel confuses Peaslee for Dr. Herbert West, a member of the faculty at Miskatonic, with whom he worked on a reagent long ago. His own reagent, Resurrectine, is based on their past work, and can bring the dead back to life. Canterel says he infuses *Vril* energy into the reagent during formulation.

Short story by Pete Rawlik in Tales of the Shadowmen Volume 10: Esprit de Corps, Jean-Marc and Randy Lofficier, eds., Black Coat Press, 2013; reprinted in French in Les Compagnons de l'Ombre (Tome 14), Jean-Marc and Randy Lofficier, eds., Rivière Blanche, 2014. Robert Peaslee, his wife Hannah, and his father, Professor Nathaniel Wingate Peaslee, are from H. P. Lovecraft's "The Shadow Out of Time." Arkham, Massachusetts and

Miskatonic University play prominent roles in Lovecraft's Cthulhu Mythos. Dr. Herbert West is from Lovecraft's "Herbert West—Reanimator." Locus Solus, Dr. Martial Canterel, and Resurrectine are from Raymond Roussel's novel Locus Solus. Jay Gatsby is from F. Scott Fitzgerald's The Great Gatsby. Captain Nemo and his Nautilus are from Jules Verne's 20,000 Leagues Under the Sea and The Mysterious Island. The Vril energy is from Edward Bulwer-Lytton's novel The Coming Race.

Summer
ROY COLT AND WINCHESTER JACK
A Russian outlaw called the Reverend refers to an Indian woman named Manila as "woman called Horse."

1970 Spaghetti Western directed by Mario Bava. Dorothy M. Johnson's story "A Man Called Horse" features a white man who is captured by Crow Indians and is eventually made a member of the tribe, taking the name Horse. The Reverend must have heard of Horse, and used his name as an ethnic slur against Manila. Since "A Man Called Horse" takes place in the CU, so does this film. The year is conjecture, though the Reverend's references to his hatred of revolutions and his friend Rasputin indicate these events take place after the Russian revolution of 1917.

EVERY ROSE
Judex, impersonating an English reporter visiting Italy, asks Magistrate Buratti to let him see the imprisoned strongman Maciste, who has been accused of murder. Judex mentions alchemists such as Paracelsus, Praetorius, Cagliostro, and Frankenstein. Buratti suggests the disguised hero visit Professor Teone. The Professor tells Judex and the Magistrate the story of a doctor named Rappaccini, whose daughter Beatrice was both immune to poisons and poisonous herself. Judex rescues a woman named Gina from the real killer, the monster named Gouroull.

Short story by Thom Brannan and Matthew Baugh in The Shadow of Judex, *Jean-Marc and Randy Lofficier, eds., Black Coat Press, 2013; reprinted in French in* L'Ombre de Judex, *Jean-Marc and Randy Lofficier, eds., Rivière Blanche, 2013. Judex is the title character of Louis Feuillade's film serial. Magistrate Buratti is an ancestor of private eye Marco Buratti, who appears in a series of novels by Massimo Carlotto. Maciste first appeared in the silent film* Cabiria *in 1914, and continued to appear in films until 1928. He was later revived for a series of films in the 1960s. Maciste must be immortal, or at least very long-lived. Gouroull is better known as Frankenstein's Monster; his nom de guerre comes from novels by Jean-Claude Carrière. Gouroull first encountered Judex in Baugh's short story "Mask of the Monster."* Dr. Praetorius is from the Universal horror film The Bride of Frankenstein. *Professor Teone is an ancestor of Dr. Hipazia Teone from* Fable of Venice, *the 25th entry in Hugo Pratt's comic book series* Corto Maltese. *Rappaccini and his daughter Beatrice are from Nathaniel Hawthorne's short story "Rappaccini's Daughter." Gina is from Hayao Miyazaki's animated film* Porco Rosso.

THE SEPIA PRINTS

A member of the security force for the American delegation to the Treaty of Versailles is on leave after an incident involving a strange estate on the outskirts of Paris and a disreputable doctor who, like him, is from Arkham. A woman gives the unnamed man a collection of photographs from the Paris Opera House's 1899 production of *The King in Yellow* before committing suicide. Rumors about the opera being haunted came to a head in the early 1880s with the strange affair of the Opera Ghost. The man meets Moncharmin, the Opera's librarian, who appeared in the play.

Short story by Pete Rawlik *in* In the Court of the Yellow King, *Glynn Owen Barrass, ed., Celaeno Press, 2014. The story's unnamed narrator is Robert Peaslee from H. P. Lovecraft's "The Shadow Out of Time." The disreputable doctor is Martial Canterel, the owner of the titular estate in Raymond Roussel's novel* Locus Solus. *Peaslee encountered Canterel in Rawlik's story "Revenge of the Reanimator." Arkham, Massachusetts is the setting of a number of Lovecraft's Cthulhu Mythos stories. The Opera Ghost and Moncharmin are from Gaston Leroux's novel* The Phantom of the Opera.

July
THE YLOURGNE ACCORDS

Lt. Peaslee has left Paris after his experiences at Locus Solus and the Paris Opera House, and is now acting as security for a conference on reanimation in the province of Averoigne, in the ruins of the ancient fortress Ylourgne. Averoigne's only city is Vyones. Peaslee hears references to a "Beast of Averoigne" he takes to be a werewolf, not unlike the tale of the Brotherhood of the Wolf which had plagued Gévaudan. Peaslee's client is industrialist Meldrum Strange, whose son Hugo is studying medicine at Peaslee's alma mater, Miskatonic University. The attendees at the conference include Dr. Astrov of Russia, General Mazovia of the Polish Republic, Dr. Lorde and General Duval of Paris, von Schelling and Dr. Miklos Sangre of Austria, Richard Steadman of Britain, and Dr. Cornelius Kramm, former leader of the Red Hand crime syndicate, of Germany. Strange gives Peaslee files that have pictures of Doctor Herbert West, Daniel Cain, and Major Doctor Sir Eric Moreland Clapham-Lee. General von Schelling says Austria's agents have obtained Herr Frankenstein's notebooks. Steadman says Frankenstein, West, Cain, Hartwell, and Tsiang should have left well enough alone. In the files, Peaslee reads about Victor Frankenstein's descendant Henry, as well as the mysterious Dr. Pretorius. The Sâr Dubnotal delivers a warning to Peaslee. Peaslee reads in Friedrich Wilhelm Von Juntz's *Unaussprechlichen Kulten* about Gaspard du Nord, a would-be wizard who in the spring of 1281 battled the necromancer Nathaire, who resurrected the bodies of dead soldiers and merged them into an unholy Colossus. Lt. Peaslee discovers "Steadman" is really the reanimated Major Sir Eric Moreland Clapham-Lee.

Short story by Pete Rawlik in Tales of the Shadowmen Volume 11: Force Majeure, *Jean-Marc and Randy Lofficier, eds., Black Coat Press, 2014; reprinted in French in* Les Compagnons de l'Ombre (Tome 16), *Jean-Marc and Randy Lofficier, eds., Rivière Blanche, 2015. Robert Peaslee is from H. P. Lovecraft's story "The Shadow Out of Time." Peaslee's experience at Locus Solus (from Raymond Roussel's titular novel) was depicted in Rawlik's story "Revenge of the Reanimator" (*Tales of the Shadowmen Volume 10: Esprit de Corps, *Jean-Marc and Randy Lofficier, eds., Black Coat Press, 2013), while the affair at the Paris Opera House was recounted in "The Sepia Prints" (*In the Court of the Yellow King, *Glynn Owen Barrass, ed., Celaeno Press, 2014). Averoigne, Ylourgne, Vyonnes, the Beast of Averoigne, Gaspard du Nord, Nathaire, and the Colossus are from the fiction of Clark Ashton Smith. The Brotherhood of the Wolf is from Christophe Gans' 2001 film of the same name. Meldrum Strange is a recurring character in the works of Talbot Mundy. Dr. Hugo Strange is one of Batman's earliest recurring foes. Miskatonic University appears in a number of Lovecraft's Cthulhu Mythos tales. Dr. Astrov is from Anton Chekhov's play* Uncle Vanya. *General Mazovia, General Duval, General von Schelling, and Tsiang are from the movie* Revolt of the Zombies. *Dr. Lorde is from Cyril-Berger's novel* L'Expérience du Dr Lorde. *Dr. Miklos Sangre is from the movie* King of the Zombies. *Dr. Cornelius Kramm and his Red Hand syndicate are from*

Gustave Le Rouge's serial novel The Mysterious Doctor Cornelius, *which is available from Black Coat Press in a three-volume edition translated by Brian Stableford. Doctor Herbert West and Major Doctor Sir Eric Moreland Clapham-Lee are from Lovecraft's story "Herbert West—Reanimator." The Major also uses the name "Richard Steadman" in Robert M. Price, Peter Cannon, Will Murray, Donald R. Burleson, and Charles Hoffman's round-robin story "Herbert West—Reanimated."Victor Frankenstein is from Mary Shelley's novel* Frankenstein. *Daniel Cain is meant to be the unnamed narrator of "Herbert West—Reanimator"; his name comes from the film* Re-Animator, *loosely based on Lovecraft's story. Dr. Stuart Asa Hartwell is a minor character from Lovecraft's story "The Dunwich Horror"; his involvement in reanimation experiments was revealed in Rawlik's novel* Reanimators, *which must take place in an alternate reality to the CU due to several continuity conflicts. Obviously, the CU version of Hartwell was involved in similar research. Henry Frankenstein and Dr. Pretorius are from Universal Studios' Frankenstein films. Mark K. Brown proposed Henry was a descendant of Victor Frankenstein in his article "The House of Frankenstein," found on the website* An Expansion of Philip José Farmer's Wold Newton Universe. *The Sâr Dubnotal was an occult detective featured in a French pulp series by an anonymous writer. Robert E. Howard created Friedrich Wilhelm Von Juntz and his book* Unaussprechlichen Kulten *as part of the Cthulhu Mythos.*

THE VALLEY OF THE LOST

Professor Challenger and Edward Malone explore a plateau in Big Hole Valley, Montana, which is inhabited by creatures from the last Ice Age, an old blind man called the Pastor who came there on a gold-hunting expedition in the 1870s, and a race of hairy wee folk.

Story by Edward Malone, edited by William Meikle in Professor Challenger: The Kew Growths and Other Stories, *Dark Renaissance Books, 2014. The plateau, the Pastor, and the wee folk are from Meikle's novel* The Valley. *This story takes place in July, shortly after the death of Professor Challenger's wife, which Rick Lai's essay "The Anomaly of Professor Challenger's Daughter" (Rick Lai's Secret Histories: Daring Adventurers, Altus Press, 2008) placed in 1919.*

November
VON BORK'S PRIORITIES

Von Bork, seeking revenge on Sherlock Holmes, gains employment in a British hotel. He and his co-worker Cartwright examine the body of one of the guests, who had in his possession plans for a super-weapon. Chief Inspector Teal arrives to investigate, as does Chantecoq, the so-called "King of Detectives." Holmes himself is aiding Teal on the case.

Short story by Nigel Malcolm in Tales of the Shadowmen Volume 10: Esprit de Corps, *Jean-Marc and Randy Lofficier, eds., Black Coat Press, 2013; reprinted in French in* Les Compagnons de l'Ombre (Tome 16), *Jean-Marc and Randy Lofficier, eds., Rivière Blanche, 2015. Von Bork is from Arthur Conan Doyle's Sherlock Holmes story "His Last Bow"; he was last seen in Win Scott Eckert's story "The Adventure of the Fallen Stone." After that story, Von Bork was evidently placed in a British prison, and released at the end of the War, only to discover his wife had remarried, prompting him to once again return to England for vengeance on the Great Detective. Cartwright is from perhaps the most famous Holmes tale,* The Hound of the Baskervilles. *Inspector Claude Eustace Teal is a foe of Leslie Charteris' dashing adventurer Simon Templar, alias the Saint. Chantecoq appears in novels by Arthur Bernède, as well as the serial* Belphégor.

THE DREAMING DEAD

Charles St. Cyprian, England's Royal Occultist, remarks "That which is not dead is eternally annoying." St. Cyprian's predecessor was Thomas Carnacki, who in turned succeeded Edwin Drood.

Short story by Josh Reynolds in Horror for the Holidays, *Scott David Aniolowski, Miskatonic River Press, 2011. St. Cyprian is paraphrasing a passage from the* Necronomicon *that appears in Lovecraft's "The Call of Cthulhu": "That is not dead which can eternal lie and with strange eons, even death may die." Thomas Carnacki is from William Hope Hodgson's* Carnacki the Ghost-Finder. *Edwin Drood is from Charles Dickens' unfinished novel* The Mystery of Edwin Drood.

November–December
PARTING THE VEIL

Edward Malone learned about the concept of Faraday cages from one of his friend Carnacki's dinner stories.

Story by Edward Malone, edited by William Meikle in Professor Challenger: The Kew Growths and Other Stories, *Dark Renaissance Books, 2014.*

November 21
FROM THE NOTEBOOKS OF DR. LYNDON PARKER

Mr. Howard Robinson, a potential client of Solar Pons, tells the detective, "I looked in on Thorndyke, but he was in Scotland. I took the liberty of coming to you without an appointment."

Story by August Derleth in A Praed Street Dossier, *Mycroft & Moran, 1968. This reference confirms Pons exists in the same universe as R. Austin Freeman's sleuth, Dr. John Evelyn Thorndyke.*

December
THE ULTIMATE PRIZE

Judex duels with Count Dracula, who has turned actress and dancer Gabrielle Deslys into a vampire like himself. Private detective Prosper Cocantin, Judex's ally, tells the vigilante Inspector Maigret is investigating the disappearances of Dracula and Gabrielle's victims.

Short story by Christofer Nigro in The Shadow of Judex, *Jean-Marc and Randy Lofficier, eds., Black Coat Press, 2013; reprinted in* The Vampire Almanac (Volume 1), *Jean-Marc and Randy Lofficier, eds., Black Coat Press, 2015; and in French in* L'Almanach des Vampires, *Jean-Marc and Randy Lofficier, eds., Rivière Blanche, 2014. Judex and Cocantin are from the classic film serial directed by Louis Feuillade. Dracula requires no explanation. Gabrielle Deslys was a real person who allegedly died in 1920 of a throat infection caused by influenza, which she contracted in December 1919. This story reveals the true circumstances of her death. Inspector Jules Maigret is the protagonist of a series of mystery novels by Georges Simenon.*

Christmas
MERRY JOHN MOCK

Charles St. Cyprian and Ebe Gallowglass visit the island of Lecach to search for Georgie Craye, the niece of the Earl of Worplesdon. St. Cyprian's acquaintance Jessop says Craye, his sweetheart, has been kidnapped. Gallowglass refers to "that dratted Wickham woman's party." When St. Cyprian says he thought she loved Bobbie's parties, Gallowglass replies she'd "rather suck on a loaded carbine than put up with Wickham and Wooster and the rest of that lot." Jessop is a former member of Thomas Carnacki's circle, as was Arkwright. St. Cyprian learned how to open his spirit-eye from a Tibetan lama with an unhealthy fascination for the color green. Jessop tells St. Cyprian about a local folk legend called Merry John Mock, a sort of friendly swineherd, prompting St. Cyprian to say "A daemon swineherd by any other name, I suppose." When Jessop doesn't understand the reference, St. Cyprian says it's something he once heard. Merry John Mock is revealed to be the Celtic god Moccus, whom Carnacki once encountered, though he only knew the deity as "the Hog." At that time, Moccus was looking to possess a man named Baines.

 Short story by Josh Reynolds in PulpWork Christmas Special, *Pulp-Work Press, 2011. The Earl of Worplesdon, Bobbie Wickham, and Bertie Wooster are from P. G. Wodehouse's Jeeves novels and short stories. Jessop, Thomas Carnacki, Arkwright, the Hog, and Baines are from William Hope Hodgson's book* Carnacki the Ghost-Finder. *The Tibetan lama with an unholy fascination for the color green is Kendell Crossen's hero Jethro Dumont, aka the Green Lama, who appeared in the pulp magazine* Double Detective. *In H. P. Lovecraft's "The Rats in the Walls," the protagonist, Delapore, has nightmares involving a "daemon swineherd."*

1920

January
THE WHITECHAPEL DEMON

 The title of Royal Occultist, once held by Thomas Carnacki, has been passed to Charles St. Cyprian, who battles a demonic being that has assumed the persona of Jack the Ripper alongside his assistant, Ebe Gallowglass. St. Cyprian quotes, "That is not dead which can eternal lie and with strange eons, even death may die." St. Cyprian accuses Robert Gladstone of using a mummy to murder Colonel Warburton and Bertie Moore. One of the members of the Whitechapel Club that summons the demon uses the name Mr. Eddowes, and tells Mr. Kelly, Mr. Nichols, and

Mr. Chapman to align themselves to three cardinal points, according to Prinn's translation of the Incantation of Raaaee. Carnacki allowed a fellow named Dodgson to write about him for *The Idler*, and once acted as an apprentice to Edwin Drood. St. Cyprian has inherited Carnacki's residence at No. 427 Cheyne Walk. Prince Rupert of the Rhine, a previous Royal Occultist, gathered a library that included books by Dee, Strange, and Subtle, as well as lost Pnakotic texts, but that collection was ultimately burned by Oliver Cromwell's men. Morris, an employee of the Ministry of Esoteric Observation, asks St. Cyprian to look into the murders of several people in Whitechapel; St. Cyprian agrees in exchange for a look at Gough-Thomas' 1867 translation of the *Livre d'Eibon*. St. Cyprian asks his apprentice, Ebe Gallowglass, if a spiritualist residing in the house where the murders occurred owned a copy of *The Revelations of Glaaki* or Harzan's monograph on lupine waveform entities. St. Cyprian traces the Voorish Sign in the air. St. Cyprian asks if Morris is familiar with the Sigsand Manuscript and Morris replies by asking if the deaths were the result of a *Saiitii* manifestation. St. Cyprian mentions an affair regarding a man named Bains Carnacki was involved in before the War. A member of the Whitechapel Club called Stack says St. Cyprian was associated with Carnacki before the war, along with Arkwright and Dodgson, and mentions St. Cyprian is a member of the Drones. Morris visits St. Cyprian and Gallowglass, accompanied by men named Mr. Haddo and Mr. Booth. Gallowglass suggests taking Aife Andraste, the medium who conjured up the *faux* Ripper, to St. Cyprian's Rosicrucian pal's place, up the road, or to "that old fraud Klaw, in the East End." St. Cyprian tells Gallowglass to go to the cabinet in his office and get some oil of Hyssop, a vial of the powder of Ibn Ghazi, and Carnacki's electric pentacle. Edwin Drood once faced a *tulpa* that served as a doppelganger to its creator; this encounter was supposedly distorted into a morality play and given a gloss of science by Robert Louis Stevenson. Attempting to remove traces of the Ripper demon from Andraste's body, Gallowglass makes the lines of the second sign of the Saaamaaa Ritual within a circle of water, and St. Cyprian traces sacred shapes from the Third and Fourth Rituals of Hloh in the air. Among the books in St. Cyprian's library are du Nord's *Liber Ivonie* in the original French, Artephous' *Key of Wisdom*, a concise collected edition of the *Seven Cryptical Books of Hsan*, Armstrong's English translation of *The Book of Minor Grotesques*, the pamphlet edition of *The Zanthu Tablets*, a partial Negus translation of *The Book of Iod*, *The Garden of Forking Paths* by Ts'ui Pen, and *The Oldest Rite* by Arkady Cottonwood. St. Cyprian refers to an acquaintance named Warren, and later mentions "those boxing lessons I got from Captain Drummond that night in Marseille." St. Cyprian does not look forward to going up against the Sisterhood of the Rats or the Si-Fan.

Novel by Josh Reynolds, Emby Press, 2013. Thomas Carnacki, the Incantation of Raaaee, Dodgson, No. 427 Cheyne Walk, Harzan, the Sigsand Manuscript, Saiitii manifestations, Bains, Arkwright, the electric pentacle, and the Saaamaaa Ritual *are from William Hope Hodgson's* Carnacki the Ghost-Finder. *The quote "That is not dead which can eternal lie and with strange eons, even death may die" is from the* Necronomicon, *as cited in H. P. Lovecraft's "The Call of Cthulhu." The Pnakotic texts are a reference to the Pnakotic Manuscripts that appear in Lovecraft's Cthulhu Mythos. The Voorish Sign and the powder of Ibn Ghazi are from Lovecraft's "The Dunwich Horror." The* Seven Cryptical Books of Hsan *are mentioned in Lovecraft's tales "The Other Gods" and "The Dream-Quest of Unknown Kadath." Harley Warren is from Lovecraft's story "The Statement of Randolph Carter." "Colonel Warburton's madness" is the subject of an unchronicled Sherlock Holmes case mentioned in "The Adventure of the Engineer's Thumb." Prinn is Ludwig Prinn, the author of* De Vermis Mysteriis, *from Robert Bloch's "The Shambler from the Stars." Edwin Drood is from Charles Dickens' unfinished novel* The Mystery of Edwin Drood. *Strange is an ancestor of the Marvel Comics magician Doctor Strange. Subtle is from Ben Jonson's play* The Alchemist. *The* Livre d'Eibon *is Gaspard du Nord's translation of the* Liber Ivonie *(Book of Eibon) into 13th century French; the tome appears in various works by Clark Ashton Smith.* The Revelations of Glaaki *are from Ramsey Campbell's contributions to the Cthulhu Mythos. The Drones Club is a recurring organization in the works of P. G. Wodehouse. Mr. Haddo must be a relative of Oliver Haddo from W. Somerset Maugham's novel* The Magician. *St. Cyprian's Rosicrucian friend is the French pulp character the Sâr Dubnotal, while "that old fraud Klaw" is Moris Klaw from Sax Rohmer's collection* The Dream Detective. *The Si-Fan is the criminal organization run by Rohmer's most famous creation, Dr. Fu Manchu. The story of Drood's encounter with the* tulpa *inspiring Stevenson must be false, since there are numerous stories bringing Dr. Henry Jekyll and his alter ego, Mr. Edward Hyde, into the CU. The Rituals of Hloh are from the Miles Pennoyer stories by Margery Lawrence.* The Book of Minor Grotesques *is mentioned in other stories by Reynolds.* The Zanthu Tablets *appear in Cthulhu Mythos stories by Lin Carter, while* The Book of Iod *and Johann Negus were added to the Mythos by Henry Kuttner.* The Garden of Forking Paths *is from Jorge Luis Borges' short story of the same name. Arkady Cottonwood is from Reynolds' story "Corn Wolf." Cottonwood's book* The Oldest Rite *appears in Reynolds' short stories set in Jackapo County, South Carolina, as do quotes attributed to him. Captain Hugh "Bulldog" Drummond is the hero of novels written by H. C. McNeile under the pen name "Sapper."*

February
THE STRIX SOCIETY

Two policemen are standing on the stoop of No. 427 Cheyne Walk as Charles St. Cyprian, Britain's Royal Occultist, speaks to Lord Curzon, the country's Foreign Minister. St. Cyprian thinks Curzon's future son-in-law Oswald Mosley is, "in the words of the honourable Freddie Threepwood, an absolutely perfect perisher." St. Cyprian asks Curzon why he does not hire a detective to investigate Mosley's involvement with the hedonistic Strix society, saying "You can find them in practically every A.B.C. teashop and Piccadilly flat. I have that fellow Blake's number, if you'd like." The two discuss an affair in Persia during the War,  one of St. Cyprian's last cases as Carnacki's assistant. Going up against the Sisterhood of the Rats or the Si-Fan when, by and large, they adequately police themselves, is not something St. Cyprian looks forward to. St. Cyprian remembers how he tried to lose himself in parties and drink after the war, snatching policemen's helmets with the Wooster crowd and swimming in the Trafalgar fountains with the Runcible set. St. Cyprian traces the sacred shape of the Voorish Sign in the air with a finger and lets his inner eye flicker open. He recalls his encounter in Seven Dials with the mummy of a pharaoh awakened by the Esoteric Order of Thoth-Ra. St. Cyprian uses the powder of Ibn Ghazi to view the members of the Strix Society, who have taken the forms of vampire-spirits. One of St. Cyprian's predecessors' journals has a few Greek flowers that turn people into such wraiths pressed between its pages, "plucked from the lonely mountain grave of Sir Francis Varney himself."

Short story by Josh Reynolds in Occult Detectives, *Ron Fortier, ed., Airship 27 Productions, 2014. No. 427 Cheyne Walk and Thomas Carnacki are from William Hope Hodgson's short story collection* Carnacki the Ghost-Finder. *Freddie Threepwood is from P. G. Wodehouse's Blandings novels, while the Wooster crowd is a reference to Bertie Wooster from Wodehouse's* Jeeves and Wooster *books. The A.B.C. teashop reference is an allusion to the titular detective from Baroness Orczy's* The Old Man in the Corner. *The*

Piccadilly flat reference is to Dorothy L. Sayers' sleuth Lord Peter Wimsey. Blake is Sexton Blake, the most famous of all British penny dreadful detectives. The Si-Fan is the criminal organization run by Sax Rohmer's Dr. Fu Manchu. The Runcible set is a reference to Agatha Runcible from Evelyn Waugh's novel Vile Bodies. The Voorish Sign and the powder of Ibn Ghazi are from H. P. Lovecraft's story "The Dunwich Horror." The pharaoh awakened by the Esoteric Order of Thoth-Ra was Nephren-Ka from Lovecraft's "The Haunter of the Dark," whom St. Cyprian battled in "The Unwrapping Party." Sir Francis Varney is from James Malcolm Rymer's serialized horror story Varney the Vampire. The year is specifically given as 1920, and Curzon refers to St. Cyprian's handling of "that disturbance at the Voyagers Club last week." In Reynolds' novel The Jade Suit of Death, set in March of the same year, the Voyagers Club affair is said to have taken place "last month." Therefore, "The Strix Society" takes place in February of 1920.

March
THE JADE SUIT OF DEATH

Charles St. Cyprian and his assistant Ebe Gallowglass battle the Order of the Cosmic Ram, which has unleashed the demon Baphomet and the ancient Chinese sage and werewolf Zhang Su. St. Cyprian uses a "devil-box" formerly used by Carnacki to subdue the Hairy Hands of Dartmoor. Soho's dockworkers are a mixture of races, including Chinese, Lascar, English and Tcho-Tcho. St. Cyprian and Gallowglass dwell at No. 427, Cheyne Walk. Carnacki, St. Cyprian's predecessor as Royal Occultist, was once the apprentice to Edwin Drood, his own predecessor. Picking up a letter, Gallowglass asks St. Cyprian, "What's a Janus House and why doesn't it have a postmark?" St. Cyprian replies, "The Sergeant has other means of posting letters than Royal Mail." St. Cyprian and Gallowglass answer a summons from William Melion, who was once a member of the Kensington Clique, a group of occultists that also included John Silence, Saxon Amadeus Dorr, Sar Dubnotal, and Flaxman Low. In Limehouse, St. Cyprian and Gallowglass meet with

Lady Molly Robertson-Kirk, formerly of Scotland Yard. St. Cyprian tells Robertson-Kirk he was sorry to hear about Hubert, and she mentions Inspector Meisures. Amelia Glossop is a member of the Order. Melion thinks of previous Royal Occultists, such as Drood and his shimmering crystal egg, and Beamish and his hunt for the worms in the earth. Philip Wendy-Smythe claims to know the hidden mysteries of Lemuria and ancient Khem, the Aklo, and how to make the Voorish Sign. St. Cyprian asks if he knows the Hloh Gestures. Wendy-Smythe, who falsely believes one of his personal curios is the idol of Chaugnar Faugn, invokes the myriad and malevolent moons of Munnapor and the roving rings of Raggadorr when he and St. Cyprian are attacked by an animated statue. Wendy-Smythe tells his servant to retrieve the cursed scepter of Ibn-Schacabao, but the butler gives notice, saying he'll be in residence at the Junior Ganymede Club. St. Cyprian's unidentified enemy is a magus in the truest sense of the word, on a level with Oliver Haddo or one of that lot. St. Cyprian uses the powder of Ibn Ghazi to expose an invisible menace. St. Cyprian tells Gallowglass to get the arbutus, which is on the third shelf, left of the statue with the head of an ibis; Gallowglass mistakes a falcon figurine for the ibis. Saxon Amadeus Dorr smokes cigarettes made from the poppies of Leng. The sorcerers of Averoigne are mentioned, as is the Westenra Fund. Melion's servant Ghale brews his tea from the blossoms of the mariphasa, a flower known only to grow in the higher altitudes of Tibet. Sadie Fleece refers to the Starry Wisdom. St. Cyprian uses the sign of Koth, which guards the Black Tower and seals the vaults of Pnath, to bind Zhang Su. Saxon Dorr tells Melion about a Polish nobleman who shares his affliction of lycanthropy, and has lived for centuries.

Novel by Josh Reynolds, Emby Press, 2014. Thomas Carnacki and No. 427, Cheyne Walk are from William Hope Hodgson's Carnacki the Ghost-Finder. *The Tcho-Tcho people are from August Derleth's contributions to the Cthulhu Mythos created by H. P. Lovecraft. Edwin Drood is the title character of Charles Dickens' unfinished novel* The Mystery of Edwin Drood. *The Sergeant is Sergeant Roman Janus, the "Spirit-Breaker," an occult detective created by Jim Beard. John Silence is the protagonist of an eponymous collection by Algernon Blackwood. The Sâr Dubnotal appeared in a French pulp series by an anonymous author. Flaxman Low is from* Ghosts; Being the Experiences of Flaxman Low *by "E. and H. Heron" (Hesketh V. Prichard and Kate O'Brien Ryall Prichard). Lady Molly Robertson-Kirk, Hubert de Mazareen, and Inspector Meisures are from Baroness Orczy's collection* Lady Molly of Scotland Yard. *Amelia Glossop is presumably a member of the Glossop family from P. G. Wodehouse's Jeeves books. The Junior Ganymede Club is a club for gentlemen's gentlemen of which Jeeves* is a member. *The shimmering crystal egg* is from H. G. Wells' "The Crystal Egg." *Worms in the Earth* are from Robert E. Howard's Bran Mak Morn story "Worms of the Earth." *Khem* and the *Starry Wisdom* are from H. P. Lovecraft's story "The Haunter of the Dark." *The Aklo language* is from Arthur Machen's "The White People," and was also used by Lovecraft in "The Dunwich Horror" and "The Haunter of the Dark." *The Voorish Sign* and the *powder of Ibn Ghazi* are also from "The Dunwich Horror." *The Plateau of Leng* is featured in Lovecraft's Cthulhu Mythos stories. *The Sign of Koth* and the *Vale of Pnath* are from Lovecraft's Dream Cycle. *The Hloh Gestures* are from Margery Lawrence's stories about occult detective Miles Pennoyer. *Chaugnar Faugn* is from Frank Belknap Long's novel The Horror from the Hills. *Munnapor (or Munnopor)* and *Raggadorr* are mystic entities from the stories of Marvel Comics' Sorcerer Supreme, Doctor Strange. *Ibn-Schacabao* is from Lovecraft's story "The Festival." *Oliver Haddo* is from W. Somerset Maugham's novel The Magician. *The falcon figurine* is the titular statue from Dashiell Hammett's The Maltese Falcon. *Averoigne* is a province of France that is the site of many supernatural events in Clark Ashton Smith's works. *The Westenra fund* is named after Lucy Westenra from Bram Stoker's Dracula. *Mariphasa* is from the 1935 horror film Werewolf of London. *The Polish nobleman* is Waldemar Daninsky, a werewolf played by Paul Naschy in a long-running series of Spanish horror films.

October
ANGEL VS. FRANKENSTEIN II: FRAGMENTS

Angel, the vampire with a soul, is working as an orderly in a New York City mental hospital when he discovers one of the patients is the Frankenstein Monster, whom he met more than a century before. Naturally, the monster escapes and rampages through the city, and Angel is compelled to fight him.

One-shot by John Byrne, IDW Publishing, 2010. Angel originally met the Frankenstein monster in 1806, as seen in the first *Angel vs. Frankenstein* one-shot, also by Byrne. It is implied the Monster has been imprisoned in the asylum for more than fifteen years; however, this contradicts several accounts set between 1905 and 1920 in which he appears. Therefore, the Monster must have been imprisoned for only a year at most, since the 1919 events of Thom Brannan and Matthew Baugh's story "Every Rose."

November
THE ARTIST AS WOLF

Charles St. Cyprian and Ebe Gallowglass attend a party where the art of Gabriel-Ernest Smythe is being displayed. St. Cyprian pronounces Smythe's work "no worse than your average Pickman." The party is hosted by Roberta "Bobbie" Wickham, who expresses surprise at St. Cyprian's attendance, having thought he "would have gone into hiding with Bertie and the rest of the Drones." St. Cyprian refers to Van Cheele and Toop.

Short story by Joshua Reynolds in Leather, Denim & Silver: Legends of the Monster Hunter, *Miles Boothe, ed., Pill Hill Press, 2011. Gabriel-Ernest Smythe, Van Cheele, and Toop are from H. H. Munro's werewolf story "Gabriel-Ernest." Richard Upton Pickman is from H. P. Lovecraft's "Pickman's Model." Bobbie Wickham appears in P. G. Wodehouse's stories about Bertie Wooster and his valet Jeeves, and is also related to the author's series character Mr. Mulliner. The Drones Club appears in the Jeeves and Wooster stories, as well as many of Wodehouse's other interconnected works.*

Autumn
DEEP RED BELLS

Charles St. Cyprian and Ebe Gallowglass try to exorcise the ghost of a shark from St. Cyprian's friend Gussie Fitzgrace's body. St. Cyprian has a tremendous amount of respect for the Society for Psychical Research, engendered in him by his mentor Thomas Carnacki. St. Cyprian describes Gussie's sister Dahlia as "this year's answer to Rosie M. Banks, producing widely read and inevitably maudlin tripe with a speed that would astound the messenger of the gods himself," and recalls an incident with an ichthyosaur skeleton in the Drones billiards room. Dahlia mentions "that business with the crystal egg." St. Cyprian mutters "By their smell can men sometimes know them near," in response to the odor Gussie is emitting. St. Cyprian asks Gallowglass if he did or did not give her Harzan's monograph on the detection of abhuman manifestations, and says no two Saaitii manifestations are the same. St. Cyprian traces the sacred shape of the Voorish sign in the air. St. Cyprian possesses a silver disc that has engraved upon its surface the signs of the Saaamaaa Ritual, crafted by the hands of the last of the ab-human priests of Raaee sometime in the 1600s, and confiscated by Dr. John Dee.

Short story by Josh Reynolds in Sharkpunk, Jonathan Green, ed., Snowbooks, 2015. Thomas Carnacki, Harzan, Saiitii manifestations, the Saaamaaa Ritual, and Raaee are from William Hope Hodgson's short story collection Carnacki the Ghost-Finder. Rosie M. Banks and the Drones Club are from the works of P. G. Wodehouse. The crystal egg is from H. G. Wells' titular story. The quote "By their smell can men sometimes know them near" and the Voorish Sign are from H. P. Lovecraft's "The Dunwich Horror."

Christmas
KRAMPUSNACHT

One of Charles St. Cyprian's predecessors as Royal Occultist was Sir Edwin Drood, in the earliest days of the late Queen Victoria's reign. St. Cyprian instructs his assistant Ebe Gallowglass to get Carnacki's Electric Pentacle.

Short story by Josh Reynolds in Horror for the Holidays, Scott David Aniolowski, Miskatonic River Press, 2011; reprinted in Psychopomp Christmas Special, Artifice Comics, 2013. Edwin Drood is the title character of Charles Dickens' unfinished novel The Mystery of Edwin Drood. Thomas Carnacki, "the Ghost-Finder," was created by William Hope Hodgson.

1921

Winter
THE ULTIMATE EVIL

A Gypsy visits Baker Street in the hopes of hiring Sherlock Holmes to investigate the disappearance of his tribe's children. Holmes being retired, he enlists the aid of Harry Dickson instead. Dickson tells the culprit his associate the Sâr Dubnotal will take him to a secluded island, where he will be given the opportunity to reform and atone for his crimes.

Short story by Matthew Dennion in Harry Dickson vs. the Spider, Jean-Marc and Randy Lofficier, eds., Black Coat Press, 2014. Harry Dickson, "the American Sherlock Holmes," appeared in pulp stories by Jean Ray and others. The Sâr Dubnotal starred in an anonymously-written pulp series.

THE FACELESS FIEND

Charles St. Cyprian and Ebe Gallowglass battle a psychically-created invisible creature that uses humans' brains and spines as host bodies. St. Cyprian asks Gallowglass if he did or did not give her Harzan's monograph on the detection of ab-human manifestations, traces the Voorish Sign in the air, and scrawls out the Sign of Koth. St. Cyprian recalls Hesselius' encounter with something like the creature: a vicar overindulged in exotic teas and accidentally forged a psychic conduit between himself and a nasty entity from elsewhere. St. Cyprian spreads the powder of Ibn Ghazi to make the creature visible.

Short story by Josh Reynolds on The Royal Occultist *website. The invisible creature is related to the one seen in Amelia Reynolds Long's short story "The Thought Monster," which appeared in* Weird Tales *in 1930, and was adapted in 1958 as the film* Fiend Without a Face. *Harzan is from William Hope Hodgson's Carnacki story "The Haunted Jarvee." The Voorish Sign and the powder of Ibn Ghazi are from H. P. Lovecraft's story "The Dunwich Horror." The Sign of Koth is from Lovecraft's story "The Dream-Quest of Unknown Kadath" and novel* The Case of Charles Dexter Ward. *Dr. Martin Hesselius is from the stories collected in J. Sheridan Le Fanu's* In a Glass Darkly, *including "Green Tea," which depicts the incident involving the vicar.*

Spring
SIGN OF THE SALAMANDER

Charles St. Cyprian is described as knowing how to draw the Yellow Sign properly. St. Cyprian reminds Ebe Gallowglass of their encounter with Nephren-Ka in Seven Dials two years ago. St. Cyprian remembers his mentor, Thomas Carnacki, and thinks of others who wear a set of rings like his, including an American, Warren. St. Cyprian mentions the Seven Stars. Edwin Drood brought the Eye of Atum back to Heliopolis.

Story by Josh Reynolds in Fantasy and Fear *#3, Pro Se Press, 2011. The Yellow Sign is from Robert W. Chambers' collection* The King in Yellow. *Nephren-Ka is from H. P. Lovecraft's "The Haunter of the Dark." Harley Warren is from Lovecraft's Dream Cycle stories. St. Cyprian and Gallowglass encountered Nephren-Ka in Reynolds' story "Unwrapping Party" (*Pro Se Presents, *August 2012). Thomas Carnacki, "the Ghost-Finder," is an occult detective created by William Hope Hodgson. The Seven Stars are from Bram Stoker's* The Jewel of Seven Stars. *Edwin Drood is from Charles Dickens' unfinished novel* The Mystery of Edwin Drood.

Summer
WINGS OF FEAR

Hugh "Bulldog" Drummond finds himself imprisoned alongside Harry Dickson. Dickson tells him about dinosaur-like creatures that have been spotted recently, one of which was killed by Major-General Sir Richard Hannay. He also says Sir Walter Bullivant received an extortion note from Drummond's nemesis Carl Peterson. Peterson has been spotted in the area, accompanied by his lover Irma. The creatures have been created by the mad vivisectionist Dr. Lerne, a former student of Dr. Moreau. Dickson speculates perhaps Lerne's creatures were based on a group of dinosaurs discovered in a valley in the Auvergne near Gambertin. When Bullivant asks Hannay if his wife will mind him investigating Dickson's disappearance, Hannay replies, "Mary's at Cannes with Janet Roylance, and Peter John's at school." He also quotes Peter Pienaar. Hannay runs surveillance alongside Archie Roylance. Battling Lerne's "diablosaurs," Drummond wonders what Phyllis is doing right now.

Short story by Nicholas Boving in Tales of the Shadowmen Volume 9: La Vie en Noir, *Jean-Marc and Randy Lofficier, eds., Black Coat Press, 2012; reprinted in French in* Les Compagnons de l'Ombre (Tome 12), *Jean-Marc and Randy Lofficier, eds., Rivière Blanche, 2013; and in* Harry Dickson vs. the Spider, *Jean-Marc and Randy Lofficier, eds., Black Coat Press, 2014. Hugh "Bulldog" Drummond, his wife Phyllis, and Carl and Irma Peterson are from the series of novels by H. C. "Sapper" McNeile and Gerard Fairlie. The exploits of Harry Dickson, "the American Sherlock Holmes," were chronicled by Jean Ray and others. Richard Hannay, his wife Mary and son Peter John, Sir Walter Bullivant, Archie Roylance and his wife Janet, and Peter Pienaar are all from the works of John Buchan. Dr. Lerne is from the novel of the same name by Maurice Renard. The Gambertin dinosaurs are from Renard's story "Monsieur Dupont's Vacation." Dr. Moreau is from H. G. Wells' classic novel* The Island of Doctor Moreau. *The year of 1923 given for this adventure must be incorrect, as Peterson was at that time believed dead after the 1922 events of McNeile's* The Final Count.

Mid Summer
A SPOTTED TROUBLE AT DOLOR-ON-THE-DOWNS

Alastair Fitzroy, the twenty-seventh Lord Calipash, enlists the services of Bertie Wooster's valet Reginald Jeeves in dealing with his sister Lady Alethea's amphibious transformation, a recurring condition that in this case was triggered and prolonged by contact with a bizarre octopoidal creature. Lord Calipash and Lady Alethea hope to harvest whatever caused this particular change and sell it as a drug. Lord Calipash tells Jeeves, "Neither Alethea nor I have any wish to end up like our American cousins, the Mortlows. Humiliated, shamed, imprisoned."

Short story by Molly Tanzer in A Pretty Mouth, *Lazy Fascist Press*, 2012. The connection to P. G. Wodehouse's Jeeves novels reinforces the Calipash family's inclusion in the CU. The Mortlow family is from Alan M. Clark's novel A Parliament of Crows, *also published by Lazy Fascist Press. A reference to "Rafael Sabatini's recently-published* Scaramouche" *places this story in 1921.*

October 31
THE GOTTERDAMMERUNG GAVOTTE

Charles St. Cyprian and Ebe Gallowglass team up with a group of occult detectives to prevent the Great Old Ones from being unleashed upon the world. Appearing or mentioned are: Semi Dual; No. 472 Cheyne Walk; Harley Warren; John Silence; Ravenwood; Sar Dubnotal; de Grandin; Thunstone; Pursuivant; Ms. Crerar; Kirowan; Zarnak; Thomas Carnacki; the Nameless One; a Tibetan lama with an unhealthy fascination for the color green; the Third Ritual of Hloh; Tserpchikopf; the Great Detective; the Hog; the Shambler; the Walker; the Lurker; the Yimghaz Sign; fire vampires; the dust of Ibn Gazi; Naacal; Thorne; openers and closers; the Drones Club; and Captain Drummond.

Story by Josh Reynolds in The Lovecraft eZine #18, Mike Davis, ed., October 2012. *Semi Dual is an occult detective created for the pulps by J. U. Giesy. Thomas Carnacki is from William Hope Hodgson's collection* Carnacki the Ghost-Finder. *Carnacki lives at No. 472 Cheyne Walk. The Hog is from the Carnacki story of the same name. Harley Warren appears in H. P. Lovecraft's "The Statement of Randolph Carter," and is mentioned in "The Silver Key" and "Through the Gates of the Silver Key." The Naacal language is also from "Through the Gates of the Silver Key." John Silence is from Algernon Blackwood's collection of the same name. Ravenwood was the hero of a series of stories by Frederick C. Davis in the pulp magazine* Secret Agent X; *the Nameless One is Ravenwood's Tibetan mystic mentor.*

The Sar Dubnotal was the subject of a French pulp series by an anonymous author who may have been Norbert Sevestre. Tserpchikopf is one of the mystic's foes. Jules de Grandin is an occult detective created by Seabury Quinn. John Thunstone is the hero of a series of stories by Manly Wade Wellman, as is Judge Keith Hilary Pursuivant. Rowley Thorne is Thunstone's archenemy. Ms. Crerar is Sheila Crerar, an occult detective appearing in stories by Ella Scrymsour. John Kirowan is a recurring character in the works of Robert E. Howard. Anton Zarnak is an occult investigator created by Lin Carter; his adventures have been continued by a number of other authors. The Tibetan lama is Kendell Crossen's pulp hero the Green Lama. The Ritual of Hloh and the Yimghaz Sign are from "The Case of the Bronze Door," one of Margery Lawrence's stories about psychic detective Miles Pennoyer. The Great Detective is Sherlock Holmes, of course. The Shambler is a reference to Robert Bloch's "The Shambler from the Stars." The Walker is Ithaqua (aka the Wind-Walker), from August Derleth's story of the same name. The Lurker is Lovecraft's Nyarlathotep; the Lurker appellation is an allusion to Derleth's The Lurker at the Threshold. Fire vampires are from Donald Wandrei's story "The Fire Vampires." The Dust of Ibn Gazi is from Lovecraft's "The Dunwich Horror." The openers and closers are from Roger Zelazny's A Night in the Lonesome October; although the events of that novel have been placed in an alternate universe, there is nothing to prevent the Crossover Universe from having openers and closers of its own. The Drones Club is a recurring London gentlemen's club in the interconnected works of P. G. Wodehouse. Captain Drummond is H. C. McNeile's hero Hugh "Bulldog" Drummond.

Christmas
THE TEETH OF WINTER

Charles St. Cyprian, hunting down a man-eating wendigo in Alberta alongside his assistant Ebe Gallowglass and the elderly Native American gunfighter Lone Crow, makes the third Hloh gesture. St. Cyprian first met the Inuit *angakkuq* Ukaleq in London, before the War, when he was an assistant to Thomas Carnacki. St. Cyprian and Lone Crow discuss Dr. Silence. St. Cyprian traces the sacred shape of the Voorish Sign in the air.

Short story by Josh Reynolds in PulpWork Christmas Special 2014, *PulpWork Press. Lone Crow appears in weird Western stories by Joel Jenkins. Hloh is from Margery Lawrence's stories about occult detective Miles Pennoyer. Thomas Carnacki is from William Hope Hodgson's collection* Carnacki the Ghost-Finder, *while Dr. Silence is from Algernon Blackwood's collection* John Silence. *The Voorish Sign is from H. P. Lovecraft's story "The Dunwich Horror."*

1922

Winter
THE CRYSTAL MINDERS

Professor Challenger suggests a scientist has "invented a machine capable of traveling through time, like that loon in Surrey, have you?"

Short story by John Takis *in* Professor Challenger: New Worlds, Lost Places, *J. R. Campbell and Charles Prepolec, eds., EDGE Science Fiction and Fantasy Publishing, 2015. "That loon in Surrey" is the Time Traveler from H. G. Wells'* The Time Machine. *This story is primarily narrated by Professor Summerlee, though a framing sequence narrated by Edward Malone involves Summerlee coming to the reporter to tell him of the adventure. Malone refers to the events of "The Disintegration Machine" as a past event. This creates a chronological conflict, as Rick Lai's essay "The Anomaly of Professor Challenger's Daughter" (Rick Lai's Secret Histories: Daring Adventurers, Altus Press, 2008) places both "The Disintegration Machine" and* The Land of Mists *in 1926. According to* The Land of Mists, *Summerlee died "last year," i.e., in 1925. Therefore, the reference to "The Disintegration Machine" must be obfuscation on Malone's part, similar to Dr. Watson providing false dates in his accounts of Sherlock Holmes' cases. The true year of the story is conjecture.*

March
ARMY OF DARKNESS/REANIMATOR

Ash Williams time-travels to this era from 2012 and meets Herbert West, who is later revealed to be the same West whom Ash has met before, having used the *Necronomicon Ex Mortis* to travel back in time.

One-shot comic by Mark Rahner *and Randy Valiente, Dynamite Entertainment, 2013. Ash previously met West in the stories* Army of Darkness vs. Re-Animator *and* Prophecy. *Jay Lindsey notes "This one takes some wrangling, since the implication is that the 2000s West is the one from Lovecraft's original story. Since the Cthulhu Mythos timeline I generally refer to claims that West disappeared in 1921, I propose that the*

2000s West attempted to use the Necronomicon *to visit his ancestor, but due to some temporal quirk, missed his demise and ended up with amnesia, assuming the identity of the previous West." Although the latter-day Herbert dies in this story, he is later resurrected via sorcery and returned to the 21st century via unrevealed means, as referenced in the* Reanimator *miniseries.*

Spring
IRON BELLS

Charles St. Cyprian and Ebe Gallowglass battle ghouls lurking in the London Underground. St. Cyprian refers to his predecessors Drood and Carnacki.

Short story by Josh Reynolds in The Trigger Reflex, Miles Boothe, ed., *Pill Hill Press, 2011; reprinted in* Both Barrels, Miles Boothe, ed., Emby Press, 2013. *The ghouls are of the same species seen in H. P. Lovecraft's "Pickman's Model." Edwin Drood, one of St. Cyprian's predecessors as Royal Occultist, is from Charles Dickens'* The Mystery of Edwin Drood. *Thomas Carnacki is an occult detective created by William Hope Hodgson.*

Summer
THE SECOND-STORY ANGEL

Female con artist Angel Grace Cardigan swindles short story writers.

Story by Dashiell Hammett in Black Mask, *November 15, 1923; reprinted in* A Man Called Thin, *1962. Angel Grace Cardigan went on to appear in Hammett's Continental Op stories "The Big Knockover" and "$106,000 Blood Money," thus bringing this story into the CU.*

October 31
THE BELLS OF NORTHAM

Harley Warren and Charles St. Cyprian discuss the death of Lord Northam. St. Cyprian mentions his predecessor as Royal Occultist. John Silence vouched for Warren. Warren and St. Cyprian are accompanied by Randolph Carter and Ebe Gallowglass, respectively. Northam was murdered by a man named Williams. Carter says he hopes their encounter with Williams won't be like Innsmouth. Carter recognizes the Sign of Koth on an altar stone. Williams identifies a coffin as that of Lunaeus Gabinius Capito, and says wherever strange folk met together and made the Elder Sign, Lunaeus would hold court. St. Cyprian thinks Williams has something that egotistical would-be power-brokers like Crowley and Karswell haven't—namely, a figurehead. Williams says he and Warren were acquaintances in their university days, but they eventually went their separate ways, Warren to Tibet and Williams to Exham. Warren tries to ward off Lunaeus' revived corpse with the Voorish Sign.

Short story by Joshua Reynolds in The Lovecraft eZine #23, Mike Davis, ed., October 2013. Harley Warren and Randolph Carter are from H. P. Lovecraft's Dream Cycle of stories. Lord Northam, Williams, and Lunaeus Gabinius Capito are from Lovecraft's story "The Descendant." St. Cyprian's predecessor is William Hope Hodgson's "ghost-finder" Thomas Carnacki. John Silence is from Algernon Blackwood's collection of the same name. Innsmouth, Massachusetts is the setting of Lovecraft's "The Shadow over Innsmouth." The Sign of Koth is mentioned in one of the Dream Cycle tales, "The Dream-Quest of Unknown Kadath," as well as another Lovecraft work, The Case of Charles Dexter Ward. The Elder Sign is mentioned in several of Lovecraft's stories. Karswell is from M. R. James' story "Casting the Runes." Exham is from Lovecraft's "The Rats in the Walls." The Voorish Sign is from Lovecraft's "The Dunwich Horror." A reference to the year being 1926 is incorrect.

Autumn
THE WHITE JADE RING
It is mentioned Francis X. Gordon and Steve Allison (aka El Borak and the Sonora Kid, respectively) recently had a "war with the Si-Fan."

Unfinished short story fragment by Robert E. Howard included in The Last of the Trunk, The Robert E. Howard Foundation Press, 2005. The reference to the Si-Fan, the criminal organization controlled by Dr. Fu Manchu, reinforces Gordon and Allison's inclusion in the CU.

LOCKED ROOM
Dr. Anton Zarnak, ex-Inspector John Raymond Legrasse, and Lieutenant Mark Thorner battle a Tindalos hound.

Short story by C. J. Henderson in The Tales of Inspector Legrasse, Mythos Books, 2005. Zarnak was created by Lin Carter, and appears in stories by Carter, Henderson, and others. Mark Thorner is his ally on the police force of the city (either New York or San Francisco) out of which Zarnak operates. Legrasse is from Lovecraft's "The Call of Cthulhu"; he and Zarnak first met during the events of Henderson's story "To Cast Out Fear." "The Hounds of Tindalos" is a story by Frank Belknap Long.

THE D'ERLETTE CONFIGURATION

Phillip Wendy-Smythe seeks Charles St. Cyprian's help in protecting him from the cursed puzzle box known as the d'Erlette Configuration. St. Cyprian tells his assistant, Ebe Gallowglass, to remember what happened in Myrdstone. The d'Erlette Configuration was one of several such boxes commissioned by the Comte d'Erlette in the 18th century; allegedly a French toymaker of dubious reputation was involved.

Short story by Josh Reynolds. Lin Carter mentioned "the Myrdstone Witches" in his Anton Zarnak story "Curse of the Black Pharaoh." The Comte d'Erlette is the author of the Cultes des Goules, *and was first mentioned in Robert Bloch's story "The Suicide in the Study." The Comte was named after Bloch's friend and fellow Lovecraft disciple August Derleth. The French toymaker is Philip Lemarchand, creator of the Lament Configuration and other unholy puzzle boxes in Clive Barker's "The Hellbound Heart" and the* Hellraiser *film series.*

December 26
FEAST OF FOOLS

Charles St. Cyprian speaks to George "Boko" Fittleworth, who resides in Steeple Bumpleigh. According to their mutual friends, Boko's successes make liver-gnawing characters like Adam Fenwick-Symes and Harold Acton grind their teeth in literary frustration. Boko remarks it's a shame none of the Trinity Tiddlers could make it, and George St. Barleigh enjoyed a touch of the polo. St. Cyprian refers to Tuppy and Bingo, and Boko asks where Bertie Wooster is. Their host Monty Wallace is a member in good standing of several London clubs, including the Drones. St. Cyprian notices a few stragglers from the Runcible set among the guests. Boko remarks he thought Finknottle was a pedantic ass, with his blasted newts. St. Cyprian mentions his predecessor Carnacki. Monty complains about a bottle of Averoigne '72 left in his burning house.

Short story by Josh Reynolds in PulpWork Christmas Special 2012, *PulpWork Press. George "Boko" Fittleworth, Steeple Bumpleigh, Tuppy Glossop, Bingo Little, Bertie Wooster, the Drones Club, and Gussie Fink-Nottle (spelled Finknottle here) are from P. G. Wodehouse's Jeeves stories. Adam Fenwick-Symes and Agatha Runcible are from Evelyn Waugh's novel* Vile Bodies. *The Trinity Tiddlers and George St. Barleigh are from the television series* Blackadder Goes Forth. *Carnacki is from William Hope Hodgson's short story collection* Carnacki the Ghost-Finder. *The French province of Averoigne appears in a number of Clark Ashton Smith's stories.*

1923

Winter
DER NEUE EXCENTRIC CLUB
  The New Eccentric Club encounters the New Robinson.
  Der Neue Excentric Club, *1924. The New Robinson must be quite elderly by now.*

IN THE DARK AND QUIET
  Ebe Gallowglass tells Charles St. Cyprian she knows worms in the earth and such hide in England. St. Cyprian has an electric pentacle set up that was designed by his predecessor, Thomas Carnacki. St. Cyprian traces a sacred shape from the Third Ritual of Hloh in the air with two fingers. St. Cyprian learned how to open his spirit-eye from a Tibetan lama of his acquaintance who has an unhealthy fascination with the color green. Earlier, St. Cyprian drew three circles as required by the Saaamaaa Ritual in chalk. He recites the Yimghaz Test. St. Cyprian thinks of saying the Dhol Chant, but realizes it will do no good. St. Cyprian suggests using either the Chant or the Incantation of Raaaee to keep the Black Nun sealed away. He identifies the Nun as a Saitii manifestation, like the one Carnacki encountered in "that business with the Whistling Room."

  Short story by Josh Reynolds in Use Enough Gun: Legends of the Monster Hunter III, *Miles Boothe, ed., Emby Press, 2013. The worms in the earth are from Robert E. Howard's Bran Mak Morn story "Worms of the Earth." The electric pentacle, Thomas Carnacki, the Saaamaaa Ritual, the Incantation of Raaaee, the Saitii, and the Whistling Room are from William Hope Hodgson's collection* Carnacki the Ghost-Finder. *The Ritual of Hloh and the Yimghaz Test are from Margery Lawrence's stories featured occult detective Miles Pennoyer. The Tibetan lama is the Green Lama, a pulp hero appearing in stories by "Richard Foster" (Kendell Foster Crossen) in the pulp magazine* Double Detective. *The Dhol Chant is from H. P. Lovecraft and Hazel Heald's story "The Horror in the Museum."*

WENDY-SMYTHE'S WORM

Charles St. Cyprian's predecessor as Royal Occultist was Thomas Carnacki. St. Cyprian refers to "the incident with the Karnstein girl." Phillip Wendy-Smythe says the man from whom he bought an egg which hatched a giant killer worm said he got it from the ruins of Castra Regis, in Lesser Hill.

Short story by Josh Reynolds at The Adventures of the Royal Occultist *website. Thomas Carnacki is from William Hope Hodgson's short story collection* Carnacki the Ghost-Finder. *"The Karnstein girl" is the title character of J. Sheridan Le Fanu's lesbian vampire tale* Carmilla. *Castra Regis is from Bram Stoker's novel* The Lair of the White Worm. *The November 1 date given in this story is incorrect.*

March 1923–March 1943
BRIDESHEAD REVISITED

Sebastian Flyte visits a nightclub on Sink Street called the Old Hundredth. The Anchorage, Chasm, and Vanbrugh families do not attend Rex Mottram's wedding to Lady Julia Flyte. "Sammy" Samgrass gets a job at *The Daily Beast*, working for Lord Copper. A woman named Margot holds a luncheon party for Charles Ryder's exhibition upon his return from South America.

Novel by Evelyn Waugh. The Old Hundredth first appeared in Waugh's novel A Handful of Dust. *Lady Anchorage and Lady Chasm appear or are mentioned in several works by Waugh, beginning with* Vile Bodies. *Lady Vanbrugh is from Waugh's first novel,* Decline and Fall. *The Daily Beast and its publisher, Lord Copper, are from* Scoop. *Margot is Margot Metroland, a recurring character in Waugh's fiction beginning with* Decline and Fall. *Waugh's fragment "Charles Ryder's Schooldays" features Ryder in his youth.*

April 22
THE RIDERS OF ST. GEORGE

Charles St. Cyprian and Ebe Gallowglass battle undead knights in Hertfordshire. Gallowglass says she is going to try the ammunition they got blessed by a vicar in Ambridge.

Short story by Josh Reynolds. The village of Ambridge is the setting of the long-running British radio soap opera The Archers. *This story takes place on the eve of St. George's Day, which falls on April 23.*

Spring
VAMPIRE IN THE FIST

Ferdinand Rezeau tells the story of how his family was robbed by their new housekeeper, who turned out to be the notorious Irma Vep, and her comrades in *Les Vampires*.

Short story by Ferdinand Rezeau, edited by Michel Stéphan in Tales of the Shadowmen Volume 9: La Vie en Noir, *Jean-Marc and Randy Lofficier, eds., Black Coat Press, 2012; reprinted in French in* Les Compagnons de l'Ombre (Tome 9), *Jean-Marc and Randy Lofficier, eds., Rivière Blanche, 2012.* Les Vampires *are from the 1915–1916 silent film serial of the same name, as is Irma Vep. Ferdinand Rezeau and his family are from Hervé Bazin's novel* Vipère au Poing *(aka* Viper in the Fist*). This crossover brings Bazin's novel into the CU.*

Summer
THE NARROWING CIRCLE
The elderly sleuth Sebastian Zambra is described as having been a contemporary and rival of Sherlock Holmes.

Novel by Headon Hill. Hill's Zambra books and short stories are already in the CU through a connection to Robert Louis Stevenson's "The Suicide Club." The reference to Holmes as a real person bolsters Zambra's inclusion.

THE HUNGRY STONES
Charles St. Cyprian and Ebe Gallowglass come to the aid of one of St. Cyprian's former classmates in the Derbyshire village of Wargus when his sister becomes a werewolf via possession. St. Cyprian says a farmer who encountered the sister is in care at the Pemberley Hospice for apoplexy. He also says of his old acquaintance's family, "Their plot wasn't quite as big as Pemberley was in its heyday, but it's quite substantial nonetheless. And unlike Pemberley's former inhabitants, they're still around and keeping a hand in the affairs of Wargus." St. Cyprian finds he is unable to use the Third Hloh Ritual or the Sign of Yimghaz against the werewolf.

Short story by Josh Reynolds in Luna's Children: Stranger Worlds, *D. Alan Lewis, ed., Dark Oak Press, 2014. Although this story seems to imply Pemberley House (from Jane Austen's novel* Pride and Prejudice*) has been converted into a hospital, this cannot be the case. In Philip José Farmer and*

Win Scott Eckert's novel The Evil in Pemberley House, Edith, the Dowager Duchess of Greystoke, resides in Pemberley House until her death in 1973, with no reference to Pemberley ever being used as a hospital. Most likely, the Pemberley Hospice was a separate building financed by the Duchess. The reference to Pemberley's former inhabitants must refer to Sir Gawain Darcy having sold the estate to his distant cousin the 6th Duke of Greystoke, Edith's husband, as first revealed by Farmer in Tarzan Alive. Hloh and Yimghaz are from Margery Lawrence's stories about psychic detective Miles Pennoyer.

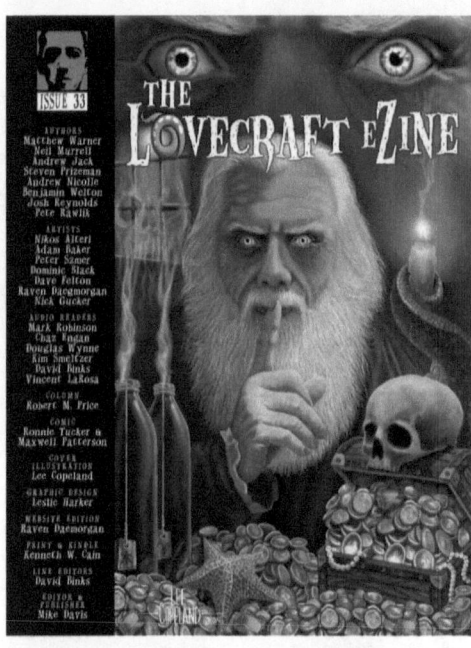

Autumn
THE PNAKOTIC PUZZLE

Charles St. Cyprian, the former assistant to Thomas Carnacki, meets Indrid Cold in the sitting room of No. 427, Cheyne Walk, whose walls are lined with fetish masks and lurid artworks by Goya, Blake and Pickman. St. Cyprian wonders if Cold is the same Indrid Cold Carnacki had a run in with during an affair with Professor Challenger and John Silence some years before the war. Cold is seeking the diary of Sir Edwin Drood, who preceded Carnacki as Royal Occultist, just as Carnacki preceded St. Cyprian in the role. St. Cyprian, who is passing fluent in Polari and the ancien Naacal alphabet, tells his assistant Ebe Gallowglass to get the Zanthu Box, which contains the Mnar fragments. Cold is described as wearing a wax mask. St. Cyprian also makes the third sign of the Hloh Ritual. Drood's exploits were allegedly fictionalized in Dickens' *The Mystery of Edwin Drood*, as well as books by Stoker (who replaced Drood with a Dutchman), Marsh, and Boothby (who added an unfortunate glamor to an otherwise monstrous individual, as well as excising Drood completely). Drood's diary contains a sketch of a crystal egg Drood had purchased in a grimy little shop near Seven Dials. Carnacki referred to the notebook as "the Pnakotic Puzzle." Drood believed alien minds from the distant past had infiltrated the human race at every stage of its evolution. Beings like Cold tried to wipe out the evidence of this, but they missed the Hoccleve translations and the Sigsand Manuscripts. Even *The Book of Eibon* wasn't much help in piecing together the puzzle. St. Cyprian refers to other foes of his, such as the Tcho-Tchos and the Brotherhood of the Golden Chrysanthemum. Cold says Earthly matter is not meant to travel along the Dho Curve. Drood refers to the Great Race that drove the creatures that are being unleashed upon the world underground.

Short story by Josh Reynolds in The Lovecraft eZine *#33*, Mike Davis, ed., January 2015. *Thomas Carnacki; No. 427, Cheyne Walk; and the Sigsand Manuscripts are from* William Hope Hodgson's collection Carnacki the Ghost-Finder. *Indrid Cold is an enigmatic, supposedly real individual who was allegedly connected to the Mothman sightings in West Virginia in the mid 1960s. Cold also appears in Reynolds' story "The Yoth Protocols," and is a member of the wax-masked race of creatures from H. P. Lovecraft's story "The Festival." Painter Richard Upton Pickman is from Lovecraft's story "Pickman's Model." The Great Race of Yith is from Lovecraft's story "The Shadow Out of Time," as are the race of flying polyps they drove underground. The ancient Naacal alphabet is from Lovecraft and E. Hoffmann Price's tale "Through the Gates of the Silver Key." Professor George Edward Challenger is from* The Lost World *and other tales by Arthur Conan Doyle. John Silence is an occult detective from Algernon Blackwood's titular collection. Edwin Drood is from Charles Dickens' unfinished novel* The Mystery of Edwin Drood. *The claim Drood, rather than Abraham Van Helsing, was involved in the events of* Dracula, *must be misinformation, since numerous stories make it clear Van Helsing was a real person in the CU. However, Drood might have been involved with Van Helsing's battle against Dracula behind the scenes, and arranged for Stoker to omit any mention of him from his fictionalized account. The Marsh and Boothby references indicate Drood was involved in the events of Richard Marsh's novel* The Beetle *and Guy Boothby's Dr. Nikola books, though both authors omitted any mention of Drood from their fictionalized accounts. The Zanthu Box is related to the Zanthu Tablets from Lin Carter's "The Dweller in the Tomb," which is part of Lovecraft's Cthulhu Mythos. The Mnar fragments come from the Star-Stones of Mnar, from August Derleth's Mythos novella* The Lurker at the Threshold. *The Hloh Ritual is from Margery Lawrence's stories of occult detective Miles Pennoyer. The Crystal Egg is from H. G. Wells' story of the same name. The Pnakotic Puzzle evokes the Pnakotic Manuscripts mentioned in Lovecraft's Mythos stories.* The Book of Eibon *is from Mythos fiction by Clark Ashton Smith. The Brotherhood of the Golden Chrysanthemum is also mentioned in Reynolds' novella* Phileas Fogg and the War of Shadows, *and may be related to the Sons of the Golden Chrysanthemum*

tong from Derrick Ferguson's Dillon novels and stories. The Dho Curve is probably related to the Dho-Nha geometry curves from Charles Stross' The Atrocity Archives.

December
THE SLYPE

Some residents of the village of Dullchester find a letter written by Mr. Mipps to Captain Collyer in 1805, which supposedly gives the location of a treasure, and engage in their own treasure hunt until they discover it is a fraud.

This novel by Russell Thorndike is connected to his Doctor Syn novels, and therefore to the Crossover Universe. Mr. Mipps is Doctor Syn's assistant, while Captain Collyer was the villain of the book Doctor Syn.

Christmas
THE JAGTOOTH LANE HORROR

Charles St. Cyprian and Ebe Gallowglass battle a Viking ghost in York. Thomas Carnacki, Edwin Drood, a Tibetan lama of St. Cyprian's acquaintance with what he considers an unhealthy predilection for the color green, and Subtle are mentioned.

Short story by Joshua Reynolds in Pro Se Presents, *Lee Houston, Jr., Nancy Hansen, and Frank Schildiner, eds., Pro Se Press, 2011. Thomas Carnacki is from William Hope Hodgson's collection* Carnacki the Ghost-Finder. *Edwin Drood is from Charles Dickens' unfinished novel* The Mystery of Edwin Drood. *The Tibetan lama is the Green Lama, a hero created by "Richard Foster" (Kendell Foster Crossen), who appeared in the pulp magazine* Double Detective. *Subtle is from Ben Jonson's play* The Alchemist.

1924

April
LOCKED ROOMS

Sherlock Holmes and Mary Russell are in San Francisco, where they cross paths with writer Dashiell Hammett, who tells Mary her former psychiatrist was murdered using "some kind of bird carving... an owl maybe, from Rhodes or Crete or something in the Mediterranean."

Novel by Mary Russell, edited by Laurie R. King. The statue used to murder Russell's psychiatrist will later become the object of a case investigated by Sam Spade, whose account will be edited by Hammett into a novel entitled The Maltese Falcon.

September
DEO VIRIDIO

Charles St. Cyprian and Ebe Gallowglass encounter Bella Mae Jobson.

Three-part serial by Josh Reynolds at The Adventures of the Royal Occultist *website. Bella Mae Jobson is from P. G. Wodehouse's Drones Club story "The Editor Regrets."*

Autumn
OWD HOB

Charles St. Cyprian and Ebe Gallowglass battle a boggart in a cottage on Dunny-on-the-Wold whose residents include Mr. Bolsom, a Member of Parliament.

Short story by Josh Reynolds at the Monster Corral *website. Dunny-on-the-Wold is from "Dish and Dishonesty," the first episode of the television series* Blackadder the Third. *Mr. Bolsom is a descendant of a character from that episode, Brigadier General Horace Bolsom.*

HAIRY SHANKS

Charles St. Cyprian and Ebe Gallowglass deal with a ghostly bear in London's sewers. St. Cyprian traces a sacred shape from the Third Ritual of Hloh in the air with two fingers. St. Cyprian's old mentor Carnacki called his third eye the spirit-eye.

A Single Shot Signature story by Josh Reynolds, Pro Se Press, 2015. The Rituals of Hloh are from Margery Lawrence's stories of occult detective Miles Pennoyer. Thomas Carnacki, another occult detective, is from William Hope Hodgson's Carnacki the Ghost-Finder.

December
BRIDE OF THE RAT GOD

Norah Blackstone came to America on a ship called the *Ruritania*.

Novel by Barbara Hambly. The Ruritania *is named after the country seen in Anthony Hope's* The Prisoner of Zenda *and* Rupert of Hentzau.

Christmas
VAULTS OF THE DARK BURGEONING GOD

On Maitress Island, Charles St. Cyprian and Ebe Gallowglass battle the God of the Dark Burgeoning Deaths. St. Cyprian notes, "Professor Moriarty Moreau is said to have possession of a fragment of the Pnakotic Manuscript which contains directions for sealing portals without the use of human blood." Bella Mae Jobson of the Royal Archaeological Society comes to St. Cyprian and Gallowglass' aid.

Short story by Joel Jenkins in PulpWork Christmas Special 2014, *PulpWork Press. St. Cyprian and Gallowglass are from the Royal Occultist stories by Josh Reynolds. Professor Moriarty Moreau's connection to Professor James Robert Moriarty and Doctor Alphonse Moreau is unknown. The Pnakotic Manuscript is from H. P. Lovecraft's Cthulhu Mythos. Bella Mae Jobson, originally from P. G. Wodehouse's Drones Club story "The Editor Regrets," first encountered St. Cyprian and Gallowglass in Reynolds' story "Deo Viridio."*

1925

Winter
LOST IN AVEROIGNE

Jules de Grandin and Professor Henry Jones Jr. discover the crypt of Azedarac in Averoigne. De Grandin mentions Saddoqua, Iogsotott and the *Book of Eibon*. Just then, the evil Azederac and the warrior woman Jirel of Joiry arrive from the year 1225. After Jirel defeats Azederac and is returned to her native time, Jones writes to de Grandin about a Pre-Columbian artifact he found, which may be connected to Hyperborea.

Short story by Olivier Legrand in Tales of the Shadowmen Volume 8: Agents Provocateurs, *Jean-Marc and Randy Lofficier, eds., Black Coat Press, 2011. Jules de Grandin is an occult investigator featured in several stories by Seabury Quinn. Professor Jones is, of course, Indiana Jones. Azedarac is from Clark Ashton Smith's story "The Holiness of Azédarac." Averoigne* appears in several other works by Smith. Iogsotott is better known as Yog-Sothoth from H. P. Lovecraft's Cthulhu Mythos. The Book of Eibon and Saddoqua (another name for Tsathoggua) appear in Smith's own Mythos fiction. Jirel of Joiry appears in several stories by Catherine L. Moore. While there is a Hyperborea in Greek myth, the Hyperborea cited here appears in a cycle of short stories by Smith.

CASTLE ATLANTE

Jules de Grandin discovers Jirel of Joiry fought the forces of darkness during many disparate centuries. De Grandin met Jirel while combating the sorcerer Azederac, and later attempted to return her to her own time using the *Book of Eibon*. De Grandin was accompanied by his friend, Henry Jones, Jr. Using a technique taught to him by his friend Randolph Carter, de Grandin places himself in a dreaming state, which he shares with Jirel, who is currently in the year 900 A.D.

Short story by Olivier Legrand in Doctor Omega and the Shadowmen, Jean-Marc and Randy Lofficier, eds., Black Coat Press, 2011. *This tale serves as a sequel to Legrand's story "Lost in Averoigne." Doctor Jules de Grandin is an occult investigator in many stories by Seabury Quinn. Jirel of Joiry was a female warrior created by C. L. Moore. Azederac is from Clark Ashton Smith's story "The Holiness of Azédarac." The* Book of Eibon *is from Smith's stories utilizing the Cthulhu Mythos created by H. P. Lovecraft. Henry Jones, Jr. is better known as Indiana Jones. Randolph Carter is from Lovecraft's Cthulhu Mythos stories.*

February
NOTHING TO FEAR BUT DUST

Inspector Legrasse gathers a group of allies to prevent Cthulhu from rising again. Among these allies are Bill Clutts and Michael Leigh, Anton Zarnak's apprentice.

Short story by C. J. Henderson in The Tales of Inspector Legrasse, *Mythos Books, 2005. Legrasse is from Lovecraft's "The Call of Cthulhu," which happens simultaneously with this story. Bill Clutts is from Robert E. Howard's story "Pay Day." Michael Leigh was created by Henry Kuttner, and appears in "The Salem Horror" and "The Black Kiss," the latter of which was cowritten with Robert Bloch. Dr. Anton Zarnak is a supernatural detective created by Lin Carter, and has appeared in stories by Henderson and a number of other authors. Legrasse's claim he and Zarnak last met twenty years ago is inaccurate, as they worked together three years ago, as recounted in Henderson's story "Locked Room." Also, references in "The Call of Cthulhu" to the death of Cthulhu cultist Castro having occurred many years* before must have been fictionalized, as he meets his fate in Henderson's tale. In addition, Legrasse's death in this story must be an exaggeration, as the Inspector appears again in 1941 during the events of Henderson's novel To Battle Beyond.

Spring
THE EMPEROR OF AMERICA
Naval officer Drake Roscoe enlists the services of a Pinkerton-like detective agency headed by Ned W. Regan.

1927 novel by Sax Rohmer. Drake Roscoe later became a Secret Service agent and recurring foe of Rohmer's villainess Sumuru. Regan also appeared in Roscoe's first appearance in the series, Sumuru, *as well as a series of short stories featuring a stage magician turned detective called Bazarada, which were presented as a short novel in* Salute to Bazarada and Other Stories. *At one point in "Salute to Bazarada," Bazarada impersonated a Scotland Yard Inspector named Grimsby. An Inspector Grimsby appears in Rohmer's* The Dream Detective, *featuring occult detective Moris Klaw. Since Sumuru and Klaw are in the CU, so are Roscoe, Regan, and Bazarada. Rohmer's story "Bazarada," reprinted in the 1970 Ace paperback* The Secret of Holm Peel, *features a Spanish adventurer in the time of Queen Elizabeth I named Don Sanchez Bazarada, presumably the magician's ancestor.*

WRESTLEMANIA
Tarzan and Jane visit Jane's cousin Anne and her son Todd, who live in Richmond. They discuss a picture of great-great-great-uncle John, who was in the Confederate Cavalry, and went west after the war and disappeared.

Tarzan *Sunday strip by Don Kraar and Gray Morrow, published January 26, 1992. John is, of course, John Carter, Edgar Rice Burroughs' most famous creation after Tarzan. In* Tarzan Alive, *Philip José Farmer identified Jane's mother as Jane Carter Lee. Therefore, Jane's genealogical connection to John Carter must be through her mother. Although this story seems to be set in the 1990s, Professor Porter is still alive at the time of its events. Farmer placed his death in March 1927 in* Tarzan Alive. *Therefore, the contemporary elements of the story must be fictionalized, and I have instead placed it in 1925, two years before the Professor's passing.*

Summer. The Crimson Clown begins his career as a modern day Robin Hood in "The Crimson Clown" by Johnston McCulley, *Detective Story Magazine,* July 1926.

Summer
THE DREADFUL CONSPIRACY (L'ABOMINABLE CONSPIRATION)
Inspector Ménardier interrogates murder suspect and medical student Francis Ardan, aka Clark Savage, Jr. Ardan instructs the Inspector to contact his lawyer, Mr. Theodore Marley Brooks of New York, and refers to the income generated by the Hidalgo Trading Company. One of the victims transferred billion of francs into Ardan's account at the Depository Bank of Zurich before he died. Judex disguises himself as Vallières, secretary to a banker who took part in a swindle in China with the murdered men. Brooks, nicknamed "Ham," and Andrew Blodgett "Monk" Mayfair walk through Paris. The duo came to France after Colonel John "Renny" Renwick received a letter revealing Ardan had been arrested. Renny passed the news on to Thomas J. "Long Tom" Roberts and William Harper "Johnny" Littlejohn. Ham is acquainted with Mr. Ferval, the head of the Police Judiciare. Ham and Monk meet with the man presiding over the autopsy of one of the victims, Doctor Jules de Grandin. Ham produces a letter from Judge Coméliau authorizing Ardan to sit in on de Grandin's analysis of an object found in the skull of the man de Grandin examined. Ham tells the surving conspirator two years ago a colleague of Ardan's, Dr. Lyndon Parker, encountered a Chinese tong called the Si-Fan. One of those who suffered a blow from the conspiracy was Ming Tsai Tsai Tsu, head of the secret society known as the Shin Tan. De Grandin tells Ardan a man known as Anton Zarnak spent twenty years in Tibet studying the occult with those he called the "Masters of A'alshirie." Chantecoq, the "king of detectives," previously identified one of the Shin Tan's few French agents, Leclerc, whose family had been in the group's service for several generations according to a report written in the last century by Chevalier Dupin. Monk, Ham, and Ménardier search the Paris catacombs, accompanied by a squad of policemen dispatched by Commissaire Valentin of the notorious *Brigades du Tigre.* The men sent by Valentin include Inspectors Pujol and Terrasson. One of Ming's subordinates is his sister, Ivana Orloff, who is related to the Counts Boehm of Germany. Ming used a "Mega Wave" to enslave his victims; an English physician named Doctor Septimus wrote a book on the device.
Short story by Vincent Jounieaux appearing as "L'Abominable Conspiration" in Les Compagnons de L'Ombre (Tome 10), *Jean-Marc and Randy Lofficier, eds., Rivière Blanche, 2012, and in English in* The Shadow of Judex, *Jean-Marc and Randy Lofficier, eds., Black Coat Press, 2013; reprinted in* L'Ombre de Judex, *Jean-Marc and Randy Lofficier, eds., Rivière*

Blanche, 2013. Inspector Ménardier, Ferval, and Chantecoq are from Arthur Bernède's novel Belphégor *and its simultaneous adaptation as a film serial. Francis Ardan is from Guy d'Armen's novel* Doc Ardan: City of Gold and Lepers. *Jean-Marc and Randy Lofficier's adaptation and translation of d'Armen's novel implied Ardan was really a young James Clarke "Doc" Wildman, Jr. Brooks, Mayfair, Renwick, Roberts, and Littlejohn will become Doc's aides in his future battles against the forces of evil. Although Jounieaux indicates Ardan/Wildman and company are based out of the Empire State Building, that structure had yet to be built in 1925. Doc uses the name of the Hidalgo Trading Company as a front for the warehouse where he stores his vehicles. Judex is from the serial of the same name directed by Louis Feuillade. Doctor Jules de Grandin appeared in several pulp tales by Seabury Quinn. Judge Ernest Coméliau is from the Maigret novels by Georges Simenon. Dr. Lyndon Parker is the best friend and biographer of August Derleth's sleuth Solar Pons. Pons and Parker's 1923 encounter with the Si-Fan (from Sax Rohmer's Fu Manchu novels) was recounted in "The Adventure of the Six Silver Spiders"; Pons and Parker would have many more encounters with the secret society in the years to come. Ming Tai Tsou, aka Monsieur Ming and the Yellow Shadow, is the leader of the Shin Tan in Henri Vernes' Bob Morane novels. Ming is aided in the Morane books by his niece Tania Orloff, Ivana's daughter. Anton Zarnak is an occult detective created by Lin Carter, whose further exploits have been chronicled by several other writers. The Masters of A'alshirie are from Zarnak stories by C. J. Henderson. Leclerc's ancestor Honoré Leclerc appeared as an agent of the Shin Tan in Dennis E. Power's story "No Good Deed . . ." (*Tales of the Shadowmen Volume 6: Grand Guignol, *Jean-Marc and Randy Lofficier, eds., Black Coat Press, 2009). The Chevalier C. Auguste Dupin appeared in a trio of stories by Edgar Allan Poe. The* Brigades du Tigre *was the subject of a titular television series from 1974–1983, which featured Valentin, Pujol, and Terrasson as its leads. The Counts Boehm are from Paul Féval's novel* John Devil. *The Mega Wave and Doctor Septimus are from* The Yellow "M," *a story in Edgar P. Jacobs' comic book series* Blake and Mortimer.

October 18–December 6
THE EXPRESS DIARIES

An unlikely assemblage of individuals travels across Europe via the Orient Express to obtain the pieces of a statue called the Sedefkar Simulacrum before the cult known as the Brothers of the Skin can do so. Professor Julius Smith, whose apparent death sets the adventurers on their course, first speaks at the Challenger Trust Banquet Lecture. One of the members of the group, Professor Alphonse Moretti, finds a reference to the Simulacrum in von

Juntz's *Unaussprechlichen Kulten*. The Duc d'Essientes is a member of the Brothers of the Skin. Moretti finds mentions of a Duc Jean Floressas d'Essientes in fashion and society papers from Paris in the 1870s. The leader of the expedition, Mrs. Betty Sunderland, writes in her diary "I suspect even the remarkable Mr. S. Holmes would find it difficult to uncover a trail grown so cold." On the Express, another member of the group, Colonel Neville Goodenough, pushes past a portly balding gentleman with a small waxed moustache, who is either French or Belgian.

Novel by Nick Marsh, Innsmouth Free Press, 2012. *The Challenger Trust is named after Professor George Edward Challenger from Arthur Conan Doyle's* The Lost World *and other works. Consulting detective Sherlock Holmes is Doyle's most famous creation. Friedrich von Juntz's* Unaussprechlichen Kulten *is a book created by Robert E. Howard as part of H. P. Lovecraft's Cthulhu Mythos. The Duc d'Essientes (originally des Esseintes) is from J.-K. Huysmans' 1884 novel* À Rebours. *The Duc appears to have extended his lifespan via supernatural means. The gentleman with the waxed moustache is Agatha Christie's detective Hercule Poirot.*

November

MRS. HUDSON AT THE CHRISTMAS HOTEL

Dr. Watson reveals Mrs. Hudson is now Professor Challenger's housekeeper.

Short story by Dr. Watson, edited by Paul Magrs in Encounters of Sherlock Holmes, *George Mann, ed., Titan Books, 2013. Mrs. Hudson is referred to as "Hettie" by her sister Nellie. However, many pastiches conflate her with Martha, Holmes' housekeeper at his Sussex cottage, from "His Last Bow." Either Hettie is a pet name, or her full name is Martha Henrietta Hudson, and her sister prefers to refer to her by the shortened version of her middle name. Mrs. Hudson was still acting as Holmes' housekeeper in 1941 (see Manly Wade Wellman's "But Our Hero Was Not Dead"), but perhaps she left his employ for a short time to work for his cousin Professor Challenger. The briefness of her tenure likely had to do with Challenger's formidable temper.*

THE TALISMAN

Jacques de Trémeuse (aka Judex) pays a call on Henry Jones, seeking his help in finding the Baroness Hilda von Einem. A mystical talisman in Judex's possession has been stolen by the Baroness, who is in an alliance with a black magician called Mocata. Hercule Poirot is a passenger on the Orient Express alongside Judex and Jones. Judex learns von Einem's location from a member of the Companions of the Rosy Hours. After defeating von Einem and Mocata and recovering the talisman, Judex tells Jones he will give it to the Sâr Dubnotal to destroy.

Short story by Nicholas Boving in The Shadow of Judex, *Jean-Marc and Randy Lofficier, eds., Black Coat Press, 2013; reprinted in French in* L'Ombre de Judex, *Jean-Marc and Randy Lofficier, eds., Rivière Blanche, 2013. Judex is the title character of Louis Feuillade's classic film serial. Dr. Henry "Indiana" Jones, Jr. needs no introduction. Baroness Hilda von Einem and the Companions of the Rosy Hours are from John Buchan's novel* Greenmantle. *Mocata is from Dennis Wheatley's novel* The Devil Rides Out. *Hercule Poirot, of course, is Agatha Christie's master detective. The Sâr Dubnotal was the subject of a French pulp magazine series penned by an anonymous author, who may have been Norbert Sevestre. The year is given in the story; the November placement is based on Nick Marsh's* The Express Diaries, *in which an unnamed Poirot has a cameo aboard the Orient Express during November of 1925.*

Mid December
THE THIRD DEATH OF HENRY ANTRIM

Charles St. Cyprian and Ebe Gallowglass investigate a dead body at a Christmas party hosted by Porthos "Porky" Caruthers, whose guests include Roberta "Bobbie" Wickham. St. Cyprian notes the bite marks on the neck of the victim are not the discreet pinpricks of Stoker's sanitized account of the last vampire outbreak, but rather the red, wide marks of a beast of prey. St. Cyprian examines Caruthers' collection of wanted posters for outlaws of the Old West, including Jesse James, John Wesley Hardin, Butch Cavendish, and Billy the Kid. Bobbie refers to an incident at an art opening, and St. Cyprian replies the artist was a lycanthrope. Caruthers owns a .45 Colt Peacemaker that allegedly belonged to Lone Crow, an Indian mystic, gunslinger, and devil-hunter mentioned in the diaries of Shotgun Ferguson. Caruthers says he has an agent trying to get access to a box of unpublished dime novels sealed away by Miskatonic University.

Short story by Josh Reynolds in PulpWork Christmas Special 2013, *PulpWork Press. Roberta "Bobbie" Wickham appears in two different series by P. G. Wodehouse, the Jeeves books and the Mr. Mulliner stories. The last* vampire outbreak in England was chronicled in Bram Stoker's Dracula. Butch Cavendish is one of the Lone Ranger's foes. The lycanthropic artist is Gabriel-Ernest Smythe from H. H. Munro's story "Gabriel-Ernest." St. Cyprian encountered Smythe in Reynolds' story "The Artist as Wolf." Lone Crow and Shotgun Ferguson appear in "weird" Western stories by Joel Jenkins. In Jenkins' stories, Lone Crow sometimes visits Miskatonic University (from H. P. Lovecraft's Cthulhu Mythos). This story takes place two weeks before Christmas.

1926

April 3, 1926–February 9, 2009
ATOMIC ROBO AND THE SHADOW FROM BEYOND TIME

Atomic Robo battles an eldritch horror that exists across time over the course of 83 years. Ro-Man appears outside Robo's office in the 1971 chapter.

Five-issue miniseries by Brian Clevinger and Scott Wegener, Red 5 Comics, April–September 2009. Robo's transtemporal foe, though not named, is unmistakably the Great Old One Yog-Sothoth. Ro-Man is from the science fiction film Robot Monster. *Although the film's ending reveals its apocalyptic events were only a dream, Ro-Man is shown coming out of a cave. Robo probably convinced Ro-Man to abandon his plans for conquest and join Tesladyne. The Moon Ro-Man hails from must be that of an alternate universe, possibly even that of the ERB-AU.*

May
ROULETABILLE AND THE NEW WORLD ORDER

The wealthy James Worth asks Joseph Rouletabille to look into the disappearance of a train. Rouletabille says this is hardly a unique problem, noting Sherlock Holmes was peripherally involved in the case of "the Lost Special." Worth tells Rouletabille his father Adam was one of the castaways on Lincoln Island alongside Cyrus West and General Herbert Brown, although all references to the elder Worth were expunged from accounts of their time on the island. Worth also says "Robin Hood is more than merely my favorite character, he is an early embodiment of the spirit of rebellion, just like Ned Ludd or the Scarecrow of Romney Marsh," and tells Rouletabille he needs to be at Vermissa Junction in Luzerne tomorrow. Aboard the train to the junction, Rouletabille meets the former Private Danner, a superstrong man who, like the detective, served under Captain Crouan during the Great War. The train is hijacked by two oddly-dressed soldiers, one of whom is a marksman wielding a weapon that resembles the pneumatic carbines used by the crew of the *Nautilus*. Rouletabille, Danner, and the other passengers find themselves at a mine that is the main enclave of the Catharus Society, of which Worth is the leader. Worth says his father was the true Captain Nemo, not Prince Dakkar. One of the Society's senior officers is Ward Baldwin. Rouletabille receives some aid from Anthony Rogers of the American Radioactive Gas Corporation, who unholsters a pistol that reminds Rouletabille of one he saw wielded by Kapitan Mors a decade ago. Worth told Danner he had a diary written by Danner's father, Professor Abednego Danner, claiming the elder Danner was rocketed to Earth from a dying planet as a child, and adopted by the Danner family, explaining Hugo's abilities. The duo, along with Danner, learns Worth was trying to charter the staff and equipment of the Maracot Diving Company for an exploration of the Pacific, after they had concluded their own excursion to the deep Atlantic. Rouletabille remembers an earlier attempt at a Maracot expedition to the Atlantic, which fell through when a man named Ian Hassett embezzled virtually all of the company's funds.

Short story by Martin Gately in Tales of the Shadowmen Volume 11: Force Majeure, *Jean-Marc and Randy Lofficier, eds., Black Coat Press, 2014. Joseph Rouletabille is a French journalist and detective in novels by Gaston Leroux. "The Lost Special" is a reference to Arthur Conan Doyle's story of the same name, which refers to "an amateur reasoner of some celebrity," implicitly Doyle's detective Sherlock Holmes. Vermissa Junction is from Doyle's Holmes novel* The Valley of Fear. *The Maracot Diving Corporation is from Doyle's novel* The Maracot Deep. *Ian Hassett and the earlier unsuccessful Maracot expedition are from Gately's story "The Petrifying Well" (*Sherlock Holmes: The Crossovers Casebook, *Howard Hopkins, ed., Moonstone Books, 2012). The* Nautilus *and Captain Nemo are from Jules Verne's novel* 20,000 Leagues Under the Sea *and* The Mysterious Island. *Lincoln Island and Herbert Brown are also from* The Mysterious Island. *Cyrus West is from John Willard's play* The Cat and the Canary; *Gately's story "Rouletabille vs. the Cat" (*Tales of the Shadowmen Volume 10: Esprit de Corps, *Jean-Marc and Randy Lofficier, eds., Black Coat Press, 2013) conflated West with Cyrus Smith (aka Cyrus Harding) from* The Mysterious Island. *The Scarecrow of Romney Marsh (Doctor Christopher Syn) appears in novels by Russell Thorndike. Hugo Danner, Captain Crouan, and Professor Abednego Danner are from Philip*

Wylie's novel Gladiator. *The Catharus Society is the precursor to THRUSH from the television series* The Man from U.N.C.L.E. *Ward Baldwin is a high-ranking member of THRUSH in David McDaniel's tie-in novels for* The Man from U.N.C.L.E. *Anthony Rogers is from Philip Francis Nowlan's novel* Armageddon 2419 A.D., *establishing the future seen in that novel as one of several possible futures for the CU. Kapitan Mors is a German pulp hero who encountered Rouletabille in Gately's story "Leviathan Creek" (*Tales of the Shadowmen Volume 8: Agents Provocateurs, *Jean-Marc and Randy Lofficier, eds., Black Coat Press, 2011). Several other accounts verify the Captain Nemo of Jules Verne's novels was indeed Prince Dakkar, so Worth's story must be at least partially false. His claims about Hugo Danner's origins are definitely false, as Danner's strength is the result of a serum which his father injected into him in utero. Hugo's alleged alien origins evoke Superman's.*

1927

Spring
LES CINQ DÉTECTIVES (THE FIVE DETECTIVES)
Bob, who was allegedly raised by Sherlock Holmes; Jonas, who was raised by Monsieur Lecoq; Scipion, a former collaborator with Nick Carter; Leonard, a former assistant to Inspector Tony; and a man named Valentin team up to solve a case.

Novel by Gabriel Bernard, 1928. All of the first four detectives' mentors are already in the CU. It is unlikely Bob was actually raised by Sherlock Holmes, but he is probably a former student of the Great Detective's.

THE GREAT BUDGET CONSPIRACY
Sexton Blake and Mr. Mist (Ian Craig, a disfigured scientist who uses an invention called the Invicta Ray to become invisible) fight Rudolph Kent, a vicious blackmailer who also runs a drug-smuggling ring in Limehouse. Assisting Blake and Mist is Inspector Red Berry.

Story by Gwyn Evans in Union Jack *#1280, April 28, 1928. This story is the third part of the "Mr. Mist" storyline starring Blake. "Berry" is clearly*

Inspector Red Kerry from Sax Rohmer's Dope, Tales of Chinatown, *and* Yellow Shadows. *The first two chapters, appearing in #1277 and #1278, were titled "The Man Who Walked by Night" and "The Phantom of Scotland Yard" respectively. The fourth and final chapter, "The Mystery of the Missing Mace," appeared in #1281, and had several references to "Berry."*

November 10–Christmas
VILE BODIES

Miles Malpractice, the ex-King of Ruritania, Lady Metroland, Pamela Popham, and Peter Pastmaster appear, and David Lennox is mentioned.

Novel by Evelyn Waugh. Miles Malpractice, Lady Metroland and her son Peter Pastmaster, Pamela Popham, and David Lennox first appeared in Waugh's novel Decline and Fall. *Ruritania is from Anthony Hope's* The Prisoner of Zenda, Rupert of Hentzau, *and* The Heart of Princess Osra. *The ex-King seen here must be the same former monarch of Ruritania seen in the works of P. G. Wodehouse.*

1928

Winter
SWEET GRASS

Saul Macartney and Camilia Lanigan are mentioned

Short story by Henry S. Whitehead in Weird Tales, *July 1929; reprinted in* Jumbee and Other Uncanny Tales, Arkham House, 1944. *Saul Macartney and Camilia Lanigan are from Whitehead's Gerald Canevin story "West India Lights." For an explanation of how the Canevin stories fit into the CU, see the 1929 entry for "The Shut Room."*

A DARK REFLECTION

Doctor Francis Ardan discovers the man known as Gurrhu and his brother are misusing his father's money to plan a takeover of the Amazon and oppress the displaced Aztecs in the area.

Short story by Matthew Dennion in Harry Dickson vs. the Spider, *Jean-Marc and Randy Lofficier, eds., Black Coat Press, 2014. Doctor Francis*

Ardan is from Guy d'Armen's novel Doc Ardan: City of Gold and Lepers, *which has been interpreted as a disguised adventure of a bronze-skinned hero of the pulps. Gurrhu battled detective Harry Dickson in Jean Ray's pulp novel* The Iron Temple.

Spring
THE DEATH OF COUNTESS CAGLIOSTRO
Faustine gives a young woman a letter from her deceased grandmother, Joséphine Balsamo, the Countess Cagliostro, which explains how she had an illegitimate child, Joseph, the girl's father, by a circus contortionist, Alexandre "Sandre" Cascabel. The Countess says if he had gone after the Moonstone, or the Hollow Needle, she could have saved Joseph from his fate, but he instead stole *The Brigand's Painting*. The Countess was visited by the Master of the Black Coats (aka the Colonel-Who-Never-Died) and his executioner, the Marchef, who instructed her to kill Joseph. The Colonel says Joseph is presently being kept in the caves of Palazzio Monteleone. If the Countess kills Joseph, the Colonel will have her taken to Sartene, near the Convent of La Merci, and she will live the rest of her life in peace. The Countess was later visited by her former second-in-command Marga.

Short story by Jean-Marc and Randy Lofficier published as an epilogue in Arsène Lupin vs. Countess Cagliostro *by Maurice Leblanc, adapted and translated by Jean-Marc and Randy Lofficier, Black Coat Press, 2010. Joséphine Balsamo is from Leblanc's Arsène Lupin novels* The Countess of Cagliostro *and* Countess Cagliostro's Revenge, *both of which are collected in* Arsène Lupin vs. Countess Cagliostro. *Faustine is also from* Countess Cagliostro's Revenge. *The Hollow Needle is from Leblanc's Lupin novel of the same name. Alexandre "Sandre" Cascabel is from Jules Verne's novel* César Cascabel. *Marga Sandorf, the niece of the title character of Verne's novel* Mathias Sandorf, *was created by Rick Lai, and appears in his collection* Sisters of the Shadows: The Cagliostro Curse. *The Moonstone is from Wilkie Collins' novel of the same name. The Brigand's Painting, the Colonel-Who-Never-Died (Colonel Bozzo-Corona), the Marchef, the Palazzio Monteleone, and the Convent of La Merci are from the Black Coats novels by Paul Féval. The year is conjecture.*

November
THE POISONED CHOCOLATES CASE
Roger Sheringham competes with the members of his Crimes Circle, all of whom share his interest in criminology, to solve a murder. The winner is the mild-mannered Ambrose Chitterwick.

Novel by Anthony Berkeley. Roger Sheringham is in the CU through an appearance in the round robin novel Ask a Policeman, *which also features Dorothy L. Sayers' Lord Peter Wimsey (a Wold Newton Family member), Gladys Mitchell's Mrs. Bradley, and Clemence Dane and Helen Simpson's Sir John Saumarez. After this case, Chitterwick went on to appear in two novels by Berkeley that did not feature Sheringham,* The Piccadilly Murder *and* Trial and Error.

1929

Winter
THE SHUT ROOM
Gerald Canevin and his friend Lord Carruth investigate a room haunted by a highwayman who died there. Carruth mentions a "parallel case" that happened years earlier in Britain. Canevin realizes the case is that of a court jester who haunted the room in which he died, and mentions the case was recorded by William Hope Hodgson in *Carnacki the Ghost-Finder.*

Short story by Henry S. Whitehead in Weird Tales, *April 1930; reprinted in* West India Lights, *Arkham House, 1946. Carruth and Canevin's comments treat the events of Hodgson's Carnacki tale "The Whistling Room" as a real occurrence. Canevin is an American writer from a Virginia family who travels the Caribbean, where he keeps encountering Voodoo manifestations and ghosts. This crossover brings him into the CU.*

Winter–Autumn
THE JUDEX CODEX
Raymond Mystère and Henrietta de Marigny explore a Mayan temple in Guatemala. When Raymond first met Henrietta at the University of Sorbonne, he thought she was too interested in visiting professors like Henry Jones, Thomas Swift, and John Kenton. Henrietta's brother Etienne-Laurent de Marigny was an archaeologist specializing in occult lore, who was inspired in his choice of profession by his friend Pierre d'Artois. Henrietta was once kidnapped by a madman named Don Jose to sacrifice to a dark god. Her twin sister Louise had been previously abducted and killed

by the Don. Etienne was able to attend Miskatonic University through d'Artois' influence. Etienne disappeared in 1926 while investigating some ruins in the swamps of Louisiana, the inhabitants of which he believed to be the remnants of a Tcho-Tcho group that had come to North America during the Asian Migration. When he resurfaced, he opened a shop in New Orleans dealing in occult artifacts. A group of five men, including two named Hernandez and Aguirre respectively, attempt to steal a stone tablet discovered by Raymond and Henrietta. Months later, Raymond, recognizing the pictoglyphs on the tablet as representing Vedic words, tells the pregnant Henrietta his grandfather, Doctor Mystère, claimed his vehicle, the Electric Hotel, was based on ancient Vedic designs. Henrietta and Raymond's student Jean Aubry introduces them to his father, Comte Jacques de Trémeuse. The two visit the Comte's estate, where they meet his wife Jacqueline and their two sons, their old family friend Prosper Cocantin, his wife Daisy, and their young son Jacques. Trémeuse tells Raymond and Henrietta his mother made his brother Roger and he swear to kill the banker Favraux for driving their father to suicide. Trémeuse shows them a tablet he discovered in Africa, one of a group of such items, almost identical to the one they discovered, which has a ring set into it. Prosper and Daisy's adopted son Michel Cocantin, formerly known as the Licorice Kid, accompanies Henrietta and Jacqueline on a trip to buy baby clothes. Henrietta is abducted by members of a group known as the Men in Black. Jacques Cocantin has been learning the martial arts from a young Annamese boy named Cato. Henrietta refers to tales of the legendary continents of Hyboria, Lemuria, Mu, and Atlantis. Raymond says the area where he and Henrietta found the temple was near the region described by Ventidius as Atala, which had ties with Atlantis, and was sometimes mistaken for it. Raymond suspects there was an African civilization that was the true parent of lost cities such as Zu-Vendis, Kôr, Opar, and Zimbabue. Raymond and Trémeuse charter *The Pious Woman*, owned and operated by Captain Owen Kettle, to take them to Easter Island. They meet the manager of the island, Señor Ortiz. Raymond and Trémeuse are confronted by the Men in Black, who are accompanied by Dr. René Belloq. Belloq claims to have trained at Rache Churan. A crystal ball emits an image of a man resembling an elderly version of Trémeuse, who tells him and Raymond Trémeuse is a member of the house of Elessar Telcontar. Trémeuse's forebear refers to the crystal ball as a *Palantir*, and charges him to take the Book of Thain, the Book of Kings, and the Book of Mazarbul to "the one who can best translate them for your people." Henrietta identifies Khokarsa as the sunken island civilization mentioned in the African tablets discovered by Trémeuse. It is mentioned some believe the tale of Numenor to be the

Oxford scholar to whom Henrietta sent the three books' own version of Atlantis, rather than the story of an island empire that existed ages before Atlantis. An epic about the hero named Hadon described in the African tablets was popularized by an American author whose work was recommended to the Mystères by the Ironcastle family. Wooden tablets discovered by Raymond on Easter Island form the epic tale of a warrior-King named Thongor who lived in ancient Lemuria. After Jacques' apparent death, his son Frédéric-Jean de Trémeuse followed in his footsteps, adopting the identity of Frédéric-Jean Orth, aka L'Ombre. Jacques Cocantin grew up to become Chief of the Sûreté after his predecessor, Chief Inspector Dreyfuss, became mentally unstable. A film version of Inspector Cocantin's famous case against Sir Charles Litton, the jewel thief known as the Phantom, portrayed him as a buffoon, causing the Inspector to demand the filmmakers change his name.

Short story by Dennis E. Power in The Shadow of Judex, *Jean-Marc and Randy Lofficier, eds., Black Coat Press, 2013; reprinted in French in* L'Ombre de Judex, *Jean-Marc and Randy Lofficier, eds., Rivière Blanche, 2013. Raymond Mystère and Henrietta de Marigny are the parents of the title character of Alfredo Castelli's comic book* Martin Mystère. *Henrietta is meant to be the same character as Yvonne Marigny from E. Hoffmann Price's Pierre d'Artois story "The Devil's Crypt." Don Jose and Louise (de) Marigny are also from "The Devil's Crypt." Etienne-Laurent de Marigny is from H. P. Lovecraft and Price's story "Through the Gates of the Silver Key." Etienne's shop will be inherited by his son Henri-Laurent de Marigny, as seen in Brian Lumley's Titus Crow novels. Henry Jones, Sr. is Indiana Jones' father. Dr. René Belloq is from the first Indiana Jones movie,* Raiders of the Lost Ark. *Thomas Swift is better known as Tom Swift from the novels by Victor Appleton. John Kenton is from A. Merritt's* The Ship of Ishtar. *Miskatonic University and the Tcho-Tcho are staples of the Cthulhu Mythos. Hernandez is a descendant of the robber Hernandez from Joseph Conrad's novel* Nostromo. *Aguirre is a descendant of the fictionalized version of the historical conquistador Don Lope de Aguirre seen in the film* Aguirre: The Wrath of God. *Doctor Mystère appeared in a series of novels by Paul d'Ivoi. The Martin Mystère comics have established Martin was the grandson of Doctor Mystère's adopted son Cigale. Jacques de Trémeuse, his brother Roger, his wife Jacqueline, Jacqueline's son Jean Aubry, Prosper Cocantin, his wife Daisy, their adopted son the Licorice Kid, and Favraux are from Louis Feuillade's film serial* Judex. *Jacques Cocantin is meant to be Inspector Jacques Clouseau from the movie* The Pink Panther *and its sequels. Cato will grow up to be the Inspector's manservant and sparring* partner. Chief Inspector Dreyfus and Sir Charles Litton are also from the Pink Panther films. The tablet found by Raymond and Henrietta in Guatemala and the one found by Jacques in Africa, when combined, describe the events of J. R. R. Tolkien's fantasy saga The Lord of the Rings. In Tolkien's books, Elessar is the name Aragorn took after assuming the throne of the Reunited Kingdoms. Telcontor is an Elvish term for his nickname of Strider. The Palantir is one of the scrying stones used by the order of Wizards. Tolkien claimed The Book of Thain was his source for The Hobbit, The Lord of the Rings, and The Silmarillion. The  Book of Kings and The Book of Mazarbul were supposedly the other two books that served as Tolkien's source for Middle Earth lore not found in The Book of Thain. The Men in Black are the subject of many conspiracy theories, but the version of the group seen here is the same one that will later battle Martin Mystère. Power reveals the Men in Black are the modern day equivalent of the Black Riders, the Nazgûl, which served the Dark Lord Sauron. Power also implies the Men in Black are connected to the Nine from Philip José Farmer's novels A Feast Unknown, Lord of the Trees, and The Mad Goblin; although the Secrets of the Nine trilogy takes place in an alternate reality to the Crossover Universe, Win Scott Eckert's story "The Wild Huntsman" establishes a version of the Nine exists in the CU. Numenor is an island that rose from the sea in The Lord of the Rings and The Silmarillion. Hyboria is from Robert E. Howard's Conan stories. Ventidius Varro and Atala are from H. Warner Munn's novel The Ship from Atlantis. Philip José Farmer, in his novels of Ancient Opar, revealed the lost cities of Zu-Vendis (from H. Rider Haggard's Allan Quatermain), Kôr (from Haggard's She and sequels), and Opar (from the books about Lord Greystoke by Edgar Rice Burroughs) were among the remnants of the destroyed Central African empire of Khokarsa, which was later mistakenly identified with Atlantis. Power's story adds Zimbabue (from Charles R.

Saunders' Imaro novels, the precursor to Zimbabwe) to the list. Hadon is the hero of the first two Ancient Opar books, Hadon of Ancient Opar *and* Flight to Opar. *Captain Owen Kettle is featured in a series of books by C. J. Cutcliffe Hyne. Señor Ortiz is meant to be an ancestor of a villain from Edgar Rice Burroughs' Moon series. Although the Moon books take place in the Edgar Rice Burroughs Alternate Universe (ERB-AU), there is no reason why Ortiz could not exist in both that universe and the CU. The Rache Churan monastery is from Sax Rohmer's Fu Manchu novels. The Ironcastle family is from Farmer's adaptation and translation of J.-H. Rosny aîné's novel* Ironcastle. *Thongor of Lemuria is the hero of a series of books by Lin Carter. Frédéric-Jean Orth, aka L'Ombre, is the hero of a series of novels by Alain Page; Jean-Marc Lofficier identified L'Ombre as Judex's son in his article "The Tangled Web: Genealogies of the Members of the French Wold Newton Families–Rocambole and Fantômas" on the website* The French Wold Newton Universe.

Spring
THE BANDIT

One of South American bandit chief Ramon Manrique's assistants turns out to be a Pinkerton detective who has been in contact with "Kennedy the Assistant Commissioner." Detective Inspector Peters arrests Ramon.

1929 novel by Leslie Charteris. Kennedy and Peters also appear in Charteris' novels featuring the Saint, as well as the non-series novels X Esquire, The White Rider, *and* Daredevil.

SWAN SONG

The tyrant known as Gurrhu is driven out of his kingdom by the jungle girl Rima and the birds she communicates with.

Short story by Matthew Dennion in Harry Dickson vs. the Spider, *Jean-Marc and Randy Lofficier, eds., Black Coat Press, 2014. Gurrhu will go on to battle Harry Dickson, "the American Sherlock Holmes," as seen in Jean Ray's pulp novel* The Iron Temple. *Rima is from W. H. Hudson's novel* Green Mansions.

Summer
TARZAN AND THE LAND THAT TIME FORGOT
Traveling back to civilization in the O-220 zeppelin after another visit to the world at Earth's core, Tarzan and the ship's crew find themselves shipwrecked on an island inhabited by prehistoric creatures.

Short story by Joe R. Lansdale in The Worlds of Edgar Rice Burroughs, *Mike Resnick and Robert T. Garcia, eds., Baen Books, 2013. The jungle lord first traveled to world at the Earth's core in the O-220 in Burroughs'* Tarzan at the Earth's Core. *The destruction of the O-220 in Lansdale's story must be an exaggeration, as Tarzan used it to travel to Pellucidar again in both 1960 and 1986, as seen in the Sunday* Tarzan *comic strip stories "Dead Moon of Pellucidar" (aka "The Jewel of Pellucidar") and "Back to Pellucidar," respectively. The jungle lord will make at least two more trips to the land that time forgot in the future, as seen in the comic book* Tarzan in the Land That Time Forgot *and the Sunday* Tarzan *strip story "Return to the Land That Time Forgot."*

Late July–October 24
PICKMAN'S OTHER MODEL (1929)
The narrator, a Mr. Blackman, says of actress Vera Endecott, who modeled nude for Richard Upton Pickman, "Later, I would come to recognize some commonality between her face and those of such movie 'vamps' and *femme fatales* as Theda Bara, Eva Galli, Musidora, and, in particular, Pola Negri."

Sequel to Lovecraft's "Pickman's Model" by Caitlín R. Kiernan in Sirenia Digest *#28, March 2008; reprinted in* New Cthulhu: The Recent Weird, *Paula Guran, ed., Prime Books, 2011. Eva Galli is from Peter Straub's novel* Ghost Story. *Rick Lai writes, "There are numerous interconnections in Peter Straub's works.* Black House, *coauthored with Stephen King, mentions the fictional town of Arden, Wisconsin, which was the setting for Straub's* If You Could See Me Now. *Miles Teagarden, the adult hero of* If You Could See Me Now, *makes a brief appearance as a high school senior in Straub's* Shadowland. *In* Black House, *there is an elderly serial killer, who is actually a worshipper of the Crimson King from King's* Dark Tower *series, living in a nursing home in Wisconsin. His bills at the nursing home are paid by an unseen woman, Althea Burnside, who pretends to be his aunt. This whole scenario had an earlier parallel in Straub's* Ghost Story, *in which an enigmatic woman, Florence de Peyser, was always pretending to be the aunt of a shape-shifting female monster posing as a human. Florence de Peyser was orchestrating a vendetta against the Wanderley family. The sole survivor of*

this vendetta appeared to be Don Wanderley, whose brother David was destroyed by the shape-shifter. Florence de Peyser appears to have survived the events of Ghost Story. In Black House, *one of the serial killer's victims is eventually revealed to have been Milton Wanderly, a school teacher and the 'kid brother' of Don Wanderly. Note that the spelling of the surname (no 'e' before the 'y') is slightly different from* Ghost Story. *If Don Wanderley of* Ghost Story *is Don Wanderly of* Black House, *then is the murder of Milton somehow related to the vendetta in* Ghost Story? *Are Althea Burnside and Florence de Peyser aliases of the same demonic female?*

"The setting of Ghost Story *is Milburn, New York. There is a brief funeral in Milburn in Straub's* Koko. *There are also some scenes in a fictional Connecticut town, Hampstead. Straub's* Floating Dragon *is set in Hampstead. Charles Daisy, a resident of Hampstead, appears in both* Floating Dragon *and* Koko. Koko *is the first of a trilogy by Straub. The other two parts are* Mystery *and* The Throat. *The connection between* Koko *and* Mystery *is fairly loose (there are references to Timothy Underhill from* Koko *in* Mystery*), but* The Throat *is closely linked to both* Koko *and* Mystery. *A few short stories also hook into the trilogy. In* Koko, *Timothy Underhill writes two short stories, 'Blue Rose' and 'The Juniper Tree.' Straub then wrote stories with those names, which can be found in* Houses without Doors. *In the afterword to* Houses without Doors, *Straub indicates that these are supposed to be the stories written by Underhill in* Koko. *'The Juniper Tree' can just be viewed as Underhill's fiction, but 'Blue Rose' features Lt. Harry Beevers from* Koko *as its main character. It is unclear whether real events from Beevers' life are described in 'Blue Rose,' or whether Beevers' life is being heavily distorted by Underhill. 'The Ghost Village' and 'Bunny is Good Bread' (also known as 'Fee') are short stories from* Magic Terror. *'The Ghost Village' features Underhill and other characters from* Koko *and* The Throat *('The Ghost Village' actually incorporates a*

Vietnam flashback from The Throat). 'Bunny is Good Bread' is the origin story of the villain from The Throat (the short story only makes sense if you read it after the novel). Both The Throat and 'Bunny is Good Bread' describe a non-existent movie, From Dangerous Depths, starring Robert Ryan, Ida Lupino, and William Bendix, and directed by Robert Siodmak. Stephen King did something similar with a fictional Western starring John Payne, Rory Calhoun, and Karen Steele in The Regulators. There are two radically different plot summaries of Straub's fictional movie. According to The Throat, From Dangerous Depths is about a child-murderer (similar to Fritz Lang's actual movie, M). According to 'Bunny is Good Bread,' From Dangerous Depths is about an embezzlement scheme with a love triangle that leads to murderous rampage. Although both versions of this bogus film have the same lead actors, they play radically different roles with radically different names. Perhaps From Dangerous Depths was an anthology movie with the main actors playing different roles in each story.

"Both Koko and The Hellfire Club feature a town called Westerholm. However, Koko has the town in New York, and The Hellfire Club has the town in Connecticut. An obscure Ohio town called Azure plays a small role in The Throat, 'Bunny is Good Bread,' and Mr. X. Mr. X could arguably be classified as a Cthulhu Mythos story. The title character is a sort of mutant born with strange powers. After reading H. P. Lovecraft, he becomes convinced that he was fathered by one of the Great Old Ones (like Wilbur Whateley in 'The Dunwich Horror.') Mr. X eventually learns that he is actually descended from a family of humans with incredible psychic abilities, but the novel's conclusion indicates that the family is descended from some sort of weird extra-dimensional ancestor. In The Throat, there is an Arkham College in Millhaven, Illinois. Like the asylum in the Batman comics, the name is homage to Lovecraft's New England town of Arkham." In addition to the connections noted by Lai, Ricky Hawthorne from Ghost Story is mentioned in Floating Dragon, and Timothy Underhill also appears in the book Lost Boy, Lost Girl and its sequel, In the Night Room. Lai also notes that an alternate version of Lamont Von Heilitz from Mystery appears in Straub's "Under Venus," included in the collection Wild Animals. The Von Heilitz seen in "Under Venus" is probably an alternate reality counterpart to the character seen in Mystery. According to Mystery, Von Heilitz was an amateur criminologist, and the inspiration for the radio version of the shadowy vigilante (the pulp version of the character is not mentioned). Presumably, at least the early episodes of The Shadow radio series were actually distorted accounts of Von Heilitz's investigations.

Autumn
EYE OF THE TIGER-MAN

A trio of operatives for the Black Coats is set upon by Judex. The hero's young ally the Licorice Kid is poisoned by one of the criminals. Doctor de Villiers-Pagan analyzes the Kid's blood sample. Judex travels to Benares to seek the antidote to the poison. He confronts the Brahman Sourina, whose knowledge of the jungles and their native flora is said to be second only to a legendary hero called Felifax. Judex once encountered a South American cannibal tribe called the Shamatari. He resolves to retrieve the healing plants, the Leaves of Mercy, and get out of the area as fast as a human who has not taken Professor Gibberne's "accelerator" drug can. Felifax himself attempts to prevent Judex from taking the Leaves. Judex confidently thinks he has survived battle with the likes of Dracula.

Short story by Christofer Nigro in The Shadow of Judex, *Jean-Marc and Randy Lofficier, eds., Black Coat Press, 2013; reprinted in French in* L'Ombre de Judex, *Jean-Marc and Randy Lofficier, eds., Rivière Blanche, 2013. Judex is from Louis Feuillade's film serial of the same name. The Black Coats are a criminal society featured in novels by Paul Féval. Doctor de Villiers-Pagan designed the artificial heart of Jean de La Hire's hero the Nyctalope. Felifax and Sourina are from Paul Féval fils' novel* Felifax the Tiger-Man. *This story takes place between Books 1 and 2 of the younger Féval's novel. The Shamatari tribe is from Ruggero Deodato's film* Cannibal Holocaust. *Professor Gibberne is from H. G. Wells' story "The New Accelerator." Judex encountered Dracula (from Bram Stoker's titular novel) in Nigro's story "The Ultimate Prize," set in 1919.*

1930

January 14
THE TOURNAMENT OF THE TREASURE

On Papeete, Sailor Steve Costigan takes shore leave from the *Sea Girl*. He runs into his old sparring partner Ned Dargan at an athletic club. Dargan tells Steve he's been hired to take part in a tournament, and he has seen

Butch "Slug" O'Leary and Mullargan in town. The men who hired Dargan are named Gutman and Cairo. Steve and Dargan go to the American Bar to meet Dargan's clients, as well as Steve's shipmates Bill O'Brian and Sven Larson. They are accosted by a woman named Virginia Harper, who tells them Gutman and Cairo have her husband. A woman named Madame Ingomar has some sort of power over both Virginia's husband, Townsend Harper, and the Harpers' Chinese cook, Sing Lee. Entering the American Bar after O'Brian and Larson come out of it somewhat the worse for wear, Steve spots a retired British fighter named "Seaman" Pallant seated at a corner table with Gutman and Cairo, Fatala and her companion Bebert, and Ingomar. Harper, who prefers to be called Bulan, is the one who attacked Steve's shipmates. Fatala and her associates have stolen the treasure of Colonel Bozzo-Corona, the head of a criminal organization. The member of the group whose champion wins the tournament will receive all of the treasure. Mullargan is the champion of a small man named Oden. Jack Holligan is fighting for a European named Marius, while a ship's captain named Bull Dawson is fighting for himself. Sing Lee is a member of the secret society called the Si-Fan. Holligan has been compared to Ace Jessel. Sing Lee tells Steve some believe Fatala is Fantômas come back in female form. He also reveals Bulan was created in a laboratory by Professor Maxon, Virginia's father. Sing Lee inserted cell samples from the real Townsend Harper, who drowned, into Bulan at the orders of Madame Ingomar's father.

Short story by Matthew Baugh in Tales of the Shadowmen Volume 9: La Vie en Noir, *Jean-Marc and Randy Lofficier, eds., Black Coat Press, 2012; reprinted in French in* Les Compagnons de l'Ombre (Tome 13), *Jean-Marc and Randy Lofficier, eds., Rivière Blanche, 2014. Sailor Steve Costigan is the protagonist of a series of stories by Robert E. Howard; Bill O'Brian and Sven Larson serve with him aboard the* Sea Girl. *Ace Jessel is the protagonist of Howard's stories "The Apparition in the Prize Ring" and "Double-Cross." Ned "Angel" Dargan is an ally of Frederick C. Davis' pulp hero the Moon Man. Butch O'Leary is an ally of Norman A. Daniels' pulp adventurer the Black Bat; here, he is conflated with Slug O'Leary from "Eando Binder's" (Earl and Otto Binder) story "Adam Link, Robot Detective." This crossover brings Adam Link into the CU. "One-Punch" Mullargan is from Edgar Rice Burroughs' "Tarzan and the Champion." Harper, Maxon and his daughter, and Sing Lee are from Burroughs' novel* The Monster Men. *In the novel, Bulan initially believes he is Maxon's creation, but discovers he is really Townsend Harper; here, it is revealed he was indeed created by Maxon using cells from the real Harper. Gutman and Cairo are Casper Gutman and Joel Cairo from Dashiell Hammett's* The Maltese Falcon. *Madame Ingomar is Fu Manchu's daughter, Fah Lo Suee, who used the Ingomar alias in Sax*

Rohmer's Daughter of Fu Manchu *and* The Trail of Fu Manchu. *The Si-Fan is the secret society run by Fu Manchu. "Seaman" Pallant is from* The Drums of Fu Manchu. *Fatala and Bebert appear in a series of novels by Marcel Allain. Fantômas is a criminal mastermind created by Allain and Pierre Souvestre. Colonel Bozzo-Corona is the head of the Black Coats in novels by Paul Féval. Oden is meant to be the villain of the Doc Savage novel* Repel *(aka* The Deadly Dwarf*). Jack Holligan is an ally of Paul Müller's German pulp hero Sun Koh. Marius is Rayt Marius from Leslie Charteris'* The Last Hero, Knight Templar, *and* The Misfortunes of Mr. Teal, *featuring Simon Templar, alias the Saint.*

Summer
THE BENEVOLENT BURGLAR

A police informant suggests to Commissaire Maigret he strike a blow to the criminal organization known as the Black Coats by stealing their Treasure. Maigret is on friendly terms with England's Detective Inspector Claud Eustace Teal, who has been fruitlessly pursuing a criminal named Simon Templar. The conversation between Maigret and his informant is overheard by Templar himself, along with his companions Patricia Holm and Roger Conway. Traveling to Britain, Maigret enlists the aid of Mr. J. G. Reeder, who works for the Public Prosecutor's office. Reeder, his reformed burglar ally Larry O'Ryan, and O'Ryan's wife, the former Lane Leonard, attempt the theft, only to find Simon Templar has beaten them to the punch.

Short story by John Peel in Tales of the Shadowmen Volume 9: La Vie en Noir, *Jean-Marc and Randy Lofficier, eds., Black Coat Press, 2012; reprinted in French in* Les Compagnons de l'Ombre (Tome 12), *Jean-Marc and Randy Lofficier, eds., Rivière Blanche, 2013. Commissaire Jules Maigret appears in a series of novels by Georges Simenon. The Black Coats are featured in books by Paul Féval. Simon Templar, alias the Saint, is featured in novels by Leslie Charteris, as are Detective Inspector Claud Eustace Teal, Patricia Holm, and Roger Conway. Mr. J. G. Reeder is from a series of books by Edgar Wallace; Larry and Lane O'Ryan also appear in the Reeder books. It is worth noting the Reeder series and many of Wallace's other books feature a fictional London newspaper called* The Daily Megaphone.

NOTHING IS AS IT SEEMS

When the Tiger-Man Felifax's wife Grace is abducted, her father Sir Eric Palmer enlists detective Harry Dickson to help Felifax find her. The trail leads them to Haley's Circus, which employs a magician called Oz the Great and Powerful. The mastermind behind the kidnapping turns out to be Felifax's former lover Lady Deborah Moorhen.

Short story by Matthew Dennion in Harry Dickson vs. the Spider, *Jean-Marc and Randy Lofficier, eds., Black Coat Press, 2014. Felifax, his wife Grace, Sir Eric Palmer, and Lady Moorhen are from Paul Féval fils' novel Felifax the Tiger-Man, which has been translated and adapted for Black Coat Press by Brian Stableford. Harry Dickson appeared in pulp stories by Jean Ray and others. Haley's Circus is the same circus that employed the Flying Graysons, the youngest of whom was Dick Grayson, who fought crime alongside the Batman as the first Robin after his parents' murder in 1939. Oz the Great and Powerful is from L. Frank Baum's* The Wonderful Wizard of Oz.

FEAR FROM ABOVE

Military intelligence officer Richard Knight battles vampires led by the Grandmaster, who once survived the fires of Mount Vesuvius, and who calls himself "Sir Fran..." before being shot at by Knight. The vampires kill all those aboard the ship *Western Star*, including Captain Edward "Evil" Larsen, the son of a sea captain with an explosive temper who traded in the Pacific and was often accused of piracy in whispers. Knight consults a judge who is an expert on the occult about vampires.

Short story by Frank Schildiner in The New Adventures of Richard Knight, *Tommy Hancock, ed., Pro Se Press, 2012. Richard Knight appeared in stories by Donald E. Keyhoe in the pulp magazine* Flying Aces. *The Grandmaster is Sir Francis Varney from James Malcolm Rymer's* Varney the Vampire. *Evil Larsen's father is Wolf Larsen from Jack London's novel* The Sea-Wolf. *The judge is Manly Wade Wellman's occult detective Judge Keith Hilary Pursuivant. All these connections bring Richard Knight into the CU. The Empire State Building is still under construction, placing this story in 1930 or early 1931.*

December
THE LESSON OF CAPTAIN DANRIT
The Nyctalope tells his son Pierre of his activities on February 20–22, 1916, which included destroying a cloaking device built for the German army by Herr Doktor Krueger.

Short story by Emmanuel Gorlier in The Nyctalope Steps In, *Jean-Marc and Randy Lofficier, eds., Black Coat Press, 2011; reprinted in French in Les Compagnons de l'Ombre (Tome 8), Jean-Marc and Randy Lofficier, eds., Rivière Blanche, 2011. The Nyctalope is the hero of a series of novels by Jean de La Hire. Herr Doktor Krueger is the archenemy of Robert J. Hogan's pulp aviator G-8.*

1931

Mid January
RETURN OF THE DUGPA
Ravenwood battles the Dweller on the Threshold, the former chief agent of the benevolent White Lodge, now an inhabitant of the Black Lodge, served by a group called the dugpas. Ravenwood is aided in his battle with the Dweller by a shadowy figure called the Dark Eminence. Actress Anne D'Arromanches grew up in an orphanage in the Midwest, where she was placed by her mother, who only spoke French.

Novel by Micah S. Harris, Airship 27 Productions, 2015. Ravenwood, "the stepson of mystery," appeared in stories by Frederick C. Davis in the pulp magazine Secret Agent X. *The Dweller on the Threshold is from Edward Bulwer-Lytton's novel* Zanoni. *The White Lodge, the Black Lodge, and the dugpas are from Talbot Mundy's novel* The Devil's Guard. *David Lynch and Mark Frost utilized the Dweller, the Lodges, and the dugpas in their television series* Twin Peaks. *Anne D'Arromanches is meant to be Ann Darrow from the classic film* King Kong. *The Dark Eminence is the pulp hero of the shadows; Harris reveals this man planted the idea into director Carl Denham's mind to ask Ann to star in his film shot on Skull Island. In his book* The Eldritch New Adventures of Becky Sharp, *Harris identified*

Ann as the daughter of Lord Eugenides (an analogue of the jungle lord) and Becky, a character from William Makepeace Thackeray's Vanity Fair. The chronology of Lord Eugenides' exploits does not fit with the timeline of the Lord Greystoke novels, which combined with other conflicts with the established CU history of characters such as Captain Nemo and Irene Adler places The Eldritch New Adventures of Becky Sharp *in an alternate universe*. The Ann Darrow/Anne D'Arromanches of the CU is probably Becky Sharp's daughter by John Gribardsun, the time-traveling future jungle lord seen in Time's Last Gift.

Mid February–October
THE HUNTERS

Jim Anthony asks his friend Eddie Phipps if he is coming to the next meeting of the Baltimore Gun Club. After Phipps is attacked by a strange man-monster, Jim tells an old man to call Healy in Homicide, and tell him he said there's been trouble at the Suydam Building. Healy refers to "that thing last year with that Yogami fellow—," to which Jim replies "Yes. The so-called Werewolf of Red Hook." One of Phipps' murderer's other victims is named Guster Wooster. A man who unsuccessfully tries to kill Jim commits suicide by taking a distillation of Mariphasa Lupinum, the Tibetan Moon Blossom. At the Gun Club, Jim and his sidekick Tom Gentry meet Count Zaroff, whom a castaway named Rainsford falsely claimed died on his island a few years ago. Another Gun Club member, Otto DeLancy, asks Jim if he was in New York when Bertie Freis left. Jim replies he was in Paris on a case involving a band of thieves, *Les Vampires*. A murderous fiend called Fantômas was also involved in this case. Jim thinks of a Gun Club member named Ironcastle. Jim and Tom battle a group of Tcho-Tcho. Zaroff says the Tcho-Tcho tried to kill him while he was in Tibet, searching for the elusive Mi-go. The word Leng pops into Jim's mind. Franklin Pike reminds Jim of their trip to Maple-White Land, and of someone named Ki-Gor who was also present. Pike refers to Leng as the Doorway to the Lost Valley of Carcosa, and tells Jim about a swami in New Orleans, "Chanda-something." Jim requests his butler Dawkins have certain tools from his laboratory delivered to the Freis family burying ground at New York's Wildwood Cemetery. A captured Tcho-Tcho claims to be a member of the royal guard of the King in Yellow. Jim sees Zaroff speaking to a man called Allardravitch, who, like Zaroff himself, was once part of the Czar of Russia's inner circle. Zaroff invites Jim to hunt with him on an uncharted island, far west of Sumatra, which is inhabited by prehistoric animals. Allardravitch sneers at Jim's use of mercy bullets, which prompts Jim to tell him not to confuse him for the bronze man. Traveling to the island, Jim and Zaroff spot a ship in the distance called the *Venture*. Zaroff tells Jim how an old German named

Lidenbrock put him up in his lodge during the Great War, and told him he and his uncle went on an expedition to the center of the earth many years earlier, where they also encountered prehistoric animals. Lidenbrock's uncle told him of a previous, aborted attempt to enter the earth's core, through an opening on the island Jim and Zaroff are visiting. That ingress was sealed, but not before creatures from the core migrated through it and settled on the island. Aboard the *Venture*, Jim and Zaroff meet filmmaker D. W. Cecil De Cent, his leading lady Dana Sparrow, the elderly captain of the ship, and Jack the first mate. Dana grew up in an orphanage, with her father unaware of her existence. Jim finds a book written by one of the Weta-people, who sailed to the island from the Gray Havens after the return of the king, but cannot read it. Zaroff tells Jim there are signs of a giant anthropoid on the island. Dana refers to "that Doctor Wildman in the pulps." The ape's unveiling in New York draws a lot of celebrity attention, including that of the Celebrated Feral Child of Africa, who has a personal interest in apes, giant or otherwise. De Cent, about to unveil the ape, tells Jim's Comanche grandfather Mephito he has filmed the strange monoliths and ruins of the Indians in Dunwich. The ape escapes thanks to Zaroff's scheming, and climbs to the top of the Empire State Building with Dana in his paw, only to be shot down by airplanes.

Jim Anthony: Super Detective Volume Two, *Airship 27 Productions, 2010, composed of two novellas, "Death in Yellow" by Joshua Reynolds and "On the Periphery of Legend" by Micah S. Harris. Jim Anthony appeared in the pulp* Super Detective. *The Baltimore Gun Club seen here is the New York branch of the club seen in Jules Verne's* From the Earth to the Moon. *The Suydam Building is named after Robert Suydam from H. P. Lovecraft's "The Horror at Red Hook." The Mi-go are a race of Yeti from Lovecraft's "The Whisperer in Darkness." Leng is a plateau in Lovecraft's Cthulhu Mythos, first described in "The Hound." Dr. Yogami and the Mariphasa Lupinum (or Mariphasa Lupina Lumina) are from the film* Werewolf of London. *Guster Wooster is presumably an American relative of P. G. Wodehouse's most famous character, Bertie Wooster. Count Zaroff, his island, and Sanger Rainsford are from Richard Connell's "The Most Dangerous Game." Xavier Mauméjean's story "The Most Exciting Game," which is set in 1930, also portrayed Zaroff as a member of the New York branch of the Gun Club. Les Vampires are from Louis Feuillade's 1915 film serial of the same name. Fantômas is a French pulp villain created by Marcel Allain and Pierre Souvestre. Hareton Ironcastle is from J.-H. Rosny aîné's* L'Étonnant Voyage d'Hareton Ironcastle, *as well as Philip José Farmer's translation and adaptation,* Ironcastle, *which revealed Ironcastle was a member of the Baltimore Gun Club. The Tcho-Tcho race were created by August Derleth as part of the Cthulhu*

Mythos. These Tcho-Tcho must have been the result of interbreeding with humans, as they are noticeably taller than the race is described to be by Derleth and other authors. Maple White Land is from Arthur Conan Doyle's The Lost World. *John Peter Drummond's jungle hero Ki-Gor's first adventure must have actually taken place years before its 1938 publication in* Jungle Stories Magazine. *Carcosa is originally from Ambrose Bierce's short story "An Inhabitant of Carcosa," but also appears in Robert W. Chambers'* The King in Yellow, *which Lovecraft incorporated into the Cthulhu Mythos. The Swami Chandraputra is an identity assumed by Randolph Carter, the protagonist of Lovecraft's Dream Cycle, in the story "Through the Gates of the Silver Key." He also appears under that alias in Lovecraft and Hazel Heald's story "Out of the Aeons." Wildwood Cemetery also hosts the grave of the allegedly deceased Denny Colt, also known as the Spirit. "Allardravitch" is actually the shadowy hero who was a spy for the Czar during the Great War. The uncharted island is Skull Island from the classic film* King Kong. *The* Venture *is also from* King Kong. *"D. W. Cecil De Cent" and "Dana Sparrow" are aliases for Carl Denham and Ann Darrow, while the captain and first mate are Captain Englehorn and Jack Driscoll; all four appear in the film. The giant ape is Kong himself, of course. The bronze man is a famous pulp hero of the 1930s and '40s, of whome Rick Lai notes, "Doc wouldn't have been using mercy bullets regularly until 1932 (*The Phantom City*). However, Doc might have experimented with mercy bullets like Anthony in early 1931. Doc would have abandoned them to avenge the deaths of his father (*The Man of Bronze*) and favorite tutor (*The Land of Terror*) during May–July 1931." Axel Lidenbrock and his uncle Otto are from Jules Verne's* Journey to the Center of the Earth. *The connection between the subterranean world visited by the Lidenbrocks and Skull Island was first proposed by Micah S. Harris in* The Eldritch New Adventures of Becky Sharp. *Although that novel takes place in an alternate universe, apparently the connection is true in the CU as well. According to* The Eldritch New Adventures of Becky Sharp,

Ann Darrow was the illegitimate daughter of Becky herself (from William Makepeace Thackeray's Vanity Fair) and Lord Eugenides, an analogue of the jungle lord. Unlike the jungle lord, Eugenides grew to adulthood during the Victorian era, with his own counterparts to Jane and La. The Ann Darrow of the CU is probably the daughter of Becky Sharp and the time-traveling future version of the jungle lord (aka John Gribardsun) seen in Farmer's Time's Last Gift. The Grey Havens (aka Mithlond) are an Elvish port from J. R. R. Tolkien's classic fantasy trilogy The Lord of the Rings. In Doc Savage: His Apocalyptic Life, Philip José Farmer revealed an iconic pulp hero's real name as James Clarke Wildman, Jr. However, Dana's reference to this man as a pulp character should not be taken literally, since his pulp magazine did not begin publication until 1933, two years after the events of this story. The Celebrated Feral Child of Africa is the jungle lord. Although Harris places Kong's unveiling in April, shortly after Denham and company return from Skull Island, Kong's rampage took place in October in the CU. More likely, Kong spent months in quarantine before being officially exhibited. Dunwich is from Lovecraft's "The Dunwich Horror."

Spring
EXCURSION IN REALITY
Simon Lent's mail includes an invitation to luncheon from Lady Metroland.

Short story by Evelyn Waugh, originally published as "An Entirely New Angle" in Harper's Bazaar, *New York, July 1932; reprinted as "This Quota Stuff: Positive Proof That the British Can Make Good Films,"* Harper's Bazaar, *London, August 1932, and as "Excursion in Reality" in* The Complete Stories of Evelyn Waugh, *Little, Brown and Company, 1998. Lady Metroland appears in many of Waugh's interconnected works, bringing this story into the CU.*

Spring 1931–Winter 1932
HARRY DICKSON VS. THE SPIDER
Baker Street detective Harry Dickson battles Georgette Cuvelier and her Spider Society. Georgette tells Dickson the Society's plans wouldn't even be limited to Earth if they had the means to leave it, like Mr. Barbicane did. Georgette tells Dickson and his young assistant Tom Wills to evade two Italian mercenaries belonging to the Black Coats. Dickson first met a money lender friend of his when he cleared the man of murder during his time as an apprentice to Sexton Blake. The Society's headquarters is located inside an opium den; the entrance to their lair can be accessed by manipulating

statuettes of the Three Madmen of Toko-Djawa, which are described in Challenger's book on the religions of Sumatra.

Originally published as La Bande de l'Araignée *in Harry Dickson #85, May 1933; translated and adapted by Jean-Marc and Randy Lofficier and collected in* Harry Dickson vs. the Spider, *Jean-Marc and Randy Lofficier, eds., Black Coat Press, 2014. Impey Barbicane is the president of the Baltimore Gun Club in Jules Verne's novels* From the Earth to the Moon *and* Around the Moon. *The Black Coats are a criminal organization appearing in novels by Paul Féval. Sexton Blake is the most famous British penny dreadful detective; G. L. Gick revealed a young Dickson served as Blake's apprentice in his novella "The Werewolf of Rutherford Grange." Professor George Edward Challenger is the protagonist of* The Lost World *and other tales by Arthur Conan Doyle.*

Summer
THE PRIVILEGE OF ADONIS
The Rama Circus Menagerie, run by Rama Tamerlane, aka Felifax the Tiger-Man, visits Paris. Accompanying Rama are his surrogate sister Djina and his valet Baber. Roland Frollo displays Bertrand Calliet, the "Werewolf of Paris," in his Freon Side Show. Calliet was recently revived under unknown circumstances after being fatally shot by Dr. Cornelius Kramm a few years ago. Djina is abducted by Quasimodo, a relative of the individual immortalized by Victor Hugo who shares his kinsman's deformity.

Short story by Christofer Nigro in Tales of the Shadowmen Volume 10: Esprit de Corps, *Jean-Marc and Randy Lofficier, eds., Black Coat Press, 2013. Rama Tamerlane, Djina, and Baber are from Paul Féval fils' novel* Felifax the Tiger-Man, *which has been translated by Brian Stableford for Black Coat Press. The earlier Quasimodo is from Victor Hugo's* The Hunchback of Notre-Dame. *Roland Frollo is related to Dom Claude Frollo from the same novel. Bertrand Calliet is the title character of Guy Endore's book* The Werewolf of Paris. *The Freon Side Show and the latter-day Quasimodo are from Sean Todd's Frankenstein stories in the comic book magazine*

Psycho. *Dr. Cornelius Kramm is from Gustave Le Rouge's* Le Mystérieux Docteur Cornélius; *his encounter with Calliet was recounted by Nigro in his story "The Beast Within" (*The Shadow of Judex, *Jean-Marc and Randy Lofficier, eds., Black Coat Press, 2013).*

Summer 1931–Autumn 1932
BLACK MISCHIEF

Basil Seal attends a party held by Lady Metroland. Another guest refers to a party held by Basil, Alastair Trumpington, Peter Pastmaster, and others. Lord Monomark is also in attendance. Basil refers to a party at Lottie Crump's. Toby Cruttwell is present at a party held by Basil's mother.

Novel by Evelyn Waugh. Lady Metroland and her son Peter Pastmaster previously appeared in Waugh's novels Decline and Fall *and* Vile Bodies. *Toby Cruttwell and Alastair Trumpington also appeared in* Decline and Fall, *while Lottie Crump and Lord Monomark first appeared in* Vile Bodies. *Waugh's story "Incident in Azania" is a follow-up to* Black Mischief, *set in the same African nation and featuring some of the same characters.*

October
THE GREAT APE CAPER

Arsène Lupin loosens the giant ape Kong's restraints in order for the beast to escape, distracting the citizens of New York while he steals a jeweled bird statue from the home base of its current custodian, a famous doctor who travels around the world with five scientist-adventurers. It is mentioned an old rival of Lupin's would say the game was afoot.

Short story by Nathan Cabaniss in Tales of the Shadowmen Volume 10: Esprit de Corps, *Jean-Marc and Randy Lofficier, eds., Black Coat Press, 2013; reprinted in French in* Les Compagnons de l'Ombre (Tome 14), *Jean-Marc and Randy Lofficier, eds., Rivière Blanche, 2014. Arsène Lupin is the gentleman thief created by Maurice Leblanc. King Kong is from the classic 1933 film of the same name. Micah S. Harris' "On the Periphery of Legend"* reveals Count Zaroff (from Richard Connell's "The Most Dangerous Game") bribed a laborer to use substandard metal in Kong's restraints. Lupin inadvertently played into Zaroff's plans. The bird statue is the Maltese Falcon, from Dashiell Hammett's titular novel. The famous doctor is otherwise called "Doc"; he and his five aides would return to their headquarters at the Empire State Building just in time to witness the aftermath of the giant ape's plunge from that very same structure, as recounted in Farmer's story "After King Kong Fell." Lupin's old rival is Sherlock Holmes. The 1933 date assigned to this story is incorrect.

NESTOR BURMA IN NEW YORK (L'ODEUR DE L'INNOMMABLE)
Nestor Burma and his friend Gouvieux journey to New York to report on the discovery of a giant ape dubbed King Kong. The ape's body is kept in a stadium that currently houses Mrs. Tetrallini's circus, whose sideshow freaks include a dwarf couple named Hans and Frieda. Hans refers to Anne Darrow. Mrs. Tetrallini's fiancé, an American named Herbert West, created an invention that brings Kong back to life, only for him to be shot down again. Burma says he'd rather deal with the likes of Riton le Nantais or Roger le Brestois than monsters performing in a circus or apes that aren't alive.

Short story by Michel Stéphan, appearing as "L'Odeur de l'Innommable" in Les Compagnons de l'Ombre (Tome 11), Jean-Marc and Randy Lofficier, eds., Rivière Blanche, 2013, and in English in Tales of the Shadowmen Volume 10: Esprit de Corps, Jean-Marc and Randy Lofficier, eds. Black Coat Press, 2013. Nestor Burma is a private detective created by author Léo Malet. Gouvieux, Riton le Nantais, and Roger le Brestois are also from the Burma novels. King Kong and Anne Darrow are from the classic 1933 film. Mrs. Tetrallini, Hans, and Frieda are from Tod Browning's film Freaks. Herbert West is from Lovecraft's "Herbert West—Reanimator." After Kong's second death, he must have been moved to an icehouse until the legal owner of the ape's body could be decided, as referred to in Farmer's "After King Kong Fell." The 1933 date given is incorrect.

1932

Winter
DEATH OF A DREAM
The tramp Bouzille, a servant of Erik, the Phantom of the Opera, is accosted by the Sons of the Red Hand, a group of young ruffians who have modeled themselves upon the criminal organization known as the Red Hand. He is saved by the Phantom's current angels of music: Ellen, an American who disables her opponents using hypodermic needles filled with anesthetic;

Joséphine Balsamo IV, the scion of a notorious family; and Mizzeia Khali, an amazon from a kingdom in the Himalayas. Ellen remarks it is for the best she sent one of the thugs to "visit that kid Nemo in his Slumberland" rather than let him battle Mizzeia. Later, Erik confers with his current assistant, who is known as the Daroga like his predecessors, though he bears no Persian blood himself. Erik plans to steal the Treasure of the Black Coats and use it to pay Doctor Ambrose Vollmer to perform surgery that will cure Erik of his deformed appearance, while still allowing him to retain all of the remarkable attributes he inherited from his progenitor. The apartment holding the Treasure is currently resided in by the Black Coats' leader, Colonel Bozzo-Corona. The apartment is guarded by the Colonel's bodyguard, the Marchef, and the Mummy Pha-ho-tep, which the Colonel controls using a golden ankh. Exploring the darkened apartment with her teammates, Mizzeia thinks how useful the Nyctalope's vision would be at this time. The Phantom and his agents are confronted by the Colonel and his henchmen, along with his paramour Jo Jo La Verne.

Short story by Christofer Nigro in Tales of the Shadowmen Volume 9: La Vie en Noir, *Jean-Marc and Randy Lofficier, eds., Black Coat Press, 2012; reprinted in French in* Les Compagnons de l'Ombre (Tome 13), *Jean-Marc and Randy Lofficier, eds., Rivière Blanche, 2014. Bouzille is the son of the character of the same name in Marcel Allain and Pierre Souvestre's Fantômas novels. The Phantom of the Opera is from the novel of the same name by Gaston Leroux, as is the original Daroga, who was also known as the Persian. The Red Hand crime syndicate is from Gustave Le Rouge's* Le Mystérieux Docteur Cornélius. *Previous incarnations of the Angels of Music have appeared in Kim Newman's stories "Angels of Music" (*Tales of the Shadowmen Volume 2: Gentlemen of the Night, *Jean-Marc and Randy Lofficier, eds., Black Coat Press, 2005) and "Angels of Music II: The Mark of Kane" (*Tales of the Shadowmen Volume 4: Lords of Terror, *Jean-Marc and Randy Lofficier, eds., Black Coat Press, 2007), as well as Nigro's own story "Patricide" (*Tales of the Shadowmen Volume 8: Agents Provocateurs, *Jean-Marc and Randy Lofficier, eds., Black Coat Press, 2011). Ellen is Ellen Patrick, who will soon become the masked vigilante known as the Domino Lady, as chronicled in stories by an anonymous author using the nom de plume Lars Anderson in the "spicy" pulps. I have moved this story from the 1931 date assigned to it to 1932 to be consistent with references in other stories to Ellen's father's death, the impetus for her adopting a costumed persona, having taken place in that year. Mizzeia Khali is an ally of Jean de La Hire's hero the Nyctalope, who possesses the ability to see in complete darkness. Joséphine Balsamo IV is the daughter of Arsène Lupin's archenemy Joséphine Balsamo. "That kid Nemo in his Slumberland" is a reference to*

Winsor McCay's classic comic strip Little Nemo. *The Black Coats, their Treasure, the Colonel,* and *the Marchef* are featured in novels by Paul Féval. *Doctor Ambrose Vollmer* is from L'Empereur du Pacifique *by Jose Moselli.* Erik's progenitor is the Frankenstein Monster, as revealed by Jean-Marc and Randy Lofficier in their story "His Father's Eyes," which was published as a bonus feature in their translation of Leroux's novel. Pha-ho-tep and the Golden Ankh are from the Spanish horror film Assignment Terror. *Jo Jo La Verne is from the 1934 film* Come On, Marines!

Spring
THE PHANTOM EXECUTIONERS

Harry Dickson once again battles Georgette Cuvelier and her Spider Society. Georgette tries to sell an underground submarine base to a member of the Lords of the Red Hand, and reveals to Harry she is the daughter of his old foe Professor Flax.

Originally published as Les Spectres Bourreaux *in* Harry Dickson *#86, June 1933; translated and adapted by Jean-Marc and Randy Lofficier and collected in* Harry Dickson vs. the Spider, *Jean-Marc and Randy Lofficier, eds., Black Coat Press, 2014. The Lords of the Red Hand are from Gustave Le Rouge's* The Mysterious Doctor Cornelius, *which has been translated by Brian Stableford in three volumes for Black Coat Press. Professor Flax was a recurring foe of Dickson, but first appeared in Louis Forest's* Someone is Stealing Children in Paris, *which has also been translated by Stableford.*

November 1932–Late Winter 1934
A HANDFUL OF DUST

Mrs. Beaver tells her son she is lunching at Viola Chasm's. Lady Metroland telephones Mrs. Beaver about putting up a new bathroom ceiling. Brenda Last's sister and brother-in-law travel aboard Lord Monomark's yacht, while her mother visits Lady Anchorage's chalet.

Novel by Evelyn Waugh. Viola Chasm and Lady Anchorage previously appeared in Waugh's novel Vile Bodies. *Lady Metroland appears in a number of Waugh's books and stories. Lord Monomark appeared prior to this in* Vile Bodies *and* Black Mischief.

Autumn
DECEIT

Boston Blackie aids the Domino Lady by luring a mobster who helped engineer the death of her father into a trap.

Short story by C. J. Henderson in the *Domino Lady: Blonde Bombshell* trade paperback, Moonstone Comics, 2012. Jewel thief Boston Blackie appeared in a series of short stories by Jack Boyle. In Jim Steranko's story "Aroused, the Domino Lady," Ellen Patrick brought the men who killed her father to justice. Martin Powell's "Masks of Madness" identified a different culprit as the murderer of Ellen's father. The murderers in "Masks of Madness" and "Deceit" must have been additional conspirators Ellen did not initially identify. The elder Patrick died less than a year ago, placing this story in 1932.

1933

Winter. The first exploit of journalist Foster Fade, also known as "the Crime Spectacularist," "Hell in Boxes" by Lester Dent, *All Detective Magazine*, February 1934.

Spring. Scientific detective I. V. "Ivy" Frost's first case, "Frost," as related by Donald Wandrei, *Clues Detective Stories*, September 1934.

Spring
OUT OF DEPTH

A man named Rip Van Winkle attends a party at Lady Metroland's mansion, where he tells Lord Metroland about his big-game hunting experiences. Rip and Alastair Trumpington drive an occultist home. The black magician gives them each a vision of other time periods.

Short story by Evelyn Waugh in Harper's Bazaar, *London*, December 1933; reprinted in The Complete Stories of Evelyn Waugh, Little, Brown and Company, 1998. This Rip Van Winkle may be a relative and namesake of the title character of Washington Irving's story. Lord and Lady Metroland appear in a number of Waugh's works. Alastair Trumpington previously appeared in Waugh's books Decline and Fall *and* Black Mischief. *The 26th century London seen by Rip represents one of many possible futures for the Crossover Universe.*

GRENDEL VS. THE SHADOW

The masked assassin and crime lord Grendel finds himself thrown back in time to the 1930s, where he takes over New York's organized crime, drawing the attention of the Shadow. Grendel's collection of treasures that once belonged to famous individuals throughout history includes Sweeney Todd's shaving razor.

Three-issue miniseries by Matt Wagner, Dark Horse Comics and Dynamite Entertainment, 2014. This crossover brings Wagner's character Grendel (aka Hunter Rose) into the CU. However, the Grendel stories set after Rose's death take place in a future timeline that is very different from the established future of the CU, and therefore must represent an alternate universe. Sweeney Todd is from the penny dreadful story "The String of Pearls," the basis for the musical Sweeney Todd: The Demon Barber of Fleet Street. *The year is based on a theater marquee advertising the movie* The Mummy, *which was released on December 22, 1932. Since none of the characters dress like it is autumn or winter, this comic likely takes place in the spring of 1933.*

MYSTERY OF THE FLAMING MEN

Injured scientific detective Lynn Lash assures Detective Captain Sam Casey he's okay, to which Casey retorts, "And I'm the Shadow."

Story by Tim Lasiuta in The New Adventures of Lynn Lash, *Tommy Hancock, Morgan McKay, and David White, eds., Pro Se Press, 2015. Lynn Lash appeared in two stories by Lester Dent in* Detective-Dragnet Magazine *in 1932, "The Sinister Ray" and "The Mummy Murders." A third story, "The Flame Horror," went unpublished until it was printed, along with the other two stories, in the collection* Hell in Boxes: The Exploits of Lynn Lash and Foster Fade, *Altus Press, 2012. The reference to the shadowy hero could be interpreted as a reference to either a pulp character or a real vigilante of whom Casey has met or heard. Since "The Sinister Ray" contained a reference to Sherlock Holmes as a real person, I am treating this as a valid crossover.*

Summer
DEAD MEN'S GUNS

One of the victims of a serial killer targeting mobsters is Kevin Howard, who works for Pete Barry. Mob enforcer Johnny "Wits" Pomatto appears. Foster Fade speaks to an unnamed police lieutenant.

Short story by Adam Lance Garcia in The New Adventures of Foster

Fade, the Crime Spectacularist, *Tommy Hancock and Morgan Minor, eds., Pro Se Press, 2013.* Foster Fade appeared in three stories by Lester Dent, which were published in All Detective Magazine *in 1934.* Pete Barry is from "The Case of the Beardless Corpse," one of "Richard Foster's" (Kendell Foster Crossen) stories about the hero called the Green Lama, which appeared in the magazine Double Detective. *The police lieutenant is John Caraway, a supporting character from the Green Lama stories. Johnny "Wits" Pomatto first appeared in Garcia's novella* The Green Lama: Horror in Clay. *Both "The Case of the Beardless Corpse" and* Horror in Clay *take place years after "Dead Men's Guns."*

THE PROMETHEUS EFFECT

Lynn Lash works a case with a Secret Service agent asked to aid him by regional supervisor Rex Bennet.

Story by Teel James Glenn in The New Adventures of Lynn Lash, *Tommy Hancock, Morgan McKay, and David White, eds., Pro Se Press, 2015. Scientific detective Lynn Lash appeared in two stories by Lester Dent in* Detective-Dragnet Magazine *in 1932. Rex Bennet (or Bennett) is from the movie serials* G-Men vs. the Black Dragon *and* Secret Service in Darkest Africa. *Bennett also appears in Glenn's story "The Coming Storm," featuring Norman Daniels' pulp hero the Eagle.*

THE DAMSEL OF DISASTER

Gia Provenzo takes over her father Gino's mob family in Buffalo, New York, after he is murdered by the Gambino Family. One of Gino's men refers to the New Orleans branch of the Gambinos' war with the Pontis last year. Don Vito Gambino tells Gino before his death, "Together, we can be bigger than the likes of Maggadino, Bonnano, Corleone, Camonte, and Morello . . . combined."

Story by Christofer Nigro in The Dame Did It, *Jessica Fleming, ed., Pro Se, Press, 2015. The New Orleans branch of the Gambinos and the Pontis are from "The Butcher," a* short-lived series by Bill DuBay and Richard Corben in Eerie #62 and 64, Warren Publishing, January and March 1975. Lucio Gambino, a member of the New York City branch of the Gambino family, appears in DuBay's "Exterminator One" stories for Eerie, which take place in an alternate future. Corleone is Don Vito Corleone from Mario Puzo's novel The Godfather, which was brought into the CU by Emmanuel Gorlier's story "Madison Square Garden." Tony Camonte is from the 1932 film Scarface, which was brought in by Stuart Shiffman's story "True Believers." Don Morello is from Mafia: The City of Lost Heaven, the first video game in the Mafia series.

CREEP, SHADOW, CREEP!
Dr. Alan Caranac battles the evil sorcerer Rene de Keradel and his daughter Dahut, who was Caranac's lover in their past lives in ancient Ys. Dr. Austin Lowell aids Caranac in his conflict with the de Keradels. De Karadel refers to Khalk-ru, the Kraken God of the Uighurs.

Novel by A. Merritt, originally serialized in Argosy, *September 8– October 20, 1934. Alan Caranac also appears in Merritt's story "The Drone." Dr. Lowell first appeared in Merritt's novel* Burn, Witch, Burn! *and is also mentioned in James Ambuehl and Simon Bucher-Jones' Anton Zarnak story "The Case of the Curiously Competent Conjurer." Khalk-ru (or Khalk'ru) is from Merritt's novel* The Dwellers in the Mirage.

Mid September–Early November
ISLE OF BLOOD
Clifton "Challenger" Storm, the head of MARDL (Miami Aerodrome Research & Development Laboratories) received the news of his parents' death after having dinner at the Mortimer Club.

Novel by Don Gates, Cornerstone Book Publishers, 2011. MARDL is mentioned in Derrick Ferguson's Dillon series, bringing Challenger Storm into the CU. The Mortimer Club is from "Dorothy's New Friend," an episode of the television series The Golden Girls, *which is set in Miami.*

Early Autumn
THE SINISTER SHADOW
Doc Savage and the Shadow join forces against a villain called the Funeral Director, who has kidnapped both Ham Brooks and Lamont Cranston.

Novel by "Kenneth Robeson" (Will Murray), Altus Press, 2015. This adventure takes place sometime between the Shadow novels The Black Falcon *and* The Cobra. *Chronologically, this novel would occur before two* comic book crossovers between Doc and the Shadow, DC Comics' The Conflagration Man and Dark Horse Comics' The Case of the Shrieking Skeletons. Both of those accounts purport to depict the heroes' first meetings, but this can easily be chalked up to fictionalization.

Autumn
PRZYGODY GENJUSZA DETEKTYWOW MAC AN TABU
The brilliant Polish detective Mac An Tabu opens an office in Warsaw. He quickly becomes known as "the Sherlock Holmes of Poland."
From Przygody Genjusza Detektywow Mac An Tabu *#1, written by "Jean Coque."*

THE SIGN OF THE SALAMANDER
The introduction to this reprint of Curtiss Stryker's first story featuring occult detective John Chance is written by Kent Allard, the well-known author of *Drive-Thru Fiction* and *The Futility of Awareness*. Among the occult matters studied by Chance are the secrets of Carsultyal and Carcosa. Chance, seeking help against his archenemy Dr. Gerhard Modred (aka Dread), sends a message to another well-known occult investigator, de Grandin, but he cannot be reached. Dread plans to raid the lost mines of the Ancients in the Appalachian Mountains.
Short story by Karl Edward Wagner in the collection Why Not You and I, 1987. Curtiss Stryker also appears as a major character in Wagner's "Blue Lady Come Back," also included in Why Not You and I. Stryker is based on author Manly Wade Wellman. Kent Allard is neither the well-known shadowy pulp hero nor H. Kenneth "Kent" Allard from Wagner's Cthulhu Mythos story "Sticks"; however, he does make a brief appearance in "At First Just Ghostly," a Kane story found in the collection Exorcisms and Ecstasies. Allard's *Drive-Thru Fiction is* also quoted in Wagner's story "Plan 10 from Inner Space," also found in Exorcisms and Ecstasies. *Carsultyal is from the Kane story "Undertow,"* while Carcosa is from Ambrose Bierce's "An Inhabitant of Carcosa" and

Robert W. Chambers' The King in Yellow. *Chambers' version of Carcosa was heavily utilized in Wagner's "The River of Night's Dreaming," found in* In a Lonely Place. *De Grandin is Seabury Quinn's occult detective Dr. Jules de Grandin; the reference to him in Wagner's tale is a nod to Manly Wade Wellman's references to de Grandin in his own stories. The lost mines of the Ancients are from Wellman's John the Balladeer story "Shiver in the Pines." We can infer Curtiss Stryker was actually the biographer of John Chance, who was a real person in the Crossover Universe. Regarding the dating of this story, Chance's adventure was supposedly originally published in the January 1934 issue of the non-existent pulp* Black Circle Mystery, *while references to the National Recovery Administration place the story's events in 1933.*

THE BLACK ROCK CONSPIRACY

Foster Fade, traveling by train, tells a man the *Sentinel*, the *Herald-Tribune*, and even the *Times* have attacked him. Dinamenta "Din" Stevens, Fade's ghostwriter, goes on a date with Luke Jaconetti, a crime reporter for the *Herald-Tribune* who sometimes moonlights at the Amalgamated Press as a writer for the late-night news hour. Din asks Luke to accompany her in coming to Fade's aid, an invitation that is described as the equivalent of getting asked to join the Freemasons, Skull and Bones, and the Diogenes Club all at once. A police lieutenant Fade recognizes from the Tipton Murders shows him the bodies of an elderly couple. A police officer tells the lieutenant there's been a gangland shooting at the navy yard. Five people are dead, and the officer says the lieutenant won't believe who is there.

Short story by Adam Lance Garcia in The New Adventures of Foster Fade, the Crime Spectacularist, *Tommy Hancock and Morgan Minor, eds., Pro Se Press, 2013. Foster Fade was the protagonist of three stories by Lester Dent which were published in* All Detective Magazine *in 1934. The* Sentinel *is from "Richard Foster's" (Kendell Foster Crossen) Green Lama pulp novels. The* New York Sentinel *may be a branch of the Detroit-based newspaper owned by Britt Reid, aka the Green Hornet. The lieutenant is John Caraway, one of the Lama's allies. In Garcia's stories, the* Herald-Tribune *is another name for the* New York Herald *from the Secret Agent X pulp novels. Another employee of the Amalgamated Press is Diane Elliott, Operator #5's girlfriend. The Diogenes Club is from the Sherlock Holmes stories. The gangland shooting was witnessed by the future Green Lama, Jethro Dumont, as depicted in flashback in Garcia's novel* The Green Lama: Unbound. *The Tipton Murders were described in Garcia's story "Dead Men's Guns," also included in* The New Adventures of Foster Fade.

THE FALSE GLOBE

The Moon Man (Steve Thatcher) remembers a reporter from the *St. Louis Clarion* telling him about the Saint, an Englishman dubbed the "Modern Robin Hood of Crime," who steals from what he calls "the ungodly." The reporter also said for some reason the *Clarion*'s home office takes a serious interest in mysterious folks like the Saint.

Story by Erwin K. Roberts in The Moon Man Vol. 1, *Ron Fortier, ed., Airship 27 Productions, 2012. The Moon Man appeared in tales by Frederick C. Davis in the pulp magazine* Ten Detective Aces *in 1933–1937. The Saint, also known as Simon Templar, is from Leslie Charteris' books. The* Clarion*'s home office is the* New York Clarion, *owned by Frank Havens, an ally of another pulp hero, the Phantom Detective.*

MANIFEST DESTINY

The Green Ghost (Danny Blaney, an ex-cop framed and kicked off the force) battles a mad bomber. The Ghost initially suspects gangster Bennecio Tommasso of having ordered the bombing, and it is stated Tommasso is suspected of funding an arsonist in Atlanta to convince stubborn property owners to sell. Danny also receives help from a private eye named Rick, who is a former beat cop himself.

Short story by Bobby Nash in The New Adventures of the Green Ghost, *Pro Se Press, 2013. The Green Ghost (not to be confused with magician George Chance, who went by both that name and simply "The Ghost") appeared in seven stories by Johnston McCulley in the magazine* Thrilling Detective *in 1934–1935. The Tommasso crime family is featured in several of Nash's stories and novels. The incident in Atlanta is a reference to his story "Where There's Smoke," featuring the Peregrine, a hero created by Barry Reese. The Peregrine stories feature the Warlike Manchu and the Revenant, characters based on Fu Manchu and the Phantom, respectively. However, the Warlike Manchu and the Revenant's personal histories do not fit with the established continuity of Fu Manchu and the Phantom's exploits, and so the Peregrine stories must take place in an* alternate reality to the CU. However, the reference in "Manifest Destiny" indicates some version of the events of "Where There's Smoke" occurred in the CU, although whether a CU version of the Peregrine was involved has yet to be confirmed. Rick is private eye Rick Ruby, who was created by Nash and Sean Taylor for a series of anthologies entitled The Ruby Files.

November 1933–January 1934
THE CURSE OF POSEIDON

Challenger Storm and the members of MARDL travel to their advanced ship the *Independence* aboard Flying Platform #1 (F.P. 1), whose skipper is Commander B. E. Droste. F.P.1 was once the subject of sabotage by a spy named Damsky, but Droste's old friend Ellissen and his future wife Claire Lennartz helped save the day. A government agent asks Storm to take on a mission related to Miskatonic University's expedition to Antarctica.

Novel by Don Gates. F.P.1, Commander Droste, Damsky, Ellissen, and Claire Lennartz are from the 1933 film F.P. 1 Doesn't Answer, based on Curt Siodmak's novel F.P. 1 Does Not Reply. The Miskatonic University expedition to Antarctica is the subject of H. P. Lovecraft's At the Mountains of Madness. Presumably, the next Challenger Storm novel will be a sequel to that classic tale.

1934

Winter
BUMP IN THE NIGHT

The Moon Man battles the Invisible Man.

Short story by Tommy Hancock in Of Monsters and Men, Tommy Hancock and Joe Gentile, eds., Moonstone Books, 2014. The Moon Man appeared in stories by Frederick C. Davis in the pulp Ten Detective Aces from 1933–1937. The Invisible Man specifically identifies himself as the same individual of whom H. G. Wells wrote. However, it seems unlikely John Hawley Griffin would have survived his brutal assault at the hands of Edward Hyde in The League of Extraordinary Gentlemen, Volume II. Most likely, this Invisible Man is an unidentified individual who has replicated Griffin's formula for his own misdeeds, and simply lied about being the original.

Spring
NEIGHBORHOOD IN PERIL

Jim Anthony works to protect the non-Anglo Saxon residents of a New York neighborhood from a racist group. Officer Burland secretly meets with Jim to discuss the situation. Gibbons, the Managing Editor of Jim's paper, the *New York Star*, tells Jim that Gunigun at the *Sentinel* says one of his delivery boys in the neighborhood got hit by a truck. FBI agent Dan Fowler asks Jim not to get involved with the investigation. Jim threatens to go to Frank Havens of the *Clarion* with the story, and suggests someone in the U.S. government may be working with a "pure America" group like the Knights of the Open Palm. Jim is later visited by G-2 agent Jeff Shannon, aka the Eagle, who refers to a man named Ashton-Kirk. After the villains are defeated, Jim shakes hands with Dan, the *Sentinel*'s elderly owner.

    Story by Erwin K. Roberts in Jim Anthony: Super Detective Volume Four, *Ron Fortier, ed., Airship 27 Productions, 2013. Officer Kip Burland is the alter ego of the comic book hero the Black Hood, whose adventures were published by MLJ, the company later known as Archie Comics. The character also appeared in a short-lived pulp magazine,* Black Hood Detective. *It is unconfirmed whether Burland ever operated as the Black Hood in the CU. "Gunigun" is a reference to Bill Gunnigan, the City Editor of the* Daily Sentinel, *the newspaper owned by Britt Reid, aka the Green Hornet. Dan is Britt's father, Dan Reid Jr. Since the Green Hornet was based out of Detroit in the CU, Gunnigan and the elder Reid must have been visiting New York to work with the paper's branch in that city. The year of this story is conjecture based on the fact it takes place before Britt took over ownership of the* Sentinel *from his father. FBI agent Dan Fowler was created by Major George Fielding Eliot and appeared in the pulp* G-Men Detective. *Frank Havens and the* Clarion *newspaper are from the pulp magazine* The Phantom Detective, *written by a number of authors using the pen names "G. Wayman Jones" and "Robert Wallace." The Knights of the Open Palm are from Carroll John Daly's short story of the same name, the first of a series of tales about P.I. Race Williams that appeared in the pulp* Black Mask. *Jeff Shannon, aka the Eagle, appeared in four stories in the pulp* Thrilling Spy Stories *and one in* Popular Detective, *all written by Norman A. Daniels as "Kerry McRoberts." Ashton-Kirk was a Sherlock Holmes-like detective (albeit based in New York) who appeared in stories by John T. McIntyre for* The Popular Magazine, *which were collected in four books.*

May
THE NYCTALOPE'S NEW YORK ADVENTURE
    Leo Saint-Clair (aka the Nyctalope) meets a man named Henry Arnaud while traveling to New York City aboard a commercial airship. They are joined by Ivor Llewellyn, head of Superba-Llewellyn Pictures in California, who wants to make a movie based on Saint-Clair's exploits, in which he would co-star with the studio's own Lotus Blossom. Llewellyn also says the Americans used to see the silent serials based on both Saint-Clair and

Judex's adventures, and he wouldn't put it past Schnellenhammer of Perfecto-Zizzbaum, F. X. Weinberg of Metropolis Pictures, or Jacques Butcher of Magna to attempt to sign the hero to a contract as well. Leo is traveling to New York at the invitation of Dr. Orestes Preson, Curator of Fossil Mammals at the Bradley Institute of Paleontology and Natural History. The other reason for his journey is some time ago, his friend Judge Coméliau was the victim of a murder attempt by a crime lord who calls himself Zigomar after the self-styled "King of Thieves" from twenty years ago, who escaped death at the hands of the policeman Broquet many times. Leo has received a tip the new Zigomar has relocated to New

York. After they land, Leo accompanies Arnaud in a cab driven by Moe Shrevnitz to the Churchill Hotel. Arnaud offers Leo the services of his friend Lamont Cranston. The manager of the Hotel argues with a man who identifies himself as Sebastian Tombs. Nero Wolfe asks Archie Goodwin if he's ever told him about Monsieur Anatole, a French chef who works for a wealthy Englishman named Thomas Travers and his wife. Archie adds Mrs. Travers publishes a magazine called *Milady's Boudoir*. Wolfe remarks Anatole is said to surpass Fritz Brenner in the culinary arts. Inspector Cramer calls Wolfe and says Detective Sgt. Purley Stebbins is escorting a Frenchman (meaning Leo) to Wolfe's brownstone. Wolfe tells Archie to call Colonel Dubois of the *Deuxième Bureau* in Paris, as well as Saul Panzer. Prosper Lepicq is mentioned in Wolfe and Dubois' conversation. Stebbins arrives with Saint-Clair in tow, and returns to his taxi, a new yellow Checker from the Sunshine Cab Company. Among the items in Wolfe's office is a framed portrait of Sherlock Holmes above Archie's desk. After breakfast at the Churchill, Leo was escorted to the Panther-Pilsner brewery by criminals named Harry the Horse, Little Isadore, and Spanish John, who work for a man called "the Big Fellow." Commissioner Wainwright Barth took Leo to see Cramer. Cramer himself arrives at the brownstone, with District Attorney William Skinner and his assistant, Anthony Quinn, in tow. Skinner says

Leo's friend Alexandre Prillant is worried about him. He also divulges the fact the previous Big Fellow was William Valcross, who was remanded into the custody of Inspector Fernack several years ago, and died in the electric chair.

Short story by Stuart Shiffman in The Nyctalope Steps In, *Jean-Marc and Randy Lofficier, eds., Black Coat Press, 2011; reprinted in French in* La Nuit du Nyctalope, *Jean-Marc and Randy Lofficier, eds., Rivière Blanche, 2012. The Nyctalope and his friend Alexandre Prillant are from French pulp novels by Jean de La Hire. Henry Arnaud is one of the many aliases of the pulp vigilante who sticks to the shadows. Cranston is a millionaire whom this vigilante frequently impersonates. Shrevnitz and Barth are also from the novels about this crimefighter. Ivor "Ikey" Llewellyn and his studio Superba-Llewellyn Pictures are from P. G. Wodehouse's novels* The Luck of the Bodkins; Frozen Assets; Pearls, Girls, and Monty Bodkin; *and* Bachelors Anonymous. *Lotus "Lottie" Blossom is also from* The Luck of the Bodkins. *Jacob Z. Schnellenhammer and the Perfecto-Zizzbaum Motion Picture Corporation are from Wodehouse's Mr. Mulliner stories. Tom Travers and his wife Dahlia are the uncle and aunt respectively of Wodehouse's most famous character, Bertie Wooster. Monsieur Anatole is their personal chef, while* Milady's Boudoir *is a magazine published by Dahlia. Judex is the title character of Louis Feuillade's film serial. F. X. Weinberg's Metropolis Pictures appears in Denis Green and Anthony Boucher's radio series* The Casebook of Gregory Hood, *as well as Boucher's novels* The Case of the Baker Street Irregulars *and* Rocket to the Morgue, *the Fergus O'Breen novels and stories, and the short story "Mystery for Christmas."* The Case of the Baker Street Irregulars *features O'Breen's sister in a prominent role, while* Rocket to the Morgue *features nun Sister Ursula and police detective Terry Marshall, who first appeared in Boucher's* Nine Times Nine. *Lt. Herman Finch from* The Case of the Baker Street Irregulars *also appears in Boucher's first Nick Noble story, "Screwball Division," while the last Noble story, "The Girl Who Married a Monster," refers to Fergus O'Breen's detective agency. Jacques Butcher and Magna Studios are from the Ellery Queen novel* The Four of Hearts. *Dr. Orestes Preson is from Frances and Richard Lockridge's Mr. and Mrs. North mystery* Dead as a Dinosaur. *All of Richard Lockridge's series are connected. Some of those links include: Lieutenant (later Captain) Heimrich appearing in two Mr. and Mrs. North novels before spinning off into his own series; police detective Nathan Shapiro, the protagonist of his own series of books, appearing in the Heimrich novel* Murder Can't Wait; *a retired college professor who appeared in both* Accent on Murder *and* Murder Can't Wait *going on to appear in* Twice Retired, *part of a series about A.D.A. Bernard Simmons; and Detective Paul Lane appearing in the novels* Night of the

Shadows *and* Quest of the Bogeyman *before becoming a recurring character in the Simmons books. Judge Ernest Coméliau appeared in several non-series novels written by Georges Simenon under pseudonyms before becoming a supporting character in the Maigret books. The original Zigomar was a gypsy crime lord and foe of policeman Paulin Broquet in stories by Léon Sazie. Nero Wolfe, Archie Goodwin, Fritz Brenner, Inspector Cramer, Sgt. Stebbins, Saul Panzer, and D.A. Skinner are from the novels by Rex Stout. The Churchill Hotel appears in both the Nero Wolfe novels and Stout's Tecumseh Fox series. Sebastian Tombs is an alias used by Simon Templar, aka the Saint. William Valcross (the original Big Fellow) and Inspector Fernack are from Leslie Charteris'* The Saint in New York. *Prosper Lepicq is featured in books by Pierre Véry. Colonel Dubois appears in novels by Pierre Nord. The Sunshine Cab Company is from the TV series* Taxi. *The painting of Sherlock Holmes above Archie Goodwin's desk is described in Stout's novels. William S. Baring-Gould identified Holmes as Nero Wolfe's father. The Panther-Pilsner brewery is from the Three Stooges short* Three Little Beers. *Harry the Horse, Little Isadore, and Spanish John are from the stories of Damon Runyon. Anthony Quinn will later become the vigilante known as the Black Bat, whose adventures appeared in the pulp* Black Book Detective.

Summer
THE SPIDER AND DOMINO LADY: THE LADY AND THE SPIDER
The Spider travels to Los Angeles to investigate cases of people bursting into flame, and teams up with the Domino Lady to set matters right.

A Return of the Originals *one-shot by Nancy Holder, Joe Gentile, and E. M. Gist, Moonstone Comics, 2011.*

VOODOO DEATH
Foster Fade attempts to prevent the death of John Brooks, a sharply-dressed lawyer who is a member of the firm Brooks, Brooks, and Mason. Brooks refers to his older brother Theodore and the latter's friend Lt. Col. A. B. Mayfair from the Great War.

Short story by Aubrey Stephens in The New Adventures of Foster Fade, the Crime Spectacularist, Tommy

Hancock and Morgan Minor, eds., Pro Se Press, 2013. Foster Fade appeared in three stories by Lester Dent in the pulp All Detective Magazine in 1934. John Brooks' brother and Mayfair are two of the five aides of Dent's most famous creation, a bronze-skinned pulp superman.

LOVE IS A BATTLEFIELD

The Domino Lady borrows a pistol that fires "mercy bullets" from her friend Andrew at Mayfair Labs in New York, who has a crush on her.

Short story by Greg Hatcher in Domino Lady Volume One, Ron Fortier, ed., Airship 27 Productions, 2015. Mayfair is an aide to a famous "Doc." Ellen Patrick's father died a year and a half ago, placing this story in 1934.

July
ONE DEATH TO A CUSTOMER

Professional entertainer and private investigator Ed Race (aka the Masked Marksman) and druggist Doc Turner come to the Spider's aid against gangsters led by a former friend of Race's.

Short story by Rich Harvey in the hardcover edition of The Spider Chronicles, Joe Gentile, Garrett Anderson, and Lori G., eds., Moonstone Books, 2013. This crossover brings Emile C. Tepperman's Ed Race, the Masked Marksman, and Arthur Leo Zagat's Doc Turner, both of whom had their own features in The Spider magazine, into the CU.

August
DEATH'S HEAD BERLIN

It is mentioned three people have recently left Germany: Mr. Norris, Herr Issyvoo, and Sally Bowles.

The first Inspector Lohmann novel by Jack Gerson. Lohmann is from Fritz Lang's films M and The Testament of Dr. Mabuse. The three individuals who have recently departed Germany appear in two short novels by Christopher Isherwood collected as The Berlin Stories, the basis for the musical Cabaret. Norris is from Mr. Norris Changes Trains, while Issyvoo (a fictionalized version of Isherwood himself whose surname was mispronounced by the Germans) and Sally Bowles appear in Goodbye to Berlin.

1935

Winter
BITTER FRUIT

A friend of Margo Lane asks her when she plans to finally marry Lamont Cranston, saying, "*You* think that marriage means the good times are over, don't you? But look at Nora! Has she slowed down any since she got hitched?" Margo retorts, "What about Dian? She and her beau are thick as thieves. Does the fact that she doesn't have a ring on her finger make a bit of difference?"

The Shadow *#19–23 by Chris Roberson, Andrea Mutti, and Giovanni Timpano, Dynamite Entertainment, November 2013–March 2014. Nora is the wealthy Nora Charles, who investigates crimes alongside her husband Nick, a former private investigator, as seen in Dashiell Hammett's novel* The Thin Man *and the subsequent film series starring William Powell and Myrna Loy. Dian is Dian Belmont, the girlfriend and companion of Wesley Dodds, aka the Sandman, whose exploits appeared in* Adventure Comics *in the 1940s. Nora and Dian are mentioned in #19.*

Early Winter
THE CURSE OF THE CRIMSON HEART

Harry Dickson and his assistant Tom Wills dine at the home of Mortimer Triggs, a bookseller whom Dickson considers a greater detective than himself. Dickson quotes the travel diary of explorer Leo Saint-Clair, who visited the most remote sections of Northern India on the Tibetan border.

Short story by Jean Ray, originally published as "Les idées de Monsieur Triggs" in Harry Dickson *#141, 1936; adapted and translated under a new title by Jean-Marc and Randy Lofficier in* Harry Dickson: The Heir of Dracula, *Black Coat Press, 2009. Mortimer Triggs would go on to appear in several non-Dickson stories by Ray. Leo Saint-Clair is better known as Jean de La Hire's hero the Nyctalope.*

Spring
GHOST SQUAD: RISE OF THE BLACK LEGION

The Ghost Squad is formed by the U.S. government to battle the Nazi society known as the Black Legion. The Squad consists of the immortal John Lazarus, pilot Alan Hale, and magician Arlene "Lady Arcane" Kane. Hale collaborates with FBI Agent Dan Fowler during the mission, and later receives aid from boxer Mad Chad Hardin, who once helped out Jim Anthony. Lazarus (who is in fact the biblical Lazarus) reveals to his teammates the Black Legion's leader, Engel von Nacht, is really Vlad Dracula.

Novel by Ron Fortier and Andrew Salmon, Cornerstone Book Publishers, 2012. Lady Arcane first appeared in Fortier's story "Lady Arcane: The Mistress of Magic." Dan Fowler appeared in the pulp G-Men Detective, while Jim Anthony's adventures were showcased in Super Detective. Dracula needs no introduction.

THE GRAY REAPERS

The Spider (aka Richard Wentworth) battles dead men brought back as zombies by an Egyptian cult. When Nita Van Sloan expresses astonishment at the idea of resurrecting the deceased, Wentworth cites a monograph on the subject by a Dr. West who works at a university in New England, and also notes Savage claims to have revived an Egyptian mummy using a process involving tana leaf extract; however, the tana plant is extinct, and Savage used the last known specimens of the extract for his experiment.

Short story by Matthew Baugh in The Spider: Extreme Prejudice, Joe Gentile and Tommy Hancock, eds., Moonstone Books, 2013. This story explains how the Spider's chauffeur and aide Ronald Jackson appeared alive and well in the pulp novel Reign of the Death Fiddler and later novels after his death in The Pain Emperor. Both of the aforementioned novels were published in 1935. Dr. West is the title character of H. P. Lovecraft's "Herbert West–Reanimator." The university West teaches at is Miskatonic University, which is featured prominently in Lovecraft's Cthulhu Mythos. Savage may be the man Philip José Farmer identified as Doc Wildman, who resurrected a mummy in the pulp novel Resurrection Day; however, both Farmer's and Rick Lai's chronologies place the events of that novel in 1936. Perhaps Doc resurrected a mummy in 1935 or earlier using the tana leaves, and turned to other methods when his supply ran out, leading to another mummy resurrection in 1936. Doc's first revived mummy probably did not live very long. Tana leaves are from Universal Studios' original cycle of Mummy films. Despite what Wentworth thinks, the leaves are not really extinct, as they appear in several works set after 1935, such as the cartoon Gargoyles, the movie Bubba Ho-Tep, and Simon R. Green's Nightside novels.

THE SCARLET COURTESAN OF SOVEREIGN CITY

The adventurer Fortune McCall and his companions settle in Sovereign City, where they battle the evil Dr. Sundown Mayhew and his sister Orchid. One of Fortune's comrades, Stephen Lapinsky, smokes Morley Cigarettes. Several snippets of conversation at a party held by the Mayhews are given: "... dahling, you simply *must* go see Victor Vail at the Croxton! The way the man plays a violin is positively *arousing*..." "... you'd think that Benson would have thrown me a little something. He'd never have found those diamonds in Brazil if it hadn't been for me..." and "... just as well that Mayhew didn't invite Lazarus Gray. The man has no sense of how things are done in this town..." Mayor Rainsford Byles refers to Sovereign City's other heroes, including Doc Daye.

Story by Derrick Ferguson in The Adventures of Fortune McCall, *Pro Se Press, 2011. Sovereign City is the setting of a book imprint by various authors, published by Pro Se. Lazarus Gray is a Sovereign City hero who appears in collections by Barry Reese. The Lazarus Gray books are set in the same continuity as most of Reese's other fiction, including his books about the vigilante known as the Peregrine. The Peregrine books have appearances by a recurring villain called the Warlike Manchu, who is meant to be Fu Manchu, and a heroine called the Revenant, who is a pastiche of the Phantom. Reese's portrayals of the Warlike Manchu and the Revenant do not fit with the continuity of Fu Manchu and the Phantom's lives and exploits in the CU, and therefore Reese's connected fiction must take place in an alternate universe. However, we can infer from this crossover Lazarus Gray has a counterpart in the CU as well. Presumably Fortune McCall also exists in both universes. Doc Daye is from Tommy Hancock's upcoming book* The Adventures of Doc Daye. *Morley Cigarettes have appeared in a number of TV shows and movies, but are most famous for their appearances on* The X-Files. *Victor Vail is a blind violinist from the Doc Savage pulp novel* The Polar Treasure. *Benson may be Paul Ernst's pulp hero. In his first appearance,* Justice, Inc., *it was mentioned that he had mined diamonds in Brazil.*

PERIOD PIECE

Lady Amelia tells her employee Miss Myers a story about her distant cousin Lord Cornphillip. Viola Chasm, Lady Anchorage, and Lady Metroland are all mentioned in the tale.

Short story by Evelyn Waugh in Mr. Loveday's Little Outing, and Other Sad Stories, *Chapman & Hall, London, 1936; reprinted in* The Complete Stories of Evelyn Waugh, *Little, Brown and Company, 1998. Viola Chasm and Lady Anchorage first appeared in Waugh's novel* Vile Bodies, *and went on to appear in several of his other books and stories. Lady Metroland debuted in* Decline and Fall, *and also reappeared in several later books and stories.*

May 19
LEGACY OF EVIL

In 1935, a man rides a motorcycle in England. In a flashback to 1925, the same man, allegedly Thomas Edward Shaw, is questioned by Sir Dennis Nayland Smith about a Chinese woman he encountered more than 10 years before. Smith was recommended to Shaw by Dr. Petrie. Smith identifies the Chinese woman as Fah Lo Suee. Smith is working with Captain Sauvin of the Deuxième Bureau, who is nicknamed *Le Poisson Chinois* (the Chinese Fish). Fah Lo Suee's father is leader of the Si-Fan. Smith mentions the Zayat's Kiss, and reveals to "Shaw" he is in fact Thomas Edward Lawrence, otherwise known as Lawrence of Arabia. Lawrence was brainwashed by Fah Lo Suee's father, Fu Manchu. Back in the present, Fah Lo Suee tells Lawrence, who is seriously injured after crashing his motorcycle, she is taking him to Fu Manchu.

Short story by T. E. Lawrence, edited by Neil Penswick in Tales of the Shadowmen Volume 7: Femmes Fatales, *Jean-Marc and Randy Lofficier, eds., Black Coat Press, 2010; reprinted in French in* Les Compagnons de l'Ombre (Tome 8), *Jean-Marc and Randy Lofficier, eds., Rivière Blanche, 2011. Fu Manchu, Fah Lo Suee, Sir Dennis Nayland Smith, Dr. Petrie, the Si-Fan, and the Zayat's Kiss are from the novels by Sax Rohmer. Captain Georges "Le Poisson Chinois" Sauvin debuted in the novel* Le Poisson Chinois *by Jean Bommart in 1934 and continued to appear in novels well into the '60s; this crossover brings him into the CU. T. E. Lawrence, better known as "Lawrence of Arabia," was a real person. Historically, he fatally crashed his motorcycle on May 19, 1935. Fah Lo Suee must have injected the badly wounded Lawrence with her father's death-simulating drug* F. Katalepsis *and pressed him into Fu Manchu's service.*

May 19–Late May
CROWN OF THE COBRA KING

The death of T. E. Lawrence causes Secret Agent X to remember his meeting with Lawrence and Auda ibu Tayi in 1917, during which they told him about the cult known as the Circle of Father Set. Back in the present, an assassin for the Circle thinks the Great Serpent controlled much of the Earth in ancient times. He also thinks of a kingdom in the north called Hyperborea that existed thousands of years ago. The Circle's High Priest says the Nazis, with whom they are allied, recognize the Circle's members are heirs to great Acheron. Secret Agent X travels to the city known as Irem of the Pillars. In another flashback to 1917, X holds off a swordsman whose unblinking stare causes him to resemble one of the waxwork figures created by Professor Henry Jarrod in the United States. In the present once more, a lesser priest of the Circle says Thoth-Amon mentioned a prophecy that a man wearing the Ring of Father Set would arise, and the Circle would rule the world. The High Priest reveals himself as a Serpent Man.

Short story by Frank Schildiner in Secret Agent X, Volume 4, *Ron Fortier*, ed., Airship 27 Productions, 2012. Father Set, his ring, and Thoth-Amon are from Robert E. Howard's first Conan story, "The Phoenix on the Sword." In their own Conan stories, L. Sprague de Camp and Lin Carter conflated Set with the Great Serpent worshipped by the Serpent Men from Howard's stories of King Kull. Acheron is from the Conan novel The Hour of the Dragon. Hyperborea is the name of a land from Greek mythology, but the Hyperborea mentioned here is from the Conan stories. Irem of the Pillars is mentioned in the Quran, but the version of the city seen here is from H. P. Lovecraft's "The Nameless City." Professor Henry Jarrod is from the 1953 horror film House of Wax. According to this story, the Circle of Father Set's assassin poisoned T. E. Lawrence, which caused his historical motorcycle crash on May 19, 1935. Lawrence's account "Legacy of Evil" (edited by Neil Penswick) indicates Fu Manchu's daughter Fah Lo Suee brought the still-living (albeit wounded) Lawrence to Fu Manchu after the crash. I have already conjectured Fah Lo Suee injected Lawrence with her father's death-simulating drug F. Katalepsis before bringing him to Fu. The Devil Doctor, being an expert in toxicology and countless other fields, most likely produced an antidote for the Circle's poison.

June
THE SKULLMASK ON ZOMBIE ISLAND
On the Caribbean island of Martinidad, the African-American Darby Townsend, an employee of Wentworth-Cranston Limited, becomes the latest to hold the mantle of the supernatural vigilante the Skullmask in order to avenge his wife's murder.

Story by Teel James Glenn in Weird Tales of the Skullmask, *BooksForABuck.com, 2009*. Wentworth-Cranston Limited must be owned by millionaires Richard Wentworth (aka the Spider) and a New Jersey millionaire named Cranston (or, more likely, Wentworth's half-brother Allard Kent Rassendyll, the shadowy hero of the pulps, posing as Cranston). This crossover brings the various Skullmasks into the CU. This story takes place after the repeal of Prohibition in 1933.

Summer. Brian O'Brien dons the suit, fedora, and mask of the Clock (*Funny Pages* #6, November 1936, Centaur).

Summer
THE CIDER KING MURDER
Foster Fade refuses to narrate his investigations over the radio. When Dinamenta "Din" Stevens, who writes up the stories Fade dictates to her for *The Planet* newspaper, asks him what the paper's owner and publisher Gubb Hackrox is supposed to do with a brand new broadcast studio and auditorium, Fade replies, "Tell him to hire King Mantell and his orchestra. I like King." Din drinks some of Fade's bottle of Black Pony Scotch to calm her nerves after a nearly fatal encounter with a murderer.
Short story by Derrick Ferguson in The New Adventures of Foster Fade, the Crime Spectacularist, *Tommy Hancock and Morgan Minor, eds., Pro Se Press, 2013. Foster Fade appeared in three stories by Lester Dent in the pulp* All Detective Magazine *in 1934. Band leader King Mantell is from the 1936 film* The Princess Comes Across, *while Black Pony Scotch is from the 1944 film noir* Laura.

THE DAY OF THE SILENT DEATH
Fortune McCall and his crew battle a fiend who has abducted a scientist and is using the virus the latter created for the government for his own evil ends. Dr. Regina Mallory, one of Fortune's comrades, admires the imposing Daye Tower that can be seen from just about anywhere in Sovereign City. Fortune's foe adopts the Third Defensive Stance of the Third Level of Llap-Goch.
Story by Derrick Ferguson in The Adventures of Fortune McCall, *Pro Se Press, 2011. Sovereign City is the setting of a New Pulp book imprint published by Pro Se. The Daye Tower is named after Doc Daye, a Sovereign*

City adventurer who will appear in an upcoming book by Tommy Hancock. Llap-Goch is a fictional Welsh martial art from the British comedy troupe Monty Python's book The Brand New Monty Python Bok.

INDIANA JONES AND THE CUP OF THE VAMPIRE

Indiana Jones and Mihail Tepes, a descendant of Dracula, hunt for the Cup of Djemsheed, which grants eternal life to those who drink human blood from it, encountering the Romanian Anti-Vampire League and other foes in the process. The Cup is buried in the grave of Dracula himself. Indy inadvertently awakens Dracula, who wipes out the League.

A Find Your Fate Adventure *novel by Andrew Helfer. This book allows you to choose what courses of action Indy takes, and gives corresponding page numbers to flip to for the outcome of those actions. Indy's awakening of Dracula is the most likely final outcome for the CU. It is implied drinking from the Cup of Djemsheed is what turned Dracula into a vampire, but there were probably more factors at work than just that.*

Summer 1935–1936
DAY OF THE DESTROYERS

Jimmie Flint, Secret Agent X-11 of the Intelligence Service Command, battles Colonel Lucian Starliss and his Medusa Council, who seek to oust President Franklin Delano Roosevelt and take over the United States. Along the way, he receives aid from the Phantom Detective (Richard Curtis Van Loan), the Black Bat (Tony Quinn), the Green Lama (Jethro Dumont), and the Gray Face (Owen Tull). *Herald-Tribune* reporter Luke Jaconetti moonlights for the Amalgamated Press, which employs Jimmie's girlfriend Kara Eastland. Luke receives a phone call from Betty Dale. After the Council is defeated, Kara says Dumont is organizing other wealthy men such as himself, including Van Loan and "that odd chap, Wentworth" for a Patriots for Progress group.

An anthology of linked stories by Gary Phillips, Tommy Hancock, Aaron Shaps, Jeri Westerson, Ron Fortier, Eric Fein, Joe Gentile, Paul Bishop, and Adam Lance Garcia, edited by Gary Phillips, Moonstone Books, 2015. Luke Jaconetti first appeared in Garcia's story "The Black Rock Conspiracy," featuring Lester Dent's pulp hero Foster Fade; he also appeared in Garcia's novel The Green Lama: Scions. *Reporter Betty Dale is the girlfriend of Secret Agent X, who has no known connection to Secret Agent X-11. "That odd chap, Wentworth" is Richard Wentworth, aka the Spider. This crossover brings Secret Agent X-11 (a character created for this anthology) and the Gray Face (another original character, created by Phillips), into the CU.*

August 31, 1935–July 2, 1961
TOROS & TORSOS

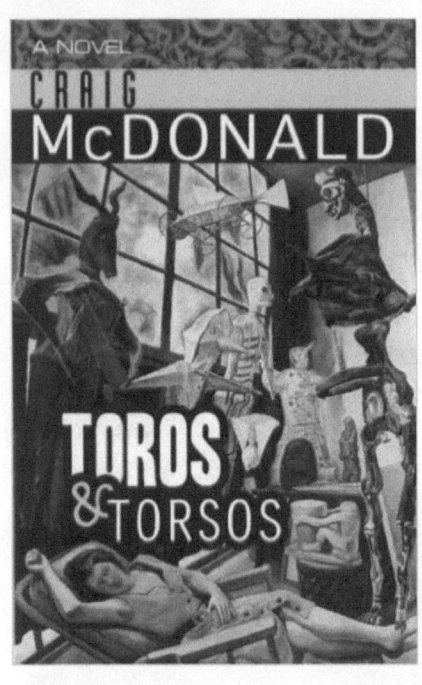

Harriet Blair tells author Hector Lassiter she has read all of his novels and Holly Martins', and she just finished Martins' *Lone Rider of Santa Fe*. The art pieces owned by Lassiter include a couple of pieces by Nick Hart and a Matisse he picked up from the estate of Bertram Stone. Hector has a friend from Paris named Libby who now has an art gallery in Cannes. At Chicote's, Hector chats with an older woman named Roslyn, who lived for many years in Alaska and met Kafka and Houdini.

Novel by Craig McDonald, Bleak House Books, 2008. Holly Martins is from the movie The Third Man, *starring Orson Welles as Harry Lime and Joseph Cotten as Holly. Interestingly, Welles himself is a recurring character in the Hector Lassiter series. The Third Man must be a slightly fictionalized account of Holly Martins and Harry Lime's real exploits in Vienna. Roslyn and her friend Cicely are the founders of the town of Cicely, Alaska on the television series* Northern Exposure. *Since* The Third Man *and* Northern Exposure *both take place in the CU, so do the Hector Lassiter novels. Nick Hart, Bertram Stone, and Libby Valentin are from the movie* The Moderns, *bringing in that film as well. The Lassiter novel* Print the Legend *introduced writer Chris Lyon, who went on to appear in his own series of novels by McDonald. Chris' cousin Tell Lyon is the main character of McDonald's standalone novel* El Gavilan.

Late Summer
THE MAGIC OF MADNESS

Fortune McCall and his crew attempt to rescue a professional magician from the clutches of the Asian criminal organization known as the Ui Kwoon Ah-How.

Short story by Derrick Ferguson in The Adventures of Fortune McCall, *Pro Se Press, 2011. The Ui Kwoon Ah-How was the secret society run by the villain Li Shoon, who appeared in stories by H. Irving Hancock in* Detective Story Magazine *in 1916–1917.*

September 4
THE TIME TRAVELERS' EX-WIFE

In Kingsport, the former Alice Peaslee is wished a happy sixtieth birthday by her son Wingate, who has just returned from an expedition in Australia with his father. Alice is brought cake and lemonade by her grandson John, the son of her daughter Hannah and Samuel Beckett. Looking in a photo album, she sees a picture of herself in London on June 5, 1931, alongside author Olaf Stapledon and the latter's young protégé, the poet Paul Tregardis. Another picture, taken on September 2, 1924, shows the members of Hannah's wedding party. Among them is Hannah's husband's supervisor at Brooklyn's Museum of Fine Arts, Dr. Halpin Chalmers, a graduate of Miskatonic University, with whom Alice reminisces about the faculty and Arkham. Chalmers is friends with a private detective named Charles. Alice marries Chalmers, and on weekends and holidays they travel to Partridgeville where he was raised. In 1910, Alice divorces her husband, Professor Nathaniel Wingate Peaslee, having experienced strange visions of the past and future when she touched him. In 1912, her son Robert finds the notebooks in which she described her visions. Robert takes large portions of the text and reorganizes them into narratives, which Alice rewrites and has published in *Whispers* magazine. The periodical forwards her a letter of praise from a man named Randolph Carter. Alice spent six years with a distant relative named Alice the Elder, wandering time and space, having breakfast in Hyperborea, dancing in Irem, and reading books in Celeano.

Short story by Pete and Mandy Rawlik in The Lovecraft eZine *#29, Mike Davis, ed., February 2014. Kingsport, Miskatonic University, Arkham, and Randolph Carter appear in a number of H. P. Lovecraft's Cthulhu Mythos stories. Alice Peaslee; her husband, Professor Nathaniel Wingate Peaslee; and their children, Wingate, Hannah and Robert, are from Lovecraft's "The Shadow Out of Time." Irem is from Lovecraft's "The Nameless City." The magazine* Whispers *appears in Lovecraft's "The Unnamable"; it is believed by many Lovecraft scholars the Carter that narrates that story is Randolph Carter. John Beckett is the father of time traveler Sam Beckett on the television series* Quantum Leap. *Paul Tregardis is from Clark Ashton Smith's story "Ubbo-Sathla." Hyperborea appears in "Ubbo-Sathla" and many other works by Smith. Dr. Halpin Chalmers and Partridgeville are from Frank Belknap Long's story "The Hounds of Tindalos." Chalmers' private detective friend is Nick Charles from Dashiell Hammett's* The Thin Man. *Celeano (or Celaeno) is mentioned in several Mythos stories by August Derleth.*

Mid October
UNDER A COMANCHE MOON

Jim Anthony is framed by an embittered albino Comanche for the murders of three female acquaintances of his. Jim was set up on a date with the first victim by the *Clarion*'s publisher, Frank Havens. Jim's butler Dawkins buys a number of newspapers for his employer, including the *Herald*.

Story by Frank Byrns in Jim Anthony: Super Detective Volume Four, *Ron Fortier, ed., Airship 27 Productions, 2013. The* New York Clarion *newspaper and its publisher, Frank Havens, are from the Phantom Detective pulp novels. The* Daily Herald *is from the Secret Agent X stories. There are two conflicting chronological references in the story. One is to Jim and the second victim having attended the Broadway premiere of* Porgy and Bess *just a week ago. Historically, the play made its Broadway debut on October 10, 1935. The other reference is to District Attorney Dodge possibly being reelected in less than a year. In real life, William C. Dodge was New York's District Attorney from January 1, 1934 to December 1, 1937, serving only one term. I have chosen to ignore the reelection reference and place this story in October 1935.*

Autumn
A TICKET FOR THULE (UN BILLET POUR THULÉ)

Judex and French Secret Service agent Georges Sauvin (aka the Chinese Fish) battle a group of thieves who are stealing a tablet in the custody of the Ironcastle Foundation. The thieves are working for Jan Mayen, a minion of Sun Koh. Hareton Ironcastle, the Foundation's head, also appears.

Short story by Romain d'Huissier appearing as "Un Billet pour Thulé" in Les Compagnons de l'Ombre (Tome 8), *Jean-Marc and Randy Lofficier, eds., Rivière Blanche, 2011, and in English in* The Shadow of Judex, *Jean-Marc and Randy Lofficier, eds., Black Coat Press, 2013; reprinted in* L'Ombre de Judex, *Jean-Marc and Randy Lofficier, eds., Rivière Blanche, 2013. Judex is from the classic film serial of the same name. The Chinese Fish appears in spy novels by Jean Bommart. Jan Mayen and Sun Koh were the subjects of two German pulp series written by Paul Müller that crossed over. Hareton Ironcastle is from J.-H. Rosny aîné's* L'Étonnant Voyage d'Hareton Ironcastle, *adapted and translated by Philip José Farmer as* Ironcastle.

THE GOLD OF BOX 850
Fortune McCall tells Tais Pennington-Smythe he has read she has been out to dinner with Lazarus Gray. Later, Police Chief Tate tells Fortune Faceless Cabrini has broken out of the detention house where he was being held awaiting transfer to Denbrook Penitentiary.

Short story by Derrick Ferguson in The Adventures of Fortune McCall, *Pro Se Press, 2011. Lazarus Gray is an adventurer created by Barry Reese; like Fortune McCall, Gray operates out of Sovereign City. The Lazarus Gray books take place in the same continuity as many of Reese's other works, including his series about the vigilante known as the Peregrine. The Peregrine's adventures are incompatible with CU continuity, so Lazarus Gray must have a CU counterpart. The city of Denbrook, created by Mike McGee, was the setting of several serialized novels on the online fiction site* Frontier Publishing.

FOR VIOLENT FIRES THAT SOON BURN OUT
The heroes of Sovereign City include Fortune McCall, Doc Daye, and Lazarus Gray. McCall's living quarters aboard his boat *The Heart of Fortune* include a wonderfully appointed lounge that looks as if it could be one of the private lounges located in the Baltimore Gun Club or New York's Cobalt Club.

A Single Shot Signature *story by Derrick Ferguson, Pro Se Press, 2015. Doc Daye was created by Tommy Hancock. Lazarus Gray appears in a series of books by Barry Reese, which are set in the same universe as his Peregrine books. The Peregrine tales are incompatible with Crossover Universe continuity, so Lazarus Gray must have a counterpart in the CU. The Baltimore Gun Club is from Jules Verne's books* From the Earth to the Moon *and* Around the Moon. *The Cobalt Club is from the pulp novels of a certain slouch-hatted vigilante.*

1936

January
UNA VOCE POCO FA
Leo Saint-Clair, the Nyctalope, attends the Paris Opera with Rose Bruyère, also known as the Phantom Angel, a friend of his deceased third wife, Sylvie Mac Duhl, whom Rose freed from the clutches of her evil stepmother Simone Desroches, aka Belphégor. Falling under a spell in the 10th Century, Rose was revived a few years ago via a kiss by Doctor Francis

Ardan. A sniper tries unsuccessfully to shoot Leo and Rose. The Nyctalope suggests the would-be assassin may have retreated to the caves where Erik, the Phantom, used to hide.

Short story by Emmanuel Gorlier in Night of the Nyctalope, *Jean-Marc and Randy Lofficier, eds., Black Coat Press, 2012; reprinted in French in* La Nuit du Nyctalope, *Jean-Marc and Randy Lofficier, eds., Rivière Blanche, 2012. The Nyctalope and his late wife Sylvie Mac Duhl are from French pulp novels by Jean de La Hire. The Phantom Angel, a character created by Randy Lofficier for the* Tales of the Shadowmen *anthology series, is also meant to be the title character of Charles Perrault's fairy tale "The Sleeping Beauty." Belphégor is from the French film serial of the same name. Doctor Francis Ardan is from Guy d'Armen's novel* Doc Ardan: City of Gold and Lepers; *Jean-Marc and Randy Lofficier's adaptation and translation of the novel implied Ardan was actually a famous "Doc" from the American pulps. Erik is better known as the Phantom of the Opera, from Gaston Leroux's novel of the same name.*

ONCE MORE, THE NYCTALOPE (LE SURHOMME EST-IL FRANÇAIS?)

An Invisible Man named Jacques enters the mansion of his friend Leo Saint-Clair, the Nyctalope, and sees an oil painting of Leo and his late wife Sylvie. Leo introduces Jacques to Briar Rose, also known as Belle and the Phantom Angel, alongside whom Leo fought Belphégor. Jacques' children have been kidnapped; the mastermind behind the abductions is Professor René Belloq. Below the house are a series of secret rooms that were used by Sylvie's stepfather Mathias Lumen in his fight against Leonid Zattan, which have been converted by Leo into a laboratory. Leo uses a device that allowed him to overcome Lucifer in the early '20s to prevent the kidnappers from tracking Jacques' aura. The three attend a lecture given by Belloq, whose other guests include archaeologist Artistide Clairembart and Tryphon Tournesol. Also in attendance are journalist Jérôme Fandor and Dutil-Parot, Jacques Roll's predecessor as President of the Council of Ministers. Belloq announces Doctor Haushofer of the Thule Society will tell the audience the results of his research on the use of *Vril* as a psychic energy source. Leo's friend Gno Mitang initiated him into the Japanese fighting disciplines.

Short story by Emmanuel Gorlier appearing as "Le Surhomme est-il français?" in Les Compagnons de l'Ombre (Tome 14), *Jean-Marc and Randy Lofficier, eds., Rivière Blanche, 2014, and in English in* Tales of the Shadowmen Volume 11: Force Majeure, *Jean-Marc and Randy Lofficier, eds., Black Coat Press, 2014. Jacques Roll (formerly known as Joe Rollon) and Dutil-Parot are from Jean de La Hire's book* Joe Rollon, the Invisible

Man. *The Nyctalope* is the hero of a series of novels by de La Hire. Sylvie, Mathias Lumen, Leonid Zattan, Lucifer, and Gno Mitang are from the Nyctalope series. The Phantom Angel has appeared in several stories by Randy Lofficier in the Tales of the Shadowmen *series, and is meant to be the title character of the French fairy tale "Sleeping Beauty."* Belphégor is the title character of a French film serial; she encountered Leo and Belle earlier in the month in Gorlier's story "Une Voce Poco Fa." Professor René Belloq encountered Indiana Jones in the film Raiders of the Lost Ark. Aristide Clairembart is from Henri Vernes' Bob Morane novels, while Tryphon Tournesol (Cuthbert Calculus in English translations) is from Hergé's Tintin comics. Jerôme Fandor is one of the greatest foes of Marcel Allain and Pierre Souvestre's villain Fantômas, and may in fact be the "Lord of Terror's" illegitimate son. Doctor Karl Haushofer was a real person whose geopolitical views may have influenced Hitler. The Vril energy is from Edward Bulwer-Lytton's novel The Coming Race.

February
GHOST PIRATES FROM THE BEYOND

Doc Savage and his assistants investigate the murder of one of Doc's friends, an adventure which draws them to Casablanca. There, they meet a potential ally at an establishment called the Blue Parrot.

Marvel Comics' Doc Savage Magazine #4 *by Doug Moench, Marie Severin, and Tony DeZuniga, April 1976. The Blue Parrot is the bar owned by Signor Ferrari in the classic film* Casablanca. *There are several confusing chronological references in this story. The tale begins on February 23, 1936, and Doc and the boys become involved on February 28. However, a later scene, which takes place after Doc's investigation begins, is dated February 24. Additionally, a woman refers to Orson Welles'* War of the Worlds *broadcast, which was not given until October 30, 1938. Renny mentions John Sunlight, whom Doc did not encounter until the August 1937 events of* The Fortress of Solitude. *These latter two references, and the exact dates given, must be considered fictional. However, it can be assumed the story does indeed take place in February of 1936.*

Spring
THE SOCIETY OF UNITED MAGICIANS

The Shadow battles a group of corrupt magicians who are attempting to force Bess Houdini to contact the spirit of her late husband Harry, seeking secrets he has learned on the other side. A poster of Mandrake the Magician is seen in the Society's headquarters.

The Shadow #0 by Cullen Bunn and Colton Worley, Dynamite Entertainment 2014. This story reveals Harry Houdini trained the future Shadow in escapology. The Houdini seen here is the CU counterpart of the real magician.

Summer
THE STAR OF AFRICA

The masked vigilante called Funny Face eavesdrops on a gangster's conversation at the crook's speakeasy, the Pink Ship in Hell's Kitchen.

Short story by Tom Johnson in Exciting Pulp Tales, *Altus Press, 2011. The Pink Ship also appears in Johnson's Phantom Detective story "The Eyes of Satan" and his story "Legends," which takes place in an alternate universe. Since the Phantom Detective is in the CU, this crossover brings in Funny Face, who originally appeared in "Masked Faces," a story by Norman A. Daniels that appeared in the February 1935 episode of the* Phantom Detective *pulp magazine.*

Mid June–September 16
SCOOP

Mrs. Stitch gives Mrs. Beaver twenty pounds for Lady Jean's wedding present, and wonders why she should attend a party held by Viola Chasm. Lady Cockpurse attends a luncheon at Lady Metroland's home.

Novel by Evelyn Waugh. Mrs. Beaver and Lady Cockpurse first appeared in Waugh's novel A Handful of Dust. *Viola Chasm and Lady Metroland also appeared in that novel, as well as several other books and stories by Waugh.*

June 21, 1936–March 16, 1944
THE HOUR OF THE GRAIL

At the castle of Montsegur, the Nyctalope encounters a group of occultists led by Otto Rahn, who refers to the hero's attempted assassination of Hitler. He is surprised, believing no one knew of the attempt, which was thwarted by the Time Patrol.

Short story by Philippe Ward in Night of the Nyctalope, *Jean-Marc* and Randy Lofficier, eds., Black Coat Press, 2012; reprinted in French in La Nuit du Nyctalope, Jean-Marc and Randy Lofficier, eds., Rivière Blanche, 2012. The Nyctalope's attempt to assassinate Hitler was depicted in Emmanuel Gorlier's story "Out of Time" (Tales of the Shadowmen Volume 6: Grand Guignol, Jean-Marc and Randy Lofficier, eds., Black Coat Press, 2010). Gorlier's story conflated Poul Anderson's Time Patrol with the identically-named group in Henri Vernes' Bob Morane novels.

August
THE AFFAIR OF THE BLOODSTAINED EGG COSY
Detective-Inspector Wilkins, investigating a theft and murder at a diplomatic conference at Alderley, the estate of the Earl of Burford, tells one of the Earl's guests, "Hercule Poirot always says that when trying to solve a mystery, any theory you evolve must explain each isolated fact and happening; they've all got to fit into a harmonious pattern with no loose ends. Of course, I'm not in the same class as him—though they do say I look a bit like him—and I can never get that far."

The first Inspector Wilkins novel by James Anderson. Wilkins' comments treat Poirot as a real person. Therefore, this crossover brings him into the CU. Regarding dating this story, Hitler is in power, but World War II has not yet begun and the fear of war is not yet widespread. Further, the third book in the series, The Affair of the 39 Cufflinks, *set in Mid August, states this case happened twelve months ago.*

September
LIFEBLOOD
Jack Fleming, a vampire P.I. in Chicago, meets fanatical vampire hunter James Braxton, who possesses a copy of the *Necronomicon*.

Novel by P. N. Elrod, Ace Books, 1990. The appearance of Lovecraft's Necronomicon *places Jack Fleming in the CU. All of Elrod's vampire series are set in the same universe. Fleming was bitten by Maureen Dumont, who was herself turned by the title character of Elrod's* Jonathan Barrett,

Gentleman Vampire *series*. *Barrett, who met Lucie Manette and a young Percy Blakeney in Elrod's story* "*Death in Dover,*" *was himself turned by Nora Jones, who also turned Quincey Morris, as seen in Elrod's novel* Quincey Morris, Vampire, *a sequel to Stoker's* Dracula *that has already been included in the CU via a reference to Colonel Sebastian Moran from the Sherlock Holmes stories*. Quincey Morris, Vampire *also has an appearance by Lord Richard d'Orleans from Elrod and Nigel Bennett's* Ethical Vampires *series*.

October
THE NOBLE FREAK

Rama Tamerlane, also known as Felifax the Tiger Man, misses his wife Grace and adopted sister Djina. Felifax's British government contact is Sir Ralph Napper. Felifax acquires the dossier of Sir Edmund Sexton, which includes information on his medical and scientific experimentation in regards to genetic splicing. Felifax seeks his sibling Felanthus, who was also the product of one of Sexton's cross-breeding experiments. Felanthus is the captive of Prof. Tornada, his protégé Lance Nolter, and Tornada's artificial man Adam Danator, named after a previous creation. The other prisoners include Gouroull, the Frankenstein Monster; the Deep Ones, fish-men from a colony off the coast of Innsmouth, Massachusetts who worship the Elder God Dagon; a man brought back from the dead by a chemical possibly derived from a re-agent first formulated by Dr. Herbert West, and later further perfected by Dr. Stuart Hartwell; and a zombie. Nolter has created a unique moss that uses the components of a dead organism to self-replicate. Tornada suggests using the remains of his old business rival Roger Kirk as one such organism.

Short story by Christofer Nigro in Tales of the Shadowmen Volume 11: Force Majeure, *Jean-Marc and Randy Lofficier, eds., Black Coat Press 2014. Rama Tamerlane, his wife Grace, his adopted sister Djina, Sir Ralph Napper, and Sir Edmund Sexton are from Paul Féval fils' novel* Felifax the Tiger Man, *which has been translated and adapted by Brian Stableford for Black Coat Press. Prof. Tornada and the first Adam Danator appeared in six novels by André Couvreur, which have also been translated and adapted by Stableford in three volumes. Lance Nolter is from the movie* The Freakmaker *(aka* The Mutations*). Gouroull is the name by which the Frankenstein Monster is known in stories by Jean-Claude Carrière. The Deep Ones and Dagon are from H. P. Lovecraft's story "The Shadow over Innsmouth." Dr. Herbert West is from another Lovecraft tale, "Herbert West—Reanimator." Dr. Hartwell, a minor character in Lovecraft's "The Dunwich Horror," was given the first name Stuart and portrayed as a rival of Herbert West's in Peter Rawlik's novel* Reanimators. *Due to several conflicts with Crossover Universe* continuity, Reanimators *must take place in an alternate universe. However, the Stuart Hartwell of the CU must have engaged in similar reanimation experiments. The zombie evokes the flesh-eating, contagious variety popularized by filmmaker George Romero in* Night of the Living Dead *and its sequels, which also take place in an alternate reality. The self-replicating moss and Roger Kirk are from Theodore Sturgeon's story "It!"*

1937

January
THE AFFAIR OF THE MUTILATED MINK

Chief Inspector Wilkins investigates another murder at the home of the Earl of Burford. The Earl tells a flattered Wilkins he recently lunched with Lord Peter Wimsey, who expressed admiration for the methods Wilkins used in his previous investigation. Wilkins' chief constable suggests calling in one of the so-called "three Great A's" of Scotland Yard: John Appleby, Roderick Alleyn, or St. John Allgood. Ultimately, he chooses Allgood. After her suitor Paul Carter is assaulted, Lord Burford's daughter Gerry offers to read to him Ariadne Oliver's *Death of a Debutante*, *The Screaming Bone* by Annette de la Tour, or Richard Eliot's *The Spider Bites Back.*

The second Inspector Wilkins novel by James Anderson. Wold Newton Family member Lord Peter Wimsey's exploits were chronicled by Dorothy L. Sayers. Sir John Appleby appears in a series of novels by Michael Innes; one of these, Stop Press, *features Richard Eliot. Inspector Roderick Alleyn appears in books by Ngaio Marsh. Ariadne Oliver is from Agatha Christie's Hercule Poirot novels, and also appears solo in Christie's* The Pale Horse, *as well as two of her Parker Pyne stories. Oliver's novel* Death of a Debutante *is mentioned in the Poirot book* Mrs. McGinty's Dead. *Annette de la Tour is the nom de plume of Mr. Judd in Edmund Crispin's Gervase Fen novel* Buried for Pleasure. *This crossover brings Fen, a crime-solving English professor at Oxford, into the CU. The* third book in this series, The Affair of the 39 Cufflinks, establishes The Affair of the Mutilated Mink *takes place less than six months after the events of the first novel,* The Affair of the Blood-Stained Egg Cosy. *Actor Rex Ransom also says the film studio United Artists was formed "fifteen—twenty years ago."* United Artists was formed in 1919, which would suggest the novel takes place between 1934 and 1939. Lord Burford refers to Nelson Eddy co-starring in films with Jeannette MacDonald; the two first worked together on the 1935 film Naughty Marietta. *Lady Burford's reference to "Monday, the 19th" is incorrect, as January 19, 1937 was a Tuesday.*

THE HEIGHT OF ARROGANCE

Ki Nam Moon, secretary to Korean businessman Kim Mu Duk, calls adventurer Anton Chadeaux "the famous Dr. Shadows the newsreel chappies are always talking about, rather as famous as that other Doc S. fellow, eh what?"

Short story by Teel James Glenn in Shadows of New York: The Mysterious Adventures of Dr. Shadows, *BooksForABuck.com, 2011. The reference to Doc S. brings Dr. Shadows into the CU.*

February
THE FIRST SYNN: THE BLOODSTONE CONFIDENTIAL

Major Gideon Synn attempts to end an alleged curse on the Bloodstone family, having failed in that task seven years ago. Synn recommends to his comrades they call Ham Brooks, since they will need a lawyer to clear them of any possible murder charges regarding the ninjas they just battled, who have committed suicide. An article about the battle by Moxie Donovan appears in the *Daily Star.* Synn often takes over teaching the martial art *Sulsa Do* to students at the Shadows Foundation building, including Suzi Duk, when his friend and teacher Anton Chadeaux is away. Synn once explained the *Sulsa Do* secret of self-concealment to his acquaintance Lamont Cranston, who seemed to understand what he was saying. Synn's sister Kathy recounts to him a dirty joke she heard from Monk Mayfair. Synn tells Kathy they'll have to lay a network of the black light/body heat sensors that Long Tom designed for him around the Bloodstone mansion.

Novel by Teel James Glenn, Pro Se Press, 2013. Brooks, Mayfair, and Long Tom are three of Doc's aides. Daily Star *reporter Moxie Donovan is another series character of Glenn's. The* Daily Star *that employs Donovan appears to be a different newspaper than the* Daily Star *owned by Jim Anthony, though both are based in New York. Anton Chadeaux (aka Dr. Shadows), the head of the Shadows Foundation, is also a series character created by Glenn. Suzi Duk is also from the Dr. Shadows series. In this context, Cranston must be the vigilante of the shadows posing as the real millionaire of that name.*

Winter
MOUNTAIN MEN OF THE LOST VALLEY
Secret Agent X travels to Kiev on a mission and sabotages an enemy stronghold where a deadly weapon is being built.

Short story by Bobby Nash in Secret Agent X, Volume 4, *Ron Fortier, ed., Airship 27 Productions, 2012. In Nash and James Burns' comic book* Lance Star: Sky Ranger–One Shot! *Star's foe Baron Otto Von Blood attempts to resurrect the weapon-making project dismantled by X.*

THE DEATH PLAGUE
The Masked Avenger's comrade Curtis Van Leif is interrupted while reading the Morning *Clarion* at the Explorer's Club by Commissioner Kirk Stanley.

Short story by Tom Johnson in Double Danger Tales *#39, Tom and Ginger Johnson, eds., Fading Shadows Publications, August 2000; reprinted in* Triple Detective *#4, Altus Press, 2010. The* Clarion *newspaper is from the* Phantom Detective *pulp stories. "Kirk Stanley" is presumably a pseudonym for Commissioner Stanley Kirkpatrick from the* Spider *pulps.*

Spring
DAWN OF THE PURPLE HOODS
Adventurer Jim Anthony is part of a charity auction where the prizes are dates with celebrities. Another of the eligible bachelors is the young publisher of the *Sentinel* newspaper chain. Jim and his date, Marinda Stubbing, are attacked by a group of men in purple hoods, during which event Marinda is wounded. Jim goes to his ally Frank Havens, publisher of the

Clarion, asking him to put out feelers for information regarding the gang. One of Havens' sources is the mysterious sleuth known as the Phantom. One of Jim's other informants is the owner of a cigar store. Jim evades a group of journalists that includes Rex Parker of the *New York Comet*. Inspector Gregg arrives at Jim's home and headquarters, the Waldorf-Anthony Hotel, in the aftermath of another attack by the Purple Hoods. Marinda is treated by Nurse Ames. When the Purple Hoods capture Jim and Marinda, a group of current and former naval officers set out to rescue them. One member of this rescue mission is Arkansas native Ruben Clampett, who mentions his nephew Jedidiah. Another officer tells Jim Commander Winslow sends his compliments.

Short story by Erwin K. Roberts in Jim Anthony: Super Detective Volume One, Ron Fortier, ed., Cornerstone Book Publishers, 2009. *Jim Anthony's adventures in the "spicy" pulp* Super Detective *were chronicled by Victor Rousseau Emanuel, Robert Leslie Bellem and W. T. Ballard. The publisher of the* Sentinel *newspaper is Britt Reid, the alter ego of the Green Hornet. The auction must have drawn Reid from his native Detroit to Anthony's stomping grounds of New York City. Frank Havens and Inspector Gregg are from the Phantom Detective pulp novels, written by various authors using the pseudonyms "G. Wayman Jones" and "Robert Wallace." The cigar store owner is Danny Blaney, formerly the Green Ghost, a creation of Johnston McCulley's who appeared in* Thrilling Detective. *Rex Parker will later become the Masked Detective, the title character of a pulp magazine written by Norman A. Daniels under the pen name "C. K. M. Scanlon" that was published beginning in Fall 1940, and ending in Spring 1943 due to wartime paper shortages. Cherry Ames, Student Nurse, appeared in a series of mystery novels written by Helen Wells and Julie Campbell Tatham. Ruben Clampett's nephew is Jed Clampett from* The Beverly Hillbillies, *bringing that show into the CU. Don Winslow of the Navy appeared in the comic strip of the same name by Lt. Cmdr. Frank V. Martinek, as well as radio and film serials and a comic book published by Fawcett.*

HOUSE PAINTING–LODGE STYLE

Vic and Sade Gook briefly meet Aunt Fanny, Lum Edwards, and Abner Peabody.

Short story by George Fowler in It's That Time Again 3: Even More New Stories of Old-Time Radio, *Jim Harmon, ed., BearManor Media, 2006. Lum Edwards and Abner Peabody, from the radio show* Lum and Abner, *are in the CU through an appearance in a 2014 Dick Tracy strip. Therefore, this crossover brings in their fellow radio characters Vic and Sade Gook (from* Vic and Sade*) and Aunt Fanny (from the variety program* The Breakfast Club*).*

May
THE DEVIL'S TIGER

An article by Moxie Donovan in *The Daily Star* says Commissioner Weston will not discuss the so-called "Green Claw Deaths" that have occurred in recent months, and several private criminologists have been called in, including Anton Chadeaux, aka Dr. Shadows. When Dr. Shadows began fighting crime, he thought Clark Savage's whole attitude towards publicity for himself was missing a chance to reach many more people. His comrade Slugger Harris says, "Even this hill ape will tell you that Clark or Dr. Pali failed now and then." Traveling to the Philippines, Dr. Shadows and Slugger have lunch with a detective acquaintance, Jo Gar, who gets them tickets to a baseball game. Dr. Shadows, using a device to short out the lights in his foe the White Tiger's headquarters, hopes Mr. Roberts is the electrical whiz he says he is. He later states George Chance, Ardini, or Dr. Pali could outdo a trick performed by the White Tiger, but it did have a flawless setup and execution. Dr. Shadows speculates maybe in time Andy Mayfair or his boss will find a way to synthesize clay used by the White Tiger as an explosive, so it can be used instead against the Japanese.

Short story by Teel James Glenn in Shadows of New York: The Mysterious Adventures of Dr. Shadows, *BooksForABuck.com, 2011.* Daily Star *reporter Moxie Donovan has been featured in two short story collections by Glenn,* Deadline Zombies: The Adventures of Maxi and Moxie *and* Headline Ghouls: The Further Adventures of Maxi and Moxie. *Commissioner Weston is from Walter Gibson's novels of a shadowy pulp vigilante. Electrical expert Roberts is one of Doc's five aides, as is Mayfair. Dr. Pali is a false identity assumed by "Richard Foster's" (Kendell Crossen) pulp hero the Green Lama. Spanish-Filipino detective Jo Gar appeared in stories by "Ramon Decolta" (Raoul Whitfield) in* Black Mask. *George Chance is the alter ego of G. T. Fleming-Roberts' pulp hero the Ghost (aka the Green Ghost). Ardini is a magician-cum-detective who appears in Walter Gibson's novel* A Blonde for Murder.

June–November
MANCHURIAN SHADOWS

Dr. Shadows is described as having traveled extensively, often with his father, Kent Allard, and Jim Wade, to many of the wild places in the world. Police detective Michael Collins tells the hero, "Despite the spider guy and that big bronze lug, we frown on vigilante action here in New York." At the Metropolitan Museum of Art, the wealthy Jan Van Groot reminds Dr. Shadows they were introduced to each other last year by Lamont Cranston, and asks if he has seen the newest addition Dr. Littlejohn brought in from one of his digs. Dr. Shadows tells the evil hypnotist Professor Gregor Zmeyaglaz "Dr. Pali or George Chance could conjure rings around you." Dr. Shadows has two throwing knives, Mike and Ike. Dr. Shadows shows a military guard United States trade representative credentials supplied to him by Ham Brooks' U.S. government contacts.

Novel by Teel James Glenn, BooksForABuck.Com, 2013; revised and expanded from "The Chinese Box Mystery," a short story in Shadows of New York: The Mysterious Adventures of Dr. Shadows, *BooksForABuck.com, 2011. Allard may be the man Farmer identified as Allard Kent Rassendyll. The Cranston who introduced Dr. Shadows to Van Groot was presumably Rassendyll posing as Cranston while the millionaire was abroad. Thunder Jim Wade is an adventurer who appeared in five stories by Henry Kuttner in the pulp magazine* Thrilling Adventure *in 1941. This crossover brings Wade into the CU. "The spider guy" is obviously the Spider, while "that big bronze lug" is a famous pulp superman. Littlejohn and Brooks are two of Doc's aides. The Buddhist priest Dr. Pali is a false identity assumed by Kendell Crossen's pulp hero the Green Lama, who appeared in* Double Detective. *Stage magician George Chance is the alter ego of the vigilante the Ghost (aka the Green Ghost), the protagonist of the pulp* The Ghost, Super-Detective *(later retitled* The Ghost Detective *and* The Green Ghost Detective*). Dr. Shadows must have named his throwing knives after the knife and pistol wielded by Paul Ernst's pulp hero, who only recently made his debut.*

Summer
MONEY SHOT

The Domino Lady (Ellen Patrick) avenges the death of a gubernatorial candidate with whom she was romantically involved. Anton Manelli has filled the void in Hollywood's organized crime scene left by Miles Prince's downfall a year ago. Ellen is friends with Nita Van Sloan. Another candidate, a former actor, once co-starred in a film with Hamilton James. Associated Press reporter A. J. Martin, who is actually Secret Agent X, writes a story about the case.

Novella by Bobby Nash, Moonstone Books, 2014. *The Domino Lady* appeared in "spicy" pulp stories by an author using the pseudonym Lars Anderson. The Manellis are a recurring crime family in Nash's fiction. Nita Van Sloan is the Spider's fiancée. Hamilton James appears in Nash's story "Lights! Camera! Sabotage!" featuring Norman A. Daniels' pulp hero the Eagle. Secret Agent X appeared in a titular pulp magazine by several authors using the pen name "Brant House," beginning with Paul Chadwick.

THE COMING RACE

Jim Anthony rescues a kidnapped scientist from the Nazi superman Sun Koh. Appearing or mentioned are: Rolf Karsten; the Black Bat; Alaska Jim; Sturmvogel; Ashanti Garuda; Ludwig Minx; Wells' time machine; Jan Mayen; the Kingscote School for Girls; St. Trinian's; the Minichin's Seminary; "a dance academy in Freiburg of dubious reputation"; Judex; the second woman to bear the name "Irma Vep"; the Gun Club; St. Cyprian; Harley Warren; and "that fellow in Kansas."

Part II of Derrick Ferguson and Josh Reynolds' novel The Vril Agenda, Airship 27 Productions, 2014, written solely by Reynolds. Jim Anthony appeared in the pulp magazine Super Detective. Sun Koh is from the German pulp magazine (heftroman) Sun Koh, die Erbe von Atlantis, *written by Paul Müller as "Lok Myler." Rolf Karsten appeared in the heftroman* Rolf Karsten, der Schrecken der Berliner Unterwelt. *The Black Bat appeared in the pulp* Black Book Detective. *Alaska Jim is from "Big Ben" and "F. L. Barwin's" heftroman* Alaska Jim, ein Held der Kanadischen Polizei. *Sturmvogel appeared in the* heftroman Sturmvögel, mit Buchse und Toboggan durch die Arktis, Abenteuer zwischen Urwald und Prairie, *also written by F. L. Barwin. Ludwig*

Minx appeared in the series Minx der Geisterbeschwörer *and* Minx der Geistersucher. *Jan Mayen appeared in Müller's magazine* Jan Mayen, der Herr der Atomkraft, *and had several crossovers with Sun Koh. Sun Koh met Alaska Jim in an issue of the former's magazine, while Alaska Jim met Sturmvögel in an issue of his own series. Ashanti Garuda is from Dr. Art Sippo's collection* Sun Koh: Heir of Atlantis Vol. 1, *which portrayed the other German pulp characters as members of the Thule Society serving Sun Koh. Although* Sun Koh: Heir of Atlantis' *take on the Atlantis Sun Koh is from is incompatible with Win Scott Eckert's story "Captain Midnight at Ultima Thule," and therefore the collection must take place in an alternate universe, there is no reason the other heftroman heroes could not have worked with Sun Koh in the CU as well. Jim indicates he has actually seen the time machine described in H. G. Wells' novel. The Kingscote School for Girls is from Antonia Forest's novels about the Marlow family. St. Trinian's appears in cartoons by Ronald Searle. The Minchin's Seminary is from Frances Hodgson Burnett's book* A Little Princess. *The dance academy in Freiburg of dubious reputation is from the Italian horror film* Suspiria. *Judex is from Louis Feuillade's silent film serial of the same name. The second woman to bear the name "Irma Vep," the daughter of the Irma Vep seen in Feuillade's serial* Les Vampires, *is from Reynolds' story "Nestor Burma Goes West." The Gun Club is the New York branch of the Baltimore Gun Club from Jules Verne's novel* From the Earth to the Moon *and* Around the Moon. *Charles St. Cyprian, the Royal Occultist, is featured in a series of novels and short stories by Reynolds. Harley Warren is from H. P. Lovecraft's Dream Cycle stories. "That fellow in Kansas" is Superman. Anthony must have met him shortly before he moved from Smallville, Kansas to Metropolis in this year. The rest of the novel's events take place in 1995.*

August–October
JAZZY

Ravenwood helps Countess Marya Dracula and her daughter Jazemara ("Jazzy") fend off the Imperial Vampire Court, which wishes to make Jazzy the ruler of their race, like her grandfather, the Count, before her. Marya was cured of her vampirism due to her deep love for Jazzy's father, Baron Manfred von Richthofen, the Red Baron. To protect both mother and daughter, Ravenwood takes them to the Hidden City, also known as Shangri-La.

Novella by Ron Fortier in Occult Detectives, *Ron Fortier, ed., Airship 27 Productions, 2014. Occult detective Ravenwood, "the stepson of mystery," was an occult detective who appeared in five stories by Frederick C. Davis* in the pulp magazine Secret Agent X *in 1936. Marya Dracula and her relationship with von Richthofen appear in Fortier and Rob Davis' graphic novel* Daughter of Dracula. *Marya appears to be the daughter of Dracula-Prime, rather than one of his many "soul-clones," and is not to be confused with Princess Marya Zaleska, the daughter of one of those clones, who was seen in the movie* Dracula's Daughter. *Presumably, Marya Zaleska was named after the true Dracula's daughter, who was turned into a vampire by her father shortly after his own undeath. Shangri-La is from James Hilton's novel* Lost Horizon.

Mid August
THE AFFAIR OF THE 39 CUFFLINKS

Inspector Wilkins once more investigates a murder at the home of the Earl of Burford. The Earl's daughter Gerry tells the family butler, Merryweather, he is a natural detective, and she will obviously need his help to unravel the mystery, just as Bunter, Lord Peter Wimsey's man, often assists him in investigations. Merryweather replies he is slightly acquainted with Bunter, whom he describes as an admirable man. However, he feels he does not share Bunter's ability at or enthusiasm for ratiocination and criminology.

The third and final Inspector Wilkins novel by James Anderson.

September 8–16
DEAD MAN'S VENGEANCE

William Stoker has an article clipped from the *New York Classic* on the wall of his hotel room.

Short story by Eric Fein in The Avenger: The Justice, Inc. Files, *Joe Gentile and Howard Hopkins, eds., Moonstone Books, 2011. The* New York Classic *is the newspaper that employs one of the agents of the pulp hero who operated in the shadows.*

Late September
DEMON SLAVES OF THE RED CLAW

The Spider and Operator #5 battle the Red Claw, who has mutated gangsters and animals into monsters. Boxer Achilles "Decimator" Smith briefly appears.

Story by Gary Phillips in *The Spider: Extreme Prejudice,* Joe Gentile and Tommy Hancock, eds., Moonstone Books, 2013. *The Spider and Operator #5 first encountered each other during the June 1935 events of the Spider novel* Master of the Death Madness, *although Phillips writes this story as if it were the heroic duo's first encounter. Achilles "Decimator" Smith also appears in Phillips' story "Decimator Smith and the Fangs of the Fire Serpent." The date of this story is based on references to the beginning of autumn and the official search for Amelia Earhart and Fred Noonan having been over for months.*

October 29–November 1
THE DEADLY PUPPETS

A doorman from the Cobalt Club is killed by what appears to be living puppets, who are having a gun battle with the vigilante known as the Skullmask. The doorman received a tip from Reid, the publisher of the *Daily Sentinel*, who was in town for a publishers' convention. Reporter Moxie Donovan's coworker Fran Striker tells him their paper, *The Daily Star*, will ignore the puppet aspect of the story because that is what Commissioner Weston wants. Donovan remembers covering "that gun fight on the pier that bronze guy had with those silver-suited guys," and taking lead in the shoulder "when the hunchback in the fright-wig stopped the take-over at Grand Central." Donovan also refers to a shootout at Chinatown in June which that Shadows guy was at.

Short story by Teel James Glenn in Weird Tales of the Skullmask, Books-ForABuck.com, 2009; *reprinted in* Deadline Zombies: The Adventures of Maxi and Moxie, BooksForABuck.com, 2010. *The Cobalt Club and Weston are from the novels of the man Farmer identified as Allard Kent Rassendyll. Britt Reid, the publisher of* The Daily Sentinel, *is also known as the Green Hornet. Moxie's reference to the* Sentinel *as a Chicago newspaper is mistaken, as Britt lived and operated in Detroit. Moxie Donovan appears in his own series of stories by Glenn, which are collected in* Deadline Zombies *and its sequel,* Headline Ghouls. *Fran Striker is named after the real radio and comic writer who worked on* The Lone Ranger *and* The Green Hornet, *among others. "That bronze guy" who battled a group of silver-suited villains in the pulp novel* Death in Silver *likely needs no further introduction here.* "The hunchback in the fright-wig" *is the Spider. A few Spider novels have action scenes set at Grand Central Station; Moxie could have received a bullet wound in the shoulder during any one of them.* "That Shadows guy" *is Glenn's hero Anton "Dr. Shadows" Chadeaux, who appears in the books* Shadows of New York: The Mysterious Adventures of Dr. Shadows *and* Manchurian Shadows. *The incident in Chinatown in June is an allusion to* Manchurian Shadows, *although Donovan does not make a physical appearance in that story.*

Autumn
THE EYE OF DARKNESS
Aboard a ship bound from Hong Kong to San Francisco, Dr. Shadows hunts a killer who is trying to get his hands on precious medallions found on an archaeological expedition led by Dr. Henry Gordon. The other surviving members of the expedition, including Gordon's daughter Nyoka, are also on the ship.

A Single Shot Signature *story by Teel James Glenn, Pro Se Press, 2015. Dr. Henry Gordon and his daughter Nyoka are from the 1942 serial* Perils of Nyoka.

1938

Winter
DRAGON'S TONGUE
A private detective employed by the Continental agency in San Francisco seeks to settle an old score with a Chinese villain called the Lord of Strange Deaths. For a time, the detective believed a shady Asian in New York named Shiwan Khan was the Lord, but Khan "ran up against some kook in a cape and a slouch hat and hadn't come out so well." The detective visits Police Detective Brad Brannigan, who was given a car by a grateful man whose daughter he helped to save. Back at the Continental office, the detective says hello to Effie as she steps out of the Spade & Archer office

down the hall, but she ignores him. The detective is lured into a trap by Fah Lo Suee, the Lord of Strange Deaths' daughter, who tells him her father is a member of a group called the Si-Fan. The Lord lists the many aliases his daughter has used, including Madame Ingomar, Queen Mamaloi, Ling Moy, and Lin Tang.

Story by F. Paul Wilson in the e-book Sex Slaves of the Dragon Tong. *The Continental detective is Dashiell Hammett's Continental Op. The Lord of Strange Deaths is Sax Rohmer's master villain Dr. Fu Manchu. Fah Lo Suee and the Si-Fan are also from the Fu Manchu novels. Fah used the name Madame Ingomar in* The Daughter of Fu Manchu *and* The Trail of Fu Manchu, *and the alias Queen Mamaloi in* The Island of Fu Manchu. *Ling Moy is the name of Fu Manchu's daughter in the 1931 film* Daughter of the Dragon, *while Lin Tang is Fu's daughter in the Fu Manchu films produced by Harry Alan Towers in the 1960s. Shiwan Khan is a recurring foe of the shadowy "kook in a cape and a slouch hat." The man who gave Brannigan the car is Oliver "Daddy" Warbucks from the classic comic strip* Little Orphan Annie; *Brannigan helped Oliver rescue the latter's adopted daughter Annie from Fu Manchu's clutches in Wilson's "Sex Slaves of the Dragon Tong," which takes place a week before this story. The Spade & Archer agency is from Dashiell Hammett's* The Maltese Falcon; *apparently Sam Spade did not bother to change the name of the agency after his partner Miles Archer's death during the 1928 events of Hammett's novel. Effie Perrine is Spade's secretary. The Op, who narrates this story, claims at the age of two he was found wandering the waterfront after the San Francisco earthquake and fire of 1906, unable to remember his family or name, and was placed in a series of foster homes, where he was regularly abused. He also claims to have revealed some of these details to Fu Manchu after being injected with a truth serum. This conflicts with Win Scott Eckert's speculations about the Op's background in his essay "Who's Going to Take Over the World When I'm Gone?: A Look at the Genealogies of Wold Newton Family Super-Villains and Their Nemeses" (*Myths for the Modern Age: Philip José Farmer's Wold Newton Universe, *Win Scott Eckert, ed., MonkeyBrain Books, 2005). Eckert argued the Op was in fact the brother of Fu Manchu's archenemy Sir Denis Nayland Smith, and he was born in 1884 or 1885, which fits much better with references to the Op being a military intelligence Captain during the Great War in Hammett's "This King Business" than a 1904 birthdate. Perhaps the Op lied to his readers about his background in order to protect himself and his brother from some of his other enemies, and actually told Fu a more accurate version of his life story. Alternatively, Wilson himself could have made the changes for reasons of his own while editing the story.*

GATEWAY MACHINE

Secret Agent X battles Dr. Miles David Alhazred, a descendant of the Mad Arab who wrote the *Necronomicon*, who is trying to bring the Old Ones into our world. A coin with the name Yog-Sothoth on it is seen, and Alhazred employs fish-eyed men from Innsmouth as henchmen.

Short story by B. C. Bell *in* Secret Agent X, Volume 2, *second edition*, Ron Fortier, ed., Airship 27 Productions, 2008, connecting Secret Agent X to the Cthulhu Mythos.

HORROR IN CLAY

The Green Lama battles a murderous golem created by a Rabbi who initially unleashed the creature on the German consulate in New York. The Rabbi has learned of the Holocaust the Nazis will soon enact against his people from hieroglyphics in an ancient temple in Jerusalem. The temple had images on the walls of the Ark of the Covenant, the Staff of Ra, and crystal skulls. Also in the temple was a statue of a horrible ancient god named Cthulhu.

Novella by Adam Lance Garcia *in* The Green Lama Volume One, Ron Fortier, ed., Cornerstone Book Publishers, 2009; revised and expanded as a standalone volume published by Moonstone Books, 2014. The Green Lama appeared in stories by "Richard Foster" (Kendell Foster Crossen) in the pulp magazine Double Detective. The Ark of the Covenant, Staff of Ra, and crystal skull references are meant to evoke the Indiana Jones films; indeed, the original version of the novella contains a reference to "Professor Jones, Jr. at Marshall College." Cthulhu needs no explanation at this point.

February
CAVEMEN OF NEW YORK

Captain Hazzard battles mad scientists Professor Marko Steil and Doctor Henry Moreau. Moreau's grandfather was the subject of a factual book by H. G. Wells that was published under the guise of fiction. FBI agent Ernest Grogan works with Hazzard to end the threat. Pulp writer Lester Dent arranges for Annie Brennan to transport one of Hazzard's vehicles aboard her tugboat, the *Narcissus*.

Novel by Ron Fortier, Cornerstone Book Publishers, 2008. Henry Moreau's grandfather was the subject of H. G. Wells' novel The Island of Doctor Moreau. *Fortier gives Wells' Moreau the same first name, Alphonse, given to him by Alan Moore and Kevin O'Neill in* The League of Extraordinary Gentlemen, Volume II. *Ernest Grogan is based on Eric Gordon from Donald E. Keyhoe's Dr. Yen Sin pulp novels. Gordon was a reporter in the original stories, but he and Michael Traile were often aided by the FBI, so it is possible he joined the Bureau after his and Traile's last recorded encounter with Yen Sin. "Grogan" first worked with Hazzard in Fortier's* The Citadel of Fear. *Annie Brennan is better known as Tugboat Annie from a series of stories by Norman Reilly Raine, and also appeared in three films and a television series, each of which had her being portrayed by a different actress. Fortier's reason for falsely claiming Dent's encounter with Hazzard inspired him to come up with the character of a bronze-skinned pulp hero is unknown. Doc's cousin eventually married Hazzard, and at any rate his pulp magazine (primarily penned by Dent) began publication in March 1933, five years before the events of this story.*

April
HOME AGAIN

Cliff Secord, aka the Rocketeer, alights outside the Bulldog Café, where he is reunited with his mechanic Peevy and his girlfriend Betty. He reveals Mr. Jonas confronted him on his way out of New York and offered Cliff a proposition, which involved Jonas replicating the rocket prototype for his own use. Jonas provides Cliff with the first replica, which is tested and works perfectly; in exchange for this backup pack, Cliff must perform certain unspecified duties for Jonas regarding "dark forces that are lining up."

Story written and illustrated by Mike Allred in Rocketeer Adventures #1, *IDW Publishing, May 2011. This story immediately follows the ending of Dave Stevens' comic* The Rocketeer: Death Stalks the Midway. *Jonas is actually the pulp hero who stays in the shadows.*

THE FOOTPRINTS ON THE CEILING

New York magician and amateur sleuth Merlini is told by Inspector Gavigan, ". . . All the amateur dicks in town are gunning for your job. When the papers hit the streets, all hell broke loose at headquarters. Philo Vance has been crowding his friend, the D.A. He wants to kick this case around. Says it's right up his bloomin' alley, don't you know. Ellery Queen's campaigning to get his old man assigned to it so he can get a look see, and Malloy says that awhile ago he saw Archie Goodwin circling the island in a speedboat, looking the situation over. Nero Wolfe's seen that mention of the eight million bucks."

Novel by Ross Harte, edited by Clayton Rawson. Merlini is already in the CU, and the references to Vance, Queen, and Wolfe and Goodwin reinforce his inclusion.

Spring. Robot Adam Link's first adventure, "I, Robot" by "Eando Binder" (Earl and Otto Binder; *Amazing Stories*, January 1939.)

Spring
JOSHUA WILLIAMS BREAKS A DATE
Adventurer Josh Williams meets with Thierry Gerothanassi, who says he and Josh's friend Dr. James Tew accompanied Dr. Littlejohn on the Tut-Ra-Med expedition. Gerothanassi is working on a project for Dr. Foot. Josh later prepares for a date, dressing in the same suit he wore when he delivered a speech to the members of the Cobalt Club in New York last year.

Short story by John Allen Small in Something in the Air: A Collection of Stories, *Ethan Books, 2011. The references to Doc's aide Littlejohn and the Cobalt Club (from the Shadow pulp novels) bring this story into the CU. Dr. Foot is an ancestor of the mad scientist Foot from the Beatles movie* Help! *which must feature the CU version of the Fab Four.*

A STYGIAN DARKNESS
Secret Agent X battles the diabolical Fantômas. A man named Dunn, who is Operative 48 for an unnamed agency, helps X by questioning a scientist.

Short story by Kevin Noel Olson in Secret Agent X, Volume 4, *Ron Fortier, ed., Airship 27 Productions, 2012. Secret Agent X appeared in the pulp magazine of the same name from February 1934–March 1939. Fantômas is the Lord of Terror created by Marcel Allain and Pierre Souvestre. Fantômas claims he is dying of cancer in this story; however, since he is still alive and well during the 1964 events of Jean-Marc Lofficier's "The Sincerest Form of Flattery," he was either lying or his cancer eventually* went into remission. *Dunn is the title character of Norman Marsh's one-shot comic book* Detective Dan, Secret Operative No. 48, *who went on to appear in his own comic strip,* Dan Dunn, *both in 1933.*

THE DEVIL'S CRATER

Pilot Jimmy Dolan, a resident of the island of Motugra in the South Seas and frequent visitor to *The Hanging Monkey*, a bar and inn on the island, flies a group from Miskatonic University to the island of Ghora to find Professor Tyler Freeborn, who proves to be a megalomaniac. The other members of the expedition include Sonia Orne, Warren Rice, Francis Morgan, John Lapham, and Freeborn's wife Sam. Freeborn refers to Warren, Legrasse, the Sanbourne Institute, Armitage, Peaslee, Dyer, the Naacal language, and the *Ponape Scriptures*. Jimmy once visited the Waldorf-Anthony Building in New York.

Short story by Joshua Reynolds in Tales from the Hanging Monkey Volume One, *Ron Fortier, ed., Airship 27 Productions, 2012. Miskatonic University is from H. P. Lovecraft's Cthulhu Mythos. Other references from Lovecraft: Tyler Freeborn and Nathaniel Wingate Peaslee from "The Shadow Out of Time"; Sonia Orne, a descendant of necromancer Simon Orne from* The Case of Charles Dexter Ward; *Warren Rice, Francis Morgan, and Henry Armitage from "The Dunwich Horror"; Harley Warren from the Dream Cycle stories; Inspector John Raymond Legrasse from "The Call of Cthulhu"; William Dyer from* At the Mountains of Madness *(it is worth noting Philip José Farmer conflated Dyer with one of Doc Wildman's five assistants in* Doc Savage: His Apocalyptic Life*); and the Naacal language from "Out of the Aeons" and "Through the Gates of the Silver Key." John Lapham is a relative of Seneca Lapham from August Derleth's* The Lurker at the Threshold. *The Sanbourne Institute of Pacific Antiquities and the* Ponape Scriptures *are both from Cthulhu Mythos stories by Lin Carter. The Waldorf-Anthony Hotel is owned by adventurer Jim Anthony, who appeared in the pulp magazine* Super Detective. *Since the Cthulhu Mythos and Jim Anthony are already connected to the CU, so are the* Tales from the Hanging Monkey *anthologies, which pay homage to several works of adventure fiction that are set in the South Seas, particularly the television series* Tales of the Gold Monkey.

MARY NOBLE: A BACKWOODS LIFE WITH LUM AND ABNER

Actor Larry Noble is tricked into taking a role in a play in Pine Ridge, Arkansas, preventing him from auditioning for the film *Gone with the Wind*. While in Pine Ridge, Larry and his wife Mary meet store owners Lum Edwards and Abner Peabody. The Nobles see a sign saying Bug Tussle is 50 miles aways, and Pine Ridge 10 miles.

Short story by John Leasure in It's That Time Again 3: Even More New

Stories of Old-Time Radio, *Jim Harmon, ed., BearManor Media, 2006.* Lum Edwards and Abner Peabody, from the radio, film, and comic strip series Lum and Abner, are in the CU through an appearance in a 2014 Dick Tracy *storyline. The town of Bug Tussle was the original home of the Clampett family on the television series* The Beverly Hillbillies, *which is also in the CU through a reference in Erwin K. Roberts' Jim Anthony story "The League of Dead Patriots." Therefore, this story brings in Mary Noble from the radio show* Backstage Wife.

THE MYSTERY OF THE BYZANTINE MOSAIC

Harry Dickson says his friend the Sâr Dubnotal would explain an aspect of the case he has just solved better than he would.

Short story by Jean-Paul Raymond in Harry Dickson vs. The Spider, *Jean-Marc and Randy Lofficier, eds., Black Coat Press 2014. Harry Dickson appeared in German, Dutch, Belgian, and French pulp stories, the latter written by Jean Ray. The Sâr Dubnotal was an occult detective featured in a French pulp series by an anonymous author.*

THE WILL TO POWER

Atomic Robo, created by Nikola Tesla, is the head of Tesladyne, a group dedicated to combating bizarre menaces, as well as conducting scientific research. He battles Baron Heinrich von Helsingard, preventing him from having the *Vril* infused into his own body.

Atomic Robo *#1 by Brian Clevinger and Scott Wegener, Red 5 Comics, October 2007. The Vril is from Edward Bulwer-Lytton's novel* The Coming Race. *This and several later crossovers bring Atomic Robo into the CU. The comics portray Robo's existence as common knowledge, but this must be an exaggeration, as both sentient robots and the kinds of scientific menaces Robo faces on a regular basis are considered mere urban legends in the CU.*

May
THE IRON PHANTOM

The Avenger learned hobo code from a man named A-Number One. Nellie and Smitty get into a fight with two men, one of whom is short and apelike, the other well-dressed and wielding a sword cane. Benson goes to the offices of the *Classic* newspaper seeking information. The editor expresses surprise Benson came to them rather than the *Times* or the *Planet*. Benson asks a *Classic* reporter named Burke about his interview with inventor Elias Martinson. Martinson at one point was working on a mechanical man, but complications caused him to seek the aid of another inventor, Charles Link. Benson later tells Nellie and Smitty the men they fought are actually in the same line of work as they are, and their battle was the result of a misunderstanding.

Short story by Matthew Baugh in The Avenger: Roaring Heart of the Crucible, *Nancy Holder and Joe Gentile, eds., Moonstone Books, 2013. A-Number One is from the movie* Emperor of the North. *Benson's aides' opponents are two aides of a famous bronze-skinned pulp hero known as "Doc." Burke, besides being a reporter for the* New York Classic, *is an agent of a certain shadowy pulp hero. The* New York Planet *is the newspaper that employs Foster Fade, "the Crime Spectacularist," who appeared in three stories by Lester Dent in* All Detective Magazine *in 1934. Elias Martinson is meant to be the unnamed inventor from Robert E. Howard's unfinished El Borak story "The Iron Terror." Charles Link is the creator of "Eando Binder's" (Earl and Otto Binder) robot Adam Link.*

June
DAMBALLA

The vigilante Damballa, the son of an African-American missionary and a native African woman, explains his origin to boxer Jackhammer Jackson's trainer, stating, "I had read with interest about the American guardians of liberty and justice who operate beyond the strictures of the law. People like the Shadow, Doc Savage, Captain Hazzard, Jim Anthony... and I became convinced that our people needed such a defender as well."

Novel by Charles R. Saunders, *Airship 27 Productions, 2011. The pulp heroes noted are referred to as real people, bringing Damballa into the CU.*

Summer
GRIM DAYS

Lord Peter Wimsey chats with Colonel Haki while on a government assignment in Istanbul. Wimsey's hostess is Mrs. Rittenhouse, and another of her guests is Captain Geoffrey Spaulding. Lord Peter asks Captain Spaulding if he knows his friend Major Brabazon-Plank. Spaulding's valet is Emanuel Ravelli. Haki asks Wimsey if his wife is with him. Sir Henry Merrivale is involved in Wimsey's mission. Wimsey meets Haki at a café owned by a Greek named Nikko Charalambides, who has an American cousin that is a famous and wealthy detective. Wimsey's hat was made by Jno. Bodmin of Vigo Street. Wimsey has two brands of cigarettes with him: Morlands and Whifflets. He did an ad campaign for the latter years before while working for Pym's Publicity, Ltd. Wimsey also quotes his friend Lord Ickenham. Lord Peter is friends with some of the "troublesome young men" that have drawn the ire of Winston Churchill and Sir Edward Leithen. Wimsey talks about British fascists like Oswald Mosley or Roderick Spode, and remarks all their movements have black clothing, such as shorts or coats. Wimsey says he shared a night train to Munich with archaeologists Professor Horatio Smith, Dr. Henry Jones, Jr., and Professeur Aristide Clairembart. Lord Peter went to Eton and Balliol with Smith's brother Sir George. Haki says Clairembart competed with Leidner for excavation permits during World War I, and he later found out the Professor was providing intelligence to Colonel Dubois of the *Deuxième Bureau*. Wimsey mentions a recent urban legend about an English governess who disappeared from the Orient Express, and that an amateur archaeologist named Mr. Bandicott allegedly discovered the tomb of the Viking chieftain Harald Blacktooth in Scotland. Smith suggested during the train ride the current situation in Europe required a new Scarlet Pimpernel to arise. Wimsey describes Reichminister Von Graum as the Chauvelin of their time. Haki had several run-ins during the War with Major James Schuyler Grim, also known as Jimgrim.

Short story by Stuart Shiffman in Tales of the Shadowmen Volume 7: Femmes Fatales, *Jean-Marc and Randy Lofficier, eds., Black Coat Press, 2010; reprinted in French in* Les Compagnons de l'Ombre (Tome 12), *Jean-Marc and Randy Lofficier, eds., Rivière Blanche, 2013. Lord Peter Wimsey and his wife, the former Harriet Vane, are from the novels by Dorothy L. Sayers. Pym's Publicity, Ltd. and Whifflets cigarettes are from the Wimsey novel* Murder Must Advertise. *Colonel Haki is from Eric Ambler's novels* The Mask of Dimitrios *and* Journey into Fear; *he is mentioned as General Haki in Ambler's* The Light of Day, *having been promoted.* The Mask of Dimitrios *features English crime novelist Charles Latimer, who also appears in Ambler's novel* The Intercom Conspiracy. *Graham, the protagonist of* Journey into Fear, *works for the British arms company Cator and Bliss, which also appears in Ambler's novels* The Dark Frontier, Uncommon Danger, *and* Cause for

Alarm. *Thief Arthur Abdel Simpson appears in both* The Light of Day *and* Dirty Story. *The Eurasian Credit Trust bank from* The Mask of Dimitrios *also appears in* The Schirmer Inheritance. *Mrs. Rittenhouse, Captain Geoffrey Spaulding, and Emmanuel Ravelli are from the Marx Bros.' film* Animal Crackers. *References from the works of P. G. Wodehouse: Lord Ickenham is from the Uncle Fred novels; Major Brabazon-Plank is from the Uncle Fred novel* Uncle Dynamite; *Jno. Bodmin is from the story* "The Amazing Hat Mystery"; *and Roderick Spode is the leader of the Black Shorts in the Jeeves novels. Sir Henry "H. M." Merrivale is from novels written by John Dickson Carr under the pen name Carter Dickson. Charalambides' cousin is Nick Charles from Dashiell Hammett's* The Thin Man; *in the novel, it is established Nick's name was originally Charalambides. In Ian Fleming's novels, James Bond's cigarettes are handmade for him by Morland of Grosvenor Street. Sir Edward Leithen appears in several novels by John Buchan. Mr. Bandicott and Harald Blacktooth are from Buchan's novel* John Macnab. *The Black Coats are from the novels by Paul Féval, although they are a European criminal organization rather than a British fascist group. Professor Horatio Smith, his brother Sir George and Reichminister Von Graum are from the film* Pimpernel Smith. *Dr. Henry Jones, Jr. is better known as Indiana Jones. Professeur Clairembart is from Henri Vernes' Bob Morane books. Dr. Erich Leidner is from Agatha Christie's Hercule Poirot novel* Murder in Mesopotamia. *Colonel Dubois appeared in novels written by Andre Brouillard under the pen name Pierre Nord. The English governess who disappeared from the Orient Express is Miss Froy from the novel* The Wheel Spins *by Ethel Lina White, the basis for Alfred Hitchcock's film* The Lady Vanishes. *The Scarlet Pimpernel and Chauvelin are from the novels by Baroness Orczy. Jimgrim appears in several novels by Talbot Mundy.*

THE EYE OF KA

The gemstone known as the Eye of Ka was stolen from Papogo Island by an archaeologist named Burke, whose university stopped paying his salary after Jones revealed his finds to be fakes. A Chinese man named Chi Pei wishes to purchase the Eye, but Burke is murdered before any sale can take place. Chi Pei has green eyes, employs a dacoit as a henchman, and is sometimes known as "the Devil Doctor."

Short story by Bill Craig in Tales from the Hanging Monkey Volume One, *Airship 27 Productions, 2012. Jones is Dr. Henry "Indiana" Jones, Jr., providing further evidence the characters appearing in the* Tales from the Hanging Monkey *anthologies exist in the CU. Chi Pei also appears in Craig's Jack Riley novels, as well as his Hardluck Hannigan series. Chi Pei's obvious similarities to Fu Manchu suggest a close connection between the two, though descriptions of Chi Pei as pale and mustachioed preclude them being the same person. Perhaps the two are related, and Chi Pei is actually one of Fu Manchu's lieutenants within the Si-Fan.*

INTERVIEW WITH A NYCTALOPE

A reporter interviews Leo Saint-Clair, also known as the Nyctalope. Saint-Clair tells the journalist, "Sad to say, unlike your Doctor Savage, I have no Arctic Fortress of Solitude." He also refers to Lupin and "that madman who murdered all those people before the Great War"; Saint-Clair once met the latter individual's nemesis, Inspector Juve. The "reporter" returns to the car driven by his chauffeur, Alfred. After the reception at Wayne Manor, Saint-Clair's next destination is Metropolis, which is allegedly the home of a man with incredible powers. Saint-Clair hopes to speak with the woman that writes fantastic stories for the *Planet*, but she is off on a different story, and the editor gives a new member of the staff the assignment.

Short story by David L. Vineyard in Tales of the Shadowmen Volume 10: Esprit de Corps, *Jean-Marc and Randy Lofficier, eds., Black Coat Press, 2013. The Nyctalope was the hero of novels by Jean de La Hire. Doctor Savage is the man Farmer identified as Doc Wildman in* Doc Savage: His Apocalyptic Life. *Lupin is Maurice Leblanc's gentleman thief Arsène Lupin. The madman who fought Inspector Juve is Fantômas, the master criminal created by Marcel Allain and Pierre Souvestre. The alleged reporter is actually millionaire Bruce Wayne, aka the Batman. Alfred Pennyworth is Wayne's butler. The man with remarkable powers in Metropolis is Superman, aka reporter Clark Kent. Although Vineyard refers to the paper Clark works for as the* Planet, *this is incorrect; the paper was originally known as* The Daily Star, *and only changed its name to* The Daily Planet *in 1939. The paper's editor is George Taylor (later replaced by Perry White), and Clark's female coworker is Lois Lane.*

FUNNY, YOU DON'T LOOK . . .

Reporter Moxie Donovan, pretending to be homeless for a story, joins a group of urchins in listening to the Dr. Shadows radio show.

Story by Teel James Glenn in Adventures in Otherwhen: Tales of Pulp

Fantastique, BooksForABuck.com, 2012. Moxie Donovan and Dr. Shadows each appear in their own series of stories by Glenn. Although "Funny, You Don't Look..." does not explicitly refer to Dr. Shadows as a real person, other stories by Glenn establish Moxie and Dr. Shadows exist in the same universe, and the doctor has had his exploits fictionalized in film serials and other media.

PROOF OF SUPREMACY

Dan Fowler and Jim Anthony team up to investigate a series of bank robberies. Millionaire Harold Oliver Graybuck, his adopted daughter Annie Sanders, and his servants Khyber and Asper appear, as does a man named Dithers. Saint Sebastian in the Caribbean, Camp Swampy, and a friend of Anthony's in Belgium are mentioned.

Short story by Josh Reynolds in Dan Fowler: G-Man Volume Two, *Ron Fortier, ed., Airship 27 Productions, 2013. Dan Fowler is from the pulp* G-Men Detective, *while Jim Anthony appeared in the magazine* Super Detective. *Although this story allegedly depicts the first meeting between the two, they previously crossed paths in Erwin K. Roberts' story "Neighborhood in Peril." Graybuck, Annie, Khyber, and Asper strongly resemble Oliver "Daddy" Warbucks, Annie, Punjab, and the Asp from Harold Gray's comic strip* Little Orphan Annie. *Since they are portrayed as villains, the quartet cannot be conflated with Gray's characters. The similarity is unexplained, but perhaps Graybuck and Khyber are the individuals resembling Warbucks and Punjab who worked with Shiwan Khan in the storyline "The Revenge of Shiwan Khan" from the DC Comic* The Shadow Strikes! *J. C. Dithers is from Chic Young's comic strip* Blondie. *The Caribbean island of Saint Sebastian is from the 1943 film* I Walked with a Zombie; *the island appears under the variant name San Sebastian in the 1945 film* Zombies on Broadway. *Camp Swampy is from Mort Walker's comic strip* Beetle Bailey. *Beetle's sister Lois Flagston and her husband Hi spun off from* Beetle Bailey *into their own strip,* Hi and Lois, *written by Walker and illustrated by Dik Browne. Anthony's Belgian friend is Agatha Christie's detective Hercule Poirot.*

WORK SUSPENDED

It is mentioned Lady Metroland once attended a showing of John Plant's father's art. At the same party, Mrs. Algernon Stitch bought a painting for 500 guineas. Plant is friends with Basil Seal. Lord Monomark is mentioned.

Unfinished novel by Evelyn Waugh; the first two chapters, "My Father's House" and "Lucy Simmonds," appeared in the collection Work Suspended and Other Stories, *1943. Lady Metroland is a recurring character in Waugh's books and stories. Mrs. Algernon Stitch is from* Scoop. *Basil Seal is the protagonist of Waugh's novels* Black Mischief *and* Put Out More Flags. *Lord Monomark previously appeared in* Vile Bodies *and* Black Mischief, *and was mentioned in* A Handful of Dust.

THE FLASHBACK FLOOZY

Moxie Donovan, now married to his actress girlfriend Maxi and living in Hollywood, is asked by an ex-girlfriend to help her recover compromising photos from a blackmailer. Moxie asks her, "Why not go to Turner or Marlow or one of the two dozen private dicks here in Lala Land?"

Story by Teel James Glenn in Headline Ghouls: The Further Adventures of Maxi and Moxie, *BooksForABuck.com, 2012. Turner is Hollywood private eye Dan Turner, who appeared in stories by Robert Leslie Bellem in* Spicy Detective Stories *and* Hollywood Detective *from 1934–1950. "Marlow" is a reference to Raymond Chandler's P.I. Philip Marlowe.*

July
HALO OF HORROR

Secret Agent X, in his assumed identity of Elisha Pond, is called to Vicksburg, Mississippi, to receive an inheritance. There, he meets Waylon Bramble, an acquaintance of the real Pond, who disappeared at the end of World War I. Agent X tells Bramble he was stricken with amnesia, but his memory was eventually restored by a brilliant neurosurgeon in New York named Savage. An awestruck Bramble asks if this is "*the* Savage?" and X replies, "the same."

Three-part serial by "Brant House" (actually Stephen Payne) in Double Danger Tales *#21–23, Tom and Ginger Johnson, eds., Fading Shadows Publications, October–December 1998, reprinted as a novel by Altus Press in 2008. Although "Pond's" story is false, Bramble's reaction establishes the neurosurgeon is a real person, thus reinforcing Secret Agent X's place in the CU. Although the first two chapters take place on November 10–11, 1918, the remainder of the novel takes place twenty years afterwards.*

Summer
KING CRIME!
Dan Fowler cracks a case that begins in Newkirk City.
Story by D. L. Champion in G-Men Detective *Vol. 2, #3, March 1936. Newkirk City was also the setting of "Alias Mr. Death," a novel by Champion serialized in nine chapters in* Thrilling Detective *in February–October 1932. Two more Mr. Death stories by George Fielding Eliot appeared in 1939. Since Dan Fowler is in the CU, so is Mr. Death, aka James Quincy Gilmore, Jr., who took on the guise to battle the Murder Club responsible for his father's death.*

September
THE DESTINY OF FU MANCHU
Dr. Petrie remembers working alongside the great Sherlock Holmes in Wales when Sir Denis Nayland Smith was abducted by Fu Manchu.
Novel by William Patrick Maynard, Black Coat Press, 2012. Petrie and Holmes saved Nayland Smith from Fu Manchu in Cay Van Ash's novel Ten Years Beyond Baker Street.

Mid September
THE COMING STORM
Secret Service agent Rex Bennett assigns Jeff Shannon (aka the Eagle) to rescue a kidnapped scientist. Shannon has read a series of articles about German Bunds by "that Donovan guy at the *Daily Star.*" Shannon's friend Lefty Kovaks tells the disguised hero he looks like a regular man of bronze, to which Shannon responds that name is taken. Shannon consulted with an old instructor of his in New York, Andrew Mayfair, a noted biochemist, to create an antidote to any truth serums or sedatives he may face.
Short story by Teel James Glenn in The New Adventures of the Eagle, *David White, ed., Pro Se Press, 2012. The Eagle was created by Norman A. Daniels under the nom de plume "Captain Kerry McRoberts" and appeared in* Thrilling Spy Stories *and* Popular Detective. *Rex Bennett is from the film serials* G-Men vs. the Black Dragon *and* Secret Service in Darkest Africa. *Donovan is Moxie Donovan, an original character created by Glenn who appears in the collections* Deadline Zombies: The Adventures of Maxi and

Moxie *and* Headline Ghouls: The Further Adventures of Maxi and Moxie. *The man of bronze needs no further introduciton; Mayfair is one of his five assistants. This story concludes on September 21, and shows the historical "Long Island Express" hurricane which occurred during that time.*

October
THE BLOOD MOON

The Avenger and the Spider join forces to battle the vampire known as the Cold Man (also referred to as Vlad), who has stolen a gem called the Blood Moon in an attempt to control his bloodlust.

Short story by David Michelinie in The Avenger: The Justice, Inc. Files, *Joe Gentile and Howard Hopkins, eds., Moonstone Books, 2011. "The Cold Man" is meant to be Dracula. However, his description of his life before becoming a vampire conflicts with the life of the historical Vlad Dracula. Since the Cold Man says he was born in 1647 (171 years after Dracula's death and turning), it is more likely he is one of Dracula's "soul-clones."*

October 27–31
THE GREAT PRETENDER

Author Hector Lassiter suggests to a mysterious woman he has just met that they go to the Cobalt Club. The woman replies it sounds better than the Pink Rat. Lassiter and the woman, Cassie Allegre, leave the Cobalt in a cab driven by a man named Moe.

Novel by Craig McDonald, Betimes Books, 2014. The Cobalt Club, the Pink Rat, and Moe are from Walter Gibson's novels about a shadowy pulp hero, further strengthening Hector Lassiter's inclusion in the CU. Although the book's events extend into December 1948, these references are all in the first section.

Autumn
LEGENDS ARE FOREVER

Jake Cutter's fellow former Flying Tiger, Gandy Dancer, recruits him to fly medical supplies to the Watusi tribe and locate the treasure of King Solomon's Mines. Initially, Jake tells Gandy whatever he's searching for, whether it is the Shinto Emerald, the Maltese Falcon, Tut's treasure, or the Fountain of Youth, he can count him out. When Bon Chance Louie refers to his past experiences at Fort Zinderneuf, Gandy wonders if Louie may know the location of the Blue Water Sapphire. Gandy says Haggard omitted from his novel the fact that after Tremain's visit, the Watusi relocated Solomon's treasure to a Pacific island.

Episode of the television series Tales of the Gold Monkey *broadcast October 20, 1982. "Tremain" is a pseudonym for Allan Quatermain, the protagonist of* King Solomon's Mines *and several other books by H. Rider Haggard. The references to the Watusi are likely another fictionalization, as the tribe Quatermain and company encountered in Haggard's novel was called the Kukuanas. The Kukuanas were substituted with the Watusi in the 1950 film version of* King Solomon's Mine, *which probably inspired their use in this story. The Maltese Falcon needs no explanation at this point. Fort Zinderneuf and the Blue Water Sapphire are from P. C. Wren's novel* Beau Geste. *Bon Chance Louie referred to his service at Zinderneuf in the episode immediately preceding this one, "Black Pearl," though there he mistakenly gave the fort's name as "Zinderman."*

THE SULTAN OF SWAT

Jake Cutter reads the book *Murder on the Footbridge* by Isobel Sedbusk.

Episode of Tales of the Gold Monkey *broadcast January 5, 1983. Isobel Sedbusk and her book* Murder on the Footbridge *are from the 1932 book* Before the Fact *by "Francis Iles" (pseudonym for Anthony Berkeley), which was adapted by Alfred Hitchcock into the 1941 film* Suspicion.

THE CRIMSON MASK TAKES OVER

The Rue Morgue in Paris is one of the many places where Robert "Doc" Clarke (aka the Crimson Mask) trained to become a crime fighter.

Short story by Terrence P. McCauley in The Crimson Mask Volume One, *Ron Fortier, ed., Airship 27 Productions, 2013. The Crimson Mask appeared in stories by "Frank Johnson" (pseudonym for Norman A. Daniels) in the pulp* Detective Novels Magazine. *Robert Clarke may be a descendant of Micah Clarke, and therefore a member of the extended Wold Newton Family. The Rue Morgue in Paris is from Edgar Allan Poe's "The Murders in the Rue Morgue."*

THE GREEN LAMA: SCIONS

The Green Lama investigates a cruise ship that has crashed on Liberty Island, all but one of those aboard having killed themselves. The Lama's ally Police Lieutenant John Caraway captures crime lord Tzu-hao Ming-yu, who claims to be "the son of Doctor Fu—" The Lama, in his civilian identity of millionaire Jethro Dumont, is interviewed by Betty Dale of the *Herald-Tribune*. One of Betty's coworkers is crime reporter Luke Jaconetti. The Lama's agents Gary Brown and Evangl Stewart-Brown have a small farm outside Black Rock. Commissioner Woods refers to the Tipton Murders. The crew and passengers of the ship were possessed by the Old Ones. Betty remarks now she knows how Din feels over at the *Planet*. Falsely suspecting Frankie Annor, Jr. of being a disguised vigilante, Betty remarks, "Next thing you're going to tell me is you prefer to be called a letter or some kind of arachnid."

Novel by Adam Lance Garcia, Moonstone Books, 2014. The Green Lama appeared in stories by "Richard Foster" (Kendell Foster Crossen) in the pulp Double Detective. *"Doctor Fu—" is Sax Rohmer's criminal mastermind Doctor Fu Manchu. Reporter Betty Dale is the girlfriend of Paul Chadwick's pulp hero* Secret Agent X. *The Tipton Murders occurred in Garcia's story "Dead Men's Guns." Luke Jaconetti and the town of Black Rock are from another story by Garcia, "The Black Rock Conspiracy." Both of the aforementioned stories appeared in the anthology* The New Adventures of Foster Fade, the Crime Spectacularist, *featuring new stories of Lester Dent's pulp hero, and both had cameos by an unnamed Caraway. Dinamenta "Din" Stevens is Fade's ghostwriter for* The New York Planet *newspaper. The Old Ones (also known as the Great Old Ones) are the malevolent alien beings worshipped as gods in H. P. Lovecraft's Cthulhu Mythos. Betty is suggesting Frankie could be either Secret Agent X or the Spider.*

MEET MISTER ALCHEMY

Moxie Donovan encounters the bizarre Nazi menace known as Mister Alchemy, who says the American Doctor Shadows serials are too fantastic. Moxie replies the actor who played him wasn't nearly as tall as the real man. Alchemy tries to sacrifice Donovan, hoping to acquire his *Vril* energy.

Story by Teel James Glenn in Headline Ghouls: The Further Adventures of Maxi and Moxie, *BooksForABuck.com, 2012. Dr. Shadows is another of Glenn's heroes, who has been featured in two books to date. The* Vril *energy is from Edward Bulwer-Lytton's* The Coming Race.

December
DEVIL'S DARK HARVEST

The Avenger and his aides battle a man named Vannicks, whose henchmen include an individual known as Rode Boeman. Boeman says he doesn't care if Vannicks is richer than a Rockefeller or a Stonecraft. Another of Boeman's henchmen is named Audson.

Short story by Christopher Paul Carey in The Avenger: The Justice, Inc. Files, *Joe Gentile and Howard Hopkins, eds., Moonstone Books, 2011. Vannicks and Rode Boeman are meant to be Vannax and Red Orc from Philip José Farmer's* The World of Tiers *series. "Rode Boeman" is Dutch for "Red Bogeyman." Millionaire James D. Stonecraft is from Farmer's* The Dark Heart of Time: A Tarzan Novel. *The name Audson is based on a seemingly mistaken reference to Jim Grimson, the protagonist of Farmer's novel* Red Orc's Rage *(which is connected to* The World of Tiers*), as Jim Audson on the dust jacket flap of the hardcover edition of that novel. The "Audson" working for Vannicks/Vannax may be Jim's grandfather, Ragnar Grimson.*

1939

Winter
MOTUGRA'S REVENGE

Miko, barmaid at *The Hanging Monkey*, says to Captain Nick Fortune they cannot go to the local gendarme on their home, the island of Motugra, seeking help in finding their missing friends. Fortune replies he heard the policeman, Gilhooley, ranting about joining the army, and he has probably already left the island.

Short story by Tommy Hancock in Tales from the Hanging Monkey Volume One, *Ron Fortier, ed., Airship 27 Productions, 2012. Thomas Aloysius "Boats" Gilhooley's later life is shown in the movie* Donovan's Reef.

THE WOMAN IN BLACK

Michael Shaw (aka the Nightmare) attends a dinner party hosted by Mrs. Rittenhouse. The Nightmare attends a meeting at the bar Moran's, where a mysterious voice tells him the Whispering Monk has been murdered. He encounters Nemesis, daughter of the night goddess Nyx, who has killed the gangster who orchestrated the Monk's death. The Nightmare was told about the man by a gunman named Cliff. Lieutenant Jerome Easton tells Shaw the murderers of his cousin Kaye Chandler's uncle were brought to justice by a woman called "The Pink Avenger or Pink Reaper or something like that."

Story by Patrick Thomas and John L. French in From the Shadows, Dark Quest, 2012. *The Nightmare is French's own creation. Mrs. Rittenhouse is from the Marx Brothers' film* Animal Crackers. *Moran's is owned by a cousin of leprechaun Paddy Moran, owner of the Bar Bulfinche's, from Thomas' Murphy's Lore books. The Whispering Monk was the title character of a story by Gordon E. Warnke in the June 1934 issue of the pulp* All Detective Magazine. *Nemesis is from Thomas' Murphy's Lore and Terrorbelle books. Cliff is an agent of the shadowy vigilante, as well as his inside man in the criminal underworld. The Pink Reaper (who is in fact Kaye Chandler) first appeared in Thomas' book* Lore and Dysorder: The Hell's Detective Mysteries. *The year is conjecture.*

THE CASE OF THE FINAL COLUMN
Jean Farrell, one of the Green Lama's aides, dreams of tentacles and wings and a man glowing in jade.

Novella by Adam Lance Garcia in *The Green Lama: The Complete Pulp Adventures Volume 3*, Altus Press, 2012. *Jean's dream is of the events of Garcia's novel* The Green Lama: Unbound, *which takes place not long after this tale. The tentacles and wings are those of H. P. Lovecraft's Great Old One Cthulhu.*

February
SNOW BLIND
The Avenger pursues two criminal brothers through a snowstorm in the mining town of Personville, Montana.

Short story by Mark Ellis in *The Avenger: The Justice, Inc. Files*, Joe Gentile and Howard Hopkins, eds., Moonstone Books, 2011. *Personville is from Dashiell Hammett's Continental Op novel* Red Harvest, *further reinforcing the Op's place in the CU.*

Spring. Bart Hill begins challenging the forces of evil as Daredevil. (*Silver Streak Comics* #6, September 1940.) Perhaps Matt Murdock adopted the costumed alias of Daredevil in 1963 as a nod to the earlier masked hero who went by that name.

Spring
THE PHANTOM DETECTIVE VS. FRANKENSTEIN

The Phantom Detective battles the Black Sun, an apocalyptic Nazi cult that has abducted Dr. Henry Cushing, a descendant of Victor Frankenstein. The Frankenstein Monster appears, also seeking Cushing. The Detective, in his secret identity of playboy Richard Curtis Van Loan, tells his confidante Frank Havens, publisher of the *Clarion*, villains have been demanding his attention, "not I. V. Frost's, or the Domino Lady's." Inspector Denham tells the Detective he never thought he'd have to deal with the threats the Detective combats, "not to mention characters like the Spider and the Black Bat."

A Return of the Monsters one-shot by Aaron Shaps and Jay Piscopo, Moonstone Comics, 2012. The Phantom Detective, Victor Frankenstein and his Monster, the Domino Lady, the Spider, and the Black Bat are already in the CU. Frost, a scientific detective, was created by Donald Wandrei and appeared in Clues Detective Stories, among other magazines; this crossover brings him into the CU. The Black Sun's leader claims Robert Walton falsified Victor Frankenstein's death, and Frankenstein had offspring later on, with that lineage eventually leading to Cushing. However, many other sources verify Victor's death. Furthermore, Robert Myers' novels The Cross of Frankenstein *and* The Slave of Frankenstein *establish Victor fathered a son, Victor Saville, prior to his death, and Mark Brown's creative mythographic essay "The House of Frankenstein" (found at the* An Expansion of Philip José Farmer's Wold Newton Universe *website) examines the younger Victor's descendants. It is more likely Cushing is descended from Victor Saville, and the Black Sun's informant only told them half-truths. This story takes place before the United States has entered World War II.*

JAZZ

Occult detective Ravenwood opens a jazz club. Guests at the grand opening party include a famed industrialist named Stark and his much younger fiancée, A. J. Martin from the Associated Press, a scientist named Dr. Erskine and his wife, and former actress Margaret Grace, who was flown to New York by ace pilot Lance Star. Ravenwood remembers a recent visit to Los Angeles where a thrilling golden-haired woman came to his aid against some shady characters.

Short story by Bobby Nash in Ravenwood: Stepson of Mystery Volume One, *Ron Fortier, ed., Cornerstone Book Publishers, 2010. Ravenwood was the subject of a series of stories by Frederick C. Davis in the pulp magazine* Secret Agent X. *Journalist A. J. Martin is one of Secret Agent X's many aliases. The industrialist named Stark and his fiancée are the future parents of Tony Stark, aka the Marvel Comics superhero Iron Man. Dr. Erskine is meant to be the same scientist who created the super-soldier serum that empowered another Marvel hero, Captain America. In the original account of Cap's origins, "Meet Captain America," the scientist's name was given as Dr. Reinstein. Later writers revealed "Reinstein" was an alias given to him by the United States government, and his true name was Dr. Abraham Erskine. However, the Dark Horse Comics miniseries* The Shadow and Doc Savage: The Case of the Shrieking Skeletons, *set in 1937, has him answering to the name Reinstein (along with his daughter Bernie) well before Doc tells him about the Super-Soldier Project at the conclusion of the adventure. In the CU, Reinstein was likely his true name and Erskine the alias, rather than vice versa as in the Marvel Universe. Also, Bernie Reinstein stated in* The Case of the Shrieking Skeletons *that her mother was long dead. Reinstein must have remarried in the two years between his encounter with the Shadow and Doc and his attendance of Ravenwood's gala opening. The year of this story is conjecture, but it must take place before Steve Rogers was injected with the serum in 1940, after which Reinstein was fatally shot by a Nazi agent. The golden-haired woman is the pulp adventuress the Domino Lady, whose stories in the "spicy" pulps were chronicled by an author using the nom de plume "Lars Anderson." Margaret Grace is mentioned in Nash's story "Target: Domino Lady," and also appears in his Box 13 story "The Mystery of the Menacing Manuscript." Ostensibly a character from the Canadian pulps, Lance Star is actually an original character created by Nash.*

ENTER: CAPTAIN NEMO

Navy Jones and Princess Coral join Captain Nemo on a quest to find a sunken Roman galley that contains a map of Atlantis.

Story written and illustrated by "Frank Pensley" (pseudonym for Bert Whitman) in Science Comics #5, Fox, 1940. *This crossover brings Navy Jones, the adventurous great-great-grandson of the legendary Davy Jones, into the CU. Nemo's 1909 death (as referred to in* The New Traveler's Almanac) *must have been staged. Nemo would be 131-years-old at the time of this story, but appears much younger due to the Capellean blood-sharing ceremony he underwent when he was young. The Captain teamed up with Jones and Coral again in* Science Comics #7 and 8. *This story ran untitled; I have used the title given on the* Grand Comics Database *website.*

A NASTY BUSINESS

Three criminals in hiding discuss the possibility of being captured by "that Doc fellow and those Justice guys." The three are gunned down by the Nightmare (Michael Shaw) and his cousin, the Pink Reaper (Kaye Chandler). The Reaper tells the Nightmare Benson objected to her calling herself the Pink Avenger. The Nightmare asks her if Clark knows she's using his mercy bullets. Later, in their civilian identities, Michael and Kaye discover the owners of a restaurant Kaye frequents have been brutalized by protection racketeers. Michael thinks of how he and a woman named Leda shut down a den of depravity not too long ago. Michael and Kaye have lunch at Moran's, where they have a discussion with the owner, who mentions his cousin Paddy. Michael goes undercover seeking information at a number of underworld dives, including the Black Ship, while Kaye does the same, albeit in costume, at others, such as the Pink Rat. Kaye visits the sister of one of the racketeers, saying they met at Mrs. Rittenhouse's last gala. Michael tells Kaye he was helping Jethro handle "that Yeti problem" at the time of the sister's wedding. Planning to break into gangster Wolf Hopkins' brownstone headquarters, the Nightmare says to himself, "I could try the bold approach . . . kick open the door, guns in hand, demanding to see Hopkins, and ready to shoot down any who oppose me. Richard would do that, he actually likes getting shot at. Kent would find a way to sneak in and surprise the Wolf at his desk." Spying on a "young man" who turns out to be the sister in disguise, Kaye thinks "Well, why not . . . it worked for Irene Adler."

Story by Patrick Thomas and John L. French in From the Shadows, Dark Quest, 2012. *"That Doc fellow" shold be well known in these pages by now; likewise, "Those Justice guys." The Nightmare and the Pink Reaper were created by French and Thomas, respectively. Leda Troy is Thomas' heroine Nemesis, who also appears in his Murphy's Lore and Terrorbelle books. The owner of Moran's is Seamus Moran. His cousin Paddy Moran is also from the Murphy's Lore series. Kent is the pulp hero whose stories were told in novels by Walter Gibson and others; the Black Ship and the Pink Rat also appear in those novels. Mrs. Rittenhouse is from the Marx Brothers movie* Animal Crackers. *Jethro is Jethro Dumont, aka the Green Lama, who appeared in stories by "Richard Foster" (a pseudonym for Kendell Crossen) in the pulp* Double Detective. *Richard is Richard Wentworth, aka the Spider. Given the other references, it is reasonable to suppose Kaye was thinking of Irene Adler as a real person.*

AGENTS OF THE NIGHT

Ravenwood and the Black Bat join forces to prevent an Outer God from being summoned into our world.

Short story by Aaron Smith in Ravenwood: Stepson of Mystery Volume Two, *Ron Fortier, ed., Airship 27 Productions, 2013. Ravenwood, an occult* detective created by Frederick C. Davis, appeared in stories in the pulp magazine Secret Agent X. *The Black Bat*, created by Norman A. Daniels, appeared in Black Book Detective. The Outer Gods are from Lovecraft's Cthulhu Mythos fiction.

THE MASK OF ANUBIS

The Crimson Mask's aide Sandra "Sandy" Gray, impersonating a reporter, interviews the curator of a museum where a murder occurred. The curator says a redheaded reporter named Steve Huston has been pestering him. Sandy says she knows Steve, the crime reporter for Mr. Havens' newspaper.

Story by Tom Johnson in *Exciting Pulp Tales*, Altus Press, 2011. The Crimson Mask appeared in stories by "Frank Johnson" (Norman A. Daniels) in Detective Novels Magazine. Steve Huston, Frank Havens, and the Clarion newspaper are from the Phantom Detective pulp stories.

THE GREEN LAMA: UNBOUND

The Green Lama battles Cthulhu. Appearing or mentioned are: Nyarlathotep; R'lyeh; Rick Masters; Twin Eagle; "that guy who lives in the Empire State Building"; Toht; Vogel; Neville Sinclair; the Great Old Ones; the Elder Gods; the Outer Gods; the *Necronomicon*; "*Nyarlathotep klaatu barada nikto*"; Foster Fade; Richard Knight; the Black Bat; the Deep Ones; Chthonians; Shudde M'ell; Abdul Alhazred; Glyyu-Uho; Baalbo; Ogntlach; Yifne; Xoth; Vhoorl; "my old detective friend in London"; flying polyps; Yaksh; Tond; the Great Race of Yith; shoggoths; Arkham, Massachusetts; Innsmouth; the Miskatonic River; Miskatonic University; Professor Randolph Carter; Zkauba; and Elisha Pond.

Novel by Adam Lance Garcia, Cornerstone Book Publishers, 2010; re-released in an expanded and revised edition published by Moonstone Books, 2015. The Green Lama was created by "Richard Foster" (Kendell Foster Crossen), and appeared in the pulp magazine Double Detective. Cthulhu; Nyarlathotep; R'lyeh; the Great Old Ones; the Outer Gods; the Necronomicon; the Deep Ones; Abdul Alhazred; Glyyu-Uho; Vhoorl; flying polyps; the Great Race of Yith; shoggoths; Arkham, Massachusetts;

Innsmouth; the *Miskatonic River;* Miskatonic University; Professor Randolph Carter; and Zkauba are from the works of H. P. Lovecraft. This novel also makes use of characters and places from Cthulhu Mythos tales by August Derleth (the Elder Gods); Brian Lumley (Chthonians and Shudde M'ell); Ramsey Campbell (Baalbo, Yifne, and Tond); Walter C. DeBill, Jr. (Ogntlach); Lin Carter (Xoth); and A. A. Attanasio (Yaksh). Rick Masters and Twin Eagle had their own feature in Spark Publications' Green Lama comic book series. "That guy who lives in the Empire State Building" is a well-known bronze-skinned pulp hero. Arnold Toht is from the first Indiana Jones film, Raiders of the Lost Ark, while Colonel Ernst Vogel is from the third film in the series, Indiana Jones and the Last Crusade. Neville Sinclair is from the film version of Dave Stevens' comic The Rocketeer. Since the comic book has already been incorporated into the Crossover Universe, the Sinclair mentioned here must be the CU counterpart of the Sinclair from the film, which follows a different continuity than the comic. The phrase "klaatu barada nikto" appears in both the science fiction film The Day the Earth Stood Still and Sam Raimi's Evil Dead films. Foster Fade, "the crime spectacularist," appeared in three stories by Lester Dent in All Detective Magazine in 1934. Richard Knight appeared in the pulp magazine Flying Aces in stories by Donald E. Keyhoe. The Black Bat was created by Norman Daniels and appeared in Black Book Detective. The Lama's old detective friend in London is Sherlock Holmes. Elisha Pond is a false identity used by Secret Agent X, who appeared in a titular magazine. The original version of the novel has a few references that were deleted from the revised version, such as a rampaging ape (King Kong), Captain Hazzard (a one-shot pulp hero created by Paul Chadwick), Dan Fowler (an FBI agent appearing in the pulp G-Men Detective), Lance Star (a Canadian pulp hero recently revived by Bobby Nash and other writers), and Jim Anthony (who appeared in the magazine Super Detective).

April
GHOST OF THUNDER ISLE

Angelica Tremaine reflects on recent events and their outcome for her older brother Winston and her ex-fiancé Tommy Bolt. When Angelica is murdered, her old friend Nellie Gray speaks to Officer Reagan and Detective Cardona about the crime. Angelica's second fiancé, Peter Russell, is the grandson of a man who saved a Mexican girl from a band of murderers who were on the run from the law when he was 18 or 19. The elder Russell married the girl and used the reward money to start his own ranch; Peter was named after him. Angelica's murder is part of a string of deaths of people connected to Winston Tremaine; another of the victims is James

Tripp, whose brother Wiggens Winston knew. The mad Tommy Bolt targeted the Tremaine siblings from a base on Thunder Island, but Winston's friend Clark came to their rescue. Mac remembers a physiobiologist from Harvard named Geresten who experimented on lab animals by introducing electrical stimulation to certain gland centers, altering them physically; Bolt used this same process on humans, including Wiggens Tripp, making them animal-like. It is mentioned actor Bruce Baxter got his start as an extra in films made in Chelsea.

Short story by *John Allen Small* in The Avenger: Roaring Heart of the Crucible, *Nancy Holder and Joe Gentile, eds., Moonstone Books, 2013.* This story serves as a sequel to the comic story "The Doom on Thunder Isle" *(*Doc Savage Magazine *#1,* Marvel Comics, August 1975; *reprinted in* DC Showcase Presents Doc Savage, DC Comics, 2011*), which is the source of Angelica Tremaine, her brother Winston, Tommy Bolt, Wiggens Tripp, Thunder Island, and Dr. Geresten. Officer Reagan is a member of the family of New York police officers named Reagan featured in the television series* Blue Bloods*; his nephew is Henry Reagan, a retired police commissioner in the 21st century. Detective Cardona is a supporting character in the tales of a slouch-hatted, twin .45-wielding pulp vigilante. Peter Russell is the grandson of Peter Russell and Monja from Small's story "Rite of Passage" (*Days Gone By: Legends and Tales of Sipokni West, Ethan Books, 2007*). Bruce Baxter is from Peter Jackson's 2005 remake of* King Kong; *Small reconciled several different Kong stories in his tour-de-force essay "The Beast" (*Glimmerglass: The Creative Writer's Annual, Volume 1, *John Allen Small, ed., 2009).*

INVISIBLE EMPIRE

The Avenger and Justice, Inc. travel to Atlanta to battle a group of Klansmen who have stolen Frank Griffin's invisibility formula, duocaine, in order to attack local African-Americans. Griffin's formula was based on his grandfather's, which was called monocaine.

Short story by Matthew Baugh in The Avenger: The Justice, Inc. Files, *Joe Gentile and Howard Hopkins, eds., Moonstone Books, 2011. The experiments of Frank Griffin's grandfather John Hawley Griffin were chronicled by H. G. Wells in* The Invisible Man. *Frank himself (aka Frank Raymond) appears in the movie* Invisible Agent; *Dennis E. Power has established his father is Jack Griffin, whose own use of the Griffin formula was told in the Universal film* The Invisible Man.

May
WHITEOUT

The Avenger and Justice, Inc. investigate the murders of several scientists, all of whom were members of the Atomic Club. The murderer, who calls himself "the Black Atom," turns out to be Billy Batson, the young, abnormally brilliant son of club member Dr. Jefferson Batson, who was murdered by the other members.

Short story by Robin Wayne Bailey in The Avenger: The Justice, Inc. Files, *Joe Gentile and Howard Hopkins, eds., Moonstone Books, 2011. This story confirms, once and for all, Billy Batson was never granted powers by the wizard Shazam in the CU. The name "Black Atom" is meant to evoke Captain Marvel's foe Black Adam.*

Summer. Fantomah begins patrolling the jungle, meting out harsh and bizarre punishments to those who would threaten it (*Jungle Comics* #2, February 1940).

Summer. The mad scientist known as Dr. Mortal begins menacing the world. (*Weird Comics* #1, April 1940.)

Summer
BUTCHY SAVES BETTY

Cliff Secord and Betty attempt to rescue Butch the dog, who has become entangled in Cliff's rocket pack and airborne thanks to the new auto-ignition feature Peevy has installed. Meanwhile, Peevy meets with Jonas, who is using Cliff and him to investigate espionage.

Story written and illustrated by Kyle Baker in Rocketeer Adventures Vol. 2 #3, *IDW Publishing, May 2012. Jonas is actually the pulp hero of the shadows. He and Cliff first met in Dave Stevens'* The Rocketeer: Death Stalks the Midway.

DEATH MASTER OF THE SECRET ISLAND

Captain Midnight and Chuck Ramsey travel to a remote island to rescue a Swedish nuclear physicist who has been kidnapped by Midnight's archnemesis Ivan Shark and his daughter Fury. The Captain speculates the lost race that built the statues on the island may have been early representatives of the cult of Cthulhu.

Short story by Trina Robbins in *The Captain Midnight Chronicles*, Christopher Mills, ed., Moonstone Books, 2010. *The reference to Cthulhu provides further confirmation Captain Midnight and his Secret Squadron are in the CU. This story takes place during the New York World's Fair.*

THE ROCKETEER: HOLLYWOOD HORROR

Cliff Secord (aka the Rocketeer) battles the nefarious Otto Rune. The inventor of Cliff's rocket pack, the Cirrus X-3, sends two of his aides to retrieve it for some tests. A married couple that used to be detectives and own a dog named Asta help Cliff out. The inventor of the Cirrus X-3 agrees to let Cliff keep it as long as he gives him regular updates on how the pack is working. Cliff briefly comes in contact with two paperhangers, one of whom is named Jeff. A friend of Betty's who had fallen victim to Rune meets two desert hillbillies.

Four-issue miniseries by Roger Langridge and J. Bone, IDW Publishing, February–May 2013. *The inventor of the Cirrus X-3 is the famous pulp hero "Doc," as shown in Dave Stevens' original comic book* The Rocketeer. *The detective couple are Nick and Nora Charles from Dashiell Hammett's novel* The Thin Man *and the subsequent film series starring William Powell and Myrna Loy. Jeff and his colleague are the title characters of Bud Fisher's comic strip* Mutt and Jeff. *The hillbillies are Snuffy Smith and his wife Loweezy from Billy DeBeck's strip* Barney Google and Snuffy Smith. *In the comic strip, the Smiths lived in the Appalachian town of Hootin' Holler, rather than California. Perhaps they were on vacation.*

THE SONS OF THOR

Several adventurers form an alliance to stop a Nazi-affiliated group seeking world conquest. Appearing or mentioned are: the Phantom Detective; Captain Midnight; Secret Agent X; the *New York Clarion*; Frank Havens;

Inspector Gregg; the world's first consulting detective; George Chance; N. Wind Investigations; Dale Foundation; B. Jonas; the Hidalgo Trading Company; Jethro Dumont; the Crimson Mask; K-9; Dr. Skull; Jim Anthony; the Waldorf-Anthony Hotel; the *Daily Star*; Mephito; Dawkins; Tom Gentry; Hack O'Hara; Tiger Standish; Harmon Ventnor; "those Purple Hooded chaps"; Snarkey; Ruben Clampett; Dave King; a friend of King's who has written a memoir called *The Challenge of the Yukon*; Dan Fowler; Carol Baldwin; the Black Bat; Butch O'Leary; Silk Kirby; McGraff; the *Sentinel*; Charles Foster Kane; the *New York Comet*; Rex Parker; Winnie Bligh; Walt Whitney; Mike Axford; the Masked Rider; Deadwood Dick; the first Nick Carter; the Celluloid Burglar; the retired Green Ghost; Sunshine Cab; Ashton-Kirk; and "Hooks" McGuire.

Two-part novella by Erwin K. Roberts in Pro Se Presents, *Don Thomas and Lee Houston, Jr.*, eds., Pro Se Press, April–May 2012. The Phantom Detective, the New York Clarion, Frank Havens, and Inspector Gregg are from the Phantom Detective pulp novels. Captain Midnight was the subject of a long-running radio show. Secret Agent X's exploits were chronicled by Paul Chadwick under the pseudonym "Brant House"; K-9 was X's handler. The world's first consulting detective is Sherlock Holmes. George Chance is the alter ego of the pulp hero the Ghost. N. Wind Investigations is owned by Bingham Harvard, aka the Night Wind, whose stories were told by "Varick Vanardy" (actually Frederic van Rensselaer Dey) in The Cavalier from 1913–1919. The Dale Foundation is owned by Jimmie Dale, alias the Gray Seal, who appeared in pulp stories by Frank L. Packard. "B. Jonas" is the name on the door of an office used as a message drop and meeting place by a shadowy pulp hero and his agents; he must have kept an additional office in a building used by several other adventurers. The Hidalgo Trading Company is the front for the hangar for Doc's vehicles. It is unclear for what purpose Doc uses the office in "The Sons of Thor." Jethro Dumont is the alter ego of the pulp hero the Green Lama. The Crimson Mask appeared in stories by "Frank Johnson" (pseudonym for Norman A. Daniels) in the pulp Detective Novels

Magazine. *Dr. Skull* is, along with the Skull Killer, one of the aliases of Dr. Jeffrey Fairchild, archenemy of the pulp villain known first as the Octopus and later as the Scorpion. *Jim Anthony, the Waldorf-Anthony Hotel, the* Daily Star, *Mephito, Dawkins, and Tom Gentry are from the Jim Anthony pulp stories. Hack O'Hara was a crimefighting taxi driver who appeared in* Crack Comics *in the 1940s. Tiger Standish is the protagonist of a series of novels by Sydney Horler. Harmon Ventnor, "those Purple Hooded chaps," Snarkey, and Ruben Clampett are from Roberts' short story "Dawn of the Purple Hoods"* (Jim Anthony–Super Detective Volume One, *Ron Fortier, ed., Cornerstone Book Publishers, 2009). Dave King is from the comic strip* King of the Royal Mounted. *His friend is Sergeant William Preston of the radio series* Challenge of the Yukon, *later renamed* Sergeant Preston of the Yukon. *Dan Fowler's exploits were chronicled by Major George Fielding Eliot and others in the pulp* G-Men. *Carol Baldwin, the Black Bat, Butch O'Leary, Silk Kirby, and McGraff (actually McGrath) are from the Black Bat stories, which appeared in* Black Book Detective *for nearly fifteen years. The* Sentinel *and Mike Axford are from* The Green Hornet, *though Axford first appeared on another radio program,* Warner Lester, Manhunter; *since the Hornet was based in Detroit, Axford must have been visiting the offices of the* Sentinel*'s New York edition. Charles Foster Kane is from Orson Welles' classic film* Citizen Kane. *Rex Parker, reporter for the* New York Comet, *will later become Norman A. Daniels' pulp hero the Masked Detective, who appeared in his own self-titled magazine beginning in 1940; columnist Winnie Bligh is his girlfriend. Walt Whitney is the alter ego of the costumed hero Bob Phantom, who appeared during the '40s in comics published by MLJ, which would later be known as Archie Comics. It is unconfirmed whether Walt ever donned the mantle of Bob Phantom in the CU, but it should be noted this reference does not bring all of MLJ/Archie continuity into the CU. The Masked Rider was the protagonist of the pulp magazine* The Masked Rider Western. *Deadwood Dick was a dime novel cowboy created by Edward L. Wheeler. Nick Carter is one of the most famous dime novel detectives; the reference to "the first Nick Carter" suggests the pulp incarnation of the character was a successor or offspring of the original Nick. The Celluloid Burglar appeared in G. T. Fleming-Roberts' story "Death from Damascus," published in the April 1938 issue of* Detective Novels Magazine. *The Green Ghost (not to be confused with George Chance, who also used that name) was created by Johnston McCulley and appeared in* Thrilling Detective. *The Sunshine Cab Company is from the television series* Taxi. *Ashton-Kirk was created by John T. McIntyre and appeared in* The Popular Magazine *and in four collections of short stories starting in 1910. "Hooks" (or rather "Hook") McGuire, Bowling Detective, appeared in stories by George Allan Moffatt in* The Shadow Magazine.

THE KNOBLOCH COLLECTION ASSIGNMENT

Provisions have been made for the secret agent known as the Magician so, in the event his superior Intelligence One does not respond to a radio transmission, he can travel to a blueberry farm in Collinsport, Maine and dig up a waterproof metal box containing fifty thousand dollars, allowing him to start a new life under a new name. A visitor to the island of Motugra, Gregory Duquesne, is described as looking like he just stepped out of New York's fabled Cobalt Club or the Baltimore Gun Club. Legend has it the long polished mahogany bar at the inn and bar known as The Hanging Monkey is from the Midnight Star Saloon that was located in the town of Silverado in the United States. Duquesne hunted tigers in Paraguay ten years ago alongside the Russian Count Zaroff.

Short story by Derrick Ferguson in Tales from the Hanging Monkey, Volume One, *Ron Fortier, ed., Airship 27 Productions, 2012. Intelligence One is mentioned in Ferguson's Fortune McCall story "The Magic of Madness." Collinsport, Maine is the primary setting of the classic television series* Dark Shadows. *The Cobalt Club is from Walter Gibson's pulp novels chronicling the adventures of a pulp hero who operates from the shadows. The Baltimore Gun Club is from Jules Verne's novels* From the Earth to the Moon, Around the Moon, *and* The Purchase of the North Pole. *The Midnight Star Saloon is from the movie* Silverado. *Count Zaroff is from Richard Connell's short story "The Most Dangerous Game."*

THE UNDEAD KILLER

The Nightmare battles the Dead Man, a zombie sent back in time from the future, who is now acting as an enforcer for gangster Wolf Hopkins. A mugger tells the Nightmare about a conversation he overheard among a group of hoods at the Black Ship. The Nightmare thinks maybe Kent can give him some pointers on phrases to use to intimidate criminals. Later, in his alter ego of Michael Shaw, the hero is approached by Lieutenant Jerome Easton at the pub Moran's. Easton refers to "gentlemen's clubs, like that one the Commissioner belongs to, what's it called? The Baltic Club?" Shaw replies, "Something like that." Contemplating the best course of action in confronting Hopkins, Shaw thinks, "Richard would charge in with guns a-blazing, taking down his quarry, but only after leveling half the city in doing so. Kent would already know where Hopkins' headquarters was. He would stealthily infiltrate it and find the clue that would lead him straight to the Dead Man. He'd go there straightaway, always assuming he didn't have to rescue an agent or two first." Considering whether he should recruit agents of his own, or an attractive female companion, he thinks, "Who am I kidding? If I had a girl like Nina or Carol, I'd marry her at once, and the Nightmare would be a memory. Sometimes we can be such damn fools."

Short story by John L. French in Zombies in Time and Space, Ron Hanna, ed., Wild Cat Books, 2010. Kent is from the series of novels about a shadowy pulp hero; the Black Ship, the Commissioner, and the club to which he belongs are from the same series. Moran's is owned by Seamus Moran, whose cousin Paddy Moran runs the bar Bulfinche's in Patrick Thomas' Murphy's Lore series. Richard is Richard Wentworth, better known as the Spider. "Nina" may be a typo, and meant to refer to Wentworth's beloved, Nita Van Sloan. Alternatively, it could be a reference to Nina Ferrera, niece and former assistant of Harold Ward's pulp villain Doctor Death, and the girlfriend of Death's foe Jimmy Holm. Carol is Carol Baldwin, girlfriend of Tony Quinn, alias the Black Bat. The central premise of Zombies in Time and Space is in the far future, the Zombie Institute of Time and Space was created, which sends the undead back in time because physically traveling through time is impossible for living beings. Since there are numerous instances of recorded time travel by living beings in the Crossover Universe, the Institute likely exists in the future of an alternate reality, and the Dead Man was sent to the 1930s of the CU rather than his native reality. This raises the possibility the other time periods in which the zombies found themselves were also alternate realities, both to their own universe and to the CU.

THE DAEMON'S KISS

The Green Lama and Jean Farrell have been a couple ever since their encounter with Cthulhu.

Short story by Adam Lance Garcia in Of Monsters and Men, Tommy Hancock and Joe Gentile, eds., Moonstone Books, 2014. The Lama and Jean encountered Cthulhu in Garcia's novel The Green Lama Unbound.

Mid June–July
THE RESURRECTION RING

Secret Agent X, attending a gangster's funeral disguised as a reporter, deflects a blow from one of the hoods in attendance, who asks if he is "Some kinda damn superman, like that laughin' mook what dresses in black and prowls around at night?" The crook also says, "You must think I'm a damn mind reader, like that Captain Whatisname, huh?" One of X's aides, Harvey Bates, tells him one of their field men planted a listening device in an underworld bar called the Pink Rat. X visits two of his men, Jim Hobart and Hiram Beckwith, who are recovering from their most recent adventure in a clinic owned by a friend of X's, an eminent neurophysician and sometime adventurer who has a larger, secret facility in upstate New York that treats criminals. X is passed by a Mutt-and-Jeff pair, one short and apish, the other wasp-waisted and rather handsome, who trade insults with each other. They are trailed by a golden-eyed giant of a man.

Novel by Stephen Payne, Altus Press, 2014. The Pink Rat is a gangland dive seen in many stories of a certain vigilante who prefers to operate in the darkness: "That laughin' mook what dresses in black and prowls around at night." "Captain Whatsisname" is Captain Hazzard, the telepathic hero of a one-shot pulp magazine written by Paul Chadwick, who also created Secret Agent X. The owner of the clinic where Hobart and Beckwith are recovering is the famous pulp hero known as "Doc," the golden-eyed giant who passes X. The Mutt-and-Jeff pair are two of Doc's aides.

July 4
VENGEANCE, INC.

The Avenger is friends with an extraordinary doctor who has an office in the Empire State Building.

Short story by Howard Hopkins in The Avenger: The Justice, Inc. Files, *Joe Gentile and Howard Hopkins, eds., Moonstone Books, 2011.* The Avenger's friend is the bronze hero commonly called "Doc."

July
THE BREATH OF DESTRUCTION
District Attorney Harry Fields bursts into flames at the Cobalt Club. One of the other members of the Club, a hawk-faced millionaire recently returned from the Orient, attempts unsuccessfully to douse the fire. At New York's docks, Smitty questions Pappy, a grizzled old sailor who once served on the *Sea Girl.*

Short story by Frank Schildiner in The Avenger: The Justice, Inc. Files, *Joe Gentile and Howard Hopkins, eds., Moonstone Books, 2011. The Cobalt Club is from the exploits of the vigilante who operates in the shadows. The hawk-faced millionaire is probably a shadowy pulp hero disguised as a certain wealthy man from New Jersey. Pappy is Poopdeck Pappy, father of Popeye the Sailor Man in E. C. Segar's comic strip* Thimble Theatre. *The comic book story "The Revenge of Shiwan Khan" portrayed Popeye as an agent of the shadowy vigilante; doubtless his exploits were greatly exaggerated by Segar. The* Sea Girl *is the ship on which Robert E. Howard's Sailor Steve Costigan serves. In the pulp novel* Tuned for Murder, *it is mentioned the Avenger had led armies in Java; this story elaborates on that reference.*

August 17
BRONZE LADY DOWN
Doctor Omega and his companion Madeline travel to the year 1939 in the *Cosmos* to attend the premiere of the film version of *The Wizard of Oz.* However, a temporal alteration causes the people around them to become poverty-stricken and hostile. They are saved by a man in black wearing a fedora and scarf and wielding submachine guns, who says, "the weed of exploitation bears bitter fruit." Omega says that he felt the timeline realign as they traveled back from Oz, but someone else has altered it again. Omega blends in with a mob led by Dick Benson, a short, thickly-built man with pale, expressionless features, who is attacked by a man wearing a fringed black cape and a mask with bat ears, who says, "commies are a superstitious and cowardly lot." Madeline learns many human beings and livestock were killed by the von Hessel plague during the Great War. With agriculture destroyed, industry boomed, and the lower classes were adversely affected by the stock market crash. Violence erupted, and criminals with scientific weaponry arose. Omega says the change to the timestream involves the Ardans and Bogg. At the Library of Congress, Omega has little luck finding reference to the names Wildman, Savage, or Ardan. Finally, he finds a story in a 1922 edition of the New York *Daily Bugle* about the marriage of Francis Ardan to Catherine Maxwell, daughter of Senator Maxwell. Omega believes he must ensure someone dies, and Madeline and he travel to the Caribbean circa June 12, 1902. In

November 2 of that year, they witness a woman being saved from an aquatic monster by a blond man. A disheartened Doctor Omega travels to 1936 to prevent the man who saved the woman from traveling to 1902. The *Cosmos* materializes on the 86th floor observation deck of the Empire State Building. There, he accosts Phineas Bogg, and reveals Bogg's actions lengthened and intensified the Great Depression. Suddenly, a talking dog named Ralph and a woman named Josie appear. When Omega says Josie is a member of an organization that polices time, Madeline asks if she knows Manse. Josie responds she does, but Manse is in the Time Patrol, whereas she is a member of the Time Police. She also states that the temporal anomaly Bogg caused drew her and Ralph there. Omega reveals Bogg was trying to save Doc Ardan's mother. Finally, they settle upon a solution: removing Ardan's mother from her proper time period and placing her in another, while merely allowing the world to believe her dead. When they retrieve Arronaxe Ardan, she asks whether they are Capellean or Eridanean. After Omega incapacitates Ardan, they deposit her in the 29th Century with false identification papers. As Omega and Madeline depart once again for 1939, Bogg asks if Madeline is Jeffrey's daughter. Josie responds in the affirmative, referring to Madeline as "Mama." Madeline asks Omega what the new alias he chose for Arronaxe was, and he replies it was Clarissa MacDougal.

Short story by Dennis E. Power in Doctor Omega and the Shadowmen, *Jean-Marc and Randy Lofficier, eds., Black Coat Press, 2011; reprinted in French in* Les Compagnons de L'Ombre (Tome 10), *Jean-Marc and Randy Lofficier, eds., Rivière Blanche, 2012. This story serves as a sequel to Power's earlier story "The Deadly Desert Gnome" (*Glimmerglass: The Creative Writer's Annual, Volume 1, *John Allen Small, ed., 2009). Doctor Omega is from the novel of the same name by Arnould Galopin; Jean-Marc and Randy Lofficier's adaptation and translation of Galopin's novel implied Omega was the CU counterpart of the time and dimension-traveling Doctor, of* Doctor Who *fame. Madeline is from the children's books by Ludwig Bemelmans. The man in black with the fedora and scarf is the shadowy hero of tales told by Walter Gibson and others. Dick Benson is better known as Paul Ernst's pulp* hero. *The bat-eared man in the cape and mask is the Batman. Von Hessel is Baron von Hessel from Philip José Farmer's Doc Savage novel* Escape from Loki. *Phineas Bogg and his companion Jeffrey Jones are from the television series* Voyagers! *Francis "Doc" Ardan Jr. is from Guy d'Armen's novel* Doc Ardan: City of Gold and Lepers. *The Lofficiers' adaptation and translation of d'Armen's novel implied Ardan was the pulp hero whose biography was told by Philip José Farmer in* Doc Savage: His Apocalyptic Life; *in that book, Farmer said that his subject's real surname was Wildman. Farmer revealed Wildman's mother was the former Arronaxe Larsen in his biographies* Tarzan Alive *and* Doc Savage: His Apocalyptic Life. *The Capelleans and the Eridaneans are the warring alien races seen in Farmer's novel* The Other Log of Phileas Fogg. *Doc's headquarters is on the 86th floor of the Empire State Building. The* Daily Bugle *is the New York newspaper Peter Parker (aka Spider-Man) works for as a photographer. Catherine Maxwell is the wife of Bingham Harvard, alias the Night Wind, from the novels by Frederic van Rennselaer Dey and others. Josie Bauer is the adopted daughter of Philip José Farmer and an agent of the Time Police in Spider Robinson's Callahan's Crosstime Saloon books. Ralph Von Wau Wau's career as a detective alongside such capable allies as Dr. Johann H. Weisstein and Cordwainer Bird was chronicled by Jonathan Swift Somers III. Manse Everard is an agent of the Time Patrol in books by Poul Anderson. Clarissa MacDougal is from E. E. "Doc" Smith's Lensmen novels.*

Late August
THE SCREAMING DEATH

The Spider and the Green Ghost join forces to rescue their respective beloveds, Nita Van Sloan and Meriem White, from the evil Dr. William Kane, who has invented a device which utilizes soundwaves to induce crippling fear in humans.

Short story by Eric Fein in The Spider: Extreme Prejudice, *Joe Gentile and Tommy Hancock, eds., Moonstone Books, 2013. This crossover with the Spider, a member of the Wold Newton Family, reinforces the inclusion of the Green Ghost (aka simply the Ghost), who appeared in stories by "George Chance" (G. T. Fleming-Roberts) in the pulp magazine* The Ghost, Super-Detective *(later* The Ghost Detective *and then* The Green Ghost Detective*) in the CU. The month is given in the story, and Kane says war is brewing in Europe, indicating these events take place shortly before the beginning of World War II in September 1939. Note that Merry White chose to go by the more grown-up sounding "Meriem" White, starting in about 1944 or '45, while George Chance was away on wartime missions for the OSS. The references to her as "Meriem" in this tale are in error, as she would still have been going by "Merry" at this point in time.*

September 3, 1939–Summer 1940
PUT OUT MORE FLAGS

The further adventures of Basil Seal during World War II. Basil visits Alastair and Sonia Trumpington. Peter Pastmaster rejoins the Household Cavalry. Sonia tells Basil Margot Metroland says the last war was absolute heaven. Basil was once leader writer for *The Daily Beast*, and also served in the personal entourage of Lord Monomark. Pappenhacker of the Hearst press is mentioned as having been informed of a Polish submarine that is said to have arrived at Scapa. Angela Lyne had her home decorated by David Lennox just before the war. It is said of Angela's public drunkenness it would scarcely have been more surprising had it been Mrs. Stitch herself. Lady Anchorage is present at Peter's marriage to Lady Granchester's daughter. Angela describes her father's friends as men like Metroland and Copper. Ambrose Silk's literary journal is published by the firm of Rampole and Bentley. In the late 1920s, Ambrose and his friends Hat and Malpractice issued the invitation to a party in the form of a manifesto.

Novel by Evelyn Waugh. Basil Seal first appeared in Waugh's Black Mischief, *and several characters from that novel reappear here. Basil also appeared in the unfinished novel* Work Suspended. *Alastair Trumpington first appeared in* Decline and Fall, *while his wife Sonia debuted in* Black Mischief. *Alastair also appears in the story "Out of Depth." Peter Pastmaster previously appeared in* Decline and Fall, Vile Bodies, *and* Black Mischief. *Peter's mother Margot Metroland also made her first appearance in* Decline and Fall, *and went on to appear in many of Waugh's other interconnected books and stories. Lord Metroland, her husband, is the Metroland mentioned as a friend of Angela's father. Lord Monomark previously appeared in* Vile Bodies *and* Black Mischief, *and was mentioned in* A Handful of Dust *and* Work Suspended. *The Daily Beast, its publisher Lord Copper, Pappenhacker, and Mrs. Stitch are from* Scoop. *David Lennox appeared in* Decline and Fall, *and was mentioned in* Vile Bodies. *Miles Malpractice appeared in both of the aforementioned novels. Lady Anchorage appeared in* Vile Bodies *and was mentioned in* A Handful of Dust. *Mr. Rampole first appeared in* Vile Bodies.

September 7–November 8
THE SCARLET IMPOSTOR

Gregory Sallust enlists the aid of his friend Major (formerly Captain) Jean de Brissac as part of a plot to overthrow Hitler.

Novel by Dennis Wheatley. Captain Jean de Brissac first appeared in a non-series novel by Wheatley, Uncharted Seas.

Late September
THE SUN KING

The Avenger and his team battle Sun Koh, an Atlantean prince allied with the Nazis. Benson's small fleet of vehicles includes a speedy Hirondel Roadster. Nellie Gray recognizes one of Sun Koh's aides, Nimba, as Jack Holligan, a former heavyweight contender who was scheduled to fight Mullargen in London a few years ago, but never showed. Rosabel calls friends of Nellie's father seeking information about Sun Koh, including Dr. Littlejohn, of a well-known Massachusetts university; Dr. Jones, of a small but prestigious New Jersey college; and Professor Smith, of Cambridge. Among the Atlantean secrets contained in papers stolen by Nazi agents are an epic ballad of Kardios and a formula that allows one to breathe underwater. Nimba claims Ace Jessel was the best fighter ever. Nellie prepared herself for her encounter with Sun Koh by reading books on Atlantis by authors like Maracot. Sun Koh claims Christ is but a reflection of Assurah, the Phoenix. Brent Waller sends Rosabel into a hypnotic trance by saying the name "Valka." Captain Jan Mayen is another of Sun Koh's allies. Josh saw Nimba fight Iron Mike Costigan back in '32. When Benson had been a teen, he befriended Steve Allison, a notorious Sonora gunfighter who had taught him the finer points of his art. Benson is served an Atlantean vintage of wine that is said to steal one's soul. The engine of Jan Mayen's ship is powered by *vril*. In Ultima Thule, Sun Koh tells Benson about the Temple of the Goddess Qawo, says the Sun God Ra was known as Resu in Atlantis, and directs Standartenführer Karl Strasser to the Temple of Hotath, God of War, which contains a guardian statue of Ghirann, the Many-armed. Benson points out to Sun Koh Warda's features resemble those of an African man.

Novel by Matthew Baugh, Moonstone Books, 2015, taking place between the original Avenger pulp novels River of Ice *and* Murder on Wheels. *Sun Koh was a German pulp character created by Paul Alfred Müller. Jan Mayen also appeared in a pulp series by Müller, and had crossovers with Sun Koh. The Hirondel is the brand of car driven by the Saint in Leslie Charteris'* novels. "Mullargen" is a reference to "One-Punch" Mullargan from Edgar Rice Burroughs' "Tarzan and the Champion." Dr. Littlejohn is one of Doc's aides. The formula that allows one to breathe underwater is from the Doc Savage novel Mystery Under the Sea. The well-known Massachusetts University is Miskatonic University, a staple of H. P. Lovecraft's Cthulhu Mythos. Philip José Farmer identified Miskatonic as the school which employed Littlejohn in Doc Savage: His Apocalyptic Life. Dr. Jones is Indiana Jones. Professor Smith is Horatio Smith from the movie Pimpernel Smith. Kardios appears in stories by Manly Wade Wellman. Ghirann is from Wellman's Hok the Mighty stories. Ace Jessel is from Robert E. Howard's stories "The Apparition in the Prize Ring" and "Double Cross." Valka and Hotath are from Howard's Kull stories. Iron Mike Costigan is the brother of Howard's series character Sailor Steve Costigan. Steve Allison is another series character of Howard's, better known as the Sonora Kid. Maracot and Warda are from Arthur Conan Doyle's novel The Maracot Deep. Assurah, the Phoenix is from Henry Kuttner's story "Beyond the Phoenix," part of a series featuring Elak of Atlantis. The Atlantean vintage is from Clark Ashton Smith's story "A Vintage from Atlantis." The Vril is from Edward Bulwer-Lytton's The Coming Race. Qawo and Resu are from Philip José Farmer's Ancient Opar series.

October
THE GAMES PEOPLE PLAY

The Pink Reaper (Kaye Chandler) cannot imagine Detective Mydnight or the Nightmare shivering in an alley in a skimpy outfit. Kaye's uncle was a brilliant inventor: "It was even said that Dash Chandler had been approached in a recruitment effort by a man with a team of experts with their headquarters in Manhattan's tallest skyscraper. The leader of that team had been shocked when Dash not only turned down his offer, but wasn't the least bit impressed by him."

Story by Patrick Thomas in Tales from the Pulp Side, Dark Quest, 2013. The Nightmare (aka Michael Shaw), the Pink Reaper's cousin, was created by John L. French. The man headquartered in Manhattan's tallest skyscraper is the pulp hero called "Doc."

Autumn
THE AFFAIR OF THE NECKLACE REVISITED
Richard Benson is in Paris to visit his friend Pierre Duchene. The outbreak of war has been reported on by *L'Echo de France* and *Le Matin*. Benson and Duchene attend the unveiling of the Queen's Necklace at the mansion of the Comte and Comtesse de Dreux-Soubise. The necklace was stolen by Arsène Lupin in 1880, but Lupin later returned it. The Comte's uncle was shot by Zigomar during another attempt to steal the necklace several years ago. The necklace is stolen, and the subsequent investigation is led by Monsieur Gilles. When the Comte is murdered, *Le Matin* suggests Fantômas, Belphégor, or Tenebras as possible culprits. Benson finds the mastermind behind the scheme is Baruch Jorgell, a member of the Red Hand, which is led by Dr. Cornelius Kramm. Jorgell says that one of the oldest mottos of the Red Hand is to always *pay the law*. Judex saves Benson from certain death.

Short story by Jean-Marc and Randy Lofficier in Tales of the Shadowmen Volume 8: Agents Provocateurs, *Jean-Marc and Randy Lofficier, eds., Black Coat Press, 2011; reprinted in French in* Les Compagnons de l'Ombre (Tome 9), *Jean-Marc and Randy Lofficier, eds., Rivière Blanche, 2012, and* L'Ombre de Judex, *Jean-Marc and Randy Lofficier, eds., Rivière Blanche, 2013; and in* The Shadow of Judex, *Jean-Marc and Randy Lofficier, eds., Black Coat Press, 2013. Richard Benson is Paul Ernst's pulp hero with the shock white hair and malleable skin. Arsène Lupin is the gentleman thief created by Maurice Leblanc;* L'Echo de France *is the newspaper Lupin uses as a mouthpiece. Lupin's original theft of the Queen's Necklace from the Dreux-Soubise family was chronicled by Leblanc in "The Queen's Necklace." Zigomar is the gypsy crime lord created by Léon Sazie. Commissaire Gilles appeared in twenty-two novels by Jacques Decrest. Fantômas is the archfiend created by Marcel Allain and Pierre Souvestre. Belphégor is from the film serial of the same name. Tenebras is from* Ténèbras le Bandite Fantome *by Arnould Galopin. Baruch Jorgell, the Red Hand, and Dr. Cornelius Kramm are from* Le Mystérieux Docteur Cornélius *by Gustave Le Rouge. The old motto of the Red Hand is meant to imply a connection between that criminal organization and Paul Féval's Black Coats. Judex is the title character of Louis Feuillade's film serial.*

FIGHT CLUB
The Black Bat and Death Angel get into a barroom shoot-out with a group of gangsters.

Story by Mike Bullock and Fernando Peniche in Return of the Originals: Black Bat, *Moonstone Comics, 2011. Death Angel is an original character* created by Mike Bullock. She is Rebekah Killian, who was raised in an orphanage by a reverend who sexually abused her. At the age of ten, she was adopted by her grandfather, Ray Killian. When Ray died mysteriously shortly before Rebekah's eighteenth birthday, she was sent back to the orphanage until the reading of her grandfather's will. Taking her revenge on the unrepentant reverend, Rebekah soon inherited her grandfather's company, Raystar Enterprises. Her grandfather's right hand man Walter, a brilliant scientist, gave Rebekah a tactical battle suit, which she used to fight crime. The suit is composed of carbon nano fibers that react to mental impulses read through electrodes inside Death Angel's mask. The suit also has tachyon and sonic pulse emitters that, when combined, produce a hypnotic effect, making Rebekah's costumed persona seem even more fearsome to the loathsome criminals she faces. This equipment seems far beyond the limits of 1940s technology, even if one takes into account Doc Wildman and Fu Manchu's remarkable inventions during that era. Perhaps Walter was an Eridanean adoptee.

HAND OF THE MONSTER

The monster hunting group known as the Aces forcibly recruits Dr. Jekyll to use hypnotism to convince the Frankenstein Monster to destroy itself, but their plans are thwarted when the Monster reveals he is not as docile as they thought and Jekyll turns into Mr. Hyde.

Short story by Jim Beard in Monster Aces, Percival Constantine, ed., Pro Se Press, 2012. This crossover brings the Monster Aces into the CU. The Aces were created by Beard, although other authors contributed stories featuring the group to the anthology. The Frankenstein Monster seen here is Dr. Henry Frankenstein's creation, made famous by Universal Studios' monster movies.

December
WOUNDS

New York private eye Rick Ruby witnesses the murder of a policeman inside a tenement, right before the building bursts into flames. Detective

Jack McGinnis tells Ruby his partner is with Mason down at the 87th coaxing witnesses to view a suspect in a robbery-homicide. The murdered cop's father hires Ruby to investigate the man's death, meeting with him at an Indian restaurant called the Gunga Diner at the corner of 40th and 7th. Ruby goes to the Keeler Mission on 21st to question the former inhabitants of the tenement building. The mission's chef, a black man named Collier, tells him the lady who started the mission is deceased: "She stepped out that front door with her beau and was run down just like that. Going on ten years now." Among the tenants interviewed by Ruby are a man named Charlie and his pregnant girlfriend, Sylvia Kovacs. The cop and his father live on the second floor of a three-story walkup next to the Rumrunner bar on 43rd.

Short story by Andrew Salmon in *The Ruby Files Vol. 1*, Ron Fortier, ed., Airship 27 Productions, 2012. Mason is Hollis Mason, a policeman who also operated as a masked vigilante known as Nite-Owl in the 1930s and 1940s; he appears in Alan Moore and Dave Gibbons' comic book series *Watchmen*. The Gunga Diner is also from *Watchmen*, as are Charlie and Sylvia Kovacs, the parents of the mentally unstable vigilante Rorschach, and the Rumrunner bar. *Watchmen* takes place in an alternate universe where the existence of a virtually omnipotent superhuman being, Doctor Manhattan, led to advanced technology such as electricity-powered cars, the United States winning the Vietnam War, and presidential term limits being repealed, so Richard Nixon still leads the country in the mid 1980s. Also, half the population of New York City is killed in the series' climax. The Mason, Gunga Diner, Charlie, Sylvia Kovacs, and Rumrunner in "Wounds" must be Crossover Universe versions of their equivalents in the *Watchmen* Universe. There is no solid evidence Hollis Mason ever operated as Nite-Owl in the CU, nor Walter Kovacs as Rorschach. The Keeler Mission was started by Edith Keeler, who died in 1930, as seen in "The City on the Edge of Forever," an episode of the original *Star Trek* series written by Harlan Ellison. Mr. Collier is the father of Impossible Missions Force member Barney Collier from the 1960s spy show *Mission: Impossible*. Since *Star Trek* and *Mission: Impossible* take place in the CU, so do Rick Ruby's cases.

Late Autumn
DEFYING THE ODDS

The Nightmare and the Pink Reaper come to Nemesis' aid when she is captured by her fellow goddess Tyche. Nemesis thinks of her allies the League of Shadows, Shargrin, the Dead Lady, the Reaper, Paddy Moran, and those at Bulfinche's Pub. Nemesis confronts a group of would-be rapists, one of whom suggests she may be "one of those crime fighting

chicks, like the Domino Dame out west." The Reaper pays a call on a wife-abusing judge, who thinks she was sent by Burger at the D.A.'s office. Referring to a family that witnessed a gangland execution which he is protecting, the Nightmare tells the Reaper, "Kent's agreed to keep them on his island until the trial. Anyone who finds them there is going to hear a whole lot of laughing before they die." During the rescue mission, the Nightmare contemplates, "Maybe Kent could sneak in. Jethro would have some salt to turn himself invisible. But the man who was called the Nightmare was not a lama, nor could he command the shadows." The Reaper refers to other allies of hers and Nightmare's, including Chester Coyle, Sarge Winston, and Dagonet.

Story by Patrick Thomas and John L. French in From the Shadows, Dark Quest, 2012. The Nightmare is French's own creation. The Pink Reaper, Nemesis, the League of Shadows, Shargrin, the Dead Lady, Paddy Moran, Bulfinche's Pub, Chester Coyle, Sarge Winston, and Dagonet are from Thomas' Murphy's Lore series and its various spin-offs. "The Domino Dame" is Lars Anderson's Domino Lady, arguably the most famous heroine in the pulps. Burger is probably a relative of Los Angeles D.A. Hamilton Burger from Erle Stanley Gardner's Perry Mason novels. Kent is the shadowy pulp hero. Jethro Dumont is better known as the Green Lama.

WOLF HUNT

The Nightmare (aka Michael Shaw) sacrifices his life to save Leda, the woman he loves. Lieutenant Jerome Easton receives the news the hero died while battling a gang war in Coast City alongside an unidentified pink-clad vigilante. Thinking vigilantes have been thought dead before and later turned up alive, Easton reminds himself the Whispering Monk did truly die. Easton goes to the bar Moran's, owned by Seamus Moran, searching for the Nightmare. Contemplating giving his equipment to Easton, Shaw, who has been resurrected, thinks, "Maybe he'd don the mask and gloves, wield the .45s, and go join Gordon in Chicago." Hannibal Tomas, a hired gun out of Harbor City, murders a witness to a crime committed by gang boss Wolf Hopkins' men, and kidnaps the man's sons in order to persuade his wife not to testify. One of the two boys asks the Nightmare, who has come out of his short-lived retirement, if he is "the guy on the radio?" The hero laughs, and thinks he'll have to tell Kent. Later, he thinks, "That's why people like Kent, Richard, and I wear the black and haunt the night. When the law fails, when justice is thwarted, there is always vengeance, and we are the ones who can mete it out." The Nightmare later confronts Tomas as he comes out of a Harbor City bar called Dave's Place.

Story by John L. French in Tales from the Pulp Side, *Dark Quest, 2013. The Nightmare is French's own creation. Leda, also known as Nemesis, is from Patrick Thomas' Murphy's Lore and Terrorbelle books. The pink-clad vigilante is the Pink Reaper, the Nightmare's cousin, who first appeared in Thomas' book* Lore and Dysorder: The Hell's Detective Mysteries. *The Nightmare worked with Nemesis and the Pink Reaper in French and Thomas' collection* From the Shadows; *the final story in that book, "Defying the Odds," featured the Nightmare and the Reaper becoming involved in a gang war in Coast City, with the Nightmare ultimately sacrificing his life to save Leda's, and being brought back from the dead. The Whispering Monk was the subject of a titular story by Gordon E. Warnke in the June 1934 issue of the pulp* All Detective Magazine. *The Nightmare avenged the Monk's death in the first story in* From the Shadows, *"The Woman in Black." Seamus Moran is the cousin of Paddy Moran from the Murphy's Lore books. Both Seamus and Paddy are leprechauns. Gordon is a police commissioner who moonlighted as a whispering vigilante in pulp novels by Laurence Donovan. The Chicago reference is incorrect, as this hero operated out of Gotham City, although he retired in 1941, leaving the city in the capable hands of the Batman. Hannibal Tomas is a member of the Tomas family from French's book* The Devil of Harbor City, *which also details Michael Shaw's final battle with Wolf Hopkins. Dave's Place is also from* The Devil of Harbor City. *Kent is the vigilante of shadows, while Richard is Richard Wentworth, aka the Spider.*

Appendix 1
The Night of the Television Crossovers That Wouldn't Die!

Since *Diff'rent Strokes* takes place in the Crossover Universe, so do the shows in the following chain of crossovers:

- *Diff'rent Strokes* & *The Facts of Life*: *The Facts of Life* is a spin-off of *Diff'rent Strokes*.

- *Diff'rent Strokes* & *Hello, Larry*: These shows have several crossovers.

- *The Facts of Life* & *Living Single*: On *Living Single*, Susan says she once attended a boarding school named Eastland, the setting of *The Facts of Life*.

- *Living Single* & *The Crew*: *Living Single*'s Regine Hunter and Synclaire James each appear in episodes of *The Crew* as passengers on Regency Airlines.

- *Living Single* & *Half & Half*: On *Half & Half*, Dee Dee's mother co-stars in a play with Kyle Barker, now married to Maxine Shaw, who was his fiancé on *Living Single*.

- *Diff'rent Strokes* & *Silver Spoons*: Arnold Jackson from *Diff'rent Strokes* appears on *Silver Spoons*.

- *Diff'rent Strokes* & *The Jeffersons* & *The Fresh Prince of Bel-Air*: On the series finale of *The Fresh Prince of Bel-Air*, Arnold and Mr. Drummond from *Diff'rent Strokes* show up interested in buying the Banks house, along with George and Weezie Jefferson from *The Jeffersons*.

- *The Jeffersons* & *The Fresh Prince of Bel-Air*: Prior to their appearance in the series finale, George and Weezie attend a couples counseling session alongside Will and his girlfriend on *The Fresh Prince of Bel-Air*.

- *The Jeffersons* & *All in the Family*: *The Jeffersons* is a spin-off of *All in the Family*.

- *All in the Family* & *Archie Bunker's Place*: *All in the Family* was retitled *Archie Bunker's Place*.

- *All in the Family* & *Gloria*: Archie Bunker's daughter Gloria Stivic gets her own spin-off.

- *All in the Family* & *Maude*: Edith Bunker's cousin Maude Findlay gets a spin-off as well.

- *Maude* & *Good Times*: Maude's maid Florida Evans and her family spin off into their own show.
- *Maude* & *Hanging In*: Maggie Gallagher, Sam Dickey, and Pinky Nolan appear in the three-part finale of *Maude* before spinning off into their own show, *Hanging In*
- *All in the Family* & *704 Hauser Street*. *704 Hauser Street* features another family living in the house that once belonged to the Bunker family.
- *The Jeffersons* & *Checking In*: The Jeffersons' maid Florence Johnston receives a spin-off where she becomes a housekeeper at a hotel.
- *The Jeffersons* & *E/R*: *E/R*'s Nurse Julie Williams is related to George Jefferson.
- *The Fresh Prince of Bel-Air* & *Blossom*: Blossom's brother Anthony goes on a date with Ashley Banks from *The Fresh Prince of Bel-Air*.
- *The Fresh Prince of Bel-Air* & *In the House*: *In the House*'s Marion Hill is friends with *The Fresh Prince of Bel-Air*'s Carlton Banks.
- *The Fresh Prince of Bel-Air* & *Out All Night*: Hilary Banks visits the club owned by *Out All Night*'s Chelsea Paige.

The Brady Bunch, Charlie's Angels, Columbo, Emergency! MacGyver, Mannix, Mission: Impossible, Starsky & Hutch, Walker, Texas Ranger, The Streets of San Francisco, The Beverly Hillbillies, Mister Ed, and *Hogan's Heroes* take place in the Crossover Universe, therefore bringing in the following chain of shows:

- *The Brady Bunch* & *Charlie's Angels* & *Columbo* & *Emergency!* & *MacGyver* & *Mannix* & *Mission: Impossible* & *Starsky & Hutch* & *Walker, Texas Ranger* & *The Streets of San Francisco* & *Barnaby Jones* & *Crazy Like a Fox* & *$weepstake$* & *What's Happening!!*: All of these shows utilize a fictional television station called KBEX-TV.
- *Charlie's Angels* & *The Love Boat*: The Angels search for a thief aboard the *Pacific Princess*.
- *The Love Boat* & *Fantasy Island*: Actress Kim Holland's struggles to attain some privacy begin on an episode of *The Love Boat* and conclude on an episode of *Fantasy Island*.
- *The Love Boat* & *Love Boat: The Next Wave*. *Love Boat: The Next Wave* features the *Pacific Princess*' new crew.

- *The Love Boat* & *Martin*: Martin takes a trip aboard the *Pacific Princess*.
- *Charlie's Angels* & *Vega$*: The Angels travel to Nevada on a case and cross paths with local P.I. Dan Tanna.
- *Quincy M.E.* & *Emergency!*: On *Quincy M.E.*, a paramedic treating a heart attack patient suggests they should take him to Rampart, the hospital from *Emergency!*
- *B. J. and the Bear* & *McCloud* & *Quincy M.E.*: An episode of *B. J. and the Bear* features Detective Rizzo from *McCloud*, as well as Drs. Robert Astin and Sam Fujiyama from *Quincy M.E.*
- *B. J. and the Bear* & *The Misadventures of Sheriff Lobo/Lobo*: *B. J. and the Bear*'s Sheriff Elroy P. Lobo spins off into his own series, *The Misadventures of Sheriff Lobo*, which later has its title shortened to simply *Lobo*.
- *Barnaby Jones* & *Cannon*: *Barnaby Jones* is a spin-off of *Cannon*, and the two shows have a crossover later on.
- *Barnaby Jones* & *The Beverly Hillbillies*: In *The Beverly Hillbillies* movie, which shows how the Clampett family first moved to California, Barnaby Jones investigates Granny's disappearance.
- *The Beverly Hillbillies* & *Green Acres* & *Petticoat Junction*: All three shows are connected by the town of Hooterville, and characters from one show frequently appear on another.
- *Green Acres* & *Hogan's Heroes*: An episode of *Green Acres* has a flashback to Oliver Wendell Douglas' time as a fighter pilot in World War II, during which his superiors advise him to contact Colonel Hogan if the Germans capture him and imprison him in Stalag 13.
- *The Beverly Hillbillies* & *Mister Ed*: *The Beverly Hillbillies*' Daisy "Granny" Moses appears on an episode of *Mister Ed*.
- *What's Happening!!* & *What's Happening Now!*: *What's Happening Now!* is a revival of *What's Happening!!*
- *What's Happening!!* & *The Brady Bunch Variety Hour*: Several characters from *What's Happening!!* appear on an episode of *The Brady Bunch Variety Hour*.

NYPD Blue is in the Crossover Universe, thus bringing these shows in as well:

- *NYPD Blue* & *The Drew Carey Show*: On *The Drew Carey Show*, Drew and his buddies get in a traffic jam investigated by *NYPD Blue's* James Martinez.

- *The Drew Carey Show* & *Coach* & *Ellen* & *Grace Under Fire*: These four shows crossover by having characters from each cross paths in Las Vegas.

- *Coach* & *Newhart*: *Coach's* Hayden Fox and Christine Armstrong meet *Newhart's* Larry, Darryl, and Darryl.

- *The Drew Carey Show* & *The Geena Davis Show*: *The Geena Davis Show's* Hillary has cyber-sex with *The Drew Carey Show's* Drew.

- *The Drew Carey Show* & *Home Improvement*: Drew Carey and friends watch a roof repair how-to video hosted by *Home Improvement's* Tim Taylor.

- *Home Improvement* & *Buddies*: Dave Carlisle and John Butler appear on an episode of *Home Improvement* before getting their own show, *Buddies*.

- *Home Improvement* & *Soul Man*: These two shows cross-over several times.

- *Home Improvement* & *Thunder Alley*: *Home Improvement's* Brad Taylor goes on a date with *Thunder Alley's* Claudine Turner.

- *Ellen* & *These Friends of Mine*: *These Friends of Mine* was revamped as *Ellen*.

- *The Drew Carey Show* & *The Norm Show*: *The Norm Show's* Norm dated *The Drew Carey Show's* Mimi in high school.

- *The Norm Show* & *Norm*: *The Norm Show* had its name shortened to simply *Norm*.

- *NYPD Blue* & *Hill Street Blues*: Exhibitionist Buck Naked appears on both shows.

- *Hill Street Blues* & *Beverly Hills Buntz*: Lt. Norman Buntz is fired in the series finale of *Hill Street Blues* and spins off as a P.I. into *Beverly Hills Buntz*.

- *Hill Street Blues* & *Cop Rock*: Lt. Howard Hunter from *Hill Street Blues* appears on *Cop Rock*. Presumably, depictions of the cops on that latter show breaking into song are fictionalized.

- *Cop Rock* & *L.A. Law*: *L.A. Law*'s Victor Sifuentes and Abby Perkins appear on *Cop Rock*.
- *L.A. Law* & *Civil Wars*: *Civil Wars*' Eli Levinson and Denise Iannello join the cast of *L.A. Law* when their own show is cancelled.
- *NYPD Blue* & *Public Morals*: Administrative Assistant John Irvin is a supporting character on both shows.
- *NYPD Blue* & *Brooklyn South*: *NYPD Blue*'s Det. Stu Morrissey and Steve Richards appear in separate episodes of *Brooklyn South*.

Knight Rider, Las Vegas, and Passions take place in the Crossover Universe, therefore bringing in the following chain of shows:

- *Knight Rider* & *Las Vegas*: The pilot for the 2008–2009 revival of *Knight Rider* has Mike Traceur gambling at the Montecito Casino from *Las Vegas*.
- *Las Vegas* & *Medium*: *Medium*'s Allison Dubois has a vision of herself as the killer she's tracking, in which she is gambling at the Montecito.
- *Medium* & *Castle*: An FBI agent on *Castle* refers to a case involving the Recapitator, a serial killer who was switching his victims' heads in Phoenix, from the Season 3 finale of *Medium*.
- *Castle* & *Missing*: A quote from author Richard Castle appears on a book cover on *Missing*.
- *Las Vegas* & *Passions*: Several characters from *Passions* visit the Montecito, where they meet employee Mary Connell.
- *Passions* & *Days of Our Lives*: *Days of Our Lives*' Stefano DiMera owns a mansion in Harmony, the town where *Passions* is set.
- *Passions* & *Bewitched*: *Bewitched*'s witch doctor (literally) Dr. Bombay appears on *Passions*.
- *Bewitched* & *Tabitha*: *Tabitha* is a spin-off of *Bewitched* featuring Darrin and Samantha Stephens' now-grown daughter, who has inherited her mother's powers.
- *Knight Rider* & *Code of Vengeance* (aka *Dalton's Code of Vengeance*): David Dalton teams up with Michael Knight on an episode of the original version of *Knight Rider* before spinning off into his own series, *Code of Vengeance*.

Ironside is in, therefore bringing in the following shows:

- *Ironside* & *Amy Prentiss*: Chief Amy Prentiss appears on an episode of *Ironside* before spinning off into her own show.
- *Ironside* & *Sarge*: *Sarge*'s Father Samuel Cavanaugh visits San Francisco, where he is consulted by Chief Robert Ironside.
- *Ironside* & *The Bold Ones: The New Doctors*: Sgt. Ed Brown is shot on *Ironside* and taken to *The Bold Ones: The New Doctors*' Craig Institute for treatment.
- *The Bold Ones: The New Doctors* & *The Bold Ones: The Lawyers* & *The Bold Ones: The Protectors* & *The Bold Ones: The Senator*: The various *The Bold Ones* series are all produced under the same umbrella.

Once Upon a Time, Lost, CSI: NY, Arrested Development, Buffy the Vampire Slayer, My Name is Earl, Leverage, Law & Order, Law & Order: Criminal Intent, Angel, CSI, Veronica Mars, The X-Files, The Office (U.S.), *Supernatural,* and *Chuck* are in the CU, bringing in the following shows as well:

- *Once Upon a Time* & *Lost* & *Scrubs*: Apollo candy bars appear in all three shows.
- *Once Upon a Time* & *Once Upon a Time in Wonderland*: *Once Upon a Time in Wonderland* is a spin-off of *Once Upon a Time*.
- *Scrubs* & *Cougar Town*: *Scrubs*' Ted Buckland appears in an episode of *Cougar Town*. Both shows also utilize a chain of coffee shops called Coffee Bucks, as well as Winston University. In *Scrubs*, Winston is in California, but in *Cougar Town*, it is in Florida, despite the campus being identical in both shows. The Winston University in Florida must be a satellite campus of the California school.
- *Cougar Town* & *CSI: NY* & *Arrested Development* & *Community* & *Orange is the New Black* & *New Girl* & *The Middle* & *2 Broke Girls* & *My Name is Earl* & *Ugly Betty* & *Switched at Birth* & *The New Adventures of Old Christine* & *Sons of Anarchy* & *10 Things I Hate About You* & *Ringer* & *Parenthood* & *Let's Stay Together* & *The Mentalist* & *Melissa & Joey* & *Dads* & *The Bill Engvall Show* & *Brothers & Sisters* & *Better Off Ted* & *Make It or Break It* & *Dollhouse* & *Miss Guided* & *Moonlight* & *Veronica Mars* & *The Crazy Ones* & *The Vampire Diaries* & *Trophy Wife* & *It's Always Sunny in Philadelphia* & *Scorpion* & *How to Get Away with*

Murder & *Gilmore Girls* & *Touch* & *Grey's Anatomy* & *Brooklyn Nine-Nine* & *Undateable* & *Awkward* & *Political Animals* & *Cristela* & *Rizzoli & Isles* & *See Dad Run*: Bags of Let's Potato Chips appear in all of these shows.

- *Arrested Development* & *Running Wilde*: Steve Wilde and Fa'ad Shaoulian's nightclub on *Running Wilde* is built by the Bluth Company from *Arrested Development*.

- *Community* & *Running Wilde*: Barrels of oil on *Community* bear the logo of Wilde Oil from *Running Wilde*.

- *Community* & *Buffy the Vampire Slayer*: On *Community*, a textbook is seen with the word "Sunnydale," the setting of *Buffy the Vampire Slayer*, written along its spine.

- *My Name is Earl* & *Raising Hope*: *Raising Hope* has made several references to *My Name is Earl*.

- *My Name is Earl* & *Raising Hope* & *Son of the Beach*: Patty the hooker from *My Name is Earl* runs a Gamblers Anonymous group on *Raising Hope*, and has Notch Johnson from *Son of the Beach* as her client in the same episode.

- *Raising Hope* & *Yes, Dear*: Jimmy and Christina Hughes from *Yes, Dear* appear on *Raising Hope*.

- *My Name is Earl* & *Leverage*: As a child, *Leverage*'s Parker witnessed a man dressed as a clown being killed by a man dressed as horse in Camden County, Illinois, the setting of *My Name is Earl*.

- *Leverage* & *Law & Order*: Sophie Devereaux, a member of the Leverage team, poses as a reporter for the *Ledger* at a press conference. Since the team was based in New York City at the time, this must be a reference to the *New York Ledger* newspaper from *Law & Order* and its spin-offs.

- *Ugly Betty* & *The Beautiful Life: TBL*: Mode Magazine from *Ugly Betty* is referenced on *The Beautiful Life: TBL*.

- *Sons of Anarchy* & *The Shield*: A black motorcycle gang called the One-Niners appears in both shows.

- *Sons of Anarchy* & *The Shield* & *The Unit*: A gang called the Byzantine Latinos (or Byz Lats) appears in all three shows.

- *Parenthood* & *About a Boy*: *About a Boy*'s Will Freeman appears on an episode of *Parenthood*, while *Parenthood*'s Crosby Braverman appears on two episodes of *About a Boy*.

- *Parenthood* & *Friday Night Lights*: In a four-part webisode, *Parenthood*'s Max Braverman and Amber Holt run into the band Crucifictorious from *Friday Night Lights*.
- *Brothers & Sisters* & *Chuck* & *Grey's Anatomy* & *In Plain Sight* & *Suburgatory*: Nuts & More cereal has appeared on all of these shows.
- *Grey's Anatomy* & *Private Practice*: Addison Montgomery spins off from *Grey's Anatomy* into her own show.
- *Grey's Anatomy* & *The O.C.*: On *The O.C.*, Dr. Neil Roberts gets a job at Seattle Grace Hospital, the setting of *Grey's Anatomy*.
- *The O.C.* & *Chuck*: *The O.C.*'s Seth Cohen and *Chuck*'s Chuck Bartowski both own posters for the movie *Yakuza Prep*.
- *In Plain Sight* & *Law & Order: Criminal Intent*: *Law & Order: Criminal Intent*'s Detectives Logan and Wheeler meet *In Plain Sight*'s Mary Shannon.
- *Law & Order: Criminal Intent* & *Jo*: Nicole Wallace, Detective Goren's archenemy on *Law & Order Criminal Intent*, also appears in an episode of *Jo*.
- *Dollhouse* & *Angel* & *Bones*: The Hyperion Hotel appears in all three shows. On *Bones*, the Hyperion is in Washington, D.C., but on *Angel* and *Dollhouse* it is in Los Angeles. The Hyperion must have become a chain since *Angel* ended. (*Bones* has also crossed over with *Sleepy Hollow*, but that series takes place in an AU).
- *Bones* & *The Finder*: An episode of *Bones* serves as a backdoor pilot for *The Finder*, while *Bones*' Lance Sweets and Jack Hodgins later appear on episodes of *The Finder*.
- *Bones* & *Modern Family*: The cereal Berry Loops has appeared on both shows.
- *Bones* & *CSI*: An episode of *Bones* set in Las Vegas mentions the Tangiers Hotel from *CSI*.
- *CSI* & *The Defenders*: A bank statement on *CSI* mentions Morelli & Kaczmarek, the Las Vegas-based law firm from *The Defenders*.
- *CSI* & *CSI: Cyber*: *CSI: Cyber* is a spin-off of *CSI*. D. B. Russell moves from *CSI* to *CSI: Cyber* when the elder show is cancelled.
- *Moonlight* & *Veronica Mars*: *Moonlight*'s vampire P.I. Mick St. John investigates the murder of a co-ed at *Veronica Mars*' Hearst College.

- *Veronica Mars* & *The X-Files* & *Supernatural* & *Breaking Bad* & *Prison Break*: Lariat Rent-a-Car appears on all of these shows, beginning with *The X-Files*.

- *Breaking Bad* & *The X-Files*: *Breaking Bad* also has appearances by Morley Cigarettes and Cradock Marine Bank, both of which are from *The X-Files*.

- *Breaking Bad* & *Weeds*: A character on *Weeds* says he once stayed at a drug rehab center in Albuquerque called Fresh Start, the same rehab center where Jesse Pinkman stayed for a time on *Breaking Bad*.

- *Breaking Bad* & *Better Call Saul*: *Better Call Saul* is a prequel to *Breaking Bad* featuring Walter White's crooked lawyer Saul Goodman.

- *Prison Break* & *Breakout Kings*: *Prison Break*'s Theodore "T-Bag" Bagwell appears on an episode of *Breakout Kings*.

- *The Vampire Diaries* & *The Originals*: *The Originals* is a spin-off of *The Vampire Diaries*.

- *It's Always Sunny in Philadelphia* & *The Office* (U.K.): On *It's Always Sunny in Philadelphia*, Frank Reynolds gets his daughter Sweet Dee a Sergio Georgini handbag for Christmas. On the British version of *The Office*, David Brent owns a Sergio Georgini leather jacket.

- *The Office* (U.K.) & *The Office* (U.S.): On the American version of *The Office*, Michael Scott briefly meets David Brent from the original British series. In a later episode, Brent appears as an interviewee for the job at Dunder-Mifflin recently vacated by Michael.

- *The Office* (U.K.) & *Lost*: On *Lost*, Charlie Pace's girlfriend mentions her father buying a paper company in Slough, a reference to Wernham Hogg from the British version of *The Office*.

- *Scorpion* & *NCIS: Los Angeles*: *NCIS: Los Angeles*' Hetty Lange appears on an episode of *Scorpion*.

- *NCIS* & *NCIS: Los Angeles* & *NCIS: New Orleans*: *NCIS: Los Angeles* and *NCIS: New Orleans* are spin-offs of *NCIS*. (It should be noted *NCIS: Los Angeles*' crossovers with the modern version of *Hawaii Five-O* must take place in an AU, as the original version of *Hawaii Five-O* is already in the CU. Also, an episode of the latter-day *Hawaii Five-O* mentions a villain from *Arrow*, bringing that series and its spin-offs, *The Flash* and *DC's Legends of Tomorrow*, into the same alternate universe, as well as *Constantine*).

- *NCIS* & *JAG*: *NCIS* is a spin-off of *JAG*.
- *JAG* & *First Monday*: Senator Edward Sheffield from *First Monday* becomes a supporting character on *JAG* after his own series is cancelled.
- *JAG* & *NCIS* & *Seven Days* & *Spy Game*: The TV news network ZNN appears in all of these shows.
- *Cristela* & *Last Man Standing*: *Last Man Standing*'s Mike Baxter and Ed Alzate guest-star on *Cristela*.

Reaper, Eli Stone, and Gilligan's Island are in the CU, thus bringing in the following chain of shows:

- *Reaper* & *Eli Stone*: A defendant on *Eli Stone* works at the Work Bench, the same home improvement store that employs Sam Oliver on *Reaper*.
- *Reaper* & *7th Heaven* & *Full House*: The cereal Oaties appears in all three shows.
- *Full House* & *Family Matters*: *Family Matters*' Steve Urkel convinces *Full House*'s Stephanie Tanner she should not be embarrassed to wear glasses.
- *Family Matters* & *Meego*: Steve Urkel appears on the first two episodes of *Meego*.
- *Meego* & *Gilligan's Island*: Gilligan, Mary Ann, and the Professor have a cameo on *Meego*.
- *Family Matters* & *Perfect Strangers*: Harriette Winslow, the elevator operator on *Perfect Strangers*, and her husband Carl spin-off into their own show, *Family Matters*.
- *Perfect Strangers* & *Happy Days*: On *Perfect Strangers*, Larry and Balki are contestants on a game show where one of the prizes is a toilet supplied by Cunningham Hardware of Milwaukee, Wisconsin, the company owned by Howard Cunningham on *Happy Days*.
- *Happy Days* & *Love, American Style*: The characters from *Happy Days* were originally introduced on an episode of the anthology series *Love, American Style*.
- *Happy Days* & *Blansky's Beauties*: Nancy Blansky is Howard Cunningham's cousin. Diner owner Arnold also appears on both shows.

- *Happy Days* & *Joanie Loves Chachi*: Chachi and Joanie Arcola from *Happy Days* spin off into their own show.
- *Happy Days* & *Laverne & Shirley*: Fonzie's friends Laverne and Shirley also get their own spin-off.
- *Happy Days* & *Mork & Mindy*: The alien Mork from Ork first appears on *Happy Days* before spinning off into *Mork & Mindy*.
- *Mork & Mindy* & *Happy Days* & *Laverne & Shirley*: In the first episode of *Mork & Mindy*, a flashback shows Fonzie arranging for Mork to date Laverne DeFazio.
- *Mork & Mindy* & *Out of the Blue*: On the first episode of *Out of the Blue*, Mork visits his old friend Random the angel.
- *Out of the Blue* & *Happy Days*: *Out of the Blue* is a spin-off of *Happy Days*.
- *Family Matters* & *Step by Step*: Steve Urkel's rocket pack carries him all the way from Chicago on *Family Matters* to Port Washington, Wisconsin on *Step by Step*.
- *Step by Step* & *Boy Meets World*: *Step by Step*'s Dana Foster appears on an episode of *Boy Meets World*.
- *Boy Meets World* & *Girl Meets World*: *Girl Meets World* is a sequel series to *Boy Meets World*.
- *Boy Meets World* & *Sabrina the Teenage Witch*: *Boy Meets World*'s Eric Matthews goes on a date with Sabrina Spellman.
- *Boy Meets World* & *Sabrina the Teenage Witch* & *Teen Angel* & *You Wish*: Sabrina pursues a rogue Time Ball across all four series, which throws the main characters of each back in time.
- *Sabrina the Teenage Witch* & *Clueless*: *Clueless*' Cher meets Sabrina Spellman.
- *Clueless* & *Moesha*: *Moesha*'s Hakeem and Niecy attend Cher's prom.
- *Moesha* & *Girlfriends*: Moesha's cousin Dorian's mother is the sister of *Girlfriends*' Maya, while on *Girlfriends* Joan gets some advice from Niecy while on a date.
- *Girlfriends* & *Eve*: Hairstylist Peaches from *Girlfriends* appears on an episode of *Eve*.
- *Girlfriends* & *The Game*: Joan Clayton's cousin Melanie Barnett appears in an episode of *Girlfriends* before spinning off into *The Game*.

- *Moesha* & *The Parkers*: Moesha's friend Kim Parker and her family spin off into their own show.
- *The Parkers* & *The Hughleys*: Darryl Hughley meets Nikki Parker on *The Parkers*, and Nikki appears on an episode of *The Hughleys* on the same night.
- *Full House* & *Hangin' with Mr. Cooper*: Mark Cooper serves as a substitute teacher for Michelle Tanner's class.

The Golden Girls takes place in the CU, bringing in the following chain of shows:

- *The Golden Girls* & *Empty Nest*: *Empty Nest* is a spin-off of *The Golden Girls*.
- *The Golden Girls* & *Empty Nest* & *Nurses*: These three shows have regular crossovers, either between two of them or all three.
- *The Golden Girls* & *The Golden Palace*: *The Golden Palace* is a revamped version of *The Golden Girls*, featuring Dorothy, Blanche, and Rose running a hotel.

The Bold and the Beautiful is in, and brings in the following shows by extension:

- *The Bold and the Beautiful* & *The Young and the Restless*: These two shows have several crossovers.
- *The Young and the Restless* & *As the World Turns*: These two shows have at least three crossovers.
- *As the World Turns* & *The Brighter Day* & *Another World*: Mitchell Dru, a character on *The Brighter Day*, moves to *As the World Turns* when his own show is cancelled, and later to *Another World*.
- *As the World Turns* & *Another World*: *Another World* is a spin-off of *As the World Turns*.
- *Another World* & *Guiding Light*: Mike Bauer from *Guiding Light* appears for six months on *Another World*. Much later, *Another World*'s Cass Winthrop appears on *Guiding Light*.
- *Guiding Light* & *One Life to Live*: On *One Life to Live*, Jack Manning mentions a woman in Springfield who was cloned, a reference to Reva Lewis from *Guiding Light*.

- *One Life to Live* & *General Hospital*: These shows have several crossovers. After *One Life to Live* is cancelled, Todd Manning and other characters from that show appear on *General Hospital* for a time.
- *General Hospital* & *Loving*: *General Hospital*'s Cesar Faison preys on *Loving*'s Ava.
- *Loving* & *The City*: *The City* is a revamp of *Loving*.
- *Loving* & *All My Children*: *Loving* is a spin-off of *All My Children*.
- *All My Children* & *One Life to Live*: These two shows have several crossovers.
- *One Life to Live* & *All My Children* & *General Hospital* & *Port Charles*: *One Life to Live*'s Gretel Rae Cummings appears on *All My Children*, *General Hospital*, and *Port Charles* as part of a major crossover event.
- *General Hospital* & *All My Children*: *All My Children*'s Alex Devane is the twin sister of *General Hospital*'s Anna Devane. Also, *General Hospital*'s Robin Scorpio appears on an episode of *All My Children*.
- *General Hospital* & *Port Charles*: *Port Charles* is a spin-off of *General Hospital*.
- *General Hospital* & *General Hospital: Night Shift*: *General Hospital: Night Shift* is another *General Hospital* spin-off.
- *General Hospital* & *The City*: *General Hospital*'s Tracy Quartermaine and her son Dillon both appear in episodes of *The City*.
- *General Hospital* & *Ryan's Hope*: *Ryan's Hope*'s Delia Ryan appears on *General Hospital* fourteen years after the end of her own series.
- *General Hospital* & *The Young Marrieds*: *The Young Marrieds* is set in Queen's Point, a suburb of Port Charles, New York, the setting of *General Hospital*.
- *Another World* & *Somerset*: *Somerset* is a spin-off of *Another World*.
- *Another World* & *Texas*: *Texas* is also a spin-off of *Another World*.
- *Another World* & *Lovers and Friends/For Richer, for Poorer*: *Lovers and Friends*, a spin-off of *Another World*, is later retooled as *For Richer, for Poorer*.
- *As the World Turns* & *Our Private World*: *Our Private World* is a short-lived spin-off of *As the World Turns*.

Appendix 2
The Anno Dracula Universe and Character Guide

In *Crossovers Volume 2*, Win Scott Eckert included an appendix entitled "The Anno Dracula Universe and Character Guide," which listed the crossover characters, places, objects, and concepts from Kim Newman's Anno Dracula series, which at the time consisted of the books *Anno Dracula*, *The Bloody Red Baron*, and *Dracula Cha Cha Cha*, which was released in the United States as *Judgment of Tears: Anno Dracula 1959*, as well as the short stories "Coppola's Dracula," "Castle in the Desert: Anno Dracula 1977," "Andy Warhol's Dracula: Anno Dracula 1978–1979," "Who Dares Wins: Anno Dracula 1980," "The Other Side of Midnight," and "You Are the Wind Beneath My Wings: Anno Dracula 1984." Since that time, Titan Books has reissued all three volumes, with *Dracula Cha Cha Cha* receiving its first U.S. release under that title rather than *Judgment of Tears*. As bonus features, the new editions of *The Bloody Red Baron* and *Dracula Cha Cha Cha* both contained new novellas set in the Anno Dracula Universe, "Anno Dracula 1923: Vampire Romance" and "Aquarius: Anno Dracula 1968." Following that, the fourth novel in the series, *Johnny Alucard*, was released. This book combined revised versions of the various short stories with new material to compose a full-length tale spanning nearly two decades. I also discovered some references upon rereading the first three books and the short stories that were not included in Win's previous appendix. Therefore, the present appendix contains not only the crossovers from "Vampire Romance" and "Aquarius" and the new material in *Johnny Alucard*, but also the references from the previous entries in the series that I discovered.

Anno Dracula 1923: Vampire Romance (in *Anno Dracula: The Bloody Red Baron*, Titan Books, 2012)

- Geneviève Dieudonné
- Dracula
- Sir Francis Varney
- Nutrax for Nerves (*Murder Must Advertise* by Dorothy L. Sayers)
- "NetherBeast gramophones" are a reference to the film *Netherbeast Incorporated*
- Edmond Cordery (*The Empire of Fear* by Brian Stableford)

- Elizabeth Báthory and Ilona Harczy (Delphine Seyrig and Andrea Rau, *Daughters of Darkness*)
- Daisy Bunting (*The Lodger* by Marie Belloc Lowndes)
- Charles Beauregard
- Percy and Polly Browne are from the stage musical *The Boy Friend*
- The Drones (recurring club in the works of P. G. Wodehouse)
- Handel Fane (*Enter Sir John* by Clemence Dane and Helen Simpson)
- Anton Phibes (Vincent Price, *The Abominable Dr. Phibes* and *Dr. Phibes Rises Again*)
- *British Pluck* (*Something Fresh* [aka *Something New*] by P. G. Wodehouse)
- The "floppy-haired male dandy" Geneviève spots is Wilde's Dorian Gray
- Dr. Sheppard and Ackroyd (*The Murder of Roger Ackroyd* by Agatha Christie)
- *Eulalie Soeurs* (*The Code of the Woosters* by P. G. Wodehouse)
- The Diogenes Club
- Mildew Manor is from Newman's vampire story "Mildew Manor, or, The Italian Smile"
- Agatha Gregson is Bertie Wooster's aunt
- Lydia Inchfawn; Kali Chattopadhyay; Verity "Smudge" Oxenford; Drearcliff Grange; Grace Ki, the Ghost Lantern Girl; Miss Downs; Walmergrave; and Crawford are from Newman's novel *The Secrets of Drearcliff Grange School*; a later Ghost Lantern Girl is mentioned in "Cold Snap"
- Miss Carlotta Francis is named after a vampire fiction author in the *Law & Order: Criminal Intent* episode "Collective"
- Norma Desmond (Gloria Swanson, *Sunset Boulevard*; Norma co-starring with Rudolph Valentino in a film adaptation of Elinor Glyn's *The Count* is similar to Swanson co-starring with Valentino in the film version of Glyn's novel *Beyond the Rocks*)
- Ralph Levé (Dean Cameron, *Rockula*)
- George Valentin (Jean Dujardin, *The Artist*)
- Rupert of Hentzau and Zenda

- Lord Godalming
- Salome Otterbourne (*Death on the Nile* by Agatha Christie)
- Rosie M. Banks (author and wife of Wodehouse's recurring character Bingo Little)
- Harriet Vane (mystery author and wife of Lord Peter Wimsey)
- Otterbourne's *Nitelite Saga* novels are analogous to Stephenie Meyer's *Twilight Saga* novels
- Banks' *Mal de Mer* mysteries are analogous to Charlaine Harris' *Southern Vampire Mysteries*, the basis for the television series *True Blood*
- Vane's *Vampyrrhic Chronicles* are analogous to *The Vampire Chronicles* by Anne Rice
- Luna Bartendale (*The Undying Monster* by Jessie Douglas Kerruish)
- Sergeant Dravot
- Edwin Winthrop
- Kate Reed
- Jennifer Chevalier is from Rob Curley, Maura McHugh, and Stephen Downey's comic book *Jennifer Wilde*
- Lady Jane Ainsley (Frieda Inescort, *The Return of the Vampire*)
- Catriona Kaye
- Mycroft Holmes
- The Cult of Saamri is a reference to the Indian horror film *Purana Mandir*
- Bigglesworth (James "Biggles" Bigglesworth, aviator in novels by W. E. Johns)
- Ultus, played by Aurelio Sidney, is the hero of a British film series from the 1910s
- Hannay (Richard Hannay, hero of several novels by John Buchan)
- The Cat is from John Willard's play *The Cat and the Canary*
- The Bat is from Mary Roberts Rinehart and Avery Hopwood's play of the same name
- The Kane papers (Charles Foster Kane; Orson Welles, *Citizen Kane*)

- Fantômas is "The Lord of Terror" created by Marcel Allain and Pierre Souvestre
- Le Rat was played by Ivor Novello in three silent films in the 1920s
- Belphégor is from the film serial of the same name
- The Frog is from Edgar Wallace's novel *The Fellowship of the Frog*
- The Ghoul is from Frank King's novel of the same name
- The Hooded Terror (Michael Larron, *Sexton Blake and the Hooded Terror*)
- Professor Jim Moriarty
- "Arsehole Lupin" (Arsène Lupin)
- The Green Archer is the title character of Edgar Wallace's novel
- The Clutching Hand (Craig Kennedy's archenemy in *The Exploits of Elaine* and *The Clutching Hand* by Arthur B. Reeve)
- Dr. Shade is from "The Original Dr. Shade" and other stories by Newman
- The Black Abbot is from Edgar Wallace's titular novel
- Zenith the Albino, aka Anthony Zenith (Sexton Blake's greatest foe)
- Nighthawk (gentleman thief created by Sydney Horler)
- Arthur Milton (*The Gaunt Stranger* [aka *The Ringer*] by Edgar Wallace)
- Lord Ruthven
- Iorga (Robert Quarry, *Count Yorga, Vampire* and *The Return of Count Yorga*)
- Mitterhouse (Robert Tayman, *Vampire Circus*)
- Vulkan (*They Thirst* by Robert McCammon)
- David, Baron Meinster (David Peel, *The Brides of Dracula*)
- Countess Marya Zaleska (Gloria Holden, *Dracula's Daughter*)
- General Karnstein and Carmilla (*Carmilla* by J. Sheridan Le Fanu)
- Mr. Hodge (Max Phipps, *Thirst*)
- Kleopatra is meant to be Queen Katrina, the vampire played by Grace Jones in *Vamp*; her stage name Akasha Kemet is a reference to Anne Rice's novel *Queen of the Damned*

- Kah Pai Mei is a composite of Kah (Chan Shen) from the Hammer Dracula film *Legend of the 7 Golden Vampires* and Pai Mei of Chinese legend and film
- Caleb Croft (Michael Pataki, *Grave of the Vampire*)
- The double murder in Sydney in 1831 is a reference to Helen Simpson's novel *Under Capricorn*
- The Théâtre des Vampires (*Interview with the Vampire* and *The Vampire Lestat* by Anne Rice)
- Master of the Flying Guillotine is a reference to the Chinese martial arts film of the same name
- The Five Deadly Venoms Discipline is a reference to the martial arts film *Five Deadly Venoms*
- Mad Monkey Kung Fu is from the martial arts film of the same name
- The Si Fan
- Greyfriars (from Frank Richards' stories about Billy Bunter and his classmates)
- Judas College (*Zuleika Dobson* by Max Beerbohm)
- Roderick Spode (British fascist from the Jeeves books)
- Matey (James Matey; *Dear Brutus* by J. M. Barrie)
- Professor Bey (Ardath Bey, the alias used by Imhotep [Boris Karloff] in the 1932 film *The Mummy*)
- Herbert, Viscount von Krolock (Iain Quarrier, *Dance of the Vampires* aka *The Fearless Vampire Killers*)
- Prince Mamuwalde (William Marshall, *Blacula* and *Scream Blacula Scream*)
- Ethelind Fionguala ("Ken's Mystery" by Julian Hawthorne)
- Schloss Adler is the fortress from the movie *Where Eagles Dare*
- Caligari (Werner Krauss, *The Cabinet of Dr. Caligari*)
- Ten Brinken and the Alraune Experiment (*Alraune* by Hanns Heinz Ewers)
- Krueger (Herr Doktor Krueger, G-8's archenemy)
- Jekyll
- Moreau

- Royston Vasey is the setting of the British television comedy *The League of Gentlemen*
- The *Beast (The Daily Beast, Scoop* by Evelyn Waugh)
- Renfield
- The Durward family is from the film *Captain Kronos, Vampire Hunter*
- Richard Lestrange (Michael Johnson, *Lust for a Vampire*)
- S (aka Nezumi and Mouse) is based on elements of various female vampires from *anime* such as *Blood: The Last Vampire, Rosario + Vampire* and *Dance in the Vampire Bund*
- Frightening Fritton is Miss Fritton from Ronald Searle's St. Trinian's cartoons
- Inspector Hound (*The Real Inspector Hound* by Tom Stoppard)
- Jack Seward
- Isolde (Dominique, *Le Frisson de Vampires*)
- Mythwrhn is from Newman's story "Mother Hen"
- Pazuzu (*The Exorcist* by William Peter Blatty)
- Shuma-Gorath is a demon from the Marvel Comics Universe, although its name is derived from Robert E. Howard's "The Curse of the Golden Skull"
- Shub-Niggurath and Azathoth are Great Old Ones from Lovecraft's Cthulhu Mythos
- Azal is from the *Doctor Who* serial "The Daemons"
- Abanazer is from the pantomime version of *Aladdin*
- Gregory von Bayern (*The Dragon Waiting* by John M. Ford)

Anno Dracula 1968: Aquarius (in *Anno Dracula: Dracula Cha Cha Cha*, Titan Books, 2012)

- Kate Reed
- Kôr (kingdom ruled by Ayesha, aka She Who Must Be Obeyed, in novels by H. Rider Haggard)
- Jerusalem's Lot (*'Salem's Lot* by Stephen King)

- Gamma Bomb (source of Dr. Bruce Banner's transformation into the Hulk in stories published by Marvel Comics)
- Bali Ha'i (*Tales of the South Pacific* by James A. Michener, adapted by Rodgers and Hammerstein as the musical *South Pacific*)
- Frank Mills is the title character of a song in the stage musical and film *Hair*
- Algernon Ford (The Reverend Alexander Algernon Ford; Gavin Reed, *The Body Beneath*)
- Horatio Stubbs is featured in a trilogy of novels by Brian Aldiss
- Seaton Begg is Michael Moorcock's alternate reality counterpart to Sexton Blake
- *Compact* magazine is from the British soap opera *Compact*
- *Bikini Girl* magazine is from the film *The Night Caller*
- *Wow Magazine* is from the film *Cover Girl Killer*
- Fred Regent (Richard Jeperson's policeman sidekick in Newman's Diogenes Club stories)
- Jim Graham (*Empire of the Sun* by J. G. Ballard; Graham is a fictionalized version of Ballard himself)
- B Division and Pickering are from R. Chetwynd-Hayes' book *The Monster Club*
- Herrick (William Herrick; Jason Watkins, *Being Human*)
- The Diogenes Club
- Detective Superintendent Bellaver, Detective Sergeant Griffin, and Keith Kenneth (Alfred Marks, Julian Holloway, and Michael Gothard, *Scream and Scream Again*)
- Premier Torgu (Ion Torgu; *Fangland* by John Marks)
- Lord Ruthven
- Lorrimer Van Helsing (Peter Cushing, *Dracula A.D. 1972* and *The Satanic Rites of Dracula*)
- Abraham Van Helsing
- Morgan Delt (David Warner, *Morgan: A Suitable Case for Treatment*)

- Nezumi
- Arthur Bryant and John May are members of the Peculiar Crimes Unit in novels by Christopher Fowler
- Mycroft Holmes
- Richard Jeperson
- Donna Rogers (Anna Massey) and the Midnight Mess restaurant are from the film *The Vault of Horror*
- Geoff Brent (Geoffrey Brent; Ian Hendry, *Police Surgeon*)
- The Crimson Executioner (Mickey Hargitay, *Bloody Pit of Horror*)
- Carol Thatcher (Janet Lynn, *Cool It Carol!*)
- Geneviève Dieudonné
- Waldo Zhernikov (Herbert Lom, *The Frightened City*)
- Hogarth, aka Big Bloodsucker Hog (Peter Egan, *Big Breadwinner Hog*)
- The Living Dead motorcycle gang is from the film *Psychomania*
- Inspector Hornleigh (protagonist of a 1930s radio show)
- George Dixon (Jack Warner, *The Blue Lamp* and *Dixon of Dock Green*)
- Jack Regan (John Thaw, *The Sweeney*)
- Timothy Lea (Robin Askwith, *Confessions of a Window Cleaner*, *Confessions of a Pop Performer*, *Confessions of a Driving Instructor*, and *Confessions of a Summer Camp Councillor*; Askwith also played Joe Sickles in *Cool It Carol!*)
- Peter Steiger (Ralph Arliss, *Blood Relations*)
- University of Watermouth (*The History Man* by Malcolm Bradbury)
- St. Bartolph's and Laura Bellows (Caroline Munro) are from *Dracula A.D. 1972*
- Walter Goodrich and Doctor Holstrom (Peter Cushing and Edward Woodward, *Incense for the Damned*)
- Caleb Croft and James Eastman (Michael Pataki and William Smith, *Grave of the Vampire*)
- Professor Bowles-Ottery (Leo McKern, *A Jolly Bad Fellow*)

- E. B. Fern is a science fiction author played by Harold Kasket in "Amazing Stories," an episode of the British television anthology *Red Letter Day*
- Tom Choley was played by Paul Angelis in a six-part adaptation of Patricia Highsmith's novel *A Dog's Ransom* on the anthology series *Armchair Thriller*
- The Winchester is from the movie *Shaun of the Dead*
- Neville Hetherington (Robert Crewdson, *Her Private Hell*)
- Sybil Waite (Patricia Haines, *Virgin Witch*)
- *Sixth Form Girls in Chains*, Zarana and Lady Celia (Lady Celia Asquith-Leaves) are from Newman's story "Soho Golem"
- *The Science of Sex* is from the movie *Deep End*
- *Bathtime with Brenda* is from the movie *Terror*
- Thomas Nolan is David Hemmings' character from the film *Blow-Up* (Newman provided him with his surname, which is the same as that of Hemmings' character in *The Charge of the Light Brigade*; Hemmings named one of his sons Nolan in honor of that role)
- Lucy Westenra
- Sir John Rowan (Peter Cushing, *Corruption*)
- Baron Meinster
- Clive Landseer (Alexis Kanner, *Goodbye Gemini*; the "white-blonde male and female twins who 'came together'" are Julian and Jacki Dewar, played by Martin Potter and Judy Geeson)
- Syrie Van Epp (Elizabeth Shepherd, *The Corridor People*)
- The *Fevre Dream* is from George R. R. Martin's vampire novel of the same name
- Sebastian Newcastle (Don Sebastian de Villanueva, from vampire novels by Les Daniels)
- Herbert von Krolock and Professor Abronsius (Iain Quarrier and Jack MacGowran, *Dance of the Vampires* aka *The Fearless Vampire Killers*)
- Mrs. Michaela Cazaret and Tom Lynn (Ava Gardner and Ian McShane, *The Ballad of Tam Lin*)

- Paul Durward (Shane Briant, *Captain Kronos–Vampire Hunter*)
- Canon Copely-Syle (*To the Devil a Daughter* by Dennis Wheatley)
- Emir Abdulla Akaba was played by Henry Soskin in the "Death a la Carte" episode of *The Avengers*
- Plainview Oil is a reference to the film *There Will Be Blood*
- Berkeley-Willoughby (Archibald Berkeley-Willoughby, *The Adventures of PC 49* radio series)
- Jack Andrus (Kirk Douglas, *Two Weeks in Another Town*)
- Byron Orlok (Boris Karloff, *Targets*; his role of Clayface is meant to evoke Basil Karlo, the first of several Batman foes to use the name Clayface, who modeled his masked persona after the character he played in the horror film *The Terror*, which is also the name of Byron Orlok's last film)
- Countess Addhema (*The Vampire Countess* by Paul Féval)
- Toby Dammit (Terence Stamp, *Spirits of the Dead*)
- The Daughter of the Dragon (Fah Lo Suee, daughter of Fu Manchu; her alias of Lin Tang is the name given to Fu's daughter in the Harry Alan Towers-produced films in the late '60s, in which she was portrayed by Tsai Chin, while her role as Thomas Nolan's personal assistant is a reference to Chin's appearance as Thomas' unnamed receptionist in *Blow-Up*)
- The Lord of Strange Deaths (Fu Manchu)
- Barbara von Weidenborn (Evelyne Kraft, *Lady Dracula*; her pseudonym Barbarushka is a reference to 1960s fashion model Veruschka, who appeared as a fictionalized version of herself in *Blow-Up*)
- Edwina (Edwina Lionheart; Diana Rigg, *Theatre of Blood*)
- Marcus Monserrat and Mrs. Monserrat (Boris Karloff and Catherine Lacey, *The Sorcerers*)
- Hugh Conway and Shangri-La (*Lost Horizon* by James Hilton)
- Shambhala is from Tibetan and Indian Buddhist mythology
- K'un-L'un is the adopted home of the Marvel Comics hero Iron Fist
- Kent Allard
- "The secret of killing via shouting" is a reference to the film *The Shout*

- Catherine Cornelius is the sister of Michael Moorcock's adventurer and secret agent Jerry Cornelius
- Moira Kent ("The Dancing Life of Moira Kent," strip in the British comic *Bunty*)
- Fontaine Khaled (*The Stud* and *The Bitch* by Jackie Collins)
- Sir Billy Langly was played by Kevin Brennan in "The Human Time Bomb," an episode of the television series *Doomwatch*
- The Steel Claw is a British comics character
- Vanessa is Richard Jeperson's lovely companion
- Charles Beauregard
- Danny Dravot
- Whitney is Whitney Gauge from Newman's "Moon Moon Moon"
- Maureen is Maureen Mountmain from Newman's "Seven Stars"
- Louise-Ésperance is Madame Louise Ésperance "Mama-Lou" d'Ailly-Guin from Newman's "The Serial Murders," which is also the source of Corri (Professor Barbara Corri) and *The Northern Barstows*
- Quelou is Mademoiselle Quelou from Newman's *Doctor Who* novel *Time and Relative*
- CI5 is from the British television series *The Professionals*
- WOOC(P) (*The Ipcress File* by Len Deighton)
- The Circus is from the George Smiley novels by John le Carré
- Universal Exports is the front for the British Secret Service in the James Bond novels
- The Section is from the TV series *Callan*; David Callan's boss is known as Colonel Hunter
- Sandbaggers are a reference to the British spy TV series *The Sandbaggers*
- Scalphunters are a reference to le Carré's Smiley novel *Tinker Tailor Soldier Spy*
- Edwin Winthrop
- Mildew Manor is from Kim Newman's story of the same name
- James Manfred, O.B.E. (James Cossins, *Raw Meat* aka *Deathline*)

- The Department of Administrative Affairs is from the British sitcom *Yes Minister*
- Nicholas Dyer (*Hawksmoor* by Peter Ackroyd)
- Professor Elwyn Clayton (George Zucco, *Dead Men Walk*)
- Faber College is from the film *National Lampoon's Animal House*
- Santonix (Rudolf Santonix; *Endless Night* by Agatha Christie)
- Harry Paget Flashman
- Horatio Hornblower
- George Edward Challenger
- Sir Francis Varney
- Prince Mamuwalde
- Dru is Drusilla (Juliet Landau) from *Buffy the Vampire Slayer*
- Ricky Strange (Steve Patterson) and Groover's are from the film *Au Pair Girls*
- Mina Harker
- Kostaki ("The Pale Lady" by Alexandre Dumas)
- Styles, the Haymarket Strangler (Edward Styles; Michael Atkinson, *Grip of the Strangler*)
- Constable Thackeray is from the Inspector Cribb novels by Peter Lovesey
- Eric DeBoys was played by Patrick Mower in *The Avengers* episode "A Sense of History"
- Cathy Castel and Pony Tricot are meant to be the vampires played by Catherine and Marie-Pierre Castel in several films directed by Jean Rollin; "Pony Tricot" is one of Marie-Pierre's stage names.
- Howard W. Campbell Jr. (*Mother Night* and *Slaughterhouse-Five* by Kurt Vonnegut)
- Miss Brabazon (Sheila Keith, *House of Mortal Sin*)
- Scrawdyke (Malcolm Scrawdyke; John Hurt, *Little Malcolm and His Struggle Against the Eunuchs*)
- Withnail (Richard E. Grant, *Withnail & I*)

- Moïse King is a combination of Moise from the film *The Party's Over* and King from the film *These Are the Damned*; both roles were played by Oliver Reed
- Simon Armstrong (*The Feast of the Wolf* by Thomas Blackburn)
- Anna Franklyn (Jacqueline Pearce, *The Reptile*; Pearce also played Marianne Gray in "A Sense of History")
- Fran (Marianne Morris, *Vampyres*)
- Roquentin (Antoine Roquentin; *Nausea* by Jean-Paul Sartre)
- Elizabeth Bathory
- Hesselius (Dr. Martin Hesselius, *In A Glass Darkly* by J. Sheridan LeFanu)
- "The vanishing police box" is the Doctor's TARDIS from *Doctor Who*
- The Mother of Tears is from Dario Argento's film trilogy consisting of *Suspiria*, *Inferno*, and *Mother of Tears*
- Carmilla
- Edward Langdon, MP (Lennard Pearce, *Face of Darkness*)
- Dr. John Hardy (Marius Goring, *The Expert*)
- Lionel St. Dubois (Lorenzo "L. S. D." St. Dubois; Dick Shawn, *The Producers*)
- Horace Rumpole (Leo McKern, *Rumpole of the Bailey*)
- Joe Hawkins is the protagonist of the *Skinhead* novels by "Richard Allen," a pen name for James Moffat
- Adam Cochran (*Dracula and the Virgins of the Undead* by "Etienne Aubin," also a Moffat pseudonym)
- Reginald Bird (Ronald "Budgie" Bird; Adam Faith, *Budgie*)
- Peter Craven (Malcolm McFee, *Please Sir!* and *The Fenn Street Gang*)
- Fullalove of the *Gazette* (James Fullalove; Paul Whitsun-Jones, *The Quatermass Experiment*; Brian Worth, *Quatermass and the Pit*)
- Stenning of the *Express* (Peter Stenning; Edward Judd, *The Day the Earth Caught Fire*)
- DCI Charlie Barlow (Stratford Johns) and New Town are from the TV series *Z Cars* and its many spin-offs
- Sergeant Lynch (James Ellis, *Z Cars*)

- Jasper Lakin was played by John Laurie in *The Avengers* episode "Brief for Murder"
- Perryman (Det. Sgt. Perryman; Michael McStay, *No Hiding Place*)
- North (Det. Sgt. Bill North; Roger Rowland, *Special Branch*)
- *The Bowmans*, from the titular episode of the British sitcom *Hancock*, is a parody of the radio soap opera *The Archers*
- Sister George is from the play and film *The Killing of Sister George*
- Jessica Van Helsing (Stephanie Beacham, *Dracula A.D. 1972*; Joanna Lumley, *The Satanic Rites of Dracula*)
- Marcus Obadiah (*The Dead Travel Fast* by Richard Tate)
- Kingstead Cemetery is from *Dracula*
- The India-Rubber Men are from Edgar Wallace's novel of the same name
- Graf von Orlok (Max Schreck, *Nosferatu*)
- John Blaylock (David Bowie, *The Hunger*)
- Orlon Kronsteen (*They Thirst* and "Makeup" by Robert McCammon)
- Mavis Weld (*The Little Sister* by Raymond Chandler)
- Biff Bailey (Roy Castle, *Dr. Terror's House of Horrors*)
- Marcel DeLange (Martin Kosleck, *House of Horrors* [no relation to the above])
- The Gorilla of Soho is from the 1968 German film of the same name
- Renfield
- St. Swithin's and Michael Upton (Barry Evans) are from the television series *Doctor in the House* and *Doctor at Large*

Anno Dracula: Johnny Alucard (Titan Books, 2013)

- Brastov (Count Gregor Brastov; *The Soft Whisper of the Dead* by Charles L. Grant)
- Magda Cuza, Dinu Pass, and the Keep (*The Keep* by F. Paul Wilson)
- Maleva (Maria Ouspenskaya, *The Wolf Man* and *Frankenstein Meets the Wolf Man*)

- Bowles-Ottery
- Whistler (Jamey Whistler; *The World on Blood* and *Shadows* by Jonathan Nasaw)
- B Division
- Bellaver
- Nezumi
- Captain Gardner (changed from Rogers in the original version of "You Are the Wind Beneath My Wings," where he was meant to be Steve Rogers, aka Captain America; the name Gardner is a reference to Grant Gardner, Cap's alter ego in the 1944 Republic serial)
- Herbert von Krolock
- Feraru (Michael Feraru; *The Lost* by Jonathan Aycliffe)
- Striescu (Aldo Striescu; *Shadows* by Jonathan Nasaw)
- Visser (Loren Visser; M. Emmet Walsh, *Blood Simple*)
- Sarah Roberts (Susan Sarandon, *The Hunger*)
- Michael Morbius (Marvel Comics' "Living Vampire")
- Opar (lost African city in Burroughs' books about Lord Greystoke)
- Holly Sargis and Kit Carruthers (Sissy Spacek and Martin Sheen, *Badlands*)
- Judd (Neville Brand, *Eaten Alive*)
- Doctor Porthos is the title character of a vampire story by Basil Copper
- Liberty Valance (Lee Marvin, *The Man Who Shot Liberty Valance*)
- John Reid (the Lone Ranger)
- John Reid's nephew, a big newspaperman (Britt Reid, aka the Green Hornet)
- Joseph Sibley appeared in the original version of George du Maurier's *Trilby*, and was based on painter James McNeill Whistler; Whistler objected to du Maurier's unflattering depiction of him, and the character of Sibley was excised from subsequent editions of the book
- C. C. Drood (Tom Hulce, *Slam Dance*)
- Gordon Gecko (Michael Douglas, *Wall Street* and *Wall Street: Money Never Sleeps*)

- The *Hope* is from James Lovegrove's novel of the same name
- Max Zorin (Christopher Walken, *A View to a Kill*)
- Rosamond Denham was played by Elizabeth Montgomery in "Masquerade," an episode of the anthology television series *Thriller*
- The Sta-Puft Marshmallow Man is from the movie *Ghostbusters*
- Bowie and Keechie (Keith Carradine and Shelley Duvall, *Thieves Like Us*)
- Bart and Laurie (Bart Tare and Annie Laurie Starr; John Dall and Peggy Cummins, *Gun Crazy*)
- Sailor and Lula (Sailor Ripley and Lula Fortune; Nicolas Cage and Laura Dern, *Wild at Heart*)
- Dirty Mary and Crazy Larry (Peter Fonda and Susan George, *Dirty Mary Crazy Larry*)
- Mickey and Mallory (Mickey and Mallory Knox; Woody Harrelson and Juliette Lewis, *Natural Born Killers*)
- Sadie and Krug (Jeramie Rain and David Hess, *The Last House on the Left*)
- Harry Martin (Harley Venton, *Blood Ties*)
- General Zaroff ("The Most Dangerous Game" by Richard Connell)
- Salvatore Macelli (Robert Loggia, *Innocent Blood*)
- Spinal Tap is from the movie *This is Spinal Tap*
- The Be-Sharps are from *The Simpsons* episode "Homer's Barbershop Quartet"
- Maple White Land (*The Lost World* by Arthur Conan Doyle)
- Nerissa Simms (Michelle Forbes, *Love Bites*)
- Scorpio (Andrew Robinson, *Dirty Harry*)
- Eric DeBoys
- Lucien Lacroix and Knight (Nigel Bennett and Geraint Wyn Davies, *Forever Knight*)
- Fitzroy (Henry Fitzroy, vampire novelist in the *Blood Books* series by Tanya Huff, as well as the TV series *Blood Ties*)
- The Crimson Executioner

- Anita Blake (vampire slayer in novels by Laurell K. Hamilton)
- Captain Kronos (Horst Janson, *Captain Kronos–Vampire Hunter*)
- Baron Samedi (Don Pedro Colley, *Sugar Hill*)
- Adam Simon is a real director and screenwriter, but Newman's version is based on Simon's fictionalized portrayal of himself in the movie *The Player*
- Glick (Sammy Glick; *What Makes Sammy Run?* by Budd Schulberg)
- Ricia "Rusty" Cadigan (*Love Bite* and *Worse Than Death* by Sherry Gottlieb)
- Hoffman (Theodore "Ted" Hoffman; Daniel Benzali, *Murder One*)
- The Brotherhood of the Bell is from the TV movie of the same name
- The lawyer killed by Kit and Holly is Henry Turner (Harrison Ford) from the movie *Regarding Henry*
- Janos Skorzeny (Barry Atwater, *The Night Stalker*)
- Ralph Rockula
- Chapman (Merrick Chapman; *Rulers of Darkness* and *Daughter of Darkness* by Stephen Spruill)
- Crispian (Crispian Grimes; Greg Wise, *House of Frankenstein*, 1997 TV miniseries)
- Sebastian Newcastle
- Rafkin (Adam Rafkin; Jarrad Paul, *Action*)
- Lugash is a fictional Middle Eastern nation from the movie *The Pink Panther* and its sequels
- Blake and Grimes (Arthur Blake and Willy Grimes; Dominic Monaghan and Larry Fessenden, *I Sell the Dead*)
- Light-skinned African-American detective who always wears a hat (Meldrick Lewis; Clark Johnson, *Homicide: Life on the Street*)
- Underfed Jewish detective (John Munch; Richard Belzer, *Homicide* and *Law & Order: Special Victims Unit* [regular character]; *Law & Order*, *The X-Files*, *The Beat*, *Law & Order: Trial by Jury*, *Arrested Development*, and *The Wire* [guest appearances])
- "Rare moth cocoons in the gullets of preserved severed heads" and the Baltimore State Hospital for the Criminally Insane are from Thomas Harris' novel *The Silence of the Lambs*

- "Mad poets walling themselves up in tribute to Edgar Allan Poe" is a reference to the *Homicide* episode "Heartbeat"
- "Giant crustacean attacks" is a reference to the film *Multiple Maniacs*
- Lorie Bryer and Dan Hanson (Elizabeth Perkins and Kevin Bacon, *He Said, She Said*)
- Emma Zoole was played by Lauren Tom in the *Homicide* episodes "A Model Citizen" and "Happy to Be Here"
- Alonzo "Drak" Fortunato was played by Kevin Thigpen in the *Homicide* episode "The Damage Done"
- Scheiner (Ralph Tabakin, *Homicide*)
- *The Jerry Langford Show* is from Martin Scorsese's film *The King of Comedy*
- Alexandra Forrest (Glenn Close, *Fatal Attraction*)
- Lydia Deetz (Winona Ryder, *Beetlejuice*)
- Wilkie Collins was played by Robert Chew in "Blood Ties," a three-part episode of *Homicide*
- The Barksdale organization is from *The Wire*
- Luther Mahoney (Erik Dellum, *Homicide*)
- Mighty Joe Young is from the film of the same name
- The CTU (Counter Terrorist Unit) is from the TV series *24*
- The BPRD (Bureau for Paranormal Research and Defense) is the organization for which Hellboy works
- Most of the regional names for Drac are also the titles of 1980s and 1990s vampire films and television series, with the exceptions of Black Lodge and Killer Bob, which are nods to *Twin Peaks*; Night Inside, named after a vampire novel by Nancy Baker; and Amarantha, a reference to Amarantha Knight, a pen name of vampire fiction author Nancy Kilpatrick
- Divorced guide-book writer (Macon Leary; William Hurt, *The Accidental Tourist*)
- Willis Daniels (Richard Lawson, *Scream Blacula Scream*)
- Prince Mamuwalde
- Corny Collins (Shawn Thompson, *Hairspray*)

- Georgia Rae Drumgo (Georgia Rae Mahoney from *Homicide* combined with Evelda Drumgo from the movie *Hannibal*, both played by Hazelle Goodman)
- Eli Cross and Lucky Cameron (Peter O'Toole and Steve Railsback, *The Stunt Man*)
- Josie Hart is the vampire protagonist of Everett Hartsoe's comic book *Embrace*
- Frank Frene ("The Transfer" by Algernon Blackwood)
- Rudolph (Rudolph Sackville-Bagg; Rollo Weeks, *The Little Vampire*)
- Kurt Barlow (*'Salem's Lot* by Stephen King)
- Monroe Stahr (*The Love of the Last Tycoon* by F. Scott Fitzgerald)
- Christopher Neville (Eric Bogosian, *Special Effects*)
- Caine (Kwai Chang Caine II; David Carradine, *Kung Fu: The Legend Continues*)
- The USS *Philip Francis Queeg* is named after Humphrey Bogart's character in *The Caine Mutiny*
- The Rocket-Man program is a reference to the serial *Radar Men from the Moon*
- Swan and Phoenix (Paul Williams and Jessica Harper, *Phantom of the Paradise*)
- The T5 space station is from the television series *Thunderbirds*
- Frozen Gold (*Espedair Street* by Iain Banks)
- Loud Shit (*Jago* by Kim Newman)
- Strange Fruit is from the movie *Still Crazy*
- Whip Hand (*The Kill Riff* by David J. Schow)
- Crucial Taunt is from the movies *Wayne's World* and *Wayne's World 2*
- The Jake Hammer Band (*The Scream* by John Skipp and Craig Spector)
- Black Roses is from the film of the same name
- The Johnny Favorite Big Band is a reference to the movie *Angel Heart*
- Steven Shorter (Paul Jones, *Privilege*)
- The Impossibles are a rock group doubling as superheroes in the 1960s cartoon of the same name

- Petya Tcherkassoff is from tie-in novels for the role-playing game *Dark Future* written by Newman under the pen name "Jack Yeovil"
- Ringo Starr's Merlin costume is an in-joke based on Starr playing Merlin in the 1974 British musical comedy film *Son of Dracula*
- Rose Murasaki (*Suckers* by Anne Billson)
- Czakyr (David Sawyer, *Children of the Night*)
- Count Boris Bolescu (vampire in children's books by Ann Jungman)
- The Nakatomi Corporation is from the movie *Die Hard*
- Henry Jekyll and Edward Hyde
- Sir Rodger Baskerville (*The Hound of the Baskervilles* by Arthur Conan Doyle)
- Dr. Pretorius (Ernest Thesiger, *Bride of Frankenstein*; also appears in stories by Paul J. McAuley)
- The Daughter of the Dragon and the Lord of Strange Deaths are Fah Lo Suee and Fu Manchu, respectively
- Herbert West
- The Swiss (Victor Frankenstein)
- "A retirement colony for spies in North Wales" is the Village from *The Prisoner*
- Moreau
- Nikola (Guy Boothby's Dr. Nikola)
- Orloff (Howard Vernon, *The Awful Dr. Orloff*)
- Illyana (Julie Strain, *Blonde Heaven*)
- Crosby (Linda Crosby; *Sweetmeats*, graphic novel by Steve Tanner and Pete Venters)
- The Alcore Institute is a reference to the film *Red Blooded American Girl*
- "A 'cleaner'—a dapper fellow with a trimmed mustache" (Winston Wolfe; Harvey Keitel, *Pulp Fiction*)
- Dragon (Peter Dragon; Jay Mohr, *Action*)
- Drakoulias (Oseary Drakoulias; Michael Gambon, *The Life Aquatic with Steve Zissou*)

- Stefan Grlsc (Jude Law, *The Wisdom of Crocodiles*)
- Countess Elisabeth Bathory

Here are the additional "borrowed" characters appearing or mentioned in previous entries in the series that had not been identified at the time *Crossovers Volume 2* was published.

Anno Dracula (1888)

- Hawkshaw (*The Ticket-of-Leave Man* by Tom Taylor)

The Bloody Red Baron (1918)

- Maranique and Lieutenant-Colonel Raymond (later Major Raymond) are from W. E. Johns' Biggles series
- Jimson (Gulley Jimson, *The Horse's Mouth* by Joyce Cary)
- Unteroffizier Paulier (Sebastian Paulier, *Progeny of the Adder* by Leslie H. Whitten)
- Dr. Krueger (G-8's nemesis in pulp novels by Robert J. Hogan)
- Dr. Orlof (Howard Vernon, *The Awful Dr. Orlof*)
- Professor Hansen is from the German film serial *Homunculus*
- The Théâtre des Vampires (*Interview with the Vampire* and *The Vampire Lestat* by Anne Rice)
- Clarimonde ("La Morte Amoureuse" by Théophile Gautier)
- The Théâtre Raoul Privache is named after the vampire from John Metcalfe's short novel *The Feasting Dead*
- Dr. Mabuse (master criminal in novels by Norbert Jacques and a German film series)
- Sebastian Newcastle
- The Hotel Transylvania (*Hotel Transylvania* by Chelsea Quinn Yarbro)
- Faustine ("Vampire's Honeymoon" by Cornell Woolrich)
- Ouran (Hans Steinke, *Island of Lost Souls*)

- Curtiss Stryker ("Sign of the Salamander" and "Blue Lady, Come Back" by Karl Edward Wagner)
- Voerman is meant to be Captain Klaus Woermann from F. Paul Wilson's *The Keep*
- Rutledge is from the film *Hell's Angels*
- The Reverend Mr. Robert Elsmere (*Robert Elsmere* by Mrs. Humphry Ward)
- Alex Brandberg (Mike Horner, *Bite!*)
- Penderel (Roger Penderel; Melvyn Douglas, *The Old Dark House*)
- Reitberg (Carl Reitberg; *The Great Airship: A Tale of Adventure* by F. S. Brereton)
- Comte Hubert de Sinestre (Hubert Noël, *Devils of Darkness*)
- George Sherston (*Memoirs of a Fox-Hunting Man*, *Memoirs of an Infantry Officer*, and *Sherston's Progress* by Siegfried Sassoon)

Dracula Cha Cha Cha (aka Judgment of Tears: Anno Dracula 1959)

- Elisabeta of Transylvania (Winona Ryder, *Bram Stoker's Dracula*)
- Patek Lioncourt is a reference to Lestat de Lioncourt from Anne Rice's *The Vampire Chronicles*
- Miss Desmond (Norma Desmond; Gloria Swanson, *Sunset Boulevard*)
- The Circus is the organization for which John le Carré's spy George Smiley works
- Kah of Ping Kuei Temple (Chan Shen, *Legend of the 7 Golden Vampires*)
- Radu the Repulsive (Radu Vladislav; Anders Hove, *Subspecies*)
- Duchess Marguerite de Grand (Gianna Maria Canale, *Lust of the Vampire*)
- Maciste (protagonist of the 1914 movie *Cabiria*, and later a series of Italian "sword-and-sandal" films in the 1960s)
- Mario Balato (Joe Dallesandro, *Blood for Dracula* aka *Andy Warhol's Dracula*)
- Satanik is the title character of an Italian comic book series by Max Bunker and Magnus
- The astronomy professor (Professor Moriarty)

- Loxley Barrett is from the British radio soap opera *The Archers*
- Madame Cassandra (Britt Ekland, *Beverly Hills Vamp*)
- Edmund Cordery (*The Empire of Fear* by Brian Stableford)
- Cathy and Pony are meant to be the vampire twins played by the Castel sisters in Jean Rollin's films
- Varelli (E. Varelli; Feodor Chaliapin, *Inferno*)
- Dr. Ravna (Noel Willman, *The Kiss of the Vampire*)
- "A vampire cracksman of our vintage" (A. J. Raffles)

"Castle in the Desert: Anno Dracula 1977"

- George the butler (John Carradine, *Blood of Dracula's Castle*)

"Andy Warhol's Dracula: Anno Dracula 1978–1979"

- Kathleen Conklin (Lili Taylor, *The Addiction*; Taylor also played Valerie Solanas in the film *I Shot Andy Warhol*)
- Niccolo Cavalanti (*The Delicate Dependency* by Michael Talbot)
- Chevalier Futaine ("I, the Vampire" by Henry Kuttner)
- Benjamin Lathem (Kevin Kindlin, *Heartstopper*)
- L. B. Jeffries (James Stewart, *Rear Window*)
- Alex Ford (Alexander Algernon Ford; Gavin Reed, *The Body Beneath*)
- Baby Jane Hudson (Bette Davis, *What Ever Happened to Baby Jane?*; her role in the Warhol Factory is analogous to Baby Jane Holzer's in the real world)
- Anders Wolleck (Stephen Lack, *Dead Ringers*)
- Helga and Heinrich (Lalla Ward and Robin Sachs, *Vampire Circus*)

"The Other Side of Midnight" (1981)

- David Henry Reid (*Stainless* by Todd Grimson)
- Psychoplasmics is a therapy technique from David Cronenberg's film *The Brood*
- Strange orchid ("The Flowering of the Strange Orchid" by H. G. Wells)

- Nico (Natasha Gregson Wagner, *Modern Vampires*)
- Mink (*Vamps* by Elaine Lee and William Simpson, Vertigo [imprint of DC Comics])
- Vampi is the Anno Dracula Universe counterpart of Vampirella
- Jonathan Gates (*Flicker* by Theodore Roszak)
- The film *Throat Sprockets* is from Tim Lucas' novel of the same name, as is Debbie W. Griffith
- "Would you care for some instant coffee? Ghastly muck, but I'm mildly addicted to it." (Anthony Stewart Head, who played Giles on *Buffy the Vampire Slayer*, did a series of Gold Blend Coffee ads)
- Miriam and John Blaylock (Catherine Deneuve and David Bowie, *The Hunger*)
- Sir Francis Varney
- Kimberly Wells (Jane Fonda, *The China Syndrome*)
- *The Duelling Cavalier* is from the film *Singin' in the Rain*
- Fedora (Hildegarde Knef, *Fedora*)
- The After Hours club (*Less Than Zero* by Bret Easton Ellis)

"You Are the Wind Beneath My Wings: Anno Dracula 1984"

- Purgatory, New Mexico is from the film *Sundown: The Vampire in Retreat*, starring David Carradine as Dracula

About the Author

Sean Lee Levin discovered Philip José Farmer's Wold Newton family writings in 2002 and has never looked back. A lifelong Chicagoan, Sean spends much of his free time reading, writing, and watching a diverse range of films. Sean was honored to serve as a continuity editor on Josh Reynolds' novella *Phileas Fogg and the War of Shadows*, published by Meteor House in 2014. *Crossovers Expanded* is his first published work, with hopefully many more to come.

Meteor House Titles

THE WORLDS OF PHILIP JOSÉ FARMER
Anthology Series edited by Michael Croteau

Volume 1: Protean Dimensions
Volume 2: Of Dust and Soul
Volume 3: Portraits of a Trickster
Volume 4: Voyages to Strange Days

WOLD NEWTON SERIES

Doc Savage: His Apocalyptic Life by Philip José Farmer

The Khokarsa Series
Exiles of Kho by Christopher Paul Carey
Flight to Opar (Restored Edition) by Philip José Farmer
The Song of Kwasin by Philip José Farmer and Christopher Paul Carey
Hadon, King of Opar by Christopher Paul Carey
Blood of Ancient Opar by Christopher Paul Carey

The Pat Wildman Series
The Evil in Pemberley House by Philip José Farmer and Win Scott Eckert
The Scarlet Jaguar by Win Scott Eckert

The Phileas Fogg Series
Phileas Fogg and the War of Shadows by Josh Reynolds
Phileas Fogg and the Heart of Osra by Josh Reynolds

SCIENCE FICTION ADVENTURE

The Abnormalities of Stringent Strange by Rhys Hughes
Airship Hunters by Jim Beard and Duane Spurlock
Dayworld: A Hole in Wednesday by Philip José Farmer and Danny Adams

NONFICTION

Crossovers Expanded, Volume 1 by Sean Lee Levin
Crossovers Expanded, Volume 2 by Sean Lee Levin

meteorhousepress.com